P9-DNI-994

COMPOSING PROCESSES
You will learn how to:

- maintain engagement with your intellectual and rhetorical problem (Chapters 1, 2, 3, 17)
- use a variety of exploratory techniques such as freewriting, idea mapping, playing the believing and doubting game, reading with and against the grain, and conversing with classmates (Chapters 2, 3, 6, 17, 23)
- reduce writer's block by lowering your expectations for early drafts (Chapter 17, writing projects chapters)
- use multiple drafts to achieve your desired result (Chapters 2, 3, 17, writing projects chapters)
- give and receive constructive feedback through peer reviews of drafts (Chapters 17, 23, writing projects chapters)
- follow the revision practices of experts (Chapter 17)
- draft and revise closed-form prose by using readers' expectations for unity, coherence, and old before new (Chapter 18)
- draft and revise open-form prose by following the principles of narration, precise detail, artistic style, and strategic violation of closed-form "rules" (Chapter 19)
- edit for gracefulness, clarity, and correctness (Chapters 17, 18, writing projects chapters)

THE CONVENTIONS OF WRITING
You will learn how to:

- follow the conventions and formats of different genres (Chapters 1, 3, 18)
- adapt the tone, structure, content, and style of your writing to different writing situations (Chapters 3, 18, 19, 23, 24, writing projects chapters)
- cite and document your sources using conventions appropriate to your audience and genre (Chapter 22)
- edit your prose for correct grammar, punctuation, and spelling (Chapters 17, 18)

Note to instructors:
These learning goals are keyed to the Council of Writing Program Administration's "Outcomes Statements for First-Year Composition" (WPA: Writing Program Administration 23.1/2 (Fall/Winter 1999): 59–63. The WPA statement places outcomes under four categories: Rhetorical Knowledge; Critical Thinking, Reading, and Writing; Processes; and Knowledge of Conventions.

The
Allyn & Bacon
Guide to Writing
Brief Edition

The Allyn & Bacon Guide to Writing
Brief Edition

FOURTH EDITION

John D. Ramage
Arizona State University

John C. Bean
Seattle University

June Johnson
Seattle University

PEARSON
Longman

New York   San Francisco   Boston
London   Toronto   Sydney   Tokyo   Singapore   Madrid
Mexico City   Munich   Paris   Cape Town   Hong Kong   Montreal

Publisher: Joseph Opiela
Vice President: Eben W. Ludlow
Development Editor: Marion B. Castellucci
Executive Marketing Manager: Megan Galvin-Fak
Senior Supplements Editor: Donna Campion
Media Supplements Editor: Jenna Egan
Production Manager: Donna DeBenedictis
Project Coordination, Text Design, and Electronic Page Makeup:
  Elm Street Publishing Services, Inc.
Cover Design Manager: Wendy Ann Fredericks
Cover Designer: Base Art Co.
Cover Art: *The Human Edge,* by Helen Frankenthaler. Acrylic on canvas. 1967.
  10' 4-5/8" × 7' 9-1/4". Everson Museum of Fine Art, Syracuse NY/Superstock.
Photo Researcher: Photosearch, Inc.
Senior Manufacturing Buyer: Alfred C. Dorsey
Printer and Binder: RR Donnelley & Sons Company, Crawfordsville
Cover Printer: Phoenix Color Corporation

For permission to use copyrighted material, grateful acknowledgment is made to the copyright
holders on pages 747 to 751, which are hereby made part of this copyright page.

Library of Congress Cataloging-in-Publication Data
Ramage, John D.
      The Allyn & Bacon guide to writing / John D. Ramage, John C. Bean, June Johnson.—
  4th ed.
            p.   cm.
      Includes bibliographical references and index.
      ISBN 0-321-29150-6
      1. English language—Rhetoric—Handbooks, manuals, etc. 2. English language—
  Grammar—Handbooks, manuals, etc. 3. Report writing—Handbooks, manuals, etc. 4.
  College readers. I. Title: Allyn and Bacon guide to writing. II. Bean, John C. III. Johnson,
  June. IV. Title.

      PE1408.R18 2006
      808'.042—dc22   2004060070

Please visit us at http://www.ablongman.com/ramage

ISBN 0-321-29150-6 (Complete Edition)
ISBN 0-321-29151-4 (Brief Edition)
ISBN 0-321-29152-2 (Concise Edition)

3 4 5 6 7 8 9 10—DOC—08 07 06

Brief Contents

PART ONE
A Rhetoric for College Writers   2

PART TWO
Writing Projects   94

➤ **WRITING TO LEARN**

➤ **WRITING TO EXPRESS**

➤ **WRITING TO EXPLORE**

➤ **WRITING TO INFORM**

➤ **WRITING TO ANALYZE AND SYNTHESIZE**

Detailed Contents

PART ONE
A Rhetoric for College Writers   2

➤   WRITING TO ANALYZE AND SYNTHESIZE

PART THREE
A Guide to Composing and Revising 504

Writing Projects

xxvi   Writing Projects

Thematic Contents

The Allyn & Bacon Guide to Writing, Fourth Edition, contains 59 essays—34 by professional writers and 25 by students. In addition, the text contains a number of visual texts (advertisements, political photographs, posters, and Web sites) that can lead to productive thematic discussions. These essays and visual texts can be clustered thematically in the following ways:

FOOD, OBESITY, AND PUBLIC WELLNESS

USA PATRIOT ACT

VIOLENCE, PUBLIC SAFETY, AND INDIVIDUAL RIGHTS

OTHER PUBLIC POLICY ISSUES

RACE AND CLASS ISSUES

IDENTITY AND VALUES

PARENTS, CHILDREN, AND FAMILY

NATURE AND ECOLOGY

Preface

We continue to be grateful for the enthusiastic reviews of *The Allyn & Bacon Guide to Writing*. Known for its groundbreaking integration of composition research and rhetorical perspective, *The Allyn & Bacon Guide to Writing* has been hailed as the most successful college rhetoric in more than a decade. In the regular, brief, and concise editions, the book has been adopted at a wide range of two- and four-year institutions where instructors admire its appeal to students, its focus on problem posing, and its distinctive emphasis on writing and reading as rhetorical acts. The book is distinguished by its lively and engaging instruction, practical classroom activities, and effective writing assignments. From all quarters, instructors have praised the book's theoretical coherence and explanatory power, which help students produce interesting, idea-rich essays and help composition teachers create pedagogically effective, challenging, and intellectually stimulating courses. This fourth edition retains the signature strengths of the third edition while making substantial improvements based on our continuing research in composition theory and practice, on the needs and interests of our students, and on the pedagogical insights and suggestions of the users of the third edition who have shared with us how they teach this text.

What's New in the Fourth Edition

Building on the text's well-established strengths, we have revised the book judiciously to increase its flexibility, clarity, usefulness, and student interest. We have particularly responded to reviewers' requests for an expanded treatment of rhetoric in Part One, for more emphasis on rhetorical context in assignments and exercises, for more attention to visuals, and for a greater range of student models. Here is what's new:

- **A revision of Part One, "A Rhetoric for College Writers," aimed at improving students' comprehension of key rhetorical principles.** Rhetorical instruction that in the third edition was dispersed throughout the writing project chapters has been consolidated into a revised Part One for easier reference and stronger focus. We have improved the explanation of question asking in Chapter 1, condensed three chapters into two, and added a new chapter on how messages persuade. Part One now provides students with a more inclusive and powerful overview to rhetoric that will ground their study of college-level writing, reading, and thinking.
- **In Chapter 1, an improved explanation of question asking and problem posing** that leads to more engaged class discussion, higher-quality questions, and improved performance on the chapter's brief writing project. Using short visual and verbal texts on a lively new topic—"automobiles,

fossil fuels, and energy choices"—the chapter now provides a cultural context for questioning while connecting with students' personal experiences. The writing prompt now offers two options, both of which ground the students' questions in a real-world context.

- **In Chapters 2 and 3, a condensing and streamlining of the third edition's Chapters 2, 3, and 4.** Improved explanations, often updated with newer or better examples, make the rhetorical concepts in these chapters easier to read, understand, and retain. The explanations of freewriting and idea mapping, formerly in Chapter 2, have been moved to Chapter 17 as part of that chapter's explanation of the writing process.

- **A new Chapter 4, "Thinking Rhetorically about How Messages Persuade."** This lively new chapter gives students the background and explanations needed to think rhetorically about a wide range of verbal and nonverbal texts. An initial section on rhetorical theory provides a framework for introducing concepts previously delayed until later in the text. Chapter 4 now introduces the classical appeals of *logos, ethos,* and *pathos,* explains angle of vision, introduces strategies for analyzing a text rhetorically, and shows students how they can think rhetorically about nonverbal texts such as images or clothing fashions. These powerful concepts can then be used to enhance rhetorical discussions of readings or assignments throughout Part Two.

- **Within Part Two, expanded options for teaching different genres to appeal to students from a wide range of majors.** Chapter 9 now includes a wider discussion of informative prose, while a new Chapter 10 introduces students to empirical report writing common in the natural and social sciences. These expanded options, which emerge from our commitment to writing-across-the-curriculum, allow teachers to introduce students to a range of genres that they will encounter in their academic and professional lives.

- **An expansion of Chapter 9, "Writing an Informative (and Surprising) Essay,"** to include informational reports as well as pieces using a surprising-reversal strategy. Several new student examples have been included to demonstrate the use of field or library research with an informational aim.

- **A new writing project chapter on "Analyzing Field Research Data from Observation, Interviews, or Questionnaires" (Chapter 10).** Aimed at appealing to students majoring in the social or natural sciences—while introducing humanities majors to the scientific method—this chapter invites students to pose a field research question, to conduct an investigation using questionnaires, interviews, or observations, and to present their findings as a scientific report. The exercises and writing project for this chapter engage students in their own original research, which can often be done in teams. Replacing the third edition's chapters on analyzing numerical data and on investigating causes and consequences, the new Chapter 10 consolidates key principles from those chapters into a useful and interesting introduction to scientific thinking and writing.

- **Throughout the text, a greatly expanded focus on visual rhetoric.** Striking visual images appear at the beginning of the major parts of the text with explanatory captions that provoke critical thinking. Examples of visual or visual-verbal texts also appear in numerous For Writing and Discussion exercises throughout the book to provoke interest in how visual images influence audiences' responses and how they contribute to social conversations and controversies. For example, in the Chapter 6 readings on Lake Powell and the Glen Canyon Dam, students can examine how the advocacy group Friends of Lake Powell uses a stunning photo on its Web page to emphasize Lake Powell's beauty and refreshing water in direct contrast to Edward Abbey's harsh criticism of Lake Powell's ugliness and the dam's environmental destructiveness. Similarly, the advertisement for the Hummer H2 at the beginning of Part One speaks to the readings on fossil fuels and the search for alternative sources of energy, while the Army recruitment advertisements in Part Two and Chapter 8 connect with the student paper on military contractors as well as with the discussion of gender in advertisements in Chapter 11.
- **Ten new student essays, selected to show a wider range of genres** as well as varying degrees of complexity and challenge. Some of the student essays are from exceptionally strong student writers while others show good work from less-skilled writers.
- **Thirteen new professional texts, many of which were selected to form thematic units.** As can be seen in the "Thematic Contents" (pp. xxvii–xxxiv), the readings in the fourth edition form a wide range of thematic groupings. New thematic units include "Automobiles, Fossil Fuels, and Alternative Energy Sources," "Public Health and the Right to Smoke," "Food, Obesity, and Public Wellness," and "USA Patriot Act." Other thematic groupings that appeared in the third edition—such as units related to race and class; gender; media and popular culture; guns and violence; and identity and values—have been updated with new readings, including both visual and verbal texts. The readings also constitute a wide range of scholarly and popular genres, as can be seen in the catalog of genres on the inside back endpapers.
- **Revised and updated instructions for doing online or library research** including explanations of documentation based on the most recent editions of the MLA and APA style manuals. An improved design greatly enhances the clarity of our examples for citing and documenting sources.

Distinctive Features of the Text

The fourth edition of *The Allyn & Bacon Guide to Writing* continues to have the following distinctive features:

- **Great flexibility for instructors.** Because the chapters on rhetoric, on writing projects, and on composing strategies have been designed as self-contained modules, users praise the ease with which they can select chapters and order them to fit the goals of their own courses.

- **Classroom-tested writing projects that guide students through all phases of reading and writing processes and make frequent use of collaboration and peer review.** Assignments are designed to promote intellectual growth and to stimulate the kind of critical thinking valued in college courses.
- **Integration of rhetorical theory with composition research.** Writing and reading are treated both as rhetorical acts and as processes of inquiry, problem posing, and critical thinking.
- **Balanced coverage of academic writing and personal and narrative forms,** placing nonfiction writing on a continuum from thesis-driven "closed-form" writing to narrative-based "open-form" writing. The text focuses on closed-form writing for entering most academic, civic, and professional conversations and on open-form writing for stylistic surprise and pleasure and for narrating ideas and experiences that resist closed-form structures.
- **Distinctive explanations of closed-form prose based on reader-expectation theory.** These explanations (Chapter 18) are arranged in a sequence of ten mini-lessons that can be easily integrated into a variety of course structures.
- **Parallel explanations of open-form prose** (Chapter 19) aimed at teaching purposeful disruptions of the conventions of closed-form prose.
- **Emphasis on teaching students to read rhetorically;** to understand the differences between print and cyberspace sources; to analyze the rhetorical occasion, genre, context, and intended audience of sources; to evaluate sources according to appropriate criteria; and to negotiate the World Wide Web with confidence.
- **Coverage of visual rhetoric and document design** with particular emphasis on Web sites, advertisements, posters, and other texts where words and images work together for rhetorical effect.
- **An attractive four-color design** that enhances the book's visual appeal and presents examples of visual rhetoric and document design in full color.
- **A sequenced skill-based approach to research** that teaches students expert strategies for conducting academic research in a rhetorical environment.
- **Instructional emphases that meet Writing Program Administrators (WPA) guidelines** for outcome goals in first-year composition courses. (See front endpapers and the fourth edition of the *Instructor's Resource Manual* revised by Susanmarie Harrington of Indiana University Purdue University Indianapolis that discusses the correlation of the WPA Outcomes Statement with the fourth edition of *The Allyn & Bacon Guide to Writing.*)
- **A friendly, encouraging tone** that respects students and treats them as serious learners.
- **Accessible readings on current and enduring questions** that illustrate rhetorical principles, represent a balance between professional and student writers, and invite thematic grouping (see the "Thematic Contents," pp. xxvii–xxxiv).

Structure of *The Allyn & Bacon Guide to Writing*

Part One, "A Rhetoric for College Writers," provides a conceptual framework for *The Allyn & Bacon Guide to Writing* by showing how inquiring writers pose problems, pursue them through dialectic thinking and research, and try to solve them within a rhetorical context shaped by the writer's purpose, audience, and genre. Chapter 1 explains how writers grapple with both subject-matter and rhetorical problems and introduces principles of question asking and the concept of a continuum from closed to open forms of prose. Chapter 2 explains college professors' desire for students to "wallow in complexity" by learning to pose engaging questions, conduct inquiry, and seek surprising thesis statements that must be supported with points and particulars. Chapter 3 shows how a writer's purpose, intended audience, and genre influence decisions about content, structure, style, and document design. Chapter 4 extends the discussion of rhetoric by showing students how messages persuade. After a brief introduction to rhetorical theory, Chapter 4 explains the classical appeals of *logos, ethos,* and *pathos* as well as the concept of angle of vision and various strategies for analyzing texts rhetorically. It concludes by showing students how to think rhetorically about visual images, clothing fashions, and other cultural texts.

Part Two, "Writing Projects," consists of twelve self-contained assignment chapters arranged according to the aims of writing: to learn, to express, to explore, to inform, to analyze and synthesize, and to persuade. Each chapter guides students through the processes of generating and exploring ideas, composing and drafting, and revising and editing. Concluding each chapter are "Guidelines for Peer Reviews," which sum up the important features in the assignments and facilitate detailed, helpful peer reviews. The heart of each chapter is a writing project designed to teach students new ways of seeing and thinking. The exploratory exercises in each assignment chapter help students generate ideas for their essays while developing their skills at posing problems, delaying closure, speaking back to texts, valuing alternative points of view, and thinking dialectically.

Part Three, "A Guide to Composing and Revising," comprises three self-contained chapters of nuts-and-bolts strategies for composing and revising along the continuum from closed to open forms. Chapter 17 explains how experienced writers use invention strategies, prewriting, and multiple drafts to manage the complexities of writing and suggests ways that students can improve their own writing processes. It also includes instruction on how to conduct peer reviews. Chapter 18 presents ten self-contained lessons—derived from reader-expectation theory—on composing and revising closed-form prose. Chapter 19 offers parallel explanations of open-form prose.

Part Four, "A Rhetorical Guide to Research," presents pedagogically sequenced instruction to help students learn how to conduct searches, evaluate sources, and incorporate sources into their own writing. Research skills are taught within a rhetorical context with special attention given to the rhetoric of Web sites. Chapter 20 introduces students to the demands of college-level research and previews seven essential skills students will learn in the next chapters. Chapter 21 covers the first five of these skills: composing and arguing one's own thesis;

understanding different kinds of sources; using purposeful search strategies; using rhetorical knowledge to read and evaluate sources; and understanding the rhetoric of Web sites. Chapter 22 explains the last two skills: how to incorporate sources into one's own writing and how to cite and document sources effectively using MLA or APA formats.

Part Five, "A Guide to Special Writing and Speaking Occasions," advises students in a number of special areas. Chapter 23 focuses on oral communication including working in groups and giving speeches and PowerPoint presentations. Chapter 24, drawing on research on timed writing, shows students how to plan and draft an exam essay by applying the principles of rhetorical assessment discussed throughout the text. Chapter 25 draws on research in reflective writing to teach students how to think metacognitively about their own composing processes, produce self-reflective evaluations of their own work, and assemble end-of-term portfolios.

Strategies for Using *The Allyn & Bacon Guide to Writing*

The text's logical organization makes it easy to design a new syllabus or adapt the text to your current syllabus. Key rhetorical concepts that students should know early in the course are developed in Part One, while explanations of compositional strategies and skills—which students will practice recursively throughout the course—are placed in Part Three. Students can work their way through assigned material in Part Three while engaged with writing assignments from Part Two. Additional instructional material related to research and to special writing occasions is included in Parts Four and Five.

Although there are many ways to use *The Allyn & Bacon Guide to Writing*, the most typical course design has students read material from Chapters 1–4 (Part One) during the opening weeks. The brief, informal write-to-learn projects in these chapters can be used either for overnight homework assignments or for in-class discussion.

For the rest of the course, instructors typically assign writing project chapters from the array of options available in Part Two, Chapters 5–16. While students are engaged with the writing projects in these chapters, instructors can assign material from the compositional chapters in Part Three, or from the additional instructional materials in Parts Four and Five selected and sequenced according to their own needs. Each of the lessons on composing and revising closed-form prose (Chapter 18) or open-form prose (Chapter 19) is designed for coverage in a half hour or less of class time. (For suggestions on how to select and sequence materials from Parts Three, Four, and Five, see the sample syllabi in the *Instructor's Resource Manual*.) While students are working on a writing project, classroom discussion can alternate between issues related directly to the assignment (invention exercises, group brainstorming, peer review workshops) and issues focusing on instructional matter from the rest of the text.

Using the Writing Projects in Part Two

Because each of the twelve assignment chapters in Part Two is self-contained, instructors can select and organize the writing projects in the way that best fits their course goals and their students' needs. The projects in Chapters 5 and 6 introduce students to the rhetorical ways of observing and reading that underpin mature academic thinking, showing students how to analyze a text, pose questions about it, and understand and resist the text's rhetorical strategies.

Chapter 7, on autobiographical narrative, is the text's primary "open-form" assignment. Introducing students to strategies of plot, character, and dramatic tension, the project often produces surprisingly sophisticated narratives. Some teachers like to give this assignment early in the course—on the grounds that personal writing should precede more academic forms. Others like to give it last—on the grounds that open-form writing is more complex and subtle than closed-form prose. We have found that either choice can work well. Teachers often pair Chapter 7 with Chapter 19, on composing and revising open-form prose.

Chapter 8's assignment, an exploratory essay, asks students to narrate their engagement with a problem and their attempts to resolve it. Teachers may want to pair this chapter with Part Four on research writing, using the exploratory essay as the first stage of a major research project. The two student essays in this chapter are, in fact, early explorations for finished projects that appear later in the text.

Chapter 9, on informative writing, urges students to think rhetorically about their readers as they contemplate writing an informative report or a "surprising-reversal" essay aimed at altering the reader's initial assumptions about a topic. Surprising reversal is a powerful rhetorical move that can be used to enliven almost any kind of informative, analytical, or persuasive prose.

The four writing projects in the analysis/synthesis section (Chapters 10–13) allow instructors to select among different kinds of phenomena for analysis. Chapter 10 focuses on field research data, inviting students to develop their own field research projects using questionnaires, interviews, or observations and introducing them to the kinds of inquiry and analysis typical of the social sciences. Chapter 11 focuses on images—photographs, drawings, advertisements—to introduce students to visual rhetoric. Its writing assignment, the analysis of advertisements, combines visual rhetoric with the analysis of popular culture. Chapter 12 focuses on analyzing a short story, introducing students to inquiry and analysis in literary studies. Chapter 13 teaches students how to analyze and synthesize ideas from two or more readings, helping them develop the advanced critical reading and thinking skills essential for success in any field.

The persuasion chapters (Chapters 14–16) teach key concepts of argumentation. Providing a strong introduction to both academic and civic argument, these chapters combine accessible Toulmin and stasis approaches while emphasizing argument as the search for the best solutions to shared problems (truth seeking, consensus seeking) rather than as a win/lose debate. Chapter 14 teaches the generic structure and procedures of classical argument. Chapter 15 focuses on evaluation arguments and Chapter 16 on proposal arguments. A distinctive feature in Chapter 16 is an assignment option to create a public affairs advocacy advertisement employing visual as well as verbal rhetoric.

Flexibility of *The Allyn & Bacon Guide to Writing*

Although *The Allyn & Bacon Guide to Writing* is a comprehensive rhetoric, it is designed to be highly teachable in a wide variety of courses and settings. Through all editions, our goal has been to offer instructors multiple possibilities for course design. To that end, *The Allyn & Bacon Guide to Writing* allows numerous options for selecting and sequencing chapters to suit courses with different writing emphases and student needs. Instructors may teach some chapters thoroughly, while assigning others largely for students' preparation outside of class.

Consider, for example, one's options for teaching Chapter 18 on composing and revising closed-form prose. The chapter consists of ten self-contained mini-lessons that can be assigned all at once for several days of class discussion or assigned one lesson at a time at appropriate moments throughout the course. The lessons can be assigned primarily as background reading, or they can be used in class as short instructional modules. Moreover, some of the lessons can be omitted or mixed and matched in a different order.

The same kind of flexibility is offered by the design of the whole text. Our intent has been to give instructors appealing choices and to equip them with pedagogical material that has both depth and breadth.

Supplements for *The Allyn & Bacon Guide to Writing*

The Allyn & Bacon Guide to Writing is supported by a variety of helpful supplements for instructors and students.

For Instructors

- The fourth edition of the *Instructor's Resource Manual* has been revised by Susanmarie Harrington of Indiana University Purdue University Indianapolis. The *Instructor's Resource Manual* integrates emphases for meeting the Writing Program Administrators guidelines for outcome goals in first-year composition courses. It continues to offer detailed teaching suggestions to help both experienced and new instructors; practical teaching strategies for composition instructors in a question-and-answer format; suggested syllabi for courses of various lengths and emphases; chapter-by-chapter teaching suggestions; suggestions for using the text with nonnative speakers; suggestions for using the text in an electronic classroom; transparency masters for class use; and annotated bibliographies.
- *The Allyn & Bacon Guide to Writing Companion Website* enables instructors to access online writing exercises, Web links keyed to specific chapters, and

teaching tips as well as receive essay assignments directly from students. (http://www.ablongman.com/ramage)

- *The Longman Instructor's Planner* includes weekly and monthly calendars, student attendance and grading rosters, space for contact information, Web references, an almanac, and blank pages for notes.
- *The Allyn & Bacon / Longman Instructor Resource Library*
  - *The Allyn & Bacon Sourcebook for College Writing Teachers,* Second Edition
  - *An Introduction to Teaching Composition in an Electronic Environment*
  - *Comp Tales*
  - *In Our Own Voice: Graduate Students Teach Writing*
  - *The Longman Guide to Community Service: Learning in the English Classroom and Beyond*
  - *Using Portfolios*
  - *Teaching in Progress: Theories, Practices, and Scenarios,* Third Edition
  - *The Longman Guide to Classroom Management*

For Students

- *The Allyn & Bacon Guide to Writing Companion Website* presents chapter summaries, writing exercises, Web links keyed to specific text sections, peer review checklists, student writing samples, and the ability to e-mail exercises to their instructor. (http://www.ablongman.com/ramage)
- NEW! *MyCompLab 2.0 Web Site* (*www.mycomplab.com*) offers all the strengths of 1.0, but adds exciting new features that makes this market-leading site even more useful for composition students and instructors. Access cards to MyCompLab 2.0 can be packaged with *The Allyn & Bacon Guide to Writing* at no additional cost to students! (MyCompLab 2.0 is available four versions: Website, CourseCompass, Blackboard, and WebCT.)

Writing Resources

- *Exchange:* Pearson's online peer and instructor writing review program. Use *Exchange* to comment on student papers at the word, sentence, paragraph, or paper level—or have your students review each other's work.
- NEW! *Process:* Guided assistance through the stages of the writing process, with interactive worksheets and in-depth exercises for each stage.
- NEW! *Activities:* Provides 100 different writing activities in which students respond to videos, images, Web sites, and writing prompts.
- NEW! *Model Documents Gallery:* Over 50 sample papers, reports, and documents from across the curriculum.

Grammar Resources

- NEW! *Diagnostics:* Two new research-based, 50-question diagnostic tests comprehensively assess student skills in basic grammar, sentence grammar, mechanics, punctuation, and style. Results pages provide overall proficiency scores as well as question-by-question feedback.

- *ExerciseZone:* Over 3,600 self-grading practice items cover all major topics of grammar, style, and usage. NEW! Sentence and paragraph editing exercises.
- NEW! *ESL ExerciseZone:* Over 650 self-grading practice exercises for students whose first language is not English.

Research Resources

- *Research Navigator:* Access to credible, reliable sources, including EBSCO's ContentSelect Database and *The New York Times* Search-by-Subject Archive, plus hundreds of pages of material on the research process itself. Includes a new bibliography-maker program!
- *Avoiding Plagiarism:* A self-guided exploration of the issue of plagiarism, these tutorials teach students to recognize plagiarism and avoid its practice in both MLA and APA formats.

Tutor Center

Students using MyCompLab receive complimentary access to Longman's English Tutor Center. Our live, qualified college instructors help students use resources in MyCompLab effectively and will review student papers for organization and consistent grammar errors.

MyDropBox

Instructors who have ordered a MyCompLab Value Pack for their course can receive complimentary access to MyDropBox, a leading online plagiarism detection service.

- *Longman Grammar and Documentation Study Card:* Packed with useful information, this colorful, laminated study card is an 8-page guide to key grammar, punctuation, and documentation skills.
- *The Longman Writer's Portfolio and Student Planner:* This unique portfolio/planner includes an assessing/organizing area (including a grammar diagnostic test, a spelling quiz, and project planning worksheets), a before and during writing area (including peer review sheets, editing checklists, writing self-evaluations, and a personal editing profile), and an after-writing area (including a progress chart, a final table of contents, and a final assessment).
- *10 Practices of Highly Successful Students:* Murphy's popular supplement helps students learn crucial study skills, offering concise tips for a successful career in college. Topics include time management, test-taking, reading critically, stress, and motivation.
- *The Longman Editing Exercises:* This print supplement allows students to practice correct English in context with dozens of paragraph editing exercises in various topic areas of grammar, style and punctuation.
- *The Longman Writer's Journal:* Written by Mimi Markus, this journal contains helpful journal writing strategies, sample journal entries by other students, and many writing prompts and topics to get students writing.

- *The Longman Researcher's Journal:* Designed to help students work through the steps involved in writing a research paper, each section contains record-keeping strategies, checklists, graphic organizers, and pages for taking notes from sources.
- *Literacy Library Series:* This series of brief booklets offers informed, detailed guidelines for writing in academic, public, and workplace communities.
- *Analyzing Literature: A Guide for Students:* This supplement provides critical reading strategies, writing advice, and sample student papers to help students interpret and discuss literary works from a variety of genres.
- *Visual Communication,* Second Edition: Susan Hilligoss' popular text introduces document-design principles and features practical discussions of space, type, organization, pattern, graphic elements, and visuals.
- *Discounted Dictionaries and Thesauruses:* The following can be packaged at a discount with *The Allyn & Bacon Guide to Writing:*
  - *The New American Webster Handy College Dictionary,* Third Edition
  - *The Oxford American Desk Dictionary and Thesaurus,* Second Edition
  - *The Oxford Essential Thesaurus*
  - *Merriam-Webster's Collegiate Dictionary,* Tenth Edition

Acknowledgments

We wish to give special thanks to several scholars who have contributed in special ways to this edition. Thanks to our longtime colleague and friend Virginia Chappell of Marquette University, who revised the research chapters in Part Four and who clarified and updated all the explanations of MLA and APA formatting and documentation. For her scholarship, library savvy, generosity, understanding of students, and graceful writing style we are particularly thankful. We also thank psychologist Erica Lilleleht and sociologist Mark Cohan of Seattle University for their thoughtful reviews of the new chapter on field research (Chapter 10) and for their generous personal conversations aimed at deepening our understanding of social science methods. We also wish to thank again various scholars who have written commissioned sections of *The Allyn & Bacon Guide to Writing* for previous editions and whose work remains in the fourth edition. Thanks to Tim McGee of Philadelphia University, who wrote our section on giving speeches and PowerPoint presentations (Chapter 23). Thanks also to Alice Gillam of the University of Wisconsin–Milwaukee, who authored the chapter on self-reflective writing (Chapter 25) and to Virginia Chappell of Marquette University, who contributed significantly to Chapter 12 on analyzing a short story. In addition Virginia Chappell wishes to thank several colleagues and friends for their insights regarding the revision of the research chapters: Roger Conner, Julie O'Keeffe, Spencer McCormick, Mark Albrecht, Brent Elrod, and Celeste McNamara. Finally, we wish to thank again Christy Friend of the University of South Carolina, Columbia, who wrote Chapter 23 on essay examinations for the first edition.

Our deep thanks and appreciation again go to Eben Ludlow, our editor, with whom we worked productively for twenty years. As vice president of Longman Publishers, Eben was one of the most experienced and insightful editors in college publishing and the best editor any textbook writer could wish for. We are also particularly grateful to our development editor, Marion Castellucci, whose superb command of both big-picture issues and essential details, combined with unfailing composure and sense of humor, made it possible for us to meet the demands of this revision. Without her extensive editorial experience, invaluable organizational skills, and steady professionalism, this revision would have been impossible.

We would also like to thank a number of students who provided invaluable research assistance for this edition as well as their student perspective on important issues: John Bean and June Johnson wish to thank Jean Bessette and Tiffany Anderson, two of Seattle University's most talented Writing Center consultants.

We would also like to thank the many scholars and teachers who reviewed *The Allyn & Bacon Guide to Writing* in its various stages. Several scholars gave us chapter-by-chapter advice at each stage of the manuscript, and to them we owe our deepest appreciation:

Larry Beason, University of South Alabama
Gregory R. Glau, Arizona State University
Jennifer Liethen Kunka, Francis Marion University
Lisa J. McClure, Southern Illinois University, Carbondale
Wendy Sharer, East Carolina University
Bill Stiffler, Harford Community College
Donna Strickland, University of Missouri—Columbia
Diane S. Thompson, Harrisburg Area Community College
Scott Weeden, Indiana University Purdue University Indianapolis
Debbie J. Williams, Abilene Christian University

Many gave us initial advice on how to proceed with the fourth edition:

Hugh Burns, Texas Woman's University
Virginia Chappell, Marquette University
Ron Christiansen, Salt Lake Community College
Gregory R. Glau, Arizona State University
Emily Golson, University of Northern Colorado
Melissa Helquist, Salt Lake Community College
Ruth M. Higgins, Mitchell College
Rosemary B. Johnson, Mitchell College
Michael Kramp, University of Northern Colorado
Bonnie Lenore Kyburz, Utah Valley State College
Lindsay Lewan, Arapahoe Community College
Phillip P. Marzluf, Kansas State University
Sharon James McGee, Southern Illinois University, Edwardsville
Carole Clark Papper, Ball State University
Irving N. Rothman, University of Houston
Wendy Sharer, East Carolina University

Linda Shelton, Utah Valley State College
Suzanne Shumway, North Central Michigan College
Donna Strickland, University of Missouri–Columbia
David Susman, Salt Lake Community College
Scott Weeden, Indiana University Purdue University Indianapolis
Carolyn Young, University of Wyoming

Most of all, we are indebted to our students, who have made the teaching of composition such a joy. We thank them for their insights and for their willingness to engage with problems, discuss ideas, and, as they compose and revise, share with us their frustrations and their triumphs. They have sustained our love of teaching and inspired us to write this book.

Finally, John Bean thanks his wife, Kit, also a professional composition teacher, whose dedication to her students as writers and individuals manifests the sustaining values of our unique profession. John also thanks his children, Matthew, Andrew, Stephen, and Sarah, who have grown to adulthood since he began writing textbooks. June Johnson thanks her husband, Kenneth Bube, for his loving support, his interest in teaching, and his expert understanding of the importance of writing in mathematics and the sciences. Finally, she thanks her daughter, Jane Ellen, who has offered encouragement and support in countless ways.

JOHN D. RAMAGE
JOHN C. BEAN
JUNE JOHNSON

The
Allyn & Bacon
Guide to Writing
Brief Edition

A Rhetoric for College Writers

This recent advertisement for the Hummer H2, taken from a surprising bird's-eye-view camera angle, depends on the viewer's memory of what the Hummer looks like from other angles—its power, size, and rugged sleekness. Note the way the bright image of the Hummer dominates the ad and reinforces the confident tone of the slogan: "Like nothing else." Consider the ad-making team's intentions in focusing exclusively on the Hummer itself, in choosing this camera angle, in creating the unusual terrain beneath the vehicle, in placing the tiny words "Lost? Cool" in the top right corner, and in relying on the Hummer's reputation as a versatile, all-terrain vehicle with top-of-the-line quality. Who seems to be the target audience for this ad?

This advertisement is part of the For Writing and Discussion exercise in Chapter 1, on page 11.

LOST? COOL

THE H2. **HUMMER**® LIKE NOTHING ELSE.™

HUMMER.COM

Part 1 A Rhetoric for College Writers

1

Posing Problems
The Demands of College Writing

It seems to me, then, that the way to help people become better writers is not to tell them that they must first learn the rules of grammar, that they must develop a four-part outline, that they must consult the experts and collect all the useful information. These things may have their place. But none of them is as crucial as having a good, interesting question.

—RODNEY KILCUP, *HISTORIAN*

Our purpose in this introductory chapter is to help you see writers as questioners and problem posers—a view of writing that we believe will lead to your greatest growth as a college-level thinker and writer. In particular, we want you to think of writers as people who pose interesting questions or problems and struggle to work out answers or responses to them. As we show in this chapter, writers pose two sorts of problems: *subject-matter problems* (for example, Should the homeless mentally ill be placed involuntarily in mental hospitals?) and *rhetorical problems* (for example, How much background about the homeless population does my audience need? What is their current attitude about mental institutions? What form and style should I use?).

We don't mean to make this focus on problems sound scary. Indeed, humans pose and solve problems all the time and often take great pleasure in doing so. Psychologists who study critical and creative thinking see problem solving as a productive and positive activity. According to one psychologist, "Critical thinkers are actively engaged with life. [. . .] They appreciate creativity, they are innovators, and they exude a sense that life is full of possibilities."* By focusing first on the kinds of problems that writers pose and struggle with, we hope to increase your own engagement and pleasure in becoming a writer.

In this chapter we introduce you to the following concepts and principles:

- Why a writing course is valuable, with special emphasis on the connection between writing and thinking

---

*Academic writers regularly document their sources. The standard method for documenting sources in student papers and in many professional scholarly articles is the MLA or the APA citation system explained in Chapter 22. In this text we have cited our sources in an "Acknowledgments" section. To find our source for this quotation (or for the quotation from Kilcup above), see the Acknowledgments at the end of the text.

- How writers pose subject-matter problems, in which they wrestle with the complexities of their topics
- How writers pose rhetorical problems, in which they must make decisions about content, organization, and style based on their purpose, audience, and genre
- How the rules of writing vary along a continuum from closed to open prose
- How to ask good subject-matter questions and show how they are problematic and significant

The chapter concludes with a brief writing assignment in which you can try your own hand at proposing a subject-matter question.

Why Take a Writing Course?

Before turning directly to the notion of writers as questioners and problem posers, let's ask why a writing course can be valuable for you.

For some people, being a writer is part of their identity, so much so that when asked, "What do you do?" they are apt to respond, "I'm a writer." Poets, novelists, scriptwriters, journalists, technical writers, grant writers, self-help book authors, and so on see themselves as writers the way other people see themselves as chefs, realtors, bankers, or musicians. But many people who don't think of themselves primarily as writers nevertheless *use* writing—often frequently—throughout their careers. They are engineers writing proposals or project reports; attorneys writing legal briefs; nurses writing patient assessments; business executives writing financial analyses or management reports; concerned citizens writing letters to the editor about public affairs; college professors writing articles for scholarly journals.

In our view, all these kinds of writing are valuable and qualify their authors as writers. If you already identify yourself as a writer, then you won't need much external motivation for improving your writing. But if you have little interest in writing for its own sake and aspire instead to become a nurse, an engineer, a business executive, a social worker, or a marine biologist, then you might question the benefits of taking a writing course.

What are these benefits? First of all, the skills you learn in this course will be directly transferable to your other college courses, where you will have to write papers in a wide variety of styles. Lower-division (general education or core) courses often focus on general academic writing, while upper-division courses in your major introduce you to the specialized writing and thinking of your chosen field. What college professors value are the kinds of questioning, analyzing, and arguing skills that this course will help you develop. You will emerge from this course as a better reader and thinker and a clearer and more persuasive writer, able to meet the demands of different academic writing situations.

Effective writing skills are also essential for most professional careers. To measure the importance of writing to career success, researchers Andrea Lunsford and Lisa Ede surveyed randomly selected members of such professional organizations as the American Consulting Engineers Counsel, the American Institute of Chemists, the American Psychological Association, and the International City

Management Association. They discovered that members of these organizations spend, on average, forty-four percent of their professional time writing, including (most commonly) letters, memos, short reports, instructional materials, and professional articles and essays.

Besides the pragmatic benefits of college and career success, learning to write well can bring you the personal pleasure of a richer mental life. As we show throughout this text, writing is closely allied to thinking and to the innate satisfaction you take in exercising your curiosity, creativity, and problem-solving ability. Writing connects you to others and helps you discover and express ideas that you would otherwise never think or say. Unlike speaking, writing gives you time to think deep and long about an idea. Because you can revise writing, it lets you pursue a problem in stages, with each new draft reflecting a deeper, clearer, or more complex level of thought. In other words, writing isn't just a way to express thought; it is a way to do the thinking itself. The act of writing stimulates, challenges, and stretches your mental powers and, when you do it well, is profoundly satisfying.

Subject Matter Problems: The Starting Point of Writing

Having made a connection between writing and thinking, we now move to the spirit of inquiry that drives the writing process. From your previous schooling, you are probably familiar with the term *thesis statement,* which is the main point a writer wants to make in an essay. However, you may not have thought much about the question that lies behind the thesis, which is the problem or issue that the writer is wrestling with. An essay's thesis statement is actually the writer's one-sentence summary answer to this question, and it is this question that has motivated the writer's thinking. Experienced writers immerse themselves in subject matter questions in pursuit of answers or solutions. They write to share their proposed solutions with readers who share their interests. As we will show in Chapter 2, introductions to academic essays typically begin with the question or problem that the writer plans to address. In this section we show you more fully the nature of subject matter questions that initiate the writing process.

Shared Problems Unite Writers and Readers

Everywhere we turn, we see writers and readers forming communities based on questions or problems of mutual interest. Perhaps nowhere are such communities more evident than in academe. Many college professors are engaged in research projects stimulated and driven by questions or problems. At a recent workshop for new faculty members, we asked participants to write a brief description of a question or problem that motivated them to write a seminar paper or article. Here are two examples of their responses.

A Biochemistry Professor During periods of starvation, the human body makes physiological adaptations to preserve essential protein mass. Unfortunately, these adaptations don't work well during long-term starvation. After the body depletes its carbohydrate storage, it must shift to depleting protein in order to produce glucose. Eventually, this loss of functional protein leads to metabolic dysfunction and death. Interestingly, several animal species are capable of surviving for extensive periods without food and water while conserving protein and maintaining glucose levels. How do the bodies of these animals accomplish this feat? I wanted to investigate the metabolic functioning of these animals, which might lead to insights into the human situation.

A Journalism Professor Several years ago, I knocked on the wooden front door of the home of an elderly woman in Tucson, Arizona. Tears of grief rolled down her cheeks as she opened the door. The tears turned to anger when I explained that I was a reporter and wished to talk with her about her son's death in jail. Her face hardened. "What right do you have coming here?" I recall her saying. "Why are you bothering me?" Those questions have haunted me throughout my journalism career. Do journalists have the right to intrude on a person's grief? Can they exercise it any time they want? What values do journalists use to decide when to intrude and violate someone's privacy?

Of course these are not new college students speaking about problems they posed; they are college professors recalling problems that fueled a piece of professional writing. We share these problems with you to persuade you that most college professors value question asking and want you to be caught up, as they are, in the spirit of inquiry.

As you progress through your college career, you will find yourself increasingly engaged with questions. All around college campuses you'll find clusters of professors and students asking questions about all manner of curious things—the reproductive cycles of worms and bugs, the surface structure of metals, the social significance of obscure poets, gender roles among the Kalahari Bushmen, the meaning of Balinese cockfighting, the effect of tax structure on economies, the rise of labor unions in agriculture, the role of prostitutes in medieval India, the properties of concrete, and almost anything else a human being might wonder about. A quick review of the magazine rack at any large supermarket reveals that similar communities have formed around everything from hot rods to model railroads, from computers to kayaks to cooking.

At the heart of all these communities of writers and readers is an interest in common questions and the hope for better or different answers. Writers write because they have something new or surprising or challenging to say in response to a question. Readers read because they share the writer's interest in the problem and want to deepen their understanding.

Posing a Problem: A Case Study of a Beginning College Writer

So far we have talked about how professional writers pose problems. In this section we show you how student writer Christopher Leigh posed a problem for an argumentative paper requiring research.

At the start of his process, Christopher was interested in the issue of school violence. Like many of his classmates, Christopher had been disturbed by the massacre at Columbine High School in Littleton, Colorado, in April 1999. When he discussed Columbine with his small group in his first-year composition course, he explained that these killings were especially unsettling for him because Columbine seemed like a safe, middle-class school with no previous record of violence. He wondered what would cause a normal-seeming group of kids to open fire on their classmates.

When he started doing research, he had formulated only a broad question: What can be done to prevent school violence? On his first trip to the library, however, he came across an article on psychological profiling. Here is what he wrote in his journal on that day:

> Today I came across an article in the *New York Times* that disturbed me. It was about psychological profiling, which means that they figure out psychological traits that are apt to indicate a person may become violent. Then they look for kids in the schools that fit those traits. After reading this article, I began to think about whether or not the use of profiles to identify potentially violent students is effective, and if it is somehow a violation of students' rights or privacy. Profiles that use signs such as "antisocial behavior" and "mood swings" may be problematic because almost any student would fit the profiles at some point. Think of all the bad, depressing days that teenagers have. And singling out a student because he or she fits the profile is never going to be able to predict for sure if that student will become violent. I know someone who was suspended for making a joke about a bomb, and even though it was a careless remark, she had no intention of doing harm. So profiling may victimize students who are not violent. Right now my feeling is that profiling in any form is wrong, but I need to learn more about how they are used and if they are effective. Also if they violate students' rights, and how other students feel about them.

After writing this journal entry, Christopher wrote out his new research question as follows: Is psychological profiling an effective way to help reduce school violence? When he discussed this question with his small group, his friends thought it was an interesting question worth researching. The group was divided about profiling. Some thought that schools should do everything they can to identify disturbed classmates and intervene with psychological counseling. Others thought profiling is a total violation of privacy. This division of opinion convinced Christopher that the question was a good one.

We will return to Christopher's story occasionally throughout this text. You can read his final paper in Chapter 22, pages 675–686, where Christopher argues against metal detectors in schools—a moderately changed focus from his initial interest in psychological profiling. You can also read his earlier exploratory paper (Ch. 8, pp. 197–202), which narrates the evolution of his thinking as he researched ways of preventing school violence.

Posing Your Own Subject-Matter Questions

Where do good questions come from and how can you learn to pose them? At the outset, we should say that the kinds of questions we discuss in this chapter may lead you toward new and unfamiliar ways of thinking. Beginning college students typically value questions that have right answers. Students ask their professors questions about a subject because they are puzzled by confusing parts of a text-book, a lecture, or an assigned reading. They hope their professors will explain the confusing material clearly. Their purpose in asking these questions is to elimi-nate misunderstandings, not to open up controversy and debate. Although basic comprehension questions are important, they are not the kinds of inquiry questions that initiate strong college-level writing and thinking.

The kinds of questions that stimulate the writing most valued in college are open-ended questions that focus on unknowns or invite multiple points of view rather than factual questions that have single right answers. These are what historian Rodney Kilcup refers to when he says that writers should begin with a "good, interesting question" (see the epigraph to this chapter, p. 5). For Kilcup, a good question sets the writer on the path of inquiry, critical thinking, analysis, and argument.

Later in your college career, many of the questions you pursue will come from your chosen major, particularly from controversies, uncertainties, and unknowns within the subject matter of that discipline. Nevertheless, you currently have many other areas of experience or knowledge that can lead to good, interesting questions. Consider, for example, the various communities to which you belong: your dorm or apartment complex; your campus; your city or region of the country; your job or volunteer work; your connection with any religious, sports, or activity group. Consider also your civic role as a citizen of a city, state, nation, and global community. If you read newspapers or magazines, watch television, listen to radio programs, or surf the Internet, you are exposed to problems that merit investigation and critical analysis. Many writers find that questions emerge when they perceive differences between their own views and those of others within a given community or when they discover confusions, gaps, and inconsistencies within information, ideas, or beliefs. Good questions can arise when you do any of the following:

- Discover holes in your knowledge of something
- Note gaps or inconsistencies in the evidence for something, or realize that you and someone else are drawing different conclusions from the same set of facts
- Think about contradictions among different perspectives and different points of view
- Consider why you are dissatisfied with someone else's explanation of a phenomenon, analysis of an event, or solution to a problem
- Feel curious about the cause, consequence, purpose, function, or value of something
- Note discrepancies between the ideal and the real, between what someone values and what he or she does, between the current state of something and your desired state of something

Once you start practicing these ways of thinking, you will see yourself as a more powerful writer able to contribute your own views to a community of readers drawn into conversation by mutual interest in a problem.

Characteristics of Good Subject-Matter Questions

Questions that lead to good college-level writing generally exhibit three main qualities:

- *A good question is problematic.* By problematic, we mean that community members do not currently know the answer or agree on the answer. A question whose answer can be looked up in a reference book or solved by applying a mathematical formula is not problematic.
- *A good question is significant.* In addition, a good question should have something at stake. Writers need to answer their readers' "So what?" question by showing that a problem is worth pursuing. Why does the problem matter? Who are its stakeholders? How will a community gain by considering the writer's answer to the question?
- *A good question is interesting to the writer.* Finally, you as writer need to be genuinely engaged with this question; it has to be a real question for you, a problem in which you feel invested. You can infuse your writing with vitality only when you, the writer, are truly curious about a question or passionately concerned about it.

Our way of thinking about problems has been motivated by the South American educator Paulo Freire, who wanted his students (often poor, illiterate villagers) to become *problematizers* instead of memorizers. Freire opposed what he called "the banking method" of education, in which students deposited knowledge in their memory banks and then made withdrawals during exams. The banking method, Freire believed, left third world villagers passive and helpless to improve their situations in life. He wanted students to ask disturbing questions and then to act on their discoveries. When students are taught to read and write through the banking method, they learn the word *water* by repeating an irrelevant, self-evident sentence such as, "The water is in the well." With Freire's method of teaching literacy, students might learn the word *water* by asking, "Why is the water dirty and who is responsible?" Freire believed that good questions have stakes and that answering the questions can make a difference in the world.

For Writing and Discussion

Your task: Working in small groups or as a whole class, create a list of problematic, significant, and interesting questions about any topic area assigned by your instructor. In the following pages we provide a context for one possible subject: the problem of the world's growing desire for automobiles in the face of a declining supply of fossil fuels. If you choose this topic, derive your questions from your personal experiences with automobiles and your energy knowledge based on reading and observation. For further context, we provide an array of data for you to examine.

(continued)

The seven visual and verbal texts in this data set present a range of perspectives on energy usage and automobiles, yet these texts represent only a small sampling of the views currently being voiced. As you read through the passages and ponder the images and graphics in light of your own personal experiences, look for controversies, inconsistencies, and gaps in knowledge that can prompt you to articulate problems worth exploring.

Some examples of questions: The range of questions you can ask is very wide. You can ask questions based on your own personal experience and observations ("What can we do to make bike riding more popular?" or "How did Hummers or Dodge Ram pickups become prestigious urban vehicles?"), or you can ask questions spinning off the exhibits ("What will happen to our way of life if oil becomes unaffordable?" or "Should the government force people into smaller cars? If so, how?") When your class shares the questions you have produced, you will begin experiencing what it is like to be drawn into inquiry—to feel the pleasure and exhilaration of doing your own critical thinking in response to a problem.

Exhibit 1: The Hummer ad that appears on page 3 as the part opener image for Part One of this text.

Exhibit 2: Excerpt from news story on China

SHIFTING INTO HIGH GEAR

From a nation of bikes and donkey carts, China has shifted to a mobile population in just a generation. Automobile sales on the mainland are doubling almost every year, with all the car makers racing to China to cash in on the world's most revved-up auto market. . . .

China really has been a dream market for the world's auto makers, who have seen profits steadily decline due to gloomy economic conditions around the globe. Except in China.

In 2002, for instance, China sales soared 37 percent, even as overall sales across Europe tumbled seven percent. And, contrary to most of the mainland products, profit margins in China are sky-high, amongst the world's biggest margins.

No wonder all the world's auto makers are established on the mainland. Most arrived less than a decade ago. All are racing to keep apace of demand.

—Source: http://www.gluckman.com/ChinaCars.html

Exhibit 3: Excerpt from the Bush Administration's *National Energy Policy*

Estimates indicate that over the next 20 years, U.S. oil consumption will increase by 33 percent, natural gas consumption by well over 50 percent, and demand for electricity will rise by 45 percent. If America's energy production grows at the same rate as it did in the 1990s we will face an ever-increasing gap.

Increases on this scale will require preparation and action today. Yet America has not been bringing on line the necessary supplies and infrastructure. . . .

A primary goal of the National Energy Policy is to add supply from diverse sources. This means [increasing the domestic production of] oil, gas, and coal. It also means [increasing our use of] hydropower and nuclear power. And it means making greater use of non-hydro renewable sources now available.

Exhibit 4: Excerpt from "Greenpeace Responds to the Bush/Cheney National Energy Policy Task Force"

The Bush/Cheney Task Force's National Energy Policy leads the nation down the wrong road. Though the administration claims to have crafted a long-term solution, the shortsighted policy includes:

- No efforts to cut the nation's global warming pollution
- Massive electric power plant construction—1,300 new polluting fossil fuel and nuclear power plants are proposed
- New oil extraction in ecologically sensitive areas such as the Arctic National Wildlife Refuge and the Rocky Mountains
- More oil refineries, pipelines and electrical transmission lines
- Additional U.S. taxpayer subsidies for the fossil fuel and nuclear industries

And in an effort to hide their true agenda, the Administration proposes:

- Minor efforts toward saving energy through energy efficiency and renewable energy sources

> —Source: http://archive.greenpeace.org/climate/climatecountdown/
> documents/bushrealitycheck.pdf

Exhibit 5: News analysis excerpt

In interviews at the New York International Auto Show this month, top executives of General Motors and the Ford Motor company, both of which make and sell a lot of cars in Europe, reiterated their support for high gasoline taxes—as opposed to stricter fuel economy regulations.

"Anything that can align the individual customer's purchase decisions with society's goals [is] the way to go," Ford's chairman and chief executive, William Clay Ford, Jr., said, adding that his company has previously supported a 50-cent increase in gas taxes. . . .

Mr. Ford said the current regulatory system, which compels automakers to make cars and trucks that meet minimum standards for fuel efficiency, "puts the manufacturer in this tug of war that's unsustainable between what the customer wants and what society says it wants."

In other words, most customers want bigger and faster cars—actually, light-duty trucks like sport utility vehicles—not efficient ones.

> —Danny Hakim, "A Fuel-Saving Proposal From Your Automaker: Tax the Gas"
> *The New York Times* (18 April 2004): BU 5

Exhibit 6: From "The Energy Guy Website" (Ray Darby, PE)

Let's look at the case for oil, our most used fuel. Data from the *Energy Information Administration (EIA)* indicates about 981.4 billion barrels of *oil reserves remain* on the planet (it was 1,033 BB when I checked a year earlier?!?). Although this may sound like a lot, the world has consumed about 800 billion barrels of oil thus far. Half of the oil we've used so far has been consumed since 1970—a mere 28 years ago. In addition to the known (verified) oil reserves on the planet, there are an estimated 547 billion more barrels of "technically feasible" oil to recover. That leaves us with a total of 1,528 billion barrels.

(continued)

The world consumed about *75 billion barrels* of oil in 1999. In another 38 years from now, at a constant 2% rate of world oil consumption growth we will have used up virtually all of the remaining oil on the planet! . . . Unfortunately, the aforementioned "current rate of world oil consumption growth" is not likely to remain constant at 2%, but increase due to world economic development. For example, the annual *percent change in world oil consumption* (over the preceding year) was 0.8% in 1998, 1.7% in 1999, and 2.4% (estimated) for 2000 . . .

Are we going to run out of oil? No. It will get very expensive long before that! It's just a matter of time and circumstances, supply and demand. As demand continues to grow while reserves continue to decline, it's simply a matter of time before a permanent oil-price spiral begins. The graphic below illustrates how supply problems will begin to limit production. The area under the curve is the total amount of (known) oil remaining on the planet (the dotted line represents production if additional discoveries, which can be reasonably anticipated, are included). Note the peak is estimated to occur around 2010 (only eight short years away)!

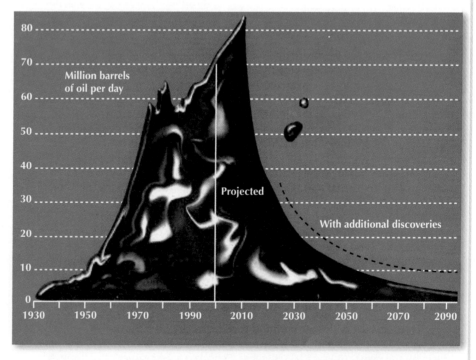

—Source: http://www.theenergyguy.com/IssuesSummary.html

Exhibit 7: Oil consumption table

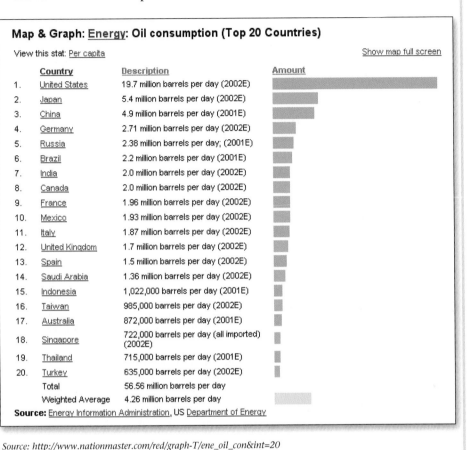

Source: http://www.nationmaster.com/red/graph-T/ene_oil_con&int=20

Rhetorical Problems: Reaching Readers Effectively

So far we have been focusing on subject-matter problems. In this section we shift our attention to rhetorical problems.

By rhetorical problems, we refer to a network of questions writers must ask about audience, purpose, and genre (a *genre* is a recurring type of writing with established conventions, such as an academic article, a personal essay, a newspaper feature story, a grant proposal, an article for *Seventeen* or *Rolling Stone,* a

Web page, and so forth). These questions often loom as large for writers as do the subject-matter problems that drive their writing in the first place. Suppose, for example, that you have asked the subject-matter question: To what extent will hydrogen cars be an effective solution to the problem of dwindling fossil fuels? Suppose further that your research casts doubt on hydrogen cars. Consider the number of rhetorical problems you must think about as you sit down to write a draft.

One of our students did a short research project on this question. You can read her paper in Chapter 9, pp. 233–235.

- Who are my readers? How much background do they need on hydrogen cell cars? Do I need to explain how hydrogen cells work?
- Are my readers already interested in the problem of dwindling supply of fossil fuels? Do they believe the world may soon run out of oil, or do they think the supply is endless? Do I need to hook them on this problem?
- Should I take a strong stand against hydrogen cars or just raise some doubts?
- How should I organize my essay to make it most effective?
- Should I write this paper as a formal college research paper or as a more popular magazine-style article?

Subject-matter problems and rhetorical problems are often so closely linked that writers can't address one without addressing the other. You would not even be able to decide on a title, for example, until you decided whether the paper should have an academic or a popular tone.

In Chapters 2 and 3 we discuss in more detail the kinds of rhetorical problems that writers must pose and solve. In this chapter we simply introduce you to one extended example of a rhetorical problem. From a student's point of view, we might call this "the problem of varying rules." From our perspective, we call it a problem of "genre"—or "what kind of prose does my audience expect me to write?"

An Example of a Rhetorical Problem: When to Choose Closed Versus Open Forms

In our experience, beginning college writers are often bothered by the ambiguity and slipperiness of rules governing writing. Many beginning writers wish that good writing followed consistent rules such as "Never use 'I' in a formal paper" or "Start every paragraph with a topic sentence." The problem is that different kinds of writing follow different rules, leaving the writer with rhetorical choices rather than with hard-and-fast formulas for success. To develop this point, we begin by asking you to consider a problem about how writing might be classified.

Read the following short pieces of nonfiction prose. The first is a letter to the editor written by a professional civil engineer in response to a newspaper editorial arguing for the development of wind-generated electricity. The second short piece is entitled "A Festival of Rain." It was written by the American poet and religious writer Thomas Merton, a Trappist monk. After reading the two samples carefully, proceed to the discussion questions that follow.

READINGS

David Rockwood
A Letter to the Editor

1   Your editorial on November 16, "Get Bullish on Wind Power," is based on fantasy rather than fact. There are several basic reasons why wind-generated power can in no way serve as a reasonable major alternative to other electrical energy supply alternatives for the Pacific Northwest power system.

2   First and foremost, wind power is unreliable. Electric power generation is evaluated not only on the amount of energy provided, but also on its ability to meet system peak load requirements on an hourly, daily, and weekly basis. In other words, an effective power system would have to provide enough electricity to meet peak demands in a situation when the wind energy would be unavailable—either in no wind situations or in severe blizzard conditions, which would shut down the wind generators. Because wind power cannot be relied on at times of peak needs, it would have to be backed up by other power generation resources at great expense and duplication of facilities.

3   Secondly, there are major unsolved problems involved in the design of wind generation facilities, particularly for those located in rugged mountain areas. Ice storms, in particular, can cause sudden dynamic problems for the rotating blades and mechanisms which could well result in breakdown or failure of the generators. Furthermore, the design of the facilities to meet the stresses imposed by high winds in these remote mountain regions, in the order of 125 miles per hour, would indeed escalate the costs.

4   Thirdly, the environmental impact of constructing wind generation facilities amounting to 28 percent of the region's electrical supply system (as proposed in your editorial) would be tremendous. The Northwest Electrical Power system presently has a capacity of about 37,000 megawatts of hydro power and 10,300 megawatts of thermal, for a total of about 48,000 megawatts. Meeting 28 percent of this capacity by wind power generators would, most optimistically, require about 13,400 wind towers, each with about 1,000 kilowatt (one megawatt) generating capacity. These towers, some 100 to 200 feet high, would have to be located in the mountains of Oregon and Washington. These would encompass hundreds of square miles of pristine mountain area, which, together with interconnecting transmission facilities, control works, and roads, would indeed have major adverse environmental impacts on the region.

5   There are many other lesser problems of control and maintenance of such a system. Let it be said that, from my experience and knowledge as a professional engineer, the use of wind power as a major resource in the Pacific Northwest power system is strictly a pipe dream.

Thomas Merton
A Festival of Rain

1   Let me say this before rain becomes a utility that they can plan and distribute for money. By "they" I mean the people who cannot understand that rain is a festival, who do not appreciate its gratuity, who think that what has no price has no value, that what cannot be sold is not real, so that the only way to make something *actual* is to place it on the market. The time will come when they will sell you even your rain. At the moment it is still free, and I am in it. I celebrate its gratuity and its meaninglessness.

2   The rain I am in is not like the rain of cities. It fills the woods with an immense and confused sound. It covers the flat roof of the cabin and its porch with insistent and controlled rhythms. And I listen, because it reminds me again and again that the whole world runs by rhythms I have not yet learned to recognize, rhythms that are not those of the engineer.

3   I came up here from the monastery last night, sloshing through the corn fields, said Vespers, and put some oatmeal on the Coleman stove for supper. . . . The night became very dark. The rain surrounded the whole cabin with its enormous virginal myth, a whole world of meaning, of secrecy, of silence, of rumor. Think of it: all that speech pouring down, selling nothing, judging nobody, drenching the thick mulch of dead leaves, soaking the trees, filling the gullies and crannies of the wood with water, washing out the places where men have stripped the hillside! What a thing it is to sit absolutely alone, in a forest, at night, cherished by this wonderful, unintelligible, perfectly innocent speech, the most comforting speech in the world, the talk that rain makes by itself all over the ridges, and the talk of the watercourses everywhere in the hollows!

4   Nobody started it, nobody is going to stop it. It will talk as long as it wants, this rain. As long as it talks I am going to listen.

5   But I am also going to sleep, because here in this wilderness I have learned how to sleep again. Here I am not alien. The trees I know, the night I know, the rain I know. I close my eyes and instantly sink into the whole rainy world of which I am a part, and the world goes on with me in it, for I am not alien to it.

For Writing and Discussion

Working in small groups or as a whole class, try to reach consensus on the following specific tasks:

1. What are the main differences between the two types of writing? If you are working in groups, help your recorder prepare a presentation describing the differences between Rockwood's writing and Merton's writing.
2. Create a metaphor, simile, or analogy that best sums up your feelings about the most important differences between Rockwood's and Merton's writing: "Rockwood's writing is like . . . , but Merton's writing is like. . . . "
3. Explain why your metaphors are apt. How do your metaphors help clarify or illuminate the differences between the two pieces of writing?

Now that you have done some thinking on your own about the differences between these two examples, turn to our brief analysis.

Distinctions between Closed and Open Forms of Writing

David Rockwood's letter and Thomas Merton's mini-essay are both examples of nonfiction prose. But as these examples illustrate, nonfiction prose can vary enormously in form and style. From the perspective of structure, we can place nonfiction prose along a continuum that goes from closed to open forms of writing (see Figure 1.1).

Of our two pieces of prose, Rockwood's letter illustrates tightly closed writing and falls at the far left end of the continuum. The elements that make this writing closed are the presence of an explicit thesis in the introduction (i.e., wind-generated power isn't a reasonable alternative energy source in the Pacific Northwest) and the

FIGURE 1.1 A Continuum of Essay Types: Closed to Open Forms

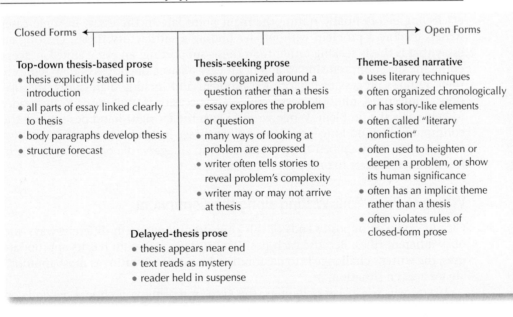

writer's consistent development of that thesis throughout the body (i.e., "First and foremost, wind power is unreliable. . . . Secondly, there are major unsolved [design] problems. . . . Thirdly, . . . "). Once the thesis is stated, the reader knows the point of the essay and can predict its structure. The reader also knows that the writer's point won't change as the essay progresses. Because its structure is transparent and predictable, the success of closed-form prose rests entirely on its ideas, which must "surprise" readers by asserting something new, challenging, doubtful, or controversial. It aims to change readers' view of the subject through the power of reason, logic, and evidence. Closed-form prose is what most college professors write when doing their own scholarly research, and it is what they most often expect of their students. It is also the most common kind of writing in professional and business contexts.

Merton's "A Festival of Rain" falls toward the right end of the closed-to-open continuum. It resists reduction to a single, summarizable thesis. Although Merton praises rain, and clearly opposes the consumer culture that will try to "sell" you the rain, it is hard to pin down exactly what he means by "festival" or by rain's "gratuity and its meaninglessness." The main organizing principle of Merton's piece, like that of most open-form prose, is a story or narrative—in this case the story of Merton's leaving the monastery to sleep in the rain-drenched cabin. Rather than announce a thesis and support it with reasons and evidence, Merton lets his point emerge suggestively from his story and his language. Open-form essays still have a focus, but the focus is more like a theme in fiction than like a thesis in argument. Readers may argue over its meaning in the same way that they argue over the meaning of a film or poem or novel.

As you can see from the continuum in Figure 1.1, essays can fall anywhere along the scale. Not all thesis-with-support writing has to be top down, stating its thesis explicitly in the introduction. In some cases writers choose to delay the thesis, creating a more exploratory, open-ended, "let's think through this together" feeling before finally stating the main point late in the essay. In some cases writers explore a problem without *ever* finding a satisfactory thesis, creating an essay that is thesis seeking rather than thesis supporting, an essay aimed at deepening the question, refusing to accept an easy answer. Such essays may replicate their author's process of exploring a problem and include digressions, speculations, conjectures, multiple perspectives, and occasional invitations to the reader to help solve the problem. When writers reach the far right-hand position on the continuum, they no longer state an explicit thesis. Instead, like novelists or short story writers, they embed their points in plot, imagery, dialogue, and so forth, leaving their readers to *infer* a theme from the text.

Where to Place Your Writing along the Continuum

Clearly, essays at opposite ends of this continuum operate in different ways and obey different rules. Because each position on the continuum has its appropriate uses, the writer's challenge is to determine which sort of writing is most appropriate for a given situation.

As you will see in later chapters, the kind of writing you choose depends on your purpose, your intended audience, and your genre (you will recall that a *genre* is a recurring type of writing with established conventions). Thus, if you were writing an analytical paper for an academic audience, you would typically choose a closed-form structure, and your finished product would include elements such as the following:

- An explicit thesis in the introduction
- Forecasting of structure
- Cohesive and unified paragraphs with topic sentences
- Clear transitions between sentences and between parts
- No digressions

But if you were writing an autobiographical narrative about, say, what family means to you, you would probably move toward the open end of the continuum and violate one or more of these conventions (note how extensively Merton violates them). It's not that open-form prose doesn't have rules; it's that the rules are different, just as the rules for jazz are different from the rules for a classical sonata.

For another perspective on how rules vary, consider two frequently encountered high school writing assignments: the five-paragraph theme and the personal-experience narrative (for example, the infamous "What I Did Last Summer" essay). The five-paragraph theme is a by-the-numbers way to teach closed-form, thesis-with-support writing. It emphasizes logical development, unity, and coherence. The five-paragraph structure may emerge naturally if you are writing an argument based on three supporting reasons—an introductory paragraph, three body paragraphs (one for each reason), and a concluding paragraph. Rockwood's letter is a real-world example of a five-paragraph theme even though Rockwood certainly didn't have that format in mind when writing.

In contrast, the "What I Did Last Summer" assignment calls for a different sort of writing, probably an open-form, narrative structure closer to Merton's piece about the night in the rain. Whether the writer chooses a closed-form or an open-form approach depends on the intended audience of the piece and the writer's purpose.

For Writing and Discussion

Do you and your classmates most enjoy writing prose at the closed or more open end of the continuum? Prior to class discussion, work individually by recalling a favorite piece of writing that you have done in the past. Jot down a brief description of the kind of writing this was (a poem, a personal-experience essay, a research paper, a newspaper story, a persuasive argument). Then, working in small groups or as a whole class, report one at a time on your favorite piece of writing and speculate where it falls on the continuum from closed to open forms. Are you at your best in closed-form writing that calls for an explicit thesis statement and logical support? Or are you at your best in more open and personal forms?

Is there a wide range of preferences in your class? If so, how do you account for this variance? If not, how do you account for the narrow range?

Chapter Summary

This chapter introduced you to the notion of writers as questioners and problem posers who wrestle with both subject-matter and rhetorical problems. We have shown how writers start with questions or problems about their subject matter rather than with topic areas, and how they take their time resolving the uncertainties raised by such questions. We saw that writers must ask questions about their rhetorical situation and make decisions about content, form, and style based on their understanding of their purpose, their audience, and their genre. We described how the rules governing writing vary as the writer moves along the continuum from closed to open forms.

The next chapter looks closely at how writers pose problems, pursue them in depth, and then pose answers that bring something new, surprising, or challenging to readers.

BRIEF WRITING PROJECT

We close this chapter with two options for a brief writing project, each aimed at helping you appreciate the value of a "good, interesting question." The first option is the easier of the two and can be done informally. The second option is more formal and yet can be completed in one page.

Option 1: Think of a recent experience in your life that has generated questions for you—for example, reading a book or magazine, watching a film or TV show, participating in a class discussion, or observing an incident in the dorms. Briefly describe the experience and then, based on your ponderings, pose several questions arising from the experience that you think are problematic, significant, and interesting.

Option 2: Write a one-page (double-spaced) essay that poses a question about automobiles and fossil fuels (or some other topic provided by your instructor). Besides explaining your question and providing needed background information, you will need to help readers see (1) why the question is problematic—that is, why it is a genuine problem with no easy right answers—and (2) why the question is significant or worth pursuing—that is, what benefit will come from solving it. Your essay should not answer the question; your purpose is only to ask it.

The goal of these brief writing project options is to give you practice at posing problematic questions. As you will see in Chapter 2, the second option, which focuses on a single question, will give you practice at writing the question-posing part of a typical academic introduction.

Either of these options will anchor your questions in a specific experience, reading, or set of data. The best kinds of questions are neither so broad that they are virtually unanswerable nor so narrow that they have only one right answer. If you can imagine several different ways to answer the questions you ask, you are on the right track. What follows are student examples for each option.

READINGS

Our first reading, by student writer Noel Gaudette, responds to Option 1.

Noel Gaudette
Questions about Genetically Modified Foods

A few weeks ago I was eating breakfast while listening to the news on the radio. One report I heard was about the political and economic tension over shipping genetically modified (GM) food to African nations. One of the concerns of Africans was the long-term safety of GM products. They worried about the food disrupting the natural biological balance we maintain in our bodies from eating traditionally grown foods. While listening to this program, I peered at my food service breakfast of reconstituted eggs, uniform hash browns, perfect-looking sausages, and little cup of bright red ketchup. My orange juice tasted fresh squeezed and my coffee seemed very ordinary. Still, I started to wonder if my breakfast contained genetically modified foods. I began to think of these questions:

1. How do I know if I am eating a GM product? How should consumers be made aware that their food contains GM products? Are these labeled on cans and boxes? If not, should they be?
2. Are the African nations correct in their assumption that GM food is unsafe?
3. What testing has been done on these new GM foods and is it sufficient?
4. To what extent should we promote the development and consumption of GM foods?

Describes the specific experience that generated the questions

Shows how details of the experience caused writer to ponder questions

States specific questions or issues that the writer feels are both problematic and significant

Our second reading, by student writer Brittany Tinker, responds to Option 2.

Brittany Tinker
Can the World Sustain an American Standard of Living?

Yesterday's class discussion about the growing demand for automobiles in China combined with all the problems of smog and air pollution in Beijing raised lots of dilemmas for me. Because the United States and other developed nations are already using up vast quantities of the world's oil, adding oil demands from China and other developing nations will cause the world to deplete its oil even sooner. Moreover, third world development adds even

Hooks reader's interest and provides background

States the question

more to the air pollution and global warming caused by consumerism in the United States and other developed countries. So I wonder, what standard of living can the whole world sustain once third world countries expand their own economies?

Begins to show that the question is problematic by presenting one side of her dilemma

Part of me hopes that the poor people in second and third world countries can one day enjoy the standard of living that I have had. The disparity between first world and second or third world countries hit me when I visited Nicaragua. Most Nicaraguans live in small, one-room homes made from corrugated tin and cinder blocks. The plumbing is underdeveloped and the electricity is inconstant. Most Nicaraguan families do not have enough food to provide adequate nutrition. But through economic development, I hope that these people can have the comforts that I and many other fortunate Americans have such as hot water, lots of nutritious food, numerous bedrooms, at least one car in the family, paved sidewalks or driveways, and a backyard, swimming pool, or hot tub.

Shows the other side of her dilemma

But another part of me sees that my own standard of living may be what's at fault; maybe this model for the good life won't work anymore. If second and third world countries attain the standard of living that I have been lucky enough to have, then air pollution, destruction of forests, global warming, and harm to wildlife, as well as the depletion of oil reserves, will pose even greater risks for the world than they already do. A lot of my classmates seem confident that scientists will discover alternative energy sources and solutions to pollution and global warming so that the whole world can live in comfort. But this pessimistic side of me doesn't share their confidence. Maybe the solution is for Americans to greatly reduce their own consumption and to begin reducing the environmental damage they have already created.

Shows why question is significant

So I am left wondering, Can the world sustain for everybody the standard of living I have enjoyed? This question is significant because there is so much at stake. If our model for the happy life is to have all the American luxuries, then the development of the third world might mean a much speedier destruction of the planet. If we hope to preserve the planet while eliminating the poverty and misery of third world people, then maybe Americans have to develop a new model for happiness. Is it possible for developing countries to find a new path to economic prosperity that shows the developed world a new model of preserving the environment?

Showing Why Your Question Is Problematic and Significant (Option 2)

If you have been assigned the second option for your brief writing project, you will need to show why your question is both problematic and significant. (Doing so helps your readers understand the puzzling nature of your problem and motivates their interest in it.) Some strategies writers can use to show that a question is problematic and significant are given in the following charts.

Strategies for Showing That a Question Is Problematic

POSSIBLE STRATEGY	EXAMPLE
Show how your own (or previous researchers') attempts to solve the problem have failed.	If your problem were "How can our university encourage more students, faculty, and staff to carpool?" you could show how the university's previous attempts to encourage carpooling (reduced-rate parking, privileged parking spots) have failed.
Show different ways that people have attempted to answer the question (different theories or competing explanations) and indicate how no one answer is fully adequate.	If you were puzzled by why Europeans accept much higher fuel prices than Americans do, you could summarize several theories presented by your classmates and show why each one isn't fully convincing.
Show the alternative points of view on an issue.	If your problem were whether to save fossil fuels by building more nuclear power plants, you could summarize the main arguments for and against nuclear power.
Show why an expected or "easy" answer isn't satisfactory.	Suppose you asked, "What is the best alternative to using fossil fuels for generating electricity?" and one of your environmentalist friends says, "All we have to do is put our money into developing wind energy." You could problematize this easy answer by summarizing engineer David Rockwood's objections to the technical feasibility of wind power (see pp. 17–18).
Narrate your own attempts to think through the problem, revealing how none of your possible answers fully satisfied you.	You might use the strategy "Part of me thinks this . . . ; but another part of me thinks this . . . " or "I used to think this, but now I think . . . ." This is the strategy used by Brittany Tinker in the example essay.

Strategies for Showing That a Question Is Significant

POSSIBLE STRATEGY	EXAMPLE
Show how solving the problem will lead to practical, real-world benefits.	If we could figure out how to get people to buy fuel-efficient cars rather than SUVs, we could cut down substantially on fossil fuel use.
Show how solving a small knowledge problem will help us solve a larger, more important knowledge problem.	If we could better understand why Europeans are willing to live with high gasoline prices, we might better understand how cultural values influence consumer behavior.

Planning Your Essay

To help you develop a plan for your Option 2 brief essay, you can make an informal outline or flowchart in which you plan out each of the required parts. Here are some examples of student plans that led to successful question-posing essays on problems other than cars and fossil fuels.

EXAMPLE 1

I would like to question the ethics of interspecies transplants and show why it is not an easy question to answer.

Illustrate question with case of a man who had a transplant of a baboon heart.

View One: Interspecies transplants are unethical. It is unethical to "play God" by taking the organs of one species and placing them into another.

View Two: Interspecies transplants may save lives. Medical research done with the intention of improving human life is ethical.

This is a significant problem because it causes us to question the limits of medical research and to ask what it means to be human.

EXAMPLE 2

I am wondering whether Eminem's music ought to be censored in some way or at least kept out of the hands of children or unknowledgeable listeners.
Show how I am conflicted by all the different points of view:

- I agree that his lyrics are vile, misogynistic, homophobic, and obscene. Children should not be allowed to listen to his music.
- Yet I believe in free speech.
- Also rap is more complex than the general public realizes. Eminem's irony and complexity are often misunderstood. Therefore, serious listeners should have access to his music.
- Additionally, there may be some value just in expressing politically incorrect thoughts, but not if doing so just leads to more hatred.

Explain how I am left with a dilemma about whether or not to censor Eminem and if so, how.
This is an important question because it involves the larger question of individual freedom versus public good.

Exploring Problems, Making Claims

"In management, people don't merely 'write papers,' they solve problems," said [business professor Kimbrough Sherman]. . . . He explained that he wanted to construct situations where students would have to "wallow in complexity" and work their way out, as managers must.

—A. KIMBROUGH SHERMAN, *MANAGEMENT PROFESSOR*

In the previous chapter we introduced you to the role of the writer as a questioner and problem poser. In this chapter, we narrow our focus to thesis-governed writing—the kind of writing most frequently required in college courses and often required in civic and professional life. Thesis-governed writing requires a behind-the-scenes ability to think rigorously about a problem and then to make a claim* that summarizes your "best solution."

In Part Three of this text, "A Guide to Composing and Revising," we give you compositional advice on the actual drafting and revising of a thesis-governed essay. Our goal in this chapter is to stand back from the nuts and bolts of writing to give you some big-picture principles of thesis-governed prose. We believe these principles, which you can transfer across most of your college courses, can significantly improve your writing. Your payoff for reading this chapter will be a marked increase in your ability to write engaging and meaningful prose targeted to the audience of your choice. In particular, you will learn the following:

- How college professors value a kind of thinking that one professor calls "wallow[ing] in complexity"
- How each academic discipline is a field of inquiry and argument, not just a repository of facts and concepts to be learned
- How the thinking process of posing questions and proposing answers is reflected in the introductions of academic articles and how an effective question must engage the interests of your intended audience
- How your thesis statement should contain a surprising element aimed at changing your reader's view of your topic

---

*In this text we use the words *claim* and *thesis statement* interchangeably. As you move from course to course, instructors typically use one or the other of these terms. Other synonyms for thesis statement include *proposition*, *main point*, or *thesis sentence*.

- How thesis statements are supported by a network of points and particulars
- How you can deepen and complicate your thinking through "the believing and doubting game" (the brief writing project for this chapter)

What Does a Professor Want?

It is important to understand the kind of thinking most college professors want in student writing. Many beginning students imagine that professors want students primarily to comprehend course concepts as taught in textbooks and lectures and to show their understanding on exams. Such comprehension is important, but it is only a starting point. As management professor A. Kimbrough Sherman explains in the epigraph to this chapter, college instructors expect students to wrestle with problems by applying the concepts, data, and thought processes they learn in a course to new situations. As Sherman puts it, students must learn to "wallow in complexity and work their way out."

Learning to Wallow in Complexity

Wallowing in complexity is not what most first-year college students aspire to do. (Certainly that wasn't what we, the authors of this text, had uppermost in our minds when we sailed off to college!) New college students tend to shut down their creative thinking processes too quickly and head straight for closure to a problem. Harvard psychologist William Perry, who has studied the intellectual development of college students, found that few of them become skilled wallowers in complexity until late in their college careers. According to Perry, most students come to college as "dualists," believing that all questions have right or wrong answers, that professors know the right answers, and that the student's job is to learn them. Of course, these beliefs are partially correct. First-year students who hope to become second-year students must indeed understand and memorize mounds of facts, data, definitions, and basic concepts.

But true intellectual growth requires the kind of problematizing we discussed in Chapter 1. It requires students to *do* something with their new knowledge, to apply it to new situations, to conduct the kinds of inquiry, research, analysis, and argument pursued by experts in each discipline. Instead of confronting only questions that have right answers, students need to confront the kinds of open-ended problems we discussed in Chapter 1. Cognitive psychologists call such problems "ill-structured" because they seldom yield a single, correct answer and often require the thinker to operate in the absence of full and complete data.* Your college professors pursue ill-structured problems in their professional writing. The kinds of problems vary from discipline to discipline, but they all require

---

*In contrast, a "well-structured" problem eventually yields a correct answer. Math problems that can be solved by applying the right formulae and processes are well structured. That's why you can have the correct answers in the back of the book.

the writer to use reasons and evidence to support a tentative solution. Because your instructors want you to learn how to do the same kind of thinking, they often phrase essay exam questions or writing assignments as ill-structured problems. They are looking not for one right answer, but for well-supported arguments that acknowledge alternative views. A C paper and an A paper may have the same "answer" (identical thesis statements), but the C writer may have waded only ankle deep into the mud of complexity, whereas the A writer wallowed in it and worked a way out.

What skills are required for successful wallowing? Specialists in critical thinking have identified the following:

1. The ability to pose problematic questions
2. The ability to analyze a problem in all its dimensions—to define its key terms, determine its causes, understand its history, appreciate its human dimension and its connection to one's own personal experience, and appreciate what makes it problematic or complex
3. The ability (and doggedness) to find, gather, and interpret facts, data, and other information relevant to the problem (often involving library, Internet, or field research)
4. The ability to imagine alternative solutions to the problem, to see different ways in which the question might be answered and different perspectives for viewing it
5. The ability to analyze competing approaches and answers, to construct arguments for and against alternatives, and to choose the best solution in light of values, objectives, and other criteria that you determine and articulate
6. The ability to write an effective argument justifying your choice while acknowledging counterarguments

We discuss and develop these skills throughout this text.

In addition to these generic thinking abilities, critical thinking requires what psychologists call "domain-specific" skills. Each academic discipline has its own characteristic ways of approaching knowledge and its own specialized habits of mind. The questions asked by psychologists differ from those asked by historians or anthropologists; the evidence and assumptions used to support arguments in literary analysis differ from those in philosophy or sociology.

What all disciplines value, however, is the ability to manage complexity, and this skill marks the final stage of William Perry's developmental scheme. At an intermediate stage of development, after they have moved beyond dualism, students become what Perry calls "multiplists." At this stage students believe that since the experts disagree on many questions, all answers are equally valid. Professors want students merely to have an opinion and to state it strongly. A multiplist believes that a low grade on an essay indicates no more than that the teacher didn't like his or her opinion. Multiplists are often cynical about professors and grades; to them, college is a game of guessing what the teacher wants to hear. Students emerge into Perry's final stages—what he calls "relativism" and "commitment in relativism"— when they are able to take a position in the face of complexity and to justify that decision through reasons and evidence while weighing and acknowledging contrary reasons and counterevidence. Professor Sherman articulates what is expected at Perry's last stages—wading into the messiness of complexity and working your way back to solid ground.

Seeing Each Academic Discipline as a Field of Inquiry and Argument

When you study a new discipline, you must learn not only the knowledge that scholars in that discipline have acquired over the years, but also the processes they used to discover that knowledge. It is useful to think of each academic discipline as a network of conversations in which participants exchange information, respond to each other's questions, and express agreements and disagreements. The scholarly articles and books that many of your instructors write (or would write if they could find the time) are formal, permanent contributions to an ongoing discussion carried on in print in your college's or university's library. Each book or article represents a contribution to a conversation; each writer agreed with some of his or her predecessors and disagreed with others.

As each discipline evolves and changes, its central questions evolve also, creating a fascinating, dynamic conversation that defines the discipline. At any given moment, scholars are pursuing hundreds of cutting-edge questions in each discipline. Table 2.1 provides examples of questions that scholars have debated over the years as well as questions they are addressing today.

As you study a discipline, you are learning how to enter its network of conversations. To do so, you have to build up a base of knowledge about the discipline, learn its terminology, observe its conversations, read its major works, see how it asks questions, and learn its methods. To help you get a fuller sense of how written "conversation" works within a discipline, the rest of this chapter shows you how a typical academic writer poses a question and then presents and supports his or her proposed answer to the question.

Posing an Engaging Question

In Chapter 1, we said that a thesis statement is the writer's answer to a thesis question. But, as we have suggested, the kinds of questions that engage audiences vary from discipline to discipline or, in popular culture, from magazine to magazine. Let's suppose, for example, that you want to write an essay on rap music. How might your essay differ if you wanted to write it for different courses you might be taking or for different popular media? Here are some examples of rap questions that would interest different audiences:

- *Psychology course:* To what extent does rap music increase misogynistic or homophobic attitudes in listeners?
- *Sociology course:* Based on a random sampling of student interview subjects, how does the level of appreciation for rap music vary by ethnicity, class, age, and gender?

TABLE 2.1 Scholarly Questions in Different Disciplines

Field	Examples of Current Cutting-Edge Questions	Examples of Historical Controversies
Anatomy	What is the effect of a pregnant rat's alcohol ingestion on the development of fetal eye tissue?	In 1628, William Harvey produced a treatise arguing that the heart, through repeated contractions, caused blood to circulate through the body. His views were attacked by followers of the Greek physician Galen.
Literature	To what extent does the structure of a work of literature, for example Conrad's *Heart of Darkness,* reflect the class and gender bias of the author?	In the 1920s, a group of New Critics argued that the interpretation of a work of literature should be based on close examination of the work's imagery and form and that the intentions of the writer and the biases of the reader were not important. These views held sway in U.S. universities until the late 1960s, when they came increasingly under attack by deconstructionists and other postmoderns, who claimed that author intentions and reader's bias were important parts of the work's meaning.
Rhetoric/ Composition	How does hypertext structure and increased attention to visual images in Web-based writing affect the composing processes of writers?	Prior to the 1970s, college writing courses in the United States were typically organized around the rhetorical modes (description, narration, exemplification, comparison and contrast, and so forth). This approach was criticized by the expressivist school associated with the British composition researcher James Britton. Since the 1980s, composition scholars have proposed various alternative strategies for designing and sequencing assignments.
Psychology	What are the underlying causes of gender identification? To what extent are differences between male and female behavior explainable by nature (genetics, body chemistry) versus nurture (social learning)?	In the early 1900s under the influence of Sigmund Freud, psychoanalytic psychologists began explaining human behavior in terms of unconscious drives and mental processes that stemmed from repressed childhood experiences. Later, psychoanalysts were opposed by behaviorists, who rejected the notion of the unconscious and explained behavior as responses to environmental stimuli.

- *Rhetoric/composition course:* What images of rap artists, urban life, and women do the lyrics of rap songs portray?
- *Local newspaper:* Should Bill Cosby be criticized or applauded for attacking "obscene rap music" as an example of bad values that keep poor African-Americans impoverished?
- *Rolling Stone Magazine:* Was the murder of Biggie used to set up a civil war in hip-hop and the Black community?

In each of these cases, the writer understands how readers in a particular community pose questions. The first three examples show differences in the way that psychologists, sociologists, and rhetoric/composition scholars might ask questions about rap music. For newspaper readers, the Bill Cosby question would interest readers who followed the public reaction to Cosby's June 2004 speech to the NAACP in which he criticized young African-Americans for wearing sagging pants, speaking in street slang, and listening to rap. The question about the murder of Biggie actually appeared in the June 7, 2004, issue of *Rolling Stone Magazine*. In all these cases, the writer poses a subject-matter question that connects in some way to the intended readers' values, beliefs, or characteristic ways of thinking.

How a Prototypical Introduction Poses a Question and Proposes an Answer

To show you how academic writers typically begin by asking a question, we will illustrate with a "prototype" introduction from a scholarly journal. A *prototype* is the most typical or generic instance of a class and doesn't constitute a value judgment. For example, a prototype bird might be a robin or blackbird (rather than an ostrich, chicken, hummingbird, or pelican) because these birds seem to exhibit the most typical features of "birdiness." Likewise, a prototype dog would be a medium-sized mutt rather than a Great Dane or toy poodle. The article we have chosen for our illustration comes from a scholarly journal called the *Journal of Popular Culture*. Other articles in this same journal are on topics ranging from *Buffy the Vampire Slayer* to international transformations of Barbie dolls in India or Mexico. In the following introduction, note how the authors first present a question and then move, at the end of the introduction, to their thesis and the overview of their argument. Note also how the question-posing part of the introduction is similar to the question-posing essay one might write for the brief writing project (Option 2) in Chapter 1.

See student writer Brittany Tinker's problem-posing essay on pp. 23–24.

PIT BULL PANIC

Provides background showing dangerous reputation of pit bulls in the media

The news media has long been criticized for being sensationalist as well as biased. One ongoing story that the media has offered their audience is a melodrama regarding the American Pit Bull Terrier (hereafter referred to as "Pit Bull"). The Pit Bull has been portrayed in the past one and a half decades as ". . . the archetype of canine evil, predators of the defenseless. Unpredictable companions that kill and maim without discretion. Walking horror shows bred with an appetite for violence (sic)" (Verzemnieks B6). This news coverage has had profound effects. Pit Bull ownership brings with it consequences not associated with most acquisitions. "These days, buying a Pit Bull means buying into a controversy; Pit Bull owners had better not be afraid of public opinion" (B6). In some places, Pit Bull ownership is not even allowed; in fact, ownership is banned in 75 communities in the United States (Sanchez-Beswick 1). Many insurance companies refuse to insure homeowners with Pit Bulls (V. Richardson 189). A survey done by the American Society for the Prevention of Cruelty to Animals found that 30% of shelters that responded do not adopt out Pit Bulls. Most of these shelters have this policy due to community bans,

Parenthetical citation of sources

but others choose not to (Schultz 36). Obviously these organizations feel that Pit Bulls are dangerous. They are, no doubt, in part influenced by media accounts. The general public also looks to the media for information to warn them of dangers that they need to avoid (De Becker 294–5). The extent to which the public has caught the wave of "Pit Bull panic" is the focus of a study that is presented in this paper.

Such a panic would be rational if, in fact, Pit Bulls were as dangerous as the media has portrayed. But is the media portrayal of Pit Bulls truly accurate? Advocates feel that Pit Bulls have been unfairly maligned by the media. As Hallum* makes painfully clear, there are always two sides to every story. Additional evidence that Pit Bulls have been unfairly demonized comes from the personal experience of the authors themselves. The authors have worked with dozens of Pit Bulls at a local animal shelter in southern New Jersey. The vast majority of these Pit Bulls have been stray dogs brought in by animal control officers from a neighborhood where residents use Pit Bulls as macho status symbols, over-breed them severely, and are alleged to hold at least occasional informal dog fights. These Pit Bulls do not belong to a special pampered minority who have been given a "genteel" upbringing. Yet, as a breed, they are consistently among the most people-friendly dogs in the shelter.

This paper examines the negative portrayal of the Pit Bull in the media. It offers a theory regarding why such a portrayal has come about. It then discusses the results of a study that examined three major issues regarding Pit Bulls: (1) people's perception of Pit Bulls; (2) attitudes towards legislation designed to place restrictions on Pit Bull ownership; and (3) whether certain variables affect these perceptions and attitudes. This research is important for several reasons. Although our primary purpose is not to prove the ultimate truth about Pit Bulls, we do offer an abundance of evidence to discredit the media's negative portrayals of Pit Bulls. Only by offering counter-evidence can we establish the existence of media bias on this topic. More importantly, we offer an innovative theory of media bias. This theory is not based on the political orientation of journalists. Indeed, many issues covered by the media can be biased for reasons other than political orientation. Furthermore, we examine, for our specific topic, whether the news media actually influences the attitudes of the people it is supposedly informing. Ultimately, media bias should only be worrisome if the public actually believes the misinformation it is exposed to.

—Judy Cohen and John Richardson

Presentation of question

Provides counterevidence that pit bulls are people friendly (shows why question is problematic)

Thesis sentences showing purpose of paper and forecasting main parts

Shows why question is significant

This introduction, like most introductions to academic articles, includes the following prototypical features:

- *Focus on a question or problem to be investigated.* In this case the question is stated explicitly: "But is the media portrayal of Pit Bulls truly accurate?" This direct question implies a further question: If the media portrayal of pit bulls is not accurate, then how do we account for the media bias? In many introductions, the question to be investigated is implied rather than stated directly.
- *An explanation of why the question is problematic.* To show that their question is problematic, Cohen and Richardson juxtapose two opposing views: the common media representation of pit bulls as dangerous, countered by their

For a detailed discussion of posing questions in closed-form introductions, see Chapter 18, "Composing and Revising Closed-Form Prose," pp. 542–546.

*Hallum is one of the "advocates" of pit bulls. He is identified in the bibliography at the end of the article as the author of a book entitled *Pit Bull Sting: The Other Side of the Story*.

own personal experience working in animal shelters and by a book by Hallum, a pit bull advocate, showing that pit bulls are "people friendly."

- *An explanation of why the question is significant.* To show the significance of their question, Cohen and Richardson see two benefits of their research and analysis: First, they hope to rectify public misunderstandings about pit bulls. Second, they hope to offer a new theory about the causes of media bias as a way of helping the public guard itself against misinformation. This explanation addresses the reader's "So what?" question.

- *The writer's tentative "answer" to this question (the essay's "thesis"), which brings something new to the audience.* In closed-form articles the thesis is usually stated explicitly at the end of the introduction. Although Cohen and Richardson do not condense their whole thesis into one sentence, such a thesis is clearly implied: The media have misrepresented pit bulls for reasons that we explain through our innovative theory of media bias.

- *[optional] A mapping statement forecasting the content and shape of the rest of the article ("First X is discussed, then Y, and finally Z").* Cohen and Richardson forecast the shape of their article by identifying its major parts Such forecasting is typical of longer articles, where readers appreciate a roadmap of what is coming. In shorter articles, writers typically omit forecasting or mapping statements.

For a detailed discussion of thesis statements, purpose statements, and blueprint statements, see Chapter 18, "Composing and Revising Closed-Form Prose," pp. 542–546.

We have used Cohen and Richardson's article to show how academic writers—in posing a problem and proposing an answer—join an ongoing conversation. The papers you will be asked to write in college will be much stronger if you create the same kind of introduction that poses a problem and then asserts a tentative, risky answer (your thesis), which you will support with reasons and evidence.

Seeking a Surprising Thesis

It is not enough to ask a good question. You also have to have a strong thesis. But what makes a thesis strong?

For one thing, a strong thesis usually contains an element of uncertainty, risk, or challenge. A strong thesis implies a naysayer who could disagree with you. According to composition theorist Peter Elbow, a thesis has "got to stick its neck out, not just hedge or wander. [It is] something that can be quarreled with." Elbow's sticking-its-neck-out metaphor is a good one, but we prefer to say that a strong thesis *surprises* the reader with a new, unexpected, different, or challenging view of the writer's topic. By surprise, we intend to connote, first of all, freshness or newness for the reader. Many kinds of closed-form prose don't have a sharply contestable thesis of the sticking-its-neck-out kind highlighted by Elbow. A geology report, for example, may provide readers with desired information about rock strata in an exposed cliff, or a Web page for diabetics may explain how to coordinate meals and insulin injections during a plane trip across time zones. In these cases, the information is surprising because it brings something new and significant to intended readers.

In other kinds of closed-form prose, especially academic or civic prose address-ing a problematic question or a disputed issue, surprise requires an argumentative, risky, or contestable thesis. In these cases also, surprise is not inherent in the mate-rial but in the intended readers' reception; it comes from the writer's providing an adequate or appropriate response to the readers' presumed question or problem.

In this section, we present two ways of creating a surprising thesis: (1) trying to change your reader's view of your subject; and (2) giving your thesis tension.

Try to Change Your Reader's View of Your Subject

To change your reader's view of your subject, you must first imagine how the reader would view the subject *before* reading your essay. Then you can articulate how you aim to change that view. A useful exercise is to write out the "before" and "after" views of your imagined readers:

Before reading my essay, my readers think this way about my topic:

_____

After reading my essay, my readers will think this different way about my

topic: _____

You can change your reader's view of a subject in several ways.* First, you can enlarge it. Writing that enlarges a view is primarily informational; it provides new ideas and data to add to a reader's store of knowledge about the subject. For example, suppose you are interested in the problem of storing nuclear waste (a highly controversial issue in the United States) and decide to investigate how Japan stores radioactive waste from its nuclear power plants. You could report your findings on this problem in an informative research paper. (Before reading my paper, readers would be uncertain how Japan stores nuclear waste. After read-ing my paper, my readers would understand the Japanese methods, possibly help-ing us better understand our options in the United States.)

Second, you can clarify your reader's view of something that was previously fuzzy, tentative, or uncertain. Writing of this kind often explains, analyzes, or interprets. This is the kind of writing you do when analyzing a short story, a painting, an historical document, a set of economic data, or other puzzling phe-nomena or when speculating on the causes, consequences, purpose, or function of something. Suppose, for example, you are analyzing the persuasive strategies used in various perfume ads and are puzzled by an advertisement for Jennifer Lopez's "Still" perfume. Your paper tries to explain how the unusual name "Still" is essential for understanding the verbal and visual aspects of the ad. (Before read-ing my paper, my readers will be puzzled by what this ad is trying to do. After reading my paper, my readers will see how the words and images of this ad are connected to different meanings of the word "Still.")

---

*Our discussion of how writing changes a reader's view of the world is indebted to Richard Young, Alton Becker, and Kenneth Pike, *Rhetoric: Discovery and Change* (New York: Harcourt Brace & Company, 1971).

Another kind of change occurs when an essay actually restructures a reader's whole view of a subject. Such essays persuade readers to change their minds or make decisions. For example, the writers of "Pit Bull Panic," the introduction to which you have just read, want to restructure their readers' thinking about pit bulls. (Before reading our article, readers would think that pit bulls are vicious animals bred to maim and kill. After reading our article, readers will regard pit bulls as people-friendly animals demonized by the media.) Likewise, engineer David Rockwood, in his letter to the editor that we reprinted in Chapter 1 (pp. 17–18), wants to change readers' views about wind power. (Before reading my letter, readers would believe that wind-generated electricity can solve our energy crisis. After reading my letter, they will see that the hope for wind power is a pipe dream.)

Surprise then is the measure of change an essay brings about in a reader. Of course, to bring about such change requires more than just a surprising thesis; the essay itself must persuade the reader that the thesis is sound as well as novel. Later in this chapter, we talk about how writers support a thesis through a network of points and particulars.

Give Your Thesis Tension

Another element of a surprising thesis is tension. By *tension* we mean the reader's sensation of being pulled away from familiar ideas toward new, unfamiliar ones or being pulled in two or more directions by opposing ideas. One of the best ways to create tension in a thesis statement is to begin the statement with an *although* or *whereas* clause: "Whereas most people believe X, this paper asserts Y." The *whereas* or *although* clause summarizes the reader's "before" view of your topic or the counterclaim that your essay opposes; the main clause states the surprising view or position that your essay will support. You may choose to omit the *although* clause from your actual essay, but formulating it first will help you achieve focus and surprise in your thesis. The examples that follow illustrate the kinds of tension we have been discussing and show why tension is a key requirement for a good thesis.

Question	What effect has the cell phone had on our culture?
Thesis without Tension	The invention of the cell phone has brought many advantages to our culture.
Thesis with Tension	Although the cell phone has brought many advantages to our culture, it may also have contributed to an increase in risky behavior among boaters and hikers.
Question	Do reservations serve a useful role in contemporary Native American culture?
Thesis without Tension	Reservations have good points and bad points.
Thesis with Tension	Although my friend Wilson Real Bird believes that reservations are necessary for Native Americans to preserve their heritage, the continuation of reservations actually degrades Native American culture.

In the first example, the thesis without tension (cell phones have brought advantages to our culture) is a truism with which everyone would agree and hence lacks surprise. The thesis with tension places this truism (the reader's "before" view) in an *although* clause and goes on to make a surprising or contestable assertion. The idea that the cell phone contributes to risky behavior among outdoor enthusiasts alters our initial complacent view of the cell phone and gives us new ideas to think about.

In the second example, the thesis without tension may not at first seem tensionless because the writer sets up an opposition between good and bad points. But *almost anything* has good and bad points, so the opposition is not meaningful, and the thesis offers no element of surprise. Substitute virtually any other social institution (marriage, the postal service, the military, prisons), and the statement that it has good and bad points would be equally true. The thesis with tension, in contrast, is risky. It commits the reader to argue that reservations have degraded Native American culture and to oppose the counterthesis that reservations are needed to *preserve* Native American culture. The reader now feels genuine tension between two opposing views.

Tension, then, is a component of surprise. The writer's goal is to surprise the reader in some way, thereby bringing about some kind of change in the reader's view. Here are some specific strategies you can use to surprise a reader:

- Give the reader new information or clarify a confusing concept.
- Make problematic something that seems nonproblematic by showing paradoxes or contradictions within it, by juxtaposing two or more conflicting points of view about it, or by looking at it more deeply or complexly than expected.
- Identify an unexpected effect, implication, or significance of something.
- Show underlying differences between two concepts normally thought to be similar or underlying similarities between two concepts normally thought to be different.
- Show that a commonly accepted answer to a question isn't satisfactory or that a commonly rejected answer may be satisfactory.
- Oppose a commonly accepted viewpoint, support an unpopular viewpoint, or in some other way take an argumentative stance on an issue.
- Propose a new solution to a problem or an unexpected answer to a question.

For Writing and Discussion

It is difficult to create thesis statements on the spot because a writer's thesis grows out of an exploratory struggle with a problem. However, in response to a question one can often propose a possible claim and treat it hypothetically as a tentative thesis statement put on the table for testing. What follows are several problematic questions that we have used as examples in this and the previous chapter, along with some possible audiences that you might consider addressing. Working individually, spend ten minutes considering possible thesis statements

(*continued*)

that you might pose in response to one or more of these questions. (Remember that these are tentative thesis statements that you might abandon after doing research.) Be ready to explain why your tentative thesis brings something new, enlightening, challenging, or otherwise surprising to the specified readers. Then, working in small groups or as a whole class, share your possible thesis statements. Finally, choose one or two thesis statements that your small group or the whole class thinks are particularly effective and brainstorm the kinds of evidence that would be required to support the thesis.

1. To what extent should the public support genetically modified foods? (possible audiences: readers of health food magazines; general public concerned about food choices; investors in companies that produce genetically modified seeds)
2. Should people be encouraged to drive more fuel-efficient cars? If so, how? (possible audiences: SUV owners; conservative legislators generally in favor of free markets; investors in the automobile industry)
3. What social views—particularly of male success and of women or gays— are promoted by rap music? (possible audiences: consumers of rap music; parents concerned about their children's exposure to rap music; black parents who read about Bill Cosby's speech to the 2004 NAACP convention— see pp. 31–32).
4. Any questions that your class might have developed through discussing Chapter 1.

Here is an example:

Problematic question: What can cities do to prevent traffic congestion?

One possible thesis: Although many people think that building light rail systems won't get people out of their cars, new light rail systems in many cities have attracted new riders and alleviated traffic problems.

Intended audience: Residents of cities concerned about traffic congestion but skeptical about light rail

Kinds of evidence needed to support thesis: Examples of cities with successful light rail systems; evidence that many riders switched from driving cars; evidence that light rail alleviated traffic problems

Supporting Your Thesis with Points and Particulars

Of course, a surprising thesis is only one aspect of an effective essay. An essay must also persuade the reader that the thesis is believable as well as surprising. Although tabloid newspapers have shocking headlines "Britney Spears Videos Contain FBI Spy Secrets!"), skepticism quickly replaces surprise when you look inside and find the article's claims unsupported. A strong thesis, then, must both surprise the reader and be supported with convincing particulars.

In fact, the particulars are the flesh and muscle of writing and comprise most of the sentences. In closed-form prose, these particulars are connected clearly to points, and the points precede the particulars. In this section, we explain this principle more fully.

How Points Convert Information to Meaning

When particulars are clearly related to a point, the point gives meaning to the particulars, and the particulars give force and validity to the point. Particulars constitute the evidence, data, details, examples, and subarguments that develop a point and make it convincing. By themselves, particulars are simply information—mere data without meaning.

In the following example, you can see for yourself the difference between information and meaning. Here is a list of information:*

- In almost all species on earth, males are more aggressive than females.
- Male chimpanzees win dominance by brawling.
- To terrorize rival troops, they kill females and infants.
- The level of aggression among monkeys can be manipulated by adjusting their testosterone levels.
- Among humans, preliminary research suggests that male fetuses are more active in the uterus than female fetuses.
- Little boys play more aggressively than little girls despite parental efforts to teach gentleness to boys and aggression to girls.

To make meaning out of this list of information, the writer needs to state a point—the idea, generalization, or claim—that this information supports. Once the point is stated, a meaningful unit (point with particulars) springs into being:

> Aggression in human males may be a function of biology rather than culture. In almost all species on earth, males are more aggressive than females. Male chimpanzees win dominance by brawling; to terrorize rival troops, they kill females and infants. Researchers have shown that the level of aggression among monkeys can be manipulated by adjusting their testosterone levels. Among humans, preliminary research suggests that male fetuses are more active in the uterus than female fetuses. Also, little boys play more aggressively than little girls despite parental efforts to teach gentleness to boys and aggression to girls.

Point

Particulars

Once the writer states this point, readers familiar with the biology/culture debate about gender differences immediately feel its surprise and tension. This writer believes that biology determines gender identity more than does culture. The writer now uses the details as evidence to support a point.

To appreciate the reader's need for a logical connection between points and particulars, note how readers would get lost if, in the preceding example, the

*The data in this exercise are adapted from Deborah Blum, "The Gender Blur," *Utne Reader* Sept. 1998: 45–48.

writer included a particular that seemed unrelated to the point ("Males also tend to be taller and heavier than women"—a factual statement, but what does it have to do with aggression?) or if, without explanation, the writer added a particular that seemed to contradict the point ("Fathers play more roughly with baby boys than with baby girls"—another fact, but one that points to culture rather than biology as a determiner of aggression).

Obviously, reasonable people seek some kind of coordination between points and particulars, some sort of weaving back and forth between them. Writing teachers use a number of nearly synonymous terms for expressing this paired relationship: *points/particulars, generalizations/specifics, claims/evidence, ideas/details, interpretations/data, meaning/support.*

How Removing Particulars Creates a Summary

What we have shown, then, is that skilled writers weave back and forth between generalizations and specifics. The generalizations form a network of higher-level and lower-level points that develop the thesis; the particulars (specifics) support each of the points and subpoints in turn. In closed-form prose, the network of points is easily discernible because points are clearly highlighted with transitions, and main points are placed prominently at the heads of paragraphs. (In open-form prose, generalizations are often left unstated, creating gaps where the reader must actively fill in meaning.)

If you remove most of the particulars from a closed-form essay, leaving only the network of points, you will have written a summary or abstract of the essay. As an example, reread the civil engineer's letter to the editor arguing against the feasibility of wind-generated power (pp. 17–18). The writer's argument can be summarized in a single sentence:

Being able to write summaries and abstracts of articles is an important academic skill. See Chapter 6 on strategies for writing summaries and strong responses, pp. 126–165.

Wind-generated power is not a reasonable alternative to other forms of power in the Pacific Northwest because wind power is unreliable, because there are major unsolved problems involved in the design of wind-generation facilities, and because the environmental impact of building thousands of wind towers would be enormous.

What we have done in this summary is remove the particulars, leaving only the high-level points that form the skeleton of the argument. The writer's thesis remains surprising and contains tension, but without the particulars the reader has no idea whether to believe the generalizations or not. The presence of the particulars is thus essential to the success of the argument.

For Writing and Discussion

Compare the civil engineer's original letter with the one-sentence summary just given and then note how the engineer uses specific details to support each point. How do these particulars differ from paragraph to paragraph? How are they chosen to support each point?

How to Use Points and Particulars When You Revise

The lesson to learn here is that in closed-form prose, writers regularly place a point sentence in front of detail sentences. When a writer begins with a point, readers interpret the ensuing particulars not as random data but rather as *evidence* in support of that point. The writer depends on the particulars to make the point credible and persuasive.

This insight may help you clarify two of the most common kinds of marginal comments that readers (or teachers) place on writers' early drafts. If your draft has a string of sentences giving data or information unconnected to any stated point, your reader is apt to write in the margin, "What's your point here?" or "Why are you telling me this information?" or "How does this information relate to your thesis?" Conversely, if your draft tries to make a point that isn't developed with particulars, your reader is apt to write marginal comments such as "Evidence?" or "Development?" or "Could you give an example?" or "More details needed."

Don't be put off by these requests; they are a gift. It is common in first drafts for main points to be unstated, buried, or otherwise disconnected from their details and for supporting information to be scattered confusingly throughout the draft or missing entirely. Having to write point sentences obliges you to wrestle with your intended meaning: Just what am I trying to say here? How can I nutshell that in a point? Likewise, having to support your points with particulars causes you to wrestle with the content and shape of your argument: What particulars will make this point convincing? What further research do I need to do to find these particulars? In Part Three of this text, which is devoted to advice about composing and revising, we show how the construction and location of point sentences are essential for reader clarity. Part Three also explains various composing and revising strategies that will help you create effective networks of points and particulars.

For more about the importance of points, see pp. 548–549, which discuss topic sentences in paragraphs.

Chapter Summary

In this chapter we looked at the kind of wallowing in complexity that professors expect from students and saw how academic writing is rooted in subject matter problems. We saw how a prototypical introduction for an academic essay poses a question, explains how the question is problematic and significant, and then states the writer's thesis. We explained how a strong thesis aims to change readers' view of a topic by bringing to the reader something new, surprising, or challenging. Finally we saw how a writer supports a thesis through a network of points and particulars.

BRIEF WRITING PROJECT

Throughout this chapter we have shown the close relationship between a thesis question and a thesis statement. We conclude this chapter with a powerful thinking exercise that will keep you from being satisfied with a thesis statement too

Strategies for doing exploratory writing, composing first drafts, revising, and editing are treated in detail in Part Three of this text, "A Guide to Composing and Revising."

soon. As we have explained, writing is an active process of problem solving involving periods of pondering, researching, note-taking, exploratory writing, talking with others, drafting, and revising. The following exercise, developed by writing theorist Peter Elbow, is called the "believing and doubting game." To play the game, you explore many sides of a problematic question by posing a possible answer and then systemically trying first to believe that answer and then to doubt it. The game, as you will see, stimulates your critical thinking, helping you resist early closure.

Playing the Believing and Doubting Game

Play the believing and doubting game with one of the assertions listed on pp. 44–46 (or another assertion provided by your instructor) by freewriting your believing and doubting responses. Spend fifteen minutes believing and then fifteen minutes doubting for a total of thirty minutes.

When you play the believing side of this game, you try to become sympathetic to an idea or point of view. You listen carefully to it, opening yourself to the possibility that it is true. You try to appreciate why the idea has force for so many people; you try to accept it by discovering as many reasons as you can for believing it. It is easy to play the believing game with ideas you already believe in, but the game becomes more difficult, sometimes even frightening and dangerous, when you try believing ideas that seem untrue or disturbing.

The doubting game is the opposite of the believing game. It calls for you to be judgmental and critical, to find fault with an idea rather than to accept it. When you doubt a new idea, you try your best to falsify it, to find counterexamples that disprove it, to find flaws in its logic. Again, it is easy to play the doubting game with ideas you don't like, but it, too, can be threatening when you try to doubt ideas that are dear to your heart or central to your own worldview.

READING

Here is how one student played the believing and doubting game with the following assertion from professional writer Paul Theroux that emphasizing sports is harmful to boys.

Just as high school basketball teaches you how to be a poor loser, the manly attitude towards sports seems to be little more than a recipe for creating bad marriages, social misfits, moral degenerates, sadists, latent rapists and just plain louts. I regard high school sports as a drug far worse than marijuana.

Believing and Doubting Paul Theroux's Negative View of Sports

Believe

1   Although I am a woman I have a hard time believing this because I was a high school basketball player and believe high school sports are *very* important. But here goes. I will try to believe this statement even though I hate it. Let's see. It would seem that I wouldn't have much first-hand experience with how society turns boys into men. I do see though that Theroux is right about some major problems. Through my observations, I've seen many young boys go through humiliating experiences with sports that have left them scarred. For example, a 7-year-old boy, Matt, isn't very athletic and when kids in our neighborhood choose teams, they usually choose girls before they choose Matt. I wonder if he sees himself as a sissy and what this does to him? I have also experienced some first-hand adverse effects of society's methods of turning boys into men. In our family, my dad spent much of his time playing football, basketball, and baseball with my brother. I've loved sports since I was very young so I was eager to play. In order to play with them, I had to play like a boy. Being told you threw or played like a girl was the worst possible insult you could receive. The phrase, "be tough" was something I heard repeatedly while I was growing up. Whenever I got hurt, my dad would say, "Be tough." It didn't matter how badly I was hurt, I always heard the same message. Today, I think, I have a very, very difficult time opening up and letting people get to know me, because for so long I was taught to keep everything inside. Maybe sports does have some bad effects.

Doubt

2   I am glad I get to doubt this too because I have been really mad at all the sports bashing that has been going on in class. I think much of what Theroux says is just a crock. I know that the statement "sports builds character" is a cliché, but I really believe it. It seems to me that the people who lash out at sports clichés are those who never experienced these aspects of athletics and therefore don't understand them. No one can tell me that sports didn't contribute to some of my best and most meaningful friendships and growing experiences. I am convinced that I am a better person because through sports I have had to deal with failure, defeat, frustration, sacrificing individual desires for the benefit of the team, and so on. After my last high school basketball game when after many years of mind games, of hating my coach one minute and the next having deep respect for him, of big games lost on my mistakes, of hours spent alone in the gym, of wondering if the end justifies the means, my coach put his arm around me and told me he was proud. Everything, all the pain, frustration, anxiety, fear, and sacrifice of the past years seemed so worthwhile. You might try to tell me that this story

is hackneyed and trite, but I won't listen because it is a part of me, and some thing you will never be able to damage or take away. I think athletes share a special bond. They know what it is like to go through the physical pain of practice time and again. They understand the wide variety of emotions felt (but rarely expressed). They also know what a big role the friendships of teammates and coaches play in an athlete's life.

We admire this writer a great deal—both for the passion with which she defends sports in her doubting section and for the courage of walking in a sports basher's shoes in the believing section. This exercise clearly engaged and stretched her thinking.

We invite you now to stretch your own thinking by playing the believing and doubting game with one of the following assertions. The first set of assertions focuses on the constellation of issues surrounding fossil fuels and energy that we introduced in Chapter 1. The last set gives you other options to explore.

Option 1: Energy Issues

For these energy issues, we have identified the source for each assertion to help you imagine yourself joining a public conversation of ideas already in print.

1. ". . . the car is the greatest modern symbol of American freedom." (John Bragg, "The American Dream: Why Environmentalists Attack the SUV," *Capitalism Magazine Online*)
2. ". . . most customers want bigger and faster cars—actually, light-duty trucks like sport utility vehicles—not efficient ones." ["A Fuel-Saving Proposal from Your Automaker: Tax the Gas," *New York Times* (April 18, 2004): BU 5]
3. "This country must immediately start phasing out its national dependence on fossil fuel [and] support policies to immediately reduce carbon emissions and greenhouse gases . . . ." ("Climate Justice: Indigenous Peoples, Global Warming and Climate Change," Indigenous Environmental Network www.ienearth.org)
4. "The best way to break the back of OPEC [Organization of Petroleum Exporting Countries] is to produce more oil here at home." [Stephen Moore, "Stick a Pump in It," *National Review Online* (May 10, 2004)]
5. "If Congress is serious about ensuring our national security, it should immediately pass legislation to raise fuel economy standards to 40 miles a gallon by 2012 and 55 by 2020." [Robert F. Kennedy, Jr., "Better Gas Mileage, Greater Security," *New York Times* (November 24, 2001)]
6. You can also play the believing and doubting game with advertisements or other visual texts. Consider using the Shell corporate ad (Figure 2.1) or the Adbusters' spoof ad (Figure 2.2) as visual commentary on the oil industry's approach to oil exploration. If you are responding to one of these visual texts, begin by stating the main point of the text in a one-sentence assertion. For example, "The Shell ad says that the oil industry, especially our company, will

FIGURE 2.1 Shell Corporate Ad

WHAT DO WE REALLY NEED IN TODAY'S ENERGY HUNGRY WORLD? MORE GARDENERS.

The Flower Gardens of the Gulf of Mexico. Home to some of the most spectacular banks of coral and sponges to be found in this part of the world.

In fact, this National Marine Sanctuary forms the most northerly reef on the U.S. continental shelf. Which is why, when Shell went looking for oil and natural gas in this region, we looked for help from Jim Ray—a marine biologist and Shell employee.

For some thirty years now, Jim and others just like him have been working to protect this magnificent area and other sensitive marine environments.

They're providing a habitat for all manner of marine life, so everyone from ecologists to school-teachers has the opportunity to study this wonderful world firsthand.

Because at Shell, we focus on energy but that's not our only focus. To find out more, see the Shell Report at www.shell.com.

FIGURE 2.2 Adbusters' Spoof Ad

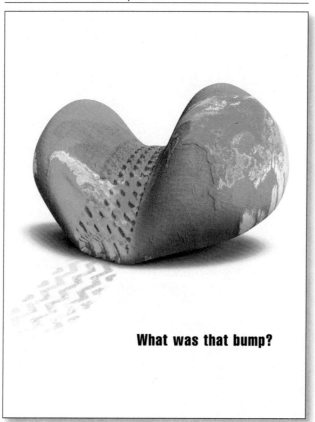

What was that bump?

solve the problem of diminishing fossil fuel reserves by using our company's innovative thinking and technological expertise." Then play the believing and doubting game with the assertion.

Option 2: Other Issues

1. Grades are an effective means of motivating students to do their best work.
2. In recent years advertising has made enormous gains in portraying women as strong, independent, and intelligent.
3. To help fight terrorism and promote public safety, individuals should be willing to give up some of their rights.
4. It is often OK to tell a lie.
5. The United States should reinstate the draft.
6. Violent video games are harmful to young people.
7. NASCAR drivers are not real athletes.
8. It is rude to talk on a cell phone in a public place.
9. Hate speech should be forbidden on college campuses.

Thinking Rhetorically about Purpose, Audience, and Genre

It is amazing how much so-called writing problems clear up when the student really cares, when he is realistically put into the drama of somebody with something to say to somebody else.

—JAMES MOFFETT, *WRITING TEACHER AND THEORIST*

In Chapters 1 and 2 we introduced you to rhetorical thinking by showing you how experienced writers think about their audience and purpose as they wrestle with subject-matter questions. They must pose questions that matter to their intended readers and propose claims that bring those readers something new, surprising, or challenging. In all these cases, the writer's subject-matter considerations are influenced by rhetorical context.

In this chapter, we extend the idea of rhetorical thinking by probing three key variables in a writer's rhetorical context: purpose, audience, and genre. While thinking about subject matter, writers also think about rhetorical issues, posing questions about their purpose (What am I trying to accomplish in this paper?), their audience (What are my readers' values and assumptions? What do they already know and believe about my subject?), and genre (What kind of document am I writing? What are its requirements for structure, style, and document design?). We show how your answers to these questions influence many of the decisions you make as a writer. We end by explaining the generic rhetorical context assumed by most teachers for college papers across the disciplines.

In this chapter you will learn the following principles:

- How to think productively about your purpose, audience, and genre
- How to make decisions about structure and style based on your analysis of these elements
- How to adjust your writing on the scale of abstraction to fit your purpose, audience, and genre
- How to recognize and employ document design features appropriate for different genres
- How to understand the generic rhetorical context for most college papers

How Writers Think about Purpose

In this section, we want to help you think more productively about your purpose for writing, which can be examined from several different perspectives: your rhetorical aim, the motivating occasion that gets you going, and your desire to change your reader's view. All three perspectives will help you make your awareness of purpose work for you and increase your savvy as a writer. Let's look at each in turn.

Purpose as Rhetorical Aim

One powerful way to think about purpose is through the general concept of "rhetorical aim." In this text, we identify six different rhetorical aims of writing: to express, to explore, to inform, to analyze and synthesize, to persuade, and to give aesthetic pleasure. Thinking of each piece of writing in terms of one or more of these rhetorical aims can help you understand typical ways that your essay can be structured and developed and can help you clarify your relationship with your audience. The writing projects in Part Two of this text are based on these rhetorical aims.* Table 3.1 gives you an overview of each of the six rhetorical aims and sketches out how the subject matter differs from aim to aim, how the writer's task and relationship to readers differ according to aim, and how a chosen aim affects the writing's genre and its position on the spectrum from open to closed forms.

Purpose as a Response to a Motivating Occasion

Another important way to think about purpose is to think about each piece of writing as a response to a particular motivating occasion. Almost all writing is compelled by some sort of motivating occasion or exigency.† This exigency can be external (someone giving you a task and setting a deadline) or internal (your awareness of a problem stimulating your desire to bring about some change in people's views). Thus, when engineer David Rockwood read a newspaper editorial supporting wind-power projects, his own belief in the impracticality of wind power motivated him to write a letter to the editor in rebuttal (see pp. 17–18). But he also knew that he had to write the letter within one or two days or else it stood no chance of being published. His exigency thus included both internal and external factors.

---

*An additional aim, not quite parallel to these others, is sometimes called "writing-to-learn." When your purpose is writing-to-learn, your writing is aimed at helping you understand an important concept or learn a skill necessary for expert performance in a discipline. Teachers often design writing-to-learn assignments focusing on specific course learning goals. In Part Two of this text, the first two writing projects (for Chapters 5 and 6) are writing-to-learn pieces.

†An *exigency* is an urgent or pressing situation requiring immediate attention. Rhetoricians use the term to describe the event or occasion that causes a writer to begin writing.

TABLE 3.1 Purpose as Rhetorical Aim

Rhetorical Aim	Focus of Writing	What Writers Do	Relationship to Audience	Form and Genres
Express or share (Chapter 7)	Your own life, personal experiences that you want to make public, reflections	You express your feelings and thoughts (even venting); you write to move others.	You ask readers to see the world your way; you invite them to see connections between your life and theirs; you surprise readers with your experiential insights.	**Form:** Tends to have many open-form features **Sample genres:** Diary or journal; personal essay; literary nonfiction, perhaps using plot, character, image, and symbol
Explore or inquire (Chapter 8)	Subject-matter problems; a significant, problematic question; shows a writer seeking to understand these problems or questions	You ask questions, wade into complexity by posing or deepening a problem, raising new questions, considering alternative views, and showing the limitations of other answers and approaches.	You invite readers on your intellectual journey; you ask readers to think with you, to collaborate in discovering a new understanding of a subject.	**Form:** Follows open form in being narrative based; seeks a thesis rather than supporting one **Sample genres:** Freewriting; idea mapping; journals; notes; formal essays in narrative form dramatizing the writer's thinking about a question
Inform or explain (Chapter 9)	Subject matter on which you present new or needed information based on your own experience or research	You provide information your readers need or want, or you arouse curiosity and then present new, surprising information.	You, as knowledgeable teacher, surprise by enlarging readers' view of a subject; you expect readers to trust your authority and information.	**Form:** Usually has a closed-form structure but could be open form **Sample genres:** Encyclopedia, newspaper, and magazine articles; brochures; instruction booklets; sales reports; technical reports; informative Web sites
Analyze, synthesize, or interpret (Chapters 10–13)	Subject matter that is problematic and complex and that you can break down into parts and put together in new ways for greater understanding	Using critical thinking and possibly research, you examine parts and their relationships to each other and the whole; you put together ideas from your analyses into a new whole that represents your enlarged, enriched understanding of a subject or issue.	You challenge readers with a new, illuminating way of seeing, thinking about, or understanding your subject; readers may be skeptical, expecting you to support your thesis with good particulars.	**Form:** Typically has a closed-form structure; introduces a question or problem, sketches an answer, and develops this answer with good supporting points and particulars **Sample genres:** Scholarly articles and much other academic writing across the disciplines; critiques; public affairs magazine articles; newspaper feature articles

(continued)

TABLE 3.1 continued

Rhetorical Aim	Focus of Writing	What Writers Do	Relationship to Audience	Form and Genres
Persuade (Chapters 14–16)	Subject-matter questions that have multiple, controversial answers	You enter a controversy in hopes of persuading readers to accept your own views on a controversial issue; you surprise your readers with reasons and evidence to change their beliefs and actions.	You try to convince your readers, who are like jurors, of the soundness of your position; you must appeal to your readers' values and beliefs and anticipate the objections and alternative views of skeptical readers.	**Form:** Anywhere on the open-to-closed-form spectrum; could be a closed-form argument consisting of logical point-by-point reasons and evidence; could also be an open-form story or collage of emotionally charged scenes **Sample genres:** Letters to the editor; op-ed pieces; policy statements for public affairs magazines and advocacy Web sites; researched academic arguments
Entertain or give aesthetic pleasure (Chapter 19)	Language itself shaped to convey experience or emotion	You explore the properties of language, using words the way artists use clay and paint; you work with sounds, rhythms, and word images to make readers see and feel.	You seek to entice and move your readers—please, delight, thrill, or disturb them.	**Form:** Open form; literary nonfiction may combine a literary purpose with an expressive or explanatory purpose **Sample genres:** Literary nonfiction; poetry; all genres of fiction

You might think that school is the only place where people are compelled to write. However, some element of external compulsion is present in nearly every writing situation, although this external compulsion is almost never the sole motivation for writing. Consider a middle manager requested by the company vice president to write a report explaining why his division's profits are down. The manager is motivated by several factors: He wants to provide a sound analysis of why profits have declined; he wants to propose possible solutions that will remedy the situation; he wants to avoid looking personally responsible for the dip in profits; he wants to impress the vice president in the hope that she will promote him to upper management; and so on.

College students' motivations for writing can be equally complex: In part, you write to meet a deadline; in part, you write to please the teacher and get a good grade. But ideally you also write because you have become engaged with an intellectual problem and want to say something significant about it. Our point here is that your purposes for writing are always more complex than the simple desire to meet an assignment deadline.

Purpose as a Desire to Change Your Reader's View

Perhaps the most useful way to think about purpose is to focus on the change you want to bring about in your audience's view of the subject. When you are given a college writing assignment, this view of purpose engages you directly with the intellectual problem specified in the assignment. This view of purpose has already been introduced in Chapter 2, where we explained the importance of surprise as a measure of what is new or challenging in your essay. For most essays, you can write a one-sentence, nutshell statement about your purpose.

See Chapter 2, pp. 34–37, for an explanation of surprise in thesis statements.

My purpose is to give my readers a vivid picture of my difficult struggle with Graves' disease.

My purpose is to raise serious doubts about the value of the traditional grading system.

My purpose is to inform my readers about the surprising growth of the marijuana industry in the Midwestern farm states.

My purpose is to explain how Thoreau's view of nature differs in important ways from that of contemporary environmentalists.

My purpose is to persuade the general public that wind-generated electricity is not a practical energy alternative in the Pacific Northwest.

In closed-form academic articles, technical reports, and other business and professional pieces, writers often place explicit purpose statements in their introductions along with the thesis. In most other forms of writing, the writer uses a behind-the-scenes purpose statement to achieve focus and direction but seldom states the purpose explicitly. Writing an explicit purpose statement for a paper is a powerful way to nutshell the kind of change you want to bring about in your reader's view of the subject.

Chapter 18, pp. 545–546, shows you how purpose statements can be included in closed-form introductions.

For Writing and Discussion

This exercise will show you how the concept of "rhetorical aim" can help you generate ideas for an essay. As a class, choose one of the following topic areas or another provided by your instructor. Then imagine six different writing situations in which a hypothetical writer would compose an essay about the selected topic. Let each situation call for a different aim. How might a person write about the selected topic with an expressive aim? An exploratory aim? An informative aim? An analytic aim? A persuasive aim? A literary aim? How would each essay surprise its readers?

automobiles	animals	hospices or nursing homes
homelessness	music	dating or marriage
advertising	energy crisis	sports injuries

(continued)

Working on your own or in small groups, create six realistic scenarios, each of which calls for prose in a different category of aim. Then share your results as a whole class. Here are two examples based on the topic "hospices."

Expressive Aim	Working one summer as a volunteer in a hospice for dying cancer patients, you befriend a woman whose attitude toward death changes your life. You write an autobiographical essay about your experiences with this remarkable woman.
Analytic Aim	You are a hospice nurse working in a home care setting. You and your colleagues note that sometimes family members cannot adjust psychologically to the burden of living with a dying person. You decide to investigate this phenomenon. You interview "reluctant" family members in an attempt to understand the causes of their psychological discomfort so that you can provide better counseling services as a possible solution. You write a paper for a professional audience analyzing the results of your interviews.

How Writers Think about Audience

In our discussion of purpose, we already had a lot to say about audience. What you know about your readers—their familiarity with your subject matter, their reasons for reading, their closeness to you, their values and beliefs—affects most of the choices you make as a writer.

The value of moving from old information to new information is explained in Chapter 18, pp. 529–530 and 556–559.

In assessing your audience, you must first consider what, to them, is old information and what is new information. You'll ask questions like these: What in my essay will be familiar and what will be new, challenging, and surprising? How much background will my readers need? What can I assume they know and don't know? What is their current view of my topic that I am trying to change?

As you think about your readers' current views on your topic, you also need to think about their methods and reasons for reading. Imagine that you want to persuade your boss to reconfigure your office's computer network. You've discussed your ideas with her briefly, and she's asked you to write a formal proposal for the next technology meeting. Knowing of her harried environment—people waiting to see her, meetings to attend, e-mails piling up, memos and reports filling her in-box—you use a tightly closed structure for your proposal. Your document must be clear, concise, summarizable, and immediately comprehensible. The same reader in a different mood and setting may turn to a more leisurely kind of prose, say, an article in her favorite magazine or a new book on her favorite subject, where she might enjoy the subtlety and stylistic pleasures of open-form prose.

Now consider how a change in audience can affect the content of a piece. Suppose you want voters in your city to approve a bond issue to build a new baseball stadium. If most members of your audience are baseball fans, you can appeal to their love of the game, the pleasure of a new facility, and so forth. But non-baseball fans won't be moved by these arguments. To reach them, you must tie the new baseball stadium to their values. You can argue that a new stadium will bring new tax revenues to the city, clean up a run-down area, revitalize local businesses, or stimulate the tourist industry. Your purpose remains the same—to persuade taxpayers to fund the stadium—but the content of your argument changes if your audience changes.

In college, you often seem to be writing for an audience of one—your instructor. However, most instructors try to read as a representative of a broader audience. To help college writers imagine these readers, many instructors try to design writing assignments that provide a fuller sense of audience. They may ask you to write for the readers of a particular magazine or journal, or they may create case assignments with built-in audiences (for example, "You are an accountant in the firm of Numbers and Fudge; one day you receive a letter from . . ."). If your instructor does not specify an audience, you can generally assume the audience to be what we like to call "the generic academic audience"—student peers who have approximately the same level of knowledge and expertise in the field as you do, who are engaged by the question you address, and who want to read your writing and be surprised in some way.

Assessing Your Audience

In any writing situation, you can use the following questions to help you make decisions about content, form, and style:

QUESTIONS TO ASK ABOUT AUDIENCE

1. Who is going to read what I write? A specific individual? A specific group with special interests? Or a general readership with wide-ranging interests and backgrounds?
2. What relationship do I have to these readers? Do I and my readers have an informal, friendly relationship or a polite, formal one? Is my readers' expertise in my general subject area greater, less, or equal to mine?
3. How much do my readers already know about the specific problem I address? How much background will I have to provide?
4. How much interest do my readers bring to my topic? Do I need to hook readers with a vivid opening and use special techniques to maintain their interest throughout? Or are they interested enough in the problem I am examining that the subject matter itself will drive their reading? (In persuasive writing, particularly in writing that proposes a solution to a problem, you may need to shock your readers into awareness that the problem exists.)
5. What are my audience's values, beliefs, and assumptions in relation to my topic? If I am writing on a controversial issue, will my readers oppose my position, be neutral to it, or support it? To which of their values, beliefs, or assumptions can I appeal? Will my position unsettle or threaten my audience or stimulate a strong emotional response? (Because a concern for audience is particularly relevant to persuasive writing, we treat these questions in more depth in Chapters 14 through 16.)

How to hook your readers' interest through an effective introduction is covered in Chapter 18, pp. 542–546.

Posing these questions will not lead to any formulaic solutions to your writing problems, but it can help you develop strategies that will appeal to your audience and enable you to achieve your purpose.

How Writers Think about Genre

The term *genre* refers to broad categories of writing that follow certain conventions of style, structure, approach to subject matter, and document design. Literary genres include the short story, the novel, the epic poem, the limerick, the sonnet, and so forth. Nonfiction prose has its own genres: the business memo, the technical manual, the scholarly article, the scientific report, the popular magazine article (each magazine, actually, has its own particular conventions), the Web page, the five-paragraph theme (a school genre), the newspaper editorial, the cover letter for a job application, the legal contract, the advertising brochure, and so forth.

The concept of genre creates strong reader expectations and places specific demands on writers. How you write any given letter, report, or article is influenced by the structure and style of hundreds of previous letters, reports, or articles written in the same genre. If you wanted to write for *Reader's Digest*, for example, you would have to use the conventions that appeal to its older, conservative readers: simple language, subjects with strong human interest, heavy reliance on anecdotal evidence in arguments, an upbeat and optimistic perspective, and an approach that reinforces the conservative *ethos* of individualism, self-discipline, and family. If you wanted to write for *Seventeen* or *Rolling Stone*, however, you would need to use quite different conventions.

To illustrate the relationship of a writer to a genre, we sometimes draw an analogy with clothing. Although most people have a variety of different types of clothing in their wardrobes, the genre of activity for which they are dressing (Saturday night movie date, job interview, wedding) severely constrains their choice and expression of individuality. A man dressing for a job interview might express his personality through choice of tie or quality and style of business suit; he probably wouldn't express it by wearing a Hawaiian shirt and sandals. Even when people deviate from a convention, they tend to do so in a conventional way. For example, teenagers who do not want to follow the genre of "teenager admired by adults" form their own genre of purple hair and pierced body parts. The concept of genre raises intriguing and sometimes unsettling questions about the relationship of the unique self to a social convention or tradition.

These same kinds of questions and constraints perplex writers. For example, academic writers usually follow the genre of the closed-form scholarly article. This highly functional form achieves maximum clarity for readers by orienting them quickly to the article's purpose, content, and structure. Readers expect this format, and writers have the greatest chance of being published if they meet these expectations. In some disciplines, however, scholars are beginning to publish more experimental, open-form articles. They may slowly alter the conventions of the scholarly article, just as fashion designers alter styles of dress.

For Writing and Discussion

1. On the previous page we offered you a brief description of the conventions governing *Reader's Digest* articles, which appeal mainly to older, conservative readers. For this exercise, prepare similar descriptions of the conventions that govern articles in several other magazines such as *Rolling Stone, Sports Illustrated, Cosmopolitan, Details, The New Yorker*, or *Psychology Today*. Each person should bring to class a copy of a magazine that he or she enjoys reading. The class should then divide into small groups according to similar interests. Your instructor may supply a few scholarly journals from different disciplines. In preparing a brief profile of your magazine, consider the following:

   - Scan the table of contents. What kinds of subjects or topics does the magazine cover?
   - Look at the average length of articles. How much depth and analysis are provided?
   - Consider the magazine's readership. Does the magazine appeal to particular political or social groups (liberal/conservative, male/female, young/old, white-collar/blue-collar, in-group/general readership)?
   - Look at the advertisements. What kinds of products are most heavily advertised in the magazine? Who is being targeted by these advertisements? What percentage of the magazine consists of advertisements?
   - Read representative pages, including the introductions, of some articles. Would you characterize the prose as difficult or easy? Intellectual or popular? Does the prose use the jargon, slang, or other language particular to a group? Are the paragraphs long or short? How are headings, inserts, visuals, and other page-formatting features used? Is the writing formal or informal?
   - Think about what advice you would give a person who wanted to write a freelance article for this magazine.

2. Imagine that someone interested in hospices (see the example in the For Writing and Discussion exercise on pp. 51–52) wanted to write an article about hospices for your chosen magazine. What approach would the writer have to take to have a hospice-related article published in your magazine? There may be no chance of this happening, but be creative. Here is an example:

   > Ordinarily *Sports Illustrated* would be an unlikely place for an article on hospices. However, *SI* might publish a piece about a dying athlete in a hospice setting. It might also publish a piece about sports memories of dying patients or about watching sports as therapy.

Rhetorical Context and Your Choices about Structure

So far in this chapter, we have examined purpose, audience, and genre as components of a writer's rhetorical context. In this section and the next, our goal is to help you appreciate how these variables influence a writer's choices regarding structure and style. Although there is no formula that allows you to determine an appropriate structure and style based on particular purposes, audiences, and genres, there are some rules of thumb that can help you make decisions. Let's look first at structure.

Because most academic, business, and professional writing uses a closed-form structure, we spend a significant portion of this text advising you how to write such prose. But open-form prose is equally valuable and is often more subtle, complex, and beautiful, so it is good to practice writing at different positions on the continuum. The following advice will help you decide when closed or open forms are more appropriate:

WHEN IS CLOSED-FORM PROSE MOST APPROPRIATE?

- When your focus is on the subject matter itself and your goal is to communicate efficiently to maximize clarity. In these cases, your aim is usually to inform, analyze, or persuade.
- When you imagine your audience as a busy or harried reader who needs to be able to read quickly and process ideas rapidly. Closed-form prose is easy to summarize; moreover, a reader can speed-read closed-form prose by scanning the introduction and then glancing at headings and the openings of paragraphs, where writers place key points.
- When the conventional genre for your context is closed-form writing and you choose to meet, rather than break, readers' expectations.
- When you encounter any rhetorical situation that asks you to assert and support a thesis in response to a problem or question.

WHEN IS A MORE OPEN FORM DESIRABLE?

- When you want to delay your thesis rather than announce it in the introduction (for example, to create suspense). A delayed-thesis structure is less combative and more friendly; it conveys an unfolding "let's think through this together" feeling.
- When your aim is expressive, exploratory, or literary. These aims tend to be served better through narrative rather than through thesis-with-support writing.
- When you imagine your audience reading primarily for enjoyment and pleasure. In this context you can often wed a literary purpose to another purpose.
- When the conventional genre calls for open-form writing—for example, autobiographical narratives, character sketches, or personal reflective pieces. Popular magazine articles often have a looser, more open structure than do scholarly articles or business reports.

- When you are writing about something that is too complex or messy to be captured in a fixed thesis statement, or when you feel constrained by the genre of thesis with support.

Rhetorical Context and Your Choices about Style

Writers need to make choices not only about structure but also about style. By *style*, we mean the choices you make about how to say something. Writers can say essentially the same thing in a multitude of ways, each placing the material in a slightly different light, subtly altering meaning, and slightly changing the effect on readers. In this section we illustrate more concretely the many stylistic options open to you and explain how you might go about making stylistic choices.

Factors That Affect Style

As we shall see, style is a complex composite of many factors. We can classify the hundreds of variables that affect style into four broad categories:

1. *Ways of shaping sentences:* long/short, simple/complex, many modifiers/few modifiers, normal word order/frequent inversions or interruptions, mostly main clauses/many embedded phrases and subordinate clauses
2. *Types of words:* abstract/concrete, formal/colloquial, unusual/ordinary, specialized/general, metaphoric/literal, scientific/literary
3. *The implied personality projected by the writer (often called* voice *or* persona): expert/layperson, scholar/student, outsider/insider, political liberal/conservative, neutral observer/active participant
4. *The writer's implied relationship to the reader and the subject matter (often called* tone): intimate/distant, personal/impersonal, angry/calm, browbeating/sharing, informative/entertaining, humorous/serious, ironic/literal, passionately involved/aloof

Recognizing Different Styles and Voices

When discussing style, rhetoricians often use related terms such as *voice* and *persona*. We can distinguish these terms by thinking of style as analyzable textual features on a page (length and complexity of sentences, level of abstraction, and so forth) and of voice or persona as the reader's impression of the writer projected from the page. Through your stylistic choices, you create an image of yourself in your readers' minds. This image can be cold or warm, insider or outsider, humorous or serious, detached or passionate, scholarly or hip, antagonistic or friendly, and so forth.

What style you adopt depends on your purpose, audience, and genre. Consider, for example, the following thought exercise: Suppose you are interested in the subject of flirting. (Perhaps you have asked a research question such as the following: How has concern about sexual harassment affected views on flirting in the workplace? Or, When is flirting psychologically and emotionally healthy?) You decide to do library research on flirting and are surprised by the different styles and genres you encounter. Here are the opening paragraphs of three different articles that discuss flirting—from a scholarly journal, from a fairly intellectual special interest magazine, and from a popular magazine devoted to women's dating and fashion. At the moment, we are considering only differences in the verbal styles of these articles. Later in this chapter, we reproduce the actual opening pages of two of these articles as they originally appeared in order to discuss document design.

SCHOLARLY JOURNAL

[*From* The Journal of Sex Research]

Sexual Messages: Comparing Findings from Three Studies

Sexual socialization is influenced by a wide range of sources, including parents, peers, and the mass media (Hyde & DeLameter, 1997). In trying to understand the process by which young people acquire their sexual beliefs, attitudes, and behaviors, the study of media provides information about potential socializing messages that are an important part of everyday life for children and adolescents (Greenberg, Brown, & Buerkel-Rothfuss, 1993). The significance of media content in this realm stems from a number of unique aspects surrounding its role in the lives of youth, including its early accessibility and its almost universal reach across the population.

Electronic media, and television in particular, provide a window to many parts of the world, such as sexually related behavior, that would otherwise be shielded from young audiences. Long before many parents begin to discuss sex with their children, answers to such questions as "When is it OK to have sex?" and "With whom does one have sexual relations?" are provided by messages delivered on television. These messages are hardly didactic, most often coming in the form of scripts and plots in fictional entertainment programs. Yet the fact that such programs do not intend to teach sexual socialization lessons hardly mitigates the potential influence of their portrayals.

—Dale Kunkel, Kirstie M. Cope, and Erica Biely

SPECIAL INTEREST MAGAZINE

[*From* Psychology Today]

The New Flirting Game

"It may be an ages-old, biologically-driven activity, but today it's also played with artful self-awareness and even conscious calculation" [opening lead in large, all-caps text].

To hear the evolutionary determinists tell it, we human beings flirt to propagate our genes and to display our genetic worth. Men are constitutionally predisposed to flirt with the healthiest, most fertile women, recognizable by their biologically correct waist-hip ratios. Women favor the guys with dominant demeanors, throbbing muscles and the most resources to invest in their offspring.

Looked at up close, human psychology is more diverse and perverse than the evolutionary determinists would have it. We flirt as thinking individuals in a particular culture at a particular time. Yes, we may express a repertoire of hardwired nonverbal expressions and behaviors—staring eyes, flashing brows, opened palms—that resemble those of other animals, but unlike other animals, we also flirt with conscious calculation. We have been known to practice our techniques in front of the mirror. In other words, flirting among human beings is culturally modulated as well as biologically driven, as much art as instinct.

—Deborah A. Lott

WOMEN'S DATING AND FASHION MAGAZINE

[*From* Cosmopolitan]

Flirting with Disaster

"I'd never be unfaithful, but . . ." [opening lead in very large type].

"You're in love and totally committed—or are you? You dirty danced with a cute guy at the office party, and make an effort to look sexy for the man in the coffee shop. Are you cheating without knowing it?" [second lead in large type]

I think I've been cheating on my partner. Let me explain. I went out clubbing recently with a really good friend, a guy I've known for years. We both love to dance. [. . .] [W]henever we get together, there comes a moment, late in the evening, when I look at him and feel myself beginning to melt. [. . .] This is not the way people who are "just friends" touch each other.

[. . .] So I suppose the question is, at what point does flirting stop being harmless fun and become an actual betrayal of your relationship?

—Lisa Sussman and Tracey Cox

For Writing and Discussion

Working in small groups or as a whole class, analyze the differences in the styles of these three samples.

1. How would you describe differences in the length and complexity of sentences, in the level of vocabulary, and in the degree of formality?
2. How do the differences in styles create different voices, personas, and tones?
3. Based on clues from style and genre, who is the intended audience of each piece? What is the writer's purpose? How does each writer hope to surprise the intended audience with something new, challenging, or valuable?
4. How are the differences in content and style influenced by differences in purpose, audience, and genre?

Rhetorical Context and Your Choices along the Scale of Abstraction

In Chapter 2, we explained how writers use particulars—examples, details, numerical data, and other kinds of evidence—to support their points. We said that strong writing weaves back and forth between points and particulars; points give meaning to particulars and particulars flesh out and develop points, making them credible and convincing. However, the distinction between points and particulars is a matter of context. The same sentence might serve as a point in one context and as a particular in another. What matters is the relative position of words and sentences along a scale of abstraction. As an illustration of such a scale, consider the following list of words descending from the abstract to the specific:

> Clothing➔footwear➔shoes➔sandals➔Birkenstocks➔my old hippie Birkenstocks with salt stains

Where you pitch a piece of writing on this scale of abstraction helps determine its style, with high-on-the-scale writing creating an abstract or theoretical effect and low-on-the-scale writing creating a more vivid and concrete effect. In descriptive and narrative prose, writers often use sensory details that are very low on the scale of abstraction. Note how shifting down the scale improves the vividness of the following passage:

> Mid-scale The awkward, badly dressed professor stood at the front of the room.
> Low on the scale At the front of the room stood the professor, a tall, gawky man with inch-thick glasses, an enormous Adam's apple, an old brown-striped jacket, burgundy and gray plaid pants, a silky vest with what appeared to be "scenes from an aquarium" printed on it, and a tie with blue koalas.

The details in the more specific passage help you experience the writer's world. They don't just tell you that the professor was dressed weirdly; they *show* you.

In closed-form prose such specific sensory language is less common, so writers need to make choices about the level of specificity that will be most effective based on their purpose, audience, and genre. Note the differences along the level of abstraction in the following passages:

PASSAGE 1: FAIRLY HIGH ON SCALE OF ABSTRACTION

Point sentence

Particulars high on scale of abstraction

Although lightning produces the most deaths and injuries of all weather-related accidents, the rate of danger varies considerably from state to state. Florida has twice as many deaths and injuries from lightning strikes as any other state. Hawaii and Alaska have the fewest.

—Passage from a general interest informative article on weather-related accidents

PASSAGE 2: LOWER ON SCALE OF ABSTRACTION

Point sentence

Florida has twice as many deaths and injuries from lightning strikes as any other state, with many of these casualties occurring on the open spaces of golf courses.

Florida golfers should carefully note the signals of dangerous weather conditions such as darkening skies, a sudden drop in temperature, an increase in wind, flashes of light and claps of thunder, and the sensation of an electric charge on one's hair or body. *Particulars at midlevel on scale*
In the event of an electric storm, golfers should run into a forest, get under a shelter, get into a car, or assume the safest body position. To avoid being the tallest object in an area, if caught in open areas, golfers should find a low spot, spread out, and crouch into a curled position with feet together to create minimal body contact with the ground. *Particulars at lower level on scale*

—Passage from a safety article aimed at Florida golfers

Both of these passages are effective for their audience and purpose. Besides sensory details, writers can use other kinds of particulars that are low on the scale of abstraction such as quotations or statistics. Civil engineer David Rockwood uses low-on-the-scale numerical data about the size and number of wind towers to convince readers that wind generation of electricity entails environmental damage. *See Rockwood's letter to the editor, pp. 17–18.*

Other kinds of closed-form writing, however, often remain high on the scale. Yet even the most theoretical kind of prose will move back and forth between several layers on the scale. Your rhetorical decisions about level of abstraction are important because too much high-on-the-scale writing can become dull for readers, while too much low-on-the-scale writing can seem overwhelming or pointless. Each of the assignment chapters in Part Two of this text gives advice on finding the right kinds and levels of particulars to support each essay.

For Writing and Discussion

The following exercise will help you appreciate how details can be chosen at different levels of abstraction to serve different purposes and audiences. Working in small groups or as a whole class, invent details at appropriate positions on the scale of abstraction for each of the following point sentences.

1. The big game was a major disappointment. You are writing an e-mail message to a friend who is a fan (of baseball, football, basketball, another sport) and missed the game; use midlevel details to explain what was disappointing.
2. Although the game stunk, there were some great moments. Switch to low-on-the-scale details to describe one of these "great moments."
3. Advertising in women's fashion magazines creates a distorted and unhealthy view of beauty. You are writing an analysis for a college course on popular culture; use high-to-midlevel details to give a one-paragraph overview of several ways these ads create an unhealthy view of beauty.
4. One recent ad, in particular, conveys an especially destructive message about beauty. Choose a particular ad and describe it with low-on-the-scale details
5. In United States politics, there are several key differences between Republicans and Democrats. As part of a service learning project, you are creating a page on "American Politics" for a Web site aimed at helping international students understand American culture. Imagine a two-columned bulleted list contrasting Republicans and Democrats and construct two or

(continued)

three of these bullets. Choose details at an appropriate level on the scale of abstraction.

6. One look at Pete's pickup, and you knew immediately he was an in-your-face Republican (Democrat). You are writing a feature story for your college newspaper about Pete, a person who has plastered his pickup with political signs, bumper stickers, and symbols. Choose details at an appropriate level on the scale of abstraction.

Rhetorical Context and your Choices about Document Design

When thinking about structure, style, and genre, writers also need to consider document design. Document design refers to the visual features of a text. The "look" of a document is closely bound to the rhetorical context, to the way writers seek to communicate with particular audiences for particular purposes, and to the audience's expectations for that genre of writing. In this section, we explain the main components of document design that you will encounter as a reader. In Chapter 18, Lesson 10, we explain some principles of document design that you can use as a writer for producing different kinds of texts.

Historically, the use of images to convey information is more important than we may realize. Alphabets, for example, derived from picture drawings, and in earlier centuries, when only a small portion of the population could read, images—such as on signs—were an important means of communication. Now in the twenty-first century, some cultural critics theorize that we are moving from a text-based culture to an image-based culture. These critics speculate that visual communication has become more important, partly because of the increased pace of life, the huge volume of information that bombards us daily, and the constantly improving technology for creating better and more varied electronic images. We rely more heavily on information transmitted visually, and we depend on receiving that information more quickly. Visual details become a shorthand code for conveying this information concisely, quickly, and vividly. The visual details of document design are part of a code for recognizing genres and part of audience expectations that writers must meet.

As a writer, you are often expected to produce manuscript (typed pages of text) rather than a publication-ready document. When your task is to produce manuscript, your concerns for document design usually focus on margins, font style and size, location of page numbers, and line spacing. As an academic writer, you generally produce manuscripts following the style guidelines of the Modern Language Association (MLA), the American Psychological Association (APA), or some other scholarly organization. In business and professional settings, you employ different kinds of manuscript conventions for writing letters, memoranda, or reports.

Chapter 22 explains MLA and APA conventions.

In contrast to manuscript, today's writers are sometimes asked to use desktop publishing software to produce camera-ready or Web-ready documents that have a professional visual appeal (such as a pamphlet or brochure, a Web page, a poster, a marketing proposal that incorporates visuals and graphics, or some other piece with a "professionally published" look). Occasionally in your manuscript documents, you may want to display ideas or information visually—for example, with graphs, tables, or images.

See Chapter 10 for suggestions about when and how to use graphics and tables.

Key Components of Document Design

The main components of document design are use of type, use of space and layout, use of color, and use of graphics or images.

Use of Type

Type comes in different typeface styles, or fonts, that are commonly grouped in three font families: serif fonts that have tiny extensions on the letters, which make them easier to read for long documents; sans serif fonts that lack these extensions on the letters and are good for labels, headings, and Web documents; and specialty fonts, often used for decorative effect, that include script fonts and special symbols. Common word processing programs usually give you a huge array of fonts. Some examples of different fonts are shown in the box on page 64.

Fonts also come in different sizes, measured in points (one point = 1/72 of an inch). Much type in printed texts is set in ten or twelve points. In addition, fonts can be formatted in different ways: boldface, italics, underlining, or shading.

Font style and size contribute to the readability and overall impression of a text. Scholarly publications use few, plain, and regular font styles that don't draw attention to the type. Their use of fonts seeks to keep the readers' focus on the content of the document, to convey a serious tone, and to maximize the readers' convenience in grappling with the ideas of the text. (Teachers regularly expect a conservative font such as CG Times, Times New Roman, or Courier New for academic papers. Were you to submit an academic paper in a specialty or scripted font, you'd make a "notice me" statement, analogous to wearing a lime green jumpsuit to a college reception.) In academic papers, boldface can be used for headings and italics for occasional emphasis, but otherwise design flourishes are seldom used.

Popular magazines, on the other hand, tend to use fonts playfully and artistically, using a variety of fonts and sizes to attract readers' attention initially and to make a document look pleasingly decorative on the page. Although the body text of articles is usually the same font throughout, the opening page often uses a variety of fonts and sizes, and font variations may occur throughout the text to highlight key ideas for readers who are reading casually or rapidly.

Examples of Font Styles

Font Style	Font Name	Example
Serif fonts	Times New Roman	Have a good day!
	Courier New	Have a good day!
Sans serif fonts	Arial	Have a good day!
	Century Gothic	Have a good day!
Specialty fonts	Monotype Corsiva	*Have a good day!*
	Symbol	Ηαϖε α γοοδ δαψ!

Use of Space and Layout of Documents

Layout refers to how the text is formatted on the page. Layout includes the following elements:

- The size of the page itself
- The proportion of text to white space
- The arrangement of text on the page (single or multiple columns, long or short paragraphs, spaces between paragraphs)
- The size of the margins
- The use of justification (alignment of text with the left margin or both margins)
- The placement of titles
- The use of headings and subheadings to signal main and subordinate ideas and main parts of the document
- The spacing before and after headings
- The use of numbered or bulleted lists
- The use of boxes to highlight ideas or break text into visual units

Academic and scholarly writing calls for simple, highly functional document layouts. Most scholarly journals use single or double columns of text that are justified at both margins to create a regular, even look. (In preparing an academic manuscript, however, justify only the left-hand margin, leaving the right margin ragged.) Layout—particularly the presentation of titles and headings and the formatting of notes and bibliographic data—is determined by the style of the individual journal, which treats all articles identically. The layout of scholarly documents strikes a balance between maximizing the amount of text that fits on a page and ensuring readability by using headings and providing adequate white space in the margins.

In contrast, popular magazines place text in multiple columns that are often varied and broken up by text in boxes or by text wrapped around photos or drawings. Readability is important, but so is visual appeal and entertainment: Readers must enjoy looking at the pages. Many popular magazines try to blur the distinction between content and advertising so that ads become part of the visual appeal. This is why, in fashion magazines, the table of contents is often buried a dozen or more pages into the magazine. The publisher wants to coax readers to look at the ads as they look for the contents. (In contrast, the table of contents for most academic journals is on the cover.)

Use of Color

Colors convey powerful messages and appeals, even affecting moods. While manuscripts are printed entirely in black, published documents often use color to identify and set off main ideas or important information. Color-tinted boxes can indicate special features or allow magazines to print different but related articles on the same page.

Academic and scholarly articles and books use color minimally, if at all, relying instead on different font styles and sizes to make distinctions in content. Popular magazines, on the other hand, use colors playfully, artistically, decoratively, and strategically to enhance their appeal and, thus, their sales. Different colors of type may be used for different articles within one magazine or within articles themselves. Some articles may be printed on colored paper to give variety to the whole magazine.

The rhetorical use of visuals is introduced in Chapter 4, pp. 85–87. More detailed discussion of tables and graphs is found in Chapter 10, pp. 261–265, and of drawings and photographs throughout Chapter 11.

Use of Graphics or Images

Graphics include visual displays of information such as tables, line graphs, bar graphs, pie charts, maps, cartoons, illustrations, and photos.

As with the use of type, space, and color, the use of graphics indicates the focus, seriousness, function, and complexity of the writing. In scientific articles and books, many of the important findings of the articles may be displayed in complex, technical graphs and tables. Sources of information for these graphics are usually prominently stated, with key variables clearly labeled. In the humanities and social sciences, content-rich photos and drawings also tend to be vital parts of an article, even the subject of the analysis.

Popular magazines typically use simple numeric visuals (for example, a colorful pie chart or a dramatic graph) combined with decorative use of images, especially photos. If photos appear, it is worthwhile to consider how they are used. For example, do photos aim to look realistic and spontaneous like documentary photos of disaster scenes, sports moments, or people at work, or are they highly constructed, aesthetic photos? (Note that many political photos are meant to look spontaneous but are actually highly scripted—for example, a photograph of the president mending a fence with a horse nearby.) Are they concept (thematic) photos meant to illustrate an idea in an article (for example, a picture of a woman surrounded by images of pills, doctors, expensive medical equipment, and wrangling employers and insurance agents, to illustrate an article on health care costs)? The use of photos and illustrations can provide important clues about a publication's angle of vision, philosophy, or political leaning. For example, the *Utne Reader* tends to use many colored drawings rather than photos to illustrate its articles. These funky drawings with muted colors suit the magazine's liberal, socially progressive, and activist angle of vision.

Understanding the political slant of magazines, newspapers, and Web sites is essential for researchers. See Chapter 21, pp. 628–631.

Examples of Different Document Designs

In our earlier discussion of style, we reprinted the opening paragraphs of three articles on flirting. Figures 3.1 and 3.2 show the opening pages of two of these articles as they appeared in *The Journal of Sex Research* and *Psychology Today* (*Cosmopolitan*

FIGURE 3.1 Opening Page from Article in The *Journal of Sex Research*

Sexual Messages on Television: Comparing Findings From Three Studies

Dale Kunkel, Kirstie M. Cope, and Erica Biely

University of California Santa Barbara

Television portrayals may contribute to the sexual socialization of children and adolescents, and therefore it is important to examine the patterns of sexual content presented on television. This report presents a summary view across three related studies of sexual messages on television. The content examined ranges from programs most popular with adolescents to a comprehensive, composite week sample of shows aired across the full range of broadcast and cable channels. The results across the three studies identify a number of consistent patterns in television's treatment of sexual content. Talk about sex and sexual behaviors are both found frequently across the television landscape, although talk about sex is more common. Most sexual behaviors tend to be precursory in nature (such as physical flirting and kissing), although intercourse is depicted or strongly implied in roughly one of every eight shows on television. Perhaps most importantly, the studies find that TV rarely presents messages about the risks or responsibilities associated with sexual behavior.

Sexual socialization is influenced by a wide range of sources, including parents, peers, and the mass media (Hyde & DeLameter, 1997). In trying to understand the process by which young people acquire their sexual beliefs, attitudes, and behaviors, the study of media provides information about potential socializing messages that are an important part of everyday life for children and adolescents (Greenberg, Brown, & Buerkel-Rothfuss, 1993). The significance of media content in this realm stems from a number of unique aspects surrounding its role in the lives of youth, including its early accessibility and its almost universal reach across the population.

Electronic media, and television in particular, provide a window to many parts of the world, such as sexually-related behavior, that would otherwise be shielded from young audiences. Long before many parents begin to discuss sex with their children, answers to such questions as "When is it OK to have sex?" and "With whom does one have sexual relations?" are provided by messages delivered on television. These messages are hardly didactic, most often coming in the form of scripts and plots in fictional entertainment programs. Yet the fact that such programs do not intend to teach sexual socialization lessons hardly mitigates the potential influence of their portrayals.

While television is certainly not the only influence on sexual socialization, adolescents often report that they use portrayals in the media to learn sexual and romantic scripts and norms for sexual behavior (Brown, Childers, & Waszak, 1990). Indeed, four out of ten (40%) teens say they have gained ideas for how to talk to their boyfriend or girlfriend about sexual issues directly from media portrayals (Kaiser Family Foundation, 1998).

Just as it is well established that media exposure influences social behaviors such as aggression and social stereotyping, there is a growing body of evidence documenting the possible effects of sexual content on television (Huston, Wartella, & Donnerstein, 1998). For example, two studies have reported correlations between watching television programs high in sexual content and the early initiation of sexual intercourse by adolescents (Brown & Newcomer, 1991; Peterson, Moore, & Furstenberg, 1991), while another found heavy television viewing to be predictive of negative attitudes toward remaining a virgin (Courtright & Baran, 1980). An experiment by Bryant and Rockwell (1994) showed that teens who had just viewed television dramas laden with sexual content rated descriptions of casual sexual encounters less negatively than teens who had not viewed any sexual material.

Another important aspect of sexual socialization involves the development of knowledge about appropriate preventative behaviors to reduce the risk of infection from AIDS or other sexually-transmitted diseases. When teenagers begin to engage in sexual activity, they assume the risk of disease as well as the risk of unwanted pregnancy, and it appears that many lack adequate preparation to avoid such negative consequences.

Two Americans under the age of 20 become infected with HIV every hour (Office of National AIDS Policy, 1996). Almost one million teenagers become pregnant every year in the United States (Kirby, 1997). In the face of these sobering statistics, it is important to consider the extent to which media portrayals engage in or overlook concerns such as these, which are very serious issues in the lives of young people today.

In summary, media effects research clearly suggests that television portrayals contribute to sexual socialization.

The Family Hour Study was supported by the Henry J. Kaiser Family Foundation (Menlo Park, CA) and Children Now (Oakland, CA). The Teen Study was the Master's Thesis for Kirstie M. Cope. The V-Chip Study was supported by the Henry J. Kaiser Family Foundation. The authors wish to thank Carolyn Colvin, Ed Donnerstein, Wendy Jo Farinola, Ulla Foehr, Jim Potter, Vicky Rideout, and Emma Rollin, each of whom made significant contributions to one or more of the studies summarized here.

Address correspondence to Dr. Dale Kunkel, Department of Communication, University of California Santa Barbara, Santa Barbara, CA 93106; e-mail: kunkel@ahshaw.ucsb.edu.

FIGURE 3.2 Opening Page from Article in *Psychology Today*

THE NEW
Flirting Game

IT MAY BE AN AGES-OLD, BIOLOGICALLY-DRIVEN ACTIVITY, BUT TODAY IT'S ALSO PLAYED WITH ARTFUL SELF-AWARENESS AND EVEN CONSCIOUS CALCULATION.

By Deborah A. Lott

To hear the evolutionary determinists tell it, we human beings flirt to propagate our genes and to display our genetic worth. Men are constitutionally predisposed to flirt with the healthiest, most fertile women, recognizable by their biologically correct waist-hip ratios. Women favor the guys with dominant demeanors, throbbing muscles and the most resources to invest in them and their offspring.

Looked at up close, human psychology is more diverse and perverse than the evolutionary determinists would have it. We flirt as thinking individuals in a particular culture at a particular time. Yes, we may express a repertoire of hardwired non-verbal expressions and behaviors—that resemble those of other animals. We flash eyes, flashing brows, opened palms—that resemble those of other animals. But unlike other animals, we also flirt with conscious calculation. We have been known to practice our techniques in front of the mirror. In other words, flirting among human beings is culturally modulated as well as biologically driven, as much art as instinct.

In our culture today, it's clear that we do not always choose as the object of our desire those people the evolutionists might deem the most biologically desirable. After all, many young women today find the pale, androgynous, scarcely muscled yet emotionally expressive Leonardo DiCaprio more appealing than the burly Tarzans (Arnold Schwarzenegger, Bruce Willis, etc.) of action movies. Woody Allen may look nerdy but he's had no trouble winning women—and that's not just because he has material resources, but because humor is also a precious cultural commodity. Though she has no breasts or hips to speak of, Ally McBeal still attracts because there's ample evidence of a quick and quirky mind.

In short, we flirt with the intent of assessing potential lifetime partners, we flirt to have easy, no-strings-attached sex, and we flirt when we are not looking for either. We flirt because, most simply, flirtation can be a liberating form of play; a game with suspense and ambiguities that brings joys of its own. As Philadelphia-based social psychologist Tim Perper says, "Some flirters appear to want to prolong the interaction because it's pleasurable and erotic in its own right, regardless of where it might lead."

Here are some of the ways the game is currently being played

TAKING The Lead

When it comes to flirting today, women aren't waiting around for men to make the advances. They're taking the lead. Psychologist Monica Moore, Ph.D. of Webster University in St. Louis, Missouri, has spent more than 2000 hours observing women's flirting maneuvers in restaurants, singles bars and at parties. According to her findings, women give non-verbal cues that get a flirtation rolling fully two-thirds of the time. A man may think he's making the first move because he is the one to literally move from wherever he is to the woman's side, but usually he has been summoned.

By the standards set out by evolutionary psychologists, the women who attract the most

PHOTOGRAPHY BY FRANK VERONSKY

Psychology Today, November/December 1999

would not permit these images in its opening two-page spread to be reproduced for this textbook. However, we describe the opening pages in some detail in the For Writing and Discussion exercise below, discussion question 4).

For Writing and Discussion

Working individually or in small groups, analyze how content, style, genre, and document design are interrelated in these articles.

1. How does the document design of each article—its use of fonts, layout, color, and graphics—identify each piece as a scholarly article or an article in a popular magazine? From your own observation, what are typical differences in the document design features of an academic article and a popular magazine article? For example, how are fonts and color typically used in articles in women's and men's fashion magazines?

2. What makes the style and document design of each article appropriate for its intended audience and purpose?

3. What is the function of the abstract (article summary) at the beginning of the academic journal article? What is the function of the large-font "leads" at the beginning of popular articles?

4. Consider the photographs that accompany popular magazine articles. To illustrate the concept of flirting as potential cheating, the opening page (not shown) of the *Cosmopolitan* article, quoted on page 59, features a two-page spread showing a beautiful, young, mysterious woman in a low-cut dress that shows her glistening tan skin. She is looking seriously but coyly at the reader, and behind her are shadowy images of handsome men in loosely buttoned white shirts and sports coats. Think about the photograph in the *Psychology Today* article shown in Figure 3.2. Is it a realistic, candid "documentary" photo? Is it a scripted photo? Is it a concept photo aimed at illustrating the article's thesis or question? What aspects of the *Psychology Today* photo appeal to psychological themes and interests and make it appropriate for the content, audience, and genre of the article? How do you think photos accompanying *Cosmopolitan* articles differ from photos accompanying articles in *Psychology Today?*

5. When you download an article from an electronic database (unless it is in pdf format), you often lose visual cues about the article's genre such as document design, visuals, and so forth. Even when an article is in pdf format, you lose cues about its original print context—the kind of magazine or journal the article appeared in, the magazine's layout and advertisements, and its targeted audience. How do these visual cues in the original print version of an article provide important contextual information for reading the article and using it in your own research? Why do experienced researchers prefer the original print version of articles rather than downloaded articles whenever possible?

- *Ethos* is the appeal to the character of the speaker/writer. It refers to the speaker/writer's trustworthiness and credibility. One can often increase the *ethos* of a message by being knowledgeable about the issue, by appearing thoughtful and fair, by listening well, and by being respectful of alternative points of view. A writer's accuracy and thoroughness in crediting sources and professionalism in caring about the format, grammar, and neat appearance of a document are part of the appeal to *ethos.*
- *Pathos* is the appeal to the sympathies, values, beliefs, and emotions of the audience. Appeals to *pathos* can be made in many ways. *Pathos* can often be enhanced through evocative visual images, frequently used in Web sites, posters, and magazine or newspaper articles. In written texts, the same effects can be created through vivid examples and details, through connotative language, and through empathy with the audience's beliefs and values.

To see how these three appeals are interrelated, you can visualize a triangle with points labeled *Message, Audience,* and *Writer* or *Speaker.* Rhetoricians study how effective communicators consider all three points of this *rhetorical triangle.* (See Figure 4.1.)

We encourage you to ask questions about the appeals to *logos, ethos,* and *pathos* every time you examine a text. For example, is the appeal to *logos* weakened by the writer's use of scanty and questionable evidence? Has the writer made a powerful appeal to *ethos* by documenting her sources and showing that she is an authority on the issue? Has the writer relied too heavily on appeals to *pathos* by

FIGURE 4.1 Rhetorical Triangle

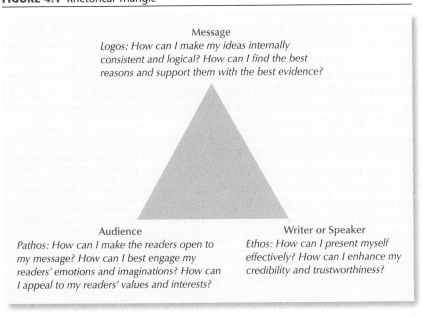

Message
Logos: How can I make my ideas internally consistent and logical? How can I find the best reasons and support them with the best evidence?

Audience
Pathos: How can I make the readers open to my message? How can I best engage my readers' emotions and imaginations? How can I appeal to my readers' values and interests?

Writer or Speaker
Ethos: How can I present myself effectively? How can I enhance my credibility and trustworthiness?

using numerous heart-wringing examples? Later chapters in this textbook will help you use these appeals well in your own writing as well as analyze these appeals in others' messages.

Angle of Vision

Another key insight of rhetoric, one that we mentioned at the beginning of this chapter, is the awareness that there is always more than one way to tell the same story and that no single way of telling it constitutes the whole truth. A writer's thesis necessarily commits a writer to a particular view of a subject that emphasizes some facts and values and de-emphasizes others. This particular point of view we call "angle of vision."

Recognizing the Angle of Vision in a Text

By saying that the writer writes from an "angle of vision," we mean that the writer cannot take a godlike stance that allows a universal, all-seeing, completely true, and whole way of knowing. Rather, the writer looks at the subject from a certain location, or, to use another metaphor, the writer wears a lens that colors or filters the topic in a certain way. The angle of vision, lens, or filter determines what part of a topic gets "seen" and what remains "unseen," what gets included or excluded from the writer's essay, what gets emphasized or de-emphasized, and so forth. It even determines what words get chosen out of an array of options—for example, whether you say "affirmative action" or "reverse discrimination," "terrorist" or "freedom fighter," "public servant" or "politician."

A good illustration of angle of vision is the political cartoon on stem cell research shown in Figure 4.2, which appeared in national newspapers in early summer 2001 when President Bush was contemplating his stance on federal funding for stem cell research. As the cartoon shows, nobody sees stem cells from a universal position. Each stakeholder has an angle of vision that emphasizes some aspects of stem cell research and de-emphasizes or censors other aspects. In the chart on page 81, we try to suggest how each of these angles of vision produces a different "picture" of the field.

In this cartoon, President Bush is cast as an inquirer trying to negotiate multiple perspectives. The cartoon treats Bush satirically—as if he were concerned only with the political implications of his decision. But if we think of him as seeking an ethically responsible stance, then his dilemma stands for all of us as writers confronting a problematic question. In such cases, we all have to forge our own individual stance and be ethically responsible for our decision, while acknowledging other stances and recognizing the limitations of our own.

FIGURE 4.2 Political Cartoon Illustrating Angle of Vision

Where do our stances come from? The stance we take on questions is partly influenced by our life experiences and knowledge, by our class and gender, by our ethnicity and sexual orientation, by our personal beliefs and values, and by our ongoing intentions and desires. But our stance can also be influenced by our rational and empathic capacity to escape from our own limitations and see the world from different perspectives, to imagine the world more fully. We have the power to take stances that are broader and more imaginative than our original limited vision, but we also never escape our own roots and situations in life.

The brief writing project at the end of this chapter will help you understand the concept of "angle of vision" more fully. Your instructor might also assign Chapter 5, which explores angle of vision in more depth.

The exercise on page 82 will help you understand the concept of "angle of vision" more fully.

Angle of Vision on Stem Cell Research

Angle of Vision	Words or Phrases Used to Refer to Stem Cells	Particulars that get "Seen" or Emphasized
Disease sufferer	Cluster of tiny cells that may help repair damaged tissues or grow new ones	The diseases that may be cured by stem cell research; the suffering of those afflicted; scientists as heroes; shelves of frozen stem cells; cells as objects that would just be thrown out if not used for research; emphasis on cures
Priest	Embryo as potential human life formed by union of sperm and egg	Moral consequences of treating human life as means rather than ends; scientists as Dr. Frankensteins; single embryo as potential baby
Scientist	Blastocysts, which are better suited for research than adult stem cells	Scientific questions that research would help solve; opportunities for grants and scholarly publication; emphasis on gradual progress rather than cures
Businessperson	New area for profitable investments	Potential wealth for company that develops new treatments for diseases or injuries
President Bush (at time of cartoon, Bush was uncertain of his stance)	Afraid to say "cluster of cells," "embryo," or "blastocyst" because each term has political consequences	Political consequences of each possible way to resolve the stem cell controversy; need to appease supporters from the Right without appearing callous to sufferers of diseases; need to woo Catholic vote

For Writing and Discussion

Background: Suppose that you are a management professor who is regularly asked to write letters of recommendation for former students. One day you receive a letter from a local bank requesting a confidential evaluation of a former student, one Uriah Rudy Riddle (U. R. Riddle), who has applied for a job as a management trainee. The bank wants your assessment of Riddle's intelligence, aptitude, dependability, and ability to work with people. You haven't seen U. R. for several years, but you remember him well. Here are the facts and impressions you recall about Riddle:

- Very temperamental student, seemed moody, something of a loner
- Long hair and very sloppy dress—seemed like a misplaced street person; often twitchy and hyperactive
- Absolutely brilliant mind; took lots of liberal arts courses and applied them to business
- Wrote a term paper relating different management styles to modern theories of psychology—the best undergraduate paper you ever received. You gave it an A+ and remember learning a lot from it yourself.
- Had a strong command of language—the paper was very well written
- Good at mathematics; could easily handle all the statistical aspects of the course
- Frequently missed class and once told you that your class was boring
- Didn't show up for the midterm. When he returned to class later, he said only that he had been out of town. You let him make up the midterm, and he got an A.
- Didn't participate in a group project required for your course. He said the other students in his group were idiots.
- You thought at the time that Riddle didn't have a chance of making it in the business world because he had no talent for getting along with people.
- Other professors held similar views of Riddle—brilliant, but rather strange and hard to like; an odd duck.

You are in a dilemma because you want to give Riddle a chance (he's still young and may have had a personality transformation of some sort), but you also don't want to damage your own professional reputation by falsifying your true impressions.

Individual task: Working individually for ten minutes or so, compose a brief letter of recommendation assessing Riddle; use details from the list to support your assessment. Role-play that you have decided to take a gamble with Riddle and give him a chance at this career. Write as strong a recommendation as possible while remaining honest. (To make this exercise more complex, your instructor might ask half the class to role-play a negative angle of vision in which you want to warn the bank against hiring Riddle without hiding his strengths or good points.)

Task for group or whole-class discussion: Working in small groups or as a whole class, share your letters. Pick out representative examples ranging from the most positive to the least positive and discuss how the letters achieve their different rhetorical effects. If your intent is to support Riddle, to what extent does honesty compel you to mention some or all of your negative memories? Is it possible to mention negative items without emphasizing them? How?

Analyzing Angle of Vision

Chapter 5, "Seeing Rhetorically," develops this connection between seeing and interpretation in more detail.

Just as there is more than one way to describe the party you went to on Friday night, there is more than one way to write a letter of recommendation for U. R. Riddle. The writer's angle of vision determines what is "seen" or "not seen" in a given piece of writing—what gets slanted in a positive or negative direction, what gets highlighted, what gets thrown into the shadows. As rhetorician Kenneth Burke claims, "A way of seeing is also a way of not seeing." Note how the writer controls what the reader "sees." As Riddle's professor, you might in your mind's eye see Riddle as long-haired and sloppy, but if you don't mention these details in your letter, they remain unseen to the reader. Note too that your own terms "long-haired and sloppy" interpret Riddle's appearance through the lens of your own characteristic way of seeing—a way that perhaps values business attire and clean-cut tidiness. Another observer might describe Riddle's appearance quite differently, thus seeing what you don't see.

In an effective piece of writing, the author's angle of vision often works so subtly that unsuspecting readers—unless they learn to think rhetorically—will be drawn into the writer's spell and believe that the writer's prose conveys the "whole picture" of its subject rather than a limited picture filtered through the screen of the writer's perspective. To understand more clearly how an angle of vision is constructed, you can analyze the language strategies at work. Some of these strategies—which writers employ consciously or unconsciously to achieve their intended effects—are as follows:

WAYS THAT WRITERS CONSTRUCT AN ANGLE OF VISION

- *Writers can state their meaning or intentions directly.* For example, your letter for U. R. Riddle might say, "Riddle would make an excellent bank manager" or "Riddle doesn't have the personality to be a bank manager."
- *Writers can select details that support their intended effect and omit those that don't.* If your intention is to support Riddle, you can include all the positive data about Riddle and omit the negative data (or vice versa if your letter opposes his candidacy). Instead of outright omission of data, you can de-emphasize some details while highlighting others.
- *Writers can choose words that frame the subject in a desired way or that have desired connotations.* For example, if you call Riddle "an independent thinker who doesn't follow the crowd," you frame him positively within a value system that favors individualism. If you call him "a loner who thinks egocentrically," you frame him negatively within a value system that favors consensus and social skills. Also, words can have connotations that serve to channel the reader's response in an intended direction. You thus could call Riddle either "forthright" or "rude" depending on your angle of vision.
- *Writers can use metaphors, similes, or analogies to create an intended effect.* For example, to suggest that Riddle has perhaps outgrown his earlier alienation from classmates, you might call him a "late-bloomer socially." But if you

see him out of place in a bank, you might say that Riddle's independent spirit would feel "caged in" by the routine of a banker's life.

- *Writers can vary sentence structure to emphasize or de-emphasize ideas and details.* Details can get emphasized or de-emphasized depending on where they appear in a sentence or paragraph. For example, material gets emphasized if it appears at the end of a long sentence, in a short sentence surrounded by long sentences, or in a main clause rather than a subordinate clause. Consider the difference between saying, "Although Riddle had problems relating to other students in my class, he is a brilliant thinker" versus "Although Riddle is a brilliant thinker, he had problems relating to other students in my class." The first sentence emphasizes his brilliance, the second his poor people skills.

The brief writing assignment at the end of this chapter will give you further practice in analyzing angle of vision.

Thinking Rhetorically about Any Cultural "Text"

To us, one of the most pleasurable aspects of rhetorical thinking is analyzing the rhetorical power of visual images or identifying rhetorical factors in people's choices about clothing, watches, cars, tattoos, and other consumer items.

Visual Rhetoric

Just as you can think rhetorically about texts, you can think rhetorically about photographs, drawings, paintings, statues, buildings, and other visual images. In Chapter 11, we deal extensively with visual rhetoric, explaining how color, perspective, cropping, camera angle, foreground/background, and other visual elements work together to create a persuasive effect. In this chapter, we intend only to introduce you to the concept of visual rhetoric and to suggest its importance. Consider, for example, the persuasive power of famous photographs from the war in Iraq. Early in the war, several widely publicized images, particularly the film footage of the toppling of the statue of Saddam Hussein and the "Mission Accomplished" photograph of President Bush wearing a pilot's flight suit on the deck of the aircraft carrier *Abraham Lincoln,* served to consolidate public support of the war. Later, certain images began eating away at public support. For example, an unauthorized picture of flag-draped coffins filling the freight deck of a military transport plane focused attention on those killed in the war. Particularly devastating for supporters of the war were the images of American prison guards sexually humiliating Iraqi prisoners in the Abu Ghraib prison. Images like these stick in viewers' memories long after specific texts are forgotten.

An illuminating example of the rhetorical power of paintings and photographs is evident in our cultural discussions of health care. In the early and middle

FIGURE 4.3 A Norman Rockwell Painting of a Family Doctor

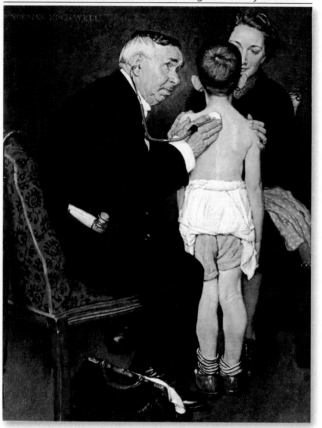

"Doc Melhorn and the Pearly Gates" by Norman Rockwell, inside illustration from
The Saturday Evening Post, December 24, 1938. Printed by permission of the Norman
Rockwell Family Agency. Copyright © 1938 the Norman Rockwell Family Entities.

decades of the twentieth century, a powerful concept of the "family doctor" emerged. This "family doctor" was envisioned as a personal, caring individual—usually a fatherly or grandfatherly male—with a stethoscope around his neck and a little black bag for making house calls. This image was deeply embedded in the American psyche through a series of paintings by Norman Rockwell, several of which were reproduced on the cover of the influential *Saturday Evening Post* (see Figure 4.3).

These paintings are now part of our cultural nostalgia for a simpler era and help explain some of the cultural resistance in the United States to impersonal HMOs, where medical decisions seem made by insurance bureaucrats. Yet, we also want our doctors to be high-tech. In the last few decades, the image of doctors in the popular imagination, especially furthered by advertising, has shifted away from idealized Norman Rockwell scenes to images of highly specialized experts

FIGURE 4.4 A Modern High-Tech Image of a Doctor

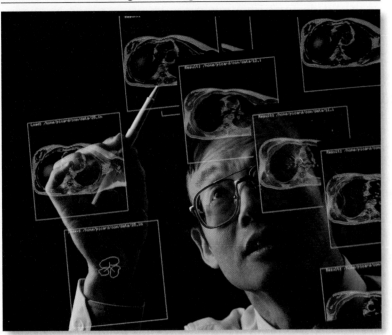

using the latest technological equipment. Figure 4.4 suggests the kinds of high-tech imagery that now characterizes popular media portrayal of doctors. However, in many current articles about health care in the United States, the Norman Rockwell paintings of the family doctor are still invoked to represent an older ideal about what people are looking for in their doctors.

   The point we want to make in this brief introduction to visual rhetoric is that images make arguments. The Norman Rockwell painting and the high-tech photograph work rhetorically to influence an audience's view of what a doctor should be. The competing images of doctors serve the interests of different groups with different views about the role of medicine in our culture.

For Writing and Discussion

Working in small groups or as a whole class, explore your answers to the following questions:

1. How do the Norman Rockwell painting and the contemporary photograph work to create different images of doctors? What are the values conveyed by the Rockwell painting? What are the values conveyed by the photograph?

(*continued*)

2. Why is it in the interest of HMOs and insurance companies to portray high-tech images of doctors? How might the influence of the Norman Rockwell view of doctors serve the interests of alternative health care providers such as naturopathic physicians?

The Rhetoric of Clothing and Other Consumer Items

Not only do visual images have rhetorical power, but so also do many of our consumer choices. We choose our clothes, for example, not only to keep ourselves covered and warm but also to project our identification with certain social groups. For example, if you want to be identified as a skate-boarder, a preppy socialite, a gang member, a pickup-driving NASCAR fan, or a junior partner in a corporate law firm, you know how to select clothes and accessories that convey that identification. The way you dress communicates where you fit (or how you want to be perceived as fitting) within a class and social structure. For the most part, clothing codes are arbitrary, based on a system of differences. For example, there is no universal "truth" saying that long baggy basketball shorts are more attractive than short basketball shorts or that cargo pants are more beautiful than stirrup pants, even though one style may feel current and one out-of-date.

How do these symbolic codes get established? They can be set by fashion designers, by advertisers, or by trendy groups or individuals. The key to any new clothing code is to make it look different in some distinctive way from an earlier code or from a code of another group. Sometimes clothing codes develop to show rebellion against the values of parents or authority figures. At other times they develop to show new kinds of group identities.

Clothing codes are played on in conscious ways in fashion advertisements so that consumers become very aware of what identifications are signaled by different styles and brands. This aspect of consumer society is so ubiquitous that one of the marks of growing affluence in third-world countries is people's attention to the rhetoric of consumer goods. Consider the second epigraph to this chapter, which indicates that villagers in India watching TV ads notice not only the soap or shampoo but also the brands of motorbikes and the lifestyles of the people in the ads. Buying a certain kind of consumer good projects a certain kind of status or group or class identity. Our point, from a rhetorical perspective, is that in making a consumer choice, many people are concerned not only with the quality of the item itself but also with the symbolic messages that the item sends to different audiences. Note that the same item can send quite different messages to different groups: A Rolex watch might enhance one's credibility at a corporate board meeting while undercutting it at a barbecue for union workers. Or consider the clothing choices of preteen girls who want to dress like female pop rock stars. They often do so to fit in with their friends, perhaps unaware of the whole array of cultural messages that these clothes convey to other social groups.

For Writing and Discussion

Working in small groups or as a whole class, do a rhetorical analysis of the consumer items shown in Figures 4.5, 4.6, 4.7, and 4.8.

1. In each case, see if you can reach consensus on why persons might have chosen a particular way of dressing. How does the clothing style project a desire to identify with certain groups or to shock or reject certain groups? How do the clothing choices help establish and enhance the wearer's sense of identity?

2. When you and your friends make consumer purchases, to what extent are you swayed by the internal quality of the item (its materials and workmanship) versus the rhetorical messages it sends to an audience (its signals about social identity and standing)? (Note: Advertisers have long known that consumers, when queried, say: "I buy to please myself." However, advertisers' extensive psychological research suggests that consumers are intensely aware of audience: "I buy to maintain and project a certain way of being perceived by others.")

3. How does the rhetoric of clothing extend to other consumer items such as cars, vacations, recreational activities, home furnishings, music, and so forth?

FIGURE 4.5

FIGURE 4.6

(continued)

FIGURE 4.7

FIGURE 4.8

Chapter Summary

In this chapter we explained Kenneth Burke's definition of *rhetoric* as the use of language and other symbols to produce cooperation among humans. We saw how rhetoric operates under the modes of inquiry and persuasion and how, under ideal conditions, an exchange of different perspectives can lead reasonable people toward better solutions to problems. We also introduced the classical appeals of *logos*, *ethos*, and *pathos* as strategies for increasing the effectiveness of messages. Next we explained the concept of angle of vision. Any text necessarily looks at its subject from a perspective that emphasizes some details while minimizing others. We also showed you how to analyze angle of vision by considering the writer's word choices and the selection and arrangement of evidence. Finally, we explained how you can apply rhetorical thinking to visual images and to various kinds of consumer choices.

BRIEF WRITING PROJECT

Background and Readings

This brief writing project will give you practice at analyzing the angle of vision in different texts. This assignment focuses on two passages about nuclear power plants. Read the two passages; then we will describe your writing task.

The first passage is from the Bush administration's *National Energy Policy: Reliable, Affordable, and Environmentally Sound Energy for America's Future*. The document was written by an energy task force chaired by Vice President Dick Cheney. This passage is an overview paragraph on nuclear power from the opening chapter of the document; the last sentence of the passage is from a later section on recommendations for increasing energy supplies:

PASSAGE 1

Nuclear power plants serve millions of American homes and businesses, have a dependable record for safety and efficiency, and discharge no greenhouse gases into the atmosphere. As noted earlier, these facilities currently generate 20 percent of all electricity in America, and more than 40 percent of electricity generated in 10 states in the Northeast, South, and Midwest. Other nations, such as Japan and France, generate a much higher percentage of their electricity from nuclear power. Yet the number of nuclear plants in America is actually projected to decline in coming years, as old plants close and none are built to replace them. . . . [Later the Cheney document makes the following recommendation:] Provide for the safe expansion of nuclear energy by establishing a national repository for nuclear waste, and by streamlining licensing of nuclear power plants.

The second passage is from an op-ed piece by columnist Marianne Means, published on April 12, 2001, by Hearst Newspapers. It was entitled "Bush, Cheney Will Face Wall of Opposition If They Try to Resurrect Nuclear Power."

PASSAGE 2

Washington—Vice President Dick Cheney, head of the presidential task force studying our energy needs, favors building new nuclear power plants—and he's oddly casual about it.

The industry has been moribund in this country since the partial meltdown at Three Mile Island more than two decades ago set off fierce emotional resistance to an unreliable technology capable of accidentally spreading deadly radiation. No new plants have been ordered since then. Only 20 percent of our electricity is generated by nuclear power.

But President Bush has instructed Cheney to look into the prospect of resurrecting and developing nuclear power as a major part of a broad new energy policy. Cheney argues that modern, improved reactors operate safely, economically and efficiently. "It's one of the safest industries around," he says unequivocally.

There remains, however, a little problem of how to dispose of the plants' radioactive waste. Cheney concedes that issue is still unsolved. "If we're going to go forward with nuclear power, we need to find a way to resolve it," he said Sunday in an NBC "Meet the Press" interview.

No state wants to be the repository of the more than 40,000 tons of high-level nuclear waste currently accumulating at 103 commercial reactor sites around the country. This spent fuel is so deadly it can remain a potential threat to public health and safety for thousands of years. A leak could silently contaminate many miles of groundwater that millions of people depend on.

Your task: Contrast the differences in angle of vision in these two passages by analyzing how they create their different rhetorical effects. Consider factors such as overt statements of meaning, selection/omission of details, connotations of words and figures of speech, and sentence emphasis. To help guide your analysis, reread the section "Analyzing Angle of Vision" on pages 84–85. Your goal here is to explain to your readers how these two passages create different impressions of nuclear power.

PART

2

Writing Projects

This ad for the United States Army highlights qualities traditionally associated with patriotic military service to the country: respect, honor, and courage. Note that this poster does not depict soldiers in uniform on a battlefield or in the midst of a drill. Consider the way the images of the father and daughter and the words in this ad connect character-building, family relationships, the Army, and success. Think about how gender functions in this ad by focusing on the young woman's long hair, tasteful makeup, and earnest manner. This advertisement is part of For Writing and Discussion exercises in Chapters 8 and 11.

**YOU TAUGHT HER ABOUT RESPECT, HONOR AND COURAGE.
IS IT ANY SURPRISE THAT NOW SHE WANTS TO USE THEM?**

She'll experience the most challenging training, use the latest technology and get the strongest support. Every drill and every mission will reinforce in her that character always leads to success. Encourage her to consider becoming a Soldier — AN ARMY OF ONE.®

AN ARMY OF ONE™

GOARMY.COM  **U.S.ARMY**

Part 2 Writing Projects

Seeing Rhetorically
The Writer as Observer

About Seeing Rhetorically

Earlier in your school career, you may have been asked in an English class to write a description of a scene as if you were painting a picture of it in words. As you observed your scene carefully, trying to use sensory details to appeal to sight, sound, touch, smell, and even taste, you might have imagined that you were creating a true and objective description of your scene. But consider what happens to a description assignment if we give it a rhetorical twist. Suppose we asked you to write *two* descriptions of the same scene from two different perspectives or angles of vision (caused, say, by different moods or intentions) and then to analyze how the two descriptions differed. We could then ask you to reflect on the extent to which any description of a scene is objective as opposed to being shaped by the observer's intentions, experiences, beliefs, or moods.

Our goal in this chapter is to help you understand more fully the rhetorical concept of "angle of vision" which we introduced in Chapter 4. Learning to ask *why* a text includes certain details and not others and to ponder *how* a text creates its dominant impression will help you analyze any text more critically and understand the complex factors that shape what a writer sees.

Angle of vision is explained on pp. 80–85.

Your writing assignment for this chapter belongs to a category that we call "writing to learn." Many instructors from across the disciplines use writing-to-learn assignments intended to help students understand important disciplinary concepts. The assignment in this chapter, while teaching you about angle of vision, also shows you some of the subtle ways that language and perception are interconnected.

Exploring Rhetorical Observation

One of the intense national debates of the last five years has been whether the federal government should permit oil exploration in the Coastal Plain of the Arctic National Wildlife Refuge (ANWR). Arguments for and against drilling in the ANWR have regularly appeared in newspapers and magazines, and numerous advocacy groups have created Web sites to argue their cases. Nearly every argument contains descriptions of the ANWR that operate rhetorically to advance the writer's position. In the following exercise, we ask you to analyze the angle of vision of these verbal and visual depictions of the ANWR—that is, to analyze how these photographs and descriptions "see" the ANWR. We ask you to consider how different descriptions of the ANWR can be used to support different views of oil exploration. After examining the following data set of five verbal or visual texts, proceed to the questions under "Analyzing the Exhibits" (p. 101).

Exhibit 1: Web Page of the Arctic Power Advocacy Group

This text, with photograph labeled "Wildlife grow accustomed to oil operations at Prudhoe Bay" (Figure 5.1), is part of a pamphlet produced by Arctic Power, an advocacy group in favor of drilling for oil. We accessed this pamphlet through the organization's Web site.

FIGURE 5.1 Bears on Pipeline

Wildlife grow accustomed to oil operations at Prudhoe Bay.

ANWR has the nation's best potential for major additions to U.S. oil supplies

Most geologists think the Coastal Plain of the Artic National Wildlife Refuge has the best prospects for major additions to U.S. domestic oil supply. This is the part of ANWR set aside by Congress in 1980 for further study of its petroleum potential. There is a good chance that very large oil and gas fields, equal to the amount found at Prudhoe Bay further west, could be discovered in ANWR's coastal plain.

The Coastal Plain has very attractive geology and lies between areas of the Alaska North Slope and the Canadian Beaufort Sea where there have been major oil and gas discoveries. Oil and gas deposits have been discovered near ANWR's western border, and a recent oil discovery may result in the first pipeline built to the western boundary of the Coastal Plain.

Although the Coastal Plain was reserved for study of its oil potential, Congress must act to open it for oil and gas exploration. Alaskans and residents of the North Slope, including the Inupiat community of Kaktovik, within ANWR, widely support exploring the Coastal Plain.

Exhibit 2: Photograph from a Pro-Environment Newspaper Op Ed Piece
The photograph of the polar bears in Figure 5.2 accompanied a newspaper op-ed column entitled "Arctic Wildlife Refuge: Protect This Sacred Place."

FIGURE 5.2 Polar Bear with Cubs

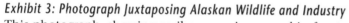

Exhibit 3: Photograph Juxtaposing Alaskan Wildlife and Industry
This photograph, showing caribou crossing a road in front of a semi, typifies the Alaskan conflict over preserving nature versus the increasing presence of people and economic development (Figure 5.3).

FIGURE 5.3 Caribou and Truck

Exhibit 4: Photograph and Description on the Arctic Power Web Site

This photograph (Figure 5.4) and passage appeared on the Web site for Arctic Power, a pro-exploration advocacy group.

FIGURE 5.4 ANWR Coastal Plain

[The facts about ANWR] are not as pretty or as emotionally appealing [as the descriptions of ANWR by anti-exploration writers]. But they are important for anyone involved in the ANWR debate. On the coastal plain, the Arctic winter lasts for 9 months. It is dark continuously for 56 days in midwinter. Temperatures with the wind chill can reach −110 degrees F. It's not pristine. There are villages, roads, houses, schools, and military installations. It's not a unique Arctic ecosystem. The coastal plain is only a small fraction of the 88,000 square miles that make up the North Slope. The same tundra environment and wildlife can be found throughout the circumpolar Arctic regions. The 1002 Area [the legal term for the plot of coastal plain being contested] is flat. That's why they call it a plain. [. . .]

Some groups want to make the 1002 Area a wilderness. But a vote for wilderness is a vote against American jobs.

Exhibit 5: Excerpt from a Newspaper Feature Article

The following passage is the opening of a newspaper feature article in which freelance writer Randall Rubini describes his bicycle tour through the Prudhoe Bay Area of Alaska.

The temperature is 39 degrees. The going is slow but finally I am in motion. The bike churns through big rocks and thick gravel that occasionally suck the wheels to a dead halt.

Sixty miles to the east lies the Arctic National Wildlife Refuge, a place ARCO [a major oil-refining company] describes as "a bleak and forbidding land where temperatures plunge to more than 40 degrees below zero and the sun is not seen for nearly two months each year." To me the refuge is 19.5 million acres of unspoiled wilderness believed to contain crude oil and natural gas fields.

Prudhoe Bay production is on the decline, and oil corporations are salivating over the prospect of drilling on the 125-mile-long stretch of coastal plain within the refuge.

The area is a principal calving ground for the 180,000-member porcupine caribou herd that annually migrates to the windswept plain, seeking relief from insects.

The refuge also provides habitat for grizzlies, wolves, musk oxen, wolverines, and arctic foxes. Polar bears hunt over the ice and come ashore. Millions of waterfowl, seabirds, and shorebirds nest here.

Analyzing the Exhibits

Working in small groups or as a whole class, try to reach consensus answers to the following questions:

1. Which photographs do you think create visual claims opposing oil exploration in the ANWR? Which create visual claims supporting oil exploration? What is the verbal argument underlying each of these photos?
2. As we explained in Chapter 4, angle of vision focuses readers' attention on some details of a scene rather than on others; it accounts for what is "seen" and "not seen" by a given writer. What do the opponents of oil exploration tend to "see" and "not see" when they describe the ANWR? What do the proponents of oil exploration tend to "see" and "not see"?
3. When opponents of oil exploration mention oil companies or oil wells, they often try to plant a quick negative picture in the reader's mind. What rhetorical strategies, such as making direct statements and using highly connotative words, do the anti-exploration writers use to give a negative impression of oil companies?
4. In contrast, how do supporters of oil exploration try to create positive feelings about drilling in the ANWR?

WRITING PROJECT

Your writing project for this chapter is to write two descriptions and a self-reflection. The assignment has two parts.*

---

*For this assignment, we are indebted to two sources: (1) Richard Braddock, *A Little Casebook in the Rhetoric of Writing* (Englewood Cliffs, NJ: Prentice-Hall, 1971); and (2) Kenneth Dowst, "Kenneth Dowst's Assignment," *What Makes Writing Good?* eds. William E. Coles, Jr., and James Vopat (Lexington, MA: D.C. Heath, 1985), pp. 52–57.

Part A: Find an indoor or outdoor place where you can sit and observe for fifteen or twenty minutes in preparation for writing a focused description of the scene that will enable your readers to see what you see. Here is the catch: You are to write *two* descriptions of the scene. Your first description must convey a favorable impression of the scene, making it appear pleasing or attractive. The second description must convey a negative, or unfavorable, impression, making the scene appear unpleasant or unattractive. Both descriptions must contain only factual details and must describe exactly the same scene from the same location at the same time. It's not fair, in other words, to describe the scene in sunny weather and then in the rain or otherwise to alter factual details. Each description should be one paragraph long (approximately 125–175 words).

Part B: Self-reflection on What You Learned (300–400 words): Attach to your two descriptions a self-reflection about what you have learned from doing this assignment. This self-reflection should include your own rhetorical analysis of your two descriptions and explain some of the insights you have gained into the concepts of "angle of vision" and "seeing rhetorically."

Strategies for doing a rhetorical analysis were introduced in Chapter 4, pp. 84–85, and are explained further on pp. 105–108.

Part A of the assignment asks you to describe the same scene in two different ways, giving your first description a positive tone and the second description a negative one. You can choose from any number of scenes: the lobby of a dormitory or apartment building, a view from a park bench or a window, a favorite (or disliked) room, a scene at your workplace, a busy street, a local eating or drinking spot, whatever. A student example of two contrasting scenes written for this assignment is found on pp. 107–108. Part B of the assignment asks you to write a self-reflection in which you do a rhetorical analysis of your two descriptions and explore what you have learned from this exercise about seeing rhetorically. An excerpt from a student self-reflection, written for this assignment, is found on p. 114. Because this assignment results in a thought exercise rather than in a self-contained essay requiring an introduction, transitions between parts, and so forth, you can label your sections simply "Descriptions" and "Self-Reflection."

Understanding Observational Writing

In this section, we elaborate on the concept of angle of vision. We explore what factors influence angle of vision and show how a writer's angle of vision shapes the language he or she chooses, or, to put it inversely, how the chosen language both conveys and creates the angle of vision. We also examine the complex relationship between perception and belief by explaining how previous knowledge, cultural background, interests, and values influence perceptions.

Considering the Factors That Shape Perception

On the face of it, terms such as *observation, perception,* and *seeing* seem nonproblematic. Objects are objects, and the process of perceiving an object is immediate and automatic. However, perception is never a simple matter. Consider what we call "the expert-novice phenomenon": Experts on any given subject notice details about that subject that the novice overlooks. An experienced bird-watcher can distinguish dozens of kinds of swallows by subtle differences in size, markings, and behaviors, whereas a non-bird-watcher sees only a group of birds of similar size and shape. Similarly, people observing an unfamiliar game (for example, an American watching cricket or a Nigerian watching baseball) don't know what actions or events have meaning and, hence, don't know what to look for.

In addition to prior knowledge, cultural differences affect perception. An American watching two Japanese business executives greet each other might not know that they are participating in an elaborate cultural code of bowing, eye contact, speech patterns, and timing of movements that convey meanings about social status. An Ethiopian newly arrived in the United States and an American sitting in a doctor's office will see different things when the nurse points to one of them to come into the examination room: The American notices nothing remarkable about the scene; he or she may remember what the nurse was wearing or something about the wallpaper. The Ethiopian, on the other hand, is likely to remember the nurse's act of pointing, a gesture of rudeness used in Ethiopia only to beckon children or discipline dogs. Again, observers of the same scene see different things.

Your beliefs and values can also shape your perceptions, often creating blind spots. You might not notice data that conflict with your beliefs and values. Or you might perceive contradictory data at some level, but if they don't register in your mind as significant, you disregard them. Consider, for example, how advocates of gun control focus on a child's being accidentally killed because the child found a loaded firearm in Dad's sock drawer, while opponents of gun control focus on burglaries or rapes being averted because the home owner had a pistol by the bedside. The lesson here is that people note and remember whatever is consistent with their worldview much more readily than they note and remember inconsistencies. What you believe is what you see.

Another factor determining what you see is mood. We know that when people are upbeat they tend to see things through "rose-colored glasses"—a cliché with a built-in reference to angle of vision. When you are in a good mood, you see the flowers in a meadow. When you are depressed, you see the discarded wrappers from someone's pack of gum.

More direct and overt is the influence of rhetorical purpose. Consider again the case of the Arctic National Wildlife Refuge mentioned earlier in this chapter. In the passage by Randall Rubini (p. 100), the author juxtaposes his own view of the ANWR as an "unspoiled wilderness" against ARCO's view of the ANWR as a "bleak and forbidding land.' " Note how each way of seeing the ANWR serves the political purposes of the author. Opponents of oil exploration focus on the unspoiled beauty of the land, listing fondly the names of different kinds of animals that live there. What remains "unseen" in their descriptions are the native villages and military installations on the Coastal Plain and any references to economic issues, the U.S. need for domestic oil, or jobs. In contrast, supporters of oil exploration shift the focus from the caribou herds (their descriptions don't "see" the animals), to the bleak and frigid landscape and the native communities that would benefit from jobs.

This example suggests the ethical dimension of description. Rhetorical purpose entails responsibility. All observers must accept responsibility for what they see and for what they make others see because their descriptions can have real-world consequences—for example, no jobs for a group of people or potential harm to an animal species and an ecosystem. We should reiterate, however, that neither perspective on the ANWR is necessarily dishonest; each is true in a limited way. In any description, writers necessarily—whether consciously or unconsciously—include some details and exclude others. But the writer's intent is nevertheless to influence the reader's way of thinking about the described phenomenon, and ethical readers must be aware of what is happening. By noting what is *not there,* readers can identify a piece's angle of vision and analyze it. The reader can see the piece of writing not as the whole truth but as one person's perspective that can seem like the whole truth if one simply succumbs to the text's rhetorical power.

Finally, let's look at one more important factor that determines angle of vision—what we might call a writer's "guiding ideology" or "belief system." We touched on this point earlier when we showed how one's belief system can create blind spots. Let's examine this phenomenon in more depth by seeing how different beliefs about the role of women in primitive societies cause two anthropologists to describe a scene in different ways. What follows are excerpts from the works of two female anthropologists studying the role of women in the !Kung tribe* of the African Kalahari Desert (sometimes called the "Bushmen"). Anthropologists have long been interested in the !Kung because they still hunt and forage for food in the manner of their prehistoric ancestors.

Here is how anthropologist Lorna Marshal describes !Kung women's work:

MARSHAL'S DESCRIPTION

Women bring most of the daily food that sustains the life of the people, but the roots and berries that are the principal plant foods of the Nyae Nyae !Kung are apt to be tasteless, harsh and not very satisfying. People crave meat. Furthermore, there is only drudgery in digging roots, picking berries, and trudging back to the encampment with heavy loads and babies sagging in the pouches of the karosses: there is no splendid excitement and triumph in returning with vegetables.

—Lorna Marshal, *The !Kung of Nyae Nyae*

*The word *!Kung* is preceded by an exclamation point in scholarly work to indicate the unique clicking sound of the language.

And here is how a second anthropologist describes women's work:

DRAPER'S DESCRIPTION

A common sight in the late afternoon is clusters of children standing on the edge of camp, scanning the bush with shaded eyes to see if the returning women are visible. When the slow-moving file of women is finally discerned in the distance, the children leap and exclaim. As the women draw closer, the children speculate as to which figure is whose mother and what the women are carrying in the karosses. [. . .]

!Kung women impress one as a self-contained people with a high sense of self-esteem. There are exceptions—women who seem forlorn and weary—but for the most part, !Kung women are vivacious and self-confident. Small groups of women forage in the Kalahari at distances of eight to ten miles from home with no thought that they need the protection of the men or of the men's weapons should they encounter any of the several large predators that also inhabit the Kalahari.

—P. Draper, "!Kung Women: Contrasts in Sexual Egalitarianism in Foraging and Sedentary Contexts"

As you can see, these two anthropologists "read" the !Kung society in remarkably different ways. Marshal's thesis is that !Kung women are a subservient class relegated to the heavy, dull, and largely thankless task of gathering vegetables. In contrast, Draper believes that women's work is more interesting and requires more skill than other anthropologists have realized. Her thesis is that there is an egalitarian relationship between men and women in the !Kung society.

The source of data for both anthropologists is careful observation of !Kung women's daily lives. But the anthropologists are clearly not seeing the same thing. When the !Kung women return from the bush at the end of the day, Marshal sees their heavy loads and babies sagging in their pouches, whereas Draper sees the excited children awaiting the women's return.

So which view is correct? That's a little like asking whether the ANWR is an "unspoiled wilderness" or a " 'bleak and forbidding land.' " If you believe that women play an important role in !Kung society, you "see" the children eagerly awaiting the women's return at the end of the day, and you note the women's courage in foraging for vegetables "eight to ten miles from home." If you believe that women are basically drudges in this culture, then you "see" the heavy loads and babies sagging in the pouches of the karosses. The details of the scene, in other words, are filtered through the observer's interpretive screen.

Conducting a Simple Rhetorical Analysis

Our discussion of two different views of the ANWR and two different views of the role of women in !Kung society shows how a seemingly objective description of a scene reflects a specific angle of vision that can be revealed through analysis. Rhetorically, a description subtly persuades the reader toward the author's angle of vision. This angle of vision isn't necessarily the author's "true self" speaking, for authors *create* an angle of vision through rhetorical choices they make while composing. We hope you will discover this insight for yourself while doing the assignment for this chapter.

In this section we describe five textual strategies writers often use (consciously or unconsciously) to create the persuasive effect of their texts. Each strategy creates textual differences that you can discuss in your rhetorical analysis.

For a more complete explanation of these five strategies, see Chapter 4's discussion of how an angle of vision is constructed on pp. 80–82.

Strategies for Creating a Persuasive Effect

Strategy 1: State your meaning or intended effect directly.

Example: The first anthropologist says that "there is only drudgery in digging roots" while the second anthropologist says, "!Kung women impress one as a self-contained people with a high sense of self-esteem." The first writer casts her view in negative terms while the second announces a more positive perspective.

Strategy 2: Select details that convey your intended effect and omit those that don't.

Example: The first anthropologist, Marshal, selects details about the tastelessness of the vegetables and the heaviness of the women's loads, creating an overall impression of women's work as thankless and exhausting. Draper, the second anthropologist, selects details about excitement of the children awaiting their mothers' return and the fearlessness of the mothers as they forage "eight to ten miles from home," creating an impression of self-reliant women performing an essential task.

Strategy 3: Choose words with connotations that convey your intended effect.

Example: Marshal chooses words connoting listlessness and fatigue such as *drudgery, trudging, heavy,* and *sagging.* Draper chooses words connoting energy: The children *scan* the bush, *leap and exclaim,* and *speculate,* while the women *forage.*

Strategy 4: Use figurative language (metaphors, similes, and analogies) that conveys your intended effect.

Example: Rubini writes that oil companies are "salivating" for new oil-drilling opportunities (p. 100). He equates oil companies with drooling dogs, giving readers an unpleasant vision of the oil companies' eagerness to get at the ANWR's oil reserves.

Strategy 5: Use sentence structure to emphasize and de-emphasize your ideas.

Example: Marshal uses sentence structure to create a negative impression of the !Kung women's plant-gathering role:

> Women bring most of the daily food that sustains the life of the people, but the roots and berries that are the principal plant foods of the Nyae Nyae !Kung are apt to be tasteless, harsh and not very satisfying. People crave meat.

The short sentence following the long sentence receives the most emphasis, giving readers the impression that meat is more important than the women's vegetables.

For Writing and Discussion

What follows is a student example of two contrasting descriptions written for the assignment in this chapter. Read the descriptions carefully. Working individually, analyze the descriptions rhetorically to explain how the writer has created contrasting impressions through overt statements of meaning, selection and omission of details, word choice, figurative language, and sentence structure. (You will do the same thing for your own two descriptions in Part B of the assignment.) Spend approximately ten minutes doing your own analysis of this example and taking notes. Then, working in small groups or as a whole class, share your analyses, trying to reach agreement on examples of how the writer has created different rhetorical effects by using the five strategies just explained.

Description 1: Positive Effect The high ceiling and plainness of this classroom on the second floor of the Administration Building make it airy, spacious, and functional. This classroom, which is neither dusty and old nor sterile and modern, has a well-used, comfortable feel like the jeans and favorite sweater you put on to go out for pizza with friends. Students around me, who are focused on the assignment, read the instructor's notes on the chalkboard, thumb through their texts, and jot down ideas in their notebooks spread out on the spacious two-person tables. In the back of the room, five students cluster around a table and talk softly and intently about the presentation they are getting ready to make to the class. Splashes of spring sunshine filtering through the blinds on the tall windows brighten the room with natural light, and a breeze pungent with the scent of newly mown grass wafts through the open ones, sweeps over the students writing at their desks, and passes out through the door to the hall. As I glance out the window, I see a view that contributes to the quiet harmony of the environment: bright pink and red rhododendron bushes and manicured beds of spring flowers ring the huge lawn where a few students are studying under the white-blossomed cherry trees.

Description 2: Negative Effect The high ceiling of this classroom on the second floor of the Administration Building cannot relieve the cramped, uncomfortable feeling of this space, which is filled with too many two-person tables, some of them crammed together at awkward angles. A third of the chalkboard is blocked from my view by the bulky television, VCR, and overhead projector that are stacked on cumbersome carts and wreathed in electrical cords. Students around me, working on the assignment, scrape their chairs on the bare linoleum floor as they try to see the chalkboard where some of the instructor's notes are blotted out by the shafts of sunlight piercing through a few bent slats in the blinds. In the back of the room, five students cluster around a table, trying to talk softly about their presentation, but their voices

(continued)

bounce off the bare floors. Baked by the sun, the classroom is so warm that the instructor has allowed us to open the windows, but the wailing sirens of ambulances racing to the various hospitals surrounding the campus distract us. The breeze, full of the smell of mown lawn, brings warm air from outside into this stuffy room. Several students besides me gaze longingly out the window at the bright pink and red rhododendrons in the garden and at the students reading comfortably in the shade under the white-blossomed cherry trees.

READINGS

The reading for this chapter consists of two eyewitness accounts of an event that occurred on the Congo River in Africa in 1877.* The first account is by the famous British explorer Henry Morton Stanley, who led an exploration party of Europeans into the African interior. The second account is by the African tribal chief Mojimba, as told orally to a Belgian missionary, Fr. Frassle, who recorded the story. The conflicting accounts suggest the complexity of what happens when different cultures meet for the first time.

Clash on the Congo: Two Eye Witness Accounts

Henry Morton Stanley's Account

1   We see a sight that sends the blood tingling through every nerve and fibre of the body . . . a flotilla of gigantic canoes bearing down upon us. A monster canoe leads the way . . . forty men on a side, their bodies bending and swaying in unison as with a swelling barbarous chorus they drive her down towards us . . . the warriors above the manned prow let fly their spears. . . . But every sound is soon lost in the ripping crackling musketry. . . . Our blood is up now. It is a murderous world, and we feel for the first time that we hate the filthy vulturous ghouls who inhabit it. . . . We pursue them . . . and continue the fight in the village streets with those who have landed, hunt them out into the woods, and there only sound the retreat, having returned the daring cannibals the compliment of a visit.

Mojimba's Account

2   When we heard that the man with the white flesh was journeying down the [Congo] we were open-mouthed with astonishment. . . . He will be one of our brothers who were drowned in the river. . . . We will prepare a feast, I

*These readings are taken from Donald C. Holsinger, "A Classroom Laboratory for Writing History," *Social Studies Review* 31.1 (1991): 59–64. The role-playing exercise following the readings is also adapted from this article.

ordered, we will go to meet our brother and escort him into the village with rejoicing! We donned our ceremonial garb. We assembled the great canoes. . . . We swept forward, my canoe leading, the others following, with songs of joy and with dancing, to meet the first white man our eyes had beheld, and to do him honor. But as we drew near his canoes there were loud reports, bang! bang! And fire-staves spat bits of iron at us. We were paralyzed with fright . . . they were the work of evil spirits! "War! That is war!" I yelled. . . . We fled into our village—they came after us. We fled into the forest and flung ourselves on the ground. When we returned that evening our eyes beheld fearful things: our brothers, dead, dying, bleeding, our village plundered and burned, and the water full of dead bodies. The robbers and murderers had disappeared.

Thinking Critically about the *Two Accounts*

Our purpose in presenting these two accounts is to raise the central problem examined in this chapter: the rhetorical nature of observation—that is, how observation is shaped by values, beliefs, knowledge, and purpose and therefore represents an angle of vision or one perspective.

1. How do the two accounts differ?

2. What is common to both accounts? Focusing on common elements, try to establish as many facts as you can about the encounter.

3. How does each observer create a persuasive effect by using one or more of the five strategies described on page 106 (overt statement of meaning, selection/omission of details, connotations of words, figurative language, ordering and shaping of sentences)?

4. What differences in assumptions, values, and knowledge shape these two interpretations of events?

5. As a class, try the following role-playing exercise:
   Background: You are a newspaper reporter who has a global reputation for objectivity, accuracy, and lack of bias. You write for a newspaper that has gained a similar reputation and prides itself on printing only the truth. Your editor has just handed you two eyewitness accounts of an incident that has recently occurred in central Africa. You are to transform the two accounts into a brief front-page article (between sixty and ninety words) informing your readers what happened. You face an immediate deadline and have no time to seek additional information.
   Task: Each class member should write a sixty- to ninety-word newspaper account of the event, striving for objectivity and lack of bias. Then share your accounts.

6. As a class, play the believing and doubting game with this assertion: "It is possible to create an objective and unbiased account of the Congo phenomenon."

Composing Your Essay

Since the assignment for this chapter has two parts—Part A, calling for two contrasting descriptions, and Part B, calling for a self-reflection—we address each part separately.

Exploring Rationales and Details for Your Two Descriptions

To get into the spirit of this unusual assignment, you need to create a personal rationale for why you are writing two opposing descriptions. Our students have been successful imagining any one of the following three rationales:

Rationales for Writing Opposing Descriptions
Different moods: One approach is to imagine observing your scene in different moods. How could I reflect a "happy" view of this scene? How could I reflect a "sad" view of this scene? Be sure, however, to focus entirely on a description of the scene, not on your mood itself. Let the mood determine your decisions about details and wording, but don't put yourself into the scene. The reader should infer the mood from the description.

Verbal game: Here you see yourself as a word wizard trying consciously to create two different rhetorical effects for readers. In this scenario, you don't worry how you feel about the scene but how you want your reader to feel. Your focus is on crafting the language to influence your audience in different ways.

Different rhetorical purposes: In this scenario, you imagine your description in service of some desired action. You might want authorities to improve an ugly, poorly designed space (for example, a poorly designed library reading room). Or you might want to commend someone for a particularly functional space (for example, a well-designed computer lab). In this scenario, you begin with a strongly held personal view of your chosen scene—something you want to commend or condemn. One of your descriptions, therefore, represents *the way you really feel*. Your next task is to see this same scene from an opposing perspective. To get beyond your current assessment of the scene—to recognize aspects of it that are inconsistent with your beliefs—you need to "defamiliarize" it, to make it strange. Artists sometimes try to disrupt their ordinary ways of seeing by drawing something upside down or by imagining the scene from the perspective of a loathsome character—whatever it takes to wipe away "the film of habit" from the object.

The student who wrote the example on pages 107–108 worked from this last rationale. She disliked one of her classrooms, which she found unpleasant and detrimental to learning. In choosing this place, she discovered that she valued college classrooms that were well equipped, comfortable, quiet, modernized, reasonably roomy, and unaffected by outside weather conditions. It was easy for her to write the negative description of this room, which used descriptive details showing how the scene violated all her criteria. However, she had trouble writing the positive description until she imagined being inside the head of someone totally different from herself.

Generating Details

Once you have chosen your scene, you need to compose descriptions that are rich in sensory detail. You might imagine yourself in descriptive partnership with a recently blinded friend in which you become your friend's eyes, while your friend—having a newly heightened sense of hearing, touch, and smell—can notice nonsight details that you might otherwise miss. In your writing, good description should be packed with sensory detail—sights, sounds, smells, textures, even on occasion tastes—all contributing to a dominant impression that gives the description focus.

After you have chosen a subject for your two descriptions, observe it intensely for fifteen or twenty minutes. One way to train yourself to notice sensory details is to create a two-column sensory chart. As you observe your scene, note details that appeal to each of the senses and then try describing them, first positively (left column) and then negatively (right column). One student, observing a scene in a local tavern, made these notes in her sensory chart:

Positive Description	Negative Description
Taste	**Taste**
salted and buttered popcorn	salty, greasy popcorn
frosty pitchers of beer	half-drunk pitchers of stale, warm beer
big bowls of salted-in-the-shell peanuts on the tables	mess of peanut shells and discarded pretzel wrappers on tables and floor
Sound	**Sound**
hum of students laughing and chatting	din of high-pitched giggles and various obnoxious frat guys shouting at each other
the jukebox playing oldies but goodies from the early Beatles	jukebox blaring out-of-date music

[She continued with the other senses of odor, touch, and sight]

Shaping and Drafting Your Two Descriptions

Once you have decided on your rationale for the two descriptions, observed your scene, and made your sensory chart, compose your two descriptions. You will need to decide on an ordering principle for your descriptions. It generally makes sense to begin with an overview of the scene to orient your reader.

From the park bench near 23rd and Maple, one can watch the people strolling by the duck pond.

By eight o'clock on any Friday night, Pagliacci's Pizzeria on Broadway becomes one of the city's most unusual gathering places.

Then you need a plan for arranging details. There are no hard-and-fast rules here, but there are some typical practices. You can arrange details in the following ways:

- By spatially scanning from left to right or from far to near
- By using the written equivalent of a movie zoom shot: begin with a broad overview of the scene, then move to close-up descriptions of specific details

Compose your pleasant description, selecting and focusing on details that convey a positive impression. Then compose your unpleasant description. Each description should comprise one fully developed paragraph (125–175 words).

Using *Show* Words Rather than *Tell* Words

In describing your scenes, use *show* words rather than *tell* words. *Tell* words interpret a scene without describing it. They name an interior, mental state, thus telling the reader what emotional reaction to draw from the scene.

TELL WORDS

There was a *pleasant* tree in the backyard.
There was an *unpleasant* tree in the backyard.

In contrast, *show* words describe a scene through sensory details appealing to sight, sound, smell, touch, and even taste. The description itself evokes the desired effect without requiring the writer to state it overtly.

SHOW WORDS

A *spreading elm* tree *bathed* the backyard with *shade*. [evokes positive feelings]
An *out-of-place elm, planted too close to the house, blocked our view* of the *mountains*. [evokes negative feelings]

The "scale of abstraction" is explained in Chapter 3, pp. 60–61.

Whereas *show* words are particulars that evoke the writer's meaning through sensory detail, *tell* words are abstractions that announce the writer's intention directly (strategy 1 on pp. 106). An occasional *tell* word can be useful, but *show* words operating at the bottom of the "scale of abstraction" are the flesh and muscle of descriptive prose.

Inexperienced writers often try to create contrasting impressions of a scene simply by switching *tell* words.

WEAK: OVERUSE OF *TELL* WORDS

The smiling merchants happily talked with customers trying to get them to buy their products. [positive purpose]
The annoying merchants kept hassling customers trying to convince them to buy their products. [negative purpose]

In this example, the negative words *annoying* and *hassling* and the positive words *smiling* and *happily* are *tell* words; they state the writer's contrasting intentions, but they don't describe the scene. Here is how the student writer revised these passages using *show* words.

STRONG: CONVERSION TO *SHOW* WORDS

One of the merchants, selling thick-wooled Peruvian sweaters, nodded approvingly as a woman tried on a richly textured blue cardigan in front of the mirror. [positive purpose]

One of the merchants, hawking those Peruvian sweaters that you find in every open-air market, tried to convince a middle-aged woman that the lumpy, oversized cardigan she was trying on looked stylish. [negative purpose]

Here are some more examples taken from students' drafts before and after revision:

Draft with *Tell* Words	Revision with *Show* Words
Children laugh and point animatedly at all the surroundings.	Across the way, a small boy taps his friend's shoulder and points at a circus clown.
The wonderful smell of food cooking on the barbecue fills my nose.	The tantalizing smell of grilled hamburgers and buttered corn on the cob wafts from the barbecue area of the park, where men in their cookout aprons wield forks and spatulas and drink Budweisers.
The paintings on the wall are confusing, dark, abstract, demented, and convey feelings of unhappiness and suffering.	The paintings on the wall, viewed through the smoke-filled room, seem confusing and abstract—the work of a demented artist on a bad trip. Splotches of black paint are splattered over a greenish-yellow background like bugs on vomit.

Revising Your Two Descriptions

The following checklist of revision questions will help you improve your first draft:

1. *How can I make my two descriptions more parallel—that is, more clearly about the same place at the same time?* The rules for the assignment ask you to use only factual details observable in the same scene at the same time. It violates the spirit of the assignment to have one scene at a winning basketball game and the other at a losing game. Your readers' sense of pleasure in comparing your two descriptions will be enhanced if many of the same details appear in both descriptions.

2. *Where can I replace* tell *words with* show *words?* Inexperienced writers tend to rely on *tell* words rather than give the reader sensory details and visual impressions. Find words that deliver prepackaged ideas to the reader (*pleasant, happy, depressing, annoying, pretty,* and so forth) and rewrite those sentences by actually describing what you see, hear, smell, touch, and taste. Pay particular attention to this advice if you are choosing "different moods" as your rationale for two descriptions.

3. *How can I make the angle of vision in each description clearer? How can I clarify my focus on a dominant impression?* Where could you use words with vividly appropriate connotations? Where could you substitute specific words for general ones? For example, consider synonyms for the generic word *shoe*. Most people wear shoes, but only certain people wear spiked heels or riding boots. Among words for kinds of sandals, *Birkenstocks* carries a different connotation from *Tevas* or *strappy espadrilles with faux-metallic finish*. Search your draft for places where you could substitute more colorful or precise words for generic words to convey your dominant impression more effectively.

Generating and Exploring Ideas for Your Self-Reflection

Writing self-reflections constitutes a powerful learning strategy. See Chapter 25 on the practice and value of self-reflective writing.

Part B of this Writing Project asks you to write a self-reflection about what you have learned. Your reflection should begin with a rhetorical analysis of your two descriptions in which you explain how you created your positive versus negative effects. Focus on how you used the strategies introduced in Chapter 4 (pages 84–85) and summarized in the chart "Strategies for Creating a Persuasive Effect" on page 106. In the rest of your self-reflection, explore what you have learned from reading this chapter and doing this exercise. You are invited to consider questions like these:

- What rationale or scenario did you use for explaining to yourself why one might write opposing descriptions (different moods? verbal game? different rhetorical purposes? something else?) Which description was easier for you to write and why?
- What new insights did you come away with? Specifically, what have you learned about the concept "angle of vision" and about ways writers can influence readers? What, if anything, was disturbing or challenging about the concepts developed in this chapter?
- Throughout this text we urge you to read rhetorically, that is, to be aware of how a text is constructed to influence readers. How has this chapter advanced your ability to read rhetorically?

To illustrate self-reflection, we reproduce here a portion of the self-reflection written by the student who wrote the two descriptions on pages 107–108.

SELECTIONS FROM A STUDENT'S SELF-REFLECTION

In writing the two descriptions, I used most of the strategies for creating rhetorical effects discussed in the text. In deliberately changing my angle of vision from positive to negative, I realized how much the connotation of individual words can convey particular ideas to readers. For example, in the positive description to get across the idea of a comfortably studious environment, I used words such as "airy," "spacious," "focused," and "quiet harmony." But in my negative description, I wanted readers to feel the unpleasantness of this room so I used words like "cramped," "crammed," "blocked," and "bulky." I also created different effects by including or excluding certain details. For example, in the positive description, I mentioned the "splashes of sunshine" coming through the window, but in the negative description

I mentioned the wailing sirens of ambulances. [She continues with this rhetorical analysis, explaining and illustrating the other strategies she used.]

I learned a lot from doing this assignment. In writing my two descriptions, I found it helpful both to imagine different moods and different rhetorical purposes. It was easy for me to write the negative view of my classroom because I often get irritated with the problems in this room—the discomfort, inconvenience, and noise. It was much harder to write the positive view. In fact, I couldn't do so until I imagined looking at the room from someone else's perspective. To do so, I imagined that a fellow student was interviewing me on the question, How could the classroom facilities on our campus be improved? I role-played telling this person what I really like in a classroom and then tried to give these features to the room.

What amazed me is that both of my descriptions are factually true but create totally different effects that depend on the observer's perspective. Writing my two descriptions made me think about how much power writers have to influence readers' thinking. . . .

[In the rest of her self-reflection, she explains further what she learned from this assignment and also notes how she has begun to notice similar rhetorical strategies being used in some of her recent reading.]

GUIDELINES FOR PEER REVIEWS

Instructions for peer reviews are provided in Chapter 17 (pp. 519–520).

For the Writer
Prepare two or three questions you would like your peer reviewer to address while responding to your draft. The questions can focus on some aspect of your draft that you are uncertain about, on one or more sections where you particularly seek help or advice, on some feature that you particularly like about your draft, or on some part you especially wrestled with. Write out your questions and give them to your peer reviewer along with your draft.

For the Reviewer
To write a peer review for a classmate, use your own paper, numbering your responses to correspond to the question numbers. At the head of your paper, place the author's name and your own name, as shown.

Author's Name: _____
Peer Reviewer's Name: _____

I. Read the draft at a normal reading speed from beginning to end. As you read, do the following:
   A. Place a wavy line in the margin next to any passages that you find confusing, that contain something that doesn't seem to fit, or that otherwise slow down your reading.
   B. Place a "Good!" in the margin next to any passages where you think the writing is particularly strong or interesting.

II. Read the draft again slowly and answer the following questions by writing brief explanations of your answers:
   A. The two descriptions
      1. How could the two descriptions be made more parallel or more detailed and vivid? How might the writer sharpen or clarify the angle of vision in each description?
      2. Where could the writer replace *tell* words with *show* words? How could the writer use *show* words more effectively? How could the writer include more sensory details appealing to more of the senses?
      3. If the writer has used only one or two of the strategies for creating contrast (direct statement of meaning, selection of details, word choice, figurative language, sentence structure), how might he or she use other strategies?
   B. Self-reflection
      1. How might the writer improve the effectiveness of the rhetorical analysis? How many strategies does the writer include? Where might the writer use more or better examples to illustrate the chosen strategies? What might the writer add or clarify?
      2. What does the writer say he or she has learned from doing this assignment? How could the writer's insights be expanded, explained more clearly, or developed more thoroughly?
III. Rhetorical considerations
   A. *Purpose, audience,* and *genre:* How do differences in organization and style in Parts A and B reveal the writer's awareness of differences in purpose, audience, and genre?
   B. *Logos, ethos,* and *pathos:* How might the writer improve the ideas in this draft, particularly in Part B? What image of the writer emerges in Parts A and B? How might the writer improve this image? How effectively does the writer appeal to the readers' feelings, emotions, and desires?
IV. If the writer has prepared questions for you, respond to his or her inquiries.
V. Sum up what you see as the chief strengths and problem areas of this draft.
   A. Strengths
   B. Problem areas
VI. Read the draft one more time. Place a check mark in the margin wherever you notice problems in grammar, spelling, or mechanics (one check mark per problem).

Reading Rhetorically
The Writer as Strong Reader

About Reading Rhetorically

Many new college students are surprised by the amount, range, and difficulty of reading they have to do in college. Every day they are challenged by reading assignments ranging from scholarly articles and textbooks on complex subject matter to primary sources such as Plato's dialogues or Darwin's *Voyage of the Beagle*.

The goal of this chapter is to help you become a more powerful reader of academic texts, prepared to take part in the conversations of the disciplines you study. To this end, we explain two kinds of thinking and writing essential to your college reading:

- Your ability to listen carefully to a text, to recognize its parts and their functions, and to summarize its ideas
- Your ability to formulate strong responses to texts by interacting with them, either by agreeing with, interrogating, or actively opposing them

To interact strongly with texts, you must learn how to read them both with and against the grain. When you read *with the grain* of a text, you see the world through its author's perspective, open yourself to the author's argument, apply the text's insights to new contexts, and connect its ideas to your own experiences and personal knowledge. When you read *against the grain* of a text, you resist it by questioning its points, raising doubts, analyzing the limits of its perspective, or even refuting its argument. We say that readers who respond strongly to texts in this manner read *rhetorically*; that is, they are aware of the effect a text is intended to have on them, and they critically consider that effect, entering into or challenging the text's intentions.

Exploring Rhetorical Reading

As an introduction to rhetorical reading, we would like you to read Dr. Andrés Martin's "On Teenagers and Tattoos," which appeared in the *Journal of the American Academy of Child and Adolescent Psychiatry*, a scholarly publication. Before reading the article, complete the following opinion survey. Answer each question using a 1–5 scale, with 1 meaning "strongly agree" and 5 meaning "strongly disagree."

1. For teenagers, getting a tattoo is like following any other fad such as wearing the currently popular kind of shoe or hairstyle.
2. Teenagers get tattoos primarily as a form of asserting independence from parents and other adults.
3. Teenagers get tattoos on the spur of the moment and usually don't consider the irreversibility of marking their skin.
4. Teenagers who get tattoos are expressing deep psychological needs.
5. A psychiatry journal can provide useful insights into teen choices to tattoo their bodies.

When you have finished rating your degree of agreement with these statements, read Martin's article, using whatever note-taking, underlining, or highlighting strategies you normally use when reading for a class. When you have finished reading, complete the exercises that follow.

READING

Andrés Martin, M.D.
On Teenagers and Tattoos

The skeleton dimensions I shall now proceed to set down are copied verbatim from my right arm, where I had them tattooed: as in my wild wanderings at that period, there was no other secure way of preserving such valuable statistics.

—Melville/*Moby Dick CII*

1   Tattoos and piercings have become a part of our everyday landscape. They are ubiquitous, having entered the circles of glamour and the mainstream of fashion, and they have even become an increasingly common feature of our urban youth. Legislation in most states restricts professional tattooing to adults older than 18 years of age, so "high end" tattooing is rare in children and adolescents, but such tattoos are occasionally seen in older teenagers. Piercings, by comparison, as well as self-made or "jailhouse" type tattoos, are not at all rare among adolescents or even among schoolage children. Like hairdo, makeup, or baggy jeans, tattoos and piercings can be subject to fad influence or peer pressure in an effort toward group affiliation. As with any other fashion statement, they can be construed as bodily aids in the inner struggle toward identity consolidation, serving as adjuncts to the defining and sculpting of the self by means of external manipulations. But unlike most other body decorations, tattoos and piercings are set apart by their irreversible and permanent nature, a quality at the core of their magnetic appeal to adolescents.

2   Adolescents and their parents are often at odds over the acquisition of bodily decorations. For the adolescent, piercings or tattoos may be seen as personal and beautifying statements, while parents may construe them as oppositional and enraging affronts to their authority. Distinguishing bodily adornment from self-mutilation may indeed prove challenging, particularly when a family is in disagreement over a teenager's motivations and a clinician is summoned as the final arbiter. At such times it may be most important to realize jointly that the skin can all too readily become but another battleground for the tensions of the age, arguments having less to do with tattoos and piercings than with core issues such as separation from the family matrix. Exploring the motivations and significance underlying tattoos (Grumet, 1983) and piercings can go a long way toward resolving such differences and can become a novel and additional way of getting to know teenagers. An interested and nonjudgmental appreciation of teenagers' surface presentations may become a way of making contact not only in their terms but on their turfs: quite literally on the territory of their skins.

3   The following three sections exemplify some of the complex psychological underpinnings of youth tattooing.

Identity and the Adolescent's Body

4   Tattoos and piercing can offer a concrete and readily available solution for many of the identity crises and conflicts normative to adolescent development. In using such decorations, and by marking out their bodily territories, adolescents can support their efforts at autonomy, privacy, and insulation. Seeking individuation, tattooed adolescents can become unambiguously demarcated from others and singled out as unique. The intense and often disturbing reactions that are mobilized in viewers can help to effectively keep them at bay, becoming tantamount to the proverbial "Keep Out" sign hanging from a teenager's door.

5   Alternatively, [when teenagers feel] prey to a rapidly evolving body over which they have no say, self-made and openly visible decorations may restore adolescents' sense of normalcy and control, a way of turning a passive experience into an active identity. By indelibly marking their bodies, adolescents can strive to reclaim their bearings within an environment experienced as alien, estranged, or suffocating or to lay claim over their evolving and increasingly unrecognizable bodies. In either case, the net outcome can be a resolution to unwelcome impositions: external, familial, or societal in one case; internal and hormonal in the other. In the words of a 16-year-old girl with several facial piercings, and who could have been referring to her body just as well as to the position within her family, "If I don't fit in, it is because *I* say so."

Incorporation and Ownership

6   Imagery of a religious, deathly, or skeletal nature, the likenesses of fierce animals or imagined creatures, and the simple inscription of names are some of the time-tested favorite contents for tattoos. In all instances, marks

become not only memorials or recipients for clearly held persons or concepts; they strive for incorporation, with images and abstract symbols gaining substance on becoming a permanent part of the individual's skin. Thickly embedded in personally meaningful representations and object relations, tattoos can become not only the ongoing memento of a relationship, but at times even the only evidence that there ever was such a bond. They can quite literally become the relationship itself. The turbulence and impulsivity of early attachments and infatuations may become grounded, effectively bridging oblivion through the visible reality of tattoos.

7   *Case Vignette.* A, a 13-year-old boy, proudly showed me his tattooed deltoid. The coarsely depicted roll of the dice marked the day and month of his birth. Rather disappointed, he then uncovered an immaculate back, going on to draw for me the great "piece" he envisioned for it. A menacing figure held a hand of cards: two aces, two eights, and a card with two sets of dates. A's father had belonged to "Dead Man's Hand," a motorcycle gang named after the set of cards (aces and eights) that the legendary Wild Bill Hickock had held in the 1890s when shot dead over a poker table in Deadwood, South Dakota. A had only the vaguest memory of and sketchiest information about his father, but he knew he had died in a motorcycle accident: the fifth card marked the dates of his birth and death.

8   The case vignette also serves to illustrate how tattoos are often the culmination of a long process of imagination, fantasy, and planning that can start at an early age. Limited markings, or relatively reversible ones such as piercings, can at a later time scaffold toward the more radical commitment of a permanent tattoo.

The Quest for Permanence

9   The popularity of the anchor as a tattoo motif may historically have had to do less with guild identification among sailors than with an intense longing for rootedness and stability. In a similar vein, the recent increase in the popularity and acceptance of tattoos may be understood as an antidote or counterpoint to our urban and nomadic lifestyles. Within an increasingly mobile society, in which relationships are so often transient—as attested by the frequencies of divorce, abandonment, foster placement, and repeated moves, for example—tattoos can be a readily available source of grounding. Tattoos, unlike many relationships, can promise permanence and stability. A sense of constancy can be derived from unchanging marks that can be carried along no matter what the physical, temporal, or geographical vicissitudes at hand. Tattoos stay, while all else may change.

10   *Case Vignette.* A proud father at 17, B had had the smiling face of his 3-month-old baby girl tattooed on his chest. As we talked at a tattoo convention, he proudly introduced her to me, explaining how he would "always know how beautiful she is today" when years from then he saw her semblance etched on himself.

11   The quest for permanence may at other times prove misleading and offer premature closure to unresolved conflicts. At a time of normative uncertain-

ties, adolescents may maladaptively and all too readily commit to a tattoo and its indefinite presence. A wish to hold on to a current certainty may lead the adolescent to lay down in ink what is valued and cherished one day but may not necessarily be in the future. The frequency of self-made tattoos among hospitalized, incarcerated, or gang-affiliated youths suggests such motivations: a sense of stability may be a particularly dire need under temporary, turbulent, or volatile conditions. In addition, through their designs teenagers may assert a sense of bonding and allegiance to a group larger than themselves. Tattoos may attest to powerful experiences, such as adolescence itself, lived and even survived together. As with *Moby Dick's* protagonist Ishmael, they may bear witness to the "valuable statistics" of one's "wild wandering(s)": those of adolescent exhilaration and excitement on the one hand; of growing pains, shared misfortune, or even incarceration on the other.

12   Adolescents' bodily decorations, at times radical and dramatic in their presentation, can be seen in terms of figuration rather than disfigurement, of the natural body being through them transformed into a personalized body (Brain, 1979). They can often be understood as self-constructive and adorning efforts, rather than prematurely subsumed as mutilatory and destructive acts. If we bear all of this in mind, we may not only arrive at a position to pass more reasoned clinical judgment, but become sensitized through our patients' skins to another level of their internal reality.

References
Brain, R. (1979). *The Decorated Body*. New York: Harper & Row.

Grumet, G. W. (1983). Psychodynamic implications of tattoos. *Am J Orthopsychiatry*, 53:482–492.

Thinking Critically about "On Teenagers and Tattoos"

1. Summarize in one or two sentences Martin's main points.

2. Freewrite a response to this question: In what way has Martin's article caused me to reconsider my answers to the opinion survey?

3. Working in small groups or as a whole class, compare the note-taking strategies you used while reading this piece. (a) How many people wrote marginal notes? How many underlined or highlighted? (b) Compare the contents of these notes. Did people highlight the same passage or different passages? (c) Individually, look at your annotations and highlights and try to decide why you wrote or marked what you did. Share your reasons for making these annotations. The goal of this exercise is to make you more aware of your thinking processes as you read.

4. Working as a whole class or in small groups, share your responses to the questionnaire and to the postreading questions. To what extent did this article

change people's thinking about the reasons teenagers choose to tattoo their bodies? What were the most insightful points in this article?

5. Assume that you are looking for substantial, detailed information about teenagers and tattooing. What parts of this article leave you with unanswered questions? Where is more explanation needed?

WRITING PROJECT

Write a "summary/strong response" essay that includes: (a) a summary (approximately 150–250 words) of a reading specified by your instructor and (b) a strong response to that reading in which you speak back to that reading from your own critical thinking, personal experience, and values. As you formulate your own response, consider both the author's rhetorical strategies and the author's ideas. Think of your response as your analysis of how the text tries to influence its readers rhetorically and how your wrestling with the text has expanded and deepened your thinking about its ideas.

The skills this assignment develops are crucial for academic writers. You will learn how to summarize an article (or book), including how to quote brief passages, how to use attributive tags to cue your reader that you are reporting someone else's ideas rather than your own, and how to cite the article using (in this case) the Modern Language Association (MLA) documentation system. Because writing summaries and producing strong responses are important writing-to-learn skills, you will draw on them any time you are asked to speak back to or critique a text. These skills are also needed for writing exploratory essays, analysis and synthesis essays, researched arguments, and any other scholarly work that uses sources. In learning how to summarize a text and interact with it in writing, you are learning how to contribute your own ideas to a conversation. Weak readers passively report what other people have said. Strong readers see themselves as contributors to the conversation, capable of analyzing and evaluating texts, speaking back to other authors, and thinking actively for themselves.

Understanding Rhetorical Reading

In this section we explain why college-level reading is often difficult for new students and offer suggestions for improving your reading process based on the reading strategies of experts. We then show you the importance of reading a text both with the grain and against the grain—skills you need to summarize a text and respond to it strongly.

What Makes College-Level Reading Difficult?

The difficulty of college-level reading stems in part from the complexity of the subject matter. Whatever the subject—from international monetary policies to the intricacies of photosynthesis—you have to wrestle with new and complex materials that might perplex anyone. But in addition to the daunting subject matter, several other factors contribute to the difficulty of college-level reading:

- *Vocabulary.* Many college-level readings—especially primary sources—contain unfamiliar technical language that may be specific to an academic discipline: for example, the terms *identity consolidation, normative, individuation,* and *object relations* in the Martin text or words like *existentialism* and *Neoplatonic* in a philosophy textbook. In academia, words often carry specialized meanings that evoke a whole history of conversation and debate that may be inaccessible, even through a specialized dictionary. You will not fully understand them until you are initiated into the disciplinary conversations that gave rise to them.
- *Unfamiliar rhetorical context.* As we explained in Part One, writers write to an audience for a purpose arising from some motivating occasion. Knowing an author's purpose, occasion, and audience will often clarify confusing parts of a text. For example, you can understand the Martin article more easily if you know that its author, writing in a scientific journal, is offering advice to psychiatrists about how to counsel tattooed teens and their families. A text's internal clues can sometimes help you fill in the rhetorical context, but often you may need to do outside research.
- *Unfamiliar genre.* In your college reading, you will encounter a range of genres such as textbooks, trade books, scholarly articles, scientific reports, historical documents, newspaper articles, op-ed pieces, and so forth. Each of these makes different demands on readers and requires a different reading strategy.
- *Lack of background knowledge.* Writers necessarily make assumptions about what their readers already know. Your understanding of Martin, for example, would be more complete if you had a background in adolescent psychology and psychiatric therapy.

For Writing and Discussion

The importance of background knowledge can be easily demonstrated any time you dip into past issues of a newsmagazine or try to read articles about an unfamiliar culture. Consider the following passage from a 1986 *Newsweek* article. How much background knowledge do you need before you can fully comprehend this passage? What cultural knowledge about the United States would a student from Ethiopia or Indonesia need?

(continued)

> Throughout the NATO countries last week, there were second thoughts about the prospect of a nuclear-free world. For 40 years nuclear weapons have been the backbone of the West's defense. For almost as long American presidents have ritually affirmed their desire to see the world rid of them. Then, suddenly, Ronald Reagan and Mikhail Gorbachev came close to actually doing it. Let's abolish all nuclear ballistic missiles in the next 10 years, Reagan said. Why not all nuclear weapons, countered Gorbachev. OK, the president responded, like a man agreeing to throw in the washer-dryer along with the house.
>
> What if the deal had gone through? On the one hand, Gorbachev would have returned to Moscow a hero. There is a belief in the United States that the Soviets need nuclear arms because nuclear weapons are what make them a superpower. But according to Marxist-Leninist doctrine, capitalism's nuclear capability (unforeseen by Marx and Lenin) is the only thing that can prevent the inevitable triumph of communism. Therefore, an end to nuclear arms would put the engine of history back on its track.
>
> On the other hand, Europeans fear, a nonnuclear United States would be tempted to retreat into neo-isolationism.
>
> —*Robert B. Cullen, "Dangers of Disarming,"* Newsweek

Working in small groups or as a class, identify words and passages in this text that depend on background information or knowledge of culture for complete comprehension.

Using the Reading Strategies of Experts

In Chapter 17, we describe the differences between the writing processes of experts and those of beginning college writers. There are parallel differences between the reading processes of experienced and inexperienced readers, especially when they encounter complex materials. In this section we describe some expert reading strategies that you can begin applying to your reading of any kind of college-level material.

Reconstruct the Text's Rhetorical Context

Before and as you read a text, ask questions about the author's audience, purpose, genre, and motivating occasion. Any piece of writing makes more sense if you think of its author as a real person writing for some real purpose in a real historical context.

If you read an article that has been anthologized (as in the readings in this textbook), note any information you are given about the author, publication data, and genre. Try to reconstruct the author's original motivation for writing. How have audience, purpose, and genre shaped this text?

Make Marginal Notes as You Read

Expert readers seldom use highlighters, which encourage passive, inefficient reading; instead, they make extensive marginal notes as they read. Advice on writing marginal notes is given throughout this chapter.

Get in the Dictionary Habit

When you can't tell a word's meaning from context, get in the habit of looking it up. One strategy is to make small check marks next to words you're unsure of; then look them up after you're done so as not to break your concentration.

Vary Your Reading Speed to Match Your Reading Goals

Unlike novices, experienced readers vary their reading speeds and strategies according to their goals. In other words, experienced readers know when to slow down or speed up. Robert Sternberg, a cognitive psychologist, discovered that novice readers tend to read everything at about the same pace, no matter what their purpose. In contrast, experienced readers vary their reading speed significantly depending on whether they are scanning for a piece of information, skimming for main ideas, reading deliberately for complete comprehension, or reading slowly for detailed analysis. Knowing when to speed up or slow down—especially if you are doing a research project and trying to cover lots of ground—can make your reading more efficient.

If a Text Is Complex, Read in a "Multidraft" Way

It may be comforting for you to know that expert readers struggle with difficult texts the same way you do. Often, experienced readers reread a text two or three times, treating their first readings like first drafts. They hold confusing passages in mental suspension, hoping that later parts of the essay will clarify earlier parts. The ironic point here is that sometimes you have to speed up to slow down. If you are lost in a passage, try skimming ahead rapidly, looking at the opening sentences of paragraphs and at any passages that sum up the writer's argument or that help clarify the argument's structure. Pay particular attention to the conclusion, which often ties the whole argument together. This rapid "first-draft reading" helps you see the text's main points and overall structure, thus providing a background for a second reading. The passage that puzzled you the first time might now be clearer.

Reading With the Grain and Against the Grain

The reading and thinking strategies that we have just described enable skilled readers to interact strongly with texts. Your purpose in using these strategies is to read texts both with the grain and against the grain, a way of reading that is analogous to the believing and doubting game we introduced in Chapter 2. This concept is so important that we have chosen to highlight it separately here.

For an explanation of the believing and doubting game, see pp. 42–46.

When you read with the grain of a text, you practice what psychologist Carl Rogers calls "empathic listening," in which you try to see the world through the author's eyes, role-playing as much as possible the author's intended readers by adopting their beliefs and values and acquiring their background knowledge. Reading with the grain is the main strategy you use when you summarize a text, but it comes into play also when you develop a strong response. When making with-the-grain points, you support the author's thesis with your own arguments and examples, or apply or extend the author's argument in new ways.

When you read against the grain of a text, you challenge, question, resist, and perhaps even rebut the author's ideas. You are a resistant reader who asks unanticipated questions, pushes back, and reads the text in ways unforeseen by the author. Reading against the grain is a key part of creating a strong response. When you make against-the-grain points, you challenge the author's reasoning, sources, examples, or choice of language. You generate counterexamples, present alternative lines of reasoning, deny the writer's values, or raise points that the writer has overlooked or specific data that the writer has omitted.

Strong readers develop their ability to read in both ways—with the grain and against the grain. Throughout the rest of this chapter, we show you different ways to practice and apply these strategies.

Understanding Summary Writing

In this section we explain techniques for writing an effective summary of a text. Summary writing fosters a close encounter between you and the text and demonstrates your understanding of it. When you write a summary, you practice reading with the grain of a text. You "listen" actively to the text's author, showing that you understand the author's point of view by restating his or her argument as completely and fairly as possible. Summary writing is an essential academic skill, regularly used in research writing of any kind, where you often present condensed views of other writers' arguments, either as support for your own view or as alternative views that you must analyze or respond to.

Reading for Structure and Content

In writing a summary, you must focus on both its structure and its content. In the following steps, we recommend a process that will help you condense a text's ideas into an accurate summary. As you become a more experienced reader and writer, you'll follow these steps without thinking about them.

Step 1:   The first time through, read the text fairly quickly for general meaning. If you get confused, keep going; later parts of the text might clarify earlier parts.

Step 2:   Reread the text carefully. As you read, write gist statements in the margins for each paragraph. A *gist statement* is a brief indication of the paragraph's function or purpose in the text or a brief summary of the paragraph's content. Sometimes it is helpful to think of these two kinds of gist statements as "what it does" statements and "what it says" statements.* A "what it does" statement specifies the paragraph's function—for example, "summarizes an opposing view," "introduces

---

*For our treatment of "what it does" and "what it says" statements, we are indebted to Kenneth A. Bruffee, *A Short Course in Writing*, 2nd ed. (Cambridge, MA: Winthrop, 1980).

another reason," "presents a supporting example," "provides statistical data in support of a point," and so on. A "what it says" statement captures the main idea of a paragraph by summarizing the paragraph's content. The "what it says" statement is the paragraph's main point, in contrast to its supporting ideas and examples. Sometimes an explicit topic sentence makes the main point easy to find, but often you have to extract the main point by shrinking an argument down to its essence. In some cases, you may be uncertain about the main point. If so, select the point that you think a majority of readers would agree is the main one.

When you first practice detailed readings of a text, you might find it helpful to write complete *does* and *says* statements on a separate sheet of paper rather than in the margins until you develop the internal habit of appreciating both the function and content of parts of an essay. Here are *does* and *says* statements for selected paragraphs of Andrés Martin's essay on teenage tattooing:

Paragraph 1: *Does:* Introduces the subject and sets up the argument. *Says:* The current popularity of tattoos and piercings is partly explained as an aid toward finding an identity, but the core of their appeal is their irreversible permanence.

Paragraph 2: *Does:* Narrows the focus and presents the thesis. *Says:* To counsel families in disagreement over tattoos, psychiatrists should exhibit a nonjudgmental appreciation of teen tattoos and use them to understand teenagers better.

Paragraph 4: *Does:* Discusses the first complex motivation behind youth tattooing. *Says:* Teens use tattoos to handle identity crises and to establish their uniqueness from others.

Paragraph 5: *Does:* Elaborates on the first motivation, the identity issue. *Says:* Tattoos provide teens with a sense of control over their changing bodies and over an environment perceived as adverse and domineering.

Paragraph 11: *Does:* Complicates the view of teens' use of tattoos to find permanence and belonging. *Says:* Although tattoos may unrealistically promise the resolution to larger conflicts, they may at least record the triumphs and miseries of adolescent turbulence, including gang and prison experience.

Paragraph 12: *Does:* Sums up the perspective and advice of the article. *Says:* Psychiatrists should regard adolescent tattoos positively as adornment and self-expression and employ tattoos to help understand teens' identities and sense of reality.

You may occasionally have difficulty writing a *says* statement for a paragraph because you may have trouble deciding what the main idea is, especially if the paragraph doesn't begin with a closed-form topic sentence. One way to respond to this problem is to formulate the question that you think the paragraph answers. If you think of chunks of the text as answers to a logical progression of questions, you can often follow the main ideas more easily. Rather than writing *says* statements in the margins, therefore, some readers prefer writing *says* questions. *Says* questions for the Martin text may include the following: What is the most constructive approach clinicians can take to teen tattooing when these tattoos have become the focus of family conflict? What psychological needs and problems are teenagers acting out through their tattoos? Why does the permanence of tattoos appeal to young people?

No matter which method you use—*says* statements or *says* questions—writing gist statements in the margins is far more effective than underlining or highlighting in helping you recall the text's structure and argument.

Step 3:   After you have analyzed the article paragraph by paragraph, try locating the article's main divisions or parts. In longer closed-form articles, writers often forecast the shape of their essays in their introductions or use their conclusions to sum up main points. Although Martin's article is short, it uses both a forecasting statement and subheads to direct readers through its main points. The article is divided into several main chunks as follows:

- Introductory paragraphs, which establish the problem to be addressed and narrow the focus to a clinical perspective (paragraphs 1–2)
- A one-sentence organizing and predicting statement (paragraph 3)
- A section explaining how tattoos may help adolescents establish a unique identity (paragraphs 4–5)
- A section explaining how tattoos help teens incorporate onto their bodies a symbolic ownership of something important to them (paragraphs 6–8)
- A section explaining how tattoos represent and satisfy teens' search for permanence (paragraphs 9–11)
- A conclusion that states the thesis explicitly and sums up Martin's advice to fellow psychiatrists (paragraph 12)

Outlines and tree diagrams are discussed in Chapter 18, pp. 538–540.

Instead of listing the sections, you might prefer to make an outline or tree diagram of the article showing its main parts.

The same basic procedures can work for summarizing a book, but you will need to modify them to fit a much longer text. For instance, you might write "what it does" and "what it says" statements for chapters or parts of a book. In summarizing a book, you might pay special attention to the introduction and conclusion of the book. In the introduction, usually authors state their motivation for writing the book and often put forth their thesis and the subtheses that the subsequent chapters of the book develop and explain. Chapter titles and chapter introductions often restate the author's subtheses and can help you identify main ideas to include in a book summary.

Producing the Summary

Once you have written gist statements or questions in the margins and clarified the text's structure by creating an outline or diagram, you are ready to write a summary. Typically, summaries range from 100 to 250 words, but sometimes writers compose summaries as short as one sentence. The order and proportions of your summary can usually follow the order and proportions of the text. However, if the original article has a delayed thesis or other characteristics of open-form writing, you can rearrange the order and begin with the thesis. With prose that has many open-form features, you may also have to infer points that are more implied than expressed.

A summary of another author's writing—when it is incorporated into your own essay—makes particular demands on you, the writer. Most of all, writing a summary challenges you to convey the main ideas of a text—ideas that are often complex—in as few and as clear words as you can. We tell our students that writing a summary is like having a word budget: you have only so many words (say, a 250- or 100-word limit), and you have to spend them wisely. In addition, a successful summary should do all of the following:

CRITERIA FOR AN EFFECTIVE SUMMARY

- Represent the original article accurately and fairly.
- Be direct and concise, using words economically.
- Remain objective and neutral, not revealing your own ideas on the subject but, rather, only the original author's points.
- Give the original article balanced and proportional coverage.
- Use your own words to express the original author's ideas.
- Keep your reader informed through attributive tags (such as *according to Martin* or *Martin argues that*) that you are expressing someone else's ideas, not your own.
- Possibly include quotations for a few key terms or ideas from the original, but quote sparingly.
- Be a unified, coherent piece of writing in its own right.
- Be properly cited and documented so that the reader can find the original text.

Some of these criteria for a successful summary are challenging to meet. For instance, to avoid interjecting your own opinions, note whether the verbs in your attributive tags reflect a bias. Consider the difference between *Smith argues* and *Smith rants* or between *Brown asserts* and *Brown leaps to the conclusion*. In each pair, the second verb, by moving beyond neutrality, reveals your own judgment of the author's ideas.

When you incorporate a summary into your own writing, it is particularly important to distinguish between the author's ideas and your own—hence the importance of frequent attributive tags, which tell the reader that these ideas belong to Smith or Jones or Brown rather than to you. If you choose to copy any of the author's words directly from the text, you need to use quotation marks and cite the quotation using an appropriate documentation system.

Chapter 22 provides additional instruction on summarizing, paraphrasing, and quoting sources. It also explains how to work sources smoothly into your own writing and avoid plagiarism.

The following example, which summarizes Martin's article on teenagers and tattoos, uses the MLA documentation system.

Summary of Martin Article

In "On Teenagers and Tattoos," published in the <u>Journal of the American Academy of Child and Adolescent Psychiatry</u>, Dr. Andrés Martin advises fellow psychiatrists to think of teenage tattooing not as a fad or as a form of self-mutilation but as an opportunity for clinicians to understand teenagers better. <u>Martin examines</u> three different reasons that teenagers get tattoos. <u>First,</u> he argues that tattoos help teenagers establish unique identities

Identification of the article, journal, and author

Thesis of article

Attributive tag

Transition

Attributive tag

Transition and attributive tag

by giving them a sense of control over their evolving bodies and over an environment perceived as adverse and domineering. <u>Second, he believes</u> that a tattooed image often symbolizes the teen's

Transition and attributive tag

relationship to a significant concept or person, making the relationship more visible and real. <u>Finally, says Martin</u>, because

Inclusion of short quotation from article. MLA documentation style; number in parentheses indicates page number of original article where quotation is found

teens are disturbed by modern society's mobility and fragmentation and because they have an "intense longing for rootedness and stability" (120), the irreversible nature of tattoos may give them a sense of permanence. <u>Martin concludes</u> that tattoos can be a

Attributive tag

meaningful record of survived teen experiences. <u>He encourages</u>

Attributive tag

therapists to regard teen tattoos as "self-constructive and

Another short quotation

adorning efforts," rather than as "mutilatory and destructive

Brackets indicate that the writer changed the material inside the brackets to fit the grammar and context of the writer's own sentence

acts" (121) and suggests that tattoos can help therapists understand "another level of [<u>teenagers'</u>] internal reality" (121). [195 words]

Works Cited

Martin article cited completely using MLA documentation form; in a formal paper, the "works cited" list begins on a new page

Martin, Andrés. "On Teenagers and Tattoos." <u>Journal of the American Academy of Child and Adolescent Psychiatry</u> 36 (1997): 860-61. Rpt. in <u>The Allyn & Bacon Guide to Writing</u>. John D. Ramage, John C. Bean, and June Johnson. 4th ed. New York: Longman, 2006. 118-121.

For Writing and Discussion

Imagine that the context of a research paper you are writing calls for a shorter summary of the Martin article than the one presented here (which is approximately 195 words, including attributive tags). To practice distilling the main ideas of an article to produce summaries of different lengths, first write a 100-word summary of "On Teenagers and Tattoos." Then reduce your summary further to 50 words. Discuss the principles you followed in deciding what to eliminate or how to restructure sentences to convey the most information in the fewest number of words.

Understanding Strong Response Writing

We have said that summary writing is an essential academic skill. Equally important is strong response writing in which you join the text's conversation and
speak back to it. If a strong reading means to engage a text actively, both assent-
ing to an author's ideas and questioning them, what exactly do you write about
when you compose a strong response? To appreciate our answer to this question,
you need to know the various ways that strong responses are assigned across the
curriculum.

Kinds of Strong Responses

A strong response is one of the most common writing assignments you will
encounter in college courses. However, teachers vary in what they mean by a
"strong response," and they often use different terms for the same basic kind of
assignment. Our conversations with instructors from across the disciplines suggest that there are three common kinds of strong response assignments:

- *Analysis or critique assignment.* Here your job is to analyze and critique
  the assigned reading. You discuss how a text is constructed, what rhetorical
  strategies it employs, and how effectively its argument is supported.
  Suppose, for example, that you are asked to critique an article, appearing in
  a conservative business journal, that advocates oil exploration in the Arctic
  National Wildlife Refuge (ANWR). For this kind of strong response, you'd
  be expected to analyze the article's rhetorical strategies (for example, How
  is it shaped to appeal to a conservative, business-oriented audience? How
  has the writer's angle of vision filtered the evidence for its arguments?) and
  evaluate its argument (for example, What are the underlying assumptions
  and beliefs on which the argument is based? Is the logic sound? Is the evidence accurate and up-to-date?). When you analyze and critique a reading,
  you focus on the text itself, giving it the same close attention that an art
  critic gives a painting, a football coach gives a game film, or a biologist
  gives a cell formation. This close attention can be with the grain, noting
  the effectiveness of the text's rhetorical strategies, or against the grain, discussing what is ineffective or problematic about these strategies. Or an
  analysis might point out both the strengths of and the problems with a
  text's rhetorical strategies.
- *"Your own views" assignment.* Here the instructor expects you to present
  your own views on the reading's topic or issue—for example, to give your
  own views on oil exploration in the ANWR, to support or challenge the
  writer's views, to raise new questions, and otherwise to add your voice to the
  ANWR conversation. This kind of strong response invites you to read both
  with and against the grain. A with-the-grain reading supports all or some of
  the article's arguments but supplies additional reasons or new evidence,

directs the argument to a different audience, extends the argument to a different context, or otherwise adds your own support to the writer's views. An against-the-grain reading attempts to challenge all or part of the writer's argument, to raise doubts in the audience, to show flaws in the writer's reasoning, and to support your own views as they arise from your personal experience, observation, other reading, and wrestling with the author's ideas.

- *A blended assignment that mixes both kinds of responses.* Here the instructor expects you to respond in both ways—to analyze and critique the article but also to engage the writer's ideas by developing your own views on the topic. As a writer, you can emphasize what is most important to you, but the paper should contain elements of analysis and critique as well as your own views on the issue. The assignment for this chapter calls for this kind of blended strong response, but your instructor can specify what kind of emphasis he or she desires.

Instructors also vary in their preferences for the tone and structure of strong response essays. Some instructors prefer the term *reflection paper* rather than *strong response*—a term that invites you to write a personal response with an open-form structure and an expressive or exploratory purpose. In a reflection paper, the instructor is particularly interested in how the reading has affected you personally—what memories it has triggered, what personal experiences it relates to, what values and beliefs it has challenged, and so forth. Other instructors prefer closed-form strong responses with an explicit thesis statement, an analytical or persuasive purpose, and a more academic tone.

The assignment in this chapter calls for a closed-form strong response with a clear thesis statement. Your instructor, however, may modify the assignment to fit the goals of his or her course or the curriculum at your university.

Student Example of a Summary/Strong Response Essay

Before giving you some tips on how to discover ideas for your strong response, we show you an example of a student essay for this chapter: a summary/strong response essay. Note that the essay begins by identifying the question under discussion: Why do teenagers get tattoos? It then summarizes the article by Andrés Martin.* Immediately following the summary, the student writer states his thesis, followed by the strong response, which contains both rhetorical points and points about the causes of teenage tattooing.

WHY DO TEENAGERS GET TATTOOS? A RESPONSE TO ANDRÉS MARTIN

Sean Barry (student)

Introduces topic and sets context

My sister has one. My brother has one. I have one. Just take a stroll downtown and you will see how commonplace it is for someone to be decorated with tattoos and hung with piercings. In fact, hundreds of teenagers, every day, allow themselves

---

*In this essay the student writer uses a shortened version of his 195-word summary that was used as an illustration on pages 129–130.

to be etched upon or poked into. What's the cause of this phenomenon? Why do so many teenagers get tattoos?

Dr. Andrés Martin has answered this question from a psychiatrist's perspective in his article "On Teenagers and Tattoos," published in the <u>Journal of the American Academy of Child and Adolescent Psychiatry</u>. Martin advises fellow psychiatrists to think of teenage tattooing as a constructive opportunity for clinicians to understand teenagers better. Martin examines three different reasons that teenagers get tattoos. First, he argues that tattoos help teenagers establish unique identities by giving them a sense of control over their evolving bodies and over an environment perceived as adverse and domineering. Second, he believes that a tattooed image often symbolizes the teen's relationship to a significant concept or person, making the relationship more visible and real. Finally, says Martin, because teens are disturbed by modern society's mobility and fragmentation and because they have an "intense longing for rootedness and stability" (120), the irreversible nature of tattoos may give them a sense of permanence. Martin concludes that tattoos can be a meaningful record of survived teen experiences. Although Martin's analysis has relevance and some strengths, I think he overgeneralizes and over-romanticizes teenage tattooing, leading him to overlook other causes of teenage tattooing such as commercialization and teenagers' desire to identify with a peer group as well as achieve an individual identity.

Summary of Martin's article

Thesis statement

Some of Martin's points seem relevant and realistic and match my own experiences. I agree that teenagers sometimes use tattoos to establish their own identities. When my brother, sister, and I all got our tattoos, we were partly asserting our own independence from our parents. Martin's point about the symbolic significance of a tattoo image also connects with my experiences. A Hawaiian guy in my dorm has a fish tattooed on his back, which he says represents his love of the ocean and the spiritual experience he has when he scuba dives.

With-the-grain point in support of Martin's ideas

Martin, speaking as a psychiatrist to other psychiatrists, also provides psychological insights into the topic of teen tattooing even though this psychological perspective brings some limitations, too. In this scholarly article, Martin's purpose is to persuade fellow psychiatrists to think of adolescent tattooing in positive rather than judgmental terms. Rather than condemn teens for getting tattoos, he argues that discussion of the tattoos can provide useful insights into the needs and behavior of troubled teens (especially males). But this perspective is also a limitation because the teenagers he sees are mostly youths in psychiatric counseling, particularly teens struggling with the absence of or violent loss of a parent and those who have experience with gangs and prison-terms. This perspective leads him to overgeneralize. As a psychological study of a specific group of troubled teens, the article is informative. However, it does not apply as well to most teenagers who are getting tattoos today.

Rhetorical point about Martin's audience, purpose, and genre that has both with-the-grain and against-the-grain elements

Besides overgeneralizing, Martin also seems to romanticize teenage tattooing. Why else would a supposedly scientific article begin and end with quotations from <u>Moby Dick</u>? Martin seems to imply a similarity between today's teenagers and the sailor hero Ishmael who wandered the seas looking for personal identity. In quoting <u>Moby Dick</u>, Martin seems to value tattooing as a suitable way for teenagers to record their experiences. Every tattoo, for Martin, has deep significance. Thus, Martin casts tattooed teens <u>as romantic outcasts, loners, and adventurers like Ishmael.</u>

Against-the-grain rhetorical point: Barry analyzes use of quotations from Moby Dick

<u>In contrast to Martin</u>, I believe that teens are influenced by the commercial nature of tattooing, which has become big business aimed at their age group. Every movie or television star or beauty queen who sports a tattoo sends the commercial message that tattoos are cool: "A tattoo will help you be successful, sexy, handsome, or attractive like us." Tattoo parlors are no longer dark dives in seedy, dangerous parts of cities, but

Transition to writer's own analysis

Against-the-grain point: writer's alternative theory

appear in lively commercial districts; in fact, there are several down the street from the university. Teenagers now buy tattoos the way they buy other consumer items.

*Against-the-grain
point: writer's second
theory*

Furthermore, Martin doesn't explore teenagers' desire not only for individuality but also for peer group acceptance. Tattooing is the "in" thing to do. Tattooing used to be defiant and daring, but now it is popular and more acceptable among teens. I even know a group of sorority women who went together to get tattoos on their ankles. As tattooing has become more mainstreamed, rebels/trendsetters have turned to newer and more outrageous practices, such as branding and extreme piercings. Meanwhile, tattoos bring middle-of-the-road teens the best of both worlds: a way to show their individuality and simultaneously to be accepted by peers.

In sum, Martin's research is important because it examines psychological responses to teen's inner conflicts. It offers partial explanations for teens' attraction to tattoos and promotes a positive, noncritical attitude toward tattooing. But I think the article is limited by its overgeneralizations based on the psychiatric focus, by its tendency to romanticize tattooing, by its lack of recognition of the commercialization of tattooing, and by its underemphasis on group belonging and peer pressure. Teen tattooing is more complex than even Martin makes it.

Works Cited

Martin, Andrés. "On Teenagers and Tattoos." <u>Journal of the American Academy of Child and Adolescent Psychiatry</u> 36 (1997): 860–61. Rpt. in <u>The Allyn & Bacon Guide to Writing</u>. John D. Ramage, John C. Bean, and June Johnson. 4th ed. New York: Longman, 2006. 118–121.

In the student example just shown, Sean Barry illustrates a blended strong response that intermixes rhetorical analysis of the article with his own views on tattooing. He analyzes Martin's article rhetorically by pointing out some of the limitations of a psychiatric angle of vision and by showing the values implications of Martin's references to *Moby Dick*. He adds his own ideas to the conversation by supporting two of Martin's points using his own personal examples. But he also reads Martin against the grain by arguing that Martin, perhaps influenced by his romantic view of tattoos, fails to appreciate the impact on teenagers of the commercialization of tattooing and the importance of peer group acceptance. Clearly, Sean Barry illustrates what we mean by a strong reader. In the next section on question-asking strategies, we help you begin developing the same skills.

Questions for Analyzing and Critiquing a Text

Now that you have read a sample student essay, let's consider questions you can ask to generate ideas for your own strong response. This section focuses on analyzing and critiquing a text and also offers ideas that can help you analyze texts that are partly or largely visual texts. The next section focuses on exploring your own views of the text's subject matter.

The concept of
"angle of vision" is
explained in Chapter
4, pp. 80–85. See also
Chapter 5 where the
concept is developed
in more detail.

You may find that analyzing and critiquing a text represents a new kind of critical thinking challenge. At this stage in your academic career, we aren't expecting you to be an expert at this kind of thinking. Rather, the strong response assignment will help you begin learning this skill—to see how texts work, how they are written from an angle of vision, how they may reinforce or clash with your own views, and so forth.

A strong response focused on the rhetorical features of a text looks at how the text is constructed to achieve its writer's purpose. Here are sample questions you can ask to help you analyze and critique a text. (We have illustrated them with examples from a variety of texts read by our own students in recent years.) Of course, you don't have to address all these questions in your strong response. Your goal is to find a few of these questions that particularly illuminate the text you are critiquing.

Sample Questions for Analyzing and Critiquing

Questions about purpose and audience.   What is the author's purpose and audience in this text? How clearly does this text convey its purpose and reach its audience?

WHAT TO WRITE ABOUT
Explain your author's purpose and intended audience and show how the author appeals to that audience. Explain how choice of language and use of examples appeal to the values and beliefs of the intended audience. In critiquing the text, you might show how the article is effective for the intended audience but has gaping holes for those who don't share these values and beliefs.

HYPOTHETICAL EXAMPLE
In "Why Johnny Can't Read, but Yoshio Can," Richard Lynn, writing for the conservative magazine the *National Review*, tries to persuade readers that the United States should adopt Japanese methods of education. He appeals to a conservative audience by using evidence and examples that support conservative beliefs favoring competition, discipline, and high academic achievement.

Questions about the text's genre.   How has the genre of the text influenced the author's style, structure, and use of evidence? How might this genre be effective for certain audiences but not for others?

WHAT TO WRITE ABOUT
Show how certain features of the text can be explained by the genre of the work. Show how this genre contributes to the effectiveness of the piece for certain audiences but also has limitations.

HYPOTHETICAL EXAMPLE
Naomi Wolf's essay "The Beauty Myth" is actually the introduction to her book *The Beauty Myth*. Therefore, it presents her major thesis and subtheses for the whole book and only begins to provide supporting evidence for these points. This lack of development might make some readers question or reject her argument.

Questions about the author's style.   How do the author's language choices contribute to the overall impact of the text?

WHAT TO WRITE ABOUT
Discuss examples of images, figures of speech, and connotations of words that draw the reader into the writer's perspective and support the writer's points. In your critique, show how language choices can be effective for some audiences but not for others.

HYPOTHETICAL EXAMPLE
In his chapter "Where I Lived, and What I Lived For" from his book *Walden*, Henry David Thoreau describes his closeness to nature in vivid poetic language. His celebration of the beauty and wonder of nature makes readers reevaluate their indifference or utilitarian attitudes toward nature. Scientific readers might be put off, however, by his romanticism.

(continued)

Sample Questions for Analyzing and Critiquing *continued*

Questions about the appeal to *logos*, the logic of the argument. Does the argument seem reasonable? Do the points all relate to the thesis? Are the points well supported? Are there any obvious flaws or fallacies in the argument?

WHAT TO WRITE ABOUT	HYPOTHETICAL EXAMPLE
Describe the argument's logical structure and analyze whether it is reasonable and well supported. Also point out places where the argument is weak or fallacious.	Lynn attributes the success of Japanese students to three main causes: (1) High competition, (2) a national curriculum, and (3) strong cultural incentives to excel in school. These points are well supported with evidence. But his argument that this system should be adopted in the United States is flawed because he doesn't see the dangers in the Japanese system or appreciate the cultural differences between the two countries.

Questions about the author's use of evidence. Does the evidence come from reputable sources? Is it relevant to the points it supports? Is it appropriately up-to-date? Is it sufficiently broad and representative?

WHAT TO WRITE ABOUT	HYPOTHETICAL EXAMPLE
Describe the sources of evidence in an argument and determine their reliability. Pay particular attention to limitations or narrowness in these data. Point out whether the information is up-to-date, relevant, and compelling. Point out whether the author actually provides data for the argument.	In his book *The McDonaldization of Society*, sociologist George Ritzer elaborates on his thesis that the fast-food industry has come to dominate all of American society. Some readers might say that Ritzer pushes his provocative thesis too far. His discussion of health care, education, and reproductive technology is brief, general, and not developed with specific data.

Questions about the appeal to *ethos* and the credibility of the author. How does the author try to persuade readers that he or she is knowledgeable and reliable? Is the author successful in appearing credible and trustworthy?

WHAT TO WRITE ABOUT	HYPOTHETICAL EXAMPLE
Discuss features of the text that increase the reader's confidence in the author's knowledge and trustworthiness or that help the intended audience "identify" with the writer. Point out problems with the author's reliability, responsible use of sources, and fair treatment of alternative views.	In her article "The Gender Blur" in the liberal magazine *Utne Reader*, Deborah Blum establishes credibility by citing numerous scientific studies showing that she has researched the issue carefully. She also tells personal anecdotes about her liberal views, establishing credibility with liberal audiences.

Sample Questions for Analyzing and Critiquing *continued*

Questions about the appeal to *pathos*.   How does the author appeal to the readers' emotions, sympathies, and values? Do these appeals to *pathos* enhance the rhetorical power of the text?

WHAT TO WRITE ABOUT
Explain how the author uses description, vivid examples, short narratives or scenarios, figurative language, or moving quotations to tap the emotions and sympathies of the audience and appeal to readers' values and beliefs. Explain whether these appeals to *pathos* are controlled and fitting or excessive and heavy-handed.

HYPOTHETICAL EXAMPLE
Compassionate Living, a brochure by the advocacy organization People for the Ethical Treatment of Animals (PETA), disturbs readers with vivid descriptions of animal suffering; however, these descriptions are so extreme in their appeals to *pathos* that they may offend readers who love animals and therefore lose their support.

Questions about the author's angle of vision.   What does the text reveal about the author's values and beliefs? What is excluded from the author's text? What other perspectives could a writer take on this topic?

WHAT TO WRITE ABOUT
Analyze the author's angle of vision or interpretive filter. Show what the text emphasizes and what it leaves out. Show how this angle of vision is related to certain key values or beliefs.

HYPOTHETICAL EXAMPLE
Dr. Andrés Martin, a psychiatrist, takes a clinical perspective on tattooed adolescents. He writes for fellow psychiatrists, and he uses his teen patients as the subject of his analysis. He does not consider more typical tattooed teenagers who do not need psychiatric therapy. If he had interviewed a wider range of teenagers, he might have reached different conclusions.

Questions for Analyzing and Critiquing a Visual-Verbal Text

In our increasingly visual world, many genres of texts—advocacy sites on the Web, public affairs advocacy ads, advertisements, posters for political and environmental campaigns, brochures, and leaflets—combine verbal and visual elements. As we discuss in Chapter 4, visual images such as photographs, drawings, and paintings can also be read rhetorically, and indeed may do much of the rhetorical work of a visual-verbal text.

Visual-verbal texts are often rhetorically complex and very interesting to examine and critique. A strong response to a visual-verbal text might examine how well the text connects with the intended audience, carries out its purposes, and fulfills readers' expectations for its genre. In critiquing a visual-verbal text, you

In Chapter 11, we explain visual rhetoric in more detail, especially such features as the composition of images, camera angle, and use of color.

might consider how well the words and images collaborate to strengthen the appeal to *logos*. For example, does this combination convey the main point clearly? The features of document design—use of type, layout, color, and images or graphics discussed in Chapter 3—are also extremely important in visual-verbal texts. Images can make powerful appeals to *pathos*, persuading through their appeal to readers' emotions, values, and beliefs. Many visual-verbal texts can also be discussed in terms of their appeal to *ethos* by focusing on how reliable and credible the creator of the text appears to be. Furthermore, these texts often reveal their angle of vision in interesting ways through the dominant impressions they convey and the ideas they ignore or exclude.

In a summary strong response essay on a visual-verbal text, the summary would capture for readers the main points of the piece and would briefly describe the text's visual features. For a strong response, most of the questions that you would ask of a verbal text could apply to a visual-verbal text; however, here are some questions that might be particularly relevant to a text with visual elements.

Sample Questions for Analyzing and Critiquing Visual-Verbal Texts

Questions about use of type, layout, color, and image.   Which of these design features is important in this text? How are these features used? How are they effective?

WHAT TO WRITE ABOUT	HYPOTHETICAL EXAMPLE
Explain what is distinctive about any or several of these visual features. Explain how these features work for the intended audience and contribute to the author's purpose. In critiquing the text, you might discuss how the visual features work to change the audience's views. You might comment on the problems or strengths of these features.	A poster on nicotine addiction by Project ALERT, a drug prevention program for middle schools, uses colors to make the poster stick in viewers' minds and create an alarmist tone. The use of unpleasant greens, oranges, and golds with the word "ADDICTING" in white overprinting gives a strong, memorable impression of illness and danger.

Questions about the relationship between image and verbal text and the appeals to *logos* and *pathos*.   How much rhetorical work do the visual images perform in this text? How do the images and words work together in this text? Are words more important than images?

WHAT TO WRITE ABOUT	HYPOTHETICAL EXAMPLE
Explain whether words comment on the images or images illustrate the words. Discuss whether the words are labels and slogans connected to the images or presentations of the author's main points. Explain how the image or images in this piece convey the main point and affect the emotions and sympathies of the audience. Discuss whether the use of image is appropriate and effective or unnecessary, unfitting, or overdone.	In the Project ALERT poster on nicotine addiction, the cartoon imaginatively illustrates the concept of addiction and does all the persuasive work of the poster. All the features of this image—the cartoon figure, the burning ramp the figure is running on, and the unreachable package of cigarettes dangling from a stick—convey the poster's idea of addiction as frustration, desperation, and insatiability. The image works equally on the viewers' emotions, evoking a sense of danger.

Sample Questions for Analyzing and Critiquing Visual-Verbal Texts *continued*

Questions about the author's angle of vision and contribution to the social conversation.   How is an angle of vision constructed in this text? Does the text make a useful contribution to a discussion of this issue?

WHAT TO WRITE ABOUT
Explain how the author's angle of vision shapes and filters the message of the text. Discuss what is included in and excluded from the text. Discuss whether the angle of vision limits the appeal of the text.

HYPOTHETICAL EXAMPLE
The brochure *Compassionate Living*, by People for the Ethical Treatment of Animals (PETA), poses and responds to eighteen questions about humans' treatment of animals. While the brochure provides clear, vivid answers to the questions and the photos illustrate these points, readers sense that the brochure emphasizes and amasses incidents of cruelty and excludes all other perspectives.

Questions for Developing Your Own Views about the Text's Subject Matter

As you are analyzing and critiquing a text, you also want to imagine how you might speak back to the text's ideas. Look for ways to join the text's conversation using your own critical thinking, personal experience, observations, reading, and knowledge.

In responding to a text's ideas, you will most likely include both with- and against-the-grain points. Strong readers know how to build on a text's ideas and extend them to other contexts. They are also open to challenging or disturbing ideas and try to use them constructively rather than simply dismiss them. Strong readers, in other words, try to believe new ideas as well as doubt them. In speaking back to a text's ideas in your strong response, you will have to decide how affirming of or resistant to those ideas you want to be.

Here are questions you can use to help you generate ideas:

Sample Questions for Generating Your Own Views on the Topic

Question: Which of the author's points do you agree with?

WHAT TO WRITE ABOUT
Build on or extend the author's points with supporting evidence from personal experience or knowledge (with the grain).

HYPOTHETICAL EXAMPLE
Build on Dr. Andrés Martin's ideas by discussing examples of acquaintances who have marked significant moments in their lives (graduation, career changes, divorces) by getting tattoos.

(continued)

Sample Questions for Generating Your Own Views on the Topic *continued*

Question: What new insights has the text given you?

WHAT TO WRITE ABOUT	HYPOTHETICAL EXAMPLE
Illustrate your insights with examples (with the grain).	Explore Martin's idea that some teens use tattoos as a form of bonding by discussing the phenomenon of women in college sororities getting tattoos together.

Question: Which of the author's points do you disagree with?

WHAT TO WRITE ABOUT	HYPOTHETICAL EXAMPLE
Provide your own counterpoints and counterexamples (against the grain).	Challenge Martin's views by showing that tattooing has become a commonplace mainstream, middle-class phenomenon among teens.

Question: What gaps or omissions do you see in the text? What has the author overlooked?

WHAT TO WRITE ABOUT	HYPOTHETICAL EXAMPLE
Point out gaps. Supply your own theory for why these gaps exist. Explain the value of your own perspective, which includes what the author has excluded or overlooked (against the grain).	Point out that Martin's views leave out the role that parents play in teens' decisions to get tattoos. Explain how rebellion has influenced some of your friends.

Question: What questions or problems does the text raise for you? How has it troubled you or expanded your views?

WHAT TO WRITE ABOUT	HYPOTHETICAL EXAMPLE
Show how the text causes you to question your own values, assumptions, and beliefs; show also how you question the author's beliefs and values (with the grain and against the grain).	Martin's highly sympathetic attitude toward tattoos portrays body modification as positive, creative, and psychologically constructive, yet he glosses over health risks and long-term costs.

Question: In what contexts can you see the usefulness of the text? What applications can you envision for it?

WHAT TO WRITE ABOUT	HYPOTHETICAL EXAMPLE
Explore the applicability and consequences of the text or explore its limitations (with the grain or against the grain).	Martin's theory that troubled teens are seeking control over their bodies and their identities through getting tattoos is one important voice in the social conversation about tattoos. However, he doesn't explore why tattooing and piercing have become so popular in the last ten years. The relationship between fads and fashions and deeper psychological factors could lead to further research.

Rereading Strategies to Stimulate Thinking for a Strong Response

Earlier in the chapter, we presented general strategies to help you become an experienced reader. Now we turn to specific rereading strategies that will stimulate ideas for your strong response. Reread your assigned text, and as you do so, try the following strategies.

Step Up Your Marginal Note Taking, Making With-the-Grain and Against-the-Grain Comments

Writing a strong response requires a deep engagement with texts, calling on all your ability to read with the grain and against the grain. As you reread your text, make copious marginal notes looking for both with-the-grain and against-the-grain responses. Figure 6.1 shows Sean Barry's marginal comments on the opening page of Martin's article. Observe how the notes incorporate with-the-grain and against-the-grain responses and show the reader truly talking back to and interacting with the text.

Identify Hot Spots in the Text

Most texts will create "hot spots" for you (each reader's hot spots are apt to be different). By "hot spot" we mean a quotation or passage that you especially notice because you agree or disagree with it or because it triggers memories or other associations. Perhaps the hot spot strikes you as particularly thought provoking. Perhaps it raises a problem or is confusing yet suggestive. Mark all hot spots with marginal notes. After you've finished reading, find these hot spots and freewrite your responses to them in a reading journal.

Write Questions Triggered by the Text

Almost any text triggers questions as you read. A good way to begin formulating a strong response is simply to write out several questions that the text caused you to think about. Then explore your responses to those questions through freewriting. Sometimes the freewrite will trigger more questions.

Articulate Your Difference from the Intended Audience

In some cases you can read strongly by articulating how you differ from the text's intended audience. As we showed in Chapter 3, experienced writers try to imagine their audience. They ask: What are my audience's values? How interested in and knowledgeable about my topic is my audience? Eventually, the author makes decisions about audience—in effect "creates" the audience—so that the text reveals both an image of the author and of its intended reader.

See pp. 52–54 for a discussion of audience analysis.

Your own experiences, arising from your gender, class, ethnicity, sexual orientation, political and religious beliefs, interests, values, and so forth, may cause

FIGURE 6.1 Student Marginal Notes on Martin's Text

Andrés Martin, M.D.
on Teenagers and Tattoos

The skeleton dimensions I shall now proceed to set down are copied verbatim from my right arm, where I had them tattooed: as in my wild wanderings at that period, there was no other secure way of preserving such valuable statistics.

—Melville/ Moby Dick CII

A strange beginning for a scientific article

What do 19th-century sailors have to do with 21st century teens?

Tattoos and piercings have become a part of our everyday landscape. They are ubiquitous, having entered the circles of glamour and the mainstream of fashion, and they have even become an increasingly common feature of our urban youth. Legislation in most states restricts professional tattooing to adults older than 18 years of age, so "high end" tattooing is rare in children and adolescents, but such tattoos are occasionally seen in older teenagers. Piercings, by comparison, as well as self-made or "jailhouse" type tattoos, are not at all rare among adolescents or even among schoolage children. Like hairdo, makeup, or baggy jeans, tattoos and piercings can be subject to fad influence or peer pressure in an effort toward group affiliation. As with any other fashion statement, they can be construed as bodily aids in the inner struggle toward identity consolidation, serving as adjuncts to the defining and sculpting of the self by means of external manipulations. But unlike most other body decorations, tattoos and piercings are set apart by their irreversible and permanent nature, a quality at the core of their magnetic appeal to adolescents.

Quotation from a novel?

Larger tattooing scene?

I like the phrase "the defining and sculpting of the self"—sounds creative, like art

Idea here: the body as a concrete record of experience?

This idea is surprising and interesting. It merits lots of discussion.

Adolescents and their parents are often at odds over the acquisition of bodily decorations. For the adolescent, piercings or tattoos may be seen as personal and beautifying statements, while parents may construe them as oppositional and enraging affronts to their authority. Distinguishing bodily adornment from self-mutilation may indeed prove challenging, particularly when a family is in disagreement over a teenager's motivations and a clinician is summoned as the final arbiter. At such times it may be most important to realize jointly that the skin can all too readily become but another battleground for the tensions of the age, arguments having less to do with tattoos and piercings than with core issues such as separation from the family matrix. Exploring the motivations and significance underlying tattoos (Grumet, 1983) and piercings can go a long way toward resolving such differences and can become a novel and additional way of getting to know teenagers. An interested and nonjudgmental appreciation of teenagers' surface presentations may become a way of making contact not only in their terms but on their turfs: quite literally on the territory of their skins.

Which teenagers? All teenagers?

Good open-minded, practical approach to teen tattoos

These terms show the main opposing views on tattoos.

Is he speaking only to psychiatrists? Does this clinical perspective have other applications?

The following three sections exemplify some of the complex psychological underpinnings of youth tattooing.

3 I like Martin's focus on complexity

you to feel estranged from the author's imagined audience. If the text seems written for straight people and you are gay, or for Christians and you are a Muslim or an atheist, or for environmentalists and you grew up in a small logging community, you may well resist the text. Sometimes your sense of exclusion from the intended audience makes it difficult to read a text at all. For example, a female student of our acquaintance once brought a class to a standstill by slamming the course anthology on her desk and exclaiming, "How can you people stand reading this patriarchal garbage!" She had become so irritated by the authors' assumption that all readers shared their male-oriented values that she could no longer bear to read the selections.

When you differ significantly from the text's assumed audience, you can often use this difference to question the author's underlying assumptions, values, and beliefs.

For Writing and Discussion

What follows is a short passage by writer Annie Dillard in response to a question about how she chooses to spend her time. This passage often evokes heated responses from our students.

> I don't do housework. Life is too short. . . . I let almost all my indoor plants die from neglect while I was writing the book. There are all kinds of ways to live. You can take your choice. You can keep a tidy house, and when St. Peter asks you what you did with your life, you can say, "I kept a tidy house, I made my own cheese balls."

Individual task: Read the passage and then briefly freewrite your reaction to it.

Group task: Working in groups or as a whole class, develop answers to the following questions:

1. What values does Dillard assume her audience holds?
2. What kinds of readers are apt to feel excluded from that audience?
3. If you are not part of the intended audience for this passage, what in the text evokes resistance?

Articulate Your Own Purpose for Reading

You may sometimes read a text against the grain if your purposes for reading differ from what the author imagined. Normally you read a text because you share the author's interest in a question and want to know the author's answer. In other words, you usually read to join the author's conversation. But suppose that you wish to review the writings of nineteenth-century scientists to figure out what they assumed about nature (or women, or God, or race, or capitalism). Or suppose that you examine a politician's metaphors to see what they reveal about his or her values, or analyze *National Geographic* for evidence of political bias. In these cases, you will be reading against the grain of the text. In a sense, you would be blindsiding the authors—while they are talking about topic X, you are observing them for topic Y. This method of resistant reading is very common in academia.

READINGS

For this chapter, we offer readings on two major controversial issues: the health and social issue of smoking and the environmental, social, and economic issue of dams. The readings on smoking include two articles, a set of posters from an anti-smoking campaign, and a mock advertisement. The readings about dams include an article and the home page of an advocacy Web site. Some of the readings for this chapter are closed form; however, the others resist easy classification in that they include many features of open-form prose: lots of narrative elements and occasional implicit—rather than explicitly stated—points. The advocacy Web site home page and the posters have distinctive features of visual texts. Each reading in this chapter will prompt your personal and intellectual grappling with the author's ideas and beliefs as well as attract your attention to the author's rhetorical strategies.

You can use these readings in various ways. Your instructor may choose one of these pieces as the subject of your assignment for this chapter. You can also use the readings to build your knowledge base on these issues. Representing a few of the many voices in these public controversies, these verbal and visual-verbal texts help form a rhetorical context for each other. We think you will find them useful in illuminating the rhetorical strategies and angle of vision of the text that you are analyzing. Because your task is to summarize your assigned piece and respond strongly to it, we omit the questions for analysis that typically accompany readings elsewhere in this text.

The first reading, by writer and journalist Florence King, first appeared in 1990 in the *National Review*, a news commentary magazine with a conservative readership.

Florence King
I'd Rather Smoke than Kiss

1   I am a woman of 54 who started smoking at the late age of 26. I had no reason to start earlier; smoking as a gesture of teenage rebellion would have been pointless in my family. My mother started at 12. At first her preferred brands were the Fatimas and Sweet Caporals that were all the rage during World War I. Later she switched to Lucky Strike Greens and smoked four packs a day.

2   She made no effort to cut down while she was pregnant with me, but I was not a low-birth-weight baby. The Angel of Death saw the nicotine stains on our door and passed over. I weighed nine pounds. My smoke-filled childhood was remarkably healthy and safe except for the time Mama set fire to my Easter basket. That was all right, however, because I was not the Easter-basket type.

3   I probably wouldn't have started smoking if I had not been a writer. One day in the drugstore I happened to see a display of Du Maurier English cigarettes in pretty red boxes with a tray that slid out like a little drawer. I thought the boxes would be ideal for keeping my paperclips in, so I bought two.

4   When I got home, I emptied out the cigarettes and replaced them with paperclips, putting the loose cigarettes in the desk drawer where the loose paperclips had been scattered. Now the cigarettes were scattered. One day, spurred by two of my best traits, neatness and thrift, I decided that the cigarettes were messing up the desk and going to waste, so I tried one.

5   It never would have happened if I had been able to offer the Du Mauriers to a lover who smoked, but I didn't get an addicted one until after I had become addicted myself. When he entered my life it was the beginning of a uniquely pleasurable footnote to sex, the post-coital cigarette.

6   Today when I see the truculent, joyless faces of anti-tobacco Puritans, I remember those easy-going smoking sessions with that man: the click of the lighter, the brief orange glow in the darkness, the ashtray between us— spilling sometimes because we laughed so much together that the bed shook.

7   A cigarette ad I remember from my childhood said: "One of life's great pleasures is smoking. Camels give you all of the excitement of choice tobaccos. Is enjoyment good for you? You just bet it is." My sentiments exactly. I believe life should be savored rather than lengthened, and I am ready to fight the misanthropes among us who are trying to make me switch.

8   A *misanthrope* is someone who hates people. Hatred of smokers is the most popular form of closet misanthropy in America today. Smokists don't hate the sin, they hate the sinner, and they don't care who knows it.

9   Their campaign never would have succeeded so well if the alleged dangers of smoking had remained a problem for smokers alone. We simply would have been allowed to invoke the Right to Die, always a favorite with democratic lovers of mankind, and that would have been that. To put a real damper on smoking and making it stick, the right of others not to die had to be invoked somehow so "passive smoking" was invented.

10   The name was a stroke of genius. Just about everybody in America is passive. Passive Americans have been taking it on the chin for years, but the concept of passive smoking offered them a chance to hate in the land of compulsory love, a chance to dish it out for a change with no fear of being called a bigot. The right of self-defense, long since gone up in smoke, was back.

Smokers on the Run

11   The big, brave Passive Americans responded with a vengeance. They began shouting at smokers in restaurants. They shuddered and grimaced and said "Ugh!" as they waved away the impure air. They put up little signs in their cars and homes: at first they said, "Thank You for Not Smoking," but now they feature a cigarette in a circle slashed with a red diagonal. Smokists even issue conditional invitations. I know—I got one. The woman said, "I'd love to have you to dinner, but I don't allow smoking in my home. Do you think you could refrain for a couple of hours?" I said, "Go—yourself," and she told everybody I was the rudest person she had ever met.

12   Smokists practice a sadistic brutality that would have done Vlad the Impaler proud. *Washington Times* columnist and smoker Jeremiah O'Leary was the target of two incredibly baleful letters to the editor after he defended the habit. The first letter said, "Smoke yourself to death, but please don't smoke me to death," but it was only a foretaste of the letter that followed:

> Jeremiah O'Leary's March 1 column, "Perilous persuaders . . . tenacious zealots," is a typical statement of a drug addict trying to defend his vice.
>
> To a cigarette smoker, all the world is an ashtray. A person who would never throw a candy wrapper or soda can will drop a lit cigarette without a thought.
>
> Mr. O'Leary is mistaken that nonsmokers are concerned about the damage smokers are inflicting on themselves. What arrogance! We care about living in a pleasant environment without the stench of tobacco smoke or the litter of smokers' trash.
>
> If Mr. O'Leary wants to kill himself, that is his choice. I ask only that he do so without imposing his drug or discarded filth on me. *It would be nice if he would die in such a way that would not increase my health-insurance rates* [my italics].

13   The expendability of smokers has also aroused the tender concern of the Federal Government. I was taking my first drag of the morning when I opened the *Washington Post* and found myself starting at this headline: NOT SMOKING COULD BE HAZARDOUS TO PENSION SYSTEM. MEDICARE, SOCIAL SECURITY MAY BE PINCHED IF ANTI-TOBACCO CAMPAIGN SUCCEEDS, REPORT SAYS.

14   The article explained that since smokers die younger than non-smokers, the Social Security we don't live to collect is put to good use, because we subsidize the pensions of our fellow citizens like a good American should. However, this convenient arrangement could end, for if too many smokers heed the Surgeon General's warnings and stop smoking, they will live too long and break the budget.

15   That, of course, is not how the government economists phrased it. They said:

> The implications of our results are that smokers "save" the Social Security system hundreds of billions of dollars. Certainly this does not mean that decreased smoking

would not be socially beneficial. In fact, it is probably one of the most cost-effective ways of increasing average longevity. It does indicate, however, that if people alter their behavior in a manner which extends life expectancy, then this must be recognized by our national retirement program.

16   At this point the reporter steps in with the soothing reminder that "the war on tobacco is more appropriately cast as a public-health crusade than as an attempt to save money." But then we hear from Health Policy Center economist Gio Gori, who says: "Prevention of disease is obviously something we should strive for. But it's not going to be cheap. We will have to pay for those who survive."

17   Something darkling crawls out of that last sentence. The whole article has a die-damn-you undertow that would make an honest misanthrope wonder if perhaps a cure for cancer was discovered years ago, but due to cost-effectiveness considerations . . .

18   But honest misanthropes are at a premium that no amount of Raleigh coupons can buy. Instead we have tinpot Torquemadas like Ahron Leichtman, president of Citizens against Tobacco Smoke, who announced after the airline smoking bans: "CATS will next launch its smoke-free airports project, which is the second phase of our smoke-free skies campaign." Representative Richard J. Durbin (D., Ill.) promised the next target will be "other forms of public transportation such as Amtrak, the inter-city bus system, and commuter lines that receive federal funding." His colleague, Senator Frank Lautenberg (D., N.J.), confessed, "We *are* gloating a little bit," and Fran Du Melle of the Coalition on Smoking OR Health, gave an ominous hint of things to come when she heralded the airline ban as "only one encouraging step on the road to a smoke-free society."

Health Nazis

19   These remarks manifest a sly, cowardly form of misanthropy that the Germans call *Schadenfreude*: pleasure in the unhappiness of others. It has always been the chief subconscious motivation of Puritans, but the smokists harbor several other subconscious motivations that are too egregious to bear close examination—which is precisely what I will now conduct.

20   Study their agitprop and you will find the same theme of pitiless revulsion running through nearly all of their so-called public-service ads. One of the earliest showed Brooke Shields toweling her wet hair and saying disgustedly, "I hate it when somebody smokes after I've just washed my hair. Yuk!" Another proclaimed, "Kissing a smoker is like licking an ashtray." The latest, a California radio spot, asks: "Why sell cigarettes? Why not just sell phlegm and cut out the middle man?"

21   Fear of being physically disgusting and smelling bad is the American's worst nightmare, which is why bathsoap commercials never include the controlled-force shower nozzles recommended by environmentalists in *their* public-service ads. The showering American uses oceans of hot water to get "ZESTfully clean" in a sudsy deluge that is often followed by a deodorant commercial.

22   "Raise your hand, raise your hand, raise your hand if you're SURE!" During this jingle we see an ecstatically happy assortment of people from all walks of life and representing every conceivable national origin, all obediently raising their hands, until the ad climaxes with a shot of the Statue of Liberty raising hers.

The New Greenhorns

23   The Statue of Liberty has become a symbol of immigration, the first aspect of American life the huddled masses experienced. The second was being called a "dirty little" something-or-other as soon as they got off the boat. Deodorant companies see the wisdom in reminding their descendants of the dirty-little period. You can sell a lot of deodorant that way. Ethnics get the point directly; WASPs get it by default in the subliminal reminder that, historically speaking, there is no such thing as a dirty little WASP.

24   Smokers have become the new greenhorns in the land of sweetness and health, scapegoats for a quintessentially American need, rooted in our fabled Great Diversity, to identify and punish the undesirables among us. Ethnic tobacco haters can get even for past slurs on their fastidiousness by refusing to inhale around dirty little smokers; WASP tobacco haters can once again savor the joys of being the "real Americans" by hurling with impunity the same dirty little insults their ancestors hurled with impunity.

25   The tobacco pogrom serves additionally as the basis for a class war in a nation afraid to mention the word "class" aloud. Hating smokers is an excellent way to hate the white working class without going on record as hating the white working class.

26   The anti-smoking campaign has enjoyed thumping success among the "data-receptive," a lovely euphemism describing the privilege of spending four years sitting in a classroom. The ubiquitous statistic that college graduates are two-and-a-half times as likely to be non-smokers as those who never went beyond high school is balm to the data-receptive, many of whom are only a generation or two removed from the lunch-bucket that smokers represent. Haunted by a fear of falling back down the ladder, and half-believing that they deserve to, they soothe their anxiety by kicking a smoker as the proverbial hen-pecked husband soothed his by kicking the dog.

27   The earnest shock that greeted the RJR Reynolds Uptown marketing scheme aimed at blacks cramped the vituperative style of the data-receptive. Looking down on blacks as smokers might be interpreted as looking down on blacks as blacks, so they settled for aping the compassionate concern they picked up from the media.

28   They got their sadism-receptive bona fides back when the same company announced plans to target Dakota cigarettes at a fearsome group called "virile females."

29   When I first saw the headline I thought surely they meant me: what other woman writer is sent off to a book-and-author luncheon with the warning, "Watch your language and don't wear your Baltimore Orioles warm-up jacket." But they didn't. Virile females are "Caucasian females, 18 to 24, with no education beyond high school and entry-level service or factory jobs."

30   Commentators could barely hide their smirks as they listed the tractor pulls, motorcycle races, and macho-man contests that comprise the leisure activities of the target group. Crocodile tears flowed copiously. "It's blue-collar people without enough education to understand what is happening to them," mourned Virginia Ernster of the University of California School of Medicine. "It's pathetic that these companies would work so hard to get these women who may not feel much control over their lives." George Will, winner of the metaphor-man contest, wrote: "They use sophisticated marketing like a sniper's rifle, drawing beads on the most vulnerable, manipulable Americans." (I would walk a mile to see Virginia Ernster riding on the back of George Will's motorcycle.)

31   Hating smokers is also a guiltless way for a youth-worshipping country to hate old people, as well as those who are merely over the hill—especially middle-aged women. Smokers predominate in both groups because we saw Bette Davis's movies the same year they were released. Now we catch *Dark Victory* whenever it comes on television just for the pleasure of watching the scene in the staff lounge at the hospital when Dr. George Brent and all the other doctors light up.

32   Smoking is the only thing that the politically correct can't blame on white males. Red men started it, but the cowardly cossacks of the anti-tobacco crusade don't dare say so because it would be too close for comfort. They see no difference between tobacco and hard drugs like cocaine and crack because they don't wish to see any. Never mind that you will never be mugged by someone needing a cigarette; hatred of smokers is the conformist's substitute for the hatred that dare not speak its name. Condemning "substance abuse" out of hand, without picking and choosing or practicing discrimination, produces lofty sensations of democratic purity in those who keep moving farther and farther out in the suburbs to get away from . . . smokers.

The second reading is a peer-reviewed research article first published in 2004 in the *American Journal of Public Health*. Its author, Lyndon Haviland, is the chief operating officer of the American Legacy Foundation, an organization devoted to the reduction of tobacco use, especially by teens. As you read this text, you might consider how Haviland's treatment of the social stigma of smoking and the issue of class differ from Florence King's view of these points. How do you think that the date of publication of these articles might affect their positions on smoking?

A Silence That Kills

Lyndon Haviland

1   Tobacco-related disease kills 178,000 women each year in the United States,[1] yet a search for the public discourse on this fact reveals a profound silence. As a nation, we have failed to mount and support an organized public response to the ongoing public health tragedy of tobacco use. The public health community must find a way to give voice to the thousands of families who will experience the premature loss of a loved one because of tobacco use. In creative new ways, we must engage a broad range of partners, both public and private, and help them raise their voices to demand comprehensive action.

2   Although many of us are activists and many are working to counteract tobacco's harm, the public remains largely silent, its lack of outrage evident in the daily news, in the public debate on smoking bans, and in the lack of pressure on our government to protect workers, families, and children. There is so little public demand for action. We must find ways to spark a national movement to demand the funding and implementation of comprehensive tobacco control programs. We must overcome apathy and public silence. Tobacco control advocates must learn from the AIDS activists that silence equals a continuing saga of disease, suffering, and death.

3   How can we as public health practitioners change this silence into a public demand for comprehensive tobacco control that includes prevention, cessation, and regulation? How can we join together to give voice to the women and men who die each year in America of tobacco-related diseases? How can we prevent the needless suffering of families across the nation that results from tobacco use?

The Facts

4   As public health practitioners, we begin planning tobacco prevention and control programs with a review of the inarguable facts. Tobacco remains the leading cause of preventable death in the United States, killing more people each year than AIDS, suicide, murder, car accidents, and drugs combined.[2] It is the only product that when used as directed kills approximately one third of its users.[3] Indeed, the facts are hard to believe—for example, passive smoking (exposure to environmental tobacco smoke) kills 53,000 people each year in the United States and puts thousands more at risk.[4] The World Bank predicts that by 2030, tobacco-related illnesses will cause 10 million deaths per year, more than any other cause,[5] yet the recently passed Framework Convention on Tobacco Control negotiated among 193 countries has been signed by 76 participants and ratified by only 3 (Matt Barry, Campaign for Tobacco-Free Kids, oral communication, November 5, 2003).

5   Given the facts about the harmfulness of tobacco, why is public silence so deafening? Why does the tobacco control community confront apathy,

silence, and seemingly insurmountable barriers when implementing scientifically sound programs designed to prevent or reduce tobacco use in the United States? Nicotine is highly addictive, yet the marketing, production, and sale of products that contain nicotine are not regulated by the Food and Drug Administration.

The Shape of Our Epidemic

6   Lung cancer is the leading cause of cancer death among men and women,[2] and the majority of its victims die within one year of diagnosis.[6] Although it has been debated by the tobacco industry for decades, the scientific evidence of tobacco's impact on health is clear and well accepted. Tobacco use is implicated in a wide range of medical conditions, both adult and pediatric, including cardiovascular diseases, pulmonary conditions, a multitude of cancers, and reproductive health outcomes.[7] Perhaps the sheer magnitude of the diverse negative health consequences precludes a targeted demand for action.

7   An additional reason for the silence is the shape and the face of the current epidemic of tobacco use in the United States. Tobacco is not an equal opportunity killer. It is the poorest and least educated Americans who smoke at the highest rates[8] and who bear a disproportionate burden of death and disease as a result of their tobacco use.[9] There is evidence that sexual minorities smoke at much higher rates than the national average, but because there are no national data for this population, the full extent of the problem—and thus the means to address it—remains unclear.[10] And while racial and ethnic minorities smoke at lower rates than White Americans, tobacco takes a dramatic toll on their communities because they have poorer access to medical care.[11]

8   To find our voice as a movement, we must confront the social and class dimensions of tobacco use. A national movement to eradicate tobacco use must encourage participation at all levels and within all communities. A successful movement must have diversity in its leadership and must manifest a commitment to identify, train, and support the diverse communities most affected by tobacco use. Diverse leadership, vision, and voice will help us win the fight against disparities in access to prevention and cessation messages as well as access to the health care services necessary to treat tobacco-related illnesses.

Smoking as a Stigmatized Behavior

9   To change the social norms around tobacco use and to build a tobacco-free world, we must recognize that tobacco use in the United States is increasingly stigmatized. As local and statewide policies are enacted that restrict the use of tobacco products in public places, smokers can be seen enclosed in small glass smoking rooms in airports or huddled outside restaurants, bars, and office buildings. They are becoming a visible and stigmatized minority. To be successful, we must add the voice of smokers to our movement and support all Americans with evidence-based cessation services.

10   The debate about tobacco use is often clouded by discourse about smoking as a personal choice or a question of civil liberties. Public debate on smoking restrictions can devolve into a discussion of paternalism and prohibition. The debate often lacks a rigorous discussion of the power of nicotine addiction and the role of the tobacco industry in supporting the concept of smoking as an "adult choice." Insufficient attention is paid to the insidious work of the tobacco industry in marketing tobacco in minority communities and to the industry's philanthropic support of leadership organizations, unions, and community-based organizations.[12]

Silence in the Government

11   Although the facts speak for themselves, the governmental response to this epidemic of death and suffering is not on a par with the impact of tobacco use on American health, either on the prevention or the treatment side. Where is the concerted effort of government commensurate with the death, disability, and suffering that tobacco causes?

12   Every US surgeon general since 1964 has known about the death and suffering linked to tobacco use, and today the government is still documenting the mortality and morbidity linked to tobacco use but not supporting comprehensive plans for its eradication. On average, 1200 people are dying each day in America as a result of tobacco use.[1] The US Public Health Service knows how to prevent these deaths,[13, 14] yet the political will to act remains absent. The government has supported the development of comprehensive plans for tobacco use prevention and control and it has supported the development of a scientific basis for action, yet collective action and a collective voice calling for sweeping change are missing.

Public Health

13   Public health must take a leadership role and demand that the health care system and public policy protect Americans from the consequences of tobacco use. We know what to do to prevent tobacco-related deaths, but we have failed to demand systemic change from our government and from our colleagues in the health care field. We have let our voices be silenced. We must speak out to prevent needless suffering. Studies have demonstrated that health care providers fail to assess patients' smoking status and advise them to quit, yet a brief intervention by a doctor is one of the most effective methods of increasing use of cessation services.[15]

14   We, the public health community, must find our voice on this issue. We must confront the social inequities of tobacco use and its burden of death and disease. We must communicate a sense of urgency and engage all Americans in the battle against tobacco use. We must demand action and we must demand scientifically sound programs and policies that will help us build a world where young people reject tobacco and where anyone who does use tobacco can quit. Our future depends on it.

References

1. Centers for Disease Control and Prevention. Annual smoking-attributable mortality, years of potential life lost, and economic costs—United States, 1995–1999. *MMWR Morb Mortal Wkly Rep.* 2002; 51:300–303.
2. Arias E, Anderson RN, Kung HC, Murphy SL, Kochanek KD. Deaths: final data for 2001. *Natl Vital Stat Rep.* 2003; 52:1–115.
3. Centers for Disease Control and Prevention. Projected smoking-related deaths among youth. *MMWR Morb Mortal Wkly Rep.* 1996; 45:971–974.
4. Glantz SA, Parmley WW. Passive smoking and heart disease: mechanisms and risk. *JAMA.* 1995; 273:1047–1053.
5. *Curbing the Epidemic: Governments and the Economics of Tobacco Control.* Washington, DC: World Bank; 1999.
6. American Cancer Society. *What are the key statistics for lung cancer?* Available at: http://www.cancer.org/docroot/CRI/CRL2_3x.asp?mav=cridg&dt=26. Accessed December 17, 2003.
7. *Reducing the Health Consequences of Smoking: 25 Years of Progress: A Report of the Surgeon General.* Atlanta, Ga: Centers for Disease Control and Prevention; 1989.
8. Centers for Disease Control and Prevention. Cigarette smoking among adults—United States, 2000. *MMWR Morb Mortal Wkly Rep.* 2002; 51:642–645.
9. Northridge MK, Morabia A, Ganz ML, et al. Contribution of smoking to excess mortality in Harlem. *Am J Epidemial.* 1998; 147:250–258.
10. Ryan H, Wortley PM, Easton A, Pederson L, Greenwood G. Smoking among lesbians, gays, and bisexuals: a review of the literature. *Am J Prev Med.* 2001; 21:142–149.
11. Bach PB, Cramer LD, Warren JL, Begg CB. Racial differences in the treatment of early-stage lung cancer. *N Engl J Med.* 1999; 341:1198–1205.
12. Siegel M. *Tobacco industry sponsorship in the United States, 1995–1999.* Available at: http://dcc2.bumc.bu.edu/tobacco. Accessed December 17, 2003.
13. *Best Practices for Comprehensive Tobacco Control Programs.* Atlanta, Ga: National Center for Chronic Disease Prevention and Health Promotion, Office on Smoking and Health; August 1999. Available at: http://www.cdc.gov/tobacco/bestprac.htm. Accessed December 17, 2003.
14. Task Force on Community Preventive Services. Recommendations regarding interventions to reduce tobacco use and exposure to environmental tobacco smoke. *Am J Prev Med.* 2001; 20(suppl 2):10–15.
15. The Tobacco Use and Dependence Clinical Practice Guideline Panel, Staff, and Consortium Representatives. A clinical practice guideline for treating tobacco use and dependence: a US Public Health Service report. *JAMA.* 2000; 283:3244–3254.

The next reading is a set of four posters created by Gasp Consultancy, Ltd., a British consulting firm that "specializes in marketing, publicising, and organising tobacco control and stop smoking projects and events" (www.gasp.org.uk/). As you examine these posters, you might think about how Gasp's approach to quitting smoking differs from other stop-smoking and anti-smoking campaigns you have seen.

Steps to Stopping Smoking

Gasp Consultancy, Ltd.

steps to stopping smoking

Reasons to stop smoking:
- Live longer and be healthier
- Lower the chances of cancer, heart attack or stroke
- Family and friends will be healthier
- Babies and children are not exposed to smoke
- More money to spend or save
- Free from nicotine addiction

Step one

Step out to stop smoking

- Set a quit date
- Retrace your steps and learn from past quit attempts
- Rid your everyday environment of tobacco and tobacco smoke
- Stop smoking completely - not a single puff!

Step three

Learn new steps to help you to stop

Step into a new way of living and change your routines.

Develop the **D** steps:
- Do things differently
- Drink plenty of water
- Distract yourself
- Do something you enjoy each day
- Deep breathe

© GASP Tel: 0117 942 5185 www.gasp.org.uk

Step two

Step up the support to stop

- Use a telephone helpline - talk to a counsellor
- Talk to your GP, nurse, midwife, pharmacist
- Ask about medications and individual or group help available
- Ask family, friends and work mates to support you
- Use the internet for stop smoking support

© GASP Tel: 0117 942 5185 www.gasp.org.uk

155

Our last text in this group is a spoof advertisement, "Welcome to Malboro Country," that appears on the Web site for Adbusters.org. Adbusters is a media foundation with a global network that sponsors a Web site and a magazine dedicated to this purpose: "We want folks to get mad about corporate disinformation, injustices in the global economy, and any industry that pollutes our physical and mental commons" (http://adbusters.org/information/guidelines/). As you think about this ad, you might recall the hallmark features of Marlboro ads. What images have made those ads famous?

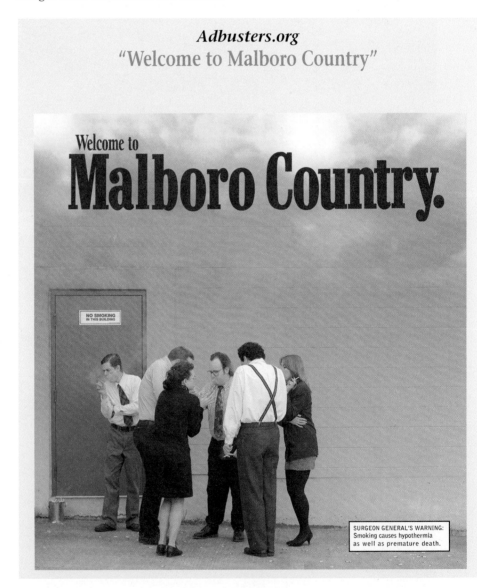

Our first reading on dams, by prolific environmental writer Edward Abbey, first appeared in 1971 in *Beyond the Wall: Essays from the Outside*. His view of Lake Powell, the reservoir formed on the border of Utah and Arizona by the damming of Glen Canyon, has helped stimulate a growing anti-dam movement among environmentalists.

Edward Abbey
The Damnation of a Canyon

1   There was a time when, in my search for essences, I concluded that the canyonland country has no heart. I was wrong. The canyonlands did have a heart, a living heart, and that heart was Glen Canyon and the golden, flowing Colorado River.

2   In the summer of 1959 a friend and I made a float trip in little rubber rafts down through the length of Glen Canyon, starting at Hite and getting off the river near Gunsight Butte—The Crossing of the Fathers. In this voyage of some 150 miles and ten days our only motive power, and all that we needed, was the current of the Colorado River.

3   In the summer and fall of 1967 I worked as a seasonal park ranger at the new Glen Canyon National Recreation Area. During my five-month tour of duty I worked at the main marina and headquarters area called Wahweap, at Bullfrog Basin toward the upper end of the reservoir, and finally at Lee's Ferry downriver from Glen Canyon Dam. In a number of powerboat tours I was privileged to see almost all of our nation's newest, biggest and most impressive "recreational facility."

4   Having thus seen Glen Canyon both before and after what we may fairly call its damnation, I feel that I am in a position to evaluate the transformation of the region caused by construction of the dam. I have had the unique opportunity to observe firsthand some of the differences between the environment of a free river and a powerplant reservoir.

5   One should admit at the outset to a certain bias. Indeed I am a "butterfly chaser, googly eyed bleeding heart and wild conservative." I take a dim view of dams; I find it hard to learn to love cement; I am poorly impressed by concrete aggregates and statistics in the cubic tons. But in this weakness I am not alone, for I belong to that ever-growing number of Americans, probably a good majority now, who have become aware that a fully industrialized, thoroughly urbanized, elegantly computerized social system is not suitable for human habitation. Great for machines, yes: But unfit for people.

6   Lake Powell, formed by Glen Canyon Dam, is not a lake. It is a reservoir, with a constantly fluctuating water level—more like a bathtub that is never drained than a true lake. As at Hoover (or Boulder) Dam, the sole practical function of this impounded water is to drive the turbines that generate electricity in the powerhouse at the base of the dam. Recreational benefits were

of secondary importance in the minds of those who conceived and built this dam. As a result the volume of water in the reservoir is continually being increased or decreased according to the requirements of the Basin States Compact and the power-grid system of which Glen Canyon Dam is a component.

7   The rising and falling water level entails various consequences. One of the most obvious, well known to all who have seen Lake Mead, is the "bathtub ring" left on the canyon walls after each drawdown of water, or what rangers at Glen Canyon call the Bathtub Foundation. This phenomenon is perhaps of no more than aesthetic importance; yet it is sufficient to dispel any illusion one might have, in contemplating the scene, that you are looking upon a natural lake.

8   The utter barrenness of the reservoir shoreline recalls by contrast the aspect of things before the dam, when Glen Canyon formed the course of the untamed Colorado. Then we had a wild and flowing river lined by boulder-strewn shores, sandy beaches, thickets of tamarisk and willow, and glades of cottonwoods.

9   The thickets teemed with songbirds: vireos, warblers, mockingbirds and thrushes. On the open beaches were killdeer, sandpipers, herons, ibises, egrets. Living in grottoes in the canyon walls were swallows, swifts, hawks, wrens, and owls. Beaver were common if not abundant: not an evening would pass, in drifting down the river, that we did not see them or at least hear the whack of their flat tails on the water. Above the river shores were the great recessed alcoves where water seeped from the sandstone, nourishing the semi-tropical hanging gardens of orchid, ivy and columbine, with their associated swarms of insects and birdlife.

10   Up most of the side canyon, before damnation, there were springs, sometimes flowing streams, waterfalls and plunge pools—the kind of marvels you can now find only in such small scale remnants of Glen Canyon as the Escalante area. In the rich flora of these laterals the larger mammals—mule deer, coyote, bobcat, ring-tailed cat, gray fox, kit fox, skunk, badger, and others—found a home. When the river was dammed almost all of these things were lost. Crowded out—or drowned and buried under mud.

11   The difference between the present reservoir, with its silent sterile shores and debris choked side canyons, and the original Glen Canyon, is the difference between death and life. Glen Canyon was alive. Lake Powell is a graveyard.

12   For those who may think I exaggerate the contrast between the former river canyon and the present man-made impoundment, I suggest a trip on Lake Powell followed immediately by another boat trip on the river below the dam. Take a boat from Lee's Ferry up the river to within sight of the dam, then shut off the motor and allow yourself the rare delight of a quiet, effortless drifting down the stream. In that twelve-mile stretch of living green, singing birds, flowing water and untarnished canyon walls—sights and sounds a million years older and infinitely lovelier than the roar of

motorboats—you will rediscover a small and imperfect sampling of the kind of experience that was taken away from everybody when the oligarchs and politicians condemned our river for purposes of their own.

13   Lake Powell, though not a lake, may well be as its defenders assert the most beautiful reservoir in the world. Certainly it has a photogenic backdrop of buttes and mesas projecting above the expansive surface of stagnant waters where the speedboats, houseboats and cabin cruisers play. But it is no longer a wilderness. It is no longer a place of natural life. It is no longer Glen Canyon.

14   The defenders of the dam argue that the recreational benefits available on the surface of the reservoir outweigh the loss of Indian ruins, historical sites, wildlife and wilderness adventure. Relying on the familiar quantitative logic of business and bureaucracy, they assert that whereas only a few thousand citizens even ventured down the river through Glen Canyon, now millions can—or will—enjoy the motorized boating and hatchery fishing available on the reservoir. They will also argue that the rising waters behind the dam have made such places as Rainbow Bridge accessible by power-boat. Formerly you could get there only by walking (six miles).

15   This argument appeals to the wheelchair ethos of the wealthy, upper-middle-class American slob. If Rainbow Bridge is worth seeing at all, then by God it should be easily, readily, immediately available to everybody with the money to buy a big powerboat. Why should a trip to such a place be the privilege only of those who are willing to walk six miles? Or if Pikes Peak is worth getting to, then why not build a highway to the top of it so that anyone can get there? Anytime? Without effort? Or as my old man would say, "By Christ, one man's just as good as another—if not a damn sight better."

16   It is quite true that the flooding of Glen Canyon has opened up to the motorboat explorer parts of side canyons that formerly could be reached only by people able to walk. But the sum total of terrain visible to the eye and touchable by hand and foot has been greatly diminished, not increased. Because of the dam the river is gone, the inner canyon is gone, the best parts of the numerous side canyons are gone—all hidden beneath hundreds of feet of polluted water, accumulating silt, and mounting tons of trash. This portion of Glen Canyon—and who can estimate how many cubic miles were lost?—*is no longer accessible to anybody*. (Except scuba divers.) And this, do not forget, was the most valuable part of Glen Canyon, richest in scenery, archaeology, history, flora, and fauna.

17   Not only has the heart of Glen Canyon been buried, but many of the side canyons above the fluctuating waterline are now rendered more difficult, not easier, to get into. This is because the debris brought down into them by desert storms, no longer carried away by the river, must unavoidably build up in the area where flood meets reservoir. Narrow Canyon, for example, at the head of the impounded waters, is already beginning to silt up and to amass huge quantities of driftwood, some of it floating on the surface, some of it half afloat beneath the surface. Anyone who has tried to

pilot a motorboat through a raft of half-sunken logs and bloated dead cows will have his own thoughts on the accessibility of these waters.

18   Second, the question of costs. It is often stated that the dam and its reservoir have opened up to the many what was formerly restricted to the few, implying in this case that what was once expensive has now been made cheap. Exactly the opposite is true.

19   Before the dam, a float trip down the river through Glen Canyon would cost you a minimum of seven days' time, well within anyone's vacation allotment and a capital outlay of about forty dollars—the prevailing price of a two-man rubber boat with oars, available at any army-navy surplus store. A life jacket might be useful but not required, for there were no dangerous rapids in the 150 miles of Glen Canyon. As the name implies, this stretch of the river was in fact so easy and gentle that the trip could be and was made by all sorts of amateurs: by Boy Scouts, Camp Fire Girls, stenographers, schoolteachers, students, little old ladies in inner tubes. Guides, professional boatmen, giant pontoons, outboard motors, radios, rescue equipment were not needed. The Glen Canyon float trip was an adventure anyone could enjoy, on his own, for a cost less than that of spending two days and nights in a Page motel. Even food was there, in the water: the channel catfish were easier to catch and a lot better eating than the striped bass and rainbow trout dumped by the ton into the reservoir these days. And one other thing: at the end of the float trip you still owned your boat, usable for many more such casual and carefree expeditions.

20   What is the situation now? Float trips are no longer possible. The only way left for the exploration of the reservoir and what remains of Glen Canyon demands the use of a powerboat. Here you have three options: (1) buy your own boat and engine, the necessary auxiliary equipment, the fuel to keep it moving, the parts and repairs to keep it running, the permits and licenses required for legal operation, the trailer to transport it; (2) rent a boat; or (3) go on a commercial excursion boat, packed in with other sightseers, following a preplanned itinerary. This kind of play is only for the affluent.

21   The inescapable conclusion is that no matter how one attempts to calculate the cost in dollars and cents, a float trip down Glen Canyon was much cheaper than a powerboat tour of the reservoir. Being less expensive, as well as safer and easier, the float trip was an adventure open to far more people than will ever be able to afford motorboat excursions in the area now.

22   All of the foregoing would be nothing but a futile exercise in nostalgia (so much water over the dam) if I had nothing constructive and concrete to offer. But I do. As alternate methods of power generation are developed, such as solar, and as the nation establishes a way of life adapted to actual resources and basic needs, so that the demand for electrical power begins to diminish, we can shut down the Glen Canyon power plant, open the diversion tunnels, and drain the reservoir.

23   This will no doubt expose a dreary and hideous scene: immense mud flats and whole plateaus of sodden garbage strewn with dead trees, sunken boats,

the skeletons of long-forgotten, decomposing water-skiers. But to those who find the prospect too appalling, I say give nature a little time. In five years, at most in ten, the sun and wind and storms will cleanse and sterilize the repellent mess. The inevitable floods will soon remove all that does not belong within the canyons. Fresh green willow, box elder and redbud will reappear; and the ancient drowned cottonwoods (noble monuments to themselves) will be replaced by young of their own kind. With the renewal of plant life will come the insects, the birds, the lizards and snakes, the mammals. Within a generation—thirty years—I predict the river and canyons will bear a decent resemblance to their former selves. Within the lifetime of our children Glen Canyon and the living river, heart of the canyonlands, will be restored to us. The wilderness will again belong to God, the people and the wild things that call it home.

Our second reading on dams is the homepage from the Web site of the advocacy organization Friends of Lake Powell (www.lakepowell.org). On its "mission link," this organization states that one of its goals is "To create awareness of and maintain the social, recreational, environmental and economic benefits of Lake Powell, Glen Canyon Dam and Glen Canyon National Recreation Area." You may want to explore some of the other links on this site, particularly its "25 Good Reasons Not to Drain Lake Powell," "Fact Sheet: Lake Powell & Glen Canyon Dam," and "Lake Powell, Habitat for Wildlife." As you browse this site, consider how the photographs and use of color contribute to the rhetorical effect. What appeals to *logos, ethos*, and *pathos* does this site make?

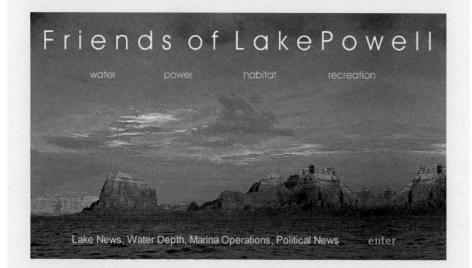

Composing Your Summary/Strong Response Essay

Generating and Exploring Ideas for Your Summary

After you have selected the piece you will use for this assignment, your first task is to read it carefully to get as accurate an understanding of the article as you can. Remember that summarizing is the most basic and preliminary form of reading with the grain of a text.

1. The first time through, read the piece for general meaning. Follow the argument's flow without judgment or criticism, trying to see the world as the author sees it.
2. Reread the piece slowly, paragraph by paragraph, writing "what it does" or "what it says" gist statements in the margins for each paragraph or writing out the question that you think each paragraph answers. We recommend that you supplement these marginal notations by writing out a complete paragraph-by-paragraph *does/says* analysis modeled after our example on page 127.
3. After you've analyzed the piece paragraph by paragraph, locate the argument's main divisions or parts and create an outline or tree diagram of the main points.

If you need to summarize a visual-verbal text such as a poster, advertisement, public affairs advocacy ad, Web page, or brochure, you can adapt the same processes you use for a verbal text piece to this kind of text. Of course, your summary will be longer for more complex texts such as Web pages and brochures than for posters. Examine the parts and record what each part contributes to the whole piece (similar to "what it does" statements). Basically, you are describing each part of the text. Imagine that you are describing the visual elements for someone who hasn't seen the document. For example, here is a brief summary of a brochure from People for the Ethical Treatment of Animals (PETA):

> The PETA brochure, *Compassionate Living*, consists of five pages. The front of the brochure states the title and shows inviting pictures of animals. The next ten panels of the brochure present questions the organization thinks its audience might ask such as, "What's wrong with animal experimentation?" and provides answers and photos of animal cruelty illustrating the answers. The final panel of the brochure describes PETA and has a membership and donation form. Its main argument is that . . . [here you would summarize the main ideas from the panels]

Shaping, Drafting, and Revising Your Summary

Once you have analyzed the article carefully paragraph by paragraph and understand its structure, you are ready to write a draft. If the piece you are summarizing is closed form, you can generally follow the order of the original article, keeping the proportions of the summary roughly equivalent to the proportions of the article. Begin the essay by identifying the question or problem that the reading addresses. Then state the article's purpose or thesis and summarize its argument point by point. If the article has a delayed thesis or some features of open-form prose, then you may have to rearrange the original order to create a clear structure for readers. For a summary of a visual-verbal text, blend your comments about the visual and verbal elements into a paragraph that enables readers to visualize the images, comprehend its parts, and understand the main points of its message.

Count the number of words in your first draft to see whether you are in the 150–250 word range specified by the assignment. When you revise your summary, follow the criteria presented on page 129. Also use the Guidelines for Peer Reviews (pp. 165–166) as a checklist for revision.

Generating and Exploring Ideas for Your Strong Response

After you have written your summary, which demonstrates your full understanding of the text, you are ready to write your strong response. Use the questions and specific reading strategies discussed on pages 134–140 to help you generate ideas. The following questions put this advice into a quick checklist. Look for the questions that most stimulate your thinking and try freewriting your responses.

- Who is the text's intended audience? How is the author trying to change that audience's view of his or her topic? What rhetorical strategies intended to influence the audience most stand out?
- How do I differ from the intended audience? How are my purposes for reading different from what the author imagined?
- How have the author's rhetorical strategies affected me?
- How have the author's ideas affected me? How have they extended or complicated my own thinking? What do I agree with? What can I support?
- How can I question the author's data, evidence, and supporting arguments? If I am not persuaded by the author's ideas and evidence, why not? What is missing? What can be called into question?
- What is excluded from the author's text? What do these exclusions tell me about the author's value system or angle of vision?
- How can I question the author's values, beliefs, and assumptions? Conversely, how does the text cause me to question my own values, beliefs, and assumptions?
- How has the author changed my view of the topic? What do I have to give up or lose in order to change my view? What do I gain?
- How can I use the author's ideas for my own purposes? What new insights have I gained? What new ways of thinking can I apply to another context?

Writing a Thesis for a Strong Response Essay

See Chapter 2, pp. 34–38 for a discussion of surprising thesis statements.

A thesis for a strong response essay should map out for readers the points that you want to develop and discuss. These points should be risky and contestable; your thesis should surprise your readers with something new or challenging. Your thesis might focus entirely on with-the-grain points or entirely on against-the-grain points, but most likely it will include some of both. Avoid tensionless thesis statements such as "This article has both good and bad points."

Here are some thesis statements that students have written for strong responses in our classes. Note that each thesis includes at least one point about the rhetorical strategies of the text.

EXAMPLES OF SUMMARY/STRONG RESPONSE THESIS STATEMENTS

- In "The Beauty Myth," Naomi Wolf makes a very good case for her idea that the beauty myth prevents women from ever feeling that they are good enough; however, Wolf's argument is geared too much toward feminists to be persuasive for a general audience, and she neglects to acknowledge the strong social pressures that I and other men feel to live up to male standards of physical perfection.
- Although Naomi Wolf in "The Beauty Myth" uses rhetorical strategies persuasively to argue that the beauty industry oppresses women, I think that she overlooks women's individual resistance and responsibility.
- Although the images and figures of speech that Thoreau uses in his chapter "Where I Lived, and What I Lived For" from *Walden* wonderfully support his argument that nature has valuable spiritually renewing powers, I disagree with his antitechnology stance and with his extreme emphasis on isolation as a means to self-discovery.
- In "Where I Lived, and What I Lived For" from *Walden*, Thoreau's argument that society is missing spiritual reality through its preoccupation with details and its frantic pace is convincing, especially to twenty-first century audiences; however, Thoreau weakens his message by criticizing his readers and by completely dismissing technological advances.
- Although the brochure *Compassionate Living* by People for the Ethical Treatment of Animals (PETA) uses the design features of layout, color, and image powerfully, its extreme examples, its quick dismissal of alternative views, and its failure to document the sources of its information weaken its appeal to *ethos* and its overall persuasiveness.

Revising Your Strong Response

In revising your strong response, you will find that peer reviews are especially helpful, both in generating ideas and in locating places that need expansion and development. As you revise, think about how well you have incorporated ideas from your initial explorations and how you can make your essay clearer and more meaningful to readers.

GUIDELINES FOR PEER REVIEWS

Instructions for peer reviews are provided in Chapter 17 (pp. 519–520).

For the Writer

Prepare two or three questions you would like your peer reviewer to address while responding to your draft. The questions can focus on some aspect of your draft that you are uncertain about, on one or more sections where you particularly seek help or advice, on some feature that you particularly like about your draft, or on some part you especially wrestled with. Write out your questions and give them to your peer reviewer along with your draft.

For the Reviewer

I. Read the draft at normal reading speed from beginning to end. As you read, do the following:
   A. Place a wavy line in the margin next to any passages where you get confused or find something that doesn't seem to fit or otherwise slowed down your reading.
   B. Place a "Good!" in the margin next to any passages where you think the writing is particularly strong or interesting.
II. Read the draft again slowly and answer the following questions by writing brief explanations of your answers.
   A. The summary
      1. How could the summary be more comprehensive, balanced, and accurate?
      2. Where could it be more fair and neutral?
      3. How could it use attributive tags more effectively?
      4. How could it include and cite quotations more effectively?
      5. What would make the summary read more smoothly?
   B. The strong response
      1. How could the writer's thesis statement be clearer in setting up several focused points about the text's rhetorical strategies and ideas?
      2. How could the body of the strong response follow the thesis more closely?
      3. How could the rhetorical points and "your own views" points engage more specifically and deeply with the text?
      4. Where do you as a reader need more clarification or support for the writer's rhetorical points and subject-matter points?
      5. How could the strong response be improved by adding points, developing points, or making points in a different way?
III. Rhetorical considerations
   A. *Purpose, audience,* and *genre*: This draft should fit the genre of academic writing. Its purpose is to summarize and critique a reading for an audience

interested in the reading's subject matter. How well does the draft fit the genre of academic writing? How effectively does it meet its purpose for its intended audience? How could the writer be more effective in communicating his or her critique and response to the intended readers?

B. *Logos, ethos,* and *pathos*: How convincing or effective is the logical or conceptual aspect of this draft? How has the writer shown his or her knowledgeable and responsible treatment of the reading? How has the writer connected with the values and sympathies of the intended readers? How could the writer improve these dimensions of the draft?

IV. If the writer has prepared questions for you, respond to his or her inquiries.

V. Sum up what you see as the chief strengths and problem areas of this draft.
   A. Strengths
   B. Problem areas

VI. Finally, read the draft one more time. This time place a check mark in the margin next to any places where you noticed problems in grammar, spelling, or mechanics. (One check mark per problem.)

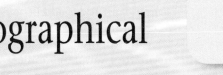

Writing an Autobiographical Narrative

About Autobiographical Narrative

This chapter focuses on the rhetorical aim we have called "writing to express or share." This chapter's assignment asks you to write an autobiographical narrative about something significant in your own life. But rather than state the significance up front in a thesis, you let it unfold in storylike fashion. This narrative structure places autobiographical writing at the open end of the closed-to-open-form continuum, making it more like literary nonfiction than a traditional academic essay. Consequently, we advise you to consult Chapter 19, which discusses the features of open-form prose, prior to writing your assignment for this chapter. The student essays in this chapter, as well as "Berkeley Blues" in Chapter 19 (pp. 574–576), were written for an assignment like the one in this chapter.

See our explanation of rhetorical aims in Table 3.1, pp. 49–50.

The closed-to-open continuum is shown in Figure 1.1, page 19.

Don't let the term *literary* scare you. It simply refers to basic techniques such as dialogue, specific language, and scene-by-scene construction that you use when sharing stories, telling jokes, or recounting experiences to friends. These are the most natural and universal of techniques, the ones that peoples of all cultures have traditionally used to pass on their collective wisdom in myths, legends, and religious narratives.

Although most academic writing is closed form, it sometimes takes an open-form structure, especially when the writer tells the story of an intellectual discovery or narrates his or her wrestling with a problem. Some of the most profound and influential science writing for general audiences—for example, the work of Loren Eiseley, Jay Gould, Rachel Carson, and others—is narrative based. Additionally, many kinds of academic prose have sections of narrative writing. Autobiographical writing can explore, deepen, and complicate our perception of the world.

In addition to telling stories to convey the complexity and significance of phenomena, we use them to reveal ourselves. In this regard, autobiographical writing, like certain forms of conversation, fills a very basic need in our daily lives—the need for intimacy or nontrivial human contact. One of the best measures we have of our closeness to other human beings is our willingness or reluctance to share with them our significant life stories, the ones that reveal our aspirations or humiliations.

We also use others' stories, particularly during adolescence, to monitor our own growth. Many of us once read (and still read) the stories of such people as

Anne Frank, Maya Angelou, Helen Keller, Malcolm X, and Laura Ingalls Wilder in search of attitudes and behaviors to emulate. Reading their stories becomes a way of critiquing and understanding our own stories.

At this point, you might be thinking that your own life lacks the high drama needed for autobiographical prose. Perhaps you're thinking that unless you've dated a movie star, won an X-Game skateboard competition, starred on a reality TV show, or convinced a venture capitalist to fund your dot-com startup company devoted to Pez dispensers, you haven't done anything significant to write about. In this chapter we try to give you another view of significance—one that gets at the heart of what it means to write a story.

To our way of thinking, significance is not a quality somewhere out there in the events of your life: It's in the sensibility that you bring to those events and the way you write about them. When you mistakenly equate significance with singularity (it never happened to anyone else) or its public importance (what happened here made history), you misunderstand the power of a good writer to render any sort of event significant.

Many of the events your audience will find most interesting are those ordinary occurrences that happen to everyone. All of us have experienced a first day at a new school or job, a rival or sibling who seemed to best us at every turn, or a conflict with a parent, lover, spouse, or employer. But everyone enjoys hearing good writers describe their unique methods of coping with and understanding these universal situations. It is precisely because readers have experienced these things that they can project themselves easily into the writer's world. This chapter shows you how to write an autobiographical story by finding a significant moment in your life and writing about it compellingly using literary techniques.

Exploring Autobiographical Narrative

One of the premises of this book is that good writing is rooted in the writer's perception of a problem. Problems are at the center not only of thesis-based writing but also of narrative writing. In effective narration, the problem usually takes the form of a *contrary*, two or more things in opposition—ideas, characters, expectations, forces, worldviews, or whatever. Three kinds of contraries that frequently form the plots of autobiographical narratives are the following:

1. *Old self versus new self.* The writer perceives changes in himself or herself as a result of some transforming moment or event.
2. *Old view of person X versus new view of person X.* The writer's perception of a person (favorite uncle, friend, childhood hero) changes as a result of some revealing moment; the change in the narrator's perception of person X also indicates growth in self-perception.
3. *Old values versus new values that threaten, challenge, or otherwise disrupt the old values.* The writer confronts an outsider who challenges

Plot

By *plot* we mean the basic action of the story, including the selection and sequencing of scenes and events. Often stories don't open with the earliest chronological moment; they may start *in medias res* ("in the middle of things") at a moment of crisis and then flash backward to fill in earlier details that explain the origins of the crisis. What you choose to include in your story and where you place it are concerns of plot. The amount of detail you choose to devote to each scene is also a function of plot. How a writer varies the amount of detail in each scene is referred to as a plot's *pacing*.

Plots typically unfold in the following stages: (a) an arresting opening scene; (b) the introduction of characters and the filling in of background; (c) the building of tension or conflict through oppositions embedded in a series of events or scenes; (d) the climax or pivotal moment when the tension or conflict comes to a head; and (e) reflection on the events of the plot and their meaning.

To help you recognize story-worthy events in your own life, consider the following list of pivotal moments that have figured in numerous autobiographical narratives:

Possible Focuses for Autobiographical Narratives

Moments of enlightenment or coming to knowledge: understanding a complex idea for the first time, recognizing what is meant by love or jealousy or justice, mastering a complex skill, seeing some truth about yourself or your family that you previously hadn't seen

Passages from one realm to the next: from innocence to experience, from outsider to insider or vice versa, from child to adult, from novice to expert, from what you once were to what you now are

Confrontation with the unknown: with people or situations that challenged or threatened your old identity and values

Moments of crisis or critical choice: moments that tested your mettle or your system of values.

Major choices: about the company you keep (friends, love interests, cliques, larger social groups) and the effects of those choices on your integrity and the persona you project to the world

Problems with people: problems maintaining relationships without compromising your own growth or denying your own needs

Problems accepting limitations and necessities: confronting the loss of dreams, the death of intimates, the failure to live up to ideals, or the difficulty of living with a chronic illness or disability

Contrasts between common wisdom and your own unique knowledge or experience: doing what people said couldn't be done, failing at something others said was easy, finding value in something rejected by society, finding bad consequences of something widely valued

For Writing and Discussion

Prior to class, use one or more of the above pivotal-moment categories as an aid to brainstorm ideas for your own autobiographical essay. Then choose one of your ideas to use for your plot, and freewrite possible answers to the following questions:

1. How might you begin your story?
2. What events and scenes might you include in your story?
3. How might you arrange them?
4. What would be the climax of your story (the pivotal moment or scene)?
5. What insights or meaning might you want your story to suggest?

Then share your ideas and explorations with classmates. Help each other explore possibilities for good autobiographical stories. Of course, you are not yet committed to any pivotal moment or plot.

Character

Which characters from your life will you choose to include in your autobiography? The answer to that question depends on the nature of the tension that moves your story forward. Characters who contribute significantly to that tension or who represent some aspect of that tension with special clarity belong in your story. Whatever the source of tension in a story, a writer typically chooses characters who exemplify the narrator's fears and desires or who forward or frustrate the narrator's growth in a significant way.

Sometimes writers develop characters not through description and sensory detail but through dialogue. Particularly if a story involves conflict between people, dialogue is a powerful means of letting the reader experience that conflict directly. The following piece of dialogue, taken from African-American writer Richard Wright's classic autobiography *Black Boy*, demonstrates how a skilled writer can let dialogue tell the story, without resorting to analysis and abstraction. In the following scene, young Wright approaches a librarian in an attempt to get a book by Baltimore author and journalist H. L. Mencken from a whites-only public library. He has forged a note and borrowed a library card from a sympathetic white coworker and is pretending to borrow the book in his coworker's name.

"What do you want, boy?"

As though I did not possess the power of speech, I stepped forward and simply handed her the forged note, not parting my lips.

"What books by Mencken does he want?" she asked.

"I don't know ma'am," I said avoiding her eyes.

"Who gave you this card?"

"Mr. Falk," I said.

"Where is he?"

"He's at work, at the M— Optical Company," I said. "I've been in here for him before."

"I remember," the woman said. "But he never wrote notes like this."

Oh, God, she's suspicious. Perhaps she would not let me have the books? If she had turned her back at that moment, I would have ducked out the door and never gone back. Then I thought of a bold idea.

"You can call him up, ma'am," I said, my heart pounding.

"You're not using these books are you?" she asked pointedly.

"Oh no ma'am. I can't read."

"I don't know what he wants by Mencken," she said under her breath.

I knew I had won; she was thinking of other things and the race question had gone out of her mind.

—Richard Wright, *Black Boy*

It's one thing to hear *about* racial prejudice and discrimination; it's another thing to *hear* it directly through dialogue such as this. In just one hundred or so words of conversation, Wright communicates the anguish and humiliation of being a "black boy" in the United States in the 1920s.

Another way to develop a character is to present a sequence of moments or scenes that reveal a variety of behaviors and moods. Imagine taking ten photographs of your character to represent his or her complexity and variety and then arranging them in a collage. Your narrative can create a similar collage using verbal descriptions. Sheila Madden uses this strategy in "Letting Go of Bart," a story in the Readings section of this chapter, pages 184–186.

For Writing and Discussion

If you currently have ideas for the story you plan to write, consider now the characters who will be in it. If you haven't yet settled on a story idea, think of memorable people in your life. Explore questions such as these: Why are these characters significant to you? What role did they play in forwarding or frustrating your progress? Given that role, which of their traits, mannerisms, modes of dress, and actions might you include in your account? Could you develop your character through dialogue? Through a collage of representative scenes? After you have considered these questions privately, share your responses to them either as a whole class or in groups. Help each other think of details to make your characters vivid and memorable.

Setting

Elements of setting are selected as characters are selected, according to how much they help readers understand the conflict or tension that drives the story. When you write about yourself, what you notice in the external world often reflects your inner world. In some moods you are apt to notice the expansive lawn, beautiful flowers, and swimming ducks in the city park; in other moods you might note the litter of paper cups, the blight on the roses, and the scum on the duck pond. The setting typically relates thematically to the other elements of a story.

In "Berkeley Blues" (pp. 574–576), for example, the author contrasts the swimming pools and sunsets of his hometown to the grit and darkness of inner-city Berkeley. The contrast in settings mirrors the contrast in the worldviews of the high school debaters and the homeless person who confronts them.

For Writing and Discussion

In writing an autobiographical narrative, one of your challenges is to use words to capture scenes so vividly that readers can see in their own minds what you are describing and can share your experience vicariously. The four photos in Figures 7.1–7.4 present four memorable scenes: a wooded stream, a busy city plaza, a steep mountain trail, and an amusement ride at a fair. For this exercise, you can either use a scene in one of these photos or move directly to a scene from your own life that might become part of your own narrative.

Your goal in this exercise is to freewrite a vivid description of a scene and to explore how the scene may be used in your own narrative. If you use one of the scenes in the photos, freewrite a description of this place, imagining that you are there. Describe the scene fully. Alternatively, use the vividness of one of these scenes to help you picture and describe a possible setting of your own to include in your narrative. What do you see? Hear? Smell? Once you have described your scene, explore how this setting might be important to your story in terms of plot, character, or theme. Can you image a second, contrasting scene that reflects the contraries or oppositions in your story? Can you imagine one of these scenes associated with one of your characters? What does the scene reveal about your character's desires, hopes, fears, or predicament? What does the scene suggest about the ideas or themes in your story?

Then, share your descriptive freewrites with classmates, discussing how your settings might be used in your autobiographical narrative.

FIGURE 7.1 A Wooded Stream

FIGURE 7.2 Busy City Plaza

FIGURE 7.3 Steep Mountain Trail   **FIGURE 7.4** Amusement Ride at a Fair

Theme

The word *theme* is difficult to define. Themes, like thesis statements, organize the other elements of the essay. But a theme is seldom stated explicitly and is never proved with reasons and factual evidence. Readers ponder—even argue about—themes, and often different readers are affected very differently by the same theme. Some literary critics view theme as simply a different way of thinking about plot. To use a phrase from critic Northrop Frye, a plot is "what happened" in a story, whereas the theme is "what happens" over and over again in this story and others like it. To illustrate this distinction, we summarize student writer Patrick José's autobiographical narrative "No Cats in America?", one of the essays in the Readings section of this chapter, from a plot perspective and from a theme perspective:

José's essay is on pp. 178–180.

> **Plot Perspective** It's the story of a Filipino boy who emigrates with his family from the Philippines to the United States when he is in the eighth grade. On the first day of school, he is humiliated when classmates snicker at the lunch his mother packed for him. Feeling more and more alienated each day, he eventually proclaims, "I hate being Filipino!"

> **Theme Perspective** It's the story of how personal identity is threatened when people are suddenly removed from their own cultures and immersed into new ones that don't understand or respect difference. The story reveals the psychic damage of cultural dislocation.

As you can see, the thematic summary goes beyond the events of the story to point toward the larger significance of those events. Although you may choose not to state your theme directly for your readers, you need to understand that theme to organize your story. This understanding usually precedes and guides your decisions about what events and characters to include, what details and dialogue to use, and what elements of setting to describe. But sometimes you need to reverse the process and start out with events and characters that, for whatever reason, force themselves on you, and then figure out your theme after you've written for a while. In other words, theme may be something you discover as you write.

For Writing and Discussion

Using the ideas you have brainstormed from previous exercises in this chapter, choose two possible ideas for an autobiographical narrative you might write. For each, freewrite your response to this question: What is the significance of this story for me? (Why did I choose this story? Why is it important to me? Why do I want to tell it? What am I trying to show my readers?)

In class, share your freewrites. All the exercises in this section are designed to generate discussion about the elements of autobiographical narrative and to encourage topic exploration.

READINGS

Now that we have examined some of the key elements of autobiographical writing, let's look at some particular examples.

The first reading is by Kris Saknussemm, an American fiction writer whose short stories have appeared in such publications as *The Boston Review, New Letters, The Antioch Review,* and *ZYZZYVA.* He is the author of an avant-garde novel to be published in 2005. This selection is taken from his autobiographical work in progress.

Kris Saknussemm
Phantom Limb Pain

1   When I was 13 my sole purpose was to shed my baby fat and become the star halfback on our football team. That meant beating out Miller King, the best athlete at my school. He was my neighbor and that mythic kid we all know—the one who's forever better than us—the person we want to be.

2   Football practice started in September and all summer long I worked out. I ordered a set of barbells that came with complimentary brochures with titles like "How to Develop a He-Man Voice." Every morning before sunrise I lumbered around our neighborhood wearing ankle weights loaded with sand. I taught myself how to do Marine push-ups and carried my football everywhere so I'd learn not to fumble. But that wasn't enough. I performed a ceremony. During a full moon, I burned my favorite NFL trading cards and an Aurora model of the great quarterback Johnny Unitas in the walnut orchard behind our house, where Miller and I'd gotten into a fight when we were seven and I'd burst into tears before he even hit me.

3   Two days after my ceremony, Miller snuck out on his older brother's Suzuki and was struck by a car. He lost his right arm, just below the elbow. I went to see him the day after football practice started—after he'd come back from the hospital. He looked pale and surprised, but he didn't cry. It was hard to look at the stump of limb where his arm had been, so I kept glancing around his room. We only lived about 200 feet away, and yet I'd never been inside his house before. It had never occurred to me that he would also have on his wall a poster of Raquel Welch from One Million Years B.C.

4   I went on to break all his records that year. Miller watched the home games from the bench, wearing his jersey with the sleeve pinned shut. We went 10-1 and I was named MVP, but I was haunted by crazy dreams in which I was somehow responsible for the accident—that I'd found the mangled limb when it could've been sewn back on—and kept it in an aquarium full of vodka under my bed.

5   One afternoon several months later, toward the end of basketball season, I was crossing the field to go home and I saw Miller stuck going over the Cyclone fence—which wasn't hard to climb if you had both arms. I guess he'd gotten tired of walking around and hoped no one was looking. Or maybe it was a matter of pride. I'm sure I was the last person in the world he wanted to see—to have to accept assistance from. But even that challenge he accepted. I helped ease him down the fence, one diamond-shaped hole at a time. When we were finally safe on the other side, he said to me, "You know, I didn't tell you this during the season, but you did all right. Thanks for filling in for me."

6   We walked home together, not saying much. But together. Back to our houses 200 feet apart. His words freed me from my bad dreams. I thought to myself, how many things I hadn't told him. How even without an arm he was more of a leader. Damaged but not diminished, he was still ahead of me. I was right to have admired him. I grew bigger and a little more real from that day on.

Thinking Critically about "Phantom Limb Pain"

Perhaps the first thing the reader realizes about Saknussemm's narrative is that the climactic event—one boy helping another climb down a Cyclone fence—is a small action; however, it has big psychological and emotional meaning for the narrator. The events leading to this moment have prepared us to understand the writer's revelation of his new relationship to his rival. Saknussemm's last paragraph comments on the preceding narrative, making connections and pulling out threads of meaning.

1. Saknussemm chooses to leave a lot unsaid, depending on his readers to fill in the gaps. Why do you suppose that he had never been inside Miller King's

See Chapter 19, pp. 582–584, for a discussion of concrete language including revelatory words and memory-soaked words. See Chapter 5, pp. 112–113, for a discussion of *show* words and *tell* words.

house before? Why does he feel "somehow responsible for the accident"? What details does Saknussemm use to sketch in Miller's admirable traits?

2. What examples can you find in this narrative of revelatory words, memory-soaked words, and other concrete words low on the ladder of abstraction? Where does Saknussemm use words that *show* what is happening in the narrative instead of simply telling readers?

3. In closed-form prose, writers seldom use sentence fragments. In open-form prose, however, writers frequently use fragments for special effects. Note the two fragments in Saknussemm's final paragraph: "But together. Back to our houses 200 feet apart." Why does Saknussemm use these fragments? What is their rhetorical effect?

4. Part of Saknussemm's style in this narrative is to use understatement and minimalistic language while also using words that resonate with multiple meanings. For example, he lets readers imagine what Miller would look like trying to climb the Cyclone fence with one arm. However, some phrases and words are figurative and symbolic. What does Saknussemm mean by the phrases "grew bigger" and "a little more real" in his final sentence? How do the ideas of size and of reality versus illusion play a role in this narrative and relate to the theme?

For a different approach to narrative, consider student writer Patrick José's "No Cats in America?" Unlike Saknussemm's narrative, José's includes plentiful description. Note also how José creates tension through contrasts in his narrative: between an ideal image of America and a factual image, between life in the Philippines and life in California.

Patrick José (student)
No Cats in America?

1   "There are no cats in America." I remember growing up watching *An American Tail* with my sisters and cousins. Ever since I first saw that movie, I had always wanted to move to America. That one song, "There Are No Cats in America," in which the Mousekewitz family is singing with other immigrating mice, had the most profound effect on me. These were Russian mice going to America to find a better life—a life without cats. At first, I thought America really had no cats. Later, I learned that they meant that America was without any problems at all. I was taught about the American Dream with its promise of happiness and equality. If you wanted a better life, then you better pack up all your belongings and move to America.

2   However, I loved living in the Philippines. My family used to throw the best parties in Angeles City. For a great party, you need some delicious food.

Of course there would be lechon, adobo, pancit, sinigang, lumpia, and rice. We eat rice for breakfast, lunch, and dinner, and rice even makes some of the best desserts. (My mom's bibingka and puto are perfect!) And you mustn't forget the drinks. San Miguel and Coke are usually sufficient. But we also had homemade mango juice and coconut milk. And a party wouldn't be a party without entertainment, right? So in one room, we had the gambling room. It's usually outside the house. Everybody would be smoking and drinking while playing mahjong. And sometimes, others would play pepito or pusoy dos. Music and dancing is always a must. And when there are firecrackers, better watch out because the children would go crazy with them.

3   Then one day, a mixed feeling came over me. My dad told us that he had gotten a job . . . in California. In the span of two months, we had moved to America, found a small apartment, and located a small private Catholic school for the kids. We did not know many people in California that first summer. We only had ourselves to depend on. We would go on car trips, go to the beach, cook, play games. In August, I thought we were living the American Dream.

4   But at the end of summer, school began. I was in the eighth grade. I had my book bag on one shoulder, stuffed with notebooks, folder paper, calculators, a ruler, a pencil box, and my lunch. I still can remember what I had for lunch on the first day of school—rice and tilapia and, in a small container, a mixture of vinegar, tomatoes, and bagoong. My mom placed everything in a big Tupperware box, knowing I eat a lot.

5   When I walked into the classroom, everyone became quiet and looked at me. I was the only Filipino in that room. Everyone was white. We began the day by introducing ourselves. When it got to my turn, I was really nervous. English was one of the courses that I took in the Philippines, and I thought I was pretty proficient at it. But when I first opened my mouth, everyone began to laugh. The teacher told everyone to hush. I sat down, smiling faintly not understanding what was so funny. I knew English, and yet I was laughed at. But it had nothing to do with the language. It was my accent.

6   Some students tried to be nice, especially during lunch. But it didn't last long. I was so hungry for my lunch. I followed a group of students to the cafeteria and sat down at an empty table. Some girls joined me. I didn't really talk to them, but they asked if they could join me. As I opened my Tupperware, I saw their heads turn away. They didn't like the smell of fish and bagoong. The girls left and moved to another table of girls. From the corner of my eye I saw them looking and laughing at me. I tried to ignore it, concentrating on eating my lunch as I heard them laugh. In the Philippines, the only way to eat fish and rice is with your hands. But that was in the Philippines. My manners were primitive here in America. I was embarrassed at the smell, was embarrassed at the way I ate, was embarrassed to be me.

7   When I got home, I lied to my parents. I told them school was great and that I was excited to go back. But deep down, I wanted to go back to the Philippines. When lunch came the next day, I was hungry. In my hand was

my lunch. Five feet away was the trash. I stood up, taking my lunch in my hands. Slowly, I walked my way towards the trashcan, opened the lid, and watched as my lunch filled the trashcan. Again, I told my parents I enjoyed school.

8 When my grades began to suffer, the teacher called my parents and scheduled an appointment. The next day, my parents came to the classroom, and when they started talking to the teacher I heard laughter in the background. It humiliated me to have my classmates hear my parents talk.

9 That night, my parents and I had a private discussion. They asked why I lied to them. I told them everything, including my humiliation. They told me not to worry about it, but I pleaded for us to return to the Philippines. My parents said no. "Living here will provide a better future for you and your sisters," they said. Then the unexpected came. I didn't know what I was thinking. I yelled to them with so much anger, "I hate being Filipino!" Silence filled the room. Teardrops rolled down my cheeks. My parents were shocked, and so was I.

10 I went to my room and cried. I didn't mean what I said. But I was tired of the humiliation. Lying on my bed, with my eyes closed, my mind began to wander. I found myself in the boat with the Mousekewitz family singing, "There are no cats in America." If only they knew how wrong they were.

Thinking Critically about "No Cats in America?"

Unlike Saknussemm, who comments explicitly on the significance of his experience, Patrick José lets the reader infer his essay's significance from the details of the narrative and from their connection to the framing story of the fictional mice and cats.

1. How do the settings help you understand José's theme at different points in the story?

2. What would you say is the story's climax or pivotal moment?

3. José's title, first paragraph, and last paragraph are about a children's movie that features the Mousekewitz's song proclaiming that there are no cats in America. How does the "no cats" image function as both part of the underlying tension of this narrative and as a symbolic vehicle for conveying the theme of José's essay? What is the insight that José has achieved at the end?

4. During a rough draft workshop, José asked his peer reviewers whether he should retain his description of parties in the Philippines, which he thought was perhaps unconnected to the rest of the story. His classmates urged him to keep those details. Do you agree with their advice? Why?

See Chapter 19, p. 584, for a discussion of the power of memory-soaked words.

5. For Filipinos and Filipinas, the specific names of foods and party games would be rich examples of memory-soaked words. For other readers, however,

these names are foreign and strange. Do you agree with José's decision to use these specific ethnic names? Why?

For Writing and Discussion

Imagine a memorable party scene from your own life and experiences. It could be a family party, a neighborhood party, or a party from high school, college, or work. What specific words, revelatory words, and memory-soaked words will most likely make this party come to life in your readers' imagination? What details about food and drink, the activities of the partygoers, clothing and mannerisms, the party's setting (furniture, pictures on the walls, arrangement of rooms), and so on will trigger associations and memories for your readers? List these details and then share them with your classmates.

The next example was written in a first-year composition course by a student writer who wishes to remain anonymous.

Masks

1   Her soft, blond hair was in piggytails, as usual, with ringlets that bounced whenever she turned her head. As if they were springs, they could stretch, then shrink, then bounce, excited by the merest movement of her head. Never was there a hair that wasn't enclosed in those glossy balls which always matched her dress. I knew the only reason she turned her head was so they'd bounce. Because it was cute. Today, she wore a pink dress with frills and lace and impeccably white tights. Her feet, which swayed back and forth underneath her chair, were pampered with shiny, black shoes without a single scuff. She was very wise, sophisticated beyond her kindergarten years.

2   I gazed at her and then looked down at my clothes. My green and red plaid pants and my yellow shirt with tiny, blue stars showed the day's wear between breakfast, lunch, and recess. Showing through the toe of my tenny runners was my red sock.

3   At paint time, I closely followed behind her, making sure I painted at the easel next to hers. She painted a big, white house with a white picket fence and a family: Mom, Dad, and Daughter. I painted my mom, my brother, and myself. I, then, painted the sky, but blue streaks ran down our faces, then our bodies, ruining the picture.

4   The next day, I wore my hair in piggytails. I had done it all by myself, which was obvious due to my craftsmanship. She pointed and giggled at me when I walked by. I also wore a dress that day but I didn't have any pretty

white tights. The boys all gathered underneath me when I went on the monkeybars to peak at my underwear to chant, "I see London, I see France, I see Tiffy's underpants."

5   When the day was done, she ran to the arms of her mother that enveloped her in a loving and nurturing hug. She showed her mother her painting, which had a big, red star on it.

6   "We'll have to put this up on the refrigerator with all of your others," her mother said. I had thrown my painting away. I looked once more at the two of them as they walked hand in hand towards their big, white house with a white picket fence. I trudged to my babysitter's house. I wouldn't see my mother until six o'clock. She had no time for me, for my paintings, for my piggytails. She was too busy working to have enough money to feed my brother and me.

7   Digging absently through books and folders, I secretly stole a glance at her, three lockers down. Today she wore her Calvins and sported a brand new pair of Nikes. As always, at the cutting edge of fashion. If I wanted Nikes, I could pay for them myself, or so said my mother. In the meantime, I had to suffer with my cheap, treadless Scats. As I searched for a pen, her giggle caught my attention. Three of her friends had flocked around her locker. I continued searching for a pen but to no avail. I thought of approaching and borrowing one but I was fearful that they would make fun of me.

8   "Jim and Brad called me last night and both of them asked me to go to the show. Which one should I pick?" she asked. My mom wouldn't let me go out on dates until I was a sophomore in high school. We were only in seventh grade and she was always going out with guys. Not that it mattered that I couldn't date, yet. Nobody had ever asked me out.

9   "My hair turned out so yucky today. Ick," she commented. She bent down to grab a book and light danced among the gentle waves of her flowing, blond mane. Her radiant brown eyes and adorable smile captivated all who saw her. Once captured, however, none was allowed past the mask she'd so artfully constructed to lure them to her. We were all so close to her, so far away. She was so elusive, like a beautiful perfume you smell but can't name, like the whisper that wakes you from a dream and turns out to belong to the dream.

10   As she walked into the library, I heard a voice whisper, "There she is. God, she's beautiful." She was wearing her brown and gold cheerleader outfit. Her pleated skirt bounced off her thighs as she strutted by. Her name, "Kathy," was written on her sweater next to her heart and by it hung a corsage. As she rounded the corner, she flicked her long, blond curls and pivoted, sending a ripple through the pleats of the skirt. She held her head up high, befitting one of her social standing: top of the high school food chain. She casually searched the length of the library for friends. When she reached the end of the room, she carefully reexamined every table, this time less casually.

Her smile shaded into a pout. She furrowed her face, knitting her eyebrows together, and saddening her eyes. People stared at her until she panicked.

11   She was bolting toward the door when she spotted me. She paused and approached my table. Putting on her biggest smile, she said, "Oh hi! Can I sit by you?" Thrilled at the possibility of at last befriending her, I was only too happy to have her sit with me. As she sat down, she again scanned the expanse of the library.

12   "So, who does the varsity basketball team play tonight?" I asked.

13   "Great Falls Central," she replied. "Make sure you're there! . . . How's the Algebra assignment today?!"

14   "Oh, it's okay. Not too tough," I said.

15   "John always does my assignments for me. I just hate Algebra. It's so hard."

16   We stood up in silence, suddenly painfully aware of our differences. She glanced in the reflection of the window behind us, checked her hair, then again scanned the room.

17   "There's Shelly! Well, I'll see you later," she said.

18   She rose from the table and fled to her more acceptable friend.

19   The next day, she walked down the hall surrounded by a platoon of friends. As we passed, I called out "Hi!" but she turned away as if she didn't know me, as if I didn't exist.

20   I, then, realized her cheerleader outfit, her golden locks, her smile were all a mask. Take them away and nothing but air would remain. Her friends and their adoration were her identity. Without them she was alone and vulnerable. I was the powerful one. I was independent.

Thinking Critically about "Masks"

1. What are the main contrarieties in this piece?

2. Where does the writer's description of the setting help to portray the characters?

3. This piece focuses on the narrator's movement toward a significant recognition. What is it she recognizes? If you were a peer reviewer for this writer, would you recommend eliminating the last paragraph, expanding it, or leaving it as it is? Why?

4. In Chapter 19, we quote writer John McPhee's advice to prefer specific words over abstract ones—brand names, for example, rather than generic names. This student writer follows this advice throughout her essay. Where does she use details and specific words with particular effectiveness?

The discussion of concrete language in Chapter 19 is on pp. 582–584.

The final example uses a collage technique. Here the emphasis is so much on the character Bart that the narrator seems relatively unimportant, and you may wonder whether this piece is biography (the story of Bart) or autobiography (the story of the narrator). We include "Letting Go of Bart" in the category of autobiographical narrative because the way in which the writer, Sheila Madden, tells the story reveals her own growth in understanding, her own deepening of character.

Sheila Madden
Letting Go of Bart

1   Bart lies stiffly in bed, toes pointed downward like a dancer's, but Bart is far from dancing. When he tries to shift position, his limbs obey spasmodically because his nervous system has been whipsawed by the medications he has been taking for years to control the various manifestations of AIDS.

2   He is wearing diapers now, for incontinence—the ultimate indignity. An oxygen tube is hooked into his nose, morphine drips into his arm; his speech is slurred.

3   But Bart is not confused. He is intensely irritable and has been the terror of his nurses. Though he has a great self-deprecating grin, I haven't seen it for weeks.

4   I can't say a proper goodbye because he is never alone. I would like to pray silently by his bedside, meditating; but even if I could, he would barely tolerate it. Bart has no god.

5   I remember the day a tall, good-looking young man popped into the open door of the downstairs apartment I was fixing up in my San Francisco home. That late afternoon, I was tiredly putting the last coat of paint on the walls with the help of a couple of friends. Bart had seen the for-rent sign in the window and just walked in. Within moments he had all three of us laughing uproariously as he put a deposit in my hand. I had asked the angels for help in finding a decent renter; the angels had responded. Bart and I would get on famously.

6   For one thing, Bart managed to fix or overlook the unfinished bits in the apartment. He and his father built a fine, much-needed deck on the back garden, charging me only for the lumber. He made the small apartment look spacious, arranging the furniture skillfully, backlighting the sofas. And he was prompt with the rent.

7   However, Bart was far more than a satisfactory renter. He was a fine singer and a member of the symphony chorus. When he practiced, his rich baritone would sail up the stairs, smoothing the airways, never ruffling them.

8   He asked permission to put a piano in his apartment, and I agreed nervously. Because he was a beginner on the instrument, I feared endless, fumbling scales disturbing my peace. It never happened. He played softly, sensitively, and always at reasonable hours.

9   I attended some of his concerts and met his friends. At times we joined forces at parties upstairs or downstairs, but somehow we never got in each other's hair.

10   He was a skillful ballroom dancer. Once he agreed to stand in as partner for my visiting sister when we attended a Friday dance at the Embarcadero Plaza—although the prospect could not have thrilled him.

11   Another time I disabled my tape deck by spraying it with WD-40 and ran downstairs for help. Bart came up immediately, scolding me roundly for putting oil on such a machine. Then he spent the better part of an hour wrapping matchsticks in cotton batting (for lack of a better tool), degreasing the heads with rubbing alcohol, and putting all to rights.

12   Bart had family problems; I had them. We commiserated. Bart was an ally, a compatriot, a brother.

13   I suspected Bart was gay; but we never talked about it, although he knew I was working in the AIDS fields as a counselor and that it was a nonissue with me.

14   Then one day he got a bad flu, which turned into a deep, wracking cough that did not go away. I worried about it, having heard such coughs in the AIDS patients I dealt with daily. I encouraged him to see a doctor, and he did, making light of his visit.

15   Finally the cough receded, but psychically so did Bart. I saw him hardly at all for the next three months. When I did, he seemed somber and abstracted.

16   However, my life was hectic at the time. I didn't pay attention, assuming his problem was job dissatisfaction; I knew his boss was a constant thorn in his side. One day he told me that he was changing jobs and moving to Napa, an hour's drive away. I rejoiced for him and cried for myself. I would miss Bart.

17   Our lives separated. Napa might as well have been the moon. Over a two-year period we talked once or twice on the phone, and I met him once for dinner in the city.

18   Then one night my doorbell rang unexpectedly, and Bart came in to tell me of his recovery from a recent bout of pneumocystis pneumonia. "I'm out of the closet, willy-nilly," he said.

19   I was stunned. I had put him in the "safe" category, stuffing my fears about the telltale cough. It must have been then that he learned his diagnosis. For the next 24 hours I cried off and on, inconsolably, for Bart and probably for all the others I had seen die.

20   Now he is at the end, an end so fierce there is nothing to do but pray it will come quickly. Bart is courageous, his anger masking fear. He has thus far refused to let the morphine dull his consciousness. His eyes, hawklike, monitor all that is going on around him. Angels, who once brought him, take him home.

Thinking Critically about "Letting Go of Bart"

1. Madden uses a series of scenes to create her portrait of Bart. Briefly list each of these scenes identifying its setting and events. How do these scenes function to reveal Bart's character? In other words, what does the reader learn through each scene?

2. How and how much does Madden as the narrator reveal about her own character? To what extent could you call this essay an "autobiographical narrative"?

3. How does Madden's collage technique create tension and resolution?

For Writing and Discussion

To generate more ideas for an autobiographical narrative, each class member should do the following exercise independently and then share the results with the rest of the class:

1. Have you ever had a moment of revelation when you suddenly realized that your own view of something (a person, a place, the world) was wrong, narrow, or distorted, as did Kris Saknussemm? If you have, freewrite about this experience.

2. Have you ever been suddenly whisked from a familiar to an unfamiliar setting and made to feel like an outsider, alienated and alone, as did Patrick José in "No Cats in America?" If so, freewrite about this experience.

3. Have you ever changed your view of a person in a way analogous to the narrator's reassessment of the cheerleader in "Masks"? If so, freewrite about this character. What details reveal this person before and after your moment of reassessment?

4. Have you ever known a person whose presence in your life made an important difference to you, as did Bart to Sheila Madden? If you have, freewrite about this character, imagining a series of scenes that might create a collage effect.

Composing Your Essay

In deciding what to write about, keep in mind the basic requirement for a good story: It must portray a sequence of connected events driven forward by some tension or conflict that results in a recognition or new understanding. Not every memorable event in your life will lend itself to this sort of structure. The most common failing in faulty narratives is that the meaning of the event is clearer to the narrator than to the audience. "You had to be there," the writer comments, when a story just doesn't have the expected impact on an audience.

But it's the storyteller's job to *put the reader there* by providing enough detail and context for the reader to *see* why the event is significant. If an event didn't lead to any significant insight, understanding, knowledge, change, or other kind of difference in your life, and if you really had to be there to appreciate its significance, then it's a poor candidate for an autobiographical narrative.

Generating and Exploring Ideas

Choosing a Plot

For some of you, identifying a plot—a significant moment or insight arising out of contrariety—will present little problem; perhaps you have already settled on an idea you generated in one of the class discussion exercises earlier in this chapter. However, if you are still searching for a plot idea, you may find the following list helpful:

- A time when you took some sort of test that conferred new status on you (Red Cross lifesaving exam, driver's test, SAT, important school or work-related test, entrance exam, team tryout). If you failed, what did you learn from it or how did it shape you? If you succeeded, did the new status turn out to be as important as you expected it would be?
- A situation in which your normal assumptions about life were challenged (an encounter with a foreign culture, a time when a person you'd stereotyped surprised you).
- A time when you left your family for an extended period or forever (going to college, getting married, entering the military, leaving one parent for another after their divorce).
- A time that plunged you into a crisis (being the first person to discover a car crash, seeing a robbery in progress, being thrown in with people who are repugnant to you, facing an emergency).
- A situation in which you didn't fit or didn't fulfill others' expectations of you, or a situation in which you were acknowledged as a leader or exceeded others' expectations of you (call to jury duty, assignment to a new committee, being placed in charge of an unfamiliar project).
- A time when you overcame your fears to do something for the first time (first date, first public presentation, first challenge in a new setting).
- A situation in which you learned how to get along amicably with another human being, or a failed relationship that taught you something about life (your first extended romantic relationship; your relationship with a difficult sibling, relative, teacher, or boss; getting a divorce).
- A time when a person who mattered to you (parent, spouse, romantic interest, authority figure) rejected you or let you down, or a time when you rejected or let down someone who cared for you.
- A time when you made a sacrifice on behalf of someone else, or someone else made a sacrifice in your name (taking in a foster child, helping a homeless person, caring for a sick person).

- A time when you were irresponsible or violated a principle or law and thereby caused others pain (you shoplifted or drank when underage and were caught, you failed to look after someone entrusted to your care).
- A time when you were criticized unjustly or given a punishment you didn't deserve (you were accused of plagiarizing a paper that you'd written, you were blamed unjustly for a problem at work).
- A time when you were forced to accept defeat or death or the loss of a dream or otherwise learned to live with reduced expectations.
- A time when you experienced great joy (having a baby, getting your dream job) or lived out a fantasy.

Thickening the Plot

Once you've identified an event about which you'd like to write, you need to develop ways to show readers what makes that event particularly story worthy. In thinking about the event, consider the following questions:

- What makes the event so memorable? What particulars or physical details come most readily to mind when you think back on the event?
- What are the major contrarieties that gave the event tension? Did it raise a conflict between two or more people? Between their worldviews? Between before and after versions of yourself?
- How can you make the contrarieties memorable and vivid to the reader?
- What scenes can you create? What words could your characters exchange? Is there a moment of insight, recognition, or resolution that would give your plot a climax?
- What is the significance of the story? How does it touch on larger human issues and concerns? What makes it something your reader will relate to? What is its theme?

Shaping and Drafting

When stuck, writers often work their way into a narrative by describing in detail a vividly recalled scene, person, or object. This inductive approach is common with many creative processes. You may or may not include all the descriptive material in your final draft, but in the act of writing exhaustively about this one element, the rest of the story may begin to unfold for you, and forgotten items and incidents may resurface. In the course of describing scenes and characters, you will probably also begin reflecting on the significance of what you are saying. Try freewriting answers to such questions as "Why is this important?" and "What am I trying to do here?" Then continue with your rough draft.

Revising

Once you've written a draft, you need to get down to the real work of writing—rewriting. Revisit your prose critically, with an eye toward helping your reader share your experience and recognize its significance. Chapter 19, as well as the following guidelines for peer reviews, will be of particular help during revision.

GUIDELINES FOR PEER REVIEWS

Instructions for peer reviews are provided in Chapter 17 (pp. 519–520).

For the Writer

Prepare two or three questions you would like your peer reviewer to address while responding to your draft. The questions can focus on some aspect of your draft that you are uncertain about, on one or more sections where you particularly seek help or advice, or on some feature that you particularly like about your draft, or on some part you especially wrestled with. Write out your questions and give them to your peer reviewer along with your draft.

For the Reviewer

I. Read the draft at normal reading speed from beginning to end. As you read, do the following:
   A. Place a wavy line in the margin next to any passages that you find confusing, that contain something that doesn't seem to fit, or that otherwise slow down your reading.
   B. Place a "Good!" in the margin next to any passages where you think the writing is particularly strong or interesting.

II. Read the draft again slowly and answer the following questions by writing down brief explanations of your answers.
   A. Plot: What are the contrarieties, tensions, or conflicts in this story?
      1. How might the writer heighten or clarify the tension in the story?
      2. How might the writer improve the structure or pacing of scenes and the connection between these events? If you were to expand or reduce the treatment given to any events, which would you change and why?
      3. How could the writer use chronological order, flashbacks, or flash-forwards more effectively?
   B. Characters: How might the writer make the characters and their functions more vivid and compelling?
      1. Where might the writer provide more information about a character or describe the character more fully?
      2. Where might the writer use dialogue more effectively to reveal character?
   C. Setting: How might the writer use setting more effectively to create contrasts or convey thematic significance? Where might the writer add or revise details about setting?
   D. Theme: What do you see as the *So what?* or significance of this story?
      1. What insight or revelation do you get from this story?
      2. How could the story's thematic significance be made more memorable, powerful, or surprising? Should the writer comment more explicitly on the meaning or significance of the story or leave more for you to grasp on your own?
   E. Title and opening paragraphs: How could the writer improve the title? How could the opening paragraphs be made more effective to hook the readers' interest and prepare them for the story to follow?

    F. Language and details: Where do you find examples of specific language, including memory-soaked or revelatory words? Where and how could the writer use specific language more effectively?

III. Rhetorical considerations

    A. *Purpose, audience,* and *genre*: Where does this draft do a good job of fulfilling its expressive purpose, reaching its intended audience, and meeting the audience's expectations for autobiographical narratives? How could the writer improve in these areas?

    B. *Logos, ethos,* and *pathos*: How effective is the conceptual part of this draft and the logic of its structure? Where could the writer improve this content? What image of the writer comes through in this narrative? How could this image be made more effective? How does the writer appeal to the audience's emotions, interests, and values?

IV. If the writer has prepared questions for you, respond to his or her inquiries.

V. Briefly summarize in a list what you see as the chief strengths and problem areas in the draft.

    A. Strengths

    B. Problem areas

VI. Read the draft one more time. Place a check mark in the margin wherever you notice problems in grammar, spelling, or mechanics (one check mark per problem).

Writing an Exploratory Essay

About Exploratory Writing

In Chapter 1, we said that to grow as a writer you need to love problems—to pose them and to live with them. Most academic writers testify that writing projects begin when they become engaged with a question or problem and commit themselves to an extensive period of exploration. During exploration, writers may radically redefine the problem and then later alter or even reverse their initial thesis.

As we noted in Chapter 2, however, inexperienced writers tend to truncate this exploratory process, committing themselves hastily to a thesis to avoid complexity. College professors say that this tendency hinders their students' intellectual growth. Asserting a thesis commits you to a position. Asking a question, on the other hand, invites you to contemplate multiple perspectives, entertain new ideas, and let your thinking evolve. As management professor A. Kimbrough Sherman puts it, to grow as thinkers, students need "to 'wallow in complexity' and work their way back out" (p. 27).

To illustrate his point, Sherman cites his experience in a management class where students were asked to write proposals for locating a new sports complex in a major U.S. city. To Sherman's disappointment, many students argued for a location without first considering all the variables—impact on neighborhoods, building costs and zoning, availability of parking, ease of access, attractiveness to tourists, aesthetics, and so forth—and without analyzing how various proposed locations stacked up against the criteria they were supposed to establish. The students reached closure without wallowing in complexity.

The assignment in this chapter asks you to dwell with a problem, even if you can't solve it. You will write an essay with an exploratory purpose; its focus will be a question rather than a thesis. The body of your paper will be a narrative account of your thinking about the problem—your attempt to examine its complexity, to explore alternative solutions, and to arrive at a solution or answer. Your exploration will generally require outside research, so many instructors will assign sections of Part Four, "A Rhetorical Guide to Research," along with this chapter. The paper will be relatively easy to organize because it follows a chronological structure, but you will have nothing to say—no process to report—unless you discover and examine your problem's complexity.

Exploratory essays can be composed in two ways—what we might call the "in-process" strategy and the "retrospective" strategy. When following the first strategy, writers compose the body of their essays during the actual process of thinking and researching. When writing page 4, for example, they don't know what they will be thinking by page 9. In contrast, when composing retrospectively, writers look back over their process from the vantage point of a completed journey. Their goal, when writing with an exploratory aim, is to reproduce their process, taking the readers, as it were, on the same intellectual and emotional journey they have just traveled. The first strategy yields genuine immediacy—like a sequence of journal entries written in the midst of the action. The second strategy, which allows for more selection and shaping of details, yields a more artistically designed essay.

Exploratory essays occur only occasionally in academic journals and almost never in business or professional life, where readers need thesis-driven arguments and reports. However, exploratory essays exist in embryo in the research journals or lab notebooks of scholars. Scholars sometimes revise their journals into stand-alone exploratory essays that take readers into the kitchen of academic discovery. The exploratory form underlies Plato's dialogues as well as the musings of the Renaissance French writer Michel de Montaigne, whose term *essai* (meaning a "try" or "attempt") leads to the English word *essay*. The power of exploratory writing as a stand-alone genre can be seen in such books as Jon Krakauer's *Into the Wild*, which recounts the author's attempt to fathom the mystery of Chris McCandless, a bright young graduate from Emory University who abandoned conventional life and "disappeared" into the Alaska wilderness, where he was eventually found dead in an abandoned school bus. Who was Chris McCandless?, Krakauer asks. What motivated him? The book records Krakauer's exploration—a collage of personal narrative intermixed with interviews, musings on his reading, and frequent theorizing. This chapter introduces you to thinking processes behind this powerful form.

Exploring Exploratory Writing

Through our work in writing centers, we often encounter students disappointed with their grades on essay exams or papers. "I worked hard on this paper," they tell us, "but I still got a lousy grade. What am I doing wrong? What do college professors want?"

To help you answer this question, consider the following two essays written for a freshman placement examination in composition at the University of Pittsburgh, in response to the following assignment:

> Describe a time when you did something you felt to be creative. Then, on the basis of the incident you have described, go on to draw some general conclusions about "creativity."

How would you describe the differences in thinking exhibited by the two writers? Which essay do you think professors rated higher?

ESSAY A

I am very interested in music, and I try to be creative in my interpretation of music. While in high school, I was a member of a jazz ensemble. The members of the ensemble were given chances to improvise and be creative in various songs. I feel that this was a great experience for me, as well as the other members. I was proud to know that I could use my imagination and feelings to create music other than what was written.

Creativity to me means being free to express yourself in a way that is unique to you, not having to conform to certain rules and guidelines. Music is only one of the many areas in which people are given opportunities to show their creativity. Sculpting, carving, building, art, and acting are just a few more areas where people can show their creativity.

Through my music I conveyed feelings and thoughts which were important to me. Music was my means of showing creativity. In whatever form creativity takes, whether it be music, art, or science, it is an important aspect of our lives because it enables us to be individuals.

ESSAY B

Throughout my life, I have been interested and intrigued by music. My mother has often told me of the times, before I went to school, when I would "conduct" the orchestra on her records. I continued to listen to music and eventually started to play the guitar and the clarinet. Finally, at about the age of twelve, I started to sit down and to try to write songs. Even though my instrumental skills were far from my own high standards, I would spend much of my spare time during the day with a guitar around my neck, trying to produce a piece of music.

Each of these sessions, as I remember them, had a rather set format. I would sit in my bedroom, strumming different combinations of the five or six chords I could play, until I heard a series which sounded particularly good to me. After this, I set the music to a suitable rhythm (usually dependent on my mood at the time), and ran through the tune until I could play it fairly easily. Only after this section was complete did I go on to writing lyrics, which generally followed along the lines of the current popular songs on the radio.

At the time of the writing, I felt that my songs were, in themselves, an original creation of my own; that is, I, alone, made them. However, I now see that, in this sense of the word, I was not creative. The songs themselves seem to be an oversimplified form of the music I listened to at the time.

In a more fitting sense, however, I *was* being creative. Since I did not purposely copy my favorite songs, I was, effectively, originating my songs from my own "process of creativity." To achieve my goal, I needed what a composer would call "inspiration" for my piece. In this case the inspiration was the current hit on the radio. Perhaps, with my present point of view, I feel that I used too much "inspiration" in my songs, but, at the time, I did not.

Creativity, therefore, is a process which, in my case, involved a certain series of "small creations" if you like. As well, it is something the appreciation of which varies with one's point of view, that point of view being set by the person's experience, tastes, and his own personal view of creativity. The less experienced tend to allow for less originality, while the more experienced demand real originality to classify something a "creation." Either way, a term as abstract as this is perfectly correct, and open to interpretation.

Working as a whole class or in small groups, analyze the differences between Essay A and Essay B. What might cause college professors to rate one essay higher than the other? What would the writer of the weaker essay have to do to produce an essay more like the stronger?

WRITING PROJECT

Choose a question, problem, or issue that genuinely perplexes you. At the beginning of your exploratory essay, explain why you are interested in this chosen problem and why you have been unable to reach a satisfactory answer. Then write a first-person, chronologically organized, narrative account of your thinking process as you investigate your question through research, talking with others, and doing your own reflective thinking. Your research might involve reading articles or other sources assigned by your instructor, doing your own library or Internet research, or doing field research through interviews and observations. As you reflect on your research, you can also draw on your own memories and experiences. Your goal is to examine your question, problem, or issue from a variety of perspectives, assessing the strengths and weaknesses of different positions and points of view. By the end of your essay, you may or may not have reached a satisfactory solution to your problem. You will be rewarded for the quality of your exploration and thinking processes. In other words, your goal is not to answer your question but to report on the process of wrestling with it.

This assignment asks you to dwell on a problem—and not necessarily to solve that problem. Your problem may shift and evolve as your thinking progresses. What matters is that you are actively engaged with your problem and demonstrate why it is problematic.

Your instructor may choose to combine this writing project with a subsequent one (for example, a research paper based on one of the assignments in the remaining chapters in Part Two) to create a sustained project in which you write two pieces on the same topic. If so, then the essay for this chapter will prepare you to write a later analytical or persuasive piece. Check with your instructor to make sure that your chosen question for this project will work for the later assignment.

Understanding Exploratory Writing

See the discussion of aims in Table 3.1, pp. 49–50.

As we have explained, this assignment calls for an essay with an *exploratory aim*. Exploratory writing generally has an open-form structure. The writer does not assert a thesis and forecast a structure in the introduction (typical features of closed-form prose) because the writer's purpose is to present the process of exploration itself—to write *thesis-seeking* rather than *thesis-supporting* prose. Instead of following a closed-form, points-first structure, the essay narrates chronologically the process of the author's thinking about the problem.

The Essence of Exploratory Prose:
Considering Multiple Solutions

The essential move of an exploratory essay is to consider multiple solutions to a problem or multiple points of view on an issue. The writer defines a problem, poses a possible solution, explores its strengths and weaknesses, and then *moves* on to consider another possible solution.

To show a mind at work examining multiple solutions, let's return to the two student essays you examined in the previous exploratory activity (p. 192). The fundamental difference between Essay A and Essay B is that the writer of Essay B treats the concept of "creativity" as a true problem. Note that the writer of Essay A is satisfied with his or her initial definition:

> Creativity to me means being free to express yourself in a way that is unique to you, not having to conform to certain rules and guidelines.

The writer of Essay B, however, is *not* satisfied with his or her first answer and uses the essay to think through the problem. This writer remembers an early creative experience—composing songs as a twelve-year-old:

> At the time of the writing, I felt that my songs were, in themselves, an original creation of my own; that is, I, alone, made them. However, I now see that, in this sense of the word, I was not creative. The songs themselves seem to be an oversimplified form of the music I listened to at the time.

This writer distinguishes between two points of view: "On the one hand, I used to think *x*, but now, in retrospect, I think *y*." This move forces the writer to go beyond the initial answer to think of alternatives.

The key to effective exploratory writing is to create a tension between alternative views. When you start out, you might not know where your thinking process will end up; at the outset you might not have formulated an opposing, countering, or alternative view. Using a statement such as "I used to think . . . , but now I think" or "Part of me thinks this . . . , but another part thinks that . . . " forces you to find something additional to say; writing then becomes a process of inquiry and discovery.

The second writer's dissatisfaction with the initial answer initiates a dialectic process that plays one idea against another, creating a generative tension. In contrast, the writer of Essay A offers no alternative to his or her definition of creativity. This writer presents no specific illustrations of creative activity (such as the specific details in Essay B about strumming the guitar) but presents merely space-filling abstractions ("Sculpting, carving, building, art, and acting are just a few more areas where people can show their creativity"). The writer of Essay B scores a higher grade, not because the essay creates a brilliant (or even particularly clear) explanation of creativity; rather, the writer is rewarded for thinking about the problem dialectically.

We use the term *dialectic* to mean a thinking process often associated with the German philosopher Hegel, who said that each thesis ("My act was creative") gives rise to an antithesis ("My act was not creative") and that the clash of these opposing perspectives leads thinkers to develop a synthesis that incorporates some features of both theses ("My act was a series of 'small creations' "). You initiate dialectic thinking any time you play Elbow's believing and doubting game or use other strategies to place alternative possibilities side by side.

See Chapter 2, pp. 42–46, for an explanation of the believing and doubting game.

Essay B's writer uses a dialectic thinking strategy that we might characterize as follows:

1. Regards the assignment as a genuine problem worth puzzling over.
2. Considers alternative views and plays them off against each other.
3. Looks at specifics.
4. Continues the thinking process in search of some sort of resolution or synthesis of the alternative views.
5. Incorporates the stages of this dialectic process into the essay.

For Writing and Discussion

1. According to writing theorist David Bartholomae, who analyzed several hundred student essays in response to the placement examination question on page 192, almost all the highest scoring essays exhibited a similar kind of dialectic thinking. How might the writer of the first essay expand the essay by using the dialectic thinking processes just described?
2. Working individually, read each of the following questions and write out your initial opinion or one or two answers that come immediately to mind.

   - Given the easy availability of birth control information and the ready availability of condoms, why do you think there are so many teenage pregnancies?
   - Why do U.S. students, on average, lag so far behind their European and Asian counterparts in scholastic achievement?
   - Should women be assigned to combat roles in the military?
   - The most popular magazines sold on college campuses around the country are women's fashion and lifestyle magazines such as *Glamour, Seventeen*, and *Cosmopolitan*. Why are these magazines being so popular? Is there a problem with these magazines being so popular? (Two separate questions, both of which are worth exploring dialectically.)

3. Choose one of the preceding questions or one assigned by your instructor and freewrite for five or ten minutes using one or more of the following to stimulate dialectic thinking:
   I used to think _____, but now I think _____.
   Part of me thinks _____, but another part of me thinks _____.
   On some days I think _____, but on other days I think _____.

The first answers that come to mind are _____, but as I think further I see _____.

My classmate thinks _____, but I think _____.

Your goal here is to explore potential weaknesses or inadequacies in your first answers, and then to push beyond them to think of new or different answers. Feel free to be wild and risky in posing possible alternative solutions.

4. As a whole class, take a poll to find out what the most common first-response answers are for each of the questions. Then share alternative solutions generated by class members during the freewriting. The goal is to pose and explore answers that go beyond or against the grain of the common answers. Remember, there is little point in arguing for an answer that everyone else already accepts.

READINGS

In this section we include two student essays that illustrate writing with an exploratory purpose. In the first essay, student writer Christopher Leigh explores the problem of preventing school violence. You read about Christopher's early exploration of this problem in Chapter 1. By the end of his first-year writing course, he had developed his ideas into a researched argument opposing metal detectors in the schools. Christopher's argument against metal detectors is our sample student research paper in Chapter 22.

Christopher's early journal entry is shown on p. 9. His researched argument is on pp. 675–686.

Christopher Leigh (student)
An Exploration of How to Prevent Violence in Schools

1   The April 20, 1999, shootings at Columbine High School in Littleton, Colorado, left me, as well as people across America, in a state of shock and disbelief. The terrifying incidents made my friends and me wonder what had driven the two high school students to commit such a horrible crime. Most of all, we wanted to know what was being done to prevent incidents like this from happening again.

2   For the exploratory paper I knew I wanted to write on some aspect of school violence, such as what causes it or what can be done to prevent it, and I decided to focus on the ways that schools are working to prevent violence.

3   While I was searching through newspaper articles on Lexis-Nexis Academic Universe, I discovered a <u>New York Times</u> article by Timothy Egan that captured my interest. The article deals with the practice of profiling in high schools to identify potentially violent students. The profiles contain a list of behaviors and warning signs that may indicate that a student is

troubled and prone to violence. Egan quotes former President Clinton, who said, "We must all do more to recognize and look for the early warning signals that deeply troubled young people send often before they explode into violence" (1). Within days, Egan writes, national organizations had distributed lists of characteristics, which included signs such as mood swings, drug/alcohol use, and fondness for violent television. I noted in my journal that the problem with these checklists is that they describe almost every person at some point in adolescence. However, I could also see why kids who fit the profiles for many of the traits should be closely watched; any adolescent who is often depressed and uses drugs or alcohol is likely to be troubled. But a kid could be depressed, troubled, and abusive of drugs or alcohol and yet pose no threat. Would being labeled as "potentially violent" only further alienate or anger the student?

4   The article really made me question how I felt about profiling. On the one hand, I believe that profiling in any form is wrong and defies the very principles upon which our country is built. Just as racial profiling singles out innocent people based on the color of their skin, profiling in schools targets those who do not fit social norms of acceptable behavior. On the other hand, I agree that violence in schools is a problem that needs to be addressed, and preventive measures that may help should be thoroughly considered.

5   After reading this article, I began to think about various issues surrounding profiling, such as whether profiling is effective and whether it violates students' rights. I decided to search for articles that specifically addressed these issues.

6   Unfortunately, after much searching I couldn't find any articles addressing whether or not profiling is effective, nor could I find any discussion of whether it violates civil rights. However, using Ebscohost I found an article in US News and World Report that raises another important issue related to profiling. Its author, Mary Lord, shows that many schools use profiling to identify kids who need counseling, but that fewer than ten percent of schools have mental health professionals available to deal with the kids once they have been identified (57). Lord also describes a student who was arrested for writing an essay about blowing up the school but then rebuilding it to make it state of the art (55). At this point I began to see more clearly why the issue of profiling is problematic. The student described in Lord's article had no intention of causing any harm, but his careless use of words in his essay resulted in an arrest and suspension, which was later rescinded when the school acknowledged its wrongdoing. The student then noted that he avoids writing essays and speaks less often in class as a result of the incident (Lord 55). I can understand that schools have good intentions—to prevent violence by providing troubled kids with counseling—but in this case, the school did not provide counseling and instead suspended him. Furthermore, if most schools do not have the resources to provide counseling, it seems pointless to try to identify potentially violent students.

7   Lord's article referred to an FBI report dealing with prevention of school violence, so I wanted to find out more about it. I found a newspaper article by David Vise and Kenneth Cooper, who write that the FBI report advises schools not to use profiling to identify potentially violent students because actual incidents of school violence are so rare. Instead, they write, the report calls for the use of profiling only when some threat of violence has already occurred (Vise and Cooper A3). I was relieved to learn that the FBI is opposed to the general use of profiling. The article by Mary Lord that I had read earlier had given me the false impression that the FBI report supported profiling, but now I see that the FBI supports profiling only in the case of an actual threat. Nevertheless, many schools still misuse the profiles.

8   I decided that I shouldn't use any more magazines or newspapers due to their potential bias and omission of important information. I next went to find the full FBI report on school violence. The report, published by the FBI Academy's National Center for the Analysis of Violent Crime, can be found on the agency's Web site and can be read in its original format using Acrobat Reader. The report is written by Mary O'Toole, PhD, who headed the investigation. She proposes that schools set up a system of professionals who can be called in to assess threats and determine their severity and risk (United States 5). I found the report impressively comprehensive, even though it does not explain how schools should go about setting up a threat-assessment program. Although the report repeatedly warns schools not to use profiles alone, it still lists pages of characteristics of potentially violent kids, which seemed to me to be an invitation to misuse the report. The way I see it, school administrators will read the report, recognize the complexity of the proposal, and simply take the easiest course of action, which is to remove the profiles from context and use them on their own.

9   One aspect of O'Toole's report really struck me. She shows how the media misrepresent school violence by treating it as a widespread, frequent phenomenon and by portraying school shooters in a stereotypical way (United States 4). I have always felt strongly about the negative power of mass media, so I decided to investigate this lead. I found a brief article in Professional School Counseling entitled "Unsafe Schools: Perception or Reality?" The article's author, Tony Del Prete, writes that people tend to "overanalyze and sensationalize [incidents] to the point of hysteria" (375). He observes that the media inaccurately portray violence as a plague in American society, when in actuality school violence has steadily declined since 1993. After reading this article, I concluded that the media devote so much coverage to incidents such as the one at Columbine High that the public adopts an it-could-happen-to-anyone view of school violence. This attitude creates a panicked need to find a simplistic and crude solution, such as profiling or installing metal detectors in schools where there are no previous incidents of violence.

10   Despite my discovery that the frequency of school violence has been exaggerated, I believe that violence is a real problem, and methods of prevention

should be implemented to maintain safe schools. Del Prete concludes his article by suggesting that the best approach is to create a more friendly community atmosphere in schools by eliminating harassment and reducing competition. Even though it too seems like a simplistic solution, I feel that making schools friendlier and educating teens about the harmful effects of a hostile environment are keys to improving the state of our schools.

11   I then began to think about how other forms of preventing school violence, such as metal detectors, might have a negative impact on the school environment. Metal detectors are a popular form of violence prevention, yet their increasing presence in schools is troubling. I began searching the Web to find out more about metal detectors. One article, entitled "Districts Should Proceed Cautiously on Metal Detectors," from the New York State School Board's Web site, points out that most schools equipped with the devices cannot check every student due to the large numbers of people arriving at once, so it is practically impossible to ensure that weapons do not enter school buildings. The article also notes that metal detectors do not address the nature of the problem of violence, and that schools should be more concerned with "creating a climate that teaches peaceful resolution" ("Districts"). However, a poll conducted by Charlotte.com, a North Carolina newspaper-affiliated Web site, showed that eighty-one percent of local residents approved of metal detectors in schools (Ly and Toosi). Despite the public demand for metal detectors in schools, I feel that they might actually have a negative effect in reducing school violence because they make schools seem like prisons and damage the feeling of community. At this point I was becoming more and more convinced that the best way to reduce violence is to make schools more friendly and less hostile.

12   I decided to try to find one more article about ways to make schools less hostile environments. I went back to the educational journals and found an article by Scott Poland, whose name appeared in many of the other sources I found. The author, who is the president of the National Association of School Psychologists, also calls for an effort to personalize our schools and hire more professionals to help counsel kids who may be troubled (45). He writes that most counselors are already overworked and are required to do things such as scheduling that take away from their attention to the students. Poland also emphasizes that it is important for teachers to form strong relationships with their students. He suggests that teachers set aside a small amount of time each day to interact with students, and he discourages schools from cutting extracurricular programs that may help students feel connected to the school (46). From my point of view, Poland's article offers the most encouraging and perhaps the most promising solution to prevent school violence. Yet Poland's solution can't be done cheaply. I remembered an article that I had scanned briefly earlier in my research process, and I decided to return to it for a closer look. This

article, "America Skips School," explains that until Americans recognize the importance of education by paying teachers higher salaries, public schools will continue to become less and less effective (Barber 45). My research on preventing violence in schools has shown me that now we have another big reason to invest more in public education. If teachers can and should play a significant role in creating a positive school community, then they should be compensated for this additional responsibility. After all, if teachers don't know the first thing about their students, there is no way they are going to be able to know who is in need of help and who is not. By developing relationships with students on a personal level, teachers will be able to sense when a student is in trouble and can take steps to reach out to that student. The need for more counselors is also crucial to provide students with help if a teacher thinks it is necessary.

13   I believe that this exploratory paper has helped me clarify my own thinking about school violence. I am now convinced that the media have instigated a panic about school violence, leading in many cases to counterproductive approaches like psychological profiling and metal detectors. When it comes time to write my major argument paper, I plan to show that these approaches only increase students' sense of alienation and hostility. The most important approach is to make schools more friendly, communal, and personal. We must ensure that troubled students are provided with the help they need, rather than treating them like criminals.

Works Cited

Barber, Benjamin. "America Skips School." <u>Harper's</u> Nov. 1993: 39–46.

Del Prete, Tony. "Unsafe Schools: Perception or Reality?" <u>Professional School Counseling</u> 3 (2000): 375–76.

"Districts Should Proceed Cautiously on Metal Detectors." <u>New York State School Boards Association</u>. 22 May 2000. 16 Aug. 2001 <http://www.nyssba.org/adnews/ employee/employee052200.3.html>.

Egan, Timothy. "The Trouble with Looking for Signs of Trouble." <u>New York Times</u> 25 Apr. 1999, sec. 4: 1.

Lord, Mary. "The Violent Kid Profile: A Controversial New Technique for Beating Violence in Schools." <u>US News & World Report</u> 11 Oct. 1999: 56–57.

Ly, Phuong, and Nahal Toosi. "Many Favor Metal Detectors." <u>Charlotte Observer</u>. 19 Nov. 2000. 16 Aug. 2001 <http://www.charlotte.com/observer/special/poll98/ 0804metal.htm>.

Poland, Scott. "The Fourth R—Relationships." <u>American School Board Journal</u> 187.3 (2000): 45–46.

United States. Dept. of Justice. Fed. Bureau of Investigation. <u>The School Shooter: A Threat Assessment Perspective</u>. By Mary O'Toole. 2000. 16 Aug. 2001 <http:// www.fbi.gov/publications/school/school2.pdf>.

Vise, David, and Kenneth Cooper. "FBI Opposes the Use of Profiling of Students." <u>Washington Post</u> 7 Sept. 2000: A3.

Thinking Critically about "An Exploration of How to Prevent Violence in Schools"

1. Exploratory papers usually narrate both the evolution of the writer's thinking and the physical actions the writer takes to do the actual research. In Christopher's case, approximately what percentage of the total paper focuses on Christopher's research processes and what percentage on ideas? When he switches from a summary of a research source to his own thinking or from his own thinking to a description of his next action, how does he write transitions that keep the reader from getting lost?

2. Trace the evolution of Christopher's ideas in this paper. Does his thinking evolve in an ordered and understandable way, or does it seem random and directionless? Explain your reasoning.

3. Read Christopher's argument against metal detectors in the schools on pages 675–686. What connections do you see between his final argument and his earlier exploratory paper? What new research did he do for his final argument? What material from his exploratory paper is omitted from the final argument? In your own words, how does the difference in purpose (exploration versus persuasion) lead to different structures for the two papers?

4. What do you see as the chief strengths and weaknesses of Christopher's exploration of how to prevent school violence?

In this next essay, also written for the assignment in this chapter, student writer Dylan Fujitani explores U.S. use of private contractors taking on military roles in the Iraq war. His interest in this topic was sparked by newspaper accounts of an incident occurring in spring 2004 (see his opening paragraph). Dylan's initial research, chronicled in this exploratory paper, eventually grew into the proposal argument that appears in Chapter 16, pages 494–499.

Dylan Fujitani (student)
Hired Guns: Uncovering the Nature of Private Militaries in the Iraq War

1   It was around March 31st, I believe, that the front page of the New York Times featured an enormous picture of mutilated corpses hanging from a bridge in Falluja. Upon seeing the images of the charred, limbless men, I was utterly shocked at the event's grotesqueness, but I was not surprised that this war had produced such a grisly scene. But what surprised me is that these corpses were not American soldiers but civilians working in Iraq. The newspaper reported that they were "civilian contractors." So I was initially under the impression that those four civilians, charred and strung up by an angry mob, were probably in Iraq transporting water, building antenna tow-

ers, or otherwise assisting reconstruction. I learned that one of the four was even from Hawaii, my home state, and that there was an outpouring of sympathy for his family. An horrific end for anyone, this revolting treatment of civilians seemed particularly tragic, and my heart went out to their families as well. How could this mob make no distinction between military and non-military personnel?

2   Then a few days later I read an article—I can't remember from where—that these contractors worked for a private security company in Iraq and were armed to the teeth. Then a thought came to my mind: *These men were mercenaries.* Having previously prided myself on being up-to-date with current events, I was dumbfounded at the thought that until that moment I had no knowledge of mercenaries being used in contemporary American warfare. Immediately, I wanted to know more about the issue and questions began to arise. Who are these contractors? How have governments legitimized their use? What are the advantages and disadvantages of using them? And most importantly, what are they allowed to do? After a discussion with my instructor about possible topics for my major research project, I decided to explore the issue of mercenaries. By this point, the Abu Ghraib prison abuse scandal had arisen, and there was talk of private contractor involvement. It occurred to me that this heretofore little discussed issue had the potential to become highly controversial. I decided to pose the following research question: Is the use of private contractors in military roles a good idea?

3   When I first started my research, I had very negative feelings about the use of mercenaries. However, my first Google search led me to an article from the Pittsburgh Post-Gazette titled, "In Iraq, Private Contractors Lighten Load on U.S. Troops." The article's author, Borzou Daragahi, presented arguments in favor of the use of private contractors: "At a time when the overstretched U.S. military is struggling to convince other nations to send troops to help secure Iraq, the private military contractors can relieve some of the pressure on American forces." I realized that indeed if our military is lacking in numbers and our military actions lack broad-based international support, the use of private military companies can help to alleviate the burden. The alternative would be to revive the draft in order to fill the military's thin ranks, a politically volatile issue. I had not yet fully developed my viewpoint on the draft, but this article certainly convinced me that more thought was necessary.

4   The same article raised another issue, however, that shows why this topic has explosive potential. Daragahi reveals how the use of private contractors disguises the war's cost to the American public because the number of American troops is kept deceptively low. Quoting a private military company security consultant, Daragahi writes, "If you're going to keep the number of troops down, this is the way to do it. The expense is the same or more. But politically, it's much less expensive." I found the consultant's casual acknowledgement of the benefits of misleading the American public disturbing. Clearly, to a mercenary, war is simply work.

5   Continuing my initial online research, I next read an article from the online magazine <u>Slate</u> entitled, "How to Discipline Private Contractors" that referred specifically to the prison abuse scandal at Abu Ghraib. In this article, former U.S. Army officer Phillip Carter argues that there are multiple ways to discipline private contractors in the event of their misbehavior. The disciplinary measures can include the termination of their contract, restriction from bidding for future contracts, criminal prosecution, and civil suits. While it was comforting to know that private contractors are not *completely* immune from punishment, I was concerned that the main form of punishment was *financial*. At this point, it occurred to me that in light of the unfolding prison abuse scandal, I have little faith in punishment that has only a financial effect. The seriousness of the situation at Abu Ghraib calls for punishment that no quantity of money could substitute for. I believe that the threat of money loss would not be an effective deterrent for crimes that would result in a court-martial and jail time for military personnel. Carter's piece left me suspicious of the level of discipline among private contractors. It seems that the penalties are, according to Carter, "at the discretion of the agency that issued the original contract," in this case the U.S. army. Civil suits provide an avenue for punishing non-military personnel, but according to Carter they are hard to pursue. Carter explains that a civil suit against government contractors in 1988 failed due to "the 'government contractor' defense, which shields government contractors from liability when they build something or provide services in accordance with governmental specifications." Although Carter appears to defend the notion that contractors can be punished, I fear that this government contractor defense will prevent meaningful discipline of private contractors and that the existing forms of punishment are inadequate.

6   At this point in my research, my curiosity about the history of private contractors was growing, so I looked for articles that were slightly older and not so heavily influenced by the war or prison scandal. I found one from <u>Washingtonpost.com</u> titled, "Thousands of Private Contractors Support U.S. Forces in Persian Gulf." It was written on March 3, 2003, during the troop buildup preceding the Iraq war. <u>Washington Post</u> staff writer Kenneth Bredemeier interviewed P. W. Singer of the Brookings Institution in Washington, who has studied the growth of private contractors in war zones. Singer attributed the growth of private contractors primarily to "the heightened reliance on civilian technology adapted for military use." Although I had initially opposed all forms of military private contractors, this article introduced a different perspective. Singer suggested that the use of private contractors was necessary because of the need for their specialized skills that the military did not teach: "The military would not be able to function without these people there. Everywhere U.S. forces are deployed, there's a contractor helping them out." I had not previously considered that the military might actually *need* these private contractors.

7   Upon reading Singer's commentary, I found myself wanting to develop more specific definitions for the types of contractors that I was looking into because there seemed to be a large degree of occupational variation. I needed to distinguish between the armed gunman of the type mutilated at Falluja and the contractors with specialized technical skills that the army needs. The recent events of the prison abuse drew most of my attention to the contractors in combat roles, but Singer revealed that the realities of warfare might necessitate civilians filling technical roles. While I do not take issue with contracting work where special skills are needed by the military, I am uncomfortable with the thought of contractors actually replacing soldiers in military roles such as guarding convoys, defending a building, or interrogating a prisoner—roles that may be dangerous to leave outside the system of military control and military justice.

8   I now felt I needed to know more about how these private security forces operate, why they are legal, and how they became such a large presence in Iraq. I decided to go to the library to use some of the licensed databases we learned about in our class's library session. Using Lexis-Nexis, I found a substantial New York Times article that responded to my questions. David Barstow, the author of this article, explained that prior to the Iraq war, there were relatively few private contractors and that people in the business often knew each other from previous jobs. With the recent upsurge in demand for security companies, however, firms are having trouble finding enough qualified people. According to Barstow, many of the contractors hired have questionable backgrounds and often do not come from the contractor's country of origin. I wondered to what extent such people would be patriotic and loyal to the United States. For example, Barstow explains that four guards working for the same subcontractor had been members of "apartheid-era security forces in South Africa" who had admitted to crimes. In addition, Barstow said that government authorities often have no oversight over who is being hired and paid for with U.S. tax dollars. These facts disturbed me. If the government is not in complete control over who is being paid by taxpayer money, the American people could be effectively funding former or future war criminals.

9   Using another licensed database, Academic Search Premier, I found two articles from the New Republic, a politically centrist publication, that deepened my concerns about using contractors. According to the 2003 article "Insecure," by Joshua Hammer, a wealthy homeowner in Baghdad pays eighteen Kurdish warriors $200 per month to guard his house—"a bargain compared with the going rate for Western companies: $1500 per guard per day" (15). Hammer states that there are at least twenty Western security companies actively working for corporations such as Halliburton and that they hire "tough-looking men" (15) from all over the world including Nepalese Gurkhas, former British SAS commandos, and retired American military personnel. Hammer's article suggested to me that using contractors is another example of the global trend of outsourcing. A second article, also

by Joshua Hammer, actually uses the term "mercenary" in talking about the contractors currently in Iraq and suggests the blurring of lines between offensive and defensive roles. This article quotes a security consultant:

> . . . most of the contractors are the hardest of the hard core—veterans of such elite outfits as the U.S. Special Forces; the Rhodesian Selous Scouts, the former special forces of the Rhodesian white regime; and Executive Outcomes, the now-disbanded South African mercenary army that fought in Sierra Leone and Angola. These men thrive on the danger of working in war zones."
> (Hammer, "Cowboy Up" 2)

It seems to me that many of these mercenary contractors search the world for armed conflicts because that's where the money is, making a living off a lifestyle of war.

10   These last articles left me thinking that allowing such a large group of people to earn enormous sums of money doing violent work while being legally unaccountable is creating huge interest groups that will *want* war in the long run. Unlike the big defense contractor companies such as Lockheed Martin and Boeing, the private security personnel have no way to support themselves when there is no war going on; peacetime will become a period of unemployment. Furthermore, because not all private contractors come from the same country, it also dawned on me that we are creating *international* interest groups that will want war.

11   After gaining a better sense of the kinds of people hired to do contracting work in Iraq, I find myself disapproving of the use of private military companies and mercenaries as a whole. This is pretty much where I stand now, against the use of "civilians" in military roles who have an interest in war and remain completely anonymous to the people who pay their salaries. I am repulsed that we outsource our combat roles to people with questionable histories who remain outside of the military justice system as a way of avoiding the political consequences of sending real troops. The American people, however, are still shouldering the financial burden without tangible information about the practices their money funds. While my research has given me a better sense of the justifications for the use of private contractors, I have come to oppose the practice because of the nature of the business and the loopholes involved. I am almost certain I will argue against their use in my final argument, but I still have a lot more thinking and research to do.

Works Cited

Barstow, David. "Security Companies: Shadow Soldiers in Iraq." <u>New York Times</u> 19 Apr. 2004: A1+. <u>Lexis-Nexis</u>. Lemieux Lib., Seattle U. 19 May 2004 <http://search.epnet.com>.

Bredemeier, Kenneth. "Thousands of Private Contractors Support U.S. Forces in Persian Gulf." <u>Washington Post</u> 3 Mar. 2003: E01. 19 May 2004 <http://www.washingtonpost.com>.

Carter, Phillip. "How to Discipline Private Contractors." Slate 4 May 2004. 19 May 2004 <http://slate.msn.com/id/2099954>.

Daragahi, Borzou. "In Iraq, Private Contractors Lighten Load on U.S. Troops." Post-gazette.com 28 Sept. 2003. 19 May 2004 <http://www.post-gazette.com/pg/pp/03271/226368.stm>.

Hammer, Joshua. "Cowboy Up." New Republic 24 May 2004: 18–19. Academic Search Premier. EBSCO. Lemieux Lib., Seattle U. 23 May 2004 <http://www.epnet.com>.

—. "Insecure." New Republic 1 and 8 Dec. 2003: 14–15. Academic Search Premier. EBSCO. Lemieux Lib., Seattle U. 19 May 2004 <http://www.epnet.com>.

Thinking Critically about "Hired Guns: Uncovering the Nature of Private Militaries in the Iraq War"

1. How does Dylan Fujitani establish the complexity and significance of his question?

2. Where does Dylan's essay exhibit dialectic thinking? What alternative views or different perspectives on contractors does he investigate?

3. Unlike an essay written to argue a thesis and persuade an audience, an exploratory essay must show the writer's intellectual journey, unfolding the writer's thoughts and insights about the question as the essay moves along. How does Dylan's wrestling with his research problem structure this essay? What transitions guide readers through this exploration?

4. In the conclusion to this essay, what synthesis or resolution does Dylan reach?

5. What do you see as the particular challenges of Dylan's question for himself and for his audience? How does he handle these challenges? What are the main strengths and weaknesses of this essay?

For Writing and Discussion

As we have shown in this chapter, seeking out alternative views and perspectives is essential to writing an exploratory essay. In this exercise, we ask you to imagine two contrasting perspectives on soldiering by comparing the values of private military contractors, as portrayed in Dylan Fujitani's exploratory essay, with the values of service in today's volunteer Army as portrayed in Army recruitment messages. Please study carefully the following visual/verbal texts:

(continued)

- The Army recruitment ad on page 95
- The "About the Army" overview page on the Army's recruitment Web site goarmy.com (Figure 8.1)

Working individually or in groups, develop responses to the following questions:

1. What image of the United States Army do these recruitment messages project? What values does the Army appeal to in these messages? How do the photos and text convey these images and values?

2. Based on Dylan's explanation of contractors and the view of the army presented in these recruitment messages, how would you say a career as a private contractor differs from a career in the Army? What motivation might cause someone to become a private military contractor? (You might try imagining a recruitment poster developed by a private contracting firm appealing to the potential commandos described in Dylan's paper—where "war is simply work" and where many contractors have "questionable backgrounds.") What motivation might cause one to join the volunteer Army? (If you want to investigate this question in more depth, you might examine the various links on the goarmy.com Web site, including the "For Parents" link, the "Careers & Jobs" link, or the links devoted to military bands, Army NASCAR racing, marksmanship competitions, or the touring "Yo Soy El Army Custom H2," which is "one tricked out vehicle.")

3. When the all-volunteer Army replaced the draft, it was imperative that many jobs formerly filled by soldiers be filled by civilian contractors. By the end of his exploratory essay, Dylan has decided that using civilian contractors in actual combat roles is bad practice (see Dylan's subsequent proposal argument in Chapter 16 where he argues against the use of these contractors—pp. 494–499). For you, to what extent do these Army recruitment messages confirm, contradict, or in some other way complicate Dylan's view of using private contractors?

4. What further questions about both the United States Army and private contractors do these recruitment messages for the Army inspire? (You might return to this question after reading the beginning pages of Sam's exploratory paper on women in combat, pp. 214–215.)

5. In paragraph 10 of his essay, Dylan mentions "big defense contractors" such as Lockheed Martin and Boeing. On page 505, you will find a corporate advertisement for Lockheed Martin. Although this advertisement focuses on the company's role in the exploration of space, the Lockheed Martin Web site (www.lockheedmartin.com) indicates that its main customer is the Department of Defense and that its main products are tactical aircraft, missiles, computerized guidance systems, government satellites, and high technology weapons. What ideas might this ad contribute to the view of military contractors that Dylan Fujitani explores in his essay?

FIGURE 8.1

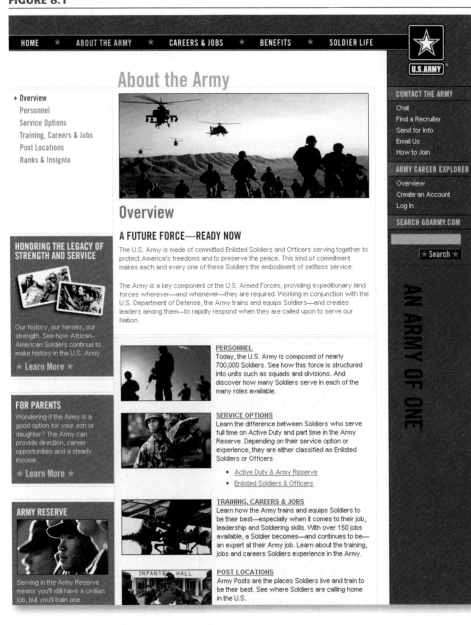

Composing Your Exploratory Essay

Generating and Exploring Ideas

Your process of generating and exploring ideas is, in essence, the *subject matter* of your exploratory paper. This section helps you get started and keep going.

Keeping a Research Log

Since this assignment asks you to create a chronologically organized account of your thinking process, you need to keep a careful, detailed record of your investigation. The best tool for doing so is a research log or journal in which you take notes on your sources and record your thinking throughout the process.

As you investigate your issue, keep a chronologically organized account that includes notes on your readings, interviews, and significant conversations, as well as explorations of how each of these sources, new perspectives, or data influence your current thinking. Many writers keep a double-entry notebook that has a "notes" section in which to summarize key points, record data, copy potentially usable quotations verbatim, and so forth and a "reflections" section in which to write a strong response to each reading, exploring how it advanced your thinking, raised questions, or pulled you in one direction or another.

For an example of double-entry notes, see "Sam's Research Log Entry on *Newsweek* Article" on pp. 212–213.

As you write your exploratory essay, your research log will be your main source for details—evidence of what you were thinking at regular intervals throughout the process.*

Exploring Possible Problems for Your Essay

Your instructor may assign a specific problem to explore. If not, then your first step is to choose a question, problem, or issue that currently perplexes you. Perhaps a question is problematic to you because you haven't studied it (How serious is the problem of global warming? How can we keep pornography on the Internet away from children?) or because the available factual data seem conflicting and inconclusive (Should postmenopausal women take supplemental estrogen?) or because the problem or issue draws you into an uncomfortable conflict of values (Should we legalize drugs? Should the homeless mentally ill be placed involuntarily in state mental hospitals?).

The key to this assignment is to choose a question, problem, or issue *that truly perplexes you*. The more clearly readers sense your personal engagement with the problem, the more likely they are to be engaged by your writing. Note: If your instructor pairs this assignment with a later one, be sure that your question is appropriate for the later assignment. Check with your instructor.

Here are several exercises to help you think of ideas for this essay:

To show how a question is problematic and significant, see Chapter 1, pp. 24–25.

Exploration Exercise 1.   In your research log, make a list of issues or problems that both interest and perplex you. Then choose two or three of your issues and freewrite about them for five minutes or so, exploring questions such as these: Why am I interested in this problem? What makes the problem problematic? What makes this problem significant? Share your list of questions and your

*For those of you majoring in science or engineering, this research log is similar to the laboratory notebooks that are required parts of any original research in science or industry. Besides recording in detail the progress of your research, these notebooks often serve as crucial data in patent applications or liability lawsuits. Doctors and nurses keep similar logs in their medical records file for each patient. This is a time-honored practice. In Mary Shelley's early-nineteenth-century novel *Frankenstein*, the monster learns about the process of his creation by reading Dr. Frankenstein's laboratory journal.

freewrites with friends and classmates. Discussing questions with friends often stimulates you to think of more questions yourself or to sharpen the focus of questions you have already asked.

Exploration Exercise 2. If your exploratory essay is paired with a subsequent assignment, look at the invention exercises for that assignment to help you ask a question that fits the context of the final paper you will write.

Exploration Exercise 3. A particularly valuable kind of problem to explore for this assignment is a public controversy. Often such issues involve complex disagreements about facts and values that merit careful, open-ended exploration. This assignment invites you to explore and clarify where you stand on such complex public issues as gay marriages, overcrowded prisons, the USA Patriot Act, racial profiling, the electoral college, Internet censorship and privacy issues, and so forth. These issues make particularly good topics for persuasive papers or formal research papers, if either is required in your course. For this exercise, look through a current newspaper or weekly newsmagazine, and in your research log make a list of public issues that you would like to know more about. Use the following trigger question:

> I don't know where I stand on the issue of _____.

Share your list with classmates and friends.

Formulating a Starting Point

After you've chosen a problem or issue, write a research log entry identifying the problem or issue you have chosen and explaining why you are perplexed by and interested in it. You might start out with a sharp, clearly focused question (for example, "Should the United States legalize the medical use of marijuana?"). Often, however, formulating the question turns out to be part of the *process* of writing the exploratory paper. Many writers don't start with a single, focused question but rather with a whole cluster of related questions swimming in their heads. This practice is all right—in fact, it is healthy—as long as you have a direction in which to move after the initial starting point. Even if you do start with a focused question, it is apt to evolve as your thinking progresses.

For this exercise, choose the question, problem, or issue you plan to investigate and write a research log entry explaining how you got interested in that question and why you find it both problematic and significant. This will be the *starting point* for your essay; it might even serve as the rough draft for your introduction. Many instructors will collect this exploration as a quick check on whether you have formulated a good question that promises fruitful results.

Here is how one student, Sam, wrote the starting point entry for his research log:

SAM'S STARTING POINT RESEARCH LOG ENTRY

I want to focus on the question of whether women should be allowed to serve in combat units in the military. I became interested in the issue of women in combat through my interest in gays in the military. While I saw that gays in the military was an important political issue for gay rights, I, like many gays, had no real desire to be in such a macho organization. But perhaps that was just the point—we had the opportunity to break stereotypes and attack areas most hostile to us.

Similarly, I wonder whether feminists see women in combat as a crucial symbolic issue for women's rights. (I wonder too whether it is a *good* symbol, since many women value a less masculine approach to the world.) I think my instinct right now is that women should be allowed to serve in combat units. I think it is wrong to discriminate against women. Yet I also think America needs to have a strong military. Therefore, I am in a quandary. If putting women in combat wouldn't harm our military power, then I am fully in favor of women in combat. But if it would hurt our military power, then I have to make a value judgment. So I guess I have a lot to think about as I research this issue. I decided to focus on the women issue rather than the gay issue because it poses more of a dilemma for me. I am absolutely in favor of gays in the military, so I am not very open-minded about *exploring* that issue. But the women's issue is more of a problem for me.

Continuing with Research and Dialectic Thinking

After you have formulated your starting point, you need to proceed with research, keeping a research log that records both your reading notes and your strong response reflections to each reading.

For instruction on how to use library databases and do research, see Chapters 20–22.

After Sam wrote his starting point entry, he created an initial bibliography by searching one of his college library's licensed databases. He decided to try keeping his research log in a double-entry, notes/reflections format. What follows is his research log entry for the first article he read, a piece from *Newsweek*.*

SAM'S RESEARCH LOG ENTRY ON *NEWSWEEK* ARTICLE

Notes

Hackworth, David H. "War and the Second Sex." *Newsweek* 5 Aug. 1991: 24–28.

- Ideals in conflict are equality and combat readiness.
- Acknowledges women's bravery, competence, and education (uses the Gulf War as an example). Admits that there are some women as strong and fit as the strongest men (gives some examples), but then argues that allowing even these women in combat is the type of experimentation that the army doesn't need right now. (He says women already have plenty of jobs open to them in noncombat units.)
- Biggest problem is "gender norming"—having different physical standards for men and women. A 22-year-old female is allowed three more minutes than a 22-year-old male to run two miles; men have to climb a 20-foot rope in 30 seconds; women can take 50 seconds.
- One of Hackworth's big values is male bonding. He points to "male bonding" as a key to unit cohesion. Men have been socialized to think that women must be protected. He uses Israel as an example:

*Note on dates: The next four pages follow Sam's research process conducted in 1996 during former President Clinton's first term of office when the issues of gays in the military and women in combat were being highly debated. Some of Sam's research data refer to combat evidence gathered during the first Gulf War (Operation Desert Storm, 1991) when U.S. and coalition forces liberated Kuwait from Iraq's occupation under Saddam Hussein.

"The Israeli Army put women on the front lines in 1948. The experiment ended disastrously after only three weeks. It wasn't that the women couldn't fight. It was that they got blown apart. Female casualties demoralized the men and gutted unit cohesion." (pp. 26–27)

- Another major problem is pregnancy causing women to leave a unit. He says that 10 to 15 percent of servicewomen wear maternity uniforms in a given year. During the Gulf War, pregnancy rates soared. 1200 pregnant women were evacuated from the gulf (p. 28) during the war. On one destroyer tender, 36 female crew members got pregnant (p. 28). These pregnancies leave vacancies in a unit that can destroy its effectiveness.
- He claims that women soldiers themselves had so many complaints about their experiences in the Gulf War (fraternization, sexual harassment, lack of privacy, primitive living conditions) that they said "don't rush to judgment on women in combat" (p. 28).

Reflections

Some challenging points, but not completely convincing. His biggest reason for opposing women in combat is harm to unit morale, but this isn't convincing to me. The Israeli example seems like unconvincing evidence seeing how those soldiers' attitudes in 1948 reflected a much different society.

Issue of pregnancy is more convincing. A pregnant woman, unlike a father-to-be, cannot continue to fill her role as a combat soldier. I was shocked by the number of pregnancies during the Gulf War and by the extent (although Hackworth doesn't give statistics) of the fraternization (he says the army passed out over a million condoms—p. 28).

I am also bothered by the gender-norming issue. It seems to me that there ought to be some absolute standards of strength and endurance needed for combat duty and the military ought to exclude both men and women who don't meet them. This would mean that a lower percentage of women than men would be eligible, but is that discrimination?

Where do I now stand? Well, I am still leaning toward believing that women should be allowed to serve in combat, but I see that there are a number of subquestions involved. Should physical standards for combat positions be the same for men and women? Will the presence of women really hurt morale in a mostly male unit? Should women be given special consideration for their roles as mothers? How serious a problem is pregnancy? I also see another problem: Should physically eligible women be *required* (e.g., drafted) to serve in combat the same way men are drafted into combat positions? And I still want to know whether this is a crucial issue for the women's rights movement.

In the next section we see how Sam converts material from his research log into a draft of his exploratory essay.

Shaping and Drafting

Your exploratory essay should offer accounts of your search procedures (useful conversations with friends, strategies for tracking down sources, use of indexes or computer searches, strokes of good fortune at stumbling on good leads, and so forth) and your thought processes (what you were discovering, how your ideas were evolving). Drawing on your research log, you can share your frustration when a promising source turned out to be off the mark or your perplexity when a conversation with a friend over late-night espresso forced you to rethink your views. Hook your readers by making your exploratory essay read like a detective story. Consider giving your account immediacy by quoting your thoughts at the very moment you wrote a log entry. The general shape of an exploratory essay can take the following pattern:

1. Starting point: You describe your initial problem, why you are interested in it, why it is problematic, why it is worth pursuing.
2. New input: You read an article, interview someone, pose an alternative solution.
   a. Summarize, describe, or explain the new input.
   b. Discuss the input, analyzing or evaluating it, playing the believing and doubting game with it, exploring how this input affects your thinking.
   c. Decide where to go next—find an alternative view, pursue a subquestion, seek more data, and so forth.
3. More new input: You repeat step 2 for your next piece of research.
4. Still more new input.
5. Ending point: You sum up where you stand at the point when the paper is due, how much your thinking about the issue has changed, whether or not you've reached a satisfactory solution.

Here is how Sam converted his starting point entry (pp. 211–212) and his first research entry (pp. 212–213) into the opening pages of his exploratory essay:

SHOULD WOMEN BE ALLOWED TO SERVE IN COMBAT UNITS?

Sam Scofield

At first, I wanted to explore the issue of gays in the military. But since I am a gay man I already knew where I stood on that issue and didn't find it truly problematic *for myself*. So I decided to shift my question to whether women should be allowed to serve in combat units. I wasn't sure whether feminists see the issue of women in combat the same way that gays see the military issue. Is it important to the feminist cause for women to be in combat? Or should feminists seek a kind of political order that avoids combat and doesn't settle issues through macho male behavior? In my initial thinking, I was also concerned about maintaining our country's military strength. In my "starting point" entry of my research log, I recorded the following thoughts:

> If putting women in combat wouldn't harm our military power, then I am fully in favor of women in combat. But if it would hurt our military power, then I have to make a value judgment.

So I decided that what I should do first is find some general background reading on the women in combat question. I went to the library, plugged the key words "woman and combat" into our online Infotrac database, and found more than a dozen entries. I went to the stacks and found the most familiar magazine in my initial list: *Newsweek*.

I began with an article by a retired Air Force colonel, David H. Hackworth. Hackworth was opposed to women in combat and focused mainly on the standard argument I was expecting—namely that women in combat would destroy male bonding. He didn't provide any evidence, however, other than citing the case of Israel in 1948:

> The Israeli Army put women on the front lines in 1948. The experiment ended disastrously after only three weeks. It wasn't that the women couldn't fight. It was that they got blown apart. Female casualties demoralized the men and gutted unit cohesion. (26–27)

However, this argument wasn't very persuasive to me. I thought that men's attitudes had changed a lot since 1948 and that cultural changes would allow us to get used to seeing both men and women as *people* so that it would be equally bad—or equally bearable—to see either men or women wounded and killed in combat.

But Hackworth did raise three points that I hadn't anticipated, and that really set me thinking. First he said that the military had different physical fitness requirements for men and women (for example, women had three minutes longer to run two miles than did men [25]). As I said in my research log, "It seems to me that there ought to be some absolute standards of strength and endurance needed for combat duty and the military ought to exclude both men and women who don't meet them." A second point was that an alarming number of female soldiers got pregnant in the Gulf War (1200 pregnant soldiers had to be evacuated [28]) and that prior to the war about ten to fifteen percent of female soldiers were pregnant at any given time (28). His point was that a pregnant woman, unlike a father-to-be, cannot continue to fill her role as a combat soldier. When she leaves her unit, she creates a dangerous gap that makes it hard for the unit to accomplish its mission. Finally, Hackworth cited lots of actual women soldiers in the Gulf War who were opposed to women in combat. They raised issues such as fraternization, sexual harassment, lack of privacy, and primitive living conditions.

Although Hackworth didn't turn me against wanting women to be able to serve in combat, he made the issue much more problematic for me. I now realized that this issue contained a lot of subissues, so I decided to focus first on the two major ones for me: (1) How important is this issue to feminists? This concern is crucial for me because I want to support equal rights for women just as I want to do so for gays or ethnic minorities. And (2) How serious are the pregnancy and strength-test issues in terms of maintaining military strength?

As I read the rest of the articles on my list, I began paying particular attention to these issues. The next article that advanced my thinking was. . . .

Revising

Because an exploratory essay describes the writer's research and thinking in chronological order, most writers have little trouble with organization. When they revise, their major concern is often to improve their essay's interest level by keeping it focused and lively. Exploratory essays grow tedious if the pace crawls too slowly or if extraneous details appear. They also tend to become too long, so that condensing and pruning become key revision tasks. The draft here is actually Sam's second draft; the first draft was a page longer and incorporated many more details and quotations from the Hackworth article. Sam eliminated these because he realized that his purpose was not to report on Hackworth but to describe the evolution of his own thinking. By condensing the Hackworth material, Sam saved room for the ideas he discovered later.

Peer reviewers can give you valuable feedback about the pace and interest level of an exploratory piece. They can also help you achieve the right balance between external details (how you did the research, to whom you talked, where you were) and mental details (what you were thinking about). As you revise, make sure you follow proper stylistic conventions for quotations and citations.

Conventions for quotations and citations are explained in Chapter 22, pp. 658–673.

GUIDELINES FOR PEER REVIEWS

Instructions for peer reviews are provided in Chapter 17 (pp. 519–520).

For the Writer

Prepare two or three questions you would like your peer reviewer to address while responding to your draft. The questions can focus on some aspect of your draft that you are uncertain about, on one or more sections where you particularly seek help or advice, on some feature that you particularly like about your draft, or on some part you especially wrestled with. Write out your questions and give them to your peer reviewer along with your draft.

For the Reviewer

I. Read the draft at a normal reading speed from beginning to end. As you read, do the following:
   A. Place a wavy line in the margin next to any passages that you find confusing, that contain something that doesn't seem to fit, or that otherwise slow down your reading.
   B. Place a "Good!" in the margin next to any passages where you think the writing is particularly strong or interesting.
II. Read the draft again slowly and answer the following questions by writing brief explanations of your answers.
   A. Posing the problem:
      1. How might the title be improved to identify the problem more accurately or to better engage your interest?
      2. How has the writer tried to show that the problem is interesting, problematic, and significant? How could the writer engage you more fully with the initial problem?
      3. How does the writer provide cues that the writer's purpose is to explore a question rather than argue a thesis? How might the opening section of the paper be improved?
   B. Narrating the exploration:
      1. Is the body of the paper organized chronologically so that you see the gradual development of the writer's thinking? Where does the writer

provide chronological transitions? Are there confusing shifts from past tense to present tense? If so, how might the chronological structure of the paper be made clearer?

2. How has the writer revealed the stages or changes in his or her thinking about the problem?

3. Part of an exploratory paper involves summarizing the argument of each new research source. Where in this draft is a summary of a source particularly clear and well developed? Where are summary passages that seem undeveloped or unclear? How could these passages be improved?

4. Another part of an exploratory paper involves the writer's strong response to each source—evidence of the writer's own critical thinking and questioning. Where are the writer's own ideas particularly strong and effective? Where are the writer's own ideas undeveloped or weak? What additional ideas or perspectives do you think the writer should consider?

5. Has the writer done enough research to explore the problem? Can you make suggestions for further research?

6. How might the ending of the paper better sum up the evolution of the writer's thinking or better clarify why the writer has or has not resolved the problem?

III. Rhetorical considerations

A. *Purpose, audience,* and *genre:* Where in this draft has the writer made a special effort to follow an exploratory purpose and to construct an essay that engages reflectively with sources? What has the writer done to interest readers in his or her dialectic exploration of this problem?

B. *Logos, ethos,* and *pathos:* How has the writer treated and structured the discussion of ideas in this essay? To what extent has the writer effectively conveyed his or her reliability, knowledge, and fairness in identifying, citing, and discussing sources throughout this draft? How does the writer connect this exploration to the interests and values of his audience? Where would you recommend improvements in appeals to *logos, ethos,* and *pathos*?

IV. If the writer has prepared questions for you, respond to his or her inquiries.

V. Sum up what you see as the chief strengths and problem areas of this draft:

A. Strengths

B. Problem areas

VI. Read the draft one more time. Place a check mark in the margin wherever you notice problems in grammar, spelling, or mechanics (one check mark per problem).

Writing an Informative (and Surprising) Essay

About Informative (and Surprising) Writing

As a reader, you regularly encounter writing with an informative aim, ranging from the instruction booklet for an MP3 player to a newspaper feature story on the African AIDS crisis. Informative documents include encyclopedias, cookbooks, news articles, instruction booklets, voters' pamphlets, and various kinds of reports, as well as informative Web sites and magazine articles. In some informative prose, visual representations of information such as diagrams, photographs, maps, tables, and graphs can be as important as the prose itself.

Informative Writing and the Audience's Reasons for Reading

A useful way to begin thinking about informative writing is to classify it according to the reader's motivation for reading. From this perspective, we can place informative prose in three categories.

In the first category, readers are motivated by an immediate need for information such as the need to program a VCR, study for a driver's test, or, in a more complex instance, make a major repair on an aircraft engine using the technical documentation supplied by the manufacturer. In these need-to-know instances, what readers want from informative prose is precision, accuracy, and clarity.

In the second category, readers are motivated by their own curiosity about a subject. For example, readers might turn to encyclopedias for information on the rings of Saturn or to newspapers or Internet news services for the latest information on the war against terror. In the academic world, scholars value annotated bibliographies and literature reviews, which provide important information that summarizes recent scholarship on a disciplinary problem.

Informative writing in these two categories does not necessarily contain a contestable thesis. Documents are organized effectively, of course, but they often follow a chronological step-by-step organization (as in a recipe) or an "all-about" topic-by-topic organization (as in an encyclopedia article on, say, Pakistan divided into "Geography," "Climate," "Population," "History," and so forth). The writer provides factual information about a subject without necessarily shaping the information specifically to support a thesis.

In contrast, the third category of informative writing *is* thesis-based and is therefore aligned with other kinds of thesis-based prose. The thesis brings new or surprising information to readers who aren't initially motivated by a need-to-know occasion or by their own curiosity. In fact, readers might not be initially interested in the writer's topic at all, so the writer's first task is to hook readers' interest—often by having an effective opening that arouses curiosity, hints that readers' current knowledge about a topic might have holes or gaps, and motivates their desire to learn something new, surprising, or different. Such pieces are commonly encountered in newspaper feature stories or in magazine articles where the reader is enticed by an intriguing title and interest-grabbing opening paragraphs. An excellent strategy for creating this motivation to read is the technique of "surprising reversal," which we explain in the next section.

The Rhetorical Power of "Surprising Reversal"

This third category of informative writing provides an excellent place to introduce a powerful rhetorical strategy that we call *surprising reversal*. Throughout this text, we have encouraged the habit of considering alternative answers to a question. The surprising-reversal strategy is directly linked to this way of thinking. Using this strategy, you contrast your new, surprising answer to a question with the targeted audience's common answer, creating tension between your own thesis and one or more alternative views. Its basic template is as follows: "Many people believe X (common view), but I am going to show Y (new, surprising view)." The concept of surprising reversal spurs the writer to go beyond the commonplace to change the reader's view of a topic.

This surprising-reversal strategy works as well for the aims of analysis and persuasion as it does for the informative aim. As we discussed in Chapter 2, writers of thesis-based prose usually try to change a reader's view in one of three ways, corresponding to three of the broadly defined aims of writing:

The broad aims of writing, including the aims of informing, analyzing, and persuading, are discussed in Table 3.1, pp. 49–50.

1. *Informative aim: enlarging* readers' views of a topic by providing new information or otherwise teaching them something about the topic they didn't know ("Many people think that security for supply lines in Iraq is provided by U.S. soldiers, but my research reveals that security is often provided by privately hired mercenaries.")
2. *Analytical or interpretive aim: clarifying* readers' views of a topic by bringing critical thinking to bear on problematic data or on a problematic text ("The students in my dorm think that this jeans ad reveals a liberated woman, but my own analysis of this ad shows that the woman fulfills traditional gender stereotypes.")
3. *Persuasive aim: restructuring* readers' views on a topic by urging them to choose the writer's position rather than a competing position on a controversial issue ("Many people believe the United States should continue to depend on an all-volunteer army, but I argue that the U.S. should reinstitute the draft.")

The concept of tension in a thesis statement is discussed in Chapter 2, pp. 36–38.

The surprising-reversal pattern occurs whenever you contrast your reader's original view of a topic with your own new or surprising view. Its power is that it automatically gives your thesis tension. It pushes your view up against the commonplace or expected views that are likely to be shared by your audience. In this chapter, the Option B writing project (pp. 224–225) invites you to use the surprising-reversal strategy for an informative aim. But this strategy also works for the aims of analysis or persuasion. You may find yourself using variations of this strategy for many of the other essays you write for this course and throughout your college career.

Exploring Informative (and Surprising) Writing

Let's say that you have just watched an old James Bond movie featuring a tarantula in Bond's bathroom. Curious about tarantulas, you do a quick Web search and retrieve the following short informative pieces. Read each one, and then proceed to the questions that follow.

READINGS

Our first mini-article comes from the Web site EnchantedLearning.com, a commercial site aimed at providing interesting, fact-filled learning lessons for children.

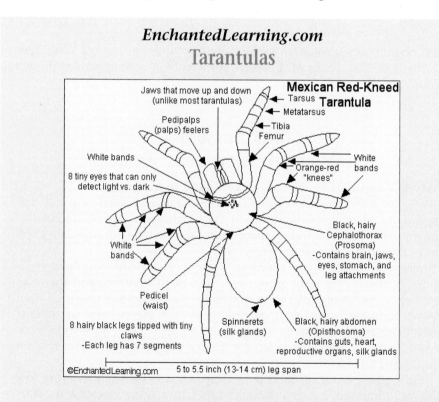

EnchantedLearning.com
Tarantulas

Mexican Red-Kneed Tarantula

Jaws that move up and down (unlike most tarantulas)
Tarsus
Metatarsus
Pedipalps (palps) feelers
Tibia
Femur
White bands
White bands
Orange-red "knees"
8 tiny eyes that can only detect light vs. dark
Black, hairy Cephalothorax (Prosoma)
-Contains brain, jaws, eyes, stomach, and leg attachments
White bands
Pedicel (waist)
8 hairy black legs tipped with tiny claws
-Each leg has 7 segments
Spinnerets (silk glands)
Black, hairy abdomen (Opisthosoma)
-Contains guts, heart, reproductive organs, silk glands
©EnchantedLearning.com   5 to 5.5 inch (13-14 cm) leg span

1   Tarantulas are large hairy spiders that live in warm areas around the world, including South America, southern North America, southern Europe, Africa, southern Asia, and Australia. The greatest concentration of tarantulas is in South America. There are about 300 species of tarantulas. The biggest

tarantula is *Pseudotherathosa apophysis,* which has a leg span of about 13 inches (33 cm). These arachnids have a very long life span; some species can live over 30 years.

2   **Habitat:** Some tarantulas live in underground burrows; some live on the ground, and others live in trees. They live in rain forests, deserts, and other habitats.

3   **Diet:** Tarantulas are carnivores (meat-eaters). They eat insects (like grasshoppers and beetles), other arachnids, small reptiles (like lizards and snakes), amphibians (like frogs), and some even eat small birds. Tarantulas kill their prey using venomous fangs; they also inject a chemical into the prey that dissolves the flesh. Tarantulas can crush their prey using powerful mouthparts. No person has ever died of a tarantula bite.

4   **Anatomy:** Tarantulas have a hairy two-part body and very strong jaws (with venomous fangs). They have eight hairy legs; each leg has 2 tiny claws at the end and a cushioning pad behind the claws. The hairs on the body and legs are sensitive to touch, temperature, and smell. Tarantulas have a hard exoskeleton and not an internal skeleton.

The second mini-article comes from the Web site of the University of Washington's Burke Museum. The author of this piece is the curator of arachnids at the Burke Museum.

Rod Crawford
Myths about "Dangerous" Spiders

1   **Myth: Tarantulas are dangerous or deadly to humans.**

2   **Fact:** Outside of southern Europe (where the name is used for a wolf spider, famous in medieval superstition as the alleged cause of "tarantella" dancing), the word tarantula is most often used for the very large, furry spiders of the family Theraphosidae.

3   Hollywood is squarely to blame for these spiders' toxic-to-humans reputation. Tarantulas are large, photogenic and easily handled, and therefore have been very widely used in horror and action-adventure movies. When some "venomous" creature is needed to menace James Bond or Indiana Jones, to invade a small town in enormous numbers, or to grow to gigantic size and prowl the Arizona desert for human prey, the special-effects team calls out the tarantulas!

4   In reality, the venom of these largest-of-all-spiders generally has **very low toxicity to humans.** I myself was once bitten by a Texan species and hardly even felt it. None of the North American species or those commonly kept as pets are considered to pose even a mild bite hazard. There are some reports that a few tropical species may have venom more toxic to vertebrates, but human bite cases haven't been reported, so we can't know for sure.

European tarantula

Lycosa tarentula
Southern Europe; body length 2–3 cm
(photo: Manuel J. Cabrero)
Click image to enlarge

Pink toe tarantula

Avicularia avicularia
Brazil to Trinidad; body length 6–7 cm
(photo by Ron Taylor)
Click image to enlarge

Both the European wolf spiders (**left**) originally called tarantulas, and the theraphosid spiders (**right**), often kept as pets and called tarantulas now, have been reputed dangerous to humans. They aren't.

5   The only health hazard posed by keeping pet tarantulas comes from the irritating chemicals on the hairs of the abdomen, which can cause skin rashes or inflammation of eyes and nasal passages. To prevent such problems, simply keep tarantulas away from your face and wash your hands after handling one.

6   Compared to common pets such as dogs, tarantulas are not dangerous at all. (For more information see the American Tarantula Society.)

Thinking Critically about "Tarantulas" and "Myths about 'Dangerous' Spiders"

1. Why do you think the reading from EnchantedLearning.com uses a diagram of a tarantula while the Burke Museum Web site uses photographs? How is each choice connected to the piece's targeted audience and purpose?

2. How would you describe the difference in organizational strategies for each of the readings? To us, one of these has an "all-about" topic-by-topic structure while the other has a thesis-based structure. Which is which? How is this difference connected to the targeted audience and purpose? How does the difference affect the way details are selected and arranged?

3. One might suppose that informational writing would be unaffected by the writer's angle of vision—that facts would simply be facts and that informational pieces on the same topic would contain the same basic information. Yet these two short pieces give somewhat different impressions of the tarantula. For example, how do these readings differ in the way they portray the bite of the tarantula? How else do they differ in overall effect?

WRITING PROJECT

To suggest some of the range of informative prose, we offer two writing project options. The first of these—which asks you to report information from a field research project—should be done in conjunction with the instructions on field research in Chapter 10.

Option A: Short Informative Report. Write a short informative report based on data you have gathered from observations, interviews, or your own questionnaire. Aim your paper at readers of a popular magazine or newspaper. The introduction of your paper should engage your readers' interest in your question. The body of your paper should present your results, which in many cases can also be displayed visually in a table or graph as well as in prose.

This assignment asks you to report the results of your own research gathered through observation, interviews, questionnaires, or other methods. Write your paper in a popular magazine style for a popular audience. For an example of a student paper written for Option A, see Kerri Ann Matsumoto's "How Much Does It Cost to Go Organic?", which Kerri Ann formatted to have the appearance of a magazine article (p. 230). Typical research questions for this assignment might be "How do college students spend their time during a typical week?" (questionnaire or interview study) or "What microorganisms are present in water samples from three area ponds?" (observation study in conjunction with an ecology class). This assignment is best accomplished when paired with the first half of Chapter 10, "Analyzing Field Research Data from Observations, Interviews, or Questionnaires," which explains techniques for asking field research questions and then doing your own field research. But whereas Chapter 10 calls for a scientific paper that both reports and analyzes field research data, Option A for this chapter asks only for a short informational report aimed at a popular audience.

Option B: Informative Paper Using Surprising Reversal. Using your personal experience or library/Internet research as a source of information, write a short informative essay using the surprising reversal pattern. Imagine an audience of readers who hold a mistaken or overly narrow view of your topic. Your purpose is to give them a new, surprising view.

Depending on the wishes of your instructor, this assignment can draw primarily on personal experience (for an example, see Cheryl Carp's essay, "Behind Stone Walls," pp. 231–232) or on library or Internet research (for an example, see Shannon King's "How Clean and Green Are Hydrogen Fuel-Cell Cars?" pp. 233–235). In either case, the assignment asks you to enlarge your reader's view of a subject in a surprising way. The introduction of your essay should engage your reader's interest in a question and provide needed context and background. Next, explain the common or popular answer to your question. Then give your own surprising answer that you develop with information derived from your personal experience or from library/Internet research. To create the "surprising-reversal" feel, consider delaying your thesis until after you have given your audience's common, expected answer to your opening question. This delay in presenting the thesis creates a more open-form feel that readers often find engaging.

For this assignment, avoid controversial issues requiring persuasive rather than informative writing. When writing persuasive prose, you imagine a resistant reader who may argue back. With informative prose, you imagine a more trusting reader, willing to learn from your experience or research. Although you hope to enlarge your reader's view of a topic, you aren't necessarily saying that your audience's original view is wrong, nor are you initiating a debate. For example, suppose a writer wanted to develop the following claim: "Many of my friends think that having an alcoholic mother would be the worst thing that could happen to you, but I will show that my mother's disease forced our family closer together." In this case the writer isn't arguing that alcoholic mothers are good or that everyone should have an alcoholic mother. Rather, the writer is simply offering readers a new, unexpected, and expanded view of what it might be like to have an alcoholic mother.

Finally, note that you do not need to be an expert on your topic, only to be more informed than your target audience. Your surprising information doesn't have to be surprising to everyone. For example, the claim that tarantula bites are harmless may be surprising to naïve viewers of a James Bond film but not to experts on spiders.

Understanding Informative (and Surprising) Writing

Informative Reports

The term *report* has numerous meanings. Students often come to college with inadequate models of what constitutes a strong academic report. For example, the "book reports" often assigned in high school aren't really "reports" in an academic sense and are quite different from professional book reviews written by scholars and critics. Likewise a "report" on Ethiopia done for a high school civics class may have been largely paraphrased from an encyclopedia, Web site, or other secondary source. In each of these cases, the report typically had an "all-about" structure rather than a problem-thesis structure—that is, the reports were organized by a sequence of topics rather than by points in support of a thesis.

Sometimes college instructors do give assignments asking primarily for repackaged all-about information. For example, a math instructor might ask you to

For further explanation of the difference between "all-about" structures and thesis-based structures, see Chapter 18, pp. 531–534.

report on a famous mathematician, or an art instructor might assign a report on cubism or impressionism—assignments that can lead primarily to paraphrasing of secondary sources. Such assignments can expand students' knowledge of a subject area, but they teach very little about the actual inquiry strategies of scholars in a discipline. As a general rule, college professors value informative reports based on the writer's own original research—reading primary documents or doing field or laboratory research—rather than on paraphrasing reference sources. The Option A assignment for this chapter, which asks you to produce new information based on your own field research, is thus a higher-level assignment than an all-about paper gleaned from secondary references.

Chapter 10, "Analyzing Field Research Data from Questionnaires, Interviews, or Observations," explains reports that have the dual function of presenting and analyzing new information.

For our purposes, we will define "report" as any document that presents the results of a fact-finding or data-gathering investigation. Some reports limit themselves to presenting newly discovered information, while others push further by analyzing or interpreting the information in an effort to understand causes, consequences, functions, or purposes. Such informative reports, which often have a thesis-driven rather than an all-about structure, can be of intense interest to researchers or decision makers. Scholars, for example, eagerly await the results of government reports on census or economic data, just as business leaders make crucial decisions based on sales or operations reports. In many disciplinary fields, scholarly writing includes informational reports as well as analyses and arguments. For example, a biologist might catalog the beetles found in a certain forest environment or an anthropologist might describe a fertility ritual in a tribal society. No report, of course, will be just pure information. The data will always be screened through the writer's angle of vision. But in informational reports, the writer's primary focus is on clear presentation of research findings.

Informative Writing Using Surprising Reversal

Because writing that uses the surprising reversal strategy has a thesis, it is useful to understand more clearly the difference between "all-about" informative writing and "thesis-based" informative writing. Consider, for example, the difference between the EnchantedLearning.com Web site on tarantulas (pp. 221–222) and the Burke Museum piece on "Myths about 'Dangerous' Spiders" (pp. 222–223). The EnchantedLearning.com piece is a short "all-about" report organized under the topic headings "Habitat," "Diet," and "Anatomy." The creator of the Web site may simply have adapted an encyclopedia article on tarantulas into a format for children. In contrast, the Burke Museum piece by Rod Crawford is thesis based. Crawford wishes to refute the myth that "[t]arantulas are dangerous or deadly to humans." He does so by providing information on the low toxicity of tarantula venom to humans and the relative painlessness of bites. All of Crawford's data focus on the potential danger of tarantulas. There are no data about habitat, diet, or other aspects of tarantula life—material that would be included if this were an all-about report. Because the piece also includes data about misconceptions of tarantulas, it follows the basic pattern of surprising reversal: "Many people believe (because of Hollywood movies) that tarantulas are toxic to humans, but I will show that tarantulas are not dangerous at all."

Because of its power to hook and sustain readers, examples of surprising-reversal essays can be found in almost any publication—from scholarly journals to easy-reading magazines. Here, for example, are abstracts of several articles from the table of contents of the *Atlantic Monthly*.

"REEFER MADNESS" BY ERIC SCHLOSSER

Marijuana has been pushed so far out of the public imagination by other drugs, and its use is so casually taken for granted in some quarters of society, that one might assume it had been effectively decriminalized. In truth, the government has never been tougher on marijuana offenders than it is today. In an era when violent criminals frequently walk free or receive modest jail terms, tens of thousands of people are serving long sentences for breaking marijuana laws.

"THE SEX-BIAS MYTH IN MEDICINE" BY ANDREW G. KADAR

A view has gained wide currency that men's health complaints are taken more seriously than those of women, and that medical research has benefited men more than it has women. "In fact," the author writes, "one sex does appear to be favored in the amount of attention devoted to its medical needs. . . . That sex is not men, however."

"MIDLIFE MYTHS" BY WINIFRED GALLAGHER

The idea that middle age is a dismal stage of life—scarred by traumas of personal crisis and physical change—is both firmly entrenched and almost completely untrue. The image in many Americans' minds, the author writes, is derived "not from the ordinary experiences of most people but from the unusual experiences of a few."

Each of these articles asserts a surprising, new position that counters a commonly held view.

Commonly Held, Narrow, or Inaccurate View	Surprising View
Because marijuana laws are no longer enforced, marijuana use has effectively become decriminalized	The government has never been tougher on marijuana offenders than it is today.
More research dollars are spent on men's diseases than on women's diseases.	The reverse is true: more money is spent on women's diseases.
Middle age is a dismal stage of life.	The widespread notion of midlife crises is a myth based on the unusual experiences of the few.

A similar pattern is often found in scholarly academic writing, which typically has the following underlying shape:

Whereas other scholars say X, Y, or Z, my research reveals Q.

Because the purpose of academic research is to advance knowledge, an academic article almost always shows the writer's new view against a background of prevailing views (what other scholars have said). This kind of tension is what often makes thesis-based writing memorable and provocative.

READINGS

The readings for this chapter include both short informational reports and surprising reversal informative essays. Our first reading is a short informative article, "Growing More Oil Dependent One Vehicle At a Time," appearing in the *New York Times* on June 20, 2004. It illustrates the power of visual graphics to complement verbal texts. Note how the bar graph, supplemented by pie charts and short text, presents important numerical information in a compact, yet dramatic form.

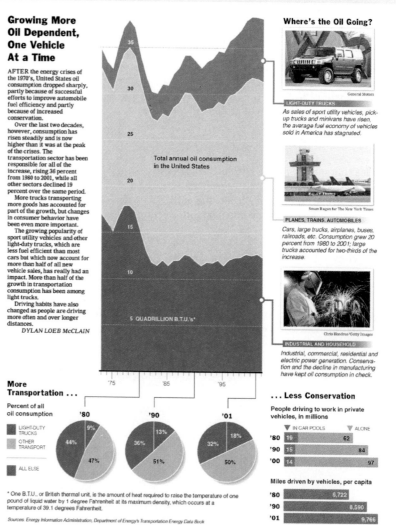

Thinking Critically about "Growing More Oil Dependent, One Vehicle At a Time"

1. Take a few moments to read the graph carefully and to note how the graph and the verbal text tell the same story. In your own words, how much did the U.S. consumption of oil decline by 1980 after a peak in the late 70s? What was the cause of this decline? From 1980 onward, the consumption of oil once again increased sharply in the transportation sector but not in the industrial and commercial sector. Why? What role do SUVs (classified as "light trucks") play in the current consumption of oil in the United States?

2. Share with classmates, your own cognitive processes in reading this article. How much extra time did you spend with this article as a result of the graphics? How do the verbal and visual text work together to tell the same story? How does your brain process verbal texts differently from visual texts?

Advice on how to construct your own graphics is found in Chapter 10, pp. 261–263.

Our second reading, by student writer Kerri Ann Matsumoto, responds to the Option A writing project for this chapter. We reproduce it on page 230 to show how Kerri Ann formatted the paper to look like a popular magazine article.

Thinking Critically about "How Much Does It Cost to Go Organic?"

1. In our teaching, we have discovered that students appreciate the concept of genre more fully if they occasionally "desktop publish" a manuscript to look like a magazine article, a poster, or a brochure rather than a standard double-spaced academic paper. If Kerri Ann had been an actual freelance writer, she would have submitted this article double-spaced with attached figures, and the magazine publisher would have done the formatting. Compare Kerri Ann's document design for "How Much Does It Cost to Go Organic?" with the document design required by the American Psychological Association for empirical research reports—the student essay on energy literacy in Chapter 10, pages 277–289. How does document design itself signal differences in genre? To what extent has Kerri Ann made this article *sound* like a popular magazine article as well as look like one?

2. Do you think Kerri Ann used visual graphics effectively in her essay? How might she have revised the graphics or the wording to make the paper more effective?

3. Do you think it is worth the extra money to go organic? How would you make your case in an argument paper with a persuasive aim?

HOW MUCH DOES IT COST TO GO ORGANIC?

Kerri Ann Matsumoto

Organic foods, grown without pesticides, weed killers, or hormone additives, are gaining popularity from small privately owned organic food stores to large corporate markets. With the cost of living rising, how much can a family of four afford to pay for organically grown food before it becomes too expensive?

To find out more information about the cost of organic foods, I went to the Rainbow Market, which is a privately owned organic food store, and to a nearby Safeway. I decided to see what it would cost to create a stir-fry for a family of four. I estimated that the cost of organic vegetables for the stir-fry would cost $3.97. Non-organic vegetables for the same stir-fry, purchased at Safeway, would cost $2.37. If we imagined our family eating the same stir fry every night for a year, it would cost $1,499 for organic and $865 for non-organic for a difference of $584.

After pricing vegetables, I wanted to find out how much it would cost to add to the stir-fry free-range chicken fed only organic feeds, as opposed to non-organic factory farmed chicken. For good quality chicken breasts, the organic chicken was $6.99 per pound and the non-organic was $3.58 per pound. Projected out over a year, the organic chicken would cost $5,103 compared to $2,613 for non-organic chicken.

My research shows that over the course of one year it will cost $6,552 per year to feed our family organic stir-fry and $3,478 for non-organic for a difference of $3,074. If a family chose to eat not only organic dinner, but also all organic meals, the cost of food would sharply increase.

Before going to the Rainbow Market I knew that the price of organic foods was slightly higher than non-organic. However, I did not expect the difference to be so great. Of course, if you did comparison shopping at other stores, you might be able to find cheaper organic chicken and vegetables. But my introductory research suggests that going organic isn't cheap.

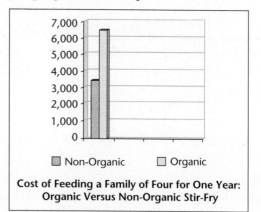

Cost of Feeding a Family of Four for One Year: Organic Versus Non-Organic Stir-Fry

Comparative Cost of Ingredients in an Organic Versus Non-Organic Stir-Fry

	Vegetables per day	Chicken per day	Total per day	Total per year
Organic	$3.97	$13.98	17.95	$6552
Non-Organic	$2.37	$ 7.16	9.53	$3478

If we add the cost of chicken and vegetables together (see the table and the graph), we can compute how much more it would cost to feed our family of four organic versus non-organic chicken stir-fry for a year.

Is it worth it? Many people today have strong concerns for the safety of the foods that they feed to their family. If you consider that organic vegetables have no pesticides and that the organic chicken has no growth hormone additives, the extra cost may be worth it. Also if you are concerned about cruelty to animals, free-range chickens have a better life than caged chickens. But many families might want to spend the $3,074 difference in other ways. If you put that money toward a college fund, within ten years you could save over $30,000. So how much are you willing to pay for organic foods?

Our next reading is by student writer Cheryl Carp, whose experience with volunteer outreach in a maximum-security prison enabled her to enlarge her readers' views of prisoners with life sentences. This paper, which uses the surprising-reversal strategy, illustrates how personal experiences can be used for an informative aim.

Cheryl Carp (student)
Behind Stone Walls

1   For about eight hours out of every month I am behind the stone walls of the Monroe State Penitentiary. No, that's not the sentencing procedure of some lenient judge; I am part of a group of inmates and outsiders who identify themselves as Concerned Lifers. Concerned Lifers is an organization operating both inside and outside of prison walls. Inside Monroe there are close to thirty men who take part in the organization and its activities, all of whom have been given life sentences. Concerned Lifers outside the prison visit the prisoners, take part in the organization's meetings, and then split into various small groups for personal conversation. I became involved in this exciting group as a personal sponsor (able to visit the prison alone for special activities) after attending my first meeting inside Monroe State Penitentiary. That first drive to Monroe seemed to take forever. Looking out the window of that twelve-seater van filled with apprehensive first-time volunteers, I kept my eyes on the evening sky and tried to imagine what it would be like to be shut up in prison for life, never to see this beautiful scenery again. I was not scared, but I was nervous and could feel my pulse rate steadily rise as I began to see the green and white road signs to the prison. As the van slowly climbed the hill to the guard tower at the top, I wondered what it would be like to visit this maximum security prison.

2   Many people believe that visiting a prison would be frightening. Most people typically picture dangerous men lurking in every corner. The guards are yelling and the men are fighting; the men are covered with tattoos, probably carrying concealed razor blades and scowling menacingly. People think that prisons are a haven for rampant homosexuality and illegal drugs. Common belief is that the inmates are like locked animals, reaching out between the iron bars of their cages. These men are seen as sex-starved, eagerly waiting for a female body to enter their domain. The atmosphere is one of suspense, with sub-human men ready at any moment to break free and run. People I've spoken to express a fear of danger to themselves and almost a threat to their lives. They wonder how I have the nerve to do it.

3   But visiting a prison to me is an uplifting experience, far from frightening. Since that initial visit, I have returned many times to organize and participate in a clown group. The clown group is made up of about twenty of the inmates in the Concerned Lifers group and myself. The prisoners meet and rehearse once a week, and I join them every other week to critique their progress, give them pointers, and do various exercises to improve their ability.

4   The only frightening part of a visit is getting through all the guards and their red tape. Last week I drove up the hill to the guard tower, identified

myself and my affiliation, and was told to "park to the left" by a disembodied voice coming from a loudspeaker. After going through many metal security doors, being checked by a metal detector that even picks up the nails in your shoes, and being escorted by numerous guards, I finally got to be with the people I had come to see.

5   The most enjoyable, exciting, and friendly time I spend at the prison is the time I spend with the boys. These people are no longer "the prisoners" or "the inmates," but are now individuals. Visiting the prison is not a frightening experience because the men inside become people, people full of emotions, creativity, and kindness. These qualities are evident in the activities and projects these men become involved in or initiate themselves. For example, one young lifer named Ken became interested in Japanese paper folding—origami. In order to pursue his interest in origami, he requested a book on the subject from the prison librarian and proceeded to teach himself. A few weeks later, I saw origami creations everywhere—flowers, dragons, and birds—all made by the guys and all done carefully and beautifully. Ken had taught his fellow inmates. Another great thing that this group has undertaken is the sponsorship of four children through an orphan relief program. The men make almost nothing at their various jobs within the prison, but what they do make they are more than willing to share, some thing many of us never seem to "get around to."

6   It is true that the men value the presence of a female, but not for sexual reasons. The men inside Monroe are hungry for outside companionship and understanding. They're hungry for a woman's viewpoint and conversation. They have treated me as a friend, valued my conversation, and never made sexual advances. The men behind the walls are reaching through their bars not menacingly, but pleadingly—begging the outside world to take a good look at them. The men need to be looked at as people and as fellow humans in this world. Most of them are aching for a second chance at life and relationships. This is not a place for outsiders to fear, but a place to which outsiders can bring light, hope, and understanding.

7   My point is not to condone the crimes that these men may have committed in the past, but to look to the present and the future by seeing these men not as "inmates," but as individual people trying to succeed in the kind of life they now have to live.

Thinking Critically about "Behind Stone Walls"

1. What is the audience that Cheryl Carp imagines?

2. For this audience, what is the common view of prisoners that Cheryl Carp attempts to reverse?

3. What is her own surprising view?

4. What are the strengths and weaknesses of Cheryl's essay?

The next reading, by student writer Shannon King, is a short research paper using the surprising-reversal strategy. Shannon's paper uses research information to enlarge her readers' understanding of hydrogen fuel cell vehicles by showing that hydrogen fuel is not as pollution-free as the general public believes.

Shannon King (Student)
How Clean and Green Are Hydrogen Fuel-Cell Cars?

1   The United States is embroiled in a controversy over energy and pollution. We are rapidly using up the earth's total supply of fossil fuels, and many experts think that children being born today will experience the end of affordable oil. One energy expert, Paul Roberts, believes that serious oil shortages will start occurring by 2015 when the world's demand for oil will outstrip the world's capacity for further oil production. An equally serious problem is that the burning of fossil fuels spews carbon dioxide into the atmosphere, which increases the rate of global warming.

2   One hopeful way of addressing these problems is to develop hydrogen fuel cell cars. According to Karim Nice, the author of the fuel cell pages on the How Stuff Works Web site, a fuel cell is "an electrochemical energy conversion device that converts hydrogen and oxygen into water, producing electricity and heat in the process." A hydrogen-fueled car is therefore an electric car, powered by an electric motor. The car's electricity is generated by a stack of fuel cells that act like a battery. In the hydrogen fuel cell, the chemicals that produce the electricity are hydrogen from the car's pressurized fuel tank, oxygen from the air, and special catalysts inside the fuel cell. The fuel cell releases no pollutants or greenhouse gases. The only waste product is pure water.

3   To what extent will these pollution-free fuel cells be our energy salvation? Are they really clean and green?

4   Many people think so. The development of hydrogen fuel cells has caused much excitement. I know people who say we don't need to worry about running out of oil because cars of the future will run on water. One recent New York Times advertisement produced by General Motors has as its headline, "Who's driving the hydrogen economy?" The text of the ad begins by saying "The hydrogen economy isn't a pipe dream. . . . The hydrogen economy is the endgame of a multifaceted strategy General Motors set in motion years ago, with steps that are real, progressive, and well-underway" (General Motors). The Web site for the Hydrogen Fuel Cell Institute includes a picture of a crystal clear blue sky landscape with a large letter headline proclaiming "At long last, a technology too long overlooked promises to transform society." At the bottom of the picture are the words, "Offering clean & abundant power, hydrogen-based fuel cells could soon end our reliance on oil and minimize emissions of pollution and global-warming gases." According to CNN News, the Bush administration has proposed devoting 1.7 billion dollars of federal funds to developing hydrogen fuel cells (CNN). The biggest nationally known proponent of hydrogen fuel cells is California Governor Arnold Schwarzenegger,

who signed an Executive Order that California's "21 interstate freeways shall be designated as the "California Hydrogen Highway Network."' (California 2). In this executive order, Schwarzenegger envisions

a network of hydrogen fueling stations along these roadways and in the urban centers that they connect, so that by 2010, every Californian will have access to hydrogen fuel, with a significant and increasing percentage produced from clean, renewable sources. (2)

Schwarzenegger's optimism about the hydrogen highway sums up the common view that hydrogen is a clean alternative energy source that is abundant throughout nature. All we have to do is bottle it up, compress it, and transport it to a network of new "gas stations" where the gas being pumped is hydrogen.

5   But what I discovered in my research is that hydrogen is not as green as most people think. Although hydrogen fuel cells appear to be an environmentally friendly alternative to fossil fuels, the processes for producing hydrogen actually require the use of fossil fuels. The problem is that pure hydrogen doesn't occur naturally on earth. It has to be separated out from chemical compounds containing hydrogen, and that process requires other forms of energy. What I discovered is that there are only two major ways to produce hydrogen. The first is to produce it from fossil fuels by unlocking the hydrogen that is bonded to the carbon in coal, oil, or natural gas. The second is to produce it from water through electrolysis, but the power required for electrolysis would also come mainly from burning fossil fuels. These problems make hydrogen fuel cell cars look less clean and green than they first appear.

6   One approach to creating hydrogen from fossil fuels is to use natural gas. According to Matthew L. Wald, writing in a New York Times article, natural gas is converted to hydrogen in a process called "steam reforming." Natural gas (made of hydrogen and carbon atoms) is mixed with steam (which contains hydrogen and oxygen atoms) to cause a chemical reaction that produces pure hydrogen. But it also produces carbon dioxide, which contributes to global warming. According to Wald, if fuel cell cars used hydrogen from steam reforming, they would emit 145 grams of global warming gases per mile compared to 374 grams an ordinary gas-powered car would emit. The good news is that using hydrogen power would cut carbon emissions by more than half. The bad news is that these cars would still contribute to global warming and consume natural gas. Moreover, Wald suggests that the natural gas supply is limited and that natural gas has many better, more efficient uses than converting it to hydrogen.

7   Another method for producing hydrogen would come from coal, which is the cheapest and most abundant source of energy. However, the current method of generating electricity by burning coal is the leading source of carbon dioxide emission. At Ohio University, engineers state we still have enough coal to last us two hundred and fifty years and that we should find some better uses for coal. The engineers have received a 4 million dollar federal grant to investigate the production of hydrogen from coal. They plan on mixing coal

with steam, air, and oxygen under high temperatures and pressure to produce hydrogen and carbon monoxide ("Ohio University"). But this too would generate greenhouse gases and is a long way off from producing results.

8   The next likely source of hydrogen is to produce it directly from water using an electrolyzer. Wald explains that the electrolyzer uses an electrical current to break down water molecules into hydrogen and oxygen atoms. Creating hydrogen through electrolysis sounds like a good idea because its only waste product is oxygen. But the hazardous environmental impact is not in the electrolysis reaction, but in the need to generate electricity to run the electrolyzer. Wald claims that if the electricity to run the electrolyzer came from a typical coal-fired electrical plant, the carbon dioxide emissions for a fuel cell car would be 17 percent worse than for today's gasoline powered cars. One solution would be to run the electrolyzer with wind-generated or nuclear-powered electricity. But wind power would be able to produce only a small fraction of what would be needed, and nuclear power brings with it a whole new set of problems including disposal of nuclear waste.

9   Although there seem to be various methods of producing hydrogen, the current sources being considered do not fulfill the claim that hydrogen fuel cell technology will end the use of fossil fuels or eliminate greenhouse gases. The problem is not with the fuel cells themselves but with the processes needed to produce hydrogen fuel. I am not arguing that research and development should be abandoned, and I hope some day that the hydrogen economy will take off. But what I have discovered in my research is that hydrogen power is not as clean and green as I thought.

Works Cited

California. Executive Department. "Executive Order S-7-04." 20 Apr. 2004. 24 May 2004 <http://www.its.ucdavis.edu/hydrogenhighway/Executive-Order.pdf>.

CNN. "The Issues/George Bush." CNN.com. 2004. 23 May 2004 <http://www.cnn.com/ELECTION/2004/special/president/issues/index.bush.html>. Path: Environment & Energy; alternative fuels.

General Motors. "Who's Driving the Hydrogen Country?" Advertisement. New York Times. 28 July 2004: A19.

Hydrogen Fuel Cell Institute. 2001. Wilder Foundation. 27 May 2004 <http://www.h2fuelcells.org>.

Nice, Karim. "How Fuel Cells Work." Howstuffworks. 27 May 2004 <http://science.howstuffworks.com/fuel-cell.htm>.

"Ohio University Aims to Use Coal to Power Fuel Cells." Fuel Cell Today. 24 Nov. 2003. 3 June 2004 <http://www.fuelcelltoday.com/FuelCellToday/IndustryInformation/IndustryInformationExternal/NewsDisplayArticle/0%2C1602%2C3678%2C00.html>.

Roberts, Paul. "Running Out of Oil—and Time." Los Angeles Times. 6 Mar. 2004. Common Dreams News Center. 23 Mar. 2004 <http://www.commondreams.org/views04/0307-02.htm>.

Wald, Matthew L. "Will Hydrogen Clear the Air? Maybe Not, Some Say." New York Times. 12 Nov. 2003: C1.

Thinking Critically about "How Clean and Green Are Hydrogen Fuel-Cell Cars?"

1. Explain how Shannon King's essay uses the surprising-reversal strategy. What question does Shannon pose? What is the common or popular answer to her question? What is Shannon's surprising answer?

2. Whereas Cheryl Carp's essay "Behind Stone Walls" (pp. 231–232) depends on personal experience for its details, Shannon's essay depends on research data. How effective is Shannon in using the surprising-reversal strategy to create an effective research paper?

3. The line between information and persuasion is often blurred. Some persons might argue that Shannon's essay has a persuasive aim that argues against hydrogen fuel cell cars rather than an informative aim that simply presents surprising information about how hydrogen is produced. To what extent do you agree with our decision to classify Shannon's aim as primarily informative rather than persuasive? Can it be both?

Our final essay, by professional writer Jonathan Rauch, appeared in the July/August 2003 issue of *The Atlantic Monthly*. Although this article focuses largely on the immigrant experience of one Chinese family, Rauch's purpose is to contrast his surprising view of Washington, D.C., as a "post-racial America" with the commonly held view of our nation's capital as a "black urban core locked in uneasy truce with it rootless white suburbs."

Jonathan Rauch
Coming to America

1   The Au family, immigrants from Hong Kong, arrived at Washington's Reagan National Airport on a sticky night late last July. I will never forget the sight of them: parents bustling after the long flight, children—three girls and a boy, ranging in age from eight to thirteen—heaped sleepily atop sixteen suitcases, as if the whole bunch had tumbled off the baggage belt.

2   They settled into a little townhouse in Arlington, Virginia, two Aus per bedroom and two more in the basement: spacious, by Hong Kong standards. The place belongs to my partner, Michael, who is brother to Mrs. Au, uncle to the children, and sponsor, for immigration purposes, of the entire family. He had applied for green cards for the Aus more than ten years ago, when he became a citizen himself. When permission to immigrate finally came, the Aus, a middle-class family headed by a recently retired civil servant, seized the chance.

3   For newcomers America is full of footholds. The Aus, Christians, immediately found a Chinese church only a couple of miles from home. Every

Sunday they attend services in Cantonese. If they want bok choy or fried dace or duck's blood, they can walk to an Asian grocery just down the block.

4   In Hong Kong—where, because of its history as a British colony, many people use English names—the girls were called Queenie, Amanda, and Cassandra, the boy Bryan. In America, Bryan has become Chi-hang. That is the name in the official records, so that is what his school calls him—and anyway, isn't it more interesting than boring old "Bryan"? Asked which he prefers, the boy says that in Hong Kong he liked Bryan and in America he likes Chi-hang. This seems to him a perfectly natural arrangement. Clearly, the melting pot has changed since my grandmother passed through Ellis Island, in 1910.

5   Still, the mysterious process known as Americanization carries on. In the public schools, the Au children struggle with English but steadily improve. True to stereotype, they are whizzes at math. Last September, when I asked Bryan, who is ten, what he thought of life in the United States, he exclaimed, "I like!" (the first English sentence I heard from him). His older sister Amanda, a seventh-grader, was soon tying up the phone talking with her American friends.

6   When I moved to the northern-Virginia suburbs from central Washington, D.C., a couple of years ago, I expected to find Confederate flags and cured hams. Instead I found the Eden Center, where the flag that flies next to Old Glory is Vietnam's, and where you can have your pho with bible tripe and soft tendon. Eden Center is an all-Vietnamese shopping mall: Vietnamese restaurants, video stores, hair salons, travel agencies, jewelers, grocers, music shops, bakeries. Even the Muzak is Vietnamese. The place is packed every day, and not much English is heard there. For a long time, though, a red banner hung beneath its gate: "Soul and heart of the Vietnamese community always with the 9-11 tragedy."

7   The long-standing meta-narrative of Washington is that of a black urban core locked in uneasy truce with its rootless white suburbs. A 2001 study by the Brookings Institution's Center on Urban and Metropolitan Policy, however, contains surprising news for people who still see the city and its environs in those terms. "Unlike some other major immigrant destinations such as Miami or Los Angeles, where one or two immigrant groups tend to predominate," says the study, "Washington's flow is diverse." Nearly two hundred countries are represented, with the top ten spanning Central America (El Salvador), South America (Peru), Asia (Vietnam, China, South Korea), Africa (Ethiopia), the Middle East (Iran), Oceania (the Philippines), and the Subcontinent (India and Pakistan).

8   Moreover, each of the ten metropolitan Washington zip codes with the most new immigrants draws from more than a hundred countries. In other words, instead of settling into separate ethnic neighborhoods, as Italians and Irish and Jews and Chinese did a century ago, the new arrivals scatter. In yet other words, they integrate. They work beside native-born Americans, they live beside them, and they suffer beside them. The third victim of the Washington-area sniper last year was a taxi driver named Premkumar

Walekar, originally from Pune, India. He was shot while pumping gas, the *Los Angeles Times* reported, "moments after buying a newspaper, a lottery ticket and a pack of gum."

9   Washington, for so long a lagging indicator of American social life—far behind edgy New York and buzzy L.A. and brazen Chicago and even upstart Atlanta and Houston—is now, of all things, a harbinger. Increasingly, the Washington area is the post-racial America that we have all been told to expect. A member of Congress who wonders what a genuinely multicultural country might look like need only rustle up taxi fare to Arlington and walk around. My immediate neighbors include a black-white couple, a Filipino psychiatrist, a Korean accountant, and two Indian families, whose kids' names I can't pronounce. I have never lived in a more neighborly neighborhood. If this is the future, it seems to work.

10   When spring finally sprang this year, I came home one Sunday afternoon to find our place aswarm with Aus, the four children bantering in Cantonese with an occasional aside to me in shy English. Under Michael's direction this Chinese task force had descended on the yard to plant flowers. Thus does new growth take root in northern Virginia, rejuvenating the soil. This Independence Day will be the Au children's first in America. Through their eyes I will see the fireworks afresh.

Thinking Critically about "Coming to America"

1. Rauch begins his article with a long anecdote about the Au family. What is the function of this anecdote within the whole article? At what point in the article do you begin to see where Rauch is going—that is, where you begin to understand his purpose and thesis?

2. What is Rauch's point in explaining that the Au son likes to be called "Chi-hang" in America but "Bryan" in Hong Kong?

3. Where in this article does Rauch explain the popular or common view of Washington, D.C.? What is that common view?

4. What is the new, surprising view of Washington, D.C., that Rauch presents? Besides the personal example of the Au family, what other data does Rauch use to support his surprising view?

5. If you had to pick out one sentence from the article as its thesis statement, what would that sentence be? Why does Rauch locate the sentence where he does?

Composing Your Essay—Option A: Informative Report

This assignment is designed to be used in conjunction with Chapter 10, "Analyzing Field Research Data from Questionnaires, Interviews, or Observations." Chapter 10 explains how to ask a field research question and how to conduct a simple field research project. The primary differences between the Option A writing project for this chapter and the writing project for Chapter 10 involve aim, genre, and audience.

- *Aim:* The Option A project has an informative aim, while the Chapter 10 project has an analytical aim. From this perspective, the assignment for this chapter is both shorter and simpler in that you need only report your newly gathered information without having to analyze it in the way that scientific papers demand.
- *Genre:* Whereas the writing project for Chapter 10 is a scientific paper in a scientific format, the Option A assignment is a popular magazine article. Imagine that you are writing for some kind of "easy-reading" magazine such as an airline travel magazine or some other popular interest magazine with short articles. In fact, your instructor may ask you to format your paper to have a "desktop-published" look, following the example of Kerri Ann Matsumoto (p. 230).
- *Audience:* The Chapter 10 project is aimed at a social science audience who expects an empirical report in scientific style. The Option A assignment for this chapter is aimed at popular audiences who might pick up an easy-reading magazine.

Generating and Exploring Ideas

Follow the advice provided in Chapter 10.

Shaping and Drafting

An informative report for a popular audience can have much the same structure as a scientific paper except that its style is more informal and there is no need to go into the kind of detail required by scientific audiences. One way to imagine shaping and drafting this paper is to see how you might "translate" a scientific article into a popular format. You will note that Kerri Ann Matsumoto's essay on the cost of organic food poses a research question (How much extra does it cost to buy organic food over nonorganic food?); explains her process (did comparison pricing for a chicken stir-fry for a family of four at organic and nonorganic stores); presents her findings in both words and graphics (organic foods cost more); and suggests the significance of her research (the advantages of organic foods versus the advantages of spending the extra money in other ways). The structure of the popular version is thus quite similar to the scientific version: problem, method, findings, significance.

If your instructor asks you to format your paper to look like a magazine article, you will get some practice in using your word processing program to form columns and import graphics. It is also possible to format the paper using scissors and paste.

Revising

As you revise, make sure that your graphics (if you use them) and your words tell the same story and reinforce each other. The principle of "independent redundancy" explained in Chapter 10 (p. 264) isn't as stringently followed in informal magazine writing as it is in scientific papers, but your text should still make explicit reference to your graphics while also explaining the same thing in words as the graphic shows visually. As you edit, try to achieve a popular easy-reading voice appropriate for a magazine article. When you have a nearly final draft, exchange it with a classmate for a peer review following the guidelines on pages 244–245.

Composing Your Essay—Option B: Informative Writing Using Surprising Reversal

The Option B assignment asks for an informative essay that surprises the reader with new information. Your new information can come either from your own personal experience (as Cheryl Carp uses her personal experience to reverse the common view of prison inmates) or from research (as Shannon King uses her research on fuel cells to complicate, if not reverse, the common view that fuel cell technology will produce pollution-free energy).

As you write your essay, keep in mind that *surprise* is a relative term based on the relationship between you and your intended audience. You don't have to surprise everyone in the world, just those who hold a mistaken or narrow view of your topic. With its emphasis on enlarging your audience's view through something unexpected or surprising, the Option B assignment teaches you to imagine an audience as you consider possible topics. The key for this task is to imagine an audience less informed about your topic than you are. Suppose, as an illustration, that you have just completed an introductory economics course. You are less informed about economics than your professor, but more informed about economics than persons who have never had an econ class. You might therefore write a surprising-reversal paper to the less informed audience:

> The average airplane traveler thinks that the widely varying ticket pricing for the same flight is chaotic and silly, but I can show how this pricing scheme makes perfect sense economically. [written to the "average airplane traveler," who hasn't taken an economics course]

This paper would be surprising to your intended audience, but not to the economics professor. From a different perspective, however, you could also write about economics to your professor because you might know more than your professor about, say, how students struggle with some concepts:

Many economics professors assume that students can easily learn the concept of "elasticity of demand," but I can show why this concept was particularly confusing for me and my classmates. [written to economics professors who aren't aware of student difficulties with particular concepts]

Additionally, your surprising view doesn't necessarily have to be diametrically opposed to the common view. Perhaps you think the common view is *incomplete* or *insufficient* rather than *dead wrong*. Instead of saying, "View X is wrong, whereas my view, Y, is correct," you can say, "View X is correct and good as far as it goes, but my view, Y, adds a new perspective." In other words, you can also create surprise by going a step beyond the common view to show readers something new.

Generating and Exploring Ideas

Your goal for the Option B assignment is to find a topic where you possess knowledge or experience that will give your targeted audience a new perspective. As you search for a subject, the key is to consider both a topic (something that you care about and that you have quite a bit of information about through personal experience or recent reading and research) and an audience (persons who have a mistaken or overly narrow view of your topic because they lack the information that you can provide).

If you do the Option B assignment as a mini-research project, start by posing a research question. As you begin doing initial research on your topic area, you will soon know more about your topic than most members of the general public. Ask yourself, "What has surprised me about my research so far? What have I learned that I didn't know before?" Your answers to these questions can suggest possible approaches to your paper. Shannon King, for example, began her research believing that fuel cell technology produced totally pollution-free energy. She didn't realize that one needed to burn fossil fuels in order to produce the hydrogen. This initial surprise shaped her paper. She decided that if this information surprised her, it should surprise others also.

What follows are two exercises you can try to generate ideas for your paper.

Part Four, on writing research papers, has many suggestions for posing good research questions. See especially pp. 607–608.

Small-Group Task to Generate Ideas

Form small groups. Assign a group recorder to make a two-column list, with the left column titled "Mistaken or Narrow View of X" and the right column titled "Groupmate's Surprising View." Brainstorm ideas for surprising-reversal essay topics until every group member has generated at least one entry for the right-hand column. Here is a sample list entry:

Mistaken or Narrow View of X	Groupmate's Surprising View
Football offensive lineman is a no-brain, repetitive job requiring size, strength, and only enough brains and athletic ability to push people out of the way.	Jeff can show that being an offensive lineman is an interesting job that requires mental smarts as well as size, strength, and athletic ability.

To help stimulate ideas, you might consider topic areas such as the following:

- *People:* computer programmers, homeless people, cheerleaders, skateboarders, gang members, priests or rabbis, feminists, house-spouses, mentally ill or developmentally disabled persons.
- *Activities:* washing dishes, climbing mountains, wrestling, modeling, gardening, living with a chronic disease or disability, owning a certain breed of dog, riding a subway at night, entering a dangerous part of a city.
- *Places:* particular neighborhoods, particular buildings or parts of buildings, local attractions, junkyards, places of entertainment, summer camps.
- *Other similar categories:* groups, animals and plants, and so forth; the list is endless.

Next, go around the room, sharing with the entire class the topics you have generated. Remember that you are not yet committed to writing about any of these topics.

Here are some examples from recent students:

A common misconception about Native Americans is that they lived in simple harmony with the earth, but my research reveals that they often "controlled" nature by setting fire to forests to make farming easier or to improve hunting.

To the average person, pawnshops are disreputable places, but my experience shows that pawnshops can be honest, wholesome businesses that perform a valuable social service.

Most of my straight friends think of the film *Frankenstein* as a monster movie about science gone amuck, but to the gay community it holds a special and quite different meaning.

Individual Task to Generate Ideas

Here are two templates that can help you generate ideas by asking you to think specifically about differences in knowledge levels between you and various audiences. Try this template:

I know more about X than [specific person or persons]

Try the exercise first by naming topics that interest you and then thinking of less informed audiences:

I know more about cars/computer games/the energy crisis than [specific persons]

Then try the exercise by naming specific audiences and then thinking of topics about which you know more than they:

I know more about X than [my mother/the college registrar/students who don't commute/my boss at work]

Shaping and Drafting

The surprising-reversal pattern requires two main writing moves: an exposition of the common or expected answers to a question, and the development of your own surprising answer to that question. In addition, your essay needs an introduction that presents the question to be addressed and a separate conclusion that finishes it off.

As a way of helping you generate ideas, we offer the following five questions. Questions 1, 2, and 4 are planning questions that will help you create broad point sentences to form your essay's skeletal framework. These questions call for one-sentence generalizations. Questions 3 and 5 are freewriting prompts to help you generate supporting details. For these questions, freewrite rapidly, either on paper or at your computer. Following each question, we speculate what Carp, King, and Rauch might have written if they had used the same questions to help them get started on their essays.

1. *What question does your essay address?* (Carp might have asked, "What is it like to visit inmates in a maximum-security prison?" King might have asked, "Are hydrogen fuel cell automobiles really clean and green?" Rauch might have asked, "What is Washington, D.C., really like in terms of ethnic diversity?")

2. *What is the common, expected, or popular answer to this question held by your imagined audience?* (Carp might have said, "Visiting these prisons will be scary because prisoners are sex-starved, dangerous people." King might have said, "Most people believe that hydrogen fuel cell cars are totally pollu-tion free." Rauch might have said, "Most people believe that Washington, D.C., is like many other American cities with a black urban core surrounded by white suburbs."

3. *What examples and details support your audience's view?* Expand on these views by developing them with supporting examples and details. (Carp might have brainstormed details about concealed razor blades, drugs, prison violence, the fear of her friends, and so on. King might have noted her research examples praising fuel cell technology such as the General Motors advertisement or California Governor Arnold Schwarzenegger's desire to build hydrogen fuel stations across the state. Rauch might have brainstormed his experiences with other American cities. His essay pro-vides the least development for the common view, which he encapsulates in his academic-sounding phrase "the long-standing meta-narrative of Washington.")

4. *What is your own surprising view?* (Carp might have answered, "Visiting the prison is uplifting because prisoners can be kind, creative, and generous." King might have said, "Although hydrogen fuel cell cars are pollution free, getting the hydrogen in the first place requires burning fossil fuels." Rauch might have said, "Many suburbs of Washington, D.C., have hundreds of dif-ferent ethnic groups all intermixed together with native-born Americans.")

5. *What examples and details support this view? Why do you hold this view? Why should a reader believe you?* Writing rapidly, spell out the evidence that supports your point. (Carp would have done a freewrite on all the experiences she had that changed her views about prisoners. Later she would have selected the most powerful ones and refined them for her read-ers. King would have done a freewrite about her research discoveries that hydrogen has to be recovered from carbon-based fossils or from electrolysis

of water—all of which mean continued use of pollution-causing fossil fuels. Rauch would have done a freewrite on his observation of the Au family, his experiences living in a Washington, D.C., suburb, and his memory of the 2001 study done by the Brookings Institute.)

After you finish exploring your responses to these five trigger questions, you will be well on your way to composing a first draft of your Option B essay. Now, finish writing your draft fairly rapidly without worrying about perfection.

Revising

Once you have your first draft on paper, the goal is to make it work better, first for yourself and then for your readers. If you discovered ideas as you wrote, you may need to do some major restructuring. Check to see that the question you are addressing is clear. Do you state it directly, as do Carp and King, or simply imply it, as does Rauch? Make sure that you distinguish between your audience's common view and your own surprising view. Do you put your meanings up front, with point sentences at the head of each section and near the beginning of every paragraph? Carp's and King's essays are more closed form than is Rauch's essay, but all three clearly contrast a surprising view with a common view.

We conclude this chapter with peer review guidelines that sum up the features to look for in your essay and remind you of the criteria your instructor will use in evaluating your work

---

GUIDELINES FOR PEER REVIEWS

Instructions for peer reviews are provided in Chapter 17 (pp. 519–520).

For the Writer
Prepare two or three questions you would like your peer reviewer to address while responding to your draft. The questions can focus on some aspect of your draft that you are uncertain about, on one or more sections where you particularly seek help or advice, on some feature that you particularly like about your draft, or on some part you especially wrestled with. Write out your questions and give them to your peer reviewer along with your draft.

For the Reviewer

I. Read the draft at a normal reading speed from beginning to end. As you read, do the following:

    A. Place a wavy line in the margin next to any passages that you find confusing, that contain something that doesn't seem to fit, or that otherwise slow down your reading.

B. Place a "Good!" in the margin next to any passages where you think the writing is particularly strong or interesting.

II. Read the draft again slowly and answer the following questions by writing down brief explanations for your answers.

A. Option A—Short Informative Report

1. Identify on the draft where the writer does each of the following: (a) explains the problem or question to be addressed; (b) explains the process for gathering information; (c) reports the findings; and (d) suggests the significance of the findings.

2. Is the draft written in a popular easy-reading style? Is the draft clear and easy to follow? Is the draft interesting? How might the writer improve the style, clarity, or interest level of the draft?

3. If the draft includes visual graphics, are they effective? Do the words and the visuals tell the same story? Are the visuals properly titled and labeled? How might the use of visuals be improved?

4. If the instructor asks writers to "desktop publish" their papers to look like popular magazine articles, is the document design effective? Are the graphics readable? How might the visual design of the paper be improved?

B. Option B—Informative Writing with Surprising Reversal

1. Do the title and introduction hook your interest? If not, how might the title and introduction be improved?

2. Where does the writer pose the question that the paper will address? Could this section of the paper be made clearer or more effective?

3. Where does the writer explain the common or popular view of the topic? Do you agree that this is the common view? How does the writer develop or support this view? What additional supporting examples, illustrations, or details might make the common view more vivid or compelling?

4. What is the writer's surprising view? Were you surprised? Identify the writer's thesis statement. Where does the writer locate the thesis? Would it be more effective to locate it elsewhere?

5. What details does the writer use to develop the surprising view? What additional supporting examples, illustrations, or details might help make the surprising view more vivid and compelling?

6. How might the writer improve the overall structure and clarity of this draft?

III. Rhetorical considerations

A. *Purpose, audience,* and *genre:* To what extent does the tone, style, and document design of the draft fit the assigned rhetorical context? How does the draft meet the demands of its genre and the needs of its audience while fulfilling the writer's purpose?

B. *Logos, ethos,* and *pathos:* How convincing or effective is the logical or conceptual part of this draft? What strategies does the writer use to construct a persona that inspires the reader's trust or confidence? How does the writer connect this study to the interests and values of the audience?

IV. Sum up what you see as the chief strengths and problem areas of this draft:
   A. Strengths
   B. Problem areas
V. Read the draft one more time. Place a check mark in the margin wherever you notice problems in grammar, spelling, or mechanics (one check mark per problem).

Analyzing Field Research Data from Observation, Interviews, or Questionnaires

About Analyzing Field Research Data

Field research—which uses strategies such as questionnaires, surveys, interviews, or direct observations—is one of the most powerful methods that scholars use to investigate our world. If you plan to major in the social or physical sciences or in professional fields such as business, nursing, or education, this chapter will introduce you to a common kind of writing in your major—the empirical research report. (By "empirical," we mean investigations based on direct observation of events or phenomena or on systematically gathered statistical data.) If your major is in the humanities, this chapter will familiarize you with ways that scientists gather and interpret research data as they investigate empirical questions. The writing project for this chapter asks you to pose an empirical research question based on a phenomenon that interests you and then to collect relevant data through direct observation, through interviews, or through a questionnaire that you design. You will present your findings within a scientific genre known as the "research report." (An alternative writing project is Option A in Chapter 9—a short informative report, p. 224.)

Our own classroom experience suggests that you will find this assignment intellectually engaging and enjoyable. You will discover that there are hundreds of interesting empirical questions that you can ask and investigate on a small scale yourself. You will actually produce new knowledge that is interesting to you and others.

Exploring the Analysis of Field Research Data

The following task, which anticipates some of the research issues discussed later in this chapter, will help you begin thinking about the analysis of field research data.

Suppose you want to find out whether there is any difference in the exercise habits of male versus female college students. (Rather than exercise habits, you might choose to investigate gender differences for other activities such as playing video games, reading magazines, watching television, surfing the Internet, or doing homework.) You might hypothesize that there are no gender differences in the percentage of male versus female students who exercise regularly or in the amount of time spent exercising by men versus women. However, you might speculate that the kinds of exercise vary by gender. For example, you might hypothesize that male students spend more time than females on muscle-building activities such as weight training or on pickup team sports such as basketball or touch football. Conversely, you might hypothesize that female students select exercises aimed at weight loss, muscle toning, and psychological well-being. Your study will help you confirm or disconfirm your initial hypotheses.

a. Working in small groups, create your own hypothesis in answer to the research question, "Are there gender differences in the exercise habits of male versus female college students?" Then create a short questionnaire (or set of interview questions) that will give you the data needed to confirm or disconfirm your hypothesis. At a minimum, your group's questionnaire will have to provide data on two variables: the respondent's gender and the amount of time each week the respondent typically spends on physical exercise. You might also wish to determine the kinds of exercise preferred by the respondents and their motivations for exercising, but try to develop an uncluttered questionnaire that yields answers that you can count and tabulate.

b. Choose one or more of the questionnaires you created in small groups and field-test them on the class. Ask class members—on a volunteer basis—to try responding to the questions. Your goal here is to discover whether the questions might be unclear or ambiguous.

c. As a class, discuss problems that arose in creating the questionnaire and then in responding to questions. Were any questions unclear? Did they yield answers that could be counted and tabulated? How would you revise your questionnaire based on difficulties you encountered?

d. Suppose on two successive days you gave one of your class's questionnaires to all students entering your college library and tabulated the results. To what extent would the results be generalizable to the whole student body at your college? Generalizable to college students overall? Generalizable to the public at large?

e. Discuss the ethics of this study. Might some students feel embarrassed or even harmed by this study if their individual answers were made public? Is it anyone's business how much a person does or does not exercise? How might safeguards be built into the study to minimize the chances of any person's being made to feel uncomfortable?

WRITING PROJECT

The assignment for this chapter is a modified version of a standard research report. (We have omitted advanced features that would be required of upper-division science majors, such as a statistical analysis of data or a review of previous research.)

Write a scientific report that presents and analyzes your research findings in response to a question about contemporary phenomena or unfolding events. The methods used for your research can include direct observations, interviews, or questionnaires. Your report should include the four main sections of a research report: Introduction, Method, Results, and Discussion. Your instructor might also ask you to prepare the report in American Psychological Association (APA) format with a title page.

Instruction on APA style and documentation is found in Chapter 22, pp. 687–693.

Later sections of this chapter describe in detail the major sections of a research report. We also provide advice for posing appropriate research questions; for conducting field research through observation, interviews, or questionnaires; for using tables and figures to report your data; for analyzing your data; and for ensuring that your research project meets appropriate ethical standards. An alternative version of this writing project is to present your findings as a short informative report written for a popular audience (see the assignment for Chapter 9, Option A, p. 224.)

Here are some suggestions for possible research projects. These should suggest a wide range of possibilities for other projects.

- Investigate students' usage patterns or levels of satisfaction with some aspect of student services on your campus (for example, computer labs, security escort service, student newspaper, recreational facilities, study skills workshops).
- Investigate the degree of gender stereotyping in randomly selected children's birthday cards from a local card store or supermarket.
- Investigate adherence to traffic rules at a chosen intersection, testing variables such as car type, weather conditions, time of day, amount of traffic, and so forth.
- Investigate the way students spend their time during a typical week (for example, studying, watching television, playing video games, participating in recreational sports, working, and so forth). You might also try to determine whether there are differences in these patterns based upon factors such as gender, major, GPA, career aspirations, job status, part-time/full-time status, or commuter/residential status.
- Investigate whether there is a correlation between the kinds of music students listen to and their choice of major, recreational habits, political views, class identification, ethnicity, age, gender, or other factors.

Understanding the Analysis of Field Research Data

The Structure of an Empirical Research Report

A flow diagram for a typical research report is shown in Figure 10.1. Formatting conventions call for prominent section headings so that readers can quickly skip ahead to find the sections labeled "Method," "Results," and "Discussion." What is

FIGURE 10.1 Structure of an Empirical Research Report*

(Title Page)	• For format of an APA title page and body of research report, see pp. 277–289.
ABSTRACT	• *Provides one-paragraph summary of report (problem, major findings, significance of study)*[†]
INTRODUCTION	• Explains the problem to be investigated • Shows importance and significance of the problem • Presents the researcher's hypothesis • *Reviews previous studies examining the same problem (called a "literature review")*[†]
METHOD	• Describes how the study was done (enables future researchers to replicate the study exactly) • Often has subheadings such as "Participants," "Materials," and "Procedure" • Often provides definitions of key concepts in the problem/hypothesis
RESULTS	• Presents the researcher's findings or results • Often displays findings in figures, charts, or graphs as well as describing them in words • Usually does not present raw data or behind-the-scenes mathematics; data focus on composite results • *Presents statistical analysis of data to show confidence levels and other advanced statistical implications or meanings*[†]
DISCUSSION	• Analyzes and evaluates the collected data in terms of the original research question and hypothesis • Speculates on causes and consequences of the findings • Shows applications and practical or theoretical significance of the study • Usually includes a section pointing out limitations and possible flaws in the study and suggests directions for future research
REFERENCES	• Bibliographic listing of any cited sources • For format of APA references, see pp. 687–693.
APPENDICES	• Provides place to include questionnaires or other materials used in study

* Based on guidelines in the *Publication Manual of the American Psychological Association,* 5th ed. (Washington, D.C.: APA, 2001) pp.10–30.
[†] Note: Material in italics is not required for the writing project in this chapter.

noteworthy about this four-part shape is that the main sections of a research report follow the logic of the scientific method, as the following explanation suggests.

The Stages of the Scientific Method and the Four Main Sections of the Research Report

Stage 1: Posing the question.   Scientists begin by posing a research question and formulating their own hypothetical answer to it based on their initial theories, assumptions, hunches, and reasoning. They wish to test this hypothesis through systematic gathering of empirical data. The "Introduction" section of the research report corresponds to this stage: It describes the research question, explains its significance, and reviews previous scientific research addressing the same or a similar question. (Note: The assignment for this chapter does not ask you to do a literature review.) Typically, the introduction ends with the scientist's hypothesis predicting what the observed data will show.

Stage 2: Collecting data.   Scientists develop a method for collecting the data needed to confirm or disconfirm the hypothesis. The materials and methods used to conduct the research, along with operational definitions of any key terms, are described in detail in the "Method" section of the report. The Method section is like a recipe that allows future researchers to replicate the research process exactly. It also allows peer reviewers to look for possible flaws or holes in the research design.

Stage 3: Determining results.   Scientists examine the collected data carefully, seeing how well the data support what was predicted in the hypothesis. These findings are reported in the "Results" section, usually displayed in tables or graphs as well as described verbally. To help determine the extent to which researchers can have confidence in the gathered data, expert researchers perform a variety of statistical tests that show, among other things, whether the results might be attributable simply to chance. (The modified assignment for this chapter does not require statistical tests.)

Stage 4: Analyzing results.   Finally, scientists interpret and analyze their findings, drawing conclusions about what the findings mean and how the research advances knowledge. This stage of the scientific process corresponds to the "Discussion" section of the research report. Typically, the Discussion section also points to limitations and flaws in the research design and suggests directions for future research.

Other Sections

In addition to the four main sections, research reports often include an abstract of 150 to 250 words that summarizes the research problem, research design, results, and major implications of the study. The abstract allows readers at a glance to get a basic understanding of the research. At the end of the report, a "References" section lists bibliographic details about any cited sources. Finally, scientists can append to the end of the report, in the "Appendices" section, copies of questionnaires used, interview questions asked, or special calculations that might interest readers.

How Readers Typically Read a Research Report

What is unusual about research reports is that readers typically don't read them in a linear fashion. The advantage of a well-marked four-part structure is that readers can skim a report first and then, if they're interested, read it carefully in an order that meets their needs. Readers will typically skim the Introduction to understand the problem under investigation and then skip directly to the Discussion section, where the researchers' findings are analyzed in depth. Readers with special interest in the question being investigated may then go back to read the Introduction, Method section, and Results section in detail to evaluate the soundness of the research design and the accuracy and reliability of the data. Some readers may follow a different order. For example, researchers primarily interested in developing new research designs might read the Method section first to learn how the research was conducted. Our point is that the conventional format of a research report allows readers to tailor their reading practices to their own interests.

We will now go back through the sections of a research report, offering you suggestions for doing the kinds of thinking needed at each stage of the research process.

Posing Your Research Question

When you pose your research question for this writing project, you need to appreciate the difference between the broad, open-ended questions we have emphasized throughout this text and the very narrow questions that scientists use when doing empirical studies. Scientists, of course, pose big, open-ended questions all the time: What is the origin of the universe? What is the role of nature versus nurture in human gender behavior? What would it be like to ride upon a beam of light (a question Einstein asked in formulating his theory of relativity)? But when they conduct actual research, scientists transform these big, speculative, indeterminate questions into narrow determinate questions. By "determinate," we mean questions that can be answered either with yes or no or with a single fact, number, or range of numbers. The kinds of determinate questions that scientists typically ask can be placed in five categories in ascending order of complexity (see Table 10.1).*

As you study Table 10.1, you will see that it moves from descriptive questions aimed at identifying, measuring, and describing a phenomenon (categories 1, 2, and 3) to explanatory questions aimed at discovering the causes or consequences of a phenomenon (categories 4 and 5). A question in the first category simply asks whether a phenomenon exists. Within the second category, researchers are interested in measuring some aspect of that existence—the phenomenon's size, temperature, frequency, and so forth. Categories three through five focus increasingly on causality. Category three determines how the phenomenon differs from other, related phenomenon, where the identification of differences would stimulate speculative thinking about causes. Category four focuses on the

---

*Table 10.1 is based on an unpublished paper by psychologist Robert Morasky, "Model of Empirical Research Questions." Morasky's model was used for the section on "Asking Empirical Research Questions for Science" in John C. Bean and John D. Ramage, *Form and Surprise in Composition: Writing and Thinking Across the Curriculum* (New York: Macmillan, 1986), pp. 183–189.

TABLE 10.1 Asking Determinate Research Questions

Question Type	Explanation	Natural Science Example	Social Science Example	Possible Question That You Might Ask for This Chapter's Writing Project
1. *Existence Questions:* "Does X exist in domain Y?"	Often researchers simply want to determine if a given phenomenon occurs or exists within a given domain	Do fragments of fungi exist in Precambrian sediments?	Do racial stereotypes exist in current world history textbooks?	Do advertisements for computers appear in women's fashion magazines?
2. *Measurement Questions:* "How large/small/fast/much/ many/bright is X?*	Here researchers want to measure the extent to which something occurs (percentages) or the degree or size of a phenomenon	How hot is the surface of Venus?	What percentage of homeless persons suffer from mental illness?	What percentage of children's birthday cards currently displayed at local stores contain gender stereotyping?
3. *Comparison Questions:* "Is X greater/less than Y or different from Y"?	Researchers frequently want to study how two events, groups, or phenomena differ according to greater or less amounts of some measure	Is radiation from Io greater in volcanic areas than in nonvolcanic areas?	Is the incidence of anorexia greater among middle-class women than among working-class women?	Do humanities majors report fewer study hours per week than nonhumanities majors?
4. *Correlation Questions:* "If X varies, does Y vary?"	This is a more complex kind of comparison question in which researchers determine whether differences in X are accompanied by corresponding differences in Y	Does the aggression level of male rats vary with testosterone levels in their blood?	Do students' evaluations of their teachers vary with the grades they expect to receive for the course?	Does students' satisfaction with university food services vary with their family size?
5. *Experimental Questions:* "Does a variation in X cause a variation in Y?"*	Here researchers move beyond correlations to try to determine the direct causes of a certain phenomenon	If male rats are forced into stress situations to compete for food, will the level of testosterone in their blood increase?	Will preschool children taken shopping after watching TV commercials for high-sugar cereals ask for such cereals at a higher rate than children in a control group who did not see the commercials?	Will persons shown a Monsanto ad promoting biotech corn reveal a more favorable attitude toward genetically modified foods than a control group not shown the ad?

*Direct experiments can be difficult to design and conduct in some of the social sciences. Also, experimental questions often raise ethical issues whenever experiments place human subjects in psychological stress, cause physical pain and suffering to laboratory animals, or otherwise bring harm to individuals. See pages 269–270 for further discussion of ethical issues in research.

discovery of how two or more phenomena are correlated—that is, how they vary together. For example, recent research has suggested that women who work night shifts and sleep during the day develop breast cancer at higher rates than women who sleep at night. However, the existence of a correlation doesn't explain what causes the correlation. Within category five, researchers try to create experiments or develop other research methods that will establish actual cause and effect.

For Writing and Discussion

This exercise encourages you to brainstorm ideas for your own research question. The goal here is not to settle on a research question but to get a feeling for the range of options you might choose for your own investigation.

Background: The following list shows how students might use the five categories in Table 10.1 to frame questions about the exercise habits of college students.

CATEGORIES OF RESEARCH QUESTIONS APPLIED TO STUDY OF EXERCISE HABITS

1. *Existence Questions ("Does X exist in domain Y?"):* Does "yoga" appear as an exercise choice among the respondents to this questionnaire?
2. *Measurement Questions ("How large/small/fast/much/many/bright is X?"):* On average, how many hours per week do female (and male) college students devote to physical exercise? Or, what percentage of females (and males) report five or more hours per week of physical exercise?
3. *Comparison Questions ("Is X greater/less than Y or different from Y?"):* Do a higher percentage of male college students than female college students report five or more hours per week of physical exercise?
4. *Correlation Questions ("If X varies, does Y vary also?"):* Do students who report studying more than thirty hours per week exercise more than students who report studying fewer than thirty hours per week?
5. *Experimental Questions ("Does a variation in X cause a variation in Y?"):* Will an experimental group of students asked to keep an exercise log exercise more regularly than a control group of students who do not keep such a log?

Individual task: Spend ten minutes thinking of possible ideas for your own research project. Try using the five categories of questions to stimulate your thinking, but don't worry whether a question exactly fits one category or the other. Remember to ask determinate questions that can be answered by yes/no or by a single number, percentage, or range of numbers.

Group task: Working in small groups or as a whole class, share your initial ideas, using your classmates' proposed research questions to stimulate more of your own thinking. Your goal is to generate a wide range of possible research questions you might like to investigate.

Collecting Data Through Observation, Interviews, or Questionnaires

Once you have formulated your research question, you need to develop a plan for collecting the needed data. In this section, we give you suggestions for conducting your research through direct observation, interviews, or questionnaires.

Using Observation to Gather Information

The key to successful observation is having a clear sense of your purpose combined with advance preparation. We offer the following practical suggestions for carrying out observational research:

1. ***Determine the purpose and scope of your observation.*** Think ahead about what you will be observing and what kinds of details, behaviors, or processes you will want to take note of. Can you observe your phenomenon only once or will you need to observe regularly over a period of days? If you plan to conduct a series of observations, the first one could provide an overview or baseline, while subsequent observations could enable you to explore parts of your subject in more detail or note changes over time.

2. ***Make timely arrangements.*** In some cases, you may need to ask permission or get special clearance for your observation. Be sure to make the necessary arrangements long before you start the observation. In making requests, state clearly who you are and what the purpose of your visit is. Be cordial in your requests and in your thanks after your observations.

3. ***Come prepared with the appropriate tools and take clear, usable notes.*** You will need note-taking materials—either a laptop computer or plenty of paper, a clipboard or binder with a hard surface for writing, and good writing utensils. Make sure that your notes are easy to read and well labeled with helpful headings. Document your notes with exact indications of location, time, and names and titles of people (if relevant).

4. ***Go through your notes soon after your observation.*** Don't count on your memory to reconstruct details or recapture thoughts you had while observing. Get your observations down on paper without regard to grammar or structure initially. You might then want to write a first draft of this segment of your paper while the results of your observation are still fresh in your mind.

Here are two examples of how students have used direct observation to conduct research:

- A student wanting to know how often people violated a "Do Not Walk on the Grass" sign on her campus observed a lawn for one week during mornings between classes and counted persons who took a shortcut across the grass rather than followed the sidewalks. She also recorded the gender of shortcut-takers to see if there were any gender differences in this behavior.
- A student hypothesized that shoppers at a local Whole Foods store would drive fewer SUVs or large pickups than shoppers at a Wal-Mart store several miles away. The student categorized cars by size ranging from large pickups or SUVs to subcompacts. Then on several different occasions, he counted the number of cars in each category at the parking lots of each store.

Conducting Interviews

Interviews can be an effective way to gather field research information. They can range from formal interviews lasting thirty or more minutes to quick, informal interviews, in which the researcher hopes only for brief answers to a few key questions. The researcher might even conduct an interview over the telephone, without a face-to-face meeting. As an example of informal interviews, consider the hypothetical case of a researcher investigating why customers at a local grocery store choose to buy or not buy organic vegetables. This researcher might ask persons buying vegetables if they would be willing to be briefly interviewed. (The researcher would need to be very polite, to keep the interviews brief, and to get the store manager's permission in advance.)

In other kinds of field research studies, you might rely on longer, formal interviews with persons whose background or knowledge was relevant to your research question. Although asking a busy professional for an interview can be intimidating, many experts are generous with their time when they encounter a student who is interested in their field. To make interviews as useful as possible, we suggest several strategies.

Preparing for Interviews   Preparing for an interview is crucial because you want to make a good first impression and not waste anyone's time. The following are some key preparatory steps:

1. *Consider your purpose.* Determine in advance what you hope to learn from the interview. Think about your research question and the aim of the paper you are planning to write.
2. *Do background reading.* Prepare for the interview by researching important subjects related to your research question and to the person you will be interviewing. Ideally, interviews should give you knowledge or perspectives unavailable in books or articles. Although you needn't be an expert at the time of the interview, you should be conversant about your subject.
3. *Formulate well-thought-out questions.* Be as thorough with your questions as possible. Most likely you will have only one chance to interview this person. Develop a range of questions, including short-answer questions like the following: How long have you been working in this field? What are the typical qualifications for this job? Give special thought to creating open-ended questions, which should be the heart of your interview. Here are some typical examples of open-ended questions: What changes have you seen in this field? What solutions have you found to be most successful in dealing with . . . ? What do you see as the causes of . . . ? Questions framed in this way will elicit the information you need but still allow the interviewee to answer freely. Avoid yes-or-no questions that can stall conversation with a one-word answer. Also, avoid leading questions. For example, instead of asking a social worker, "What do you think about infringing on the rights of the homeless by making them take antipsychotic medication?" ask instead, "What are your views on requiring the mentally ill homeless to take antipsychotic medica-

tions as a condition for welfare assistance?" The more you lead the interviewee to the answers you want, the less valid your research becomes.

4. *Gather your supplies.* Before the interview, decide how you plan to record the information. Many people like to use a portable tape or digital recorder, but be sure to get your interviewee's permission if you plan to do so. If you plan to record the session electronically, spend time familiarizing yourself with the recorder, checking for fresh batteries, or making sure you have a power cord long enough to reach an outlet. If you use a tape recorder, make sure you have plenty of blank tapes. Using a recorder allows you to focus your attention on the substance of the interview, following the speaker's train of thought and planning in your head what else you need to ask. Most likely, you will want to take notes even if you are recording.

Managing the Interview   Here are some practical suggestions for conducting successful interviews:

1. *Be prompt and agree on the length of the interview.* Arrive for the interview on time. Also agree to a time limit for the interview and stick to it. (If necessary, you can request a second interview, or your interviewee may be willing to stay longer.) You will show a lack of professionalism if you are not particularly careful to respect the interviewee's time.
2. *Be courteous and alert.* Your attitude during the interview can help set up a cordial and comfortable relationship between you and the person you are interviewing.
3. *Take brief but clear notes.* Try to record all the main ideas and to be accurate with quoted material. Don't hesitate to ask if you are unsure about a fact or statement or if you need to double-check what the person intended to say.
4. *Have your questions clearly in mind but be flexible.* Ask your questions in a logical order, but also be sensitive to the flow of the conversation. If the interviewee rambles away from the question, don't jump in too fast. You may learn something valuable from the seeming digression. You may even want to ask unanticipated questions if you have delved into new ideas.

Processing and Using Material from Interviews   You will probably leave the interview feeling immersed in what you heard. No matter how vivid the words are in your mind, take time *very* soon after the interview to go over your notes or to transcribe your tape. What may seem unforgettable at the moment is all too easy to forget later. If you do your reviewing soon after, you can usually fill in gaps in your notes or explain unclear passages on the tape. Do not trust your memory alone.

Using Questionnaires

In constructing a questionnaire, your goal is to elicit responses that are directly related to your research question and that will give you the data you need to answer the question. The construction of a questionnaire—both its wording and its arrangement on the page—is crucial to its success. As you design your questionnaire, imagine respondents with only limited patience and time. Keep your questionnaire clear, easy to complete, and as short as possible, taking care to avoid ambiguous sentences. Proofread it carefully, and pilot it on a few volunteer respondents so that you can eliminate confusing spots. Some specific examples of types of questions often found on questionnaires are shown in Figure 10.2.

When you have designed the questions you will ask, write an introductory comment that explains the questionnaire's purpose. If possible, encourage responses by explaining why the knowledge gained from the questionnaire will be beneficial to others. Make your completed questionnaire as professionally attractive and easy to read and fill out as possible. As an example, Figure 10.3 shows a questionnaire, introduced with an explanatory comment, prepared by a student investigating the parking problems of commuter students on her campus.

When you distribute your questionnaire, try to obtain a random sample. For example, if you assessed student satisfaction with a campus cafeteria by passing out questionnaires to those eating in the cafeteria at noon on a particular day, you might not achieve a random sampling of potential cafeteria users. You would miss those who avoid the cafeteria because they hate it; also, the distribution of noon users of the cafeteria might be different from the distribution of breakfast or dinner users. Another problem with sampling is that people who feel strongly about an issue are more likely to complete a questionnaire than those who don't feel strongly. The student who prepared the parking questionnaire, for example, is likely to get a particularly high rate of response from those most angry about parking issues, and thus her sample might not be representative of all commuter students. In some situations, random sampling may be unfeasible. For the assignment for this chapter, check with your instructor whether a "convenience sample" would be acceptable (for example, you would pass out questionnaires to persons in your dorm or in your class as a matter of convenience, even though these persons would not represent a random sample of the larger population).

For Writing and Discussion

Write out a possible research question that you might investigate for your project. Working individually, consider ways that you might use one of the research methods just discussed—observation, interviews, or questionnaires—to answer your question. Begin designing your research plan, including procedures for observations or formulation of questions for your questionnaire or interviews. Then, working in small groups or as a whole class, share your brainstorming. Your goal is to develop the beginnings of a research plan. Help each other talk through the stages of a possible investigation.

FIGURE 10.2 Types of Questions Used in Questionnaires

Fixed-choice question
Compared to other campuses with which you are familiar, this campus's use of alcohol is (mark one):

—— greater than other campuses'
—— less than other campuses'
—— about the same as other campuses'

Open-ended question
How would you say alcohol use on this campus compares to other campuses?
Comment: Fixed-choice questions are easier to tabulate and report statistically; open-ended questions can yield a wider variety of insights but are impractical for large numbers of respondents.

Question with operationally defined rather than undefined term
Undefined term: Think back over the last two weeks. How many times did you engage in binge drinking?
Operationally defined term: Think back over the last two weeks. How many times have you had four or more drinks in a row?
Comment: An "operational definition" states empirically measurable criteria for a term. In the first version of the question, the term "binge drinking" might mean different things to different persons. Moreover, respondents are apt to deny being binge drinkers given that it is an unflattering categorization. In the revised question, the term "binge drinking" is replaced with an observable and measurable behavior; respondents are more apt to give an honest response.

Category question
What is your current class standing?

—— freshman
—— sophomore
—— junior
—— senior
—— other (please specify)
Comment: In category questions, it is often helpful to have an "Other" category for respondents who do not fit neatly into any of the other categories.

Scaled-answer question
This campus has a serious drinking problem (circle one):

strongly agree	agree	neither agree nor disagree	disagree	strongly disagree
5	4	3	2	1

How much drinking goes on in your dormitory on Friday or Saturday nights?

a lot	some	not much	none

Comment: Although scaled-answer questions are easy to tabulate and are widely used, the data can be skewed by the subjective definitions of each respondent (one person's "a lot" may be another person's "not much").

FIGURE 10.3   Example of a Questionnaire

Dear Commuter Student:

I am conducting a study aimed at improving the parking situation for commuter students. Please take a few moments to complete the following questionnaire, which will provide valuable information that may lead to specific proposals for easing the parking problems of commuters. If we commuter students work together with the university administration, we may be able to find equitable solutions to the serious parking issues we face. Please return the questionnaires to the box I have placed at the south entrance to the Student Union Building.

1. When do you typically arrive on campus?

   Before 8 A.M. _____   Between 1 P.M. and 5 P.M. _____
   Between 8 A.M. and 9 A.M. _____   Between 5 P.M. and 7 P.M. _____
   Between 9 A.M. and noon _____   After 7 P.M. _____
   During noon hour _____

2. How frequently do you have problems finding a place to park?

   Nearly every day ____
   About half the time ____
   Occasionally ____
   Almost never ____

3. When the first lot you try is full, how long does it typically take you to find a place to park (for those who buy a commuter parking permit)?

   Less than 10 minutes ___
   10–15 minutes ___
   More than 15 minutes ___

4. For those who use street parking only, how long does it take you to find a place to park?

   Less than 10 minutes ___
   10–15 minutes ___
   More than 15 minutes ___

5. Do you currently carpool?

   Yes ____
   No ____

6. The university is considering a proposal to raise parking fees for single-driver cars and lower them for car pools. If you don't currently carpool, how difficult would it be to find a car-pool partner?

   Impossible ___
   Very difficult ___
   Somewhat difficult ___
   Fairly easy ___

7. If finding a car-pool partner would be difficult, why?

   Few fellow students live in my neighborhood ___
   Few fellow students match my commuting hours ___
   Other ___

8. What suggestions do you have for improving the parking situation for commuter students?

Reporting Your Results in Words and Graphics

Once you have completed your research and tabulated your findings, you are
ready to write the "Results" section of your paper, which reports your findings in
words often supplemented with tables and graphs.* Do not report raw data.
Rather, create composite results by tabulating totals or calculating averages and
report these results in words and in appropriate graphics. Try to report your data
in such a way that readers can quickly see whether the data support or do not
support your hypothesis. In reporting results, your aim is to create a scientific
ethos that is objective and unbiased. Your purpose is to help readers understand For a discussion of
ethos, see pp. 78–80.
your findings concisely and clearly. In this section we will first explain the kinds
of graphics you might choose for your report. Then we'll explain some of the
skills needed to make sure that your words and graphics tell the same story in a
clear, easy-to-follow manner.

Tables

Halfway between a picture and a list, a table presents data in columns (vertical
groupings) and rows (horizontal groupings), thereby allowing readers to see relationships relatively quickly. Table 10.2 displays data of a student researcher who
was investigating the number of people who bought "impulse items" in the
checkout line at a local grocery store. She wanted to see how often people added
to their carts items such as magazines, tabloids, candy, novelty toys, or convenience goods like mini-flashlights or nail files.

Line Graphs

A line graph can tell a story more dramatically than a table because it makes the
relationship between two variables immediately visible. It achieves this effect by
converting numerical data into a series of points on a grid and connecting them

TABLE 10.2 Number, Percentage, and Purchase Choices of Impulse Buyers

	Total Shoppers	Impulse Buyers		Number of Shoppers Who Purchased Each Item (Some shoppers bought more than one item.)				
		Number	Percent	Magazine	Tabloid	Candy/gum/ cigarettes	Toy	Other
Day 1	75	22	29	18	10	10	5	7
Day 2	107	38	36	26	12	20	9	11
Day 3	90	29	30	21	12	17	8	10
Total	272	89	33	65	34	47	22	28

*In professional reports, the "Results" section also includes a statistical analysis of the data to determine confidence levels and
statistical significance. For your assignment for this chapter, you do not need to do a statistical analysis, which requires a course
in statistics.

FIGURE 10.4 International Student Enrollment in Humanities College, 1994–2004

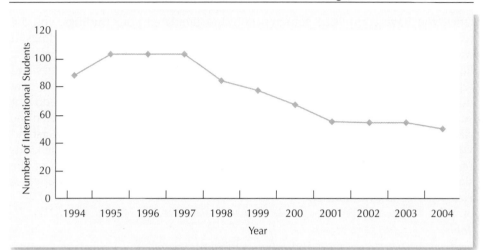

to create flat, rising, or falling lines. Figure 10.4 shows a line graph created by a student interested in interviewing international students about their experiences in the humanities college at his university. As background, he obtained registration data from his university's Web site and created this graph, which shows enrollment patterns for international students from 1994 to 2004 within the humanities college. By convention, the horizontal axis contains the predictable, known variable, such as time or some other sequence, arranged in a predictable order. The vertical axis contains the unpredictable variable that forms the graph's story.

Bar Graphs

Bar graphs use columns of varying lengths to contrast two or more quantities. They quickly allow readers to make comparisons between different groups across a variable such as time. The key to clarity is the wording of the title (which tells the reader what the bar graph is supposed to show), the labels on the horizontal and vertical axes, and the legend, which tells readers what each column represents. The legends often make use of color, shadings, or different patterns of hash marks. Figure 10.5 was created by a student investigating students' responses to the question, "If you were to achieve the 'good life,' what would be your ideal car?" (The phrase "N = 40" in the title indicates that the number of respondents was forty.)

Pie Charts

Pie charts, as their name suggests, depict different percentages of a total (the pie) in the form of slices. Pie charts tell the story of how the whole is divided into different-sized parts. Pie charts can tell a particularly dramatic story if one piece of the pie is larger or smaller than one would expect. Two pie charts placed side by

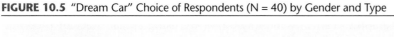

FIGURE 10.5 "Dream Car" Choice of Respondents (N = 40) by Gender and Type

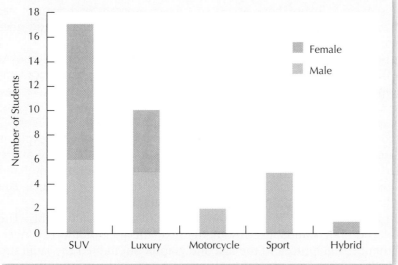

FIGURE 10.6 Factors That Are Important to Customers When Choosing Starbucks or Café Vita

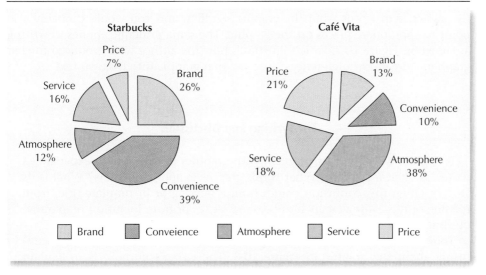

side can often tell the story of how two different cases divide up the pie different-ly. Figure 10.6 was created by a team of students investigating why customers chose a Starbucks coffee shop close to their campus as opposed to a locally owned coffee shop several blocks away. They used side-by-side pie charts to show the importance of "atmosphere" at the locally owned shop, Café Vita, versus "con-venience" for customers at Starbucks.

Incorporating Graphics into Your Research Report

Quantitative graphics can now be made quickly using spreadsheet or presentation programs. If you do not have access to such a program or have not yet learned how to use them, you can also make your graphics with pencil and ruler and tape them into your document.

In newspapers and popular magazines, writers often include graphics in boxes or sidebars without specifically referring to them in the text. However, in academic papers, graphics are always labeled, numbered, titled, and referred to in the text. By convention, tables are listed as "Tables," while line graphs, bar graphs, pie charts, or any other kinds of drawings or photographs are labeled as "Figures." In addition to numbering and labeling, each graphic needs a title that explains fully what information is being displayed. In the title for a bar graph, for example, some part of the title has to correspond to the labels on the horizontal and vertical axes and to the legends that show what each column represents. The same principle applies to other kinds of quantitative graphics.

When you insert a graphic into your own text, the general rule is this: The graphic should be understandable without the text; the text should be understandable without the graphic; and the text and graphic should tell the same story. Refer explicitly to each of your graphics and explain to your readers what you want them to see in the graphic—a referencing convention called "independent redundancy." You can easily understand this principle if you imagine giving a PowerPoint presentation. When a graphic comes on the screen, you would tell the audience in words what the graphic signifies, and you would probably also point to appropriate places on the graphic. The same principle applies in writing as shown in Figure 10.7, which illustrates how the author who produced the bar graph on "dream car preferences" inserted that graphic into his own text.

For Writing and Discussion

Background: A frequent problem with graphics designed by inexperienced writers is unclear purpose (What is this graphic supposed to show? What is its story?). Often this confusion comes from a missing or incomplete title, from missing or misleading labels for the x-and y-axes or from inclusion of extraneous information.

Your task: Working in small groups or as a whole class, explain what is confusing about the graphic in Figure 10.8. The writer's purpose is to explain respondents' answers to the question, "Which fast-food restaurant produces the best chicken nuggets?" What do you think the x- (horizontal) axis and y-(vertical) axis are supposed to represent? How could you rewrite the title and the axis labels in order to make the graphic easier to comprehend at a glance? Assuming that the vertical axis represents number of respondents, try telling this story using a pie chart (based on percentages) rather than a bar graph.

FIGURE 10.7 Example of a Student Text with Referenced Graphic

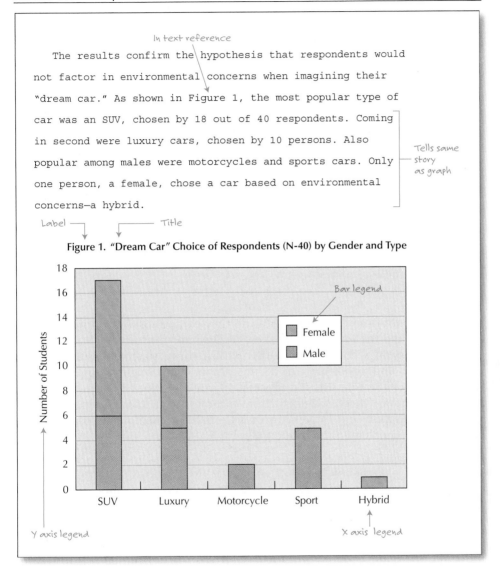

In text reference

The results confirm the hypothesis that respondents would not factor in environmental concerns when imagining their "dream car." As shown in Figure 1, the most popular type of car was an SUV, chosen by 18 out of 40 respondents. Coming in second were luxury cars, chosen by 10 persons. Also popular among males were motorcycles and sports cars. Only one person, a female, chose a car based on environmental concerns—a hybrid.

Tells same story as graph

Label   *Title*

Figure 1. "Dream Car" Choice of Respondents (N-40) by Gender and Type

Bar legend

■ Female
■ Male

Number of Students

18
16
14
12
10
8
6
4
2
0

SUV   Luxury   Motorcycle   Sport   Hybrid

Y axis legend   *X axis legend*

Analyzing Your Results

The "Discussion" section of a research report is devoted to the writer's analysis of the results. This section most resembles a thesis-governed essay addressing an open-ended problem. Think of your Discussion section as answering the following question: Now that I have reported my results, what do these results mean?

FIGURE 10.8 Example of an Unclear Student Graphic

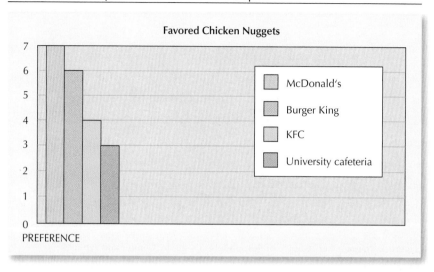

(What do I learn from the results? How do they confirm or disconfirm my initial assumptions and theories? How are these results important or significant?)

The Discussion section should open with a thesis statement that indicates whether your findings support or do not support your original hypothesis and that summarizes or forecasts the other main points of your analysis. Here is an example of how a thesis statement from a professional research report entitled "Marital Disruption and Depression in a Community Sample" is connected to their research problem in the Introduction:

DESCRIPTION OF PROBLEM FROM "INTRODUCTION"

Explanation of problem: "Researchers have long known that recently divorced persons tend to show high degrees of depression, but the direction of causation is unknown: Does divorce cause depression or does depression cause divorce?"

Research question: "Does marital disruption contribute to higher levels of depression in recently divorced persons?"

Hypothesis: "Marital disruption contributes to higher levels of depression in recently divorced persons."

Early in the Discussion section, the authors create an explicit thesis statement that directly responds to the hypothesis:

THESIS STATEMENT FROM THE "DISCUSSION" SECTION

"According to the results, marital disruption does in fact cause a significant increase in depression compared to pre-divorce levels within a period of three years after the divorce."

Although there are no formulas for the Discussion section of a research report, most reports contain the following four conventional features:

- Identification of significant patterns and speculation about causes
- Implications and significance of the results
- Limitations of the study
- Suggestions for further research

Let's look at each in turn.

Identification of Significant Patterns and Speculation about Causes

The first part of a Discussion section often points out patterns that the researcher considers significant. The most important patterns are those that bear directly on the researcher's hypothesis. For example, in studying exercise habits of college students, you might find that, contrary to your hypothesis, women exercise more than men. Depending on other findings derived from your questionnaire, you might note additional patterns—for example, that persons claiming to be on a diet exercise more than those who don't or that persons who are regular runners tend to spend more time studying than do persons who play lots of pickup team sports.

The discovery of significant patterns leads naturally to speculation about causes. Understanding how a certain event or condition leads to other events or conditions contributes to our knowledge of the world and often may have practical consequences for improving the world or our situation in it. Because of scientists' interest in the underlying causes of a phenomenon, researchers typically use the Discussion section of a report to speculate about the causes of significant patterns. Often a researcher suggests several different, alternative explanations of the data, each explanation opening up avenues for further research. As you contemplate questions raised by your research, consider the following ways that data may suggest causality:

- *Causality induced from a recurring pattern:* If you regularly start to sneeze after petting a cat but not after petting a dog, you can induce, as an initial hypothesis, that you are allergic in some way to cats even though you can't directly explain the mechanism. You were able to make this induction only after you recognized a pattern. In the social sciences, descriptive studies help reveal such patterns. For example, psychologists attempting to understand the causes of anorexia have discovered that many (but not all) anorexics come from perfectionist, highly work-oriented homes that emphasize duty and responsibility. This frequently recurring element is thus a suspected causal factor leading to anorexia.
- *Causality hypothesized from correlations: Correlation* is a statistical term indicating the probability that two events or phenomena will occur together. For example, various studies have shown a correlation between creativity and left-handedness. (The percentage of left-handed people within a sample of highly creative people is considerably higher than the percentage of left-handed people in the general population.) But does being left-handed

cause a person to be more creative? Or does some other factor cause both left-handedness and creativity? The presence of this puzzling correlation leads scientists to speculate about its causes and to design further research that might pin down an answer.

- *Causality demonstrated through experimental control of variables:* In some cases, scientists try to resolve causal questions through direct experiment. By controlling variables and testing them one at a time, scientists can sometimes isolate causal factors quite precisely. For example, through experimentation, scientists now know that a particular bacterium causes typhoid fever and that particular antibiotics will kill that bacterium. Controlled experiments in psychology have demonstrated that prolonged deprivation of sunlight can cause depression in certain individuals (a condition known as *seasonal affective disorder*).

We have mentioned these approaches to causal analysis to stimulate your thinking about possible patterns you might see in your data or about interesting or puzzling correlations. These in turn might lead you to speculate why your findings turned out as they did or suggest implications for further study.

For Writing and Discussion

Working in small groups or as a whole class, speculate on possible explanations for each of the following phenomena:

1. White female teenagers are seven times more likely to smoke than African-American female teenagers (a finding based on several professional studies).
2. When asked about the "car of their dreams" ninety-five percent of students polled listed an SUV, luxury car, or high-performance sports car. Only five percent specifically mentioned a fuel-conserving vehicle such as a hybrid.

Implications and Significance of the Results

Another typical portion in the Discussion section focuses on the implications and significance of your research—the "So what?" question. What is important about this research? How does it advance our knowledge? What, if any, are its practical applications? For example, the discovery that white female teenagers smoke at a higher rate than African-American female teenagers could lead to speculation on ways to reduce teenage smoking among white females or offer clues into the psyches of white versus African-American women. (One theory proposed in the scientific literature is that white women are more obsessed with weight and body image than African-American women and see smoking as a way to suppress appetite). Or, to take our other example, the study showing that only five percent of students mentioned a fuel-conserving car as their "dream car" could lead to speculation on how consumer preferences might be changed to promote the goal of environmental preservation.

Limitations of the Study

Another common feature of the Discussion section is the researcher's skeptical analysis of his or her own research methods and data. It may seem counterintuitive that authors would explicitly point out problems with their own research, but this honesty is part of the scientific *ethos* aimed at advancing knowledge. By nature, scientists are skeptical and cautious. Typically, authors go out of their way to mention possible flaws and other limitations of their studies and to caution other scholars against overgeneralizing from their research. They might refer to problems in sample size or duration of the study, flaws in the research design that might contaminate results, possible differences between an experimental group and a control group, or lack of statistical confidence in the data.

Your own research for this assignment will probably exhibit a number of problems that would limit other researchers' confidence in your findings. To increase your own *ethos* as a scientific writer, you should make these objections yourself as part of the Discussion section.

Suggestions for Further Research

At the conclusion of their Discussion sections, researchers often suggest avenues for future research. Typically they show how their own research raises new questions that could be profitably explored. You might try this approach at the conclusion of your own Discussion section by mentioning one or more questions that you think would be the logical next steps for researchers interested in your area of study.

Following Ethical Standards

When research involves human subjects, researchers must be scrupulous in adhering to ethical standards. In the past, there have been horrible cases of unethical research using human subjects. Among the most notorious are Nazi medical experiments on Jews in concentration camps during World War II or the Tuskegee syphilis study in which four hundred low-income African-American males with syphilis were denied treatment—even though a cure for syphilis had been discovered—because the researchers wanted to continue studying the progress of the untreated disease. Likewise, certain psychological experiments, once highly regarded in the middle of the twentieth century, are now considered by many to have been unethical. For example, the famous Milgram experiments on obedience to authority revealed the extent to which research subjects would administer what they thought were painful electric shocks to another human being when told to do so by an authority figure. This experiment depended on deception: The research subjects were unsuspecting participants in a faked laboratory scenario designed by the researchers (the authority figure and the screaming human being receiving the shock were really actors).

As a response to problems like these, in 1979 the National Institutes of Health (a federal agency) established ethical guidelines for biomedical research, instigating widespread efforts among all scientific organizations to develop ethical standards for any kind of research using human subjects. Today, almost all colleges and universities have Institutional Review Boards that provide oversight for such research. In the case of your own research, for example, consider how certain items on a questionnaire might cause stress to a potential respondent or be considered an invasion of his or her privacy. It's one thing to ask persons if they prefer a Mac to a PC; it is quite another to ask them if they have ever cheated on an exam or gotten drunk at a party. As a general rule, the kind of first-time research that you do for this writing project will not require oversight from your university's Institutional Review Board, but you should nevertheless adhere to the following guidelines:

ETHICAL GUIDELINES FOR INTERVIEWS AND QUESTIONNAIRES USED IN EMPIRICAL RESEARCH

- *Obtain informed consent.* Explain to potential respondents the purpose of your research, your methods for collecting data, and the way your data will be used. In the case of interviews, reach agreement on whether the respondent will be named or anonymous. Obtain direct permission for recording the session.
- *Explain that participation in your study is voluntary.* Do not apply any kind of personal or social pressure that would make it difficult for a respondent to say no.
- *In the case of questionnaires, explain that no respondent will be individually identified and that results will be reported as statistical aggregates.* If possible, ensure that all responses are anonymous to you (don't try to identify handwriting or otherwise match responses to an identified individual). If such anonymity is impossible (for example, you might be conducting an oral survey), then assure the respondent that you will keep all answers confidential.
- *If any of your respondents are minors, check with your instructor because human-subject regulations are particularly strict in such instances.* Parents or guardians generally have to give consent for interviews with children.

READINGS

The following two readings show a professional and a student example of a scientific research report. The first reading, by authors from the Department of Health and Social Behavior in the Harvard School of Public Health, was published in the peer-reviewed scholarly journal *The American Journal of Public Health* in March 2000. You should find this article generally accessible even though the specific meaning of terms such as "odds ratios" or "confidence levels" may be unclear. As with most scientific articles, you can skim those portions of "Results" that focus on statistical analyses, moving on to those parts of the article that you can understand.

Gina Escamilla, BA, Angie L. Cradock, MS, and
Ichiro Kawachi, MD, PhD

Women and Smoking in Hollywood Movies:

A Content Analysis

1   According to the Centers for Disease Control and Prevention, over one third (34.7%) of female high school students in a national survey reported smoking at least 1 cigarette in the previous month, up 10% since 1993 and 32% since 1991.[1] Cigarette smoking is initiated primarily in adolescence. Among adult regular smokers, 71% reported having formed the habit before the age of 18 years.[2]

2   Television and popular films have contributed to the allure of smoking. A recent study found that young adults smoked in about 75% of music videos.[3] Although tobacco industry documents suggest that manufacturers have not engaged in deliberate product placement in Hollywood movies since the late 1980s,[4] recent evidence indicates that smoking continues to be depicted at very high levels. Moreover, the gap between the prevalence of tobacco use in movies and in actual life has steadily widened through the 1990s.[5] A recent analysis of G-rated children's animated films found that more than two thirds featured tobacco or alcohol use in story plots, with no clear reference made to the adverse health consequences associated with these substances.[6]

3   Popular film actresses are likely to be role models for young women and adolescent girls. The way that movie stars portray cigarette smoking on the screen may influence young girls' attitudes toward the habit. In this study, we analyzed the portrayal of smoking by 10 leading Hollywood actresses.

Methods

Selection of Actresses

4   We selected 10 leading Hollywood actresses by surveying the 1997 issues of 5 popular magazines that had the highest readership among women aged 18 to 24 years, according to *Simmons Study of Media and Markets*.[7] Magazine titles from the "Special Interest" and "Women's Magazines" categories were selected if the editorial descriptions taken from *Bacon's Magazine Directory*[8] included 1 or more of the following key words or phrases: entertainment, contemporary or current, Hollywood, celebrity, film or movie, personality profiles, women in their 20s, or young women. All issues for the period January 1997 through December 1997 were obtained for the magazines *Cosmopolitan, Glamour, Vogue, Vanity Fair,* and *Rolling Stone.* Each issue was analyzed for the appearance of female film stars. Advertisements were excluded, and the search was limited to women whose careers are primarily

in film. The number of magazine appearances was tallied for each actress, and the 10 actresses with the greatest number of appearances were selected.

Selection of Films

5   A list of films starring each selected actress was generated from the Web site www.tvguide.com. This Web site, maintained by TV Guide Entertainment Network, provides information on the cast, credits, and reviews for some 35,000 movies. Five titles released between 1993 and 1997 were randomly selected for each of the 10 actresses. We excluded period dramas as well as movies in which the actresses did not play a lead or major supporting role. The title, year of release, rating (R, NC-17, PG, PG-13, G), and genre of each film were recorded.

Content Analysis

6   We followed the analytic approach described by Hazan et al.[9] Each film was divided into 5-minute intervals. The occurrence of smoking episodes in each interval was recorded on a coding sheet. We recorded both actual and implied smoking behavior (e.g., holding or smoking a lit or unlit tobacco product); the presence of cigarettes or other smoking paraphernalia (e.g., cigars, matches, and ashtrays); and environmental messages, including "no smoking" signs, tobacco advertising, and tobacco merchandise. Additionally, we recorded smoker characteristics (e.g., gender; whether lead, supporting, or other character); location (i.e., outdoors or in a bar, restaurant, home, or car); the social context of the event (i.e., smoking alone or with others and whether consideration was shown to nonsmokers). We also noted verbal and nonverbal tobacco messages (i.e., positive or negative consequences of smoking behavior and discussion about tobacco products, including positive, negative, or mixed reference to tobacco use). To establish interrater reliability, 5 films (10% of total sample) were randomly selected and independently rated by graduate student coders (G. Escamilla and A. L. Cradock). The coders had 99% agreement on all of the parameters examined regarding the depiction of smoking.

7   After viewing each film, the coders also completed a qualitative assessment of smoking themes and behaviors, addressing contextual issues such as the emotional valence attached to the smoking behavior and the significance of smoking for the character portrayed. All statistical analyses were performed with Stata.[10]

Results

8   The 50 films, representing approximately 96 hours of footage, were broken down into 1116 5-minute intervals (excluding introductions and credits). Of these, 317 (28.4%) of the intervals depicted smoking behavior (Table 1). Cigarettes were the most common tobacco product shown (23.9%). Over half of the smoking episodes (58.7%) occurred in the presence of others who were not smoking.

9   As Table 2 indicates, smoking was significantly more likely to be depicted in R-rated or unrated films than in PG/PG-13-rated films ($P < .001$). Although the percentage of lead actors or supporting actors shown smoking

TABLE 1 Depiction of Smoking Behavior and Paraphernalia, Smoking Context, and Location of Smoking Behaviors in 50 Hollywood Movies

	No. of 5-Min Intervals	Total 5-Min Movie Intervals, % (n = 1116)	Intervals Containing Smoking Behavior, % (n = 317)
Smoking behavior and paraphernalia			
Smoking (actual or implied) behavior	317	28.4	—
Cigarettes	267	23.9	—
Cigarette packs	64	5.7	—
Matches/lighter	108	9.7	—
Cigars, pipes, or smokeless tobacco	71	6.4	—
Ashtray	105	9.4	—
Social context of smoking behavior[a]			
Alone	46	—	14.5
With others (nonsmokers)	186	—	58.7
With others, including smokers and nonsmokers	71	—	22.4
Consideration shown to nonsmokers	5	—	1.6
Location of smoking behavior[b]			
Bar/lounge	25	—	7.9
Home/apartment	84	—	26.5
Restaurant	28	—	8.8
Car	40	—	12.6
Outside	103	—	32.5
Other location	69	—	21.8

[a]A total of 4.4% of intervals depicted incidental smoking of characters other than the lead/supporting actors.
[b]Percentages total more than 100 as smoking may have occurred in more than one context in the same interval.

TABLE 2 Odds Ratios (ORs) and 95% Confidence Intervals (95% CIs) for the Occurrence of Smoking Behavior in R-Rated/Unrated Movies

	OR[a]	95% CI
Overall smoking behavior	1.62	1.20–2.14
Smoking by male lead or supporting actor	2.48	1.55–3.97
Smoking by female lead or supporting actor	1.23	0.88–1.86

[a]Referent is PG/PG-13 movies.

was similar for men and women (38% and 42%, respectively), sex differences were apparent according to the film's rating. Males in lead or supporting roles were 2.5 times more likely to be shown smoking in R-rated/unrated movies than in PG/PG-13-rated films (P < .001). By contrast, the portrayal of smoking by a female lead or supporting character was not significantly different according to the movie's rating; that is, female actresses were *equally likely* to light up in movies aimed at juvenile audiences as in those aimed at mature audiences.

10   Smoking was also more likely to be depicted in the movies starring younger actresses. The mean age of the 10 actresses was 29.3 years (range = 21–40 years). When we categorized actresses according to quartiles by age, movies starring actresses in the youngest quartile featured 3.6 times as many intervals depicting smoking as did movies starring actresses in the oldest age group (95% confidence interval [95% CI] = 2.4, 5.4).

11   Negative messages regarding tobacco product use (e.g., depictions of the consequences of the use of tobacco products, such as coughing or grimacing at the smell of smoke) were more common than positive messages (30 vs 23) among the 50 films viewed. However, only 9 of 22 messages in PG/PG-13 films depicted smoking in a negative light, compared with 21 of 31 messages in R-rated/unrated films; that is, movies aimed at young audiences were *less* likely (odds ratio = 0.33; 95% CI = 0.11, 1.01) to carry negative messages associated with tobacco use than were movies made for mature audiences.

12   In a qualitative analysis of the social context of smoking, sex differences were detected in the themes associated with tobacco use. Women were likely to be portrayed using tobacco products to control their emotions, to manifest power and sex appeal, to enhance their body image or self-image, to control weight, or to give themselves a sense of comfort and companionship. Men were more likely to be depicted using tobacco products to reinforce their masculine identity; to portray a character with power, prestige, or significant authority; to show male bonding; or to signify their status as a "protector" (the last 3 themes were associated with cigar smoking).

Discussion

13   The results of this study raise concerns about exposure to smoking in popular movies. According to social learning theory, by paying attention to the behaviors of a person who possesses the qualities, skills, and capacities one hopes to achieve, a young observer learns to model these behaviors.[11] Among third- through sixth-grade students who had smoked, having role models who smoked was more common, and having beliefs about the adverse consequences of smoking was less common than among their peers who never smoked.[12]

14   The prevalence of smoking by both female (42%) and male (38%) lead or supporting actors was substantially higher than the national smoking prevalence for females (24.3%) and males (29.2%) aged 18 to 44.[13] This discrep-

ancy is significant, given that adolescents who overestimate smoking prevalence among young people and adults are more likely to become smokers themselves.[2] In the films viewed, over half of the smoking episodes occurred in the presence of others who were not smoking, and in fewer than 2% of the intervals was consideration shown to nonsmokers (e.g., smoker leaves the room or asks permission to smoke). The depiction of smoking in Hollywood would thus appear to reinforce smoking as an acceptable and normative behavior in society. While most young people older than 18 years are able to acknowledge that on-screen smoking is part of a movie role, this may be more difficult for younger females aged 12 to 17 years, among whom smoking initiation is taking place.

15   Our qualitative analysis of smoking identified several themes related to smoking. One of the most prominent themes was using smoking to control emotion, which was specific to female characters and occurred during times of stress or difficulty, when the character was trying to regain or establish control, to repress or deny emotion, or to exit a negative or threatening situation.

16   Important limitations of this study should be noted. First, the sampling of magazine titles was limited to those with the highest readership among women aged 18 to 24 years. On the other hand, given the content and focus of the magazines, it is highly likely that they are widely read by adolescent girls. Surveying the issues of only 5 magazines may have biased our sample of actresses. However, a recent study on the influence of movie stars on adolescent smoking identified 6 of the 10 actresses in our sample as being the "most favorite" among girls.[14] Given that African American and Latina women have become targets for tobacco advertisements, it would also be informative to survey movies starring actresses of different racial/ethnic backgrounds. Future studies need to be extended to popular male actors as well. Finally, replication of our findings through the use of raters who are unaware of the hypotheses would be desirable, since the smoking-related themes emerging from our qualitative analyses may have been biased.

17   Our findings, in conjunction with those of others,[14] suggest the need for the development of policies—such as the adoption of a voluntary code of ethics by the entertainment industry—to eliminate the depiction of smoking in ways that appeal to adolescent audiences.

References

1. Centers for Disease Control and Prevention. Tobacco use among high school students—United States, 1997. *MMWR Morb Mortal Wkly Rep.* 1998; 47:229–233.

2. *Preventing Tobacco Use Among Young People: A Report of the Surgeon General.* Atlanta, Ga: National Center for Chronic Disease Prevention and Health Promotion, Office on Smoking and Health; 1994.

3. DuRant, RH, Rome ES, Rich M, Allred E, Emans SJ, Woods ER. Tobacco and alcohol use behaviors portrayed in music videos: a content analysis. *Am J Public Health,* 1997; 87:1131–1135.

4. http://www.philipmorris.com/getallimg.asp. DOC_ID=2025863645/3659. Accessed July 1998.

5. Stockwell TF, Glantz SA. Tobacco use is increasing in popular films. *Tob Control.* 1997; 6:282–284.

6. Goldstein AO, Sobel RA, Newman GR. Tobacco and alcohol use in G-rated children's animated films. *JAMA.* 1999; 281:1131–1136.

7. Simmons Market Research Bureau. *Simmons Study of Media and Markets, M1.* New York, NY: Simmons Market Research Bureau; 1994; 0162–0163.

8. *Bacon's Magazine Directory: Directory of Magazines and Newsletters.* Chicago, Ill: Bacon's Information Inc; 1988.

9. Hazan AR, Lipton HL, Glantz S. Popular films do not reflect current tobacco use. *Am J Public Health.* 1994; 84:998–1000.

10. *Stata Statistical Software: Release 5.0.* College Station, Tex: Stata Corporation; 1997.

11. Greaves L. *Mixed Messages: Women, Tobacco and the Media.* Ottawa, Ontario: Health Canada; 1996.

12. Greenlund KJ, Johnson CC, Webber LS, Berenson GS. Cigarette smoking attitudes and first use among third-through sixth-grade students: the Bogalusa Heart Study. *Am J Public Health* 1997; 87:1345–1348.

13. Centers for Disease Control and Prevention. Cigarette smoking among adults— United States, 1995. *MMWR Morb Mortal Wkly Rep.* 1997; 46:1217–1220.

14. Distefan JM, Gilpin EA, Sargent JD, Pierce JP. Do movie stars encourage adolescents to start smoking? Evidence from California. *Prev Med.* 1999; 28:1–11.

Thinking Critically about "Women and Smoking in Hollywood Movies: A Content Analysis"

1. The introduction to this article doesn't state its research question directly, even though a question is clearly implied. In your own words, what is the question these researchers are asking? Why is this question significant?

2. How did the researchers determine which actresses they were going to study? How did they select the films for each actress? How did they analyze smoking behavior within the films selected for study?

3. What were their findings?

4. In the Discussion section, where do the researchers (a) analyze causes and effects connected to their findings, (b) suggest the significance of their study, (c) point out limitations of their study, and (d) suggest areas for further research?

Our second reading, which was written for this chapter's writing project, was jointly authored by a team of three students. We have reproduced it in manuscript format to illustrate the form and documentation style of the APA (American Psychological Association) system for research papers. For further explanation of APA style, see Chapter 22, pages 687–693.

Energy Literacy   1

Energy Literacy: A Comparative Study of Seattle

University Students

Against a National Sample

Brittany Tinker, Trevor Tsuchikawa, and Tatiana Whizar

May 10, 2004

Energy Literacy   2

Energy Literacy: A Comparative Study of Seattle
University Students Against a National Sample

The United States may soon be facing a
global energy crisis as the world's demand for
energy outstrips the production of fossil fuels
(Roberts, 2004). Yet many Americans do not seem
to be aware of this crisis. They assume either
that the world's supply of fossil fuels will
last indefinitely or that scientists and
engineers will find alternative sources of
equally cheap energy. According to the National
Environmental Education and Training Foundation
(NEETF), Americans suffer from a "low energy IQ"
(2002, p. ii)—that is, Americans lack basic
knowledge about where our energy comes from and
how much of it we use. NEETF's claim is based on
survey results of 1,503 adult Americans who were
given a 10-question energy quiz testing basic
energy knowledge. Only 12% of those surveyed
were able to answer 7 of the 10 questions
correctly (p. 3). In his forward to the NEETF
report, Kevin J. Coyle, the president of NEETF,
writes, "America needs a refresher course on

Energy Literacy   3

energy management and conservation. Lack of knowledge about energy in America wastes fuel and money and puts our energy security at risk" (p. i). The report writers argue that energy illiteracy has negative consequences because "Americans are less likely to make energy-smart decisions" (p. v) in their consumer choices, thereby propelling increased energy consumption and reliance on foreign oil.

Because of the importance of energy literacy for our nation's future, we were inspired to give the NEETF energy quiz to students on the Seattle University campus to compare our students' energy literacy against the national results established by NEETF. We also wanted to determine whether persons in different majors had different levels of energy literacy. We posed two research questions:

1. Would a random selection of Seattle University students exceed the national pass rate of 12%?

2. Would there be a difference in pass rates depending on students' area of study?

For Question 1, we hypothesized that Seattle University students would exceed the national norms on the energy IQ quiz. Because the Northwest is legendary for environmental protection and energy conservation and because various campus organizations regularly put on informational events about the environment, conservation, and energy, we reasoned that our students' energy knowledge would exceed that of average citizens.

For Question 2 we focused on three areas of study: majors in the College of Arts and Sciences (which at Seattle University means the humanities and social sciences), in the College of Science and Engineering, and in the Albers School of Business. We hypothesized that the Science and Engineering majors would score highest due to their technical knowledge and interest in scientific questions about energy and pollution; that Business majors would score the next highest because of their economic interest in the costs of energy and pollution; and that majors in the College of Arts and Sciences would

Energy Literacy   5

score the lowest because they might have less
direct interest in energy issues.

Method

To assess energy literacy, we used the 10-
question energy quiz developed by NEETF (pp.
4-5). A copy of this instrument is attached as
Appendix A. We gave the energy quiz to a
convenience sample of 46 students from Seattle
University. To administer the quiz, we
approached students eating lunch in a campus
cafeteria and asked them their major. If they
majored in one of the three areas of study we
had chosen, we told them the purpose of our
study and asked them if they would be willing to
complete the quiz. We gave them time to complete
the quiz and then immediately collected it.
Afterwards, if they wished to see their score,
we corrected the quiz and showed them their
right or wrong answers.

Results

The results for the first research question
can be seen in Table 1, which shows the number
of students scoring in each of three score

Energy Literacy   6

Table 1

Energy Literacy Score of Seattle University

Students (N = 46)

Score range (number of correct answers)	Number	Percent of total
Passing: 7-10	5	11%
Failing: 6	4	9%
Failing: 0-5	37	80%

ranges. As Table 1 shows, 11% of students received a passing score of seven or more correct answers, 9% received a score of six, and 80% received a score of five or fewer. A comparison of Seattle University scores versus national scores reported in NEETF is shown in Figure 1, which reveals that Seattle University students did slightly poorer than the national sample. Our results thus did not confirm our hypothesis for Research Question 1 that Seattle University students would exceed the national pass rate of 12%.

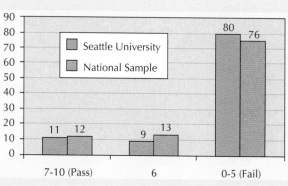

Figure 1

*Percentage of Scores by Number of Correct
Answers: Seattle University Versus
National Sample*

The results for our second research
question are shown in Table 2. These data confirm
our hypothesis that students majoring in science
and engineering would score the highest,
although the differences are very small. Science
and Engineering students averaged 4.7 correct
answers while those in business or in the
humanities and social sciences averaged 3.6
correct answers. Our related hypothesis that
business majors would score the second highest

Energy Literacy   8

Table 2

Energy Literacy Scores of Seattle University

Students by Field of Study

Field of study	Number of respondents	Average number of correct answers
Humanities and Social Sciences	22	3.6
Business	12	3.6
Science and Engineering	12	4.7

was not confirmed because their scores were the same as those in humanities and social sciences.

Discussion

The main hypothesis of this study—that Seattle University students would reveal a higher energy IQ than the national average—was not confirmed. One must be cautious, however, in generalizing from our results because our sample size of 46 students is very small. A larger, randomized sample would be required to make generalized statements about Seattle University

Energy Literacy   9

students. Nevertheless, our results do tend to
confirm the conclusions of the NEETF report that
Americans have a low rate of energy literacy.
Our results suggest that neither living in the
environmentally liberal Northwest nor being a
college student raises one's energy IQ. Even
being a major in science and engineering seems
to make little difference.

     What particularly puzzles us about our
results is the fact that Seattle University is a
very liberal campus on environmental issues.
Students generally show strong commitment to
environmental causes. Why do environmentally
conscious students have such a low knowledge
about energy production and consumption? We
suggest two possible reasons. First, the
environmental movement tends to blame
environmental problems on "industrial polluters"
or "multinational corporations" rather than on
our own habits as consumers of energy. When
students think of environmental problems, they
tend to think of acid rain, polluted rivers, or
belching smokestacks rather than their own
preferences for SUVs or air-conditioned

Energy Literacy   10

buildings. Second, science and math curricula at the high school and college levels do not focus on basic energy issues such as how much of our electricity comes from burning coal or how a small improvement in automobile gasoline mileage could lead to a significant cumulative reduction in our nation's fuel consumption. The kinds of material covered in the NEETF energy quiz do not show up in classrooms.

Developing ways to increase Americans' energy literacy is an important concern. Our nation's increasing demand for energy could be slowed, or even reversed, if more people were committed to energy conservation. Increasing Americans' energy literacy could lead to wiser consumer choices. But what kinds of approaches for increasing energy literacy might work? Something as simple as the NEETF energy literacy test might help. We discovered in administering the energy quiz that students were interested in learning the correct answers to the quiz questions. Information about energy literacy could also be included in general education courses in science and math. We also recommend

Energy Literacy   11

further studies based on the NEETF quiz. For example, it might be possible to identify students who score high on the energy quiz and then interview them to find out where they gained their energy knowledge.

Better energy education may help us postpone the day when we run out of fossil fuels so that scientists will have time to develop alternative energy sources.

Energy Literacy   12

References

National Environmental Education and Training Foundation. (2002, August). *Americans' low "energy IQ": A risk to our energy future.* Retrieved April 27, 2004, from http:www.neetf.org/roper/Roper2002.pdf

Roberts, P. (2004, March 6). Running out of oil— and time. *Los Angeles Times.* Retrieved March 23, 2004, from Common Dreams News Center: http://www.commondreams.org/views04/ 0307-02.htm

Energy Literacy   13

Appendix A

Test Your Energy IQ!

1. How is most electricity in the United States generated? Is it . . .
   a. By burning oil, coal, and wood
   b. With nuclear power
   c. Through solar energy, or
   d. At hydroelectric power plants?
   e. Don't know

2. Which of the following uses the most energy in the average home? Is it . . .
   a. Lighting rooms
   b. Heating water
   c. Heating and cooling rooms, or
   d. Refrigerating food?
   e. Don't know

3. Which of the following sectors of the U.S. economy consumes the greatest percentage of the nation's petroleum? Is it . . .
   a. The residential sector
   b. The commercial sector
   c. The transportation sector, or
   d. The industrial sector?
   e. Don't know

4. Which fuel is used to generate the most energy in the U.S. each year? Is it . . .
   a. Petroleum
   b. Coal
   c. Natural gas, or
   d. Nuclear?
   e. Don't know

5. Though the U.S. has only 4% of the world's population, what percentage of the world's energy does it consume? Is it . . .
   a. 5%
   b. 15%
   c. 20%, or
   d. 25%?
   e. Don't know

6. In the last 10 years, which of the following industries in the U.S. economy has increased its energy demands the most? Is it . . .
   a. The food industry
   b. The transportation industry
   c. The computer and technology industry, or
   d. The health care industry?
   e. Don't know

7. In the past 10 years, has the average miles per gallon of gasoline used by vehicles in the U.S. . . .
   a. Increased
   b. Remained the same
   c. Gone down, or
   d. Not been tracked?
   e. Don't know

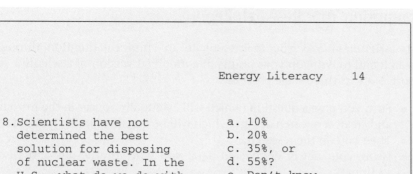

Energy Literacy   14

8. Scientists have not
determined the best
solution for disposing
of nuclear waste. In the
U.S., what do we do with
it now? Do we . . .
a. Use it as nuclear
   fuel
b. Sell it to other
   countries
c. Dispose of it in
   landfills, or
d. Store and monitor the
   waste?
e. Don't know

9. The U.S. currently uses
oil from both domestic
and foreign sources. What
percentage of the oil is
imported? Is it . . .

a. 10%
b. 20%
c. 35%, or
d. 55%?
e. Don't know

10. Scientists say the
fastest and most cost-
effective way to address
our energy needs is
to . . .
a. Develop all possible
   domestic sources of
   oil and gas
b. Build nuclear power
   plants
c. Develop more
   hydroelectric power
   plants, or
d. Promote more energy
   conservation?
e. Don't know

Thinking Critically about "Energy Literacy: A Comparative Study of Seattle University Students Against a National Sample"

1. In your own words, explain how this paper follows the genre conventions for a scientific report.

2. Students in this particular class had spent several weeks discussing energy issues. For example, the whole class had read the Roberts article listed in "References." The class therefore had more background on energy literacy than most readers. Do you think that these authors provided enough background for the general reader to understand the research questions and to see the significance of the study?

3. Have everyone in the class take the energy literacy quiz shown in Appendix A. Then have someone look up the correct answers by going to the Web site listed in the URL (see the first entry under "References"; the answers are on p. 5). Score the results and compare your class's energy literacy against the national sample.

Composing Your Research Report

This assignment asks you to investigate an empirical question through field research and to write up your results in a modified version of a scientific research report. Note its three-stage process:

- First, you pose a question (which will eventually appear in the Introduction) and create a research design (which will be described in the Method section).
- Then you do the research.
- Using your newly discovered data, you write the Results and Discussion sections.

Many researchers recommend writing the Method section before you actually do the research. Writing the Method section first not only gets it out of the way but also helps you think through your whole research process. Many researchers also write the Introduction early on to help them understand more clearly their purpose and to focus their research questions and hypotheses.

A particularly confusing problem for novice science writers is uncertainty about what goes in the Results section versus the Discussion section of a report. Our advice is to think of "Discussion" as the place where you present your own thesis and argument in response to the question: "What do my findings mean?" In contrast, the Results section simply presents the findings. The Results section is factual while the Discussion section is analytic and speculative—it is where you bring your own critical thinking to bear on your results.

Writing in Teams

Because professional field research is often done in teams, resulting in jointly authored articles, your instructor may ask you to work in teams to plan and carry out your research projects. In such cases, instructors sometimes ask team members to write their own individual reports and sometimes require jointly authored reports. If you are assigned to write in teams, consider our advice for team-writing as shown in Figure 10.9.

GUIDELINES FOR PEER REVIEWS

Instructions for peer reviews are provided in Chapter 17 (pp. 519–520).

For the Writer
Prepare two or three questions you would like your peer reviewer to address while responding to your draft. The questions can focus on some aspect of your draft that you are uncertain about, on one or more sections where you particularly seek help or advice, on some feature that you particularly like about your draft, or on some part you especially wrestled with. Write out your questions and give them to your peer reviewer along with your draft.

FIGURE 10.9 Suggestions for Team-Writing of Documents

Do as a group what teams do best. Do as individuals what individuals do best.
Teams are good at the following:

- Brainstorming for ideas
- Planning and organizing activities/setting goals
- Developing research questions and methods for gathering data
- Dividing up the work, tabulating results
- Analyzing what the results mean
- Serving as readers who give feedback on drafts

Teams are *not* good at the following:

- Writing drafts
- Editing for uniform voice and style

Talk your document before you write it.

- As a team, talk your way through each section of the report.
- Taking notes on a large sheet of drawing paper, plan what will go into each section. Each team member should feel qualified to write any section of the report.

Draft individually; revise as a team.

- Assign a different section of the report to each team member for the first draft.
- For the "Results" section, the team member most skilled at spreadsheets might volunteer to make the figures.
- Make copies of individual drafts for the whole team.
- At a team meeting all members should review drafts for accuracy, completeness, clarity, development, and style.
- Individual writers should then revise their sections. (Or an alternate process is to exchange drafts so that everyone revises someone else's first draft.)
- Repeat the team-review process.
- One group member should do final editing of the document so that it seems written in one voice.

Agree from the start on document design.

- Agree early on about a word processing program, font style, and APA design features.
- Assign one person to be design guru who really studies APA formatting and style (see pp. 687–693).

For the Reviewer

I. Read the draft at a normal reading speed from beginning to end. As you read, do the following:

  A. Place a wavy line in the margin next to any passages that you find confusing, that contain something that doesn't seem to fit, or that otherwise slow down your reading.

  B. Place a "Good!" in the margin next to any passages where you think the writing is particularly strong or interesting.

II. Read the draft again slowly and answer the following questions by writing brief explanations of your answers.

  A. Introduction

   1. Can you suggest improvements to the title to better focus the paper and pique interest?

2. Where does the writer present the research question(s) and hypothesis(es)? Are they stated as determinate questions? Can you suggest ways to improve the focus of the research questions and hypotheses?

3. Where does the writer suggest the importance or significance of the research question? What overall suggestions might you make to improve the Introduction?

B. Method

1. Will the writer's research process provide the data necessary to answer the research question? How might you improve the overall research design to provide clearer or more focused findings?

2. If you had to replicate the writer's research, where might you have problems? Explain possible confusing passages or omitted details that might be important.

C. Results

1. Are the writer's results clearly stated in both words and graphics? Where does the writer indicate whether the results confirmed or disconfirmed the hypothesis?

2. Where does the writer demonstrate "independent redundancy" by explaining what a graphic is supposed to show? Where does the writer reference graphics in the text?

3. Are the graphics well designed so that you can interpret them without reference to the text? What suggestions might you have for improving the titles, labels, legends, and overall design of graphics?

D. Discussion

1. Where is the thesis statement for the Discussion? Can you suggest ways to improve the thesis?

2. Where does the writer (a) Identify significant patterns in the data and speculate about possible causes? (b) Show the significance and importance of the study? (c) Describe the limitations of the study? (e) Suggest ideas for future research or next steps?

3. What can you suggest to improve the writer's discussion of possible causes, significance, limitations, or future research? What additional ideas or insights can you offer?

III. Rhetorical considerations

A. *Purpose, audience,* and *genre:* How well has the writer focused on a research purpose, targeted an audience interested in the investigation, and used the conventions of the research report?

B. *Logos, ethos,* and *pathos:* How convincing is the logical part of this report—the empirical data and writer's analysis? What strategies does the writer use to construct a scientific and trustworthy persona? How does the writer connect this study to the interests and values of the audience?

IV. Sum up what you see as the chief strengths and problem areas of this draft:

A. Strengths

B. Problem areas

V. Read the draft one more time. Place a check mark in the margin wherever you notice problems in grammar, spelling, or mechanics (one check mark per problem).

Analyzing Images

About Analyzing Images

This chapter asks you to analyze images in order to understand their persuasive power—a skill often called "visual literacy." By *visual literacy,* we mean your awareness of the importance of visual communication and your ability to interpret or make meaning out of images and graphics (photos, pictures, illustrations, icons, charts, graphs, and other visual displays of data). In this chapter, we seek to enhance your visual literacy by focusing on the way that images influence our conceptual and emotional understanding of a phenomenon and the way that they validate, reveal, and construct the world.

This chapter is the second of four assignment chapters on writing to analyze and synthesize. As you may recall from Chapter 3, when you write to analyze and synthesize, you apply your own critical thinking to a puzzling object or to puzzling data and offer your own new ideas to a conversation. Your goal is to raise interesting questions about the object or data being analyzed—questions that perhaps your reader hasn't thought to ask—and then to provide tentative answers to those questions, supported by points and particulars derived from your own close examination of the object or data. The word *analysis* derives from a Greek word meaning "to dissolve, loosen, undo." Metaphorically, analysis means to divide or dissolve the whole into its constituent parts, to examine these parts carefully, to look at the relationships among them, and then to use this understanding of the parts to better understand the whole—how it functions, what it means. Synonyms for writing to analyze might be *writing to interpret, clarify,* or *explain.* In this chapter, the objects being analyzed are photographs or other images as they appear in a rhetorical context—for example, as part of a news story, a television documentary, a public relations brochure, or an advertisement.

See Table 3.1, pp. 49–50 for an explanation of the aims of writing.

To appreciate the cultural importance of images, consider how British cultural critic John Berger, in his book *About Looking,* sketches the pervasive use of photographs shortly after the invention of the camera.

> The camera was invented by Fox Talbot in 1839. Within a mere 30 years of its invention as a gadget for an elite, photography was being used for police filing, war reporting, military reconnaissance, pornography, encyclopedic documentation, family albums, postcards, anthropological records (often, as with the Indians in the United States, accompanied by genocide), sentimental moralizing, inquisitive probing (the wrongly named "candid camera"), aesthetic effects, news reporting and formal portraiture. The speed with which the possible uses of photography were seized upon is surely an indication of photography's profound, central applicability to industrial capitalism.

One of photography's purposes—as Berger hints—is to create images that "have designs on" us, that urge us to believe ideas, buy things, go places, or otherwise alter our views or behaviors. Information brochures use carefully selected photographs to enhance a product's image (consider how the photographs in your college's catalog or view book have been selected); news photographs editorialize their content (during the Vietnam War a newspaper photograph of a naked Vietnamese child running screaming toward the photographer while a napalm bomb explodes behind her turned many Americans against the war; and recently, the images of weeping Iraqi mothers and houses reduced to rubble shown in newspapers, and documentary films have raised questions about U.S. tactics in Iraq); social issue posters urge us to protest capital punishment or contribute money to save the salmon or sponsor a child in a third world country; and advertisements urge us not only to buy a certain product but to be a certain kind of person with certain values.

Visual literacy is so important in our world that we have already introduced it elsewhere in this text. In Chapter 4, we showed how stakeholders in the current controversy over medical care enlist competing images of doctors such as Norman Rockwell's image of the family doctor who makes house calls versus images of physicians in lab coats surrounded by high technology equipment. In Chapter 5, we showed how specially selected photographs of the Arctic National Wildlife Refuge (ANWR) could be used to advance arguments for or against opening the ANWR to oil exploration (pp. 98–100). And for the Part Openers in this text, we have chosen examples of striking visual texts that grew out of particular rhetorical contexts and were created to have a specific rhetorical effect.

For the images in this chapter, we have selected those directly related to Berger's assertion that photographs often have a "profound, central applicability to industrial capitalism." We look specifically at how photographs and other images are used in "corporate image" advertisements and in product advertisements. We focus on advertisements because they are a wonderful source of images for analysis and because they raise important questions about how our own lives intersect with the processes of a free market economy. In addition to enhancing your visual literacy, studying advertising has other values as well. We suggest four benefits you will gain from your study of advertisements:

- You will appreciate more fully the fun, pleasure, and creativity of advertisements.
- You will become a more savvy consumer, better able to critique ads and make wise buying decisions.
- You will learn rhetorical strategies that you can use in your own career and civic life. (Your understanding of the relationship between words and images in advertising can be readily transferred to other rhetorical settings—for example, when you design a brochure or Web site or write any kind of document that incorporates images and depends on document design.)
- You will become a more perceptive cultural critic who understands how ads both convey and help construct our cultural values, our self-image, our sense of what is normal or ideal, and our ideas about gender, race, and class. A study of advertisements can raise viewers' consciousness to counter prejudice, injustice, and discrimination.

Exploring Image Analysis

To introduce you to the concept of image analysis, we provide two exercises to stimulate your thinking and discussion.

Task 1: Working on your own, freewrite your responses to the following questions:

1. Can you recall a time when a magazine or TV advertisement directly influenced you to buy a product? Describe the occasion and try to recall the specifics of how the ad influenced you.
2. Have the images in a magazine or TV advertisement ever caused you to desire a certain experience or style of life? For example, an ad might not have influenced you to buy a particular product, but it may have sparked a desire to ride a horse through a pounding surf, have a romantic encounter in a European café, or live in a certain kind of house or apartment. To what extent have the images of advertising shaped any of your values, longings, or desires?

In small groups or as a whole class, share your freewrites. From the ensuing discussion, create a list of specific ways in which magazine or TV advertisements have been successful in persuading members of your class to buy a product or to desire certain experiences or lifestyles.

Task 2: For further exploration, we invite you to imagine that you are an advertising consultant hired by the United States Army. Your mission is to create an advertisement recruiting women. Working in small groups, brainstorm ideas for the design of an advertisement that would cause women to consider enlisting in the Army. What photograph or drawing might be placed on your ad? What would the words say? Each group should propose one or two possible design ideas and explain why you think they might appeal to women.

Then look closely at an actual advertisement designed for this purpose. (See the Part Opener on page 95.) As a class, analyze this advertisement by responding to the following questions:

1. To what extent do you think this is an effective ad? Why or why not?
2. Why do you think the ad designers aimed the ad at fathers as well as daughters instead of directly at women? Why did the ad designers write the verbal part of the ad focusing on respect, honor, and courage rather than, say, on adventure or career?
3. Try playing the "what if they changed . . . ?" game. Try looking at specific details of the ad and asking how the effect of the ad would be different if the ad designers had made slight changes. For example:
   a. What if the girl in the picture were blonde rather than brunette? (Why did the ad designers decide against a blonde?)
   b. What if her hair style, makeup, or clothing were different in some way?
   c. What if the father were dressed differently—say wearing a suit—or had a different physical appearance—say the rugged, handsome type? Why is he wearing a plaid flannel shirt? Why is he clean-shaven rather than bearded?

How would the impact be different if the father and daughter were black or Asian rather than white?

d. Why did they frame the father and daughter in a window and pose them as they did with the daughter in front looking out the window instead of toward her father? How would the impact be different if the father and daughter were walking in the woods, sitting beside a tennis court, or going for a drive?

e. What if they had used a mother and daughter instead of a father and daughter?

4. Finally, why or why not do you think questions like these are worth asking? Do you think ad designers make choices as consciously and purposefully as we have suggested?

WRITING PROJECT

Choose two print advertisements—or use the two sport-utility ads shown in the For Writing and Discussion exercise on pages 301–302—that sell the same kind of product but appeal to different audiences (for example, a car advertisement aimed at men and one aimed at women; a cigarette ad aimed at upper-middle-class consumers and one aimed at working-class consumers; a clothing ad from *The New Yorker* and one from *Rolling Stone*). Describe the ads in detail so that an audience can easily visualize them without actually seeing them. Analyze the advertisements and explain how each appeals to its target audience. To what values does each ad appeal? How is each ad constructed to appeal to those values? In addition to analyzing the rhetorical appeals made by each ad, you may also wish to evaluate or criticize the ads, commenting on the images of our culture that they convey.

This writing assignment asks you to analyze how advertisers use words and images together to appeal to different audiences. By comparing ads for the same product targeted at different demographic groups, you learn how every aspect of an ad is chosen for an audience-specific rhetorical effect. You will discover, for example, that advertisers often vary their ads for female versus male audiences and that certain products or services are targeted at a specific socioeconomic class. Similarly, advertisers often vary their appeals to reach African-American, Hispanic, or Asian markets. This assignment asks you to explain how these appeals are targeted and created.

As a variation of this assignment, your instructor might ask you to analyze two photographs of a politician from magazines with different political biases; two news photographs from articles addressing the same story from different angles of vision; the images on the home pages of two Web sites presenting different perspectives on heated topics such as global warming, medical research using animals, and environmental protection; or two advocacy ads for corporations or political causes that represent opposing views. Although these images, articles, and Web sites are not selling you a product per se, they are "selling" you a viewpoint on an issue, and thus this chapter's explanations of how to analyze camera techniques and the use of details, props, and the posing of human figures in photographs can also be applied to visual images other than commercial advertisements.

Understanding Image Analysis

Before we turn directly to advertising, let's look at some strategies you can use to analyze any image intended to have a specific rhetorical effect.

How Images Create a Rhetorical Effect

An image can be said to have a rhetorical effect whenever it moves us emotionally or intellectually. We might identify with the image or be repelled by it; the image might evoke our sympathies, trigger our fears, or call forth a web of interconnected ideas, memories, and associations. When the image is a photograph, its rhetorical effect derives from both the camera techniques that produced it and the composition of the image itself. Let's look at each in turn.

Analyzing Camera Techniques

The rhetorical effect of a photographic image often derives from skillful use of the camera and from the way the film is developed or the digital image is manipulated.* To analyze a photograph, begin by considering the photographer's choices about the camera's relationship to the subject:

- *Distance of camera from subject:* Note whether the photograph is a close-up, medium shot, or long shot. Close-ups tend to increase the intensity of the photograph and suggest the importance of the subject; long shots tend to blend the subject into the environment.
- *Orientation of the image and camera angle:* Note whether the camera is positioned in front of or behind the subject; note also whether the camera is positioned below the subject, looking up (a low-angle shot), or above the subject, looking down (a high-angle shot). Front-view shots tend to emphasize the persons being photographed; rear-view shots often emphasize the scene or setting. A low-angle camera tends to grant superiority, status, and power to the subject, while a high-angle camera can comically reduce the subject to childlike status. A level angle tends to imply equality.
- *Eye gaze:* Note which persons in the photograph, if any, gaze directly at the camera or look away. Looking directly at the camera implies power; looking away can imply deference or shyness.

*Our ideas in this section are indebted to Paul Messaris, *Visual Persuasion: The Role of Images in Advertising* (Thousand Oaks, CA: Sage, 1997).

- *Point of view:* Note whether the photographer strives for an "objective effect," in which the camera stands outside the scene and observes it, or a "subjective effect," in which the camera seems to be the eyes of someone inside the scene. Subjective shots tend to involve the viewer as an actor in the scene.

In addition, photographers often use other highly artistic film or digital techniques: making parts of an image crisp and in focus and others slightly blurred; using camera filters for special effects; distorting or merging images (a city that blends into a desert; a woman who blends into a tree); and creating visual parodies (a Greek statue wearing jeans).

There are also various ways that a photographic image can be manipulated or falsified. Be aware of the following devices used to create visual deception: staging images (scenes that appear to be documentaries but are really staged); altering images (for example, airbrushing, reshaping body parts, or constructing a composite image such as putting the head of one person on the body of another); selecting images or parts of images (such as cropping photographs so that only parts of the body or only parts of a scene are shown); and mislabeling (putting a caption on a photograph that misrepresents what it actually is).

For Writing and Discussion

Look at three photographic images of bears: Figure 5.1 (Chapter 5, p. 98), Figure 5.2 (Chapter 5, p. 99), and the Nikon camera advertisement (p.299). Then, working in small groups or as a whole class, analyze the camera techniques of each photograph, and explain how these techniques are rhetorically effective for the purpose of the message to which each is attached.

Analyzing the Compositional Features of the Image

In addition to analyzing camera and film or digital techniques, you need to analyze the compositional features of the photograph's subject. When photographs are used in ads, every detail down to the props in the photograph or the placement of a model's hands are consciously chosen.

1. ***Examine the settings, furnishings, and props.***
   a. List all furnishings and props. If the photograph pictures a room, look carefully at such details as the kind and color of the rug; the subject matter of the paintings on the walls; furniture styles; objects on tables; and the general arrangement of the room. (Is it neat and tidy, or does it have a lived-in look? Is it formal or casual?) If the photograph is outdoors, observe the exact features of the landscape. (Why a mountain rather than a meadow? Why a robin rather than a crow or pigeon?)
   b. What social meanings are attached to the objects you listed? In a den, for example, duck decoys and fishing rods create a different emotional effect than computers and fax machines do. The choice of a breed of dog can signal differences in values, social class, or lifestyle—a Labrador retriever ver-

FIGURE 11.1 Nikon Ad

> *The camera for those who look at this picture and think, "Gosh, how'd
> they open up the shadows without blowing out the highlights?"*

When staring into the mouth of a 10 ft. grizzly bear, you tend to think about life. Limbs. And how handy legs are. Not the fill-flash ratio needed to expose teeth about to rip your leg off.

Nikon created the N90 specifically for complicated situations like this. When you have no time to think. A brown bear on brown earth, about to mangle a brown shoe. So instead of overexposing this picture like other cameras might, the N90™ works for you, properly analyzing the situation and delivering an accurate exposure.

Here's how it does it. The 3D Matrix Meter divides the scene into eight segments. It measures the brightness in each one of the segments and then compares them for contrast. D-type lenses incorporate the subject's distance which allows the N90 to calculate the proper ambient light exposure.

The SB-25 Speedlight fires a rapid series of imperceptible pre-flashes to determine the bear's reflectance. And then provides the precise amount of fill-flash needed to lighten the bear's dark brown fur, without overexposing his slightly yellow teeth.

The N90 can give you near-perfect exposures when other cameras would be fooled. Or, for that matter, eaten.

Professionals trust the N90. So you can too. Because it works just as well on children eating ice cream as it does on bears eating people.

The N90 System

Nikon
We take the world's
greatest pictures.

See the Nikon N90 at authorized dealers where you see this symbol. Nikon Date Link System available Winter '93. For more on our MasterCard, call 1-800-NIKON-35.

---

sus a groomed poodle; an English sheepdog versus a generic mutt. Even choice of flowers can have symbolic significance: A single rose connotes romance or elegance, a bouquet of daisies suggests freshness, and a hanging fuchsia suggests earthy naturalness.

2. ***Consider the characters, roles, and actions.***
   a. Create the story behind the image. Who are these people in the photograph? Why are they here? What are they doing? In advertisements, models can be either *instrumental,* in which case they are acting out real-life

roles, or *decorative,* in which case they are eye candy. A female model working on a car engine in grungy mechanics clothes would be instrumental; a female model in a bikini draped over the hood would be decorative.

b. Note every detail about how models are posed, clothed, and accessorized. Note facial expressions, eye contact, gestures, activities, posed relationships among actors and among actors and objects, and relative sizes. (Who is looking at whom? Who is above or below whom? Who or what is in the foreground or background?) Pay special attention to hairstyles because popular culture endows hair with great significance.

c. Ask what social roles are being played and what values appealed to. Are the gender roles traditional or nontraditional? Are the relationships romantic, erotic, friendly, formal, uncertain? What are the power relationships among characters?

3. *Analyze the rhetorical context of the image.*

a. Images are always encountered in a rhetorical context: They accompany a news story, are part of a poster or Web site, or are used in an advertisement. Consider how the image functions within that context and how it contributes to the rhetorical effect of the whole to which it is a part.

b. In advertisements, consider carefully the relationship between the image and the words in the copy. The words in advertisements are chosen with the same care as the details in the image. Pay special attention to the document design of the copy, the style of the language, and the connotations, double entendres, and puns. Also note the kind of product information that is included or excluded from the ad.

See Chapter 3, pp. 62–68, for a discussion of document design.

For Writing and Discussion

This exercise asks you to consider both the camera and film techniques and the compositional features of two Jeep advertisements. Figure 11.2 shows an ad for Jeep Grand Cherokee that appeared in the March 2004 edition of *Brio,* an upscale, elegant, glamorous Japanese magazine. Figure 11.3 shows an ad for the Jeep Wrangler from the May 2004 edition of *Spin,* an American magazine about the contemporary rock music scene. An examination of these ads will help you see how an automobile company with a global reputation targets very different audiences through different publications.

Working individually or in groups, study these ads and answer the following questions:

1. Analysis of the composition of the ads

a. Describe the Jeep Grand Cherokee ad. In the full-size version of this ad, two shadowy figures are visible—the driver and the woman looking down on the Jeep from the lighted window high up in the building. How would you describe the building and the strange effect with water on the right side of the picture? Is the water coming from a fountain, or is the effect the result of composite trick photography? Then describe the Jeep Wrangler ad. Describe the setting and note the contents of the hiker's "backpack."

FIGURE 11.2 Jeep Grand Cherokee Ad

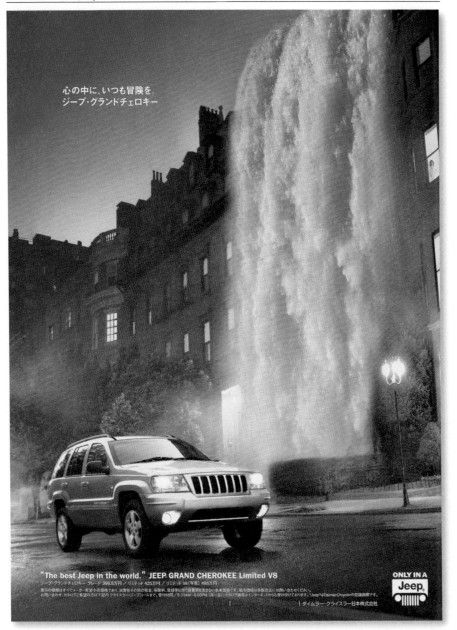

b. How is each ad composed? Note how the vehicle is positioned with regard to the viewer; also note the vehicle's size in relation to the setting. What is the relative importance of image versus verbal text in these ads?

(*continued*)

FIGURE 11.3 Jeep Wrangler Ad

c. What story does each ad tell? What roles do persons and vehicle play in each story? (In the Japanese ad, the words in the upper left part of the ad can be translated as "Always have adventure in your heart. Jeep Grand Cherokee.")

2. Analysis of the appeal of the ads
   a. To what values does each ad appeal?
   b. What connections do you see between the images and appeals of the ads and the nationality, age, class, and economic status of the audiences? How do these ads illustrate the concept of targeting different audiences?
   c. How do the features of each ad create their appeals? How would you explain the function of the setting in the Grand Cherokee ad, particularly the blended effect of an elegant building in a courtyard and an apparent waterfall? What effect is created by the woman looking down on the driver from a lighted window? Why is she behind the waterfall? Why is it a night scene rather than a day scene? In the Jeep Wrangler ad, why did the ad designers opt for humor? Why do they have the hiker carrying all the "stuff" rather than showing it packed in the Wrangler? Why is the setting a dry desert rather than a mountaintop or beach?
3. Sport-utility vehicles are at the center of the public controversy over global warming, pollution of the environment, and the growing shortage of fossil fuel. Critics of SUVs commonly point out two ironies: (1) these vehicles, which are designed to take people out into nature, are contributing disproportionately to the destruction of nature; and (2) these all-terrain vehicles are often used in urban driving that does not call for the size, power, or features of SUVs. How do these ads work to deflect these criticisms and "hide" these ironies?

How to Analyze an Advertisement

It is now time to examine advertising in more detail. In the previous section, we said that you should always analyze images within their specific rhetorical context. To analyze ads, you need to understand the context in which advertisers work—their specific goals and strategies.

Understanding an Advertiser's Goals and Strategies

Although some advertisements are primarily informational—explaining why the company believes its product is superior—most advertisements involve parity products such as soft drinks, deodorants, breakfast cereals, toothpaste, and jeans. (*Parity* products are products that are roughly equal in quality to their competitors and so can't be promoted through any rational or scientific proof of superiority.)

Advertisements for parity products usually use psychological and motivational strategies to associate a product with a target audience's (often subconscious) dreams, hopes, fears, desires, and wishes, suggesting that the product will magically dispel these fears and anxieties or magically deliver on values, desires, and dreams. Using sophisticated research techniques, advertisers study how people's fears, dreams, and values differ according to their ethnicity, gender, educational level, socioeconomic class, age, and so forth; this research allows advertisers to tailor their appeals precisely to the target audience.

Furthermore, advertisers often focus on long-range advertising campaigns rather than on just a single ad. Their goal is not simply to sell a product but to build brand loyalty or a relationship with consumers that will be long lasting. (Think of how the brand Marlboro has a different image from the brand Winston, or how Calvin Klein's "heroin chic" of the late 1990s differed from Tommy Hilfiger's "American freedom" image.) Advertisers try to convert a brand name from a label on a can or on the inside of a sweater to a field of qualities, values, and imagery that lives inside the heads of its targeted consumers. An ad campaign, therefore, uses subtle repetition of themes through a variety of individual ads aimed at building up a psychological link between the product and the consumer. Advertisers don't just want you to buy Nikes rather than Reeboks, but also to see yourself as a Nike kind of person who attributes part of your identity to Nikes. Some ad campaigns have been brilliant at turning whole segments of a population into loyal devotees of a brand. Among the most famous campaigns are the Volkswagen ads of the 1950s and early 1960s, the long-lived Marlboro cowboy ads, the independent female theme of Virginia Slims ads, and more recently, the dairy farmers and milk processors' "Got Milk?" ads in magazines and on billboards that feature all kinds of celebrities with milk mustaches, making it "cool" to drink milk.

How Advertisers Target Specific Audiences

When advertisers produce an ad, they create images and copy intended to appeal to the values, hopes, and desires of a specific audience. How do they know the psychological attributes of a specific audience? Much of the market research on which advertisers rely is based on an influential demographic tool developed by SRI Research called the "VALS" (Values And Lifestyle System).* This system divides consumers into three basic categories with further subdivision:

1. *Needs-driven consumers.* Poor, with little disposable income, these consumers generally spend their money only on basic necessities.
   - *Survivors:* Live on fixed incomes or have no disposable income. Advertising seldom targets this group.
   - *Sustainers:* Have very little disposable income, but often spend what they have impulsively on low-end, mass-market items.
2. *Outer-directed consumers.* These consumers want to identify with certain in-groups, to "keep up with the Joneses," or to surpass them.
   - *Belongers:* Believe in traditional family values and are conforming, nonexperimental, nostalgic, and sentimental. They are typically blue-collar or

*Our discussion of VALS is adapted from Harold W. Berkman and Christopher Gibson, *Advertising,* 2nd ed. (New York: Random House, 1987), pp. 134–137.

lower middle class, and they buy products associated with Mom, apple pie, and the American flag.

- *Emulators:* Are ambitious and status conscious. They have a tremendous desire to associate with currently popular in-groups. They are typically young, have at least moderate disposable income, are urban and upwardly mobile, and buy conspicuous items that are considered "in."
- *Achievers:* Have reached the top in a competitive environment. They buy to show off their status and wealth and to reward themselves for their hard climb up the ladder. They have high incomes and buy top-of-the-line luxury items that say "success." They regard themselves as leaders and persons of stature.

3. **Inner-directed consumers.** These consumers are individualistic and buy items to suit their own tastes rather than to symbolize their status.

- *I-am-me types:* Are young, independent, and often from affluent backgrounds. They typically buy expensive items associated with their individual interests (such as mountain bikes, stereo equipment, or high-end camping gear), but may spend very little on clothes, cars, or furniture.
- *Experiential types:* Are process-oriented and often reject the values of corporate America in favor of alternative lifestyles. They buy organic foods, make their own bread, do crafts and music, value holistic medicine, and send their children to alternative kindergartens.
- *Socially conscious types:* Believe in simple living and are concerned about the environment and the poor. They emphasize the social responsibility of corporations, take on community service, and actively promote their favorite causes. They have middle to high incomes and are usually very well educated.

No one fits exactly into any one category, and most people exhibit traits of several categories, but advertisers are interested in statistical averages, not individuals. When a company markets an item, it enlists advertising specialists to help target the item to a particular market segment. Budweiser is aimed at belongers, while upscale microbeers are aimed at emulators or achievers. To understand more precisely the fears and values of a target group, researchers can analyze subgroups within each of these VALS segments by focusing specifically on women, men, children, teenagers, young adults, or retirees or on specified ethnic or regional minorities. Researchers also determine what kinds of families and relationships are valued in each of the VALS segments, who in a family initiates demand for a product, and who in a family makes the actual purchasing decisions. Thus, ads aimed at belongers depict traditional families; ads aimed at I-am-me types may depict more ambiguous sexual or family relationships. Advertisements aimed at women can be particularly complex because of women's conflicting social roles in our society. When advertisers target the broader category of gender, they sometimes sweep away VALS distinctions and try to evoke more deeply embedded emotional and psychological responses.

For Writing and Discussion

You own a successful futon factory that has marketed its product primarily to experiential types. Your advertisements have associated futons with holistic health, spiritualism (transcendental meditation, yoga), and organic whole-someness (all-natural materials, gentle people working in the factory, incense and sitar music in your retail stores, and so forth). You have recently expanded your factory and now produce twice as many futons as you did six months ago. Unfortunately, demand hasn't increased correspondingly. Your market research suggests that if you are going to increase demand for futons, you have to reach other VALS segments.

Working in small groups, develop ideas for a magazine or TV advertisement that might sell futons to one or more of the other target segments in the VALS system. Your instructor can assign a different target segment to each group, or each group can decide for itself which target segment constitutes the likeliest new market for futons.

Groups should then share their ideas with the whole class.

Sample Analysis of an Advertisement

With an understanding of possible photographic effects and the compositional features of ads, you now have all the background knowledge needed to begin doing your own analysis of ads. To illustrate how an analysis of an ad can reveal the ad's persuasive strategies, we show you our analysis of an ad for Coors Light (Figure 11.4) that ran in a variety of women's magazines. First, consider the contrast between the typical beer ads that are aimed at men (showing women in bikinis fulfilling adolescent male sexual fantasies or men on fishing trips or in sports bars, representing male comradeship and bonding) and this Coors Light ad with its "Sam and Me" theme.

Rather than associating beer drinking with a wild party, this ad associates beer drinking with the warm friendship of a man and a woman, with just a hint of potential romance. The ad shows a man and a woman, probably in their early- to mid-twenties, in relaxed conversation; they are sitting casually on a tabletop, with their legs resting on chair seats. The woman is wearing casual pants, a summery cotton top, and informal shoes. Her braided, shoulder-length hair has a healthy, mussed appearance, and one braid comes across the front of her shoulder. She is turned away from the man, leans on her knees, and holds a bottle of Coors Light. Her sparkling eyes are looking up, and she smiles happily, as if reliving a pleasant memory. The man is wearing slacks, a cotton shirt with the sleeves rolled up, and scuffed tennis shoes with white socks. He also has a reminiscing smile on his face, and he leans on the woman's shoulder. The words "Coors Light. Just between friends." appear immediately below the picture next to a Coors Light can.

This ad appeals to women's desire for close friendships and relationships. Everything about the picture signifies long-established closeness and intimacy—

FIGURE 11.4 Beer Ad Aimed at Women

S am and Me.

Me and Sam? We're just friends.
Best friends, actually, since Mrs.
Ainsley's first grade class when
I let the hamster loose and Sam
took the rap for me. I mean Sam's
seen me in braces and I've seen
him eat pizza. There's just way
too much history here. Sam's my
friend. The one I go to when I
really need someone to talk to.
I bring the Coors Light and Sam
brings his shoulder. And sometimes it's Sam bringing the Coors
Light and I'm doing the listening.
Me and Sam? Together? I've
never even thought about it.
Okay, so I've thought about it.

Coors Light.
Just between friends.

old friends rather than lovers. The way the man leans on the woman shows her strength and independence. Additionally, the way they pose, with the woman slightly forward and sitting up more than the man, results in their taking up equal space in the picture. In many ads featuring male-female couples, and man appears larger and taller than the woman; this picture signifies mutuality and equality.

The words of the ad help interpret the relationship. Sam and the woman have been friends since the first grade, and they are reminiscing about old times. The relationship is thoroughly mutual. Sometimes he brings the Coors Light and sometimes she brings it; sometimes she does the listening and sometimes he does; sometimes she leans on his shoulder and sometimes he leans on hers. Sometimes the ad says, "Sam and me"; sometimes it says, "me and Sam." Even the "bad grammar" of "Sam and me" (rather than "Sam and I") suggests the lazy, relaxed absence of pretense or formality.

These two are reliable, old buddies. But the last three lines of the copy give just a hint of potential romance: "Me and Sam? Together? I've never even thought about it. Okay, so I've thought about it." Whereas beer ads targeting men portray women as sex objects, this ad appeals to many women's desire for relationships and for romance that is rooted in friendship rather than sex.

And why the name "Sam"? Students in our classes have hypothesized that Sam is a "buddy" kind of name rather than a romantic-hero name. Yet it is more modern and more interesting than other buddy names such as "Bob" or "Bill" or "Dave." "A 'Sam,'" said one of our students, "is more mysterious than a 'Bill.'" Whatever associations the name strikes in you, be assured that the admakers spent hours debating possible names until they hit on this one. For an additional example of an ad analysis, see the sample student essay (pp. 320–323).

For Writing and Discussion

1. Examine any of the ads reprinted in this chapter or magazine ads brought to class by students or your instructor, and analyze them in detail, paying particular attention to setting, furnishings, and props; characters, roles, and actions; photographic effects; and words and copy. Prior to discussion, freewrite your own analysis of the chosen ad.

2. An excellent way to learn how to analyze ads is to create your own advertisement. Read the following introduction to a brief article with the headline "Attention Advertisers: Real Men Do Laundry." This article appeared in an issue of *American Demographics,* a magazine that helps advertisers target particular audiences based on demographic analysis of the population.

> Commercials almost never show men doing the laundry, but nearly one-fifth of men do at least seven loads a week. Men don't do as much laundry as women, but the washday gap may be closing. In the dual-career 1990's laundry is going unisex.
>
> Forty-three percent of women wash at least seven loads of laundry a week, compared with 19 percent of men, according to a survey conducted for Lever Brothers Company, manufacturers of Wisk detergent. Men do 29 percent of the 419 million loads of laundry Americans wash each week. Yet virtually all laundry-detergent advertising is aimed at women.

Working in small groups, create an idea for a laundry-detergent ad to be placed in a men's magazine such as *Men's Health, Sports Illustrated, Field and Stream,* or *Esquire.* Draw a rough sketch of your ad that includes the picture, the placement of words, and a rough idea of the content of the words. Pay particular attention to the visual features of your ad—the models, their ages, ethnicity, social status or class, and dress; the setting, such as a self-service laundry or a home laundry room; and other features. When you have designed a possible approach, explain why you think your ad will be successful.

Cultural Perspectives on Advertisements

There isn't space here to examine in depth the numerous cultural issues raised by advertisements, but we can introduce you to a few of them and provide some thought-provoking tasks for exploratory writing and talking. The key issue we want you to think about in this section is how advertisements not only reflect the cultural values and the economic and political structures of the society that produces them but also actively construct and reproduce that society.

For example, look at the 1924 advertisement for the Hoover vacuum cleaner shown in Figure 11.5. This ad appealed to a middle class that was becoming more dependent on household inventions as the use of domestic help became less common. In this ad, a well-dressed wife with carefully-styled hair embraces her well-dressed husband as he returns from a day of work in the business world. Notice that the image and the words reinforce the idea of distinct gender roles while promoting pride in a comfortable, clean, and aesthetically pleasing home. The ad sells more than Hoover vacuum cleaners; it sells a vision of middle class domestic harmony in which the wife's "natural" role is housecleaning.

In its depiction of gender roles, the Hoover ad now strikes us as very old-fashioned. However, cultural critics often argue that contemporary advertisements continue to depict women in culturally subordinate ways. In 1979, the influential sociologist and semiotician* Erving Goffman published a book called *Gender Advertising,* arguing that the way in which women are pictured in advertisements removes them from serious power. In many cases, Goffman's point seems self-evident. Women in advertisements are often depicted in frivolous, childlike, exhibitionistic, sexual, or silly poses that would be considered undignified for a man, such as the "Of Sound Body" Zenith Ad (Figure 11.6). Women in advertisements are often fun to look at or enthralling to "gaze" at, but are seldom portrayed in positions of power. What distinguishes Goffman's work is his analysis of apparently positive portrayals of women in advertisements. He points out tiny details that differentiate the treatment of men from that of women. For example, when men hold umbrellas in an ad, it is usually raining, but women often hold umbrellas for decoration; men grip objects tightly, but women often caress objects or cup them in a gathering in or nurturing way. Female models dance and jump and wiggle in front of the camera (like children playing), whereas male models generally

---

*A *semiotician* is a person who studies the meanings of signs in a culture. A *sign* is any human-produced artifact or gesture that conveys meaning. It can be anything from a word to a facial expression to the arrangement of silverware at a dinner table.

FIGURE 11.5   Hoover Ad

you darling!

"Give her a Hoover and you give her the Best"

The **HOOVER**

It BEATS ... as it Sweeps   as it Cleans

ANOTHER year has slipped by since you last thought of giving her a Hoover.

But *she* has thought of it many times.

As cleaning days come and go she struggles resolutely with the only "tools" she has in her "workshop," your home.

And they are woefully inadequate, wasteful of time and strength.

As she wields her broom foot by foot across the dusty, dirty rugs her arms rebel and her back seems near to breaking.

Yet she tries to greet you with a smile when you come home at night.

In your heart you pay her tribute. "She's a brave little woman," you say.

But why put her courage to such an unfair test?

Why ask her to bear her burdens patiently when they can so easily be lifted?

The Hoover will save her strength.

The Hoover will speed her work.

The Hoover will safeguard her pride in a clean home.

You cannot afford to deny her these things for the small monthly payments which The Hoover costs.

Don't disappoint her again this Christmas!

Show her that you really do care, and throughout her lifetime your thoughtfulness will be ever in her mind.

FIGURE 11.6   Zenith Audio Products Ad

stand or sit in a dignified manner. Even when trying to portray a powerful and independent woman, ads reveal cultural signs that the woman is subordinate.

A decade later, another cultural critic, researcher Jean Kilbourne, made a more explicit argument against the way advertisements negatively construct women. In her films *Still Killing Us Softly* (1987) and *Slim Hopes: Advertising and the Obsession with Thinness* (1995), Kilbourne argues that our culture's fear of powerful women is embodied in advertisements that entrap women in futile pursuit of an impossible, flawless standard of beauty. Advertisements help construct the social values that pressure women (particularly middle-class white women) to stay thin, frail, and little-girlish and thus become perfect objects. In *Slim Hopes,* she claims that basically only one body type is preferred (the waif look or the waif-made-voluptuous-with-reconstructed-breasts look). Further, the dismemberment of women in ads—the focus on individual body parts—both objectifies women and intensifies women's anxious concentration on trying to perfect each part of their bodies. Kilbourne asserts that ads distort women's attitudes toward food through harmful and contradictory messages that encourage binging while equating moral goodness with thinness and control over eating. Ads convert women into lifelong consumers of beauty and diet products while undermining their self-esteem.

To what extent do the criticisms of Goffman or Kilbourne still apply to the most current advertisements? To what extent has advertising made gains in portraying women as strong, independent, intelligent, and equal with men in their potential for professional status? The picture painted by Goffman and Kilbourne is complicated by some new ads—for example, the new genre of physical fitness ads that emphasize women's physical strength and capabilities as well as their sexuality and femininity. Ads for athletic products feature models with beautiful hair and faces and strong, trim, and shapely bodies. These ads strike different balances between female athleticism and sexuality, perhaps creating a more powerful view of women. (See the ad for Adidas "Adrenaline" Figure 11.7.) It is also more common today to find ads picturing women in professional "business executive" roles. For example, how much cultural power is possessed by the woman in the AT&T calling card ad in Figure 11.8?

For Writing and Discussion

To test for yourself the extent to which Goffman and Kilbourne's claims about ads still apply, we invite you to explore this issue in the following sequence of activities, which combine class discussion with invitations for exploratory writing.

1. Examine again the four ads discussed in the previous section: the Hoover ad (Figure 11.5); the "Of Sound Body" Zenith ad (Figure 11.6); the Adidas "Adrenaline" ad (Figure 11.7); and the AT&T Calling Card ad (Figure 11.8). To what extent does each of these ads construct women as lacking in power in the economic, political, and professional structures of our culture? Which ads, if any, treat women as powerful? Using these ads as your evidence, draw some conclusions about how the social roles for women have changed in the last eighty years. Freewrite your responses to the way women are constructed in these ads as preparation for class discussion.

FIGURE 11.7 Adidas "Adrenaline" Ad

2. Consider again the AT&T Calling Card ad (Figure 11.8). To what extent would you call the woman in this ad an empowered professional? How might Goffman or Kilbourne argue that this ad subtly subordinates women? Try playing the "What if they changed . . . .?" game with this ad. What would be different if this ad featured a man rather than a woman to advertise the calling card? How would the image change? How would the verbal text change?

3. Bring to class advertisements for women's clothing, perfumes, or accessories from recent fashion and beauty magazines such as *Glamour, Elle, InStyle,* and *Vogue.* Study the ways that female models are typically posed in these ads. Then have male students assume the postures of the female models. How many of the postures, which look natural for women, seem ludicrous when adopted by men? To what extent are these postures really

The "What if they changed . . . ?" game is explained earlier in this chapter on pp. 295–296.

(continued)

FIGURE 11.8 AT&T Calling Card Ad

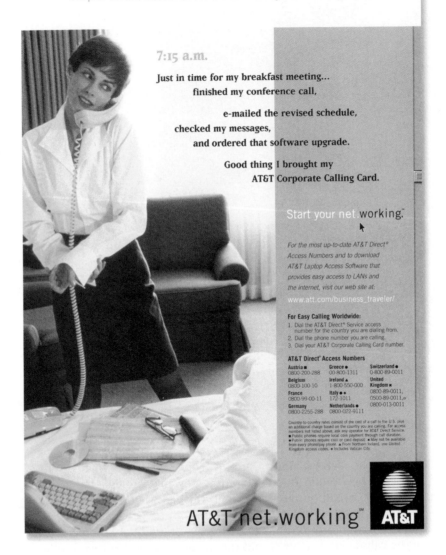

natural for women? To what extent do these postures illustrate Goffman's point that advertisements don't take women seriously?

4. Bring to class some examples of recent advertisements that you think portray women in a particularly positive and empowered way—ads that you think neither Goffman nor Kilbourne could deconstruct to show the subordination of women in our culture. Share your examples with the class and see whether your classmates agree with your assessment of these ads.

READINGS

Our first reading is an excerpt from Paul Messaris's book *Visual Persuasion: The Role of Images in Advertising*. Messaris, a communications professor at the University of Pennsylvania, intended this book for an academic audience (hence his frequent parenthetical references to other scholars). His purpose is to analyze the distinctive features of visual communication and to examine the role of visual images in political campaigns and commercial advertising. In the following excerpt, Messaris explains his position on the ethical responsibility of advertisers. The particular question at issue is whether advertisers are being unethical when they display certain groups of people—in this passage, adolescents and African-Americans—in ways that are stereotypical, unrealistic, or potentially harmful to individuals or society.

Paul Messaris
From Visual Persuasion:
The Role of Images in Advertising

1   As we have seen, the iconicity* of images makes it possible for ads to elicit our attention and emotions by simulating various significant features of our real-world visual experiences. By virtue of their iconicity, visual ads are able to erect before our eyes a mirror world, with whose inhabitants we are invited to identify or to imagine that we are interacting. These acts of identification and imaginary interaction have real-world consequences. Some of the most revealing analyses of advertising have described the ways in which viewers use the characters they see in ads as reference points for their own evolving identities (Barthel, 1988; Ewen, 1988; Ewen & Ewen, 1982). For example, Carol Moog (1990) recalls how, as a young girl, she studied the posture of a woman in a refrigerator commercial to learn how to carry herself as an adult (p. 13). Together with fictional movies and TV programs, ads are a major source of images that young people can use to previsualize their places in the world of sexual and status relationships. It can be argued that advertisers have an ethical responsibility to take these circumstances into account in fashioning the images that they place before the public.

2   What might constitute a violation of this ethical responsibility? Critics of advertising images often focus on the discrepancy between the vision of life offered in ads and the needs or abilities of real people. Drawing on her practice as a psychotherapist, Moog (1990) cites the story of a young lawyer who expressed dissatisfaction with her life because she had not lived up to her potential as a member of "the Pepsi generation"—that is, "beautiful, sexy, happy, young people . . . a generation that didn't slog through law school, work twelve-hour days, or break up with fiancés" (p. 15). Moog presents this

---

Iconicity is an academic term (related to *icon*, meaning "image") referring to the power of images to influence a viewer. When you desire, for example, to meet a stranger in a Parisian café or to ride a horse through the pounding surf because you saw characters do these things in an ad, you experience the *iconic power* of the image.

vignette as a reminder of the fact that "advertisers are not in the business of making people feel better about themselves, they're in the *selling* business" (p. 16). As this statement implies, commercial advertising often does create a vision of a fantasy world that may become a source of dissatisfaction in people's real lives, and this is especially true of ads that use sex or status as part of their appeal. Some people may find this practice objectionable in and of itself, although in my view it would be rather fatuous, as well as somewhat puritanical, to suggest that advertisers should stop purveying the images of "beautiful, sexy, happy young people" that led to Moog's client's distress. However, there is a related trend in advertising that does seem to me to raise especially troublesome ethical issues.

3   In recent years, ads aimed at young people have increasingly sought to appeal to an adolescent sense of frustration and resentment at the constricting demands of adult society. There may be a lingering element of this type of sentiment in the dissatisfaction expressed by Moog's client, but the kind of advertising to which I am referring is quite different from the old, Pepsi-generation style of happy, carefree images. Instead, these more recent ads, for products such as athletic shoes, off-road vehicles, or video games, often make a point of displaying abrasive, belligerent behavior and physical recklessness (cf. Lull, 1995, pp. 73–81). A defender of such ads might argue that they are simply being honest. Adolescents often have good reason to chafe at the standards imposed on them by older people and to recoil from the vision of the future that many of them face. The aggression and recklessness depicted in some of these ads are no doubt authentic expressions of how many young people feel. To put a happy face on those feelings could be considered hypocritical. Nevertheless, with due respect for such views, I would argue that the type of resentment exploited in these ads is unproductive at best, counterproductive at worst. Dissatisfaction that leads to impulsiveness and disregard for other people gains nothing from being expressed openly. In that sense, I would say that the ethics of this genre of advertising are certainly questionable.

4   This is not to say, however, that advertising aimed at young people should necessarily revert to the untroubled imagery of earlier times. It should be possible to portray and address youth honestly without pandering to the irresponsible tendencies that are sometimes associated with adolescence. For instance, despite the criticism that has recently been directed at the advertising of Calvin Klein, it seems to me that there are many Calvin Klein ads that manage to strike this balance quite effectively. In particular, the print ads for cK one fragrance have generated record-breaking sales while presenting a view of youthful sexuality that is remarkably unglamorized (compared to most other ads) and, furthermore, notably inclusive both racially and in terms of sexual orientation. This inclusiveness deserves special mention. The cK one ads are among the few examples of mass-produced imagery in which the mingling of people from different backgrounds appears relatively natural, rather than an artificial (albeit well-meaning) concoction of the media.

5   But, again, this comment should not be interpreted as a blanket endorsement of unvarnished naturalism in all of advertising. In a recent discussion of the portrayal of blacks and whites in the mass media, DeMott (1995) has argued that movies and ads present a phony picture of harmony between the races that serves to obscure the unpleasant truth about race relations in the United States. I do not find this argument persuasive. For one thing, information about racial friction is abundantly available elsewhere in the media. More importantly, though, I think it is a mistake to assume that people always look at advertising images expecting to see the way things really are in society. Almost by definition, the portrayals of the good life presented in ads carry with them the implicit understanding that they are idealizations, not documentary reports (cf. Schudson, 1984). What people look for in such ads is a vision of the way things ought to be. Furthermore, when an ad is produced by a large corporation, people are likely to see this vision as an indicator of socially approved values—even though it also may be understood tacitly that those values do not correspond very closely to current social reality. From this perspective, the kinds of advertisements that DeMott criticizes—depictions of people from different racial and ethnic backgrounds living together in harmony and prosperity—are actually highly desirable. For example, an American Express Gold Card ad (attacked by DeMott) shows elegantly dressed blacks and whites occupying adjacent box seats in an opulent-looking theater or concert hall, while an ad for Chubb Insurance portrays two suburban families, one black, one white, posing together in a setting of obvious wealth. Such ads should be praised, not subjected to carping objections. In my view, they are models of the responsible use of advertising's iconic powers.

Thinking Critically about *Visual Persuasion*

1. Messaris seeks to establish a middle position between two extreme views of advertisers' responsibility to viewers and consumers. How would you describe his view and the extremes he is reacting against?
2. Can you find examples of adolescent-directed ads portraying, in Messaris's words, "abrasive, belligerent behavior and physical recklessness"? What points can you raise in support of or against his censure of this type of ad?
3. Over the last two decades, the number of magazine ads featuring persons of color has increased substantially. Sometimes ads show multiracial groups. At other times, especially in middlebrow magazines such as *Parents' Magazine, Working Mother, Good Housekeeping,* or *Sports Illustrated,* ads now feature models from minority groups, where formerly the models would have been white. Observe closely the ads shown in Figures 11.9 through 11.12. Although we will call Figure 11.12 an "ad," it is actually a photograph of a huge poster placed on the wall of a youth-oriented clothing store in an urban shopping mall. To what extent do these ads present a harmonious multiracial and multicultural society?

FIGURE 11.9 MetLife Ad

Courtesy of MetLife. PEANUTS © United Feature Syndicate, Inc.

FIGURE 11.10 PINE-SOL® Household Cleaner Ad

FIGURE 11.11 Vokal by Nelly Ad

FIGURE 11.12 Wall Poster in Clothing Store

Do any of them contain racial or ethnic stereotypes? What vision of social reality, race, and class are these ads constructing?

4. Messaris refers to the argument of Benjamin DeMott that buddy movies featuring pals from different races or "happy harmony" ads showing blacks and whites together create a false sense that America no longer has a race problem. How do you think Messaris and DeMott would analyze the ads in Figures 11.9 through 11.12? Do you think the clothing store poster (Figure 11.12) illustrates DeMott's idea of a "happy harmony" ad? How would you describe the difference in the image of black males in the MetLife ad (Figure 11.9) and the Vokal ad (Figure 11.11)? How would the effect of the MetLife ad differ if the model were dressed like Nelly? Why doesn't Nelly dress like the MetLife model?

5. Messaris distinguishes between ads that include people of different races "naturally" and those that appear "artificial" and "concocted." Do the ads in Figures 11.9 and 11.11 seem to you to be natural or artificially concocted? Why or why not?

6. These ads also raise questions about the intersection of race and gender. We have asked how Messaris and DeMott might analyze these ads. Now ask how Goffman and Kilbourne might analyze them. Imagine the PINE-SOL Household Cleaner ad (Figure 11.10) using a white model rather than a black model (same pose, clothing, and body type with only the skin color changed). Would the ad work? Why or why not? Also consider the clothing store poster (Figure 11.12). The poster image features three women and two men. Why did the poster designers choose that ratio rather than, say, three men and two women or an even number of men and women? Would the effect of the ad be different if the models were placed in a different order? What impression of young people do you think the poster designers were trying to achieve? How is that impression dependent upon the arrangement and posing of the models by gender and race?

The final reading is a student essay written in response to the assignment in this chapter. It contrasts the strategies of two different cigarette ads to make smoking appear socially desirable despite public sentiment to the contrary.

Stephen Bean (Student)

How Cigarette Advertisers Address the Stigma Against Smoking:

A Tale of Two Ads

1   Any smoker can tell you there's a social stigma attached to smoking in this country. With smokers being pushed out of restaurants, airports, and many office buildings, how could anyone not feel like a pariah lighting up? While never associated with the churchgoing crowd, smoking is increasing-

ly viewed as lower class or as a symbol of rebellion. Smoking has significantly decreased among adults while increasing among teenagers and young adults in recent years—a testament to its growing status as an affront to middle- and upper-class values. Cigarette advertisers are sharply tuned into this cultural attitude. They must decide whether to overcome the working-class/rebellious image of smoking in their advertisements or use it to their advantage. The answer to this question lies in what type of people they want an ad to target—the young? the rich? the poor?—and in what values, insecurities, and desires they think this group shares. Two contrasting answers to these questions are apparent in recent magazine ads for Benson & Hedges cigarettes and for Richland cigarettes.

2   The ad for Benson & Hedges consists of a main picture and a small insert picture below the main one. The main picture shows five women (perhaps thirty years old) sitting around, talking, and laughing in the living room of a comfortable and urbane home or upscale apartment. The room is filled with natural light and is tastefully decorated with antique lamps and Persian rugs. The women have opened a bottle of wine, and a couple of glasses have been poured. They are dressed casually but fashionably, ranging from slightly hip to slightly conservative. One woman wears a loose, black, sleeveless dress; another wears grungesque boots with a sweater and skirt. One of the women, apparently the hostess, sits on a sofa a bit apart from the others, smiles with pleasure at the conversation and laughter of her friends, and knits. Two of the women are smoking, and three aren't. No smoke is visible coming from the cigarettes. Underneath the main picture is a small insert photograph of the hostess—the one knitting in the main picture—in a different pose. She is now leaning back in pleasure, apparently after the party, and this time she is smoking a cigarette. Underneath the photos reads the slogan "For people who like to smoke."

3   The ad for Richland cigarettes shows a couple in their late twenties sitting in a diner or perhaps a tavern off the freeway. The remains of their lunch—empty burger and fries baskets, a couple of beer bottles—lie on the table. They seem to be talking leisurely, sharing an after-meal smoke. The man is wearing black jeans and a black T-shirt. The woman is wearing a pinkish skirt and tank top. Learning back with her legs apart she sits in a position that signals sexuality. The slogan reads, "It's all right here." And at the bottom of the ad, "Classic taste. Right price." Outside the window of the diner you can see a freeway sign slightly blurred as if from heated air currents.

4   Whom do these different advertisements target? What about them might people find appealing? Clearly the Benson & Hedges ad is aimed at women, especially upper-middle-class women who wish to appear successful. As the media have noted lately, the social stigma against smoking is strongest among middle- and upper-class adults. My sense of the B&H ad is that it is targeting younger, college-educated women who feel social pressure to quit smoking. To them the ad is saying, "Smoking makes you no less sophisticated; it only shows that you have a fun side too. Be comfortable doing whatever makes you happy."

5   What choices did the advertisers make in constructing this scene to create this message? The living room—with its antique lamps and vases, its Persian rugs and hardcover books, and its wall hanging thrown over what appears to be an old trunk—creates a sense of comfortable, tasteful, upscale living. But figuring out the people in the room is more difficult. Who are these women? What is their story? What brought them together this afternoon? Where did their money come from? Are these professional women with high-paying jobs, or are they the wives of young bankers, attorneys, and stockbrokers? One woman has a strong business look—short hair feathered back, black sleeveless dress—but why is she dressed this way on what is apparently a Saturday afternoon? In contrast, another woman has a more hip, almost grunge look—slightly spiky hair that's long in the back, a loose sweater, a black skirt, and heavy black boots. Only one woman wears a wedding ring. It seems everything about these women resists easy definition or categorization. The most striking image in the ad is the hostess knitting. She looks remarkably domestic, almost motherly, with her knees drawn close, leaning over her knitting and smiling to herself as others laugh out loud. Her presence gives the scene a feeling of safety and old-fashioned values amidst the images of independence. Interestingly, we get a much different image of the hostess in the insert picture placed just above the B&H logo. This picture shows the hostess leaning back pleasurably on the couch and smoking. The image is undeniably sexual. Her arms are back; she's deeply relaxed; the two top buttons of her blouse are open; her hair is slightly mussed; she smokes languidly, taking full pleasure in the cigarette, basking in the party's afterglow.

6   The opposing images in the advertisement (knitting/smoking, conservative/hip, wife/career, safe/independent, domestic/sexual) mean that these women can't easily be defined—as smokers or as anything else. For an ad promoting smoking, the cigarettes themselves take a back seat. In the main picture the cigarettes are hardly noticeable; the two women holding cigarettes do so inconspicuously and there is no visible smoke. The ad doesn't say so much that it is good to smoke, but that it is okay to smoke. Smoking will not make you less sophisticated. If anything, it only shows that you have an element of youth and fun. The slogan, "For people who like to smoke," targets nonsmokers as much as it does smokers—not so much to take up smoking but to be more tolerant of those who choose to smoke. The emphasis is on choice, independence, and acceptance of others' choices. The ad attacks the social stigma against smoking; it eases the conscience of "people who like to smoke."

7   While the B&H ad hopes to remove the stigma attached to smoking, the Richland ad feasts on it. Richland cigarettes aren't for those cultivating the upper-class look. The ad goes for a rebellious, gritty image, for beer drinkers, not wine sippers. While the story of the women in the B&H ad is difficult to figure out, the Richland ad gives us a classic image: a couple on the road who have stopped at a diner or tavern. Here the story is simpler: a man and

woman being cool. They are going down the freeway to the big city. I picture a heavy American cruising car parked out front. Everything about the ad has a gritty, blue-collar feel. They sit at a booth with a Formica tabletop; the walls are bare, green-painted wood. The man is dressed in black with a combed-back, James Dean haircut. The woman wears a pink skirt with a tank top; her shoulder-length hair hasn't been fussed over, and she wears a touch of make-up. Empty baskets and bottles cluttering the table indicate they had a classic American meal—hamburgers, fries, and a beer—eaten for pleasure without politically correct worries about calories, polyunsaturated fats, cruelty to animals, or cancer. While the sexual imagery in the B&H ad is subtle, in the Richland ad it is blatant. The man is leaning forward with his elbows on the table; the woman is leaning back with her legs spread and her skirt pushed up slightly. Her eyes are closed. They smoke leisurely, and the woman holds the cigarette a couple of inches from her expecting lips. The slogan, "It's all right here," is centered beneath the woman's skirt. Smoking, like sex, is about pure pleasure—something to be done slowly. Far from avoiding working-class associations with smoking, this ad aims to reinforce them. The cigarettes are clearly visible, and, unlike the cigarettes in the B&H ad, show rings of rising smoke. This ad promotes living for the moment. The more rebellious, the better.

8   So we see, then, two different ways that cigarette companies address the stigma against smoking. The B&H ad tries to eliminate it by targeting middle-class, college-educated women. It appeals to upscale values, associating cigarette smoking with choice, and showing that "people who like to smoke" can also knit (evoking warm, safe images of domestic life) or lean back in postparty pleasure (evoking a somewhat wilder, more sexual image). In contrast, the Richland ad exploits the stigma. It associates smoking with on-the-road freedom, rebellion, sexuality, and enjoyment of the moment. The smoke visibly rising from the cigarettes in the Richland ad and noticeably absent from the Benson & Hedges ad tells the difference.

Thinking Critically about "How Cigarette Advertisers Address the Stigma Against Smoking"

1. Stephen Bean argues that the Benson & Hedges and the Richland ads use very different appeals to encourage their target audiences to smoke. What are the appeals he cites? Do you agree with Stephen's analysis?
2. Collect a variety of cigarette ads from current magazines, and analyze their various appeals. How do the ads vary according to their intended audiences? Consider ads targeted at men versus women or at audiences from different VALS segments.
3. What do you see as the strengths and weaknesses of Stephen's essay?

Composing Your Essay

Generating and Exploring Ideas

Your first task is to find two ads that sell the same general product to different target audiences or that make appeals to noticeably different value systems. Look for ads that are complex enough to invite detailed analysis. Then, analyze the ads carefully, using the strategies suggested earlier in this chapter. The sample student essay (pp. 320–323) provides an example of the kind of approach you can take.

If you get stuck, try freewriting your responses to the following questions: (a) What attracted your attention to this ad? (b) Whom do you think this ad targets? Why? (c) What photographic techniques, visual devices, and camera angles are used in this ad? (d) What props and furnishings are in this ad, and what values or meanings are attached to them? (e) What are the characters like, what are they doing, and why are they wearing what they are wearing and posed the way they are posed? (f) How do the words of the ad interplay with the picture? (g) How would the ad be less effective if its key features were changed in some way? (h) Overall, to what fears, values, hopes, or dreams is this ad appealing?

Shaping and Drafting

Your essay should be fairly easy to organize at the big-picture level, but each part will require its own organic organization depending on the main points of your analysis. At the big-picture level, you can generally follow a structure like this:

    I. Introduction (hooks readers' interest, gives background on how ads vary their appeals, asks the question your paper will address, and ends with initial mapping in the form of a purpose or thesis statement)
    II. General description of the two ads
        A. Description of ad 1
        B. Description of ad 2
    III. Analysis of the two ads
        A. Analysis of ad 1
        B. Analysis of ad 2
    IV. Conclusion (returns to the big picture for a sense of closure; makes final comments about the significance of your analysis or touches in some way on larger issues raised by the analysis)

We recommend that you write your rough draft rapidly, without worrying about gracefulness, correctness, or even getting all your ideas said at once. Many people like to begin with the description of the ads and then write the analysis before writing the introduction and the conclusion. After you have written your draft, put it aside for a while before you begin revising. We recommend that you ask classmates for a peer review of your draft early in the revising process.

Revising

Most experienced writers make global changes in their final drafts when they revise, especially when they are doing analytical writing. The act of writing a rough draft generally leads to the discovery of more ideas. You may also realize that many of your original ideas aren't clearly developed or that the draft feels scattered and unorganized.

GUIDELINES FOR PEER REVIEWS

Instructions for peer reviews are provided in Chapter 17 (pp. 519–520).

For the Writer

Prepare two or three questions you would like your peer reviewer to address while responding to your draft. The questions can focus on some aspect of your draft that you are uncertain about, on one or more sections where you particularly seek help or advice, on some feature that you particularly like about your draft, or on some part you especially wrestled with. Write out your questions and give them to your peer reviewer along with your draft.

For the Reviewer

I. Read the draft at a normal reading speed from beginning to end. As you read, do the following:
   A. Place a wavy line in the margin next to any passages that you find confusing, that contain something that doesn't seem to fit, or that otherwise slow down your reading.
   B. Place a "Good!" in the margin next to any passages where you think the writing is particularly strong or interesting.
II. Read the draft again slowly and answer the following questions by writing brief explanations of your answers.
   A. Introduction:
      1. Is the title appropriate for an academic analysis? Does it suggest the thesis and focus of the paper and pique your interest? How might the title be improved?
      2. What does the writer do to capture your interest, provide needed background, and set up the question to be addressed?
      3. How does the thesis statement, purpose statement, or forecasting statement provide the big picture for both the description and the analysis of the two ads? How might the writer improve the introduction?
   B. Description of the ads:
      1. Does the writer describe the ads in an interesting and vivid manner? How could this description help you "see" the ads more clearly?
      2. In what ways do the ads appeal to different audiences or have different value systems? What makes the ads complex enough to justify an analysis?

C. Analysis of the ads:
  1. How does the analysis of the ads shed light on and build on the description of the ads?
  2. How many of the following features does the writer discuss? Which could be added to deepen and complicate the analysis?
      a. Setting, props, and furnishings: how they indicate lifestyle and socioeconomic status; appeal to certain values; carry certain cultural associations or meanings; serve as symbols.
      b. Characters, roles, and actions: the story of the ad; power relationships and status of the characters; gender, age, or ethnic roles followed or violated; the significance of clothing and accessories, of hair and facial expressions, and of posing, positioning, and gestures.
      c. Photographic effects: lighting, camera angle, cropping, focus.
      d. Language and wording of the ad's copy: its overt message; feelings, mood, and values communicated through connotations, double entendres, and so forth; visual layout of copy.
  3. What portions of the analysis are convincing? Which details of the ads contradict the analysis? Do you disagree with the writer's view of these ads?
  4. How could the body of the paper be made clearer, better organized, or easier to follow? Where might the writer better apply the principles of clarity from Chapter 18 (starting with the big picture; putting points before particulars; using transitions; following the old/new contract)?
III. Rhetorical considerations
  A. *Purpose, audience,* and *genre:* Your purpose is to write an academic paper analyzing two advertisements for an audience who hasn't seen them. How effectively does this paper describe and analyze these ads for this audience? How effectively does it meet the genre expectations for an academic paper?
  B. *Logos, ethos,* and *pathos:* How convincing or effective is the logical or conceptual part of this draft? How does the writer build an *ethos* that readers will find reliable, fair, and authoritative? How does the writer connect this analysis to the interests and values of the audience?
IV. If the writer has prepared questions for you, respond to his or her inquiries.
 V. Sum up what you see as the chief strengths and problem areas of this draft:
  A. Strengths
  B. Problem areas
VI. Read the draft one more time. Place a check mark in the margin wherever you notice problems in grammar, spelling, or mechanics (one check mark per problem).

Analyzing a Short Story

About Literary Analysis

You've no doubt had more than one experience analyzing literature. For some students, such analysis is fun. It gives you a welcome break from densely packed textbook pages while stimulating your imagination. For others, the very word *literary* might trigger memories of mystifying class discussions and teachers' seemingly arbitrary decrees about the "hidden meaning" of something. Our goal in this chapter is to demonstrate that analyzing literature need not be either mystifying or arbitrary. In fact, analyzing literature is quite similar to analyzing just about any type of text or event: asking questions that you think will intrigue your reader as well as yourself and studying the text to find what answers it provides. What's different about literary analysis is that it opens up imaginative possibilities that can entertain and delight readers as well as inform them.

To begin understanding literary analysis, try to think of literature not so much as a collection of great books to be read, but rather as a way of reading. Or, put another way, you can choose to read anything literally or literarily. When you read something *literally*, you attempt to reduce its meaning to one clear set of statements and disregard other possible ways of reading the text. When you read something *literarily*, you read it playfully and openly, trying to see in it a wide range of possible meanings.

To help you understand the distinction we're drawing, consider the following analogy: A literal reading of an imaginative text is like a packaged bus tour of an unfamiliar city. Picture a bus filled with out-of-town conventioneers going from one landmark to the next, but missing the details of the city's lived life. The bus turns here and there, sweeping past a neighborhood market, past cemeteries dotted with crumbling headstones, past the smells of coffee, fish, spicy foods, and bakery goods. These tourists may catch a brief glimpse of a vibrant city waiting to be explored, but mostly they are looking ahead to the standardized comforts of their Quality Inn, Hilton, or Sheraton rooms.

The first step in moving beyond a literal to a literary understanding of a text, or a city, is to get off the bus. Stop being a tourist and become instead a traveler. Open yourself up to the otherness of a text the way travelers on foot open up to the sights and sounds of a new place to understand the diverse ways that humans create their lives. Reading literarily, experience the text on its own terms; that is, read it carefully, noticing and examining your reactions to what you have read. Travelers aren't driven by a desire to have been somewhere so they can tell others that they were there. Instead, they are driven by curiosity, a sense of wonder, a knack for recognizing resemblances in a world of apparent differences, and a capacity for being enthralled by the differences they do find.

To be a traveler rather than a tourist, you need to be an active participant in the process of constructing meaning from a text. Whereas tourists tend to write brief "We're here!" notes on postcards to friends, travelers are more likely to keep extensive journals to help them remember and understand their experiences. They reflect on what they see and on relationships between what they see, do, and feel one day to what they've seen, done, or felt in the past or to what others have reported seeing, doing, and feeling in the same place.

In this way, travelers interpret what they experience. Interpretive writing differs from other forms of writing most notably in its degree of tentativeness. An interpretation focuses on an ambiguous aspect of a text or experience and says, "Here's what I think is most probable." Unlike a traditional argument, which obligates the writer to refute other points of view, an interpretation may simply point out alternative explanations of the ambiguity and then focus on the writer's own interpretation and the evidence that supports it.

Exploring Literary Analysis

As we have noted, any sort of text can be read either literally or literarily. However, texts do tend to invite one kind of reading over another. The following Navajo legend contains several signals that invite us to read literarily rather than literally. As you read through this piece, note where those signals occur.

READING

Retold by Evelyn Dahl Reed
The Medicine Man

1   There is a telling that, in the beginning, when the animals first came up from the darkness to live above the ground, Coyote was sent ahead by Thought Woman to carry a buckskin pouch far to the south.

2   "You must be very careful not to open the pouch," she told him, "or you will be punished."

3   For many days, Coyote ran southward with the pouch on his back. But the world was new, and there was nothing to eat along the way, so he grew very hungry. He wondered if there might be food in the pouch. At last, he took it from his back and untied the thongs. He looked inside and saw nothing but stars. Of course, as soon as he opened the pouch the stars all flew up into the sky, and there they are to this day.

4   "Now look what you've done," said Thought Woman. "For now you shall always get into trouble everywhere you go."

5   And because Coyote disobeyed, he was also made to suffer with the toothache. When the other animals were asleep, he could only sit and howl at the stars. Thus, he has been crying ever since the beginning of the world.

6   Sometimes he would ask the other animals to cure him, but they would only catch the toothache from him, and they, too, would cry.

7   One day he met Mouse, who lived in a little mound under the chaparral bush. "Friend Mouse," begged Coyote, "can you cure me of this toothache?"

8   Now it happened that while digging underground, as is his habit, Mouse had come upon a sweet-smelling root and had put it with the other herbs in the pouch he always carried. He was said to be very wise in the use of herbs.

9   "I don't know," said Mouse, "but I have just found a new root, and it may be that it will help you." He rubbed the root on Coyote's swollen cheek, and in a little while the toothache was gone.

10   This is how it happened that coyotes never hunt or kill field mice.

Thinking Critically about "The Medicine Man"

1. List the signals in the text that led you to read this story literarily as opposed to literally. Summarize the most important differences between how you read this story and how you read the introduction to this chapter.
2. Devise questions about the legend that you think might produce different responses among your classmates. For example: Why is the woman named Thought Woman? Why is Thought Woman a female and not a male?
3. Explain why you think these questions will evoke different responses.

WRITING PROJECT

Your writing project for this chapter has two parts—a formal essay about a short story and a series of reading log entries that will prepare you to write your essay. Your entries in your reading log will give you an opportunity to explore your own understanding of the story, pose questions about it, and then compare your ways of reading and responding to it with your classmates' experiences of it. This process of writing about and discussing the story will help you find places in the text where readers' understandings differ, where ambiguities lead to uncertainties about some aspect of the story. These places will prompt *interpretive questions*— that is, questions for which the text contains evidence that supports more than one good thesis regarding, for example, events, motives, or meaning. Such questions are the perfect starting points for an interpretive paper like the one called for in the following assignment.

Essay Assignment

For help choosing or
framing such
questions, you may
wish to review the
advice in Chapter 1
about posing
interesting,
problematic, and
significant questions.

Pose an interpretive question about a short story and respond to it analytically, showing your readers where and how the text of the story supports your interpretation. In the introduction to your essay, pose an interesting, problematic, and significant question about the story, one that can be answered several different ways according to the evidence in the text. Look for a question that might lead to differences in opinion among your classmates and that offers readers new insights into the story. Your task in this assignment is not to discover the right way to interpret the text, but to explain *your* way of reading some aspect of it.

Using a closed-form structure, present your thesis about the story and your supporting arguments. Before you give your thesis, make clear just what question you are putting to the text and why. It is this question that engages your readers' interest and makes them look forward to your analysis. Then, in the body of your paper, explain your own responses to this question, contrasting your answer with other possible interpretations that have been proposed by your classmates or that you yourself have considered. Without disputing the alternative interpretations, concentrate on showing your reader how you arrived at *your* interpretation and why you think that that interpretation is valuable. Use details from the story for support.

Reading Log Assignment

To help you settle on a good question for your paper and to develop and share ideas, we have interspersed throughout the chapter a series of reading log questions for you to use in exploring the text. Your reading log will help you the most if you write in response to each freewriting task when you come to it in the text. (There are fifteen in all.) The sequence and timing of the early entries are important, so do not read ahead. Keep your notebook and pen with you as you read, and when you come to a reading log question, stop and respond to it at that time.

The reading log entries will help you pose a good question about your assigned short story. Good literary questions call attention to problematic details of the text, stimulate conversation, and provoke readers to return to the text to reread and rethink. You know you have a good question if your classmates disagree about the answer and contribute their own differing views to the conversation. Sharing your reading log entries with classmates will help you generate and sustain a productive discussion about the short story.

Understanding Literary Analysis

The Truth of Literary Events

As an introduction to literary analysis, let's return to "The Medicine Man" and consider several questions that it, and other texts of its sort, pose to the reader. First, in what sense is the story true? What advantages are there to expressing a view of truth in a literary, rather than in a literal, way? Why might someone choose to tell such a story rather than approach the world scientifically? What other stories does "The Medicine Man" remind you of? How is it different from those stories? How are the characters in the story like and unlike characters you've known in real life?

"The Medicine Man" is immediately recognizable as literary; it's difficult, if not impossible, to read it literally. Animals can't talk, and galaxies can't be carted about in a buckskin pouch. We either make a leap of faith and license the author to play fast and loose with our conventional understanding of reality, or we put the story down, dismayed that anyone could think we'd be gullible enough to buy this twaddle.

The events of the story are presented to us as if they actually happened. We know better, but we go along with the ruse in order to enjoy the story. We know that when we read these sorts of texts, we can't demand a one-to-one correspondence between the words we read and the things, persons, and events to which they supposedly refer. We must read instead with what the poet Coleridge called "a Willing Suspension of Disbelief."

Suspending disbelief does not mean erasing it. While we're reading literarily, we are to some degree consciously suppressing skepticism and nagging doubts, leftovers of our literal-minded selves. Both ways of looking at the story—literal and literary—are open to us, and we consciously choose one over the other. While we're reading "The Medicine Man," we never really forget that coyotes can't talk. But if coyotes could talk, we can imagine them talking as this coyote talks.

Choosing between a literary and a literal reading is similar to looking at an optical illusion. Consider, for example, the photograph in Figure 12.1 of painter Richard Haas's *trompe l'oeil* (fool-the-eye) mural on the Brotherhood Building in downtown Cincinnati. In the center of one of the seven-story building's flat walls, Haas has used paint to "carve out" an alcove complete with marble statue and eternal flame honoring Roman general Cincinnatus. Passersby (and people who view the photo) know that the alcove's curves—its sweeping staircase, multiple columns, domed roof, and upward curling smoke—are an illusion. (*This can't be classical Rome. Look at all the cars driving by.*) Yet the images persuade onlookers to set aside their skepticism and see something other than what they know to be physical reality. As we gaze, we conspire with the artist to compose the illusory image he designed for us. The façade is flat, but as we look, it curves inward; the tension between these perceptions makes looking itself pleasurable.

So it is with the language of literature. The both/and principle that allows us to see the roundness of images carved into a flat façade allows us to become

FIGURE 12.1 Muralist Richard Haas's 1983 *Trompe l'oeil* Classical Alcove on Cincinnati's Brotherhood Building

Courtesy of Richard Haas, Inc. Photography by Peter Mauss/Esto Photographics.

engrossed in the events in a fictional story, while at the same time standing back from the story to analyze how it works. To read literally isn't to cease reading literally as much as it is to read both/and—*both* literally *and* literarily. The image that fools the eye in Figure 12.1 is both a painted wall of an ordinary building in present-day Cincinnati and a deep marble alcove honoring a hero of ancient Rome.

Reading the Story

We ask you now to read the short story your instructor has designated for this assignment. Let the following reading log tasks help you become a traveler in the story rather than a tourist. Task 1 asks you to stop several times along the way as you read. Tasks 2 and 3 should be written immediately after you finish reading.

Reading Log Task 1: As you read your assigned story, stop at several points and predict what you think will happen in the rest of the story. Make your first stop fairly early in the story, choose a second stopping place in the middle, and stop a third time near the end. In each case, predict what is going to happen next and note what in the text causes you to make your prediction. Freewrite for three or four minutes each time you stop.

Reading Log Task 2: As soon as you finish your reading, write down your immediate responses to the text—how it made you feel or think, what emotions it triggered, what issues it raised. Freewrite for five minutes.

Reading Log Task 3: Write down (a) what most interested you about the story and (b) the most important question you're left with after reading the text. Freewrite for a couple of minutes after several minutes of reflecting.

For Writing and Discussion

As a whole class or in small groups, share your responses to the reading log tasks. Because you need to begin your formal essay for this assignment with a problematic question, pay particular attention to your classmates' responses to (b) in Task 3—the most important question raised by the text. Perhaps you have a tentative answer that you would like to propose to someone else's question.

Writing (about) Literature

We put "about" in parentheses in this heading because in a sense, to write about literature is to write literature. When you read literarily you are an active cocreator of the text just as a musician is a cocreator of a concerto. Musicians and literary readers don't completely reinvent composers' notes and authors' words every time they play or read them. Composers and writers provide abundant cues to signal how they wish their works to be played or read and to limit possible interpretations of their works. But in the process of performing another's text or music, readers and musicians give those words and notes a meaning unique to that particular performance. And in some cases, their renditions may depart considerably from the originators intentions.

This reading as performance is quite different from the more passive process of literal reading. Whereas the literal reader expects to find unambiguous, universally shared meaning in the text, the literary reader anticipates having to create meaning, which then must be justified to other readers and modified by them. For the literal reader, meaning is a commodity that is extracted intact from the text much as gold nuggets are sluiced from a stream. For the literary reader, meaning is more like a quilt constructed from bits and pieces of the text by many people who consult and argue and admire each other's skill and change each other's minds about which pieces to include and where to put them.

For additional discussion of these elements and of open-form writing in general, refer to Chapter 7 and Chapter 19.

To participate in the reading process actively, to "write" your version of a text, you need to know the kinds of questions you might ask of it. To help you, we briefly summarize five critical elements of a literary text and the kinds of questions each element suggests.

Asking Questions about Plot

Plot refers to the sequence of critical events in the story. The key term here is *critical*. A plot summary does not include everything that happens in a story; it focuses on the elements that most directly move the action of the story forward. One method of analyzing the plot is to begin by identifying what you see as the most critical single event or moment in a story. What is the most pivotal point, the one that prior events lead up to and that subsequent events derive from? Different readers are apt to pick different moments, indicating differences in the way they read the story. Your task is to identify your own choice and to be prepared to defend it. Remember, you are *performing* the story, not trying to figure out some unambiguous right meaning. As long as you have a rationale for your decision, you are acting as a literary critic.

> **Reading Log Task 4:** What is the single most important moment or event in your assigned story? Why do you see this moment as important or crucial? Freewrite for about ten minutes.

For Writing and Discussion

As a whole class or in small groups, share your responses to Task 4. Which events did you choose and what are your arguments for selecting them? Take notes about how your classmates' interpretations differ.

Asking Questions about Setting

Although a setting is sometimes little more than a backdrop, like a black curtain behind a speaker on a stage, it can also serve to amplify or help explain the events and motivations of a story. Sometimes the setting acts as a symbol or serves the same function in a story that theme music serves in a movie, underscoring the text's primary themes and moods. A story could be set at the edge of a dark forest, on an ascent up a mountain, or in an inner city, with action moving back and forth between remote vacant lots and a warm kitchen. Sometimes setting plays an active role in the text, functioning almost as a character. A setting could thwart the protagonist's efforts to bring about change or to survive; for example, the collapse of a bridge could prevent a character from crossing a river. Does setting play a role in the story you are analyzing? If so, how would you characterize that role? Could you picture the events of the text taking place in a significantly different setting? Why or why not?

Reading Log Task 5: What is worth noting about your assigned story's setting? What is the setting? How does it change? Consider multiple aspects of time, location, atmosphere, and so forth to discern the role that setting plays in the unfolding events. Freewrite for ten minutes on your ideas about the importance of setting in the story.

Asking Questions about Characters

Characters are the people who make the decisions that forward the plot and whose fortunes change as a result of the plot. You can understand characters in a text only in relationship to each other and to the direction of change in the text. The major character, sometimes called the *protagonist*, is typically the one most responsible for forwarding the plot. In action stories, these characters are pretty static: Dirty Harry or Batman may undergo occasional physical changes and disguises, but their characters tend not to grow or deepen. In other kinds of stories, the major character may change significantly in terms of fortune, insight, or understanding. Which characters change in the story you are examining? How do they change? Which characters do not change? Why do the characters change or not change?

To examine the characters' relationships with each other, you might start with the protagonist and consider the other characters according to how they help or hinder the protagonist. Characters may contribute to the plot by overt action or inaction, by recognizing or failing to recognize something of significance, by adapting to the situation of the story or by being inflexible. They can guide or misguide the protagonist, be a friend or foe, share or threaten the protagonist's values or beliefs, and so forth. What tensions, contrasts, and differing points of view do you see among the characters?

Reading Log Task 6: Who do you think is the most important character in the story? How does this character change or grow as the story progresses? How do the other characters promote or inhibit change in the main character? How do they help you see and understand the changes? Freewrite for ten to fifteen minutes.

For Writing and Discussion

Share your reading log entries and note differences in the interpretations of various members of the class. Remember that you are not seeking the one right answer to these questions. You are trying to determine how *you* read this story.

Asking Questions about Point of View

Perhaps the toughest element to perceive in a fictional work is point of view. It does not exist out there on the page as do character and plot. Point of view is the filter through which the reader views the action of a story. In some cases the impact of point of view on your perception of a character or event is obvious; in other cases it is not. The point of view can trick you into seeing an event in a particular way that you will have to revise when you realize that the narrator's perspective was limited, biased, or ironic. Often the narrator's values and perceptions are different from those of the author; you should never assume that the narrator of the story and the author are the same.

The two primary elements of point of view are time and person. Most stories are told in the past tense, a significant number in the present tense, and a few in the future tense. An almost equal number of stories are told in the first person (in which case the narrator is usually an actor in the story, although not always the main character) as in the third person (in which case the narrator tells the story from a position outside the tale). All choices of tense and person affect the reader's perception of a story. For example, a story told in the first-person present tense ("We ride back from the hunt at dusk") has an immediacy that a story told in the third-person past ("They rode back from the hunt at dusk") does not have. You learn about a first-person narrator both from what the narrator does or says in the plot and from how the narrator tells the story—what he or she includes or omits, the sentence structure, tone, or figures of speech that he or she adopts, and so forth. A third-person narrator may be objective (the narrator sees only the external actions of characters) or omniscient (the narrator can enter the minds and feelings of various characters). Sometimes a third-person narrator is omniscient with respect to one character but objective toward others.

Narrators can provide a full and complete sense of a given character (by entering that character's mind as an omniscient narrator) or a partial view only (by observing the character from the outside). Some stories feature multiple points of view through multiple narrators. For example, one character may discover a journal written by another character or may listen to a story told by another character.

The surest path to understanding point of view is to start with your feelings and attitudes toward characters and events and then to examine the extent to which point of view contributes to those attitudes. Do you trust the narrator? Do you like the narrator? Has the narrator loaded the dice, causing you to see characters or events in strongly slanted ways? Is the narrator scrupulously objective or ironic to the point that you're not quite sure what to make of his or her observations?

To ask questions about point of view, begin by asking whether the narrative is first or third person. Then ask whether the narrator's perspective is omniscient or limited. Does the narrator reveal bias or irony? Do you feel that there is more to the story than the narrator is telling you? What does the narrator leave out? How are the narrator's perceptions different from your own?

Reading Log Task 7: What is the story's point of view? What is the narrator's role in the unfolding of events? How do the narrator's perceptions filter your understanding of the story? Do you consider the narrator's perceptions reliable, or does the text suggest alternative understandings? Is the narrator's way of seeing part of what the story is about? Freewrite for ten minutes on ideas you generate by contemplating the story's point of view.

For Writing and Discussion

Share your reading log entries with your class and note differences in interpretations.

Asking Questions about Theme

If a plot is what happens in a story, then theme is the significance of what happens. Your response to the question "So what?" after reading a story represents your notion of the story's theme. Sometimes, a theme is obvious—the main characters might discuss it, or the author might even state it outright. Often, however, a theme is veiled, and you have to infer it from the words and deeds of the characters.

One way to discover theme is simply to reflect on your immediate responses to characters or on passages that affected you particularly strongly. Consider questions such as these: How did this story change your view of something or the way you feel about something? Is this story trying to reveal something about racism? About endurance in time of trial? About growth from one phase of life to another? About appearance versus reality? About conflicts between the individual and family? About exterior loss and interior gain? About rebellion from society? About what's really valuable versus what appears to be valuable? About establishing values in a confusing world?

Reading Log Task 8: Reread your response to Task 2, your first attempt to articulate ideas related to the story's theme. Then complete one of the following statements: (a) After further reflection on my assigned story, I think the author is trying to say something to readers about _____. (b) Here is what this story makes me think about and see: _____. Freewrite for ten minutes.

You can often gain valuable insights into a story's theme by examining the connections among the various literary elements we have been discussing. These points of intersection may also help you generate significant interpretive questions.

Reading Log Task 9: Look again at the place in the story that you identified in Task 4 as its most important moment or event. (a) What role do the elements of *character* that you identified in Task 6 play in this crucial passage? (b) Do elements of the story's *setting* contribute to your understanding of the importance of this passage? How do these details add to its impact? (c) How does *point of view* contribute to a reader's sense of the importance of the events and/or description in this passage? (d) Does your analysis of the interconnections of these literary elements give you new ideas or raise new questions for you about the story's *theme?* Freewrite for ten minutes.

For Writing and Discussion

Share your responses to Reading Log Tasks 8 and 9 with your class and note differences in the ways members of the class read this story.

Readings

We include in this section two short stories to test your analytical skills. Because analyzing short stories requires you to pose your own interesting questions about a text, we do not provide any analysis questions following the stories. In addition, we include a student essay written for this chapter's assignment.

The first reading is "Everyday Use (for Your Grandmama)" by contemporary African-American writer Alice Walker. It appeared in *In Love and Trouble: Stories of Black Women* in 1973.

Alice Walker
Everyday Use (For Your Grandmama)

1   I will wait for her in the yard that Maggie and I made so clean and wavy yesterday afternoon. A yard like this is more comfortable than most people know. It is not just a yard. It is like an extended living room. When the hard clay is swept clean as a floor and the fine sand around the edges lined with tiny, irregular grooves, anyone can come and sit and look up into the elm tree and wait for the breezes that never come inside the house.

2   Maggie will be nervous until after her sister goes: she will stand hopelessly in corners, homely and ashamed of the burn scars down her arms and legs, eying her sister with a mixture of envy and awe. She thinks her sister has held life always in the palm of one hand, that "no" is a word the world never learned to say to her.

3   You've no doubt seen those TV shows where the child who has "made it" is confronted, as a surprise, by her own mother and father, tottering in weakly from backstage. (A pleasant surprise, of course: What would they do if parent and child came on the show only to curse out and insult each other?) On TV mother and child embrace and smile into each other's faces. Sometimes the mother and father weep; the child wraps them in her arms and leans across the table to tell how she would not have made it without their help. I have seen these programs.

4   Sometimes I dream a dream in which Dee and I are suddenly brought together on a TV program of this sort. Out of a dark and soft-seated limousine I am ushered into a bright room filled with many people. There I meet a smiling, gray, sporty man like Johnny Carson who shakes my hand and tells me what a fine girl I have. Then we are on the stage and Dee is embracing

me with tears in her eyes. She pins on my dress a large orchid, even though she has told me once that she thinks orchids are tacky flowers.

5   In real life I am a large, big-boned woman with rough, man-working hands. In the winter I wear flannel nightgowns to bed and overalls during the day. I can kill and clean a hog as mercilessly as a man. My fat keeps me hot in zero weather. I can work outside all day, breaking once to get water for washing; I can eat pork liver cooked over the open fire minutes after it comes steaming from the hog. One winter I knocked a bull calf straight in the brain between the eyes with a sledge hammer and had the meat hung up to chill before nightfall. But of course all this does not show on television. I am the way my daughter would want me to be: a hundred pounds lighter, my skin like an uncooked barley pancake. My hair glistens in the hot bright lights. Johnny Carson has much to do to keep up with my quick and witty tongue.

6   But that is a mistake. I know even before I wake up. Who ever knew a Johnson with a quick tongue? Who can even imagine me looking a strange white man in the eye? It seems to me I have talked to them always with one foot raised in flight, with my head turned in whichever way is farthest from them. Dee, though. She would always look anyone in the eye. Hesitation was no part of her nature.

7   "How do I look, Mama?" Maggie says, showing just enough of her thin body enveloped in pink skirt and red blouse for me to know she's there, almost hidden by the door.

8   "Come out into the yard," I say.

9   Have you ever seen a lame animal, perhaps a dog run over by some careless person rich enough to own a car, sidle up to someone who is ignorant enough to be kind to him? That is the way my Maggie walks. She has been like this, chin on chest, eyes on ground, feet in shuffle, ever since the fire that burned the other house to the ground.

10   Dee is lighter than Maggie, with nicer hair and a fuller figure. She's a woman now, though sometimes I forget. How long ago was it that the other house burned? Ten, twelve years? Sometimes I can still hear the flames and feel Maggie's arms sticking to me, her hair smoking and her dress falling off her in little black papery flakes. Her eyes seemed stretched open, blazed open by the flames reflected in them. And Dee. I see her standing off under the sweet gum tree she used to dig gum out of; a look of concentration on her face as she watched the last dingy gray board of the house fall in toward the red-hot brick chimney. Why don't you do a dance around the ashes? I'd wanted to ask her. She had hated the house that much.

11   I used to think she hated Maggie, too. But that was before we raised the money, the church and me, to send her to Augusta to school. She used to read to us without pity; forcing words, lies, other folks' habits, whole lives upon us two, sitting trapped and ignorant underneath her voice. She washed us in a river of make-believe, burned us with a lot of knowledge we didn't necessarily

need to know. Pressed us to her with the serious way she read, to shove us away at just the moment, like dimwits, we seemed about to understand.

12   Dee wanted nice things. A yellow organdy dress to wear to her graduation from high school; black pumps to match a green suit she'd made from an old suit somebody gave me. She was determined to stare down any disaster in her efforts. Her eyelids would not flicker for minutes at a time. Often I fought off the temptation to shake her. At sixteen she had a style of her own: and she knew what style was.

13   I never had an education myself. After second grade the school was closed down. Don't ask me why: in 1927 colored asked fewer questions than they do now. Sometimes Maggie reads to me. She stumbles along good-naturedly but can't see well. She knows she is not bright. Like good looks and money, quickness passed her by. She will marry John Thomas (who has mossy teeth in an earnest face) and then I'll be free to sit here and I guess just sing church songs to myself. Although I never was a good singer. Never could carry a tune. I was always better at a man's job. I used to love to milk till I was hooked in the side in '49. Cows are soothing and slow and don't bother you, unless you try to milk them the wrong way.

14   I have deliberately turned my back on the house. It is three rooms, just like the one that burned, except the roof is tin; they don't make shingle roofs any more. There are no real windows, just some holes cut in the sides, like the portholes in a ship, but not round and not square, with rawhide holding the shutters up on the outside. This house is in a pasture, too, like the other one. No doubt when Dee sees it she will want to tear it down. She wrote me once that no matter where we "choose" to live, she will manage to come see us. But she will never bring her friends. Maggie and I thought about this and Maggie asked me, "Mama, when did Dee ever *have* any friends?"

15   She had a few. Furtive boys in pink shirts hanging about on washday after school. Nervous girls who never laughed. Impressed with her they worshipped the well-turned phrase, the cute shape, the scalding humor that erupted like bubbles in lye. She read to them.

16   When she was courting Jimmy T she didn't have much time to pay to us, but turned all her faultfinding power on him. He *flew* to marry a cheap city girl from a family of ignorant flashy people. She hardly had time to recompose herself.

17   When she comes I will meet—but there they are!

18   Maggie attempts to make a dash for the house, in her shuffling way, but I stay her with my hand. "Come back here," I say. And she stops and tries to dig a well in the sand with her toe.

19   It is hard to see them clearly through the strong sun. But even the first glimpse of leg out of the car tells me it is Dee. Her feet were always neat-looking, as if God himself had shaped them with a certain style. From the other side of the car comes a short, stocky man. Hair is all over his head a foot long and hanging from his chin like a kinky mule tail. I hear Maggie

suck in her breath. "Uhnnnh," is what it sounds like. Like when you see the wriggling end of a snake just in front of your foot on the road. "Uhnnnh."

20   Dee next. A dress down to the ground, in this hot weather. A dress so loud it hurts my eyes. There are yellows and oranges enough to throw back the light of the sun. I feel my whole face warming from the heat waves it throws out. Earrings gold, too, and hanging down to her shoulders. Bracelets dangling and making noises when she moves her arm up to shake the folds of the dress out of her armpits. The dress is loose and flows, and as she walks closer, I like it. I hear Maggie go "Uhnnnh" again. It is her sister's hair. It stands straight up like the wool on a sheep. It is black as night and around the edges are two long ponytails that rope about like small lizards disappearing behind her ears.

21   "Wa-su-zo-Tean-o!" she says, coming in on that gliding way the dress makes her move. The short stocky fellow with the hair to his navel is all grinning and he follows up with "Asalamalakim, my mother and sister!" He moves to hug Maggie but she falls back, right up against the back of my chair. I feel her trembling there and when I look up I see the perspiration falling off her chin.

22   "Don't get up," says Dee. Since I am stout it takes something of a push. You can see me trying to move a second or two before I make it. She turns, showing white heels through her sandals, and goes back to the car. Out she peeks next with a Polaroid. She stoops down quickly and lines up picture after picture of me sitting there in front of the house with Maggie cowering behind me. She never takes a shot without making sure the house is includ-ed. When a cow comes nibbling around the edge of the yard she snaps it and me and Maggie *and* the house. Then she puts the Polaroid in the back seat of the car, and comes up and kisses me on the forehead.

23   Meanwhile Asalamalakim is going through the motions with Maggie's hand. Maggie's hand is as limp as a fish, and probably cold, despite the sweat, and she keeps trying to pull it back. It looks like Asalamalakim wants to shake hands but wants to do it fancy. Or maybe he don't know how peo-ple shake hands. Anyhow, he soon gives up on Maggie.

24   "Well," I say. "Dee."

25   "No, Mama," she says. "Not 'Dee,' Wangero Leewanika Kemanjo!"

26   "What happened to 'Dee'?" I wanted to know.

27   "She's dead," Wangero said. "I couldn't bear it any longer, being named after the people who oppress me."

28   "You know as well as me you was named after your aunt Dicie," I said. Dicie is my sister. She named Dee. We called her "Big Dee" after Dee was born.

29   "But who was she named after?" asked Wangero.

30   "I guess after Grandma Dee," I said.

31   "And who was she named after?" asked Wangero.

32   "Her mother," I said, and saw Wangero was getting tired. "That's about as far back as I can trace it," I said. Though, in fact, I probably could have car-ried it back beyond the Civil War through the branches.

33   "Well," said Asalamalakim, "there you are."

34   "Uhnnnh," I heard Maggie say.

35   "There I was not," I said, "before 'Dicie' cropped up in our family, so why should I try to trace it that far back?"

36   He just stood there grinning, looking down on me like somebody inspecting a Model A car. Every once in a while he and Wangero sent eye signals over my head.

37   "How do you pronounce this name?" I asked.

38   "You don't have to call me by it if you don't want to," said Wangero.

39   "Why shouldn't I?" I asked. "If that's what you want us to call you, we'll call you."

40   "I know it might sound awkward at first," said Wangero.

41   "I'll get used to it," I said. "Ream it out again."

42   Well, soon we got the name out of the way. Asalamalakim had a name twice as long and three times as hard. After I tripped over it two or three times he told me to just call him Hakim-a-barber. I wanted to ask him was he a barber, but I didn't really think he was, so I didn't ask.

43   "You must belong to those beef-cattle peoples down the road," I said. They said "Asalamalakim" when they met you, too, but they didn't shake hands. Always too busy: feeding the cattle, fixing the fences, putting up salt-lick shelters, throwing down hay. When the white folks poisoned some of the herd the men stayed up all night with rifles in their hands. I walked a mile and a half just to see the sight.

44   Hakim-a-barber said, "I accept some of their doctrines, but farming and raising cattle is not my style." (They didn't tell me, and I didn't ask, whether Wangero (Dee) had really gone and married him.)

45   We sat down to eat and right away he said he didn't eat collards and pork was unclean. Wangero, though, went on through the chitlins and corn bread, the greens and everything else. She talked a blue streak over the sweet potatoes. Everything delighted her. Even the fact that we still used the benches her daddy made for the table when we couldn't afford to buy chairs.

46   "Oh, Mama!" she cried. Then turned to Hakim-a-barber. "I never knew how lovely these benches are. You can feel the rump prints," she said, running her hands underneath her and along the bench. Then she gave a sigh and her hand closed over Grandma Dee's butter dish. "That's it!" she said. "I knew there was something I wanted to ask you if I could have." She jumped up from the table and went over in the corner where the churn stood, the milk in it clabber by now. She looked at the churn and looked at it.

47   "This churn top is what I need," she said happily. "Didn't Uncle Buddy whittle it out of a tree you all used to have?"

48   "Yes," I said.

49   "Uh huh," she said happily. "And I want the dasher, too."

50   "Uncle Buddy whittle that, too?" asked the barber.

51   Dee (Wangero) looked up at me.

52   "Aunt Dee's first husband whittled the dash," said Maggie so low you almost couldn't hear her. "His name was Henry, but they called him Stash."

53   "Maggie's brain is like an elephant's," Wangero said, laughing. "I can use the churn top as a centerpiece for the alcove table," she said, sliding a plate over the churn, "and I'll think of something artistic to do with the dasher."

54   When she finished wrapping the dasher the handle stuck out. I took it for a moment in my hands. You didn't even have to look close to see where hands pushing the dasher up and down to make butter had left a kind of sink in the wood. In fact, there were a lot of small sinks; you could see where thumbs and fingers had sunk into the wood. It was beautiful light yellow wood, from a tree that grew in the yard where Big Dee and Stash had lived.

55   After dinner Dee (Wangero) went to the trunk at the foot of my bed and started rifling through it. Maggie hung back in the kitchen over the dishpan. Out came Wangero with two quilts. They had been pieced by Grandma Dee and then Big Dee and me had hung them on the quilt frames on the front porch and quilted them. One was in the Lone Star pattern. The other was Walk Around the Mountain. In both of them were scraps of dresses Grandma Dee had worn fifty and more years ago. Bits and pieces of Grandma Jarrell's Paisley shirts. And one teeny faded blue piece, about the size of a penny matchbox, that was from Great Grandpa Ezra's uniform that he wore in the Civil War.

56   "Mama," Wangero said sweet as a bird. "Can I have these old quilts?"

57   I heard something fall in the kitchen, and a minute later the kitchen door slammed.

58   "Why don't you take one or two of the others?" I asked. "These old things was just done by me and Big Dee from some tops your grandma pieced before she died."

59   "No," said Wangero. "I don't want those. They are stitched around the borders by machine."

60   "That'll make them last better," I said.

61   "That's not the point," said Wangero. "These are all pieces of dresses Grandma used to wear. She did all this stitching by hand. Imagine!" She held the quilts securely in her arms, stroking them.

62   "Some of the pieces, like those lavender ones, come from old clothes her mother handed down to her," I said, moving up to touch the quilts. Dee (Wangero) moved back just enough so that I couldn't reach the quilts. They already belonged to her.

63   "Imagine!" she breathed again, clutching them closely to her bosom.

64   "The truth is," I said, "I promised to give them quilts to Maggie, for when she marries John Thomas."

65   She gasped like a bee had stung her.

66   Maggie can't appreciate these quilts!" she said. "She'd probably be backward enough to put them to everyday use."

67   "I reckon she would," I said. "God knows I been saving 'em for long enough with nobody using 'em. I hope she will!" I didn't want to bring up

how I had offered Dee (Wangero) a quilt when she went away to college. Then she had told me they were old-fashioned, out of style.

68   "But they're *priceless!*" she was saying now, furiously; for she has a temper. "Maggie would put them on the bed and in five years they'd be in rags. Less than that!"

69   "She can always make some more," I said. "Maggie knows how to quilt."

70   Dee (Wangero) looked at me with hatred. "You just will not understand. The point is these quilts, *these* quilts!"

71   "Well," I said, stumped. "What would *you* do with them?"

72   "Hang them," she said. As if that was the only thing you *could* do with quilts.

73   Maggie by now was standing in the door. I could almost hear the sound her feet made as they scraped over each other.

74   "She can have them, Mama," she said, like somebody used to never winning anything, or having anything reserved for her. "I can 'member Grandma Dee without the quilts."

75   I looked at her hard. She had filled her bottom lip with checkerberry snuff and it gave her face a kind of dopey, hangdog look. It was Grandma Dee and Big Dee who taught her how to quilt herself. She stood there with her hands hidden in the folds of her skirt. She looked at her sister with something like fear but she wasn't mad at her. This was Maggie's portion. This was the way she knew God to work.

76   When I looked at her like that something hit me in the top of my head and ran down to the soles of my feet. Just like when I'm in church and the spirit of God touches me and I get happy and shout. I did something I never had done before: hugged Maggie to me, then dragged her on into the room, snatched the quilts out of Miss Wangero's hands and dumped them into Maggie's lap. Maggie just sat there on my bed with her mouth open.

77   "Take one or two of the others," I said to Dee.

78   But she turned without a word and went out to Hakim-a-barber.

79   "You just don't understand," she said, as Maggie and I came out to the car.

80   "What don't I understand?" I wanted to know.

81   "Your heritage," she said. And then she turned to Maggie, kissed her, and said, "You ought to try to make something of yourself, too, Maggie. It's really a new day for us. But from the way you and Mama still live you'd never know it."

82   She put on some sunglasses that hid everything above the tip of her nose and her chin.

83   Maggie smiled; maybe at the sunglasses. But a real smile, not scared. After we watched the car dust settle I asked Maggie to me bring me a dip of snuff. And then the two of us sat there just enjoying, until it was time to go in the house and go to bed.

The second reading is David Updike's story "Summer." Updike, the son of novelist John Updike, has published several children's books as well as stories and essays in magazines such as *The New Yorker* and *Doubletake*. "Summer" is from his 1988 collection *Out on the Marsh*.

David Updike
Summer

1   It was the first week in August, the time when summer briefly pauses, shifting between its beginning and its end: the light had not yet begun to change, the leaves were still full and green on the trees, the nights were still warm. From the woods and fields came the hiss of crickets; the line of distant mountains was still dulled by the edge of summer haze, the echo of fireworks was replaced by the rumble of thunder and the hollow premonition of school, too far off to imagine though dimly, dully felt. His senses were consumed by the joy of their own fulfillment: the satisfying swat of a tennis ball, the dappled damp and light of the dirt road after rain, the alternating sensations of sand, mossy stone, and pine needles under bare feet. His days were spent in the adolescent pursuit of childhood pleasures: tennis, a haphazard round of golf, a variant of baseball adapted to the local geography: two pine trees as foul poles, a broomstick as the bat, the apex of the small, secluded house the dividing line between home runs and outs. On rainy days they swatted bottle tops across the living room floor, and at night vented budding cerebral energy with games of chess thoughtfully played over glasses of iced tea. After dinner they would paddle the canoe to the middle of the lake and drift beneath the vast, blue-black dome above them, looking at the stars and speaking softly in tones which, with the waning summer, became increasingly philosophical: the sky's blue vastness, the distance and magnitude of stars, an endless succession of numbers, gave way to a rising sensation of infinity, eternity, an imagined universe with no bounds. But the sound of the paddle hitting against the side of the canoe, the faint shadow of surrounding mountains, the cry of a nocturnal bird brought them back to the happy, cloistered finity of their world, and they paddled slowly home and went to bed.

2   Homer woke to the slant and shadow of a summer morning, dressing in their shared cabin, and went into the house where Mrs. Thyme sat alone, looking out across the flat, blue stillness of the lake. She poured him a cup of coffee and they quietly talked, and it was then that his happiness seemed most tangible. In this summer month with the Thymes, freed from the complications of his own family, he had released himself to them and, as interim member—friend, brother, surrogate son—he lived in a blessed realm between two worlds.

3   From the cool darkness of the porch, smelling faintly of moldy books and kerosene and the tobacco of burning pipes, he sat looking through the screen to the lake, shimmering beneath the heat of a summer afternoon: a dog lay sleeping in the sun, a bird hopped along a swaying branch, sunlight came in through the trees and collapsed on the sandy soil beside a patch of moss, or mimicked the shade and cadence of stones as they stepped to the edge of a lake where small waves lapped a damp rock and washed onto a sandy shore. An inverted boat lay decaying under a tree, a drooping

American flag hung from its gnarled pole, a haphazard dock started out across the cove toward distant islands through which the white triangle of a sail silently moved.

4   The yellowed pages of the book from which he occasionally read swam before him: ". . . Holmes clapped the hat upon his head. It came right over the forehead and settled on the bridge of his nose. 'It is a question of cubic capacity' said he . . ." Homer looked up. The texture of the smooth, unbroken air was cleanly divided by the sound of a slamming door, echoing up into the woods around him. Through the screen he watched Fred's sister Sandra as she came ambling down the path, stepping lightly between the stones in her bare feet. She held a towel in one hand, a book in the other, and wore a pair of pale blue shorts—faded relics of another era. At the end of the dock she stopped, raised her hands above her head, stretching, and then sat down. She rolled over onto her stomach and, using the book as a pillow, fell asleep.

5   Homer was amused by the fact that although she did this every day, she didn't get any tanner. When she first came in her face was faintly flushed, and there was a pinkish line around the snowy band where her bathing suit strap had been, but the back of her legs remained an endearing, pale white, the color of eggshells, and her back acquired only the softest, brownish blur. Sometimes she kept her shoes on, other times a shirt, or sweater, or just collapsed onto the seat of the boat, her pale eyelids turned upward toward the pale sun and then, as silently as she arrived, she would leave, walking back through the stones with the same, casual sway of indifference. He would watch her, hear the distant door slam, the shower running in the far corner of the house; other times he would just look up and she would be gone.

6   On the tennis court she was strangely indifferent to his heroics. When the crucial moment arrived—Homer serving in the final game of the final set—the match would pause while she left, walking across the court, stopping to call the dog, swaying out through the gate. Homer watched her as she went down the path—her pale legs in the mottled light—and, impetus suddenly lost, he double faulted, stroked a routine backhand over the back fence and the match was over.

7   When he arrived back at the house she asked him who won, but didn't seem to hear his answer. "I wish I could go sailing," she said, looking distractedly out over the lake.

8   At night, when he went out to the cottage where he and Fred slept, he could see her through the window as she lay on her bed, reading, her arm folded beneath her head like a leaf. Her nightgown, pulled and buttoned to her chin, pierced him with a regret that had no source or resolution, and its imagined texture floated in the air above him as he lay in bed at night, suspended in the surrounding darkness, the scent of pine, the hypnotic cadence of his best friend's breathing.

9   Was it that he had known her all his life, and as such had grown up in the shadow of her subtle beauty? Was it the condensed world of the lake, the silent reverence of surrounding woods, mountains, which heightened his

sense of her and brought the warm glow of her presence into soft, amorous focus? She had the hair of a baby, the freckles of a child, and the sway of motherhood. Like his love, her beauty rose up in the world that spawned and nurtured it, and found in the family the medium in which it thrived, and in Homer distilled to a pure distant longing for something he had never had.

10   One day they climbed a mountain, and as the components of family and friends strung out along the path on their laborious upward hike, he found himself tromping along through the woods with her with nobody else in sight. Now and then they would stop by a stream, or sit on a stump, or stone, and he would speak to her, and then they would set off again, he following her. But in the end this day exhausted him, following her pale legs and tripping sneakers over the ruts and stones and a thousand roots, all the while trying to suppress a wordless, inarticulate passion, and the last mile or so he left her, sprinting down the path in a reckless, solitary release, howling into the woods around him. He was lying on the grass, staring up into the patterns of drifting clouds when she came ambling down. "Where'd you go? I thought I'd lost you," she said, and sat heavily down in the seat of the car. On the ride home, his elbow hopelessly held in the warm crook of her arm, he resolved to release his love, give it up, on the grounds that it was too disruptive to his otherwise placid life. But in the days to follow he discovered that his resolution had done little to change her, and her life went on its oblivious, happy course without him.

11   His friendship with Fred, meanwhile, continued on its course of athletic and boyhood fulfillment. Alcohol seeped into their diet, and an occasional cigarette, and at night they would drive into town, buy two enormous cans of Australian beer and sit at a small cove by the lake, talking. One night on the ride home Fred accelerated over a small bridge, and as the family station wagon left the ground their heads floated up to the ceiling, touched, and then came crashing down as they landed, and Fred wrestled the car back onto course. Other times they would take the motorboat out onto the lake and make sudden racing turns around buoys, sending a plume of water into the air and everything in the boat, including them, crashing to one side. But always with these adventures Homer felt a pang of absence, and was always relieved when they headed back toward the familiar cove, and home.

12   As August ran its merciless succession of beautiful days, Sandra drifted in and out of his presence in rising oscillations of sorrow and desire. She worked at a bowling alley on the other side of the lake, and in the evening Homer and Fred would drive the boat over, bowl a couple of strings, and wait for her to get off work. Homer sat at the counter and watched her serve up sloshing cups of coffee, secretly loathing the leering gazes of whiskered truck drivers, and loving her oblivious vacant stare in answer, hip cocked, hand on counter, gazing up into the neon air above their heads. When she was finished, they would pile into the boat and skim through darkness the four or five miles home, and it was then, bundled beneath sweaters and blankets, the white hem of her waitressing dress showing through the darkness, their

hair swept in the wind and their voices swallowed by the engine's slow, steady growl, that he felt most powerless to her attraction. As the boat rounded corners he would close his eyes and release himself to gravity, his body's warmth swaying into hers, guising his attraction in the thin veil of centrifugal force. Now and then he would lean into the floating strands of her hair and speak into her fragrance, watching her smile swell in the pale half-light of the moon, the amber glow of the boat's rear light, her laughter spilling backward over the swirling "V" of wake.

13   Into the humid days of August a sudden rain fell, leaving the sky a hard, unbroken blue and the nights clear and cool. In the morning when he woke, leaving Fred a heap of sighing covers in his bed, he stepped out into the first rays of sunlight that came through the branches of the trees and sensed, in the cool vapor that rose from damp pine needles, the piercing cry of a blue jay, that something had changed. That night as they ate dinner—hamburgers and squash and corn on the cob—everyone wore sweaters, and as the sun set behind the undulating line of distant mountains—burnt, like a filament of summer into his blinking eyes—it was with an autumnal tint, a reddish glow. Several days later the tree at the end of the point bloomed with a sprig of russet leaves, one or two of which occasionally fell, and their lives became filled with an unspoken urgency. Life of summer went on in the silent knowledge that, with the slow inexorable seepage of an hourglass, it was turning into fall. Another mountain was climbed, annual tennis matches were arranged and played. Homer and Fred became unofficial champions of the lake by trouncing the elder Dewitt boys, unbeaten in several years. "Youth, youth," glum Billy Dewitt kept saying over iced tea afterward, in jest, though Homer could tell he was hiding some greater sense of loss.

14   And the moment, the conjunction of circumstance that, through the steady exertion of will, minor adjustments of time and place, he had often tried to induce, never happened. She received his veiled attentions with a kind of amused curiosity, as if smiling back on innocence. One night they had been the last ones up, and there was a fleeting, shimmering moment before he stepped through the woods to his cabin and she went to her bed that he recognized, in a distant sort of way, as the moment of truth. But to touch her, or kiss her, seemed suddenly incongruous, absurd, contrary to something he could not put his finger on. He looked down at the floor and softly said good night. The screen door shut quietly behind him and he went out into the darkness and made his way through the unseen sticks and stones, and it was only then, tripping drunkenly on a fallen branch, that he realized he had never been able to imagine the moment he distantly longed for.

15   The Preacher gave a familiar sermon about another summer having run its course, the harvest of friendship reaped, and a concluding prayer that, "God willing, we will all meet again in June." That afternoon Homer and Fred went sailing, and as they swept past a neighboring cove Homer saw in its sullen shadows a girl sitting alone in a canoe, and in an eternal, melancholy signal of parting, she waved to them as they passed. And there was something in the way that she raised her arm which, when added to the dis-

tant impression of her fullness, beauty, youth, filled him with desire but their boat moved inexorably past anyway, slapping the waves, and she disappeared behind a crop of trees.

16   The night before they were to leave they were all sitting in the living room after dinner—Mrs. Thyme sewing, Fred folded up with the morning paper, Homer reading on the other end of the couch where Sandra was lying—when the dog leapt up and things shifted in such a way that Sandra's bare foot was lightly touching Homer's back. Mrs. Thyme came over with a roll of newspaper and hit the dog on the head and he leapt off. But to Homer's surprise Sandra's foot remained, and he felt, in the faint sensation of exerted pressure, the passive emanation of its warmth, a distant signal of acquiescence. And as the family scene continued as before it was with the accompanying drama of Homer's hand, shielded from the family by a haphazard wall of pillows migrating over the couch to where, in a moment of breathless abandon, it settled softly on the cool hollow of her arch. She laughed at something her mother had said, her toe twitched, but her foot remained. It was only then, in the presence of the entire family, that he realized she was his accomplice, and that, though this was as far as it would ever go, his love had been returned.

The following student essay on Walker's "Everyday Use (for Your Grandmama)" was written in response to this chapter's assignment. As you read it, consider what questions and comments you would have for its writer if you were in a peer review session together.

Betsy Weiler (student)
Who Do You Want to Be?
Finding Heritage in Walker's "Everyday Use"

"You just don't understand."
"What don't I understand?"
"Your heritage" (344).*

1   Whose heritage is Dee talking about? Is it her family's heritage or her ethnic heritage?

2   This exchange takes place near the end of Alice Walker's short story, "Everyday Use," when Dee is saying goodbye to her mother and her sister Maggie after a brief visit and an argument about some quilts. That visit was almost like a treasure hunt for Dee. It seems that Dee, who now has the name Wangero Leewanika Kemanjo, came to visit because she wants to try to identify herself with the past. She wants to take parts of a butter churn

*Numbers in parentheses indicate page numbers on which the quotation is found (in this case, page numbers in this text). This parenthetical citation system follows the MLA format. See Chapter 22 for a complete explanation.

and some family quilts back home with her, but Mama says "no" about the quilts because she promised them to Maggie. Dee thinks that Maggie can't "appreciate" the quilts and is "backward enough to put them to everyday use" (343). This confrontation over the quilts suggests that Dee may have learned a lot in college about her ethnic background as an African American, but she does not understand or appreciate her own family's heritage.

3   At first, a reader might think that Dee/Wangero has come home to express her appreciation for her family's heritage. While Mama is waiting for her, she expects that Dee will want to tear down the family house because it is just like the one that burned down when she was a child there. Dee hated that house. But when Dee arrives, before she even tells her mother her new name, she begins taking "picture after picture" of her mother and Maggie, "making sure the house is included" in every one (341). It seems that Dee is proud to include the house in her heritage—but is it her ethnic heritage or her family heritage? What will she do with the pictures? Are they something to remember her family with or are they something "artistic" that she will use to display her ethnic heritage?

4   When Dee explains her new name to her mother, she seems to have forgotten part of her family heritage. Wangero says that "Dee" is "dead" because "I couldn't bear it any longer, being named after the people who oppress me" (341). After her mother explains that she is actually named after Aunt Dee and Grandma Dee, Wangero Leewanika Kemanjo may gain some appreciation of the family tradition because she says that Mama doesn't have to call her the new name "if you don't want to." But Mama shows her own respect for her own daughter by saying "I'll get used to it."

5   When the treasure hunt part of the visit begins after the dinner, Dee's concern for ethnic heritage becomes clear. Dee wants items from the past that she identifies with her ethnic heritage. She jumps up from the table and declares that she needs the churn top. She asks, "Didn't Uncle Buddy whittle it [the churn] out of a tree you all used to have?" (342). She is talking about the churn top in terms of family heritage, but when she says that she intends to use it as a centerpiece on an alcove table, the reader understands that for Dee the churn is more significant for the ethnic heritage it represents. Many blacks could not afford to buy butter, so they had to make it themselves. (In fact, her mother is still using that churn to make butter.) She also wants the dasher from the churn. For Maggie and Mama, it is a tool in the present that represents family history. Maggie explains that Aunt Dee's first husband, Stash, whittled it; when Mama (the narrator) looks it over she notices the "small sinks" in the wood from the hands of people who had used it (including her own, no doubt). There is a strong contrast between their attitude toward the heirloom and Dee/Wangero's. She laughs at Maggie's story (family heritage), saying Maggie has a "brain . . . like an elephant's" and announces that she herself will "think of something artistic to do with the dasher" (343). For all of them, the dasher represents the hard work blacks have had to struggle through, but for Mama and Maggie, it is a

tool made by a family member to help with that work today. For Wangero it is an ethnic heritage object to display.

6   The final two items that Dee wants are the hand-stitched quilts that she digs out of Mama's trunk. They represent family heritage because they contain pieces of her ancestors' clothing, including a tiny piece from the blue uniform of a great-grandfather who fought in the Civil War. That family heritage is very strong for Mama, who was planning to give the quilts to Maggie as a wedding present. She remembers, but doesn't say anything, that Dee/Wangero had refused to take a quilt with her to college because they were old fashioned. Dee loses her temper over the idea of Maggie using the quilts on a bed because "in five years they'd be in rags" (344). Mama says that then Maggie would make new ones. But Dee wants "*these* quilts," the ones with pieces of her own family's clothing. This may appear to be an appreciation of family heritage, but since Dee/Wangero wants to hang the quilts on the wall, not use them for a practical purpose, it seems that she wants to display a heritage that she doesn't want to live anymore.

7   Maggie is willing to give up the quilts, saying she can remember Grandma Dee without them, but Mama grabs the quilts back from Dee. The conflict here is not only about remembering but also about how to remember. Although Dee wants to preserve the original quilts with their antique pieces, she keeps separating herself from the family heritage that created them.

8   As Dee gets into the car to leave, she puts on a pair of sunglasses that hide "everything above the tip of her nose and her chin" (344). If, as the saying goes, the eyes are the windows to the soul, then Dee is hiding her soul. By wearing the sunglasses, Dee is hiding who she truly is and just wants to be identified with the color of her skin, her ethnic heritage. She tells Maggie that "[i]t's really a new day for us" although "from the way you . . . live, you'd never know it" (344).

9   Mama and Maggie may live in a very old-fashioned setting, using old-fashioned tools every day, but Dee/Wangero's attitude about her family and its heirlooms shows that actually she is the person who does not understand her heritage.

Thinking Critically about "Who Do You Want to Be? Finding Heritage in Walker's 'Everyday Use'"

1. The assignment for this chapter asks for an essay built around a problematic and significant interpretive question. Do you think that Betsy Weiler adequately addresses the assignment? Has she been successful in articulating a problematic question and indicating its importance for our understanding of the story?

2. Does Weiler's thesis statement respond adequately to the question? Does she supply enough details from the Walker story as evidence to support her

analysis? Would the paper be better with more analysis of literary elements? What would you suggest that she add? Should she cut some material?

3. What alternative answers to Weiler's interpretive question occur to you besides the ones she brings up? What evidence do you find in the text to support your analysis and interpretation?

4. What are the strengths and weaknesses of Weiler's essay? What recommendations would you have for improving this draft of the essay?

Composing Your Essay

The reading log entries you've completed in conjunction with your assigned story should help you considerably when you start planning your essay. Begin that planning by writing out the question you will pose and explore in your paper. As we have seen, a good question, one that is problematic and significant, is one that promotes engaged conversation and differing points of view. To help you decide on a question, the reading log tasks in this section ask you to freewrite in response to several different "starter questions." After you decide on a question, you will need to explore ways to answer it, using textual details for support.

Generating and Exploring Ideas

To help you settle on a good problematic question for the introduction of your formal essay, we list several starter questions that focus on *turning points*—major changes in a story's character, plot, language, and point of view. You may want to begin with one of these questions and then refine it to make it more specific to the story.

After reviewing these questions, complete the two reading log tasks that follow.

Turning-Point Starter Questions about a Short Story
1. Changes in character
   a. How do circumstances change for each character? What sets each change of circumstance in motion?
   b. How does each character's understanding or knowledge change?
   c. How does your attitude toward each character change?
   d. How does each character's relationship to other characters change?
2. Changes in language
   a. How does the dialogue change? Do characters talk to each other differently at any point?
   b. How does the tone of the language change? Does it become lighter or darker at given points?
   c. How do the metaphors and similes change? Is there a pattern to that change?

3. Changes in point of view
   a. How does the narrator's attitude toward the characters and events change? Does the narrator move closer or farther away from characters and events at any point?
   b. How trustworthy or credible is the narrator? If the narrator is not credible, at what point do you first suspect him or her of unreliability?
4. Changes in setting
   a. How does the time or place depicted in the text change? How are other changes in the text related to these changes?

Reading Log Task 10: Using the turning-point starter questions to stimulate your thinking, pose five or six specific turning-point questions about your assigned story.

Reading Log Task 11: Choose one of our turning-point questions and explore your own answer to it.

Looking at turning points is not the only way to pose questions about a text. A second list of starter questions focuses on other considerations, such as theme, values, and character. Review the questions and then complete the two reading log tasks that follow.

Additional Starter Questions

1. How does the story's title contribute to your understanding of the story?
2. What does each of the major characters seek and want? What are each character's values?
3. Which character's beliefs and values are closest to your own? How so?
4. What are the main conflicts in the story? What or who blocks the characters from reaching their goals (remember, sometimes what blocks them may be inside them), and how much control do they have over achieving their ends?
5. How successful are the characters in achieving their goals and how do they respond to the outcome?
6. Among all the characters, who seems best to understand what happens and why?

Reading Log Task 12: Use these additional starter questions to post two or three specific questions about your assigned story.

Reading Log Task 13: Choose one of your questions and explore your responses to it.

Choosing Your Problematic Question and Exploring Your Answer

You're now ready to choose the question that will initiate your essay and to explore your answer. For the final reading log tasks, freewrite rapidly to spill your ideas onto the paper and avoid writer's block. Before you begin, read over what you have written so far in your reading log to help you get the juices flowing.

Reading Log Task 14: Write out the question that you want to ask in your essay about your assigned short story. What makes this an interesting and significant question? Why don't you and your classmates immediately agree on the answer?

Reading Log Task 15: Freewriting as rapidly as you can, explore your answer to the question you asked in Task 14. Use textual details and your own critical thinking to create an argument supporting your answer.

Shaping and Drafting

Reading Log Tasks 14 and 15 give you a head start on a rough draft. The best way to organize your literary analysis is to follow the problem-thesis pattern of closed-form prose:

First, begin with an introduction that poses your question about the text and shows readers why it is an interesting, problematic, and significant question. To show why your question is problematic, you may want to refer briefly to differing interpretations your classmates have suggested or you have considered. At the end of your introduction, be sure to include a thesis statement—a one-sentence summary answer to your question. Early in the introduction you may need to supply background about the story so that readers can understand your question.

Second, write the main body of your essay, in which you develop and support your thesis using textual details and argument. There is no formula for organizing the body. The major sections depend on your argument and the steps needed to make your case. If you haven't already summarized alternative interpretations in the introduction, you may choose to do so in the body. The key here is to create tension for your thesis and to demonstrate the significance of your interpretation.

Conclude by returning to your essay's big picture and suggesting why your answer to your opening question is significant. What larger implications does your analysis have for the story? What kind of changed view of the story do you want to bring about in your readers' minds? Why is this view important? You may choose to write about different value systems or different ways of reading that distinguish *your* analysis of the story from that of some of your classmates.

Revising

After you have produced a good rough draft, let it sit for a while. Then try it out on readers, who can follow the Guidelines for Peer Reviews. Based on your readers' advice, begin revising your draft, making it as clear as possible for your readers. Remember to start with the big issues and major changes and then work your way down to the smaller issues and minor changes.

GUIDELINES FOR PEER REVIEWS

Instructions for peer reviews are provided in Chapter 17 (pp. 519–520).

For the Writer

Prepare two or three questions you would like your peer reviewer to address while responding to your draft. The questions can focus on some aspect of your draft that you are uncertain about, on one or more sections where you particularly seek help or advice, on some feature that you particularly like about your draft, or on some part you especially wrestled with. Write out your questions and give them to your peer reviewer along with your draft.

For the Reviewer

I. Read the draft at a normal reading speed from beginning to end. As you read, do the following:

   A. Place a wavy line in the margin next to any passages that you find confusing, that contain something that doesn't seem to fit, or that otherwise slow down your reading.

   B. Place a "Good!" in the margin next to any passages where you think the writing is particularly strong or interesting.

II. Read the draft again slowly and answer the following questions by writing down brief explanations of your answers.

   A. Introduction:

      1. Does the title arouse interest and forecast the problem to be addressed? How might the author improve the title?

      2. How does the introduction capture your interest, explain the question to be addressed, and suggest why it is both problematic and significant?

      3. Does the introduction conclude with the writer's thesis? Is the thesis surprising? How might the author improve the introduction?

   B. Analysis and interpretation:

      1. How has the writer shown that his or her thesis is in tension with alternative interpretations or views?

      2. How is the essay organized? Does the writer helpfully forecast the whole, place points before particulars, use transitions, and follow the old/new contract as explained in Chapter 18? How might the author improve or clarify the organization?

      3. Where does the author quote from the story (or use paraphrase or other specific references to the text)? How are each of the author's points grounded in the text? What passages not cited might better support the argument? What recommendations do you have for improving the author's use of supporting details?

4. Where do you disagree with the author's analysis? What aspects of the story are left unexplained? What doesn't fit?

III. Rhetorical considerations

A. *Purpose, audience,* and *genre:* How well does this draft accomplish its purpose of helping readers achieve a new understanding of the short story? How effectively does it follow the conventions of closed-form academic prose?

B. *Logos, ethos,* and *pathos:* How effectively does the draft provide textual detail to support its points? How effective is the draft conceptually? To what extent does the writer reveal himself or herself to be a perceptive and credible reader? How has the writer shown awareness of the audience's interests, needs, and points of view?

IV. If the writer has prepared questions for you, respond to his or her inquiries.

V. Sum up what you see as the chief strengths and problem areas of this draft:

A. Strengths

B. Problem areas

VI. Finally, read the draft one more time. Place a check mark in the margin next to any places where you notice problems in grammar, spelling, or mechanics (one check mark per problem).

Analyzing and Synthesizing Ideas

About the Analysis and Synthesis of Ideas

In many of your college courses, you'll be asked to explore connections and contradictions among groups of texts. Distilling main points from more than one text, seeing connections among texts, commenting on meaningful relationships, and showing how the texts have influenced your own thinking on a question are all part of the thinking and writing involved in synthesis.

Synthesis, which is a way of seeing and coming to terms with complexities, is a counterpart to *analysis.* When you analyze something, you break it down into its parts to see the relationships among them. When you synthesize, you take one more step, putting parts together in some new fashion. The cognitive researcher Benjamin Bloom has schematized "synthesis" as the fifth of six levels of thinking processes, ranked in order of complexity and challenge: knowledge, comprehension, application, analysis, *synthesis,* and evaluation. Bloom defined synthesis in these terms: "putting together of constituent elements or parts to form a whole requiring original creative thinking."* Synthesis drives those light-bulb moments when you exclaim, "Ah! Now I see how these ideas are related!"

A second useful and related way to think of synthesis is as a dialectical thinking process. Throughout this text, we have explained that college writing involves posing a significant question that often forces you to encounter clashing or contradictory ideas. Such conflicts intrigued the German philosopher Hegel, who posited that thinking proceeds dialectically when a thesis clashes against an antithesis, leading the thinker to formulate a synthesis encompassing dimensions of both the original thesis and the antithesis. When you write a synthesis essay, your interaction with a group of related texts exemplifies this dialectical process. From your encounter with alternative perspectives on an issue, you emerge with a new, enlarged perspective of your own.

This Hegelian view is also discussed in Chapter 8, pp. 195–197.

Synthesis is an especially important component of research writing, where you use synthesis to carve out your own thinking space on a research question while sifting through the writings of others. Synthesis, then, is the skill of wrestling with ideas from different texts or sources, trying to forge a new whole out of potentially confusing parts. It is the principal way you enter into a conversation on a social, civic, or scholarly issue.

---

*Benjamin Bloom, *Taxonomy of Educational Objectives: Handbook I: Cognitive Domain* (New York: David McKay, 1956).

College synthesis assignments sometimes specify the readings and the questions you are to explore, or they may, as in the case of research assignments, ask you to originate your own questions and find your own readings. Here are examples of synthesis assignments that you might encounter in different disciplines. In these sample assignments, note that the readings and focusing questions are provided in each case.

ENVIRONMENTAL POLITICS COURSE

Texts to Be Analyzed

Garrett Hardin's essay on over-population, "The Tragedy of the Commons," from *Science* (1968)

Kenneth E. Boulding's essay "Economics of the Coming Spaceship Earth" (1966)

A chapter from Dixie Lee Ray's *Trashing the Planet* (1992)

A chapter from Ron Bailey's *The True State of the Planet* (1995)

Synthesis Questions

Are there any common assumptions about the world's environment in these readings

What problems and solutions appear in these readings?

What direction would you take in proposing a solution?

AMERICAN LITERATURE SURVEY COURSE

Texts to Be Analyzed

Selections from the *Lowell Offering,* a publication produced in Lowell, Massachusetts, in the 1840s, featuring the writings of young female factory workers

Historian Gerda Lerner's essay "The Lady and the Mill Girl: Changes in the Status of Women in the Age of Jackson 1800–1840" (1969)

Herman Melville's short story "The Paradise of Bachelors and the Tartarus of Maids" (1835)

Synthesis Questions

What common questions about changes in women's social roles in the 1800s emerge in these texts?

Which text gives you the clearest understanding of the problems with women's changing roles and why?

FILM CRITICISM COURSE

Films to Be Analyzed

Drums along the Mohawk (1939)

Fort Apache (1948)

Dances with Wolves (1990)

Smoke Signals (1998)

Synthesis Questions

What similarities and differences do you see in these films' representations of Native Americans?

How do you explain these differences?

The assignment for this chapter is modeled after assignments like those just shown and draws on the kinds of readings you will typically be asked to synthesize in your college courses. As an introduction to synthesis thinking, this chapter provides extended examples of student writers who are analyzing and synthesizing readings on the impact of technology. Specifically, the students are asked to address a focusing question that many cultural critics are pondering: *To what extent does technology enrich or dehumanize our lives?* As one contemporary critic puts it, "Does technology liberate or enslave us?"*

Exploring the Analysis and Synthesis of Ideas

In this exercise, we ask you to read two pieces about the value and effects of technology. The first reading, "Young Entrepreneurs' Disdain for Time Off" by John Gallagher, appeared in the Business section of *The Seattle Times,* July 4, 2001. The second, "The Late, Great Outdoors" by Keith Goetzman, is from the September–October 2001 *Utne Reader.* Read these pieces carefully and then do the exercises that follow.

READINGS

John Gallagher
Young Entrepreneurs' Disdain for Time Off

1   A weeklong cruise in the Caribbean this spring left Detroit software executive John Lauer feeling so cut off from his work that he couldn't wait to get to an island.

2   "I'll pull into the port and all of a sudden get a voice-mail alert because they had cellular connectivity and I'd be, like, 'Thank God!'" He recalled, "The only reason I was glad to be on land is because my cell phone was working again."

3   The 26-year-old Lauer typifies the gigabyte lifestyle of young entrepreneurs. It's a life gladly given to stretched workdays and little time off.

4   "I hate to not be at the office," said the sandal- and T-shirt-clad chief executive and founder of Rootlevel, a Web application-service firm based in Detroit. "Fortunately, I'm as connected at home now as I am at work."

5   A compulsive workaholic? Not necessarily. Some experts think working on vacation is growing more common. Lauer's disdain for time off reflects not just a choice of the computer elite but a growing trend for many Americans, for good or for ill.

6   Once conceived of as an extended time of renewal and exploration, vacation today too often means a cramped few days juggling kids at the beach and calls to the office.

---

*This quotation come from Bernd Herzogenrath, "The Question Concerning Humanity: Obsolete Bodies and (Post)Digital Flesh" in the online journal *Enculturation: A Journal of Rhetoric, Writing, and Culture* 3.1 (Fall 2000). We accessed this article on March 27, 2002 at http://www.uta.edu/huma/enculturation/3_1/herzogenrath/.

7   The New York-based Families and Work Institute reported in May that 26 percent of 1,003 adults surveyed do not take all the vacation to which they are entitled. They blamed the demands of their jobs.

8   Among the managerial class, the toll looks even worse. A 1999 survey of 5,000 executives by the Cleveland-based Management Recruiters International reported that 82 percent said they checked in with their office while on vacation.

9

Vacation Time
Average annual vacation days per employee, by country:

U.S.	13
Japan	25
S. Korea	25
Canada	26
Britain	28
Brazil	34
Germany	35
France	37
Italy	42

Such behavior can take a toll. Some 55 percent of employees who skip some or all of their vacation say they experience feelings of being overworked, vs. 27 percent of those who use all their vacation, the Families and Work Institute study found.

10   Perhaps worst of all, paid vacation isn't even an option for most of the nation's working poor.

11   Eileen Appelbaum, an economist with the Washington, D.C.-based Economic Policy Institute, a think tank that studies poverty issues, said that of the people who make less than $10 an hour—roughly one in five workers—two-thirds either have had no paid vacation for the past five years or had some years with no time off.

12   When the working poor do get paid time off, it's usually one week or less per year.

13   "Paid vacation is definitely a middle-class-or-better benefit," Appelbaum said.

14   Americans clearly are of two minds about working during vacation. Many bemoan the trend. Others, like Lauer, don't seem to care.

15   "I cannot be disconnected," Lauer said. "Going on vacation is horrible. It's absolutely miserable."

16   Today's connectivity encourages working on vacation. Vince Webb, senior vice president of marketing and strategy for Management Recruiters, said the profusion of laptops, cell phones, pagers and other devices makes it too easy to stay plugged in thousands of miles from the office.

17   "You can get sucked in so easily 365 days a year, 24/7," Webb said.

18   And it's only going to get worse. Airline maker Boeing said last month that it's going into business with three major airlines to let fliers access e-mail and the Internet in aircraft cabins.

19   American Airlines, United Airlines and Delta Air Lines—the nation's three largest carriers—are the first three to sign up, but Boeing is also in talks with 30 other airlines. . . .

20   If technology helps the overworked stay plugged in, it can also help would-be vacationers tune out. E-mail programs like Microsoft's Outlook

have an "out-of-office" feature that responds to incoming e-mails with an announcement that the recipient is away.

21   Ron Watson, vice president of human resources for Compuware, the Farmington Hills, Mich.-based software firm, urges employees to use such features to smooth the transition to time off.

22   "At Compuware, we really encourage people to separate themselves when they go on vacation," Watson said. "In order to be effective, they really need to get out and recharge."

23   But even those who know better sometimes get caught up in vacation work. Gary Baker, an Ann Arbor, Mich.-based partner with the Andersen consulting firm and host of the radio show "Internet Adviser," recalls the sideways glances his wife shot him when he made cell-phone calls in between rides at Walt Disney World in Florida.

24   "There's so much going on that you need to stay in touch with," he explained.

25   Baker said he tries to schedule his work time on vacation when it will least disrupt his family. "Your kids are playing in the surf, so you go upstairs and make the call."

26   But like many a New Year's Eve resolution, promising to take more time off doesn't always stick. "We have the same kind of rules that everybody else has," Baker said. "Leave the cell phone at home; take the time off." Yet Baker left unused all but a day and a half of his four weeks of vacation last year.

27   For those truly dedicated to work, vacationing may always be more burden than boon.

28   Describing plans for his wedding, Lauer outlines a three-week honeymoon with Ribiat in Europe this fall. The itinerary includes Britain, France, Spain, Italy and Greece. But then Lauer added, "Once that's done, there's no way we're going to be taking any huge vacations like that until we're old and gray."

29   His voice dropped, and he added softly, "Kind of sad, in a way."

Keith Goetzman
The Late, Great Outdoors

1   In the 2000 Sydney Olympics, whitewater kayaking competitors bucked through an artificial channel surging with machine-pumped water, then rode conveyor belts back upstream without ever getting out of their boats. In Chamonix, France, gateway to the Alps and a mountaineering mecca, ice climbers in the 2001 Ice World Cup ascended not nearby peaks but an elaborate ice-covered structure erected in the middle of town.

2   The artificial outdoors isn't just for world-class competitors, though. At the $130 million Gotcha Glacier sports complex being built in Anaheim, California, everyone will be able to surf faux waves, climb imitation cliffs, "skydive," ski, snowboard, skateboard—and, of course, shop—under one gigantic roof.

3   Gotcha may be just the tip of the glacier when it comes to the future of recreation. Increasingly, the great outdoors are being brought indoors or altered considerably to produce more accessible venues for adventure seekers. Indoor climbing walls are sprouting everywhere, artificial whitewater courses are on the drawing boards in dozens of cities, and several "snowdomes" are being built in Europe and the United States.

4   The phenomenon is generating considerable debate within the outdoor sports world. Some feel that something is lost when the rapids are always just right and the view at the top of the climb is the checkout line. Many of these are conservationists who oppose manipulating or re-creating natural environments. But for the "extreme" sports crowd—whose allies include much of the outdoor gear industry—the more places to play, the better.

5   Witness a recent exchange between paddlers on an Internet message board. "I am opposed to taking a backhoe and cement truck to the river, to supposedly make it more 'fun.' It strikes me as obscene," wrote "dancewater."

6   But "paddleboy" was unapologetic: "Artificial courses are for convenience, not getting in touch with the flow. We don't eat at McDonald's because the burgers taste good. Most 'natural' rivers aren't natural. . . . We paddle what's wet."

7   Similar differences exist among rock climbers, says Lloyd Athearn, deputy director of the American Alpine Club in Golden, Colorado. "For some people, climbing is about achieving the greatest level of technical difficulty they can achieve. There are people who climb at just obscene levels of difficulty, and they may not care at all about the scenery," he explains. "Others prefer being out on a remote peak someplace where they've bushwhacked 10 miles to get to the base of it. To them the inspiration of the environment is as important as the technical difficulties, if not more so."

8   Artificial environments have caught on for various reasons, says Professor Alan Ewert, who teaches outdoor leadership at Indiana University. For some participants, they are simply places to train for "real" outdoor experiences. Others are seeking a nontraditional athletic workout in a controlled, safe setting. And a growing number of people are using climbing walls and the like as social gathering spots. Says Athearn: "As the whole climbing gym scene evolved, there ended up being some people who like that environment, and they don't really climb outside."

9   Proponents of artificial environments, which are usually in metropolitan areas, say it's all about access, convenience, and a good time. "This is a fun sport. Why should we have to drive 200 miles to participate?" says Damon Peters, an avid kayaker and owner of L'eau Vive Paddlesports, a kayak accessory distributor based in Portland, Maine.

10   Backers of artificial environments often point out that they're helping expose urban dwellers to outdoor recreation. Gotcha Glacier's marketing and operations chief, Mike Gerard, told the *Los Angeles Times* he's performing a service. "It costs money to get to the mountains," he said. "Snowboarding is a sport with huge growth potential. We just need to get it to the people. I want to see kids of all ages and ethnic groups have a chance to do this."

11   Ewert says it's not yet clear whether artificial environments are instilling a desire for real wilderness experience in city dwellers. "We hope that's happening, but we're not really sure," he says. What is happening, he believes, is that indoor adventurers are being connected with organizations that can take them to the next step, and they may be more likely to develop an environmental consciousness.

12   And the outdoors may need some help in attracting new enthusiasts. Athearn points to a recent study that attempted to determine why younger people weren't as interested in wilderness experiences as the previous generation. One teen responded, "If I'm in the mountains, I'm out of cell-phone coverage, and I can't do that."

Individual Tasks

1. How would you describe each writer's perspective or angle of vision on technology? In one or two sentences, summarize each writer's main points in these passages.
2. List ideas that these pieces have in common.
3. List any contradictions or differences you see in these pieces.
4. Freewrite your own response to these readings for five minutes, exploring what questions they raise for you or personal experiences that they might remind you of.

Group or Whole-Class Tasks

1. Working in small groups or as a whole class, try to reach consensus answers to questions 1, 2, and 3.
2. Share your individual responses to question 4. What are the major questions and issues raised by your group or the whole class? What different views of technology emerged?

WRITING PROJECT

Write a synthesis essay that meets the following criteria:

- Addresses a focusing question that your instructor provides or that you formulate for yourself
- Summarizes and analyzes the views of at least two writers on this question
- Shows how you have wrestled with different perspectives on the question and have synthesized these ideas to arrive at your own new view of the question

To help you generate ideas for this assignment, your instructor may ask you to write your own exploratory pieces in response to some or all of the chapter's five learning log tasks.

This assignment asks you to take apart, make sense of, assess, and recombine—that is, synthesize—the ideas from two or more readings. In the introduction to your essay, present the focusing question to your readers so that they become interested in it, see its problematic nature, and appreciate its significance. Then present your own thesis that grows out of your analysis and synthesis of your chosen or assigned readings. At appropriate places in your essay, you need to summarize these readings briefly because you should assume that your audience has not read them.

In the body of your paper, you have two main goals: (1) through analysis, show how the pieces you have selected provide different perspectives on the focusing question based on differing values, assumptions, beliefs, or framing of the question; and (2) through synthesis, add your own perspective and independent thinking by making your own connections among the ideas in the readings. In other words, create a new view by combining ideas gathered from readings with your own ideas.

To help you develop ideas for your synthesis essay, we have included five learning log tasks. These tasks will guide you gradually from understanding through analysis to synthesis and will provide thinking that you can use directly in your formal essay. On several occasions you will have an opportunity to share your learning log explorations with classmates and to use them for the basis of discussions that will help you generate more ideas for your formal essay. Your instructor will specify whether you are to complete these learning logs and, if so, how much time to spend on them. If you do the learning log tasks, keep your writing informal and exploratory with an emphasis on idea generation rather than correctness and polish.

Suggested Ideas for Synthesis Questions and Readings

This text provides a number of options from which your instructor can choose. Many instructors will follow our own approach, which is to assign both the readings and the focusing question. Others may assign the readings but invite students to formulate their own focusing questions. Still others may leave both the focusing question and the readings up to the student.

The articles in the "Readings" section of this chapter raise questions about the causes of obesity and possible lifestyle changes needed for better health. But other readings throughout the text can be successfully combined for a synthesis essay. What follows is list of possible focusing questions and readings. In addition, your instructor might assign readings not found in this text.

Further suggestions for combinations of readings can be found in the "Thematic Table of Contents" in the front of the book.

Reading Options for This Assignment

Focusing Question	Possible Readings
What can we do to combat obesity in children and adults and attain better health?	• Ellen Goodman, "The Big Fat Case Against Big Macs," pp. 377–378 • Dale Buss, "Is the Food Industry the Problem or the Solution?" pp. 378–381 • Marilyn Larkin, "Can Cities Be Designed to Fight Obesity?" pp. 381–385
What social attitude should we take toward smoking?	• Florence King, "I'd Rather Smoke Than Kiss," pp. 144–149 • Lyndon Haviland, "A Silence That Kills, pp. 150–153 • Gasp Consultancy, Ltd. "Steps to Stop Smoking," pp. 154–155 • Welcome to Malboro Country," spoof ad, p. 156 • Gina Escamilla, Angie L. Cradock, and Ichiro Kawachi, "Women and Smoking in Hollywood Movies: A Content Analysis," pp. 271–276
What position should we take on the Patriot Act?	• Clay Bennett, "USA PATRIOT ACT," p. 418 • John Ashcroft, "Prepared Remarks of Attorney General Ashcroft at the Federalist Society National Convention," pp. 419–425 • James Bovard, "Surveillance State," pp. 426–432
How can we appreciate, enjoy, and preserve nature?	• Edward Abbey, "The Damnation of a Canyon," pp. 157–161 • Friends of Lake Powell, Home page, p. 161 • Thomas Merton, "A Festival of Rain," p. 18 • Annie Dillard, "Living Like Weasels," pp. 594–597 • Keith Goetzman, "The Late, Great Outdoors," pp. 361–363 • Photographs of the Arctic National Wildlife Refuge, pp. 98–101 • Selected excerpts on automobiles and energy consumption, pp. 12–15

An Explanation of the Student Examples in This Chapter

The student examples in this chapter focus on the technological question "To what extent does technology enrich or dehumanize our lives?" These examples enable you to role-play the same sort of audience stipulated in the assignment—readers who have not read the articles being discussed. You will need to depend, then, on the writers' summaries of these readings. The two student writers, Kara Watterson and Kate MacAulay, are working with the following texts:

- George Ritzer, "The Irrationality of Rationality: Traffic Jams on Those 'Happy Trails.'" This is a chapter from Ritzer's widely discussed book *The McDonaldization of Society,* New Century Edition (Thousand Oaks, CA: Pine Forge Press, 2000).
- Sherry Turkle, "Who Am We?" published in the magazine *Wired* 4.1 (January 1996): 148–52, 194–99.

Understanding Analysis and Synthesis

The Challenge of Synthesizing Ideas

The need to synthesize ideas usually begins when you pose a problematic question that sends you off on an intellectual journey through a group of texts. Your goal is to achieve your own informed view on that question, a view that reflects your intellectual wrestling with the ideas in your sources and in some way integrates ideas from these sources with your own independent thinking.

The most efficient and productive way to handle this multitask challenge is to break it into a series of incremental thinking steps that take you gradually from understanding your chosen texts, to an analysis of them, to a synthesis of their ideas with your own. The learning log tasks in each of the sections that follow show you a series of thinking steps to guide you through this process.

Understanding Your Texts Through Summary Writing

Learning Log Task 1: Write a 200–250-word summary of each of the main texts you will use in your final paper.

As a starting point for grappling with a writer's ideas, writing careful summaries prompts you to read texts with the grain, adopting each text's perspective and walking in each author's shoes. When you summarize a text, you try to achieve an accurate, thorough understanding of it by stating its main ideas in a tightly distilled format.

Instructions on how to write a summary are found on pp. 126–130.

What follows are Kara's summary of the book chapter by Ritzer and Kate's summary of Turkle's article—the two readings they will use in their synthesis essays.

Notice how they use attributive tags to show that they are representing Ritzer's and Turkle's ideas as objectively as they can and that these ideas belong to Ritzer or Turkle, not to them.

Instructions on how to use attributive tags are found on pp. 129 and 652–655.

KARA'S SUMMARY OF RITZER'S CHAPTER

In "The Irrationality of Rationality," the seventh chapter in <u>The McDonaldization of Society</u>, sociologist George Ritzer identifies a major sociological and economic problem: in an effort to find the most efficient way to run a business (what Ritzer calls "rationalizing"), more and more companies are following the franchise model pioneered by McDonald's. Although McDonaldization is efficient and economical for the companies, Ritzer argues it can be irrational, inconvenient, inefficient, and costly for consumers who often stand in long lines at fast-food restaurants and supermarkets. Ritzer also claims that McDonaldized systems cause people to forfeit real fun for manufactured fun and illusion. He cites the example of fake international villages at amusement parks and the fake friendliness of the "scripted interactions" (138) that employees are supposed to have with customers. Ritzer explains that our McDonaldized society has begun focusing more on quantity than quality. He believes that McDonaldized systems are dehumanizing: jobs "don't offer much in the way of satisfaction or stability" (137) and families hardly ever eat together any more, a situation that is contributing to the "disintegration of the family" (141). Ritzer also argues that by franchising everywhere, we are losing cultural distinctions. Whether you are in Japan or the United States, products are beginning to look the same. Finally, Ritzer shows that when companies become rationalized, they limit the possibility of connection between human beings. Citing examples from fast-food restaurants to hospitals, he states that there are many serious drawbacks to "our fast-paced and impersonal society" (140).

KATE'S SUMMARY OF TURKLE'S ARTICLE

In her <u>Wired</u> article "Who Am We?" psychologist and MIT professor Sherry Turkle explores how computers and the Internet are transforming our views of ourselves and the way we interact socially. Turkle believes that the Internet is moving us toward a "decentered" (149) sense of the self. She says that computers used to be thought of as "calculating machines" (149), but they are increasingly now seen as intelligent objects capable of interaction and simulation. She uses children's interactive computer games to illustrate how some people now think of computers as having personalities and psyches, which make them "fitting partners for dialog and relationship" (150). In the second half of her article, she argues that virtual life raises new moral issues. She uses the example of MUDs (multiuser domains), which allow people to create multiple and often simultaneous virtual identities by playing different characters. She presents examples of the relationships of cyber characters—often cyber-sex—that raise the question of whether cyber-sex is an act of real-life infidelity or adultery. Turkle concludes that it is easy for people to lose themselves between the real world and these virtual worlds. Because we have the ability to create better "selves" in the virtual world, it is possible to become addicted to virtual life and be "imprisoned by the screens" (199). According to Turkle, we are moving toward a "postmodernist culture of simulation" (149), and she cautions that it is more important than ever that we are very self-aware.

For Writing and Discussion

> Working in small groups or as a whole class, share your summaries of your two chosen or assigned readings. What important main ideas does your group agree must be included in a summary of each text? What points are secondary and can be left out?

Examining the Rhetorical Strategies Used in Your Texts

Explanations of these terms and concepts are found in Chapters 3 and 4.

Learning Log Task 2: Analyze the rhetorical strategies used in each of your texts (for example, the way your texts handle purpose, audience, genre, angle of vision, appeals to *logos, ethos,* and *pathos,* and use of evidence).

In order to analyze a text and synthesize its ideas, you need to consider the text rhetorically. To whom is the author writing and why? Do you see how the genre of each text influences some of the author's choices about language and structure? What angle of vision shapes each text and accounts for what is included and excluded? Do you share the values of the author or of his or her intended audience?

Instructions on how to write a rhetorical analysis of a text are found in Chapter 6 on pp. 134–137.

Here is Kara's learning log entry exploring the rhetorical contexts of the Ritzer and Turkle texts:

KARA'S RESPONSE TO LEARNING LOG TASK 2

Although both George Ritzer and Sherry Turkle are scholars, their texts are not really written for scholarly audiences. Both would fall in the category of nonfiction books (articles) written for general audiences and both are written to raise audience awareness of sociological/cultural problems—in this case, the way that technological advances and the fast-food model of business are affecting the quality of life and the way that the Internet is affecting our sense of ourselves and our relationships.

Both Ritzer and Turkle have chosen to write in accessible language so that their ideas can easily be understood by a general audience, and both use many examples to build credibility. Still, because I had no previous personal background with multi-user domains, I found it challenging to imagine some of Turkle's descriptions of the virtual world of MUDs, but I did have previous experience with all of Ritzer's examples so I never felt in over my head while reading his chapters.

Kara defines "rationalization" in the opening sentences of her summary of Ritzer, p. 367.

From Ritzer's angle of vision, McDonaldization has had a damaging and irreversible effect on the quality of contemporary life, and he is trying to prompt people to slow down this destructive process. His approach is quite one-sided, though. He does admit that "we undoubtedly have gained much from the rationalization of society in general" (132), but he does not develop this idea any further. He refuses to make any further concessions to the rationalization he is fighting. Instead of acknowledging contradicting ideas, Ritzer hammers his point strongly with example after example. By the end of the chapter, the reader is left with a glazed-over feeling, not really taking in the information.

Turkle's angle of vision seems to include curiosity and exploration as well as concern about the way computers are transforming society. She seems to analyze more than argue. She is trying to get across her notion that the Internet lets people adopt many different characters and have multiple selves, for example when they play in MUDs and simulation games. So maybe, in claiming that computers are no longer calculating machines, Turkle, like Ritzer, is only presenting one limited view of her subject, the view that interests her as a psychologist who has written many books and articles on computers, and our changing sense of identity and community.

For Writing and Discussion

Working in small groups or as a whole class, share what each of you discovered in Learning Log Task 2. Try to reach consensus on the most important rhetorical features of each of the texts you are using for your synthesis essay.

Identifying Main Themes and Examining Similarities and Differences in the Ideas in Your Texts

Learning Log Task 3: Identify main issues or themes in your assigned or chosen texts. Then explore the similarities and differences in their ideas.

This learning log task asks you to identify main issues, ideas, or themes that surface in your texts as preparation for looking for similarities and differences among your texts. This process of thinking—comparison and contrast—will help you clarify your understanding of each reading and promote analysis of the underlying values, assumptions, and ideas of each author. Here are some questions that can guide your learning log writing at this stage of your thinking:

QUESTIONS TO HELP YOU GRAPPLE WITH SIMILARITIES AND DIFFERENCES IN YOUR TEXTS

- What main ideas or themes do you see in each text?
- What similarities and differences do you see in the way the authors choose to frame the issues they are writing about? How do their theses (either implied or stated) differ?
- What are the main similarities and differences in their angles of vision?
- What commonalities and intersections do you see in their ideas? What contradictions and clashes do you see in their ideas?

- What similarities and differences do you see in the authors' underlying values and assumptions?
- What overlap, if any, is there in these authors' examples and uses of terms?
- How would Author A respond to Author B?

Here are excerpts from Kara's and Kate's learning logs, showing their exploratory analyses of Ritzer's and Turkle's texts. Note how they each begin to organize comparisons by points, to make analytical connections among them, and to push themselves to think out exactly where these authors agree and differ.

EXCERPT FROM KARA'S RESPONSE TO LEARNING LOG TASK 3

Both Ritzer and Turkle make strong comments about health problems that may be caused by the particular type of technology they are dealing with. For Ritzer, the dangers that arise from McDonaldization can most easily be seen in fast-food restaurants and their fatty, unhealthy foods: "such meals are the last things many Americans need, suffering as they do from obesity, high cholesterol levels, high blood pressure, and perhaps diabetes" (133). He also considers the high level of stress created by our high-speed society that can cause heart attacks, panic attacks, maybe nervous breakdowns. Turkle, too, is concerned about the effects of technology on people's health, but her focus is people's psyches and minds. One person in her research study who creates different identities on the Internet thinks that "MUDding has ultimately made him feel worse about himself" (196). For Turkle, the Internet can be dangerous for what it can do to a person's psyche.

Both authors agree that technological advances are causing a loss of real human connection. McDonaldization fosters fake contact; employees are given guidelines about how to interact with customers and are programmed with what to say and what not to say: "rule Number 17 for Burger King workers is 'Smiles at all times' " (Ritzer 130). Quick sales, not real customer relations, are the main concern. For Turkle too, this loss of human contact is a dilemma. MUDs are not places where you truly get to know a person; they are places where people are acting out characters. These are not real friends that can aid you when you are feeling ill or down. Also, people are spending vast quantities of time logging on, spending time with a computer screen instead of family and friends. . . .

EXCERPT FROM KATE'S RESPONSE TO LEARNING LOG TASK 3

. . . Last, I think that Turkle and Ritzer have very different attitudes about what they observe and claim is happening to society. Turkle seems to be a little more optimistic than Ritzer. While she sees the changes that advanced technology is causing in society, she seems to think that we, as human beings, have the ability to adjust to the changes facing us and to change ourselves in order to preserve our humanity. In contrast to that view, Ritzer seems to take the position that we are on a downward spiral and McDonaldized systems are destroying us and society as a whole. Ritzer and Turkle would have a really great discussion about all the negative effects that technology and rationality are having on individuals and society, but they would probably largely disagree on society's ability to bounce back and fix itself.

For Writing and Discussion

Working as a whole class or in small groups, share your analyses of similarities and differences in your chosen or assigned texts. Pay close attention to these two overarching questions: How are the texts similar and different? How do each author's assumptions, beliefs, purposes, and values account for these similarities and differences?

Moving Toward Your Own Views

Learning Log Task 4: In light of what you have read and thought about so far, explore your own views on the original focusing question that has guided your probing of the texts.

One of your biggest challenges in writing a synthesis essay is to move beyond analysis to synthesis. A successful synthesis essay incorporates ideas from your texts and yet represents your own independent thinking, showing evidence of the dialectic process. You need to think about how the differing perspectives of Texts A and B have led you to new realizations that will let you enter the conversation of these texts. As you begin to formulate your synthesis views, you will also need to reassert your personal/intellectual investment in the conversation of the texts. You will need to take ownership of the ideas and to emerge with a clearer sense of your own views. You may also want to consider which text—in your mind—makes the most significant contribution to the question you are exploring. You may want to evaluate the texts to determine which has influenced your thinking the most and why. The following questions should help you think of ideas for Learning Log 4:

QUESTIONS TO HELP YOU DEVELOP YOUR OWN VIEWS

- What do I agree with and disagree with in the texts I have analyzed?
- How have these texts changed my perception and understanding of an issue, question, or problem? You might want to use these prompts: "I used to think _____, but now I think _____." "Although these texts have persuaded me that _____, I still have doubts about _____."
- What do I see or think now that I didn't see or think before I read these texts?
- What new, significant questions do these texts raise for me?
- What do I now see as the main controversies?
- What is my current view on the focusing question that connects my texts and that all my texts explore?
- How would I position myself in the conversation of the texts?
- If I find one author's perspective more valid, accurate, interesting, or useful than another's, why is that?

To illustrate this learning log task, we show you excerpts from the explorations of both Kara and Kate.

EXCERPT FROM KARA'S RESPONSE TO LEARNING LOG TASK 4

When I was in Puerto Rico one spring break, I remember how excited my friend and I were to go to a burger place for dinner one night. It was so nice to have American food after days of eating fajitas and enchiladas. At the time, I did not think about how this American restaurant got to Puerto Rico; I was just glad it was there. However, after reading "The Irrationality of Rationality" by George Ritzer, I began to take a closer look at this experience. Both this article and "Who Am We?" have caused me to take a closer look at our society. . . . What is it that causes people to surf the Internet for hours on end, to chat with people they have never met? What is this doing to our culture? Are we losing the distinctions evident when you travel from one region to the next, from one country to another? . . .

EXCERPT FROM KATE'S RESPONSE TO LEARNING LOG TASK 4

Reading the articles by Ritzer and Turkle made me much more aware of a social problem that I didn't really pay attention to before. I didn't realize how much modern technology is changing our human relationships. For example, the other night I was at a family gathering, and some of my cousins began discussing the idea of purchasing a new car. After talking for a short while about how much it would cost and how to get the best deal, one of my cousins had that modern craving for wanting to know the answer immediately. He logged on to the Internet and spent the remainder of the evening looking at cars and prices, and had limited interaction with the family. It made me think about the articles and how things were becoming more immediate and less personal, and how interactions between machines and humans are decreasing the interactions between people. Why speak with another person who might not know the answer to a question or the solution to a problem when you can just log on to the Internet and find the right answer immediately? It makes me wonder what the Internet does not offer. . . .

Taking Your Position in the Conversation: Your Synthesis

Learning Log Task 5: Reread your first four learning logs and consider how your own views on the focusing question have evolved and emerged. Think about the risky, surprising, or new views that you can bring to your readers. In light of your reading and thinking, explore what you want to say in your own voice to show the connections you have made and the new insights you now have.

After you have discovered what you think about the texts you have analyzed—what ideas you accept and reject, what new questions you have formulated, how your ideas have been modified and transformed through your reading experience—you need to find a way to pull your ideas together. Your synthesis view should be the fruit of your intellectual work, a perspective that you have come to after reading the ideas of other writers, pondering them reflectively and keenly. Here are some synthesis questions that can help you articulate the points that you want to develop in your essay:

QUESTIONS TO HELP YOU FORMULATE AND DEVELOP YOUR SYNTHESIS VIEWS

- What discoveries have I made after much thought?
- What are the most important insights I have gotten from these readings?
- What is my intellectual or personal investment with the focusing question at this point?
- Where can I step out on my own, even take a risk, in my thinking about the ideas discussed in these texts?
- What new perspective do I want to share with my readers?

What follows is an excerpt from Kara's learning log. Note how she is beginning to find her stance on the focusing question of whether technology enriches or dehumanizes our lives.

EXCERPT FROM KARA'S RESPONSE TO LEARNING LOG TASK 5

What is technology doing to our relationships with one another? Both Ritzer and Turkle seem to be urging us away from dependency on technology, and these authors have made me aware of my complacence in accepting technology, but still I see value in technology that these writers don't discuss. . . .

I find myself questioning these writers' views. Ritzer seems to believe that families go to McDonald's rather than eat family meals together. He doesn't consider that it is when people are on the road or out already that these restaurants are visited, not when they are sitting at home deciding what is for dinner. Turkle also speaks of the loss of connection that can arise from people constantly at their computers. She raises some very important questions about what technology is doing to our relationships and self-image, but I think she focuses too much on MUDs. How many people actually are doing this MUDding? Also, there are some valid things that come out of relationships on the Internet. I know of several examples of people who have met their future spouses through chat rooms. When I left for college, I was not sure whom I would stay in touch with, but because of the Internet, I am able to stay connected to people I would have drifted away from otherwise.

Also, while we note the dangers of technology, I think we need to remember the benefits as well. I agree that cell phones are overused, but how often have cell phones saved people in emergencies or aided people stranded on the road with car problems? I hope to be a doctor. I have great appreciation for the way that cameras can see inside a patient as surgeons are operating and thus reduce the risk of many surgeries. . . .

For Writing and Discussion

Prior to the start of this task, work individually to write two or three main points that you want to make in the synthesis portion of your final essay. Working in small groups or as a whole class, share your short list of main points. Briefly explain to your group or to the whole class why these points interest you. Take notes on group ideas.

Student Example of a Synthesis Essay

We conclude this section by showing you Kate's final synthesis essay. Note that Kate begins by presenting the focusing question that connects the texts she is analyzing. She then summarizes these texts and presents her mapping thesis statement. She devotes more than half of the body of the essay to a close analysis of the texts before she moves on to present her own independent thinking in the synthesis section of the essay.

TECHNOLOGY'S PERIL AND POTENTIAL

Kate MacAulay (student)

Introduces focusing questions and context

Recently in English class, we have been focusing on the question, What effect is technology having on humanity and the quality of life in the twenty-first century? We have had heated discussions about the use of cell phones, palm pilots, beepers, e-mail, chat rooms, and the Web. As part of my investigation of this question, I read

Introduces the texts to be analyzed

two texts: a chapter from George Ritzer's book The McDonaldization of Society, entitled "The Irrationality of Rationality: Traffic Jams on Those 'Happy Trails,' " and an article published in the magazine Wired entitled "Who Am We?", by Sherry Turkle.

Brief summary of Ritzer's text

In his chapter, Ritzer, a sociology professor, explains how technology has rationalized businesses and many facets of society following the McDonald's model. He argues that modern technology is causing loss of quality products, time, and relationships. In the McDonaldized system, where everything is designed logically for economy and convenience, things have become more artificial, and our relationships have become more superficial. In her article "Who Am We?", Sherry Turkle, a

Brief summary of Turkle's text

psychology professor at MIT, shows how computers and the Internet are transforming our views of ourselves and the way we interact socially. Focusing on computers' capacities for simulation and promoting interaction, Turkle has explored MUDs (multiuser domains), which allow people to create virtual identities. MUDs, Turkle believes, contribute to the formation of postmodern multiple selves and raise new

Thesis statement with analytical points and synthesis points

questions about personal identity and morality. Although both Turkle and Ritzer identify problems in technology's influence and in society's responses to it, Turkle sees more potential and gain where Ritzer sees mostly peril and loss. Both articles made me question how we define our values and morality in this postmodern, technologically advanced world and persuaded me of the need for caution in embracing technology.

Analytical point: compares and contrasts Ritzer's and Turkle's ideas

Although Ritzer and Turkle both see technology as having some negative effects on human relations and the quality of life, they disagree about exactly where the most interesting and serious problems lie. Ritzer believes that the problems caused by technology are not problems within the individual, but problems imposed on the individual by McDonaldized systems. For example, Ritzer claims that fast-food

Analyzes and elaborates on Ritzer's ideas

restaurants encourage us to eat unhealthy food quickly and also contribute to "the disintegration of the family" (141) by taking away family time. He also believes that rationalized systems create illusions of fun, reality, and friendliness. He talks about the "scripted interactions" (138) that employees are supposed to have with customers, where they are told exactly what to say to every customer, making interactions less real. Further, rationalized systems are dehumanizing in the kinds of jobs they create that "don't offer much in the way of satisfaction or stability" (137), benefiting only stockholders, owners, and employers.

In contrast, Turkle responds to technology's threat by focusing inward on technology's effect on the self and on relationships. While she is clearly intrigued by such Internet capabilities as multiuser domains, she acknowledges that this potential for multiple simultaneous identities threatens the wholeness of individuals, possibly damaging our emotional and psychological selves. Her concern is that people become addicted to these games because in the virtual world it is easy to create better "selves," to be what you wish you were. Turkle shows that people can lose themselves between the real world and the virtual world and be "imprisoned by the screens" (199). Although the virtual world is exciting and fun, she notes that "[o]ur experiences there are serious play" (199). She also examines cases of virtual characters who get into relationships with other characters, including cyber-sex relationships. She ponders the issue of cyber-sex immorality and adultery.

Analyzes, contrasts, and elaborates on Turkle's ideas

Despite Turkle and Ritzer's agreement that technology can damage us as a society, they disagree on their overall outlook and on our power to respond positively to technology's influence. I find Ritzer's views almost entirely negative. He believes that we are irreversibly damaged by technological advances because we are completely caught up in the McDonaldized system, with few parts of society left unchanged. Almost all of the family-owned neighborhood restaurants or mom-and-pop grocery stores have been taken over by franchises like Red Robin or Safeway. The costs of these rationalized systems, he says, are "inefficiency, illusions of various types, disenchantment, dehumanization, and homogenization" (124). In this chapter of his book, Ritzer doesn't mention any ways that our lives could be improved by these systems; he gives only examples of the way we are misled and damaged by them.

Analytical point: compares and contrasts Ritzer's and Turkle's ideas

Analyzes and elaborates on Ritzer's ideas

Presents writer's independent thinking

Turkle's approach strikes me as much more positive and balanced than Ritzer's. Optimistically, she explains that MUDs can give people self-knowledge that they can apply to real life: "[t]he anonymity of MUDs gives people the chance to express multiple and often unexplored aspects of the self, to play with their identity and to try out new ones" (152). Turkle sees an opportunity for us to grow as individuals and to learn to use technology in a positive way: "If we can cultivate awareness of what stands behind our screen personae, we are more likely to succeed in using virtual experience for personal transformation" (199). I think Turkle's views are more complex than Ritzer's. She believes that we have to take responsibility for our own habits and psychological responses to technology. She encourages us to be aware of how we interact with technology and believes that we can grow as individuals using this technology.

Analyzes, contrasts, and elaborates on Turkle's ideas

Presents writer's independent thinking

After reading these articles, I have realized how the continuing advancement of technology raises new moral questions. In a McDonaldized system, where everything is designed for convenience, there seem to be many places for morals to be left out of the picture. For example, is it okay for us to exchange real human interaction for convenience and saving time? Is there something wrong with our ethics when interesting and fulfilling jobs are eliminated by machines or replaced by dead-end, low-paying Mcjobs? Turkle too shows us how virtual worlds pose new moral questions for us. In MUDs, people can form virtual relationships, even cyber-sex relationships. The people behind the characters are real people, even if they are acting as someone else. If a married person has a cyber-sex relationship on a MUD, is he or she cheating? If a person commits a virtual assault or other crime that has no real-world, physical effects, should he or she feel guilty or sinful for the intention? Ritzer and Turkle have made me see how important these questions are.

Transition to writer's synthesis. Synthesis point discusses writer's own view

Elaborates on the connections the writer is making

Reading the articles made me strongly believe that we must use this technology in moderation in order to preserve individual qualities and our relationships. From our

Synthesis point discusses writer's own view

class discussions, I remember what Scott said about the way that the Internet connects people. He said that people like his uncle, who was severely injured on the job, use the Internet as a way of "getting out" to meet people and socialize. He pointed out how the Microsoft Gaming Zone has brought his uncle into an ongoing backgammon tournament through which he has made friends. Meanwhile his aunt has gotten a lot of pleasure out of playing and problem solving in the world of MUDs.

Synthesis point discusses writer's own view

But my own experience has left me concerned about the danger we face as emotional, social beings in the face of technology. The other night at a family gathering, one of my cousins, after discussing car buying with some of the relatives, got the urge to research new car prices. He left the room, logged onto the Internet, and spent the rest of the evening looking at cars and prices. We saw him only once the whole evening when he came out to get a slice of pie. My cousin's withdrawal from the conversation made me think about Ritzer's and Turkle's concerns that technology decreases real interactions among people.

Transition and final connections

Ritzer and Turkle offer us a warning that technology can be damaging if we don't recognize and overcome its dangers. I would encourage us not to let ourselves become dominated by technology, not to let it take our full attention just because it is there,

Conclusion

and not to overlook the complex moral questions that technology poses. The convenience that technology offers—our e-mail, cell phones, and debit cards—should help us save time that can be spent in nurturing our relationships with other people. The real challenge is to find ways to become even better people because of technology.

Works Cited

Complete citation of articles in MLA format

Ritzer, George. <u>The McDonaldization of Society</u>. Thousand Oaks: Pine Forge, 2000.
Turkle, Sherry. "Who Am We?" <u>Wired</u> Jan. 1996: 148+.

READINGS

The readings in this chapter immerse you in the network of issues related to obesity in industrialized countries, particularly the United States. In the last few years, public speculations have proliferated over the causes of obesity with blame targeting an array of social phenomena: Americans' love of fast food; the seductive and relentless advertising of the food industry; our fondness for watching television, playing video games, surfing the Web, and spending hours at our computers; our lack of physical exercise; corporate promotions of fast food and soft drinks in schools; the stress of our lives; and even low-fat food itself. Public voices have also warned about the serious consequences of the obesity crisis, consequences including higher rates of diseases such as diabetes, shorter lives, and higher insurance costs. For example, the documentary film *Super Size Me* (2004) exposes the dangers of a regular diet of fast food. Lately the controversy has also raged over possible solutions to help children, teens, and adults achieve healthier lives. The readings that follow explore some of these proposals for constructive action. We have framed several focusing questions for synthesis essays on these readings: What is the most promising solution or combination of solutions to the health crisis of obesity? What should we do to help our children avoid obesity and lead healthier lives? To avoid influencing your own analysis of these readings, we omit the discussion questions that typically follow readings in other chapters.

The first reading, by highly reputed syndicated columnist Ellen Goodman, appeared in *The Washington Post* in December 2002. Goodman is known for her insightful delving into complex issues.

Ellen Goodman
The Big Fat Case Against Big Macs

1   I don't believe there's any magical mathematical equation between the speed of the food and the circumference of the waistline. After all, you can gain weight eating slow food as well as fast food. You can bulk up with haute cuisine as well as Big Macs. And you can, alas, trust me on this.

2   So I was inclined to scoff at the Conspiracy Theory of Obesity. This is the idea that McDonald's dunnit. That Burger King and Wendy's and their speed-eating cohorts are responsible for the Incredible Expanding American.

3   Right before Thanksgiving, some lawyers went to court in pursuit of this theory. They filed a class action against McDonald's on behalf of New York children with health problems. These plaintiffs ate at Ronald McDonald's more than at Mom's. One 13-year-old weighed 278 pounds, while a 15-year-old weighed in at 400.

4   I would have called the case frivolous, except my dictionary defines frivolous lawsuits as "of little or no weight." Nevertheless, the story was enough to make me want to cross lawyers off my dinner party list. Who wants to be sued for serving cheesecake?

5   Now I'm not so sure. I think the lawyers have made their point, if not their case.

6   Consider the toy in my hand. It comes with the Happy Meal at my neighborhood McDonald's. The yellow rattle has a safety warning on the plastic wrapper. But the nutritional information for this beginner meal—20 fat grams and 36 sugar grams—is nowhere to be seen. It is stashed under the counter and printed in agate that's off the eye chart.

7   Then there is the Mighty Kids meal, sold with a collection of Disney "Treasure Planet" toys. This newer, bigger, presumably "happier" meal for little kids totals around 1,160 calories. The Burger King version, dubbed the "Big Kids Meal," is marketed with a question for the 4-and-over eater: "Do you want to be a Big Kid?" It cheerfully supplies answers: "You Should." Indeed eat this often enough and you will.

8   A few facts? On any given day, one-quarter of Americans eat at a fast-food restaurant. In any given month, 90 percent of American children between the ages of 3 and 9 eat at a McDonald's.

9   They're not forcing hamburgers down open gullets. But if people have their share of personal responsibility for what they eat, is it really frivolous to expect some responsibility on the part of corporations for what and how they market? If parents are supposed to protect their little kids' health, is it really okay for Big Food to market and advertise in and around and over the heads of parents?

10   In a motion to dismiss the case, the lawyers for McDonald's wrote. "Every responsible person understands what is in products such as hamburgers and fries." They sound more than vaguely like all those tobacco moguls who righteously announced that "everyone knows" smoking is dangerous while they sent Joe Camel out on a recruiting mission.

11   Of course, food and tobacco are not the same, though some of the same lawyers who fought big tobacco have turned their sights to a big fat target. As Dick Daynard, head of Northeastern University's Tobacco Products Liability Project, says, "Nobody needs to smoke cigarettes unless they're hooked, but everyone needs food. And there's no such thing as secondhand eating."

12   But a deep, dark secret of the fast-food industry is that it makes most of its money from the people targeted as, ahem, "heavy users." Like the tobacco companies, says Daynard, "food companies have very sophisticated motivational people on their payroll to figure out how to get kids to use their product."

13   That's fine if there aren't any health problems associated with the product. But if fast food is good for you, how come Mickey D's took out an ad in France telling parents that kids shouldn't eat les hamburgers more than once a week?

14   I don't like to talk about the obesity epidemic; fat isn't exactly contagious. But today 61 percent of adults and 14 percent of adolescents from 12 to 19 are overweight, an increase of 300 percent over three decades.

15   That's not just a Big Mac mistake. Blame it on a sedentary lifestyle. Blame it on portion (out of) control, from candy bars on steroids to the bagels that ate New York. Blame it on schools selling soda pop in the hallway. If we are what we do and what we eat, we're potatoes: couched and fried.

16   I don't think the best lawyers in town can prove that the fast-food industry fattened its customers. But they may prove it fooled its customers. Especially the young ones.

17   Mark my words and label your lunch. This is just the beginning of a big, fat food fight.

Our second reading examines the food industry's response to public criticism and legal attacks like the one mentioned by Ellen Goodman. This piece, by journalist and author Dale Buss, first appeared in the *New York Times* on August 29, 2004.

Dale Buss
Is the Food Industry the Problem or the Solution?

1   Diet trends aren't just for adults anymore. A new obsession of America's food, beverage and restaurant companies is thwarting childhood obesity. With more nutritious products, healthier menus and new activity programs, the companies have begun a big push aimed at the youngest generation.

2   Frito-Lay is offering reduced-fat Doritos in school lunch rooms. Oscar Mayer has added apple sauce and other healthy choices to its Lunchables meal-kit line. Kraft has come out with a sugarless Kool-Aid that is being marketed in magazines like Diabetic Cooking and Diabetes Forecast.

3   Among restaurant chains, Wendy's has slipped orange slices into children's meals, and Denny's has made French fries much harder to find on its menu than new side dishes of fruits and vegetables.

4   And, this fall, Coca-Cola is helping finance a new after-school fitness program. "The big idea is to give kids education, motivation and access to ways to change," said Brock Leach, the chief innovations officer at PepsiCo, which owns Frito-Lay. "The food business can play a very constructive role in that, making these foods available to kids and marketing them in ways that make a healthier lifestyle more attractive."

5   For decades, of course, the industry has been known for serving up sugary or fat-laden products, promoted with ceaseless advertising. And despite all the new, healthier options, that will not change. "If they stop, their competitors are right there and will fill the void," said Dr. Walter Willett, chief of the nutrition department at the Harvard School of Public Health.

6   Critics say these companies are taking a new direction only to escape or mitigate possible court verdicts that could blame the food industry for the fact that about 15 percent of American youth now are plumper than they should be, more than double the proportion of 25 years ago. "There are hordes of lawyers looking at the industry's marketing practices in a way that's never happened before," said Marion Nestle, a nutrition professor at New York University.

7   Food, drink and restaurant executives are quick to place blame on video games, television watching and the recent decline of physical education programs in schools.

8   "Blaming industry is not going to get us any closer to a solution," said Richard Martin, a spokesman for the Grocery Manufacturers of America. "The only way to get there is to work collaboratively, not by pointing fingers."

9   Even more important, according to nutritionists and child psychologists, is the confounding truth that parents—whether distracted, oblivious or both—are ultimately to blame for what their children eat. "Parents were created for that function," said Dan Jaffe, executive vice president for government relations at the Association of National Advertisers, an organization based in Washington whose members include food companies. "I don't know of any little child who jumps in the car and drives to a supermarket and buys their own food."

10   So the industry is trying to shake up both generations. Subway restaurants, for example, have new 30-second commercials, aimed at adults, that highlight the weight-loss success stories of three real children. The $20 million national campaign does not mention Subway products and refers to the chain primarily with shots of the children with Jared Fogle, who lost 250 pounds while eating mostly Subway sandwiches.

11   But there were obstacles along the way for Subway, which is based in Milford, Conn. Critics inside the company found the background choral music too ponderous and reminiscent of political advertising, so the advertising agency Fallon Worldwide changed to a lighter, more inspirational tone. At first, the ads mentioned the actual number of pounds each youngster had shed, but officials of the American Heart Association, which was consulting on the project, balked and suggested that the spots focus more on the fact that the children felt better.

12   Then standards executives at two networks refused at first to broadcast the ads. "They felt as though Jared represented an extreme weight loss and that we shouldn't teach kids that they needed to have an extreme loss like that," said Chris Carroll, senior vice president for marketing at Subway's franchise-marketing group. "I didn't think we should back off, though, because kids' obesity is a real issue. And we didn't." Instead, it added disclaimers that spelled out the complexity of children's weight loss.

13   Innovative Candy Concepts Inc., based in Atlanta, has gone further, replacing its entire main product line, Too Tarts, with a new brand called Too Tarts Smart Choice, which contains only fruit juice as sweeteners and up to 60 percent fewer calories than the original. The company's chief executive, Armand Hammer (not related to the oil company executive of the same name), said he was motivated in part by a twinge of guilt last year at distributing sugar-laden products to his own grandchildren.

14   "For us to make that kind of statement, we thought, was responsible and would be well accepted," said Mr. Hammer, whose company is donating 5 percent of net earnings from the new line to the American Diabetes Association. "And we were hoping that by doing so, we would make sort of a mission statement for the industry."

15   PepsiCo has also changed focus. Some 56 percent of the growth in its North American revenue in the first half of this year came from fare that PepsiCo defines as healthful, like Quaker Oats cereals, Gatorade sports drinks, Aquafina bottled waters and baked and reduced-fat Frito-Lay snacks. The company has started a program called Smart Spot, in which healthier products across all its brands carry a green logo.

16   Yet the way some critics see it, PepsiCo has a lot to change, considering the role that soft drinks and high-calorie salty snacks have played in childhood obesity. And while the practice has declined recently, they also note that some Pepsi bottlers still make big cash payments to win exclusive on-campus vending contracts from school districts that may be short on money.

17   Mr. Leach said Pepsi had embraced the idea that "it's in our interest for kids to be able to make sustainable health choices." Last year, Pepsi introduced 30 reduced-calorie products that are sold at schools, like SoBe Synergy, which is 50 percent fruit juice and has fewer calories than all-juice alternatives. The Quaker Oats division is test-marketing a flavored-milk product called Chillers that is sweetened without sugar and has vitamins and minerals added. Frito-Lay has reformulated its snack-food recipes to

eliminate nearly all trans-fats, which contribute to coronary problems like blocked arteries. And PepsiCo said it had placed 17,000 new Aquafina and Gatorade vending machines in schools last year.

18   Like Coca-Cola, Kraft, McDonald's and others, PepsiCo is also aiming to make children more active. Gatorade, for example, is working with the University of North Carolina on ideas that include simple things like promoting construction of more sidewalks where children can play. And PepsiCo has committed $2 million a year for three years to an in-school program beginning this fall called Balance First, whose goal is to have 2.5 million students eat 100 fewer calories each day and burn off 100 calories more, mainly through walking; several hundred elementary schools around the country have committed to introducing the program through science or health classes.

19   "The idea is to prevent kids from accumulating that excess one or two pounds each year," said James O. Hill, a professor at the health sciences center of the University of Colorado, who developed Balance First. "We can look at the industry as the enemy," he added, "but we're only going to change this problem with kids if we actually engage the private sector in helping."

20   Still, skeptics say all this can be a smokescreen for food, beverage and restaurant companies.

21   Their role first and foremost should be producing and promoting only healthy-as-possible kinds of foods, especially when it comes to children," said Dr. Willett of Harvard.

22   Even with the new products, it remains difficult for the industry to resist the profits offered by the status quo. As part of an effort called Kids Smart Eating that it introduced in June, Ruby Tuesday, a restaurant chain based in Maryville, Tenn., took grilled-cheese sandwiches and macaroni-and-cheese casserole off its new children's menu in favor of entrees like whole-grain tortillas with turkey and cheese.

23   But by mid-August—thanks to popular demand—grilled cheese and mac-and-cheese were back on the menu.

Our third reading, from the September 27, 2003, edition of the British medical journal the *Lancet,* looks beyond the food industry to architecture and city planning as a means to change our lifestyle and improve our health. The author of this piece, Marilynn Larkin, is a well-known journalist and contributing editor to the *Lancet.*

Marilynn Larkin
Can Cities Be Designed to Fight Obesity?

1   In the USA, one in three adults is obese—as are roughly one in seven children and adolescents—and Europeans are not far behind. Even China has seen the prevalence of overweight double in women and triple in men from 1989 to 1997.

2   According to research in the USA, we tend to put on weight gradually. Adults in one study, for example, added about 2 pounds (0.9 kg) a year from age 20 to 40 years. This means they were taking in an excess of only about 100 kcal of energy a day—suggesting that if people could be induced to eat just a little less—or to move around just a little more, it might be possible to prevent obesity. And not much activity would be required, according to a new US fitness campaign called America on the Move, which maintains that Americans could burn off the extra calories by taking only 2000 extra steps a day—about 15–20 min of walking. Sounds easy enough, but the problem, experts say, is that in many modern cities, cut by busy streets and roaring expressways, it can be difficult to find a place to walk.

3   "Many people do not have safe and easy access to activity-friendly environments", says Richard Killingsworth, director of Active Living by Design (http://www.activelivingbydesign.org), a programme of the University of North Carolina's School of Public Health and the Robert Wood Johnson Foundation looking at ways communities can be designed to encourage more physical activity. "In the USA, most communities have a transportation system that is built around the automobile. And so our research asks which elements will draw people outside and entice them to engage in physical activity: Is it sidewalks? Bikeways? Aesthetics? Traffic speed around them? Perception of crime? Weather? We're going to try to influence these variables to improve health outcomes."

4   The philosophy behind the programme, says Killingsworth, "is recognising that physical activity does not necessarily begin and end in the gym or fitness centre; it can be simple things such as gardening, walking instead of driving, and taking stairs instead of the elevator. Incorporating these activities into a daily routine can serve as a gateway to more vigorous activity." To accomplish

this, changes need to be made not just in thinking, but also in physical structures, he says.

5   "The idea is that as communities are built or rebuilt, the design standard is to build to the human scale, instead of to the automotive scale", he explains. An important step in this direction was taken in July, 2003, when the Pedestrian and Cyclists Equity Act was introduced in the US Congress. The bill would funnel US$350 million per year for 6 years to fund active-living strategies—building safe routes to schools, bicycle trails, and community demonstration projects that provide incentives for people to become more physically active.

6   Much of the impetus for such projects comes from a shift in thinking on the part of the US Centers for Disease Control and Prevention (CDC), says Marya Morris, head of the Planning and Designing the Physically Active Community project at the American Planning Association. "The CDC has realised over the past few years that individual interventions simply aren't getting people moving. And it turns out that a lot of the solutions city planners are looking at for solving 'sprawl'—scattered development that increases traffic and destroys open space—are also appropriate for solving issues related to physical activity. This convergence of priorities represents a remarriage of city planning and public health. Planners come at it with the imperative of solving congestion or lack of open-space issues, and health professionals are asking, 'what is it about these same patterns that are making people fat?'"

7   For the "remarriage" to work, city planners must recognise the need to partner with advocacy groups and city councils to push the agenda through on a public policy level, says Morris. "Physicians also need to shift away from an individualistic approach and ask what in the environment prevents people from incorporating activity into their daily lives and what changes can they recommend to policy makers to make the changes happen."

8   Demonstration projects in a variety of communities are under way. In New York City, Majora Carter, executive director of the Sustainable South Bronx project, is overseeing a feasibility study for a greenway that would extend along 5 miles of the area's shoreline, creating a public waterfront with cycling and walking paths and recreational activities.

9   The South Bronx, explains Carter, "is among the poorest districts in the USA, with a large minority population and some of the largest concentrations

of waste facilities, diesel trucks, and environmental burdens. Trees, green parks—you name it, and we don't have it. In terms of active living, it's not just the air quality that's dangerous, but also the streets themselves. When people are selling drugs on the street, it's hard to say, 'let's go out and play'."

10   A recent pilot project showed that the South Bronx waterway could be used for something other than waste facilities and industry, by creating a small park that has become a focal point of activity, notes Carter. "People do things because the doctor tells them to", she emphasises, and so her group is partnering with physicians at Montefiore Medical Center's Children's Hospital, as well as local schools, to ensure that young people, in particular, take advantage of the evolving waterfront.

11   At the other end of the spectrum, Helen Thompson, programme and research liaison in the Center for Human Nutrition (University of Colorado Health Sciences Center), is involved with Stapleton, a planned community near Denver being built from the ground up to support active living. Stapleton is located on 4700 acres of land where Denver's old airport used to be. "We're making it a learning lab and model community for health and active living", says Thompson.

12   The community now has about 1000 residents, although eventually there will be 20,000–30,000, plus another 30 000 people working in the area. Design plans call for smaller housing lots but with more parks, and open space and with shops, restaurants, theatres, and workplaces within walking distance of homes and apartments. Even now, with a handful of stores and a

Panel 1: UK and Australia already on the move

The UK and Australia are far ahead of the USA and already have several well-developed programmes for promoting fitness-friendly environments. The UK's Walking the Way to Health Initiative (http://www.whi.org.uk), which is a project of the British Heart Foundation and the Countryside Agency, is an example. "We started with the idea of pulling together information about health and the accessibility and availability of the countryside—everything from local green space, parks, and gardens to the wildest and remotest areas that we have in the UK", explains project coordinator Mitch Counsell. Pilot projects in the south of England "showed good returns in terms of people accessing the countryside. In addition, we had a great deal of feedback regarding social interaction benefits; aside from feeling better, people were getting out and meeting other people. One of the byproducts has been improvement in mental wellbeing."

Panel 2. Websites for the projects discussed in this feature

Active Living by Design: http://www.activelivingbydesign.org

American Planning Association: http://www.planning.org/physicallyactive

American on the Move: http://www.americaonthemove.org

National Recreation and Parks Association: http://www.nrpa.org

Walking the Way to Health: http://www.whi.org.uk

Stapleton: http://www.stapletondenver.com

Text of the Pedestrian and Cyclists Equity Act: http://www.house.gov/transportation_democrats/Of_Interest/030612_PACESummary.htm

town centre, "everything's accessible, and it's easy to walk or bike to do what you need to", says Thompson. About 80% of people now working in Stapleton use alternative modes of transportation, she says.

13   Karen Donato, coordinator of the US National Heart, Lung, and Blood Institute (NHLBI)'s Obesity Education Initiative, notes that many communities already have venues that are conducive to physical activity. "Many people aren't even aware of what might be available locally", says Donato, who works with Hearts n' Parks, an initiative of the NHLBI and the National Parks and Recreation Association. The programme recently reported results from written questionnaires given to children and adults in 36 sites ("magnet centers") regarding knowledge, behaviour, and attitudes towards healthy eating and physical activity before and after participating in a Hearts n' Parks programme. Participants improved on almost all indicators.

14   The initiative sets forth certain principles, and communities are free to implement suitable programmes. "Some are quite inventive", says Donato. "The Roswell, New Mexico, site had an alien chase. In Arizona, young people performed in a play that modelled what it feels like to be heavy and carry around a lot of weight, and what happens when they take off the pounds. In Nevada, we worked with the local university to implement a public health curriculum that involved students in a Hearts n' Parks internship." Gathering reliable data for outcomes measures is a challenge, says Donato. "These are nonprofessionals doing before-and-after outcomes studies against enormous odds—older people, for example, are reluctant to fill out anything and often have vision problems; children come in and out of the programme, and so they're not exposed every day." NHLBI ultimately developed scripts to help local health and activity personnel ask the right questions and gather as much reliable information on the effects of the programme as possible.

15   "Now that parks and recreation departments are being geared up to recognising their role in health, there's a receptivity that physicians can take advantage of," notes Donate. "We've seen studies showing that overweight people are not even told by their doctors that they have a problem, and that they need to do something about it. Now physicians can say, go to your park and recreation centre."

References

Anderson, C. L., & Nickols, S. Y. (2001). The essence of our being: A synopsis of the 2001 Commemorative Lecture. Journal of Family and Consumer Sciences, 93, 15–18.

Braet, C., Mervielde, I., & Vandereycken, W. (1997). Psychological aspects of childhood obesity: A controlled study in a clinical and nonclinical sample. Journal of Pediatric Psychology, 22, 59–71.

Bruce, G. M. (1993). Implementing a university campus wellness model. American Association of Occupational Health Nurses Journal, 41, 120–123.

Epstein, L. H. (1996). Family-based behavioural intervention for obese children. International Journal of Obesity and Related Metabolic Disorders, 20, S14–S21.

Composing Your Synthesis Essay

The main project of composing your synthesis essay is to move from the kernels of good ideas that you generated in your learning logs or personal reflection to the fully developed and logically organized discussion of these ideas.

Generating and Exploring Ideas

If you have speculated about, responded to, and explored your texts using the progression of learning logs, you should now have a body of ideas to use in the development of your synthesis essay. Your task in the production of your essay is to sort through, make decisions about, and pursue further both the analysis ideas and the synthesis ideas that you have generated.

If you did the learning logs, look again at your reflections. For the analysis part of your essay, identify the points in Learning Logs 2 and 3 that strike you as the most interesting, lively, profound, or significant. For the synthesis part of your essay, identify the points in Learning Logs 4 and 5 that you feel most excited about or interested in. In both cases, add new ideas generated by class discussion and further reflection.

Shaping and Drafting

Both focusing and organizing your ideas for a synthesis essay are challenging writing tasks. We offer some suggestions for formulating a thesis that will direct and hold together your essay. There are also several plans you can use for developing your essay.

Analysis section: About two-thirds of your essay should focus on analyzing the texts. This part of the body of your essay should compare and contrast what the texts claim and argue, how they frame the problem you are exploring, how they present different angles of vision, and where they intersect or differ in their perspectives or approaches. The analysis part of your essay should show how you have wallowed in the complexity of the texts. What do the authors of the texts do to make their readers think? How rhetorically effective are these texts? How and how well do the authors' examples and approaches support their theses and advance their views?

Synthesis section: About one-third of your essay should be your synthesis. Where do the texts and their authors leave you in your thinking? What have you discovered or realized after studying these texts? What new perspectives have you gained through the contrast and/or clash of different ideas? How much or how little have these texts changed your views and why?

Writing a Thesis for a Synthesis Essay

It is often difficult to write a one-sentence, high-level thesis statement for a synthesis essay that encompasses all your analysis and synthesis points. In such cases you can write two lower-level thesis statements—one for your analysis section and one for your synthesis section—and simply join them together. What is important is that your thesis forecasts your main analysis and synthesis points and creates a map for your reader. This is the strategy used by Kate at the end of her introduction:

For a full explanation of thesis statements, purpose statements, and mapping statements, see pp. 545–546.

KATE'S THESIS

Although both Turkle and Ritzer identify problems in technology's influence and in society's responses to it, Turkle sees more potential and gain where Ritzer sees mostly peril and loss. Both articles made me question how we define our values and morality in this postmodern, technologically advanced world and persuaded me of the need for caution in embracing technology.

Lower-level thesis for analysis

Lower-level thesis for synthesis

Your thesis statement should be clear, specific, focused, and risky. It should be the product of earnest intellectual work, insights achieved through serious reflection, and your own original connecting of ideas. Avoid noncontestable thesis statements such as "These articles have both good points and bad points." Try to formulate your thesis so that it challenges or surprises your reader.

See pp. 34–37 for a discussion of how to avoid unsurprising, noncontestable thesis statements.

Here are some more examples:

EXAMPLE 1

Whereas Ritzer focuses on the way high-tech society makes us homogeneous and superficial, Turkle focuses on how the Internet unsettles traditional views of the self. Although I agree with Ritzer's argument that McDonaldization is dehumanizing, I think that role-playing in MUDs is actually a healthy way to oppose McDonaldization and expresses human desire to be creative, to develop the self, and to make human connections.

Lower-level thesis for analysis

Lower-level thesis for synthesis

EXAMPLE 2

Ritzer's attack on technological society and Turkle's more optimistic belief that it offers opportunity for growth and discovery have together forced me to consider the superficiality and vulnerability of human relationships in our high-tech society.

Writer chooses high-level, one-sentence thesis rather than two lower-level theses

Possible Organizations for Synthesis Essays

The biggest organizational decision you have to make in writing a synthesis essay is how much to summarize your texts and how to incorporate these summaries into your essay. Your decision should be guided by your audience's familiarity with the texts you are discussing and the complexity of the points you are making.

PLAN 1

- Introductory paragraph that presents the focusing question and hooks the reader

- Summaries of the texts you are examining (unless your instructor posits that readers have already read the texts, in which case you can omit the summaries or reduce them to one or two sentences each)
- A thesis that maps out your main analytical points and your main synthesis points. Your thesis can come at the end of the paragraph(s) with your summaries or in a mini-paragraph of its own.
- Paragraphs discussing and developing your analytical points
- Synthesis section consisting of paragraphs discussing and developing your synthesis points
- Concluding paragraph that reiterates the values and limitations of the texts you have analyzed, pulls together your new insights, and leaves readers thinking about your views

PLAN 2

- Introductory paragraph that presents the focusing question and hooks the reader
- A thesis that maps out your main analytical points and your main synthesis points
- Summary and analysis of the first text
- Summary and analysis of the second text
- Synthesis section that develops several main synthesis points
- Concluding paragraph that reiterates the values and limitations of the texts you have analyzed, pulls together your new insights, and leaves readers thinking about your views

Revising

As you revise your synthesis essay, make sure that you have set up the focusing question effectively. Then work on clarifying and developing your analytical points while striving for an engaging style. Also consider how to make your synthesis views more clearly reflect your wrestling with the texts' ideas. Think about finding the most interesting ways to show how these texts have enlarged and deepened your own views on technology's effect on us. The following Guidelines for Peer Reviews can both help your peer reviewers and direct you as you think of ways to revise your paper.

GUIDELINES FOR PEER REVIEWS

Instructions for peer reviews are provided in Chapter 17 (pp. 519–520).

For the Writer
Prepare two or three questions you would like your peer reviewer to address while responding to your draft. The questions can focus on some aspect of your draft

that you are uncertain about, on one or more sections where you particularly seek help or advice, on some feature that you particularly like about your draft, or on some part you especially wrestled with. Write out your questions and give them to your peer reviewer along with your draft.

For the Reviewer

I. Read the draft at a normal reading speed from beginning to end. As you read, do the following:
  A. Place a wavy line in the margin next to any passages that you find confusing, that contain some idea or word that doesn't seem to fit, or that otherwise slow down your reading.
  B. Place a "Good!" in the margin next to any passages where you think the writing is particularly strong or interesting.

II. Read the draft again slowly and answer the following questions by writing brief explanations of your answers.
  A. Introduction and summaries of the texts:
    1. How could the introduction present the focusing question more powerfully, showing its significance, relevance, and problematic nature?
    2. How could the summaries be expanded or condensed to suit more closely the audience's knowledge of these texts? In other words, does this audience need longer or shorter summaries of the texts in order to understand the writer's analysis and synthesis?
    3. How could the placement of the summaries—in the introductory paragraph or woven into the analysis section of the paper—be improved?
    4. How could the summaries be made more accurate, fair, and clear?
    5. How could the thesis be made more focused, risky, and clear in setting up the writer's analytical and synthesis points?
  B. Analytical section of the essay:
    1. How could the analytical points more clearly compare and contrast the authors' values, assumptions, angles of vision, or rhetorical strategies in addressing the question of the problem of technology?
    2. What further textual evidence could the writer add to develop these analytical points and make them more interesting or comprehensive?
  C. Synthesis section of the essay:
    1. How could the writer's synthesis points more clearly demonstrate the writer's thoughtful interaction with these texts and with the question of technology's influence?
    2. What examples or other specifics could the writer include to develop these synthesis points more effectively?
    3. How could the writer conclude this essay more effectively to leave readers with a new perspective on the texts and on the underlying question?

III. Rhetorical considerations
  A. *Purpose, audience,* and *genre:* Your purpose is to write an academic paper that analyzes two or more texts and synthesizes its ideas. How effectively does this paper summarize and analyze these texts for an audience who

hasn't read them? Where does this draft do a good job at synthesizing ideas to show the writer's own original thinking? How effectively does this draft meet the genre expectations for an academic paper?

B. *Logos, ethos,* and *pathos:* How effectively does this draft present and develop its ideas? Where or how does the writer establish credibility as a thoughtful and knowledgeable person? How has the writer connected this analysis and synthesis with the values and interests of the audience?

IV. If the writer has prepared questions for you, respond to his or her inquiries.

V. Sum up what you see as the main strengths and problem areas of the draft:

A. Strengths

B. Problem areas

VI. Read the draft one more time. Place a check mark in the margin wherever you notice problems in grammar, spelling, or mechanics (one check mark per problem).

Writing a Classical Argument

About Classical Argument

The assignment for this chapter introduces you to a classical way of arguing in which you take a stand on an issue, offer reasons and evidence in support of your position, and summarize and respond to alternative views. Your goal is to persuade your audience, who can be initially perceived as either opposed to your position or undecided about it, to adopt your position or at least to regard it more openly or favorably.

The need for argument arises whenever members of a community disagree on an issue. Classical rhetoricians believed that the art of arguing was essential for good citizenship. If disputes can be resolved through exchange of perspectives, negotiation of differences, and flexible seeking of the best solutions to a problem, then nations won't have to resort to war or individuals to fisticuffs.

The study of argumentation involves two components: truth seeking and persuasion. By *truth seeking,* we mean a diligent, open-minded, and responsible search for the best course of action or solution to a problem, taking into account all the available information and alternative points of view. By *persuasion,* we mean the art of making a claim* on an issue and justifying it convincingly so that the audience's initial resistance to your position is overcome and they are moved toward your position.

These two components of argument seem paradoxically at odds: Truth seeking asks us to relax our certainties and be willing to change our views; persuasion asks us to be certain, to be committed to our claims, and to get others to change their views. We can overcome this paradox if we dispel two common but misleading views of argument. The most common view is that argument is a fight as in "I just got into a horrible argument with my roommate." This view of argument as a fist-waving, shouting match in which you ridicule anyone who disagrees with you (popularized by radio and television talk shows) entirely disregards argument as truth seeking, but it also misrepresents argument as persuasion because it polarizes people, rather than promoting understanding, new ways of seeing, and change.

Another common but misleading view is that argument is a pro/con debate modeled after high school or college debate matches or presidential debates. Although debating can be an excellent way to develop critical thinking skills, it misrepresents argument as a two-sided contest with winners and losers. Because controversial issues involve many different points of view, not just two, reducing

---

*By longstanding tradition, the thesis statement of an argument is often called its "claim."

an issue to pro/con positions distorts the complexity of the disagreement. Instead of thinking of *both* sides of an issue, we need to think of *all* sides. Equally trouble some, the debate image invites us to ask, "Who won the debate?" rather than "What is the best solution to the question that divides us?" The best solution might be a compromise between the two debaters or an undiscovered third position. The debate image tends to privilege the confident extremes in a controversy rather than the complex and muddled middle.

From our perspective, the best image for understanding argument is neither "fight" nor "debate" but the deliberations of a committee representing a wide spectrum of community voices charged with finding the best solution to a problem. From this perspective, argument is both a *process* and a *product*. As a process, argument is an act of inquiry characterized by fact finding, information gathering, and consideration of alternative points of view. As a product, it is someone's contribution to the conversation at any one moment—a turn taking in a conversation, a formal speech, or a written position paper such as the one you will write for this chapter. The goal of argument as process is truth seeking; the goal of argument as product is persuasion. When members of a diverse committee are willing to argue persuasively for their respective points of view but are simultaneously willing to listen to other points of view and to change or modify their positions in light of new information or better arguments, then both components of argument are fully in play.

We cannot overemphasize the importance of both truth seeking and persuasion to your professional and civic life. Truth seeking makes you an informed and judicious employee and a citizen who delays decisions until a full range of evidence and alternative views are aired and examined. Persuasion gives you the power to influence the world around you, whether through letters to the editor on political issues or through convincing position papers for professional life. Whenever an organization needs to make a major decision, those who can think flexibly and write persuasively can wield great influence.

Exploring Classical Argument

An effective way to appreciate argument as both truth seeking and persuasion is to address an issue that is new to you and then watch how your own views evolve. Your initial position will probably reflect what social scientists sometimes call your personal *ideology*—that is, a network of basic values, beliefs, and assumptions that tend to guide your view of the world. However, if you adopt a truth-seeking attitude, your initial position may evolve as the conversation progresses. In fact, the conversation may even cause changes in some of your basic beliefs, since ideologies aren't set in stone and since many of us have unresolved allegiance to competing ideologies that may be logically inconsistent (for example, a belief in freedom of speech combined with a belief that hate speech should be banned). In this exercise we ask you to keep track of how your views change and to note what causes the change.

The case we present for discussion involves ethical treatment of animals.

Situation: A bunch of starlings build nests in the attic of a family's house, gaining access to the attic through a torn vent screen. Soon the eggs hatch, and every morning at sunrise the family is awakened by the sound of birds squawking and wings beating against rafters as the starlings fly in and out of the house to feed the hatchlings. After losing considerable early morning sleep, the family repairs the screen. Unable to get in and out, the parent birds are unable to feed their young. The birds die within a day. Is this cruelty to animals?

1. Freewrite your initial response to this question. Was the family's act an instance of cruelty to animals (that is, was their act ethically justifiable or not)?
2. Working in small groups or as a whole class, share your freewrites and then try to reach a group consensus on the issue. During this conversation (argument as process), listen carefully to your classmates' views and note places where your own initial views begin to evolve.
3. So far we have framed this issue as an after-the-fact yes/no question: Is the family guilty of cruelty to animals? But we can also frame it as an open-ended, before-the-fact question: "What should the family have done about the starlings in the attic?" Suppose you are a family member discussing the starlings at dinner, prior to the decision to fix the vent screen. Make a list of your family's other options and try to reach class consensus on the two or three best alternative solutions.
4. At the end of the discussion, do another freewrite exploring how your ideas evolved during the discussion. What insights did you get about the twin components of argument, truth seeking and persuasion?

WRITING PROJECT

Write a position paper that takes a stand on a controversial issue. Your introduction should present your issue, provide background, and state the claim you intend to support. The body of your argument will summarize and respond to opposing views as well as present reasons and evidence in support of your own position. You need to choose whether to summarize and refute opposing views before or after you have made your own case. Try to end your essay with your strongest arguments.

We sometimes call this assignment an argument in the *classical style* because it is patterned after the persuasive speeches of ancient Greek and Roman orators. In the terms of ancient rhetoricians, the main parts of a persuasive speech are the *exordium,* in which the speaker gets the audience's attention; the *narratio,* which provides needed background; the *propositio,* the speaker's proposition or thesis; the *partitio,* a forecast of the main parts of the speech, equivalent to a blueprint statement; the *confirmatio,* the speaker's arguments in favor of the proposition; the *confutatio,* the refutation of opposing views; and the *peroratio,* the conclusion that sums up the argument, calls for action, and leaves a strong, lasting impression.

We cite these tongue-twisting Latin terms only to assure you that in writing a classical argument you are joining a time-honored tradition that links you to Roman senators on the capitol steps. From their discourse arose the ideal of a democratic society based on superior arguments rather than on superior weaponry. Although there are many other ways to persuade audiences, the classical approach is a particularly effective introduction to persuasive writing.

Understanding Classical Argument

Having introduced you to argument as both process and product, we now turn to the details of effective argumentation. To help orient you, we begin by describing the typical stages that mark students' growth as arguers.

Stages of Development: Your Growth as an Arguer

We have found that when we teach argument in our classes, students typically proceed through identifiable stages as their argumentative skills increase. While these stages may or may not describe your own development, they suggest the skills you should strive to acquire.

- *Stage 1: Argument as personal opinion.* At the beginning of instruction in argument, students typically express strong personal opinions but have trouble justifying their opinions with reasons and evidence and often create short, undeveloped arguments that are circular, lacking in evidence, and insulting to those who disagree. The following freewrite, written by a student first confronting the starling case (p. 393), illustrates this stage:

    The family shouldn't have killed the starlings because that is really wrong! I mean that act was disgusting. It makes me sick to think how so many people are just willing to kill something for no reason at all. How are these parents going to teach their children values if they just go out and kill little birds for no good reason?!! This whole family is what's wrong with America!

This writer's opinion is passionate and heartfelt, but it provides neither reasons nor evidence why someone else should hold the same opinion.

- *Stage 2: Argument structured as claim supported by one or more reasons.* This stage represents a quantum leap in argumentative skill because the writer can now produce a rational plan containing point sentences (the reasons) and particulars (the evidence). The writer who produced the previous freewrite later developed a structure like this:

The family's act constituted cruelty to animals

- because the starlings were doing minimal harm.
- because other options were available.
- because the way they killed the birds caused needless suffering.

- *Stage 3: Increased attention to truth seeking.* In stage 3 students become increasingly engaged with the complexity of the issue as they listen to their classmates' views, conduct research, and evaluate alternative perspectives and stances. They are often willing to change their positions when they see the power of other arguments.
- *Stage 4: Ability to articulate the unstated assumptions underlying their arguments.* As we show later in this chapter, each reason in a writer's argument is based on an assumption, value, or belief (often unstated) that the audience must accept if the argument is to be persuasive. Often the writer needs to state these assumptions explicitly and support them. At this stage students identify and analyze their own assumptions and those of their intended audiences. Students gain increased skill at accommodating alternative views through refutation or concession.
- *Stage 5: Ability to link an argument to the values and beliefs of the intended audience.* In this stage writers are increasingly able to link their arguments to their audience's values and beliefs and to adapt structure and tone to the resistance level of their audience. Writers also appreciate how delayed-thesis arguments or other psychological strategies can be more effective than closed-form arguments when addressing hostile audiences.

The rest of this chapter helps you progress through these stages. Although you can read the remainder in one sitting, we recommend that you break your reading into sections, going over the material slowly and applying it to your own ideas in progress. Let the chapter's concepts and explanations sink in gradually, and return to them periodically for review. This section on "Understanding Classical Argument" contains the chapter's key instructional material and comprises a compact but comprehensive course in argumentation.

Creating an Argument Frame: A Claim with Reasons

Somewhere in the writing process, whether early or late, you need to create a frame for your argument. This frame includes a clear question that focuses the argument, your claim, and one or more supporting reasons. Often your reasons, stated as *because* clauses, can be attached to your claim to provide a working thesis statement.

Finding an Arguable Issue
At the heart of any argument is an issue, which we can define as a question that invites more than one reasonable answer and thus leads to perplexity or disagreement. This requirement excludes disagreements based on personal tastes, where no shared criteria could be developed ("Baseball is more fun than soccer"). It also

excludes purely private questions because issues arise out of disagreements in communities. When you are thinking of issues, ask what questions are currently being contested in one of the communities to which you belong (your family, neighborhood, religious or social group, workplace, classroom, dormitory, campus, hometown, state, region, nation, and so forth).

Issue questions are often framed as yes/no choices, especially when they appear on ballots or in courtrooms: Should gay marriage be legalized? Should the city pass the new school bond proposal? Is this defendant guilty of armed robbery? Just as frequently, they can be framed openly, inviting many different possible answers: What should our city do about skateboarders in downtown pedestrian areas? How can children be kept from pornography on the Internet?

It is important to remember that framing an issue as a yes/no question does not mean that all points of view fall neatly into pro/con categories. Although citizens may be forced to vote yes or no on a proposed ballot initiative, they can support or oppose the initiative for a variety of reasons. Some may vote happily for the initiative, others vote for it only by holding their noses, and still others oppose it vehemently but for entirely different reasons. To argue effectively, you need to appreciate the wide range of perspectives from which people approach the yes/no choice.

How you frame your question necessarily affects the scope and shape of your argument itself. In our exploratory exercise we framed the starling question in two ways: (1) Was the family guilty of cruelty to animals? and (2) What should the family do about the starlings? Framed in the first way, your argument would have to develop criteria for "cruelty to animals" and then argue whether the family's actions met those criteria. Framed in the second way, you could argue for your own solution to the problem, ranging from doing nothing (waiting for the birds to grow up and leave, then fixing the screen) to climbing into the attic and drowning the birds so that their deaths are quick and painless. Or you could word the question in a broader, more philosophical way: When are humans justified in killing animals? Or you could focus on a subissue: When can an animal be labeled a "pest"?

For Writing and Discussion

1. Working individually, make a list of several communities that you belong to and then identify one or more questions currently being contested within those communities. (If you have trouble, get a copy of your local campus and city newspapers or an organizational newsletter; you'll quickly discover a wealth of contested issues.) Then share your list with classmates.

2. Pick two or three issues of particular interest to you, and try framing them in different ways: as broad or narrow questions, as open-ended or yes/no questions. Place several examples on the chalkboard for class discussion.

Stating a Claim

Your claim is the position you want to take on the issue. It is your brief, one-sentence answer to your issue question:

> The family was not ethically justified in killing the starlings.

> The city should build skateboarding areas with ramps in all city parks.

You will appreciate argument as truth seeking if you find that your claim evolves as you think more deeply about your issue and listen to alternative views. Be willing to rephrase your claim to soften it or refocus it or even to reverse it as you progress through the writing process.

Articulating Reasons

Your claim, which is the position you take on an issue, needs to be supported by reasons and evidence. A *reason* (sometimes called a "premise") is a subclaim that supports your main claim. In speaking or writing, a reason is usually linked to the claim with such connecting words as *because, therefore, so, consequently,* and *thus.* In planning your argument, a powerful strategy for developing reasons is to harness the grammatical power of the conjunction *because;* think of your reasons as *because* clauses attached to your claim. Formulating your reasons in this way allows you to create a thesis statement that breaks your argument into smaller parts, each part devoted to one of the reasons.*

Suppose, for example, that you are examining the issue "Should the government legalize hard drugs such as heroin and cocaine?" Here are several different points of view on this issue, each expressed as a claim with *because* clauses:

ONE VIEW

Cocaine and heroin should be legalized

- because legalizing drugs will keep the government out of people's private lives.
- because keeping these drugs illegal has the same negative effects on our society that alcohol prohibition did in the 1920s.

ANOTHER VIEW

Cocaine and heroin should be legalized

- because the subsequent elimination of the black market would cut down on muggings and robberies.

---

*The thesis statement for your essay could be your claim by itself or you could include in your thesis statement your main supporting reasons. For advice on how much of your supporting argument you should summarize in your thesis statement, see Chapter 18, pp. 545–546.

- because decriminalization would cut down on prison overcrowding and free police to concentrate on dangerous crime rather than on finding drug dealers.
- because elimination of underworld profits would change the economic structure of the underclass and promote shifts to socially productive jobs and careers.

STILL ANOTHER VIEW

The government should not legalize heroin and cocaine

- because doing so will lead to an increase in drug users.
- because doing so will send the message that it is okay to use hard drugs.

Although the yes/no framing of this question seems to reduce the issue to a two-position debate, many different value systems are at work here. The first pro-legalization argument, libertarian in perspective, values maximum individual freedom. The second argument—although it too supports legalization—takes a community perspective valuing the social benefits of eliminating the black market. In the same way, individuals could oppose legalization for a variety of reasons.

For Writing and Discussion

Working in small groups or as a whole class, generate a list of reasons for and against one or more of the following yes/no claims. State your reasons as *because* clauses. Think of as many *because* clauses as possible by imagining a wide variety of perspectives on the issue.

1. The school year for grades 1 through 12 should be lengthened to eleven months.
2. The war against terrorism requires Americans to relinquish some of their freedoms.
3. Women's fashion and style magazines (such as *Glamour* and *Seventeen*) are harmful influences on teenage females.
4. The United States should replace its income tax with a national sales tax.
5. Medical insurance should cover alternative medicine (massage therapy, acupuncture, herbal treatments, and so forth).

Articulating Unstated Assumptions

So far, we have focused on the frame of an argument as a claim supported with one or more reasons. Shortly, we will proceed to the flesh and muscle of an argument, which is the evidence you use to support your reasons. But before turning to evidence, we need to look at another crucial part of an argument's frame: its *unstated assumptions*.

What Do We Mean by an Unstated Assumption?

Every time you link together a claim with a reason, you make a silent assumption that may need to be articulated and examined. Consider this argument:

The family was justified in killing the starlings because starlings are pests.

To support this argument, the writer would first need to provide evidence that starlings are pests (examples of the damage they do and so forth). But the persuasiveness of the argument rests on the unstated assumption that it is okay to kill pests. If an audience doesn't agree with that assumption, then the argument flounders unless the writer articulates the assumption and defends it. The complete frame of the argument must therefore include the unstated assumption.

Claim: The family was justified in killing the starlings.

Reason: Because starlings are pests.

Unstated assumption: It is ethically justifiable to kill pests.

It is important to examine the unstated assumption behind any claim with reason *because you must determine whether your audience will accept that assumption. If not, you need to make it explicit and support it.* Think of the unstated assumption as a general principle, rule, belief, or value that connects the reason to the claim. It answers your reader's question, "Why, if I accept your reason, should I accept your claim?"

Here are a few more examples:

Claim with reason: Women should be allowed to join combat units because the image of women as combat soldiers would help society overcome gender stereotyping.

Unstated assumption: It is good to overcome gender stereotyping.

Claim with reason: The government should not legalize heroin and cocaine because doing so will lead to an increase in drug users.

Unstated assumption: It is bad to increase the number of drug users.

Claim with reason: The family was guilty of cruelty to animals in the starling case because less drastic means of solving the problem were available.

Unstated assumption: A person should choose the least drastic means to solve a problem.

For Writing and Discussion

Identify the unstated assumptions for each of the following claims with reasons.

1. Cocaine and heroin should be legalized because legalizing drugs will keep the government out of people's private lives.
2. The government should eliminate welfare payments to unwed mothers because doing so will reduce the illegitimacy rate.
3. The government is justified in detaining suspected terrorists indefinitely without charging them with a crime because doing so may prevent another terrorist attack.
4. We should strengthen the Endangered Species Act because doing so will preserve genetic diversity on the planet.

(continued)

5. The Endangered Species Act is too stringent because it severely damages the economy.

Using Toulmin Terminology to Describe an Argument's Structure

Our explanation of argument structure is influenced by the work of philosopher Stephen Toulmin, who viewed argumentation as a dynamic courtroom drama where opposing attorneys exchange arguments and cross-examinations before a judge and jury. The terms used by Toulmin to describe the structure of argument are widely accepted in rhetoric and composition studies and provide a handy vocabulary for discussing arguments. Toulmin called the unstated assumption behind a claim with reason the argument's *warrant,* based on our common word *warranty* for guarantee. If the audience accepts your warrant—that is, if they agree with your unstated assumption—then your argument is sound, or guaranteed. To put it another way, if your audience accepts your warrant, and if you can convince them that your reason is true, then they will accept your claim.

Besides the term *warrant,* Toulmin also uses the terms *grounds, backing, conditions of rebuttal,* and *qualifier.* We will explain these terms to you at the appropriate moments as we proceed.

Using Evidence Effectively

In Chapter 2 we showed you that the majority of words in a closed-form essay are particulars used to support points. If you think of reasons and warrants as the main points of your argument, then think of evidence as the supporting particulars. Each of your reasons needs to be supported by evidence. Toulmin's term for evidence in support of a reason is *grounds,* which we can think of as all the facts, data, testimony, statistics, subarguments, and other details a writer can find to support a reason. Toulmin calls the evidence and arguments used to support a warrant its *backing.* In this section we survey different kinds of evidence and show you how to incorporate that evidence into an argument, either as grounds to support a reason or as backing to support a warrant. Some arguments can be fleshed out with evidence based on your personal experience and observations. But most arguments require more formal evidence—the kind you gather from library or field research.

Part Four, "A Rhetorical Guide to Research," treats research writing in detail.

Kinds of Evidence

The kinds of evidence most often used for the grounds and backing are the following:

Examples.   An example from personal experience can often be used to support a reason. Here is how one student writer, arguing that her church building needs to be remodeled, used a personal example to support a reason.

Finally, Sacred Heart Church must be renovated immediately because the terrazzo floor that covers the entire church is very dangerous. Four Sundays ago, during 11:00 Mass, nine Eucharistic Ministers went up to the altar to prepare for distributing communion. As they carefully walked to their assigned post on the recently buffed terrazzo floor, a loud crash of crystal echoed through the church. A woman moving to her post slipped on the recently buffed floor, fell to the ground, hit her head on the marble, and was knocked unconscious. People rushed to her aid, thinking she was dead. Fortunately she was alive, only badly hurt. This woman was my mother.

Besides specific examples like this, writers sometimes invent hypothetical examples, or *scenarios,* to illustrate an issue or hypothesize about the consequences of an event. (Of course, you must tell your reader that the example or scenario is hypothetical.)

Summaries of Research.   Another common way to support an argument is to summarize research articles. Here is how a student writer, investigating whether menopausal women should use hormone replacement therapy to combat menopausal symptoms, used one of several research articles in her paper. The student began by summarizing research studies showing possible dangers of hormone replacement therapy. She then made the following argument:

> Another reason not to use hormone replacement therapy is that other means are available to ease menopausal symptoms such as hot flashes, irritability, mood changes, and sleep disturbance. One possible alternative treatment is acupuncture. One study (Cohen, Rousseau, & Carey, 2003) revealed that a randomly selected group of menopausal women receiving specially designed acupuncture treatment showed substantial decreases in menopausal symptoms as compared to a control group. What was particularly persuasive about this study was that both the experimental group and the control group received acupuncture, but the needle insertion sites for the experimental group were specifically targeted to relieve menopausal symptoms whereas the control group received acupuncture at sites used to promote general well-being. The researchers concluded that "acupuncture may be recommended as a safe and effective therapy for reducing menopausal hot flushes as well as contributing to the reduction in sleep disruptions" (p. 299).*

Statistics.   Another common form of evidence is statistics. Here is how one writer uses statistics to argue that the federal government should raise fuel-efficiency standards placed on auto manufacturers:

> There is very little need for most Americans to drive huge SUVs. One recent survey found that 87 percent of four-wheel-drive SUV owners had never taken their SUVs off-road (Yacobucci). . . . By raising fuel-efficiency standards, the government would force vehicle manufacturers to find a way to create more earth-friendly vehicles that would lower vehicle emissions and pollution. An article entitled "Update:

---

*This student is using the APA (American Psychological Association) style for documenting sources. At first mention of the article, the writer names the authors and the date of publication in parentheses. The page number for the quotation is placed in parentheses immediately after the closing quotation mark. Full bibliographic information about the article will be found in the "References" list at the end of the essay, alphabetized under the first author, "Cohen." See Chapter 22 for full explanations of how to use both the APA and the MLA (Modern Language Association) systems for citing and documenting sources.

What You Should Know Before Purchasing a New Vehicle" states that for every gallon of gasoline used by a vehicle, 20 to 28 pounds of carbon dioxide are released into the environment. This article further states that carbon dioxide emissions from automobiles are responsible for 20 percent of all carbon dioxide released into the atmosphere from human causes.*

Testimony.   Writers can also use expert testimony to bolster a case. The following passage from a student essay arguing in favor of therapeutic cloning uses testimony from a prominent physician and medical researcher. Part of the paragraph quotes this expert directly; another part paraphrases the expert's argument.

> As Dr. Gerald Fischbach, Executive Vice President for Health and Biomedical Sciences and Dean of Medicine at Columbia University, said in front of a United States Senate subcommittee: "New embryonic stem cell procedures could be vital in solving the persistent problem of a lack of genetically matched, qualified donors of organs and tissues that we face today." Along with organ regeneration, therapeutic cloning could potentially cure many diseases that currently have no cure. Fischbach goes on to say that this type of cloning could lead to the discovery of cures for diseases such as ALS, Parkinson's disease, Alzheimer's disease, diabetes, heart disease, cancer, and possibly others.†

Subarguments.   Sometimes writers support reasons not directly through data but through sequences of subarguments. Sometimes these subarguments develop a persuasive analogy, hypothesize about consequences, or simply advance the argument through a chain of connected points. In the following passage, taken from a philosophic article justifying torture under certain conditions, the author uses a subargument to support one of his main points—that a terrorist holding victims hostage has no "rights":

> There is an important difference between terrorists and their victims that should mute talk of the terrorist's "rights." The terrorist's victims are at risk unintentionally, not having asked to be endangered. But the terrorist knowingly initiated his actions. Unlike his victims, he volunteered for the risks of his deed. By threatening to kill for profit or idealism, he renounces civilized standards, and he can have no complaint if civilization tries to thwart him by whatever means necessary.

Rather than using direct empirical evidence, the author supports his point with a subargument showing how terrorists differ from victims and thus relinquish their claim to rights.

---

*This writer is using the MLA (Modern Language Association) style for documenting sources. The full bibliographic information about the off-road usage statistic will be found in the "Works Cited" list at the end of the paper alphabetized under "Yacobucci," the last name of the author of the article. The bibliographic information for the source of the carbon dioxide statistics will also be found in "Works Cited" alphabetized under "Update"—the first word of the article title. The writer cites the title rather than an author because the author is anonymous. See Chapter 22.

†This writer is also using the MLA style for documenting sources. Because there is no page number cited in parentheses for the direct quotation, the source is probably from a Web site. Readers will find an entry under "Fischbach" in the "Works Cited" list at the end of the essay. See Chapter 22.

Reliability of Evidence

When you use empirical evidence, you can increase its persuasiveness by monitoring its recency, relevance, impartiality, and sufficiency.

Recency. As much as possible, and especially if you are addressing current issues in science, technology, politics, or social trends, use the most recent evidence you can find.

Relevance. Ensure that the evidence you cite is relevant to the point you are making. For example, for many decades the medical profession offered advice about heart disease to their female patients based on studies of male patients. No matter how extensive or how recent those studies, some of their conclusions were bound to be irrelevant for female patients.

Impartiality. While all data must be interpreted and hence are never completely impartial, careful readers are aware of how easily data can be skewed. Newspapers, magazines, and journals often have political biases and different levels of respectability. Generally, evidence from peer-reviewed scholarly journals is more highly regarded than evidence from secondhand sources. Particularly problematic is information gathered from Internet Web sites, which can vary wildly in reliability and degree of bias.

Sufficiency. One of the most common reasoning fallacies is to make a sweeping generalization based on only one or two instances. The criterion of sufficiency (which means having enough examples to justify your point) helps you guard against hasty generalizations.

See pp. 628–631 for a discussion of political slant in the media and for advice on evaluating sources for reliability and bias. See pp. 631–642 for help on evaluating Web sites.

Addressing Objections and Counterarguments

Having looked at the frame of an argument (claim, reasons, and warrants) and at the kinds of evidence used to flesh out the frame, let's turn now to the important concern of anticipating and responding to objections and counterarguments. In this section, we show you an extended example of a student's anticipating and responding to a reader's objection. We then describe a planning schema that can help you anticipate objections and show you how to respond to counterarguments, either through refutation or concession. Finally, we show how your active imagining of alternative views can lead you to qualify your claim.

Anticipating Objections: An Extended Example

In our earlier discussions of the starling case, we saw how readers might object to the argument "The family was justified in killing the starlings because starlings are pests." What rankles these readers is the unstated assumption (warrant) that it is okay to kill pests. Imagine an objecting reader saying something like this:

It is *not* okay to get annoyed with a living creature, label it a "pest," and then kill it. This whole use of the term *pest* suggests that humans have the right to dominate nature. We need to have more reverence for nature. The ease with which the family solved their problem by killing living things sets a bad example for children. The family could have waited until fall and then fixed the screen.

Imagining such an objection might lead a writer to modify his or her claim. But if the writer remains committed to that claim, then he or she must develop a response. In the following example in which a student writer argues that it is okay to kill the starlings, note (1) how the writer uses evidence to show that starlings are pests; (2) how he summarizes a possible objection to his warrant; and (3) how he supports his warrant with backing.

STUDENT ARGUMENT DEFENDING REASON AND WARRANT

Claim with reason

The family was justified in killing the starlings because starlings are pests. Starlings are nonindigenous birds that drive out native species and multiply rapidly. When I searched "starlings and pests" on the Alta Vista search engine, I discovered 161 Web sites dealing with starlings as pests. Starlings are hated by farmers and gardeners because huge flocks of them devour newly planted seeds in spring as well as fruits and berries at harvest. A flock of starlings can devastate a cherry orchard in a few days. As invasive nesters, starlings can also damage attics by tearing up insulation and defecating on stored items. Many of the Web site articles focused on ways to kill off starling populations. In killing the starlings, the family was protecting its own property and reducing the population of these pests.

Evidence that starlings are pests

Summary of a possible objection

Many readers might object to my argument, saying that humans should have a reverence for nature and not quickly try to kill off any creature they label a pest. Further, these readers might say that even if starlings are pests, the family could have waited until fall to repair the attic or found some other means of protecting their property without having to kill the baby starlings. I too would have waited until fall if the birds in the attic had been swallows or some other native species without starlings' destructiveness and propensity for unchecked population growth. But starlings should be compared to rats or mice. We set traps for rodents because we know the damage they cause when they nest in walls and attics. We don't get sentimental trying to save the orphaned rat babies. In the same way, we are justified in eliminating starlings as soon as they begin infesting our houses. Think of them not as chirpy little songsters but as rats of the bird world.

Response to the objection

In the preceding example, we see how the writer uses grounds to support his reason and then, anticipating his readers' objection to his warrant, summarizes that objection and offers backing. One might not be convinced by the argument, but the writer has done a good job trying to support both the reason and the warrant.

Using a Planning Schema to Anticipate Objections

The arguing strategy used by the previous writer was triggered by his anticipation of objections—what Toulmin calls *conditions of rebuttal*. Under conditions of rebuttal, Toulmin asks arguers to imagine various ways skeptical readers might object to a writer's argument or specific conditions under which the argument might not hold. The Toulmin system lets us create a planning schema that can help writers develop a persuasive argument.

This schema encourages writers to articulate their argument frame (reason and warrant) and then to imagine what could be used for grounds (to support the reason) and backing (to support the warrant). Equally important, the schema encourages writers to anticipate counterarguments by imagining how skeptical readers might object to the writer's reason or warrant or both. To create the schema, simply make a chart headed by your claim with reason and then make slots for grounds, warrant, backing, and conditions of rebuttal. Then brainstorm ideas to put into each slot. Here is how another student writer used this schema to plan an argument on the starling case:

CLAIM WITH REASON

The family showed cruelty to animals because the way they killed the birds caused needless suffering.

GROUNDS

I've got to show how the birds suffered and also how the suffering was needless. The way of killing the birds caused the birds to suffer. The hatchlings starved to death, as did the parent birds if they were trapped inside the attic. Starvation is very slow and agonizing. The suffering was also needless since other means were available such as calling an exterminator who would remove the birds and either relocate them or kill them painlessly. If no other alternative was available, someone should have crawled into the attic and found a painless way to kill the birds.

WARRANT

If it is not necessary to kill an animal, then don't; if it is necessary, then the killing should be done in the least painful way possible.

BACKING

I've got to convince readers it is wrong to make an animal suffer if you don't have to. Humans have a natural antipathy to needless suffering—our feeling of unease if we imagine cattle or chickens caused to suffer for our food rather than being cleanly and quickly killed. If a horse is incurably wounded, we put it to sleep rather then let it suffer. We are morally obligated to cause the least pain possible.

CONDITIONS OF REBUTTAL

How could a reader object to my reason? A reader could say that killing the starlings did not cause suffering. Perhaps hatchling starlings don't feel pain of starvation and die very quickly. Perhaps a reader could object to my claim that other means were available: There is no other way to kill the starlings—impossibility of catching a bunch of adult starlings flying around an attic. Poison may cause just as much suffering. Cost of exterminator is prohibitive.

How could a reader object to my warrant? Perhaps the reader would say that my rule to cause the least pain possible does not apply to animal pests. In class, someone said that worrying about the baby starlings was sentimental. Laws of nature condemn millions of animals each year to death by starvation or by being eaten alive by other animals. Humans occasionally have to take their place within this tooth-and-claw natural system.

How many of the ideas from this schema would the writer use in her actual paper? That is a judgment call based on the writer's analysis of the audience. In every case, the writer should support the reason with evidence because supporting a claim with reasons and evidence is the minimal requirement of argument. But it is not necessary to state the warrant explicitly or provide backing for it unless the writer anticipates readers who doubt it.

The same rule of thumb applies to the need for summarizing and responding to objections and counterarguments: Let your analysis of audience be your guide. If we imagined the preceding argument aimed at readers who thought it was sentimental to worry about the suffering of animal pests, the writer should make her warrant explicit and back it up. Her task would be to convince readers that humans have ethical responsibilities that exclude them from tooth-and-claw morality.

For Writing and Discussion

Working individually or in small groups, create a planning schema for the following arguments. For each claim with reason: (a) imagine the kinds of evidence needed as grounds to support the reason; (b) identify the warrant; (c) imagine a strategy for supporting the warrant (backing); and (d) anticipate possible objections to the reason and to the warrant (conditions of rebuttal).

1. *Claim with reason*: We should buy a hybrid car rather than an SUV with a HEMI engine because doing so will help the world save oil. (Imagine this argument aimed at your significant other, who has his or her heart set on a huge HEMI-powered SUV.)
2. *Claim with reason*: Gay marriage should be legalized because doing so will promote faithful, monogamous relationships among lesbians and gay men. (Aim this argument at supporters of traditional marriage.)
3. *Claim with reason*: The government should eliminate welfare payments for unwed mothers because doing so would reduce the illegitimacy rate. (Imagine this argument aimed at liberals who support welfare payments to single mothers.)
4. *Claim with reason*: The war in Iraq was justified because it rid the world of a hideous and brutal dictator. (Aim this argument at a critic of the war.)

Responding to Objections, Counterarguments, and Alternative Views Through Refutation or Concession

We have seen how a writer needs to anticipate alternative views that give rise to objections and counterarguments. Surprisingly, one of the best ways to approach counterarguments is to summarize them fairly. Make your imagined reader's best case against your argument. By resisting the temptation to distort a counterargument, you demonstrate a willingness to consider the issue from all sides. Moreover, summarizing a counterargument reduces your reader's tendency to say, "Yes, but have you thought of . . .?" After you have summarized an objection or counterargument fairly and charitably, you must then decide how to respond to it. Your two main choices are to rebut it or concede to it.

Rebutting Opposing Views

When rebutting or refuting an argument, you can question the argument's reasons/grounds or warrant or both. In the following student example, the writer summarizes her classmates' objections to abstract art and then analyzes shortcomings in their reasons and grounds.

> Some of my classmates object to abstract art because it apparently takes no technical drawing talent. They feel that historically artists turned to abstract art because they lacked the technical drafting skills exhibited by Remington, Russell, and Rockwell. Therefore these abstract artists created an art form that anyone was capable of and that was less time consuming, and then they paraded it as artistic progress. But I object to the notion that these artists turned to abstraction because they could not do representative drawing. Many abstract artists, such as Picasso, were excellent draftsmen, and their early pieces show very realistic drawing skill. As his work matured, Picasso became more abstract in order to increase the expressive quality of his work. *Guernica* was meant as a protest against the bombing of that city by the Germans. To express the terror and suffering of the victims more vividly, he distorted the figures and presented them in a black and white journalistic manner. If he had used representational images and color—which he had the skill to do—much of the emotional content would have been lost and the piece probably would not have caused the demand for justice that it did.

Conceding to Counterarguments

In some cases, an alternative view can be very strong. If so, don't hide that view from your readers; summarize it and concede to it.

Making concessions to opposing views is not necessarily a sign of weakness; in many cases, a concession simply acknowledges that the issue is complex and that your position is tentative. In turn, a concession can enhance a reader's respect for you and invite the reader to follow your example and weigh the strengths of your own argument charitably. Writers typically concede to opposing views with transitional expressions such as the following:

admittedly	I must admit that	I agree that	granted
even though	I concede that	while it is true that	

After conceding to an opposing view, you should shift to a different field of values where your position is strong and then argue for those new values. For example, adversaries of drug legalization argue plausibly that legalizing drugs would increase the number of users and addicts. If you support legalization, here is how you might deal with this point without fatally damaging your own argument:

> Opponents of legalization claim—and rightly so—that legalization will lead to an increase in drug users and addicts. I wish this weren't so, but it is. Nevertheless, the other benefits of legalizing drugs—eliminating the black market, reducing street crime, and freeing up thousands of police from fighting the war on drugs—more than outweigh the social costs of increased drug use and addiction, especially if tax revenues from drug sales are plowed back into drug education and rehabilitation programs.

The writer concedes that legalization will increase addiction (one reason for opposing legalization) and that drug addiction is bad (the warrant for that reason). But then the writer redeems the case for legalization by shifting the argument to another field of values (the benefits of eliminating the black market, reducing crime, and so forth).

Qualifying Your Claim

The need to summarize and respond to alternative views lets the writer see an issue's complexity and appreciate that no one position has a total monopoly on the truth. Consequently, in the argument schema that we have adapted from Toulmin, there is one final term that is important to know: the *qualifier.* This term refers to words that limit the scope or force of a claim to make it less sweeping and therefore less vulnerable. Consider the difference between the sentences "After-school jobs are bad for teenagers" and "After-school jobs are often bad for teenagers." The first claim can be refuted by one counterexample of a teenager who benefited from an after-school job. Because the second claim admits exceptions, it is much harder to refute. Unless your argument is airtight, you will want to limit your claim with qualifiers such as the following:

perhaps	maybe
in many cases	generally
tentatively	sometimes
often	usually
probably	likely
may *or* might (*rather than* is)	

You can also qualify a claim with an opening *unless* clause ("*Unless* your apartment is well soundproofed, you should not buy such a powerful stereo system").

Appealing to *Ethos* and *Pathos*

When the classical rhetoricians examined ways that orators could persuade listeners, they focused on three kinds of proofs: *logos,* the appeal to reason; *ethos,* the appeal to the speaker's character; and *pathos,* the appeal to the emotions and the sympathetic imagination. We introduced you to these appeals in Chapter 4 (pp. 78–80) because they are important rhetorical considerations in any kind of writing. Understanding how arguments persuade through *logos, ethos,* and *pathos* is particularly helpful when your aim is persuasion. So far in this chapter we have focused on *logos.* In this section we examine *ethos* and *pathos.*

Appeal to *Ethos*

A powerful way to increase the persuasiveness of an argument is to gain your readers' trust. You appeal to *ethos* whenever you present yourself as credible and trustworthy. In Chapter 3 we discussed how readers develop an image of the writer—the writer's *persona*—based on features of the writer's prose. For most readers to accept your argument, they must perceive a persona that's knowledgeable, trustworthy, and fair. We suggest three ways to enhance your argument's *ethos:*

1. Demonstrate that you know your subject well. If you have personal experience with the subject, cite that experience. Reflect thoughtfully on your subject, citing research as well as personal experience, and accurately and carefully summarize a range of viewpoints.
2. Be fair to alternative points of view. Scorning an opposing view may occasionally win you favor with an audience predisposed toward your position, but it will offend others and hinder critical analysis. As a general rule, treating opposing views respectfully is the best strategy.
3. Build bridges toward your audience by grounding your argument in shared values and assumptions. Doing so will demonstrate your concern for your audience and enhance your trustworthiness. Moreover, rooting your argument in the audience's values and assumptions has a strong emotional appeal, as we explain in the next section.

Appeals to Pathos

Besides basing your argument on appeals to *logos* and *ethos,* you might also base it on an appeal to what the Greeks called *pathos.* Sometimes *pathos* is interpreted narrowly as an appeal to the emotions. This interpretation effectively devalues *pathos* because popular culture generally values reason above emotion. Although appeals to *pathos* can sometimes be irrational and irrelevant ("You can't give me a C! I need a B to get into medical school, and if I don't it'll break my ill grandmother's heart"), they can also arouse audience interest and deepen understanding of an argument's human dimensions. Here are some ways to use *pathos* in your arguments:

Use Vivid Language and Examples.   One way to create *pathos* is to use vivid language and powerful examples. If you are arguing in favor of homeless shelters, for example, you can humanize your appeal by describing one homeless person:

> He is huddled over the sewer grate, his feet wrapped in newspapers. He blows on his hands, then tucks them under his armpits and lies down on the sidewalk with his shoulders over the grate, his bed for the night.

But if you are arguing for tougher laws against panhandling, you might let your reader see the issue through the eyes of downtown shoppers intimidated by "ratty, urine-soaked derelicts drinking fortified wine from a shared sack."

Find Audience-Based Reasons.   The best way to think of *pathos* is not as an appeal to emotions but rather as an appeal to the audience's values and beliefs. With its emphasis on warrants, Toulmin's system of analysis naturally encourages this kind of appeal. For example, in engineer David Rockwood's argument against wind-generated power, Rockwood's final reason is that constructing wind-generation facilities will damage the environment. To environmentalists, this reason has

Rockwood's argument appears in Chapter 1, pp. 17–18.

emotional as well as rational power because its warrant ("Preserving the environment is good") appeals to their values. It is an example of an audience-based reason, which we can define simply as any reason whose warrant the audience already accepts and endorses. Such reasons, because they hook into the beliefs and values of the audience, appeal to *pathos*.

When you plan your argument, seek audience-based reasons whenever possible. Suppose, for example, that you are advocating the legalization of heroin and cocaine. If you know that your audience is concerned about their own safety in the streets, then you can argue that legalization of drugs will cut down on crime:

> We should legalize drugs because doing so will make our streets safer: It will cut down radically on street criminals seeking drug money, and it will free up narcotics police to focus on other kinds of crime.

If your audience is concerned about improving the quality of life for youths in inner cities, you might argue that legalization of drugs will lead to better lives for the current underclass:

> We should legalize drugs because doing so will eliminate the lure of drug trafficking that tempts so many inner-city youth away from honest jobs and into crime.

Or if your audience is concerned about high taxes and government debt, you might say:

> We should legalize drugs because doing so will help us balance federal and state budgets: It will decrease police and prison costs by decriminalizing narcotics; and it will eliminate the black market in drugs, allowing us to collect taxes on drug sales.

In each case, you move people toward your position by connecting your argument to their beliefs and values.

Some Advanced Considerations

You have now finished reading what we might call a "basic course in argumentation." In this final section, we briefly discuss some more advanced ideas about argumentation. Your instructor may want to expand on these in class, simply ask you to read them, or not assign this section at all. The three concepts we explore briefly are argument types, delayed-thesis and Rogerian arguments, and informal fallacies.

Argument Types

The advice we have given you so far in this chapter applies to any type of argument. However, scholars of argumentation have categorized arguments into several different types, each of which uses its own characteristic structures and ways of development. One way to talk about argument types is to divide them into truth issues and values issues.

Truth issues stem from questions about the way reality is (or was or will be). Unlike questions of fact, which can be proved or disproved by agreed-on empirical measures, issues of truth require interpretation of the facts. "Does Linda smoke an average of twenty or more cigarettes per day?" is a question of fact, answerable with a yes or a no. But "Why did Linda start smoking when she was fifteen?" is a question of truth with many possible answers. Was it because of cigarette advertising? Peer pressure? The dynamics of Linda's family? Dynamics in the culture (for example, white American youths are seven times more likely to smoke than are African-American youths)? Truth issues generally take one of the three following forms:

1. ***Definitional issues.*** Does this particular case fit into a particular category? (Is bungee jumping a "carnival ride" for purposes of state safety regulations? Is tobacco a "drug" and therefore under the jurisdiction of the Federal Drug Administration?)
2. ***Causal issues.*** What are the causes or consequences of this phenomenon? (Does the current welfare system encourage teenage pregnancy? Has the war in Iraq made America safer against terrorists?)
3. ***Resemblance or precedence issues.*** Is this phenomenon like or analogous to some other phenomenon? (Is U.S. involvement in Iraq like U.S. involvement in Vietnam? Is killing a starling like killing a rat?)

Rational arguments can involve disputes about values as well as truth. Family disagreements about what car to buy typically revolve around competing values: What is most important? Looks? Performance? Safety? Economy? Comfort? Dependability? Prestige? Similarly, many public issues ask people to choose among competing value systems: Whose values should be adopted in a given situation: Those of corporations or environmentalists? Of the fetus or the pregnant woman? Of owners or laborers? Of the individual or the state? Values issues usually fall in one of the following two categories:

1. ***Evaluation issues.*** How good is this particular member of its class? Is this action morally good or bad? (Was Ronald Reagan a great president? Which computer system best meets the company's needs? Is the death penalty morally wrong?)
2. ***Policy issues.*** Should we take this action? (Should Congress pass stricter gun control laws? Should health insurance policies cover eating disorders?)

See Chapter 15 for a fuller discussion of evaluation arguments and Chapter 16 for more on policy issues.

Delayed-Thesis and Rogerian Arguments

Classical arguments are usually closed form with the writer's thesis stated prominently at the end of the introduction. Classical argument works best for neutral audiences weighing all sides of an issue or for somewhat-opposed audiences who are willing to listen to other views. However, when you address a highly resistant audience, one where your point of view seems especially threatening to your audience's values and beliefs, classical argument can seem too blunt and aggressive. In such cases, a *delayed-thesis argument* works best. In such an argument you don't state your actual thesis until the conclusion. The body of the paper extends your sympathy to the reader's views, shows how troubling the issue is to you, and leads the reader gradually toward your position.

A special kind of delayed-thesis argument is called *Rogerian argument,* named after psychologist Carl Rogers, who specialized in helping people with widely divergent views learn to talk to each other. The principle of Rogerian communication is that listeners must show empathy toward each other's worldviews and make every attempt to build bridges toward each other. In planning a Rogerian argument, instead of asking, "What reasons and evidence will convince my reader to adopt my claim?", you ask, "What is it about my view that especially threatens my reader? How can I reduce this threat?" Using a Rogerian strategy, the writer summarizes the audience's point of view fairly and charitably, demonstrating the ability to listen and understand the audience's views. The writer then reduces the threat of his or her own position by showing how both writer and resistant audience share many basic values. The key to successful Rogerian argument, besides the art of listening, is the ability to point out areas of agreement between the writer's and the reader's positions. Then the writer seeks a compromise between the two views.

As an example, if you support a woman's right to choose abortion and you are arguing with someone completely opposed to abortion, you're unlikely to convert your reader, but you may reduce the level of resistance. You begin this process by summarizing your reader's position sympathetically, stressing your shared values. You might say, for example, that you also value babies; that you also are appalled by people who treat abortion as a form of birth control; that you also worry that the easy acceptance of abortion diminishes the value society places on human life; and that you also agree that accepting abortion lightly can lead to lack of sexual responsibility. Building bridges like these between you and your readers makes it more likely that they will listen to you when you present your own position.

Avoiding Informal Fallacies

Informal fallacies are instances of murky reasoning that can cloud an argument and lead to unsound conclusions. Because they can crop up unintentionally in anyone's writing, and because advertisers and hucksters often use them intentionally to deceive, it is a good idea to learn to recognize the more common fallacies.

Post Hoc, Ergo Propter Hoc (After This, Therefore Because of This).   This fallacy involves mistaking sequence for cause. Just because one event happens before another event doesn't mean the first event caused the second. The connection may be coincidental, or some unknown third event may have caused both of these events.

> **Example**   For years I suffered from agonizing abdominal itching. Then I tried Smith's pills. Almost overnight my abdominal itching ceased. Smith's pills work wonders.

Hasty Generalization.   Closely related to the *post hoc* fallacy is the hasty generalization, which refers to claims based on insufficient or unrepresentative data.

> **Example**   The food stamp program supports mostly freeloaders. Let me tell you about my worthless neighbor.

False Analogy.   Analogical arguments are tricky because there are, almost always, significant differences between the two things being compared. If the two things differ greatly, the analogy can mislead rather than clarify.

> **Example**   You can't force a kid to become a musician any more than you can force a tulip to become a rose.

Either/Or Reasoning.   This fallacy occurs when a complex, multisided issue is reduced to two positions without acknowledging the possibility of other alternatives.

> **Example**   Either you are pro-choice on abortion or you are against the advancement of women in our culture.

***Ad Hominem* ("Against the Person").**   When people can't find fault with an argument, they sometimes attack the arguer, substituting irrelevant assertions about that person's character for an analysis of the argument itself.

> **Example**   Don't pay any attention to Fulke's views on sexual harassment in the workplace. I just learned that he subscribes to *Playboy*.

Appeals to False Authority and Bandwagon Appeals.   These fallacies offer as support the fact that a famous person or "many people" already support it. Unless the supporters are themselves authorities in the field, their support is irrelevant.

> **Example**   Buy Freeble oil because Joe Quarterback always uses it in his fleet of cars.

> **Example**   How can abortion be wrong if millions of people support a woman's right to choose?

***Non Sequitur* ("It Does Not Follow").**   This fallacy occurs when there is no evident connection between a claim and its reason. Sometimes a *non sequitur* can be repaired by filling in gaps in the reasoning; at other times, the reasoning is simply fallacious.

> **Example**   I don't deserve a B for this course because I am a straight-A student.

Circular Reasoning.   This fallacy occurs when you state your claim and then, usually after rewording it, you state it again as your reason.

> **Example**   Marijuana is injurious to your health because it harms your body.

Red Herring.   This fallacy refers to the practice of raising an unrelated or irrelevant point deliberately to throw an audience offtrack. Politicians often employ this fallacy when they field questions from the public or press.

> **Example**   You raise a good question about my support of companies' outsourcing jobs to find cheaper labor. Let me tell you about my admiration for the productivity of the American worker.

Slippery Slope.   The slippery slope fallacy is based on the fear that one step in a direction we don't like inevitably leads to the next step with no stopping place.

> **Example**   If we allow embryonic stem cells to be used for medical research, we will open the door for full-scale reproductive cloning.

READINGS

Our first reading, by student writer Ross Taylor, aims to increase appreciation of paintball as a healthy sport. An avid paintballer, Ross was frustrated by how many of his friends and acquaintances didn't appreciate paintball and had numerous misconceptions about it. The following argument is aimed at those who don't understand the sport or condemn it for being dangerous and violent.

Ross Taylor (Student)
Paintball:
Promoter of Violence or Healthy Fun?

1   Glancing out from behind some cover, I see an enemy soldier on the move. I level my gun and start pinching off rounds. Hearing the incoming fire, he turns and starts to fire, but it is far too late. His entire body flinches when I land two torso shots, and he falls when I hit his leg. I duck back satisfied with another good kill on my record. I pop up this time again to scan for more enemy forces. Out of the corner of my eye I see some movement and turn to see two soldiers peeking out from behind a sewer pipe. I move to take cover again, but it's futile. I feel the hits come one by one hitting me three times in the chest and once on the right bicep before I fall behind the cover. I'm hit. It's all over—for me at least. The paintball battle rages on as I carefully leave the field to nurse my welts, which are already showing. Luckily, I watch my three remaining teammates trample the two enemy soldiers who shot me to win the game. This is paintball in all its splendor and glory.

2   Paintball is one of the most misunderstood and generally looked down upon recreational activities. People see it as rewarding violence and lacking the true characteristics of a healthy team sport like ultimate Frisbee, soccer, or pickup basketball. Largely the accusations directed at paintball are false because it is a positive recreational activity. Paintball is a fun, athletic, mentally challenging recreational activity that builds teamwork and releases tension.

3   Paintball was invented in the early 1980s as a casual activity for survival enthusiasts, but it has grown into a several hundred million dollar industry. It is, quite simply, an expanded version of tag. Players use a range of CO_2 powered guns that fire small biodegradable marbles of paint at approximately 250–300 feet per second. The result of a hit is a small splatter of oily paint and a nice dark bruise. Paintball is now played nationwide in indoor and outdoor arenas. Quite often variants are played such as "Capture the Flag" or "Assassination." In "Capture the Flag" the point is to retrieve the heavily guarded flag from the other team and return it to your base. The game of "Assassination" pits one team of "assassins" against the "secret service." The secret service men guard an unarmed player dubbed the "president." Their goal is get from point A to point B without the president's getting tagged.

Contrary to popular belief, the games are highly officiated and organized. There is always a referee present. Barrel plugs are required until just before a game begins and must be reinserted as soon as the game ends. No hostages may be taken. A player catching another off guard at close range must first give the player the opportunity to surrender. Most importantly there is no physical contact between players. Punching, pushing, or butt-ending with the gun is strictly prohibited. The result is an intense game that is relatively safe for all involved.

4   The activity of paintball is athletically challenging. There are numerous sprint and dives to avoid being hit. At the end of a game, typically lasting around 20 minutes, all the players are winded, sweaty, and ultimately exhilarated. The beginning of the game includes a mad dash for cover by both teams with heavy amounts of fire being exchanged. During the game, players execute numerous strategic moves to gain a tactical advantage, often including quick jumps, dives, rolls, and runs. While undercover, players crawl across broad stretches of playing field often still feeling their bruises from previous games. These physical feats culminate in an invigorating and physically challenging activity good for building muscles and coordination.

5   In addition to the athletic challenge, paintball provides strong mental challenge, mainly the need for constant strategizing. There are many strategic positioning methods. For example, the classic pincer move involves your team's outflanking an opponent from each side to eliminate his or her mobility and shelter. In the more sophisticated ladder technique, teammates take turns covering each other as the others move onward from cover to cover. Throughout the game, players' minds are constantly reeling as they calculate their positions and cover, their teammates' positions and cover, and their opponents' positions and strength. Finally, there is the strong competitive pull of the individual. It never fails to amaze me how much thought goes into one game.

6   Teamwork is also involved. Paintball takes a lot of cooperation. You need special hand signals to communicate with your teammates, and you have to coordinate, under rapidly changing situations, who is going to flank left or right, who is going to charge, and who is going to stay back to guard the flag station. The importance of teamwork in paintball explains why more and more businesses are taking their employees for a day of action with the intent of creating a closer knit and smooth-functioning workplace. The value of teamwork is highlighted on the Web site of a British Columbia facility, Action and Adventure Paintball, Ltd, which says that in paintball,

> as in any team sport, the team that communicates best usually wins. It's about thinking, not shooting. This is why Fortune 500 companies around the world take their employees to play paintball together.

An advantage of paintball for building company team spirit is that paintball teams, unlike teams in many other recreational sports, can blend very skilled and totally unskilled players. Women like paintball as much as men, and the game is open to people of any size, body type, and strength level. Since a game usually takes no more than seven to ten minutes, teams can run a series of different games with different players to have lots of different match-ups. Also families like to play paintball together.

7   People who object to paintball criticize its danger and violence. The game's supposed danger gets mentioned a lot. The public seems to have received the impression that paintball guns are simply eye-removing hardware. It is true that paintball can lead to eye injuries. An article by medical writer Cheryl Guttman in a trade magazine for ophthalmologists warns that eye injuries from paintball are on the rise. But the fact is that Guttman's article says that only 102 cases of eye injuries from paintballs were reported from 1985 to 2000 and that 85 percent of those injured were not wearing the required safety goggles. This is not to say that accidents don't happen. I personally had a friend lose an eye after inadvertently shooting himself in the eye from a very close range. The fact of the matter is that he made a mistake by looking down the barrel of a loaded gun and the trigger malfunctioned. Had he been more careful or worn the proper equipment, he most likely would have been fine. During my first organized paintball experience I was hit in the goggles by a very powerful gun and felt no pain. The only discomfort came from having to clean all the paint off my goggles after the game. When played properly, paintball is an incredibly safe sport.

8   The most powerful argument against paintball is that it is inherently violent and thus unhealthy. Critics claim paintball is simply an accepted form of promoting violence against other people. I have anti-war friends who think that paintball glorifies war. Many new parents today try to keep their kids from playing cops and robbers and won't buy them toy guns. These people see paintball as an upgraded and more violent version of the same antisocial games they don't want their children to play. Some people also point to the connections between paintball and violent video games where participants get their fun from "killing" other people. They link paintball to all the other violent activities that they think lead to such things as gangs or school shootings. But there is no connection between school shootings and paintball. As seen in Michael Moore's <u>Bowling for Columbine</u>, the killers involved there went bowling before the massacre; they didn't practice their aim by playing paintball.

9   What I am trying to say is that, yes, paintball is violent to a degree. After all, its whole point is to "kill" each other with guns. But I object to paintball's being considered a promotion of violence. Rather, I feel that it is a healthy release of tension. From my own personal experience, when playing the game, the players aren't focused on hurting the other players; they are focused on winning the game. At the end of the day, players are not full of violent urges, but just the opposite. They want to celebrate together as a team, just as do softball or soccer teams after a game. Therefore I don't think paintball is an unhealthy activity for adults. (The only reason I wouldn't include children is because I believe the pain is too intense for

them. I have seen some younger players cry after being shot.) Paintball is simply a game, a sport, that produces intense exhilaration and fun. Admittedly, paintball guns can be used in irresponsible manners. Recently there have been some drive-by paintballings, suggesting that paintball players are irresponsible and violent. However, the percentage of people who do this sort of prank is very small and those are the bad apples of the group. There will always be those who misuse equipment. For example, baseball bats have been used in atrocious beatings, but that doesn't make baseball a violent sport. So despite the bad apples, paintball is still a worthwhile activity when properly practiced.

10   Athletic and mentally challenging, team-building and fun—the game of paintball seems perfectly legitimate to me. It is admittedly violent, but it is not the evil activity that critics portray. Injuries can occur, but usually only when the proper safety equipment is not being used and proper precautions are ignored. As a great recreational activity, paintball deserves the same respect as other sports. It is a great way to get physical exercise, make friends, and have fun.

Thinking Critically about "Paintball: Promoter of Violence or Healthy Fun?"

1. Before reading this essay, what was your own view of paintball? To what extent did this argument create for you a more positive view of paintball? What aspects of the argument did you find particularly effective or ineffective?
2. How effective are Ross's appeals to *ethos* in this argument? Does he create a persona that you find trustworthy and compelling? How does he do so or fail to do so?
3. How effective are Ross's appeals to *pathos*? How does he appeal to his readers' values, interests, and emotions in trying to make paintball seem like an exhilarating team sport? To what extent does he show empathy with readers when he summarizes objections to paintball?
4. How effective are Ross's appeals to *logos*? How effective are Ross's reasons and evidence in support of his claim? How effective are Ross's responses to opposing views?
5. What are the main strengths and weaknesses of Ross's argument?

Our second reading is a political cartoon commenting on the USA Patriot Act. Entitled "Patriots" by its creator, Clay Bennett, this cartoon joins the civic debate over the clash between freedom versus security following the September 11, 2001, terrorist attacks on the World Trade Center and the Pentagon. Clay Bennett joined the staff of *The Christian Science Monitor* in 1998. He produces five full-color print cartoons each week and also creates fully animated cartoons for the Internet. He is a 1980 graduate of North Alabama University, where he majored in art and history.

We use this cartoon to introduce two arguments about the Patriot Act: a speech supporting the Patriot Act by former Attorney General John Ashcroft and an article opposing it by libertarian James Bovard. The Patriot Act was quickly enacted with bipartisan legislative approval in the months following the September 11 attacks. The title—USA PATRIOT ACT—is an acronym for "Uniting and Strengthening America by Providing Appropriate Tools Required to Intercept and Obstruct Terrorism." According to the Justice Department, the Act improves the government's ability to fight terrorism by providing better surveillance techniques that don't tip off suspected terrorists; by allowing different government agencies to share information; by allowing easier procedures for obtaining warrants to access business, library, and personal records of suspected terrorists; and by providing harsher penalties for terrorists or those who harbor terrorists. Critics of the Patriot Act say that these powers infringe on the rights of law-abiding citizens in sinister ways. For arguments in support of the Patriot Act, see the Justice Department's Web site, *Preserving Life and Liberty,* at http://www. lifeandliberty.gov/. For a good introduction to criticisms of the Patriot Act, see the "Safe and Free" link on the Web site of the American Civil Liberties Union, http://www.aclu.org/SafeandFree/SafeandFreeMain.cfm.

Clay Bennett
Patriots

Thinking Critically about "Patriots"

1. What is this cartoon's argument or thesis?
2. Clay Bennett has drawn other cartoons critical of the Patriot Act. One of his animated cartoons simply has the words "USA PATRIOT ACT" written in large, bold letters across the page. But he has converted the "O" in "PATRIOT" into a peephole through which a huge unblinking eyeball slowly scans its field of vision. Reflected in the pupil of the spying eyeball is the seal of the U.S. Department of Justice. (You can see this cartoon at http://www.claybennett.com/pages/peephole.html.) In what ways are cartoons like these effective political arguments? Compare the effect of a political cartoon to a roughly equivalent written text that makes the same claim. How does visual argument differ from verbal argument in its impact on an audience?

Our next reading is the text of a speech delivered by former Attorney General John Ashcroft to the Federalist Society National Convention on November 15, 2003. According to its Web site, the Federalist Society, founded in 1982, "is a group of conservatives and libertarians dedicated to reforming the current legal order. We are committed to the principles that the state exists to preserve freedom, that the separation of governmental powers is central to our Constitution, and that it is emphatically the province and duty of the judiciary to say what the law is, not what it should be." Ashcroft's speech, which was posted on a special Justice Department Web site defending the Patriot Act (http://www.lifeandliberty.gov/), presents his passionate defense of the Act's purpose, goals, and legal provisions.

John Ashcroft
Prepared Remarks of Attorney General Ashcroft at the Federalist Society National Convention

1   Thank you for the invitation to join you here this morning, I would like to know when the Federalist Society began keeping farmers' hours. I mean, a speech at 8 AM on a Saturday?

2   When your friends at the American Constitution Society for Law and Policy held their inaugural event, they let Janet Reno speak at a far more civilized hour. How do you expect me to do this *and* be fresh for tonight's John Ashcroft Dance Party?

3   I do appreciate your invitation to speak to you this morning. The Federalist Society and its membership have been resolute defenders of our nation's founding ideals: liberty, the rule of law, limited government. It is in this capacity that the Federalist Society is so necessary today.

4   For the past two years, you have been part of the debate about how best to preserve and protect our liberty in the face of a very real terrorist threat.

5   America has an honored tradition of debate and dissent under the First Amendment. It is an essential piece of our constitutional and cultural fabric. As a former politician, I have heard a few dissents in my time, and even expressed a couple of my own.

6   The Founders believed debate should enlighten, not just enliven. It should reveal truth, not obscure it. The future of freedom demands that our discourse be based on a solid foundation of facts and a sincere desire for truth. As we consider the direction and destiny of our nation, the friends of freedom must practice for themselves . . . and demand from others . . . a debate informed by fact and directed toward truth.

7   Take away all the bells and whistles . . . the rhetorical flourishes and occasional vitriol . . . and the current debate about liberty is about the rule of law and the *role* of law.

8   The notion that the law can enhance, not diminish, freedom is an old one. John Locke said the end of law is, quote, ". . . not to abolish or restrain but to preserve and enlarge freedom." George Washington called this, "ordered liberty."

9   There are some voices in this discussion of how best to preserve freedom that reject the idea that law can enhance freedom. They think that passage and enforcement of any law is necessarily an infringement of liberty.

10   Ordered liberty is the reason that we are the most open and the most secure society in the world. Ordered liberty is a guiding principle, not a stumbling block to security.

11   When the first societies passed and enforced the first laws against murder, theft and rape, the men and women of those societies unquestionably were made more free.

12   A test of a law, then, is this: does it honor or degrade liberty? Does it enhance or diminish freedom?

13   The Founders provided the mechanism to protect our liberties and preserve the safety and security of the Republic: the Constitution. It is a document that safeguards security, but not at the expense of freedom. It celebrates freedom, but not at the expense of security. It protects us *and* our way of life.

14   Since September 11, 2001, the Department of Justice has fought for, Congress has created, and the judiciary has upheld, legal tools that honor the Constitution . . . legal tools that are making America safer while enhancing American freedom.

15   It is a compliment to all who worked on the Patriot Act to say that it is not constitutionally innovative. The Act uses court-tested safeguards and time-honored ideas to aid the war against terrorism, while protecting the rights and lives of citizens.

16   Madison noted in 1792 that the greatest threat to our liberty was centralized power. Such focused power, he wrote, is liable to abuse. That is why he concluded a distribution of power into separate departments is a first principle of free governments.

17   The Patriot Act honors Madison's "first principles" . . . giving each branch of government a role in ensuring both the lives and liberties of our citizens are protected. The Patriot Act grants the executive branch critical tools in the war on terrorism. It provides the legislative branch extensive oversight. It honors the judicial branch with court supervision over the Act's most important powers.

18   First, the executive branch.

19   At the Department of Justice, we are dedicated to detecting, disrupting, and dismantling the networks of terror before they can strike at our nation. In the past two years, no major terrorist attack has been perpetrated on our soil.

20   Consider the bloodshed by terrorism elsewhere in that time:

- Women and children slaughtered in Jerusalem;
- Innocent, young lives snuffed out in Indonesia;
- Saudi citizens savaged in Riyadh;
- Churchgoers in Pakistan murdered by the hands of hate.

21   We are using the tough tools provided in the USA Patriot Act to defend American lives and liberty from those who have shed blood and decimated lives in other parts of the world.

22   The Patriot Act does three things:

23   *First,* it closes the gaping holes in law enforcement's ability to collect vital intelligence information on terrorist enterprises. It allows law enforcement to use proven tactics long used in the fight against organized crime and drug dealers.

24   *Second,* the Patriot Act updates our anti-terrorism laws to meet the challenges of new technology and new threats.

25   *Third,* with these critical new investigative tools provided by the Patriot Act, law enforcement can share information and cooperate better with each other. From prosecutors to intelligence agents, the Act allows law enforcement to "connect the dots" and uncover terrorist plots before they are launched.

26   Here is an example of how we use the Act. Some of you are familiar with the Iyman Faris case. He is a naturalized American citizen who worked as a truck driver out of Columbus, Ohio.

27   Using information sharing allowed under the Patriot Act, law enforcement pieced together Faris's activities:

- How Faris met senior Al Qaeda operatives in a training camp in Afghanistan.
- How he was asked to procure equipment that might cause train derailments and sever suspension systems of bridges.
- How he traveled to New York to scout a potential terrorist target.

28   Faris pleaded guilty on May 1, 2003, and on October 28, he was sentenced under the Patriot Act's tough sentences. He will serve 20 years in prison for

providing material support to Al Qaeda and conspiracy for providing the terrorist organization with information about possible U.S. targets for attack.

29   The Faris case illustrates what the Patriot Act does. One thing the Patriot Act does not do is allow the investigation of individuals, quote, ". . . solely upon the basis of activities protected by the first amendment to the Constitution of the United States."

30   Even if the law did not prohibit it, the Justice Department has neither the time nor the inclination to delve into the reading habits or other First Amendment activities of our citizens.

31   Despite all the hoopla to the contrary, for example, the Patriot Act . . . which allows for court-approved requests for business records, including library records . . . has never been used to obtain records from a library. Not once.

32   Senator Dianne Feinstein recently said, quote, "I have never had a single abuse of the Patriot Act reported to me. My staff e-mailed the ACLU and asked them for instances of actual abuses. They e-mailed back and said they had none."

33   The Patriot Act has enabled us to make quiet, steady progress in the war on terror.

34   Since September 11, we have dismantled terrorist cells in Detroit, Seattle, Portland, Tampa, Northern Virginia, and Buffalo.

35   We have disrupted weapons procurement plots in Miami, San Diego, Newark, and Houston.

36   We have shut down terrorist-affiliated charities in Chicago, Dallas and Syracuse.

37   We have brought criminal charges against 286 individuals. We have secured convictions or guilty pleas from 155 people.

38   Terrorists who are incarcerated, deported or otherwise neutralized threaten fewer American lives. For two years, our citizens have been safe. There have been no major terrorist attacks on our soil. American freedom has been enhanced, not diminished. The Constitution has been honored, not degraded.

39   Second, the role Congress plays.

40   In six weeks of debate in September and October of 2001, both the House of Representatives and the Senate examined studiously and debated vigorously the merits of the Patriot Act. In the end, both houses supported overwhelmingly its passage.

41   Congress built into the Patriot Act strict and structured oversight of the Executive Branch. Every six months, the Justice Department provides Congress with reports of its activities under the Patriot Act.

42   Since September 24, 2001, Justice Department officials, myself included, have testified on the Patriot Act and other homeland security issues more than 115 times. We have responded to hundreds of written and oral questions and provided reams of written responses.

43   To date, no congressional committee has found any evidence that law enforcement has abused the powers provided by the Patriot Act.

44   Legislative oversight of the executive branch is critical to "ordered liberty." It ensures that laws and those who administer them respect the rights and liberties of the citizens.

45   There has not been a major terrorist attack within our borders in the past two years. Time and again, Congress has found the Patriot Act to be effective against terrorist threats, and respectful and protective of citizens' liberties. The Constitution has been honored, not degraded.

46   Finally, the judiciary.

47   The Patriot Act provides for close judicial supervision of the executive branch's use of Patriot Act authorities.

48   The Act allows the government to utilize many long-standing, well-accepted law enforcement tools in the fight against terror. These tools include delayed notification, judicially-supervised searches, and so-called roving wiretaps, which have long been used in combating organized crime and in the war on drugs.

49   In using these tactics to fight terrorism, the Patriot Act includes an *additional* layer of protection for individual liberty. A federal judge supervises the use of each of these tactics.

50   Were we to seek an order to request business records, that order would need the approval of a federal judge. Grand jury subpoenas issued for similar requests by police in standard criminal investigations are issued without judicial oversight.

51   Throughout the Patriot Act, tools provided to fight terrorism require that the same predication be established before a federal judge as with similar tools provided to fight other crime.

52   In addition, the Patriot Act includes yet *another* layer of judicial scrutiny by providing a civil remedy in the event of abuse. Section 223 of the Patriot Act allows citizens to seek monetary damages for willful violations of the Patriot Act. This civil remedy serves as a further deterrent against infringement upon individual liberties.

53   Given our overly litigious society, you are probably wondering how many such civil cases have been filed to date. It is a figure as astronomical as the library searches. Zero.

54   There is a simple reason for this . . . the Patriot has *not* been used to infringe upon individual liberty.

55   Many of you have heard the hue and cry from critics of the Patriot Act who allege that liberty has been eroded. But more telling is what you have not heard. You have not heard of one single case in which a judge has found an abuse of the Patriot Act because, again, *there have been no abuses.*

56   It is also important to consider what we have not *seen* . . . no major terrorist attacks on our soil over the past two years.

57   The Patriot Act's record demonstrates that we are protecting the American people while honoring the Constitution and preserving the liberties we hold dear.

58   While we are discussing the judiciary, allow me to add one more point. To be at its best, the judiciary requires a full bench. This is not like football or basketball, where the bench consists of reserves who might not see action. The judicial bench, to operate best for the people, must be at full strength.

59   Let me say this . . . President Bush has performed his duties admirably in selecting and nominating highly qualified jurists to serve.

60   The language in a judge's commission reads, and I quote, "George W. Bush, President of the United States of America . . . to all who shall see this, presents greeting: Know ye that reposing special confidence and trust in the wisdom, uprightness and learning, I have nominated . . .", you can fill in the blank, with the name Janice Rogers Brown, or Bill Pryor, or Priscilla Owen, or Carolyn Kuhl [Cool].

61   The commission's language may seem anachronistic. The ideals the men and women of the bench must uphold are not: Wisdom. Uprightness. Learning.

62   The president's nominees personify those noble ideals. They are proven defenders of the rule of law. They should be treated fairly. They deserve to be treated with the dignity that befits the position to which they seek to serve our country and its citizens.

63   You may think that some of the best of the president's nominees are being treated unfairly. In that case, *you* may want to exercise *your* right to dissent. The future of freedom and the rule of law depend on citizens informed by fact and directed toward truth.

64   To be sure, the law depends on the integrity of those who make it, enforce it, and apply it. It depends on the moral courage of lawyers like you . . . and our citizens . . . to insist on being heard, whether in town hall meetings, county council meetings, or the Senate.

65   There is nothing more noble than fighting to preserve our God-given rights. Our proven tactics against the terrorist threat are helping to do just that.

66   For more than two years, we have protected the lives of our citizens here at home. Again and again, Congress has determined and the courts have determined that our citizens' rights have been respected.

67   Twenty-six months ago, terrorists attacked our nation thinking our liberties were our weakness. They were wrong. The American people have fulfilled the destiny shaped by our forefathers and founders, and revealed the power of freedom.

68   Time and again, the spirit of our nation has been renewed and our greatness as a people has been strengthened by our dedication to the cause of liberty, the rule of law and the primacy and dignity of the individual.

69   I know we will keep alive these noble aspirations that lie in the hearts of all our fellow citizens, and for which our young men and women are at this moment fighting and making the ultimate sacrifice.

70   What we are defending is what generations before us fought for and defended: a nation that is a standard, a beacon, to all who desire a land that promises to uphold the best hopes of all mankind. A land of justice. A land of liberty.

71   Thank you. God bless you. And God bless America.

Thinking Critically about "Prepared Remarks of Attorney General Ashcroft at the Federalist Society National Convention"

1. What do you think Ashcroft means by "ordered liberty"? Why would "ordered liberty" be a phrase particularly valued by the conservative and libertarian Federalist Society? How does the USA Patriot Act, in Ashcroft's view, increase liberty ("enhance freedom") by preserving order? (Note that critics of the Patriot Act believe it diminishes liberty.)

2. As a conservative and a strict constructionist in settling constitutional issues, John Ashcroft comes to the Federalist Society with a positive reputation and strong credentials that appeal to Federalist Society values—unlike, for example, his predecessor, Janet Reno, who was Attorney General under former President Clinton. How does Ashcroft further enhance his standing with the Federalist Society through appeals to *ethos*? As one example, how does he establish rapport with this group through the joke about Janet Reno and the reference to a "John Ashcroft Dance Party"? Why later in the speech does he point out that the Patriot Act is "not constitutionally innovative"?

3. How does Ashcroft make appeals to *pathos*? Consider his use of examples, references, and word choices that particularly resonate with the values and beliefs of Federalist Society members. Point to specific passages in the speech.

4. How effective do you find Ashcroft's appeals to *logos*? What reasons and evidence does he provide to argue that the Patriot Act has been effective in fighting terrorism? What reasons and evidence does he provide to argue that the Patriot Act doesn't degrade the liberties of American citizens?

5. One way to construct the angle of vision of any document is to ask, "What is not being said here? What is being omitted or censored?" Ashcroft refers to "all the hoopla" being raised by critics of the Patriot Act, but he doesn't refer specifically to any of the arguments such persons might make against the Act. From what you have heard about the way suspected terrorists are treated, what does Ashcroft try to keep invisible in this speech? (Note: You might return to this question after you have finished the next reading.)

For a discussion of angle of vision see Chapter 4, pp. 80–85.

6. At the end of his talk, Ashcroft switches topics briefly to complain about the way Congress is holding up the confirmations of President Bush's appointments

to federal court positions. Try doing an Internet search on any one of the nominees mentioned by Ashcroft to see what objections to Bush's judicial appointments were being made by liberal members of Congress at the time of this speech (November 2003).

Our next reading, by libertarian James Bovard, takes a position on the USA Patriot Act very different from that of former Attorney General John Ashcroft. Although conservatives and libertarians are often closely allied (see the description of the Federalist Society in our headnote to Ashcroft's speech), Bovard here departs company with Ashcroft in significant ways. Bovard serves as a policy advisor to the Future of Freedom Foundation, whose mission, as stated on its Web site, is "to advance freedom by providing an uncompromising moral and economic case for individual liberty, free markets, private property, and limited government." Bovard's article "Surveillance State" was published in the May 19, 2003, issue of *The American Conservative,* one of the editors of which is well-known conservative and former presidential candidate Pat Buchanan. James Bovard is the author of six books and dozens of articles published in magazines as diverse as *Reader's Digest, New Republic, Newsweek,* and *Playboy.*

James Bovard
Surveillance State

1   Perhaps you've visited your local library to keep speed with the War on Terror: borrowed a few books on Islamic fundamentalism or did web research on biochemical weapons. Beware.

2   Last January, an FBI agent entered a branch of the St. Louis Public Library and requested a list of all the sign-up sheets showing names of people who used library computers on Dec. 28, 2002. Even though the FBI agent did not have a warrant or subpoena, the library quickly surrendered the list of all users. The FBI acted because someone phoned in a tip that they "smelled something strange" about a library patron of Middle Eastern descent.

3   Welcome to America under the Patriot Act. One person claims to "smell something," and the feds can round up everyone's records. From books you check out to credit card purchases, money transfers to medications, your activities are now subject to federal surveillance. Uncle Sam now has a blank check to search and pry—all in the name of security.

4   Last October, then House Majority Leader Dick Armey branded our own Justice Department "the biggest threat to personal liberty in the country." And while that characterization of a Republican Justice Department makes many conservatives cringe, the DOJ has been working overtime to expand its power—and the biggest danger may be yet to come.

5   When John Ashcroft was in the U.S. Senate, he was a leader in the fight to protect Americans' privacy. In an August 1997 op-ed, Ashcroft declared, "This is no reason to hand Big Brother the keys to unlock our e-mail diaries, open our ATM records, read our medical records, or translate our international communications." His early days as attorney general showed a keen appreciation for the Bill of Rights' constraints. That changed on 9/11.

6   Within days of the Twin Towers' collapse, Ashcroft began strong-arming Congress to enact sweeping anti-terrorism legislation—and Americans seemed ready to trade a measure of liberty to restore their shaken security. The month of the attacks, an NBC/*Wall Street Journal* poll found 78 percent willing to have Internet activity monitored. The administration took this as free rein, moving swiftly to enact the Patriot (Provide Appropriate Tools Required to Intercept and Obstruct Terrorism) Act. Some of its provisions were simply updates to existing law. As Sen. Russell Feingold (D-Wis.), the only senator to vote against the act observed, "It made sense to stiffen penalties and lengthen or eliminate statutes of limitation for certain terrorist crimes." But the Patriot Act goes far beyond "good government" amendments.

7   It empowers federal agents to cannibalize Americans' e-mail with Carnivore wiretaps, allows federal agents to commandeer library records, and requires banks to surrender personal account information. It also authorizes federal agents to confiscate bulk cash from travelers who fail to fill out Customs Service forms disclosing how much money they are taking out of or into the U.S. and allows the attorney general to order long-term detentions if he has "reasonable grounds to believe that the alien is engaged in any activity that endangers the national security of the United States." Last year alone, Ashcroft personally issued 170 emergency domestic spying warrants, permitting agents to carry out wiretaps and search homes and offices for up to 72 hours before requesting a search warrant from the Foreign Intelligence Surveillance Court.

8   When privacy-minded legislators question these new powers, the Justice Department stonewalls. House Judiciary Chairman James Sensenbrenner (R-Wis.) threatened to subpoena the DOJ last summer to get information to which his committee is specifically entitled. Justice eventually divulged a few fragments of information but has refused to reveal the number of secret searches, the number of libraries whose records have been seized, and how often Carnivore e-mail wiretaps have been used. Freedom has apparently become so fragile that citizens can no longer be permitted to know how often their government invades their privacy.

9   Some intrusive provisions of the Patriot Act were temporary—set to expire in 2005 absent Congressional reauthorization. But Sen. Orrin Hatch (R-Utah), chairman of the Senate Judiciary Committee, recently proposed making the federal prying powers permanent.

The Wrong Response

10   The Patriot Act was rushed into law before any effort was made to understand why the feds failed to stop the 9/11 attacks. The government could have done a better job of tracking the terrorist suspects, but the feds had all the relevant information to detect and block the conspiracy to hijack four airplanes. The Joint House-Senate Intelligence Committee observed that the FBI's negligence "contributed to the United States becoming, in effect, a sanctuary for radical terrorists." Its investigation concluded, "It is at least a possibility that increased analysis, sharing and focus would have drawn greater attention to the growing potential for a major terrorist attack in the United States involving the aviation industry."

11   But the administration rewarded failure by the FBI and intelligence agencies with bigger budgets, more power, and presidential commendations. There is nothing in the Patriot Act that can solve the problem of FBI agents who do not understand the Foreign Intelligence Surveillance Act or solve the shortage of CIA and National Security Agency employees who can read intercepted messages in the languages of prime terrorist threats. Neither does the legislation compensate for lackadaisical federal agents who failed to add promptly the names of al-Qaeda members to terrorism watch-lists or of analysts who ignored the cascading warnings of terrorists using stolen airplanes as flying bombs. The success of the 9/11 hijackers was due far more to a lack of government competence than to a shortfall in government power. Yet the Bush administration has successfully suppressed investigations and revelations of federal failures, thereby permitting Ashcroft and others to portray new government powers as the key to national safety.

12   The Justice Department isn't the only agency taking aim at American liberties. The Department of Transportation has compiled secret "no fly" lists of passengers suspected of terrorist ties—or at least those critical of the administration. In one instance, two dozen members of a peace group, students chaperoned by a priest and nun, were detained en route to a teach-in, thus missing their flight.

13   The Department of Defense is piling on with its Total Information Awareness program. TIA's goal is to stockpile as much information as possible about everyone on Earth—thereby allowing government to protect everyone from everything. *New York Times* columnist William Safire warned, "Every purchase you make with a credit card, every magazine subscription you buy and medical prescription you fill, every Web site you visit and e-mail you send or receive, every academic grade you receive, every bank deposit you make, every trip you book and every event you attend—all these transactions and communications will go into what the Defense Department describes as 'a virtual, centralized grand database.'" Columnist Ted Rall noted that the feds will even scan "veterinary records. The TIA believes that knowing if and when Fluffy got spayed—and whether your son stopped torturing Fluffy after you put him on Ritalin—will help the military stop terrorists before they strike."

14   Congress passed a law seeking to rein in TIA. The Pentagon, however, is barging forward, and the congressional provision specifies that if Bush formally certifies that TIA is necessary for national security, the law is null and void.

Coming Soon: Patriot II

15   In February, the Center for Public Integrity obtained and released an 86-page draft version of the Domestic Security Enhancement Act—quickly dubbed Patriot II. Notations on the Justice Department document—stamped "Confidential—Not for Distribution" on every page—showed that it had already been sent to Vice President Cheney and House Speaker Dennis Hastert (R-Ill). Justice Department spokesman Mark Corallo dismisses DSEA as a benign sequel, "filling in the holes" in the Patriot Act.

16   Section 101 of the proposed bill, titled "Individual Terrorists as Foreign Powers," would revise the Foreign Intelligence Surveillance Act (FISA) to permit the U.S. government to label individuals who are suspected terrorists—including American citizens—as "foreign powers" for the purpose of conducting total surveillance of their activities. This alteration nullifies all Fourth Amendment rights of the target, allowing the government to tap phones, search computers, and read e-mail—even when there is no evidence that a citizen is violating any statute. If Section 101 becomes law, the more people the feds wrongfully accuse of being terrorists, the more power federal agents will receive.

17   Americans suspected of gathering information for a foreign power could be subject to FISA surveillance even though they were violating no law and the information gathered did not pertain to national security. The administration's confidential explanation of proposed Section 102 notes, "Requiring the additional showing that the intelligence gathering violates the laws of the United States is both unnecessary and counterproductive, as such activities threaten the national security regardless of whether they are illegal." But, as the ACLU noted, "This amendment would permit electronic surveillance of a local activist who was preparing a report on human rights for London-based Amnesty International, a 'foreign political organization,' even if the activist was not engaged in any violation of law."

18   While some parts of the new bill would overturn federal court decisions, Section 106 is more visionary, seeking to negate principles established in the Nuremberg trials: that following orders is no excuse for violating the law. As proposed, it would permit federal agents illegally to wiretap and surveil and leak damaging personal information on Americans—as long as they are following orders from the president or the attorney general. The Senate COINTELPRO investigation revealed how President Johnson and top Nixon aides personally ordered federal agents to conduct illegal surveillance of political opponents and others, though neither the FBI nor LBJ was ever held accountable. This proposal is a further attempt to make federal agents legally untouchable and could encourage law-breaking at every level of the federal government.

19   Section 129, entitled "Strengthening Access to and Use of Information in National Security Investigations," would empower federal agents to issue "national security letters" that compel businesses and other institutions to surrender confidential or proprietary information without a court order. Anyone hit with such a letter will be obliged to remain forever silent on the demand with disclosure punishable by up to five years in prison. The ACLU noted that this provision would "reduce judicial oversight of terrorism investigations by relegating the role of the judge to considering challenges to orders already issued, rather than ensuring such orders are drawn with due regard for the privacy and other interests of the target." This turns the Fourth Amendment on its head by creating a presumption that the government is entitled to personal or confidential information unless the citizen or business can prove to a federal judge that the "national security letter" should not be enforced against them. But few Americans can afford the cost of litigating against the world's largest law firm—the U.S. Justice Department—to preserve their privacy.

20   Secret mass arrests could be the result of Section 201. The provision notes, "Although existing Freedom of Information Act (FOIA) exemptions . . . permit the government to protect information relating to detainees, defending this interpretation through litigation requires extensive Department of Justice resources, which would be better spent detecting and incapacitate [sic] terrorists." In the wake of 9/11, the feds locked up over 1,200 "special interest" detainees and continually insisted that none of their names or details of their cases could be disclosed without endangering national survival, though federal courts denounced the secret arrests as "odious to democracy" or "profoundly undemocratic." To save the Justice Department the bother of having to defend secret round-ups, the Bush administration now seeks to amend the federal statute book to imitate repressive dictatorships around the globe.

21   Section 312, "Appropriate Remedies with Respect to Law Enforcement Surveillance Activities," would unleash local law enforcement to spy on Americans, nullifying almost all federal, state, and local court "consent decrees" that restrict the power of local and state police. The administration complains that such decrees result in police lacking "the ability to use the full range of investigative techniques that are lawful under the Constitution, and that are available to the FBI." But, in every case, consent decrees were imposed after gross abuses of citizens' rights by the police. The administration draft bill explanation declares, "All surviving decrees would have to be necessary to correct a current and ongoing violation of a Federal right, extend no further than necessary to correct the violation of the Federal right, and be narrowly drawn and the least intrusive means to correct the violation." Historically, the Supreme Court has required the federal government to use the "least intrusive means" to achieve some policy in cases involving the First Amendment, in order to prevent any unnecessary

restriction of freedom of speech. The administration now demands the "least intrusive" restrictions on government intrusions.

22   Section 402 would permit U.S. attorneys to prosecute Americans for aiding terrorist organizations even if they made donations to organizations that the U.S. government did not publicly label as terrorist groups. Yale Law School professor Jack Balkin said, "Give a few dollars to a Muslim charity Ashcroft thinks is a terrorist organization and you could be on the next plane out of this country." Robert Higgs of the Independent Institution warns that the feds "can categorize the most innocent action"—such as "signing a petition"—as an act of terrorism.

23   Users of Pretty Good Privacy and other common encryption software could face greater perils from Section 404, which creates "a new, separate crime of using encryption technology that could add five years or more to any sentence for crimes committed with a computer," the ACLU notes. Encryption software is routinely included on new computers and is commonly used for business transactions. The Justice Department thus seeks to treat use of encryption software the same way that the federal government treats gun possession—something sinister enough to justify routinely doubling or tripling prison sentences for people who violate other federal statutes, regardless of whether the gun was actually used.

24   Critics label Section 501 of the bill the "citizenship death penalty." Under existing law, an American must state his intent to relinquish his citizenship in order to lose it. Under this provision, intent "need not be manifested in words but can be inferred from conduct," thus empowering the Justice Department to strip Americans of their citizenship if the feds accuse them of supporting terrorism—either domestic or international. The American Immigration Lawyers Association cautions that, under this provision, "targeted [U.S. citizens] potentially could find themselves consigned to indefinite detention as undocumented immigrants in their own country."

25   Shortly after the text of Patriot II surfaced, the attorney general was asked at a press conference about this expansion of federal power. He refused to confirm plans formally to propose Patriot II but did declare, "Every day we are asking each other, what can we do to be more successful in securing the freedoms of America and sustaining the liberty, the tolerance, the human dignity that America represents, and how can we do a better job in defeating the threat of terrorism."

26   Despite Ashcroft's reassurances, resistance is building. Eighty-nine cities have passed resolutions condemning the Patriot Act, and a coalition is stretching across ideological lines to oppose it. Recently the ACLU drafted a letter to Congress and found 67 organizations from the conservative Gun Owners of America to the liberal La Raza eager to sign on. They accuse Patriot II of "new and sweeping law enforcement and intelligence gathering powers, many of which are not related to terrorism, that would severely dilute, if not undermine, basic constitutional rights."

27   Three months after 9/11, Ashcroft announced, "To those who scare peace-loving people with phantoms of lost liberty, my message is this, your tactics only aid terrorists for they erode our national unity and . . . give ammunition to America's enemies." Ashcroft is wrong to portray any criticism of Bush administration civil liberties policies as aiding and abetting terrorism. America is overdue for a searching examination of the powers the Bush administration has seized and the powers it is seeking.

Thinking Critically about "Surveillance State"

1. Legal arguments are often conceptually difficult to follow because they proceed step-by-step through different sections of an intricate, complex law. You will thus need to read closely to understand Bovard's appeals to *logos*. In your own words, what are the main reasons and evidence Bovard uses to critique the USA Patriot Act? (Note: The student arguments in this chapter have very clear, closed-form structures—a result of our own teaching strategies that emphasize *because* clauses attached to a claim. Professional essays such as Bovard's often have a much looser structure. In examining the *logos* of this article, you might imagine that Bovard has to reorganize his essay into a *because* clause frame: "The USA Patriot Act endangers Americans' freedoms because . . . , because . . . , because . . . , and so on. How might Bovard word his *because* clauses?)

2. Analyze Bovard's angle of vision. What is not said in Bovard's article? What does Bovard keep invisible or censor? Consider also Bovard's choice of language in such phrases as "the feds can round up everyone's records . . . all in the name of security" or the feds can "cannibalize American's e-mail with Carnivore wiretaps." How might Ashcroft make the same points in language more favorable to his own views?

3. Analyze Bovard's appeals to *ethos* in this argument. Does he seem reasonable and trustworthy?

4. Analyze Bovard's appeals to *pathos*. Point to specific passages where Bovard's choice of words or his use of examples stirs emotions favorable to his views. Focus also on how he appeals to the beliefs and values of his audience. Often critiques of the Patriot Act come from liberals and other left-leaning opponents of the Bush administration. But Bovard's argument appears in a conservative, very-right-of-center journal. How might this article appeal to both libertarians on the right and liberals on the left?

5. How do you think John Ashcroft would reply to the criticisms raised by Bovard?

Our next reading changes pace, moving from global issues of terrorism to the family issue of how we should discipline our children. "Spare the Rod, Spoil the Parenting" is an op-ed piece by *Miami Herald* columnist Leonard Pitts, Jr., which appeared in newspapers across the country in September 2001. In this editorial, Pitts jumps into the ongoing controversy over corporal punishment, children's rights, child-rearing practices, and spanking. Leonard Pitts, one of the nation's foremost African-American opinion writers, won the Pulitzer Prize for commentary in 2004. He is the author of *Becoming Dad: Black Men and the Journey to Fatherhood.*

Leonard Pitts, Jr.
Spare the Rod, Spoil the Parenting

1   I hate to tell you this, but your kid is spoiled. Mine aren't much better.

2   That, in essence, is the finding of a recent Time/CNN poll. Most of us think most of our kids are overindulged, materialistic brats.

3   If you're waiting for me to argue the point, you're in the wrong column.

4   No, I only bring it up as context to talk about a controversial study released late last month. It deals with corporal punishment—spanking—and it has outraged those who oppose the practice while rearming those who support it.

5   It seems that Dr. Diana Baumrind, a psychologist at the University of California at Berkeley, followed 164 middle-class families from the time their children were in preschool until they reached their 20s. She found that most used some form of corporal punishment. She further found that, contrary to what we've been told for years, giving a child a mild spanking (defined as open-handed swats on the backside, arm or legs) does not leave the child scarred for life.

6   Baumrind, by the way, opposes spanking. Still, it's to her credit as an academic that her research draws a distinction other opponents refuse to. That is, a distinction between the minor punishments practiced by most parents who spank and the harsher variants practiced by a tiny minority (shaking and blows to the head or face, for example).

7   Yes, children whose parents treat them that severely are, indeed, more likely to be maladjusted by the time they reach adolescence. And, yes, the parents themselves are teetering dangerously close to child abuse.

8   But does the same hold true in cases where corporal punishment means little more than swatting a misbehaving backside?

9   For years, the official consensus from the nation's child-rearing experts was that it did. Maybe that's about to change. We can only hope.

10   For my money, there was always something spurious about the orthodoxy that assured us all corporal punishment, regardless of severity, was defacto abuse. Nevertheless, we bought into it, with the result being that parents who admitted to spanking were treated as primitive dolts and

heaped with scorn. They were encouraged to negotiate with misbehaving children in order to nurture their self-esteem.

11   But the orthodoxy was wrong on several fronts.

12   In the first place, it's plainly ridiculous—and offensive—to equate a child who has been swatted on the butt with one who has been stomped, scalded or punched. In the second, the argument that reasonable corporal punishment leads inevitably to mental instability always seemed insupportable and has just been proven so by Baumrind's study. And in the third, have you ever tried to "negotiate" with a screaming 5-year-old? It may do wonders for the child's self-esteem, but, I promise, it's going to kill yours. Your sanity, too.

13   Don't get me wrong, contrary to what its proponents sometimes claim, corporal punishment is not a panacea for misbehavior. Rearing a child requires not just discipline, but also humor, love and some luck.

14   Yet the very fact that spanking must be exonerated by a university study suggests how far afield we've wandered from what used to be the central tenet of family life: parents in charge. Ultimately, it probably doesn't matter whether that tenet is enforced by spanking or other corrective measures, so long as it is enforced.

15   I've seen too many children behave with too grand a sense of entitlement to believe that it is. Heard too many teachers tell horror stories of dealing with kids from households where parents are not sovereign, adult authority not respected. As a culture, we seem to have forgotten that the family is not a democracy, but a benign dictatorship.

16   Small wonder our kids are brats.

17   So the pertinent question isn't: To spank or not to spank? Rather, it's: Who's in charge here? Who is teaching whom? Who is guiding whom?

18   The answer used to be obvious. It's obvious no more. And is it so difficult to see where that road leads? To understand that it is possible to be poisoned by self-esteem, and that a spoiled child becomes a self-centered adult ill-equipped to deal with the vagaries and reversals of life?

19   Some folks think it's abuse when you swat a child's backside. But maybe, sometimes, it's abuse when you don't.

Thinking Critically about "Spare the Rod, Spoil the Parenting"

1. In the introductory paragraphs of this op-ed piece, Leonard Pitts, Jr., mentions the rhetorical situation that has called forth his argument. What contemporary research is prompting Pitts's column?

2. Pitts's argument takes a stand on the issue question, "Is spanking a good child-rearing practice?" What claim does he make in this argument? What reasons and evidence does he offer to support this claim?

3. Where does Pitts acknowledge and respond to opposing views?

4. To understand the intensity of the social controversy on this issue, we suggest that you search the key words "spanking" and "corporal punishment" using an online database and the Web. What different positions do you find represented in articles and by advocacy Web sites such as the site for the Center for Effective Discipline? How would these sources challenge Pitts's position and evidence?

The last reading is by student writer A. J. Chavez, who wrote this paper for the classical argument assignment in this chapter. In proposing the legalization of gay marriage, A. J. Chavez draws on personal knowledge and experience, some Internet research, and information from an anthropology course he was taking simultaneously with first-year composition.

A. J. Chavez (Student)
The Case for (Gay) Marriage

1   "What if it was a gay world? And you were straight?" a recent TV spot asks (the ad can be viewed at commercialcloset.org—see "What If" in Works Cited). The camera pans across a hospital waiting room, filled with gay and lesbian couples. There, a middle-aged man sits, waiting. "Your partner's in a coma. She's not responding," a young male doctor says to him. "Unfortunately, since the state doesn't recognize your marriage, I can't grant you spousal visitation. If she were to wake, or a family member gave consent—I wish there was more I could do. I'm sorry." After that, the camera quickly zooms out from the man's heartbroken face. The scene blurs, and a female voiceover reads the fact that appears on the screen: "hospital visitation: just one of over 1000 rights granted to a legally married couple." Next, the scene fades into a black screen with a blue rectangle that has a yellow equal sign on it. The female voiceover continues, "Support equality for all Americans. Millionformarriage.org." This spot, sponsored by the Human Rights Campaign, the largest queer political organization in the United States, shows a scenario that undoubtedly happens every day in America, just with the tables turned. According to a report from the United States General Accounting Office, released after the passage of the federal Defense of Marriage Act of 1996, there are at least 1,049 federal laws in the U.S. code that relate to rights specific to marriage (2). Some are obvious, like Social Security or Veterans' Administration benefits upon the death of a spouse for the surviving spouse and children. Others are not so obvious, but equally important, such as the federally guaranteed right of an employee to take time off from work to care for an ill spouse or the so-called "spousal privilege" of not having to testify against a husband or wife in court. Currently, marriage rights are denied to a small, but still significant

group in America—gays and lesbians, a group of which I am a part. We are denied the same rights enjoyed by straight people, simply because we are attracted to and love members of our own sex and have chosen to live open, honest lives, instead of closeted ones.

2   In opposition to the current Congressional proposal to amend the Constitution by defining marriage as a union between a man and a woman, I am proposing the nationwide legalization of same-sex marriage. First of all, gay marriage is the easiest way to ensure equality for all. Civil unions can only go part of the way. Secondly, the government must define marriage through a secular framework that respects the spirit of laws already in place, not a religious one that would violate separation between church and state. Third, the costs to taxpayers for legalizing gay marriage would be negligible. Some studies even suggest it would save taxpayer money. Finally, anthropological evidence exists for the existence of what we would refer to today as "gay marriage" across a long time span and wide range of cultures, demonstrating that it is not abnormal or perverted.

3   There are many arguments against gay marriage. Some are definitional, such as "Marriage is between a man and a woman." Other claims against gay marriage stem from concern for the well-being of children raised by gay or lesbian couples from previous straight marriages, adoption, or reproductive assistance. Still others arise out of respect for the Hebrew and Christian scriptures, the moral code from which most of Western civilization has lived by for thousands of years—certain passages in them prohibit homosexual relations. Another objection is that marriage is reserved for procreation, and that gay marriage, obviously, cannot serve this end. Additionally, there is the argument that legal options already exist for gay couples that offer some of the benefits of marriage, such as power of attorney or living will. Some politicians claim that marriage is something that should be left to the states to decide how to define and deal with individually. Furthermore, there is the argument that the legalization of gay marriage will open the doors to the legalization of more radical unions, such as adult-child unions or polygamy. Last, some members of America's queer community oppose gay marriage because they see it as just an attempt to copy and live a hetero lifestyle.

4   My first reason for legalizing gay marriage is that it is the easiest and most effective way to ensure equal rights for all in this country. Currently, sexual minorities receive no explicit protection from federal anti-discrimination acts, such as Title VII from the Civil Rights Act of 1964, which only prohibits discrimination in employment based on "race, color, religion, sex, or national origin." Employers are not required to offer the same benefits to the significant others of gay employees as they do to straight employees. With gay marriage, they would be obliged under laws that protect the rights of married couples to do so. Civil unions relegate gays and lesbians to second-class status. Civil unions or domestic partnerships are offered only by a few states, but can be disregarded by neighboring anti-gay states because of the federal Defense of Marriage Act. Civil unions can guarantee protections only at the state level,

and at that, only the state they were issued in. Gay marriage, with its protections, would help prevent discrimination toward sexual minorities from prejudiced individuals. Here, it becomes clear that marriage laws should not just be left to the states, as some politicians who would rather not take a stand on the issue suggest, because if they are, patchwork laws will continue to develop across the nation. Some states will prohibit same-sex marriages and civil unions, while others will provide civil unions, and, perhaps in the future, gay marriage. A clear, federal standard for the inclusion of gay marriage will also prevent possible loopholes in marriage or civil union laws for inappropriate unions between adults and children or among more than two partners.

5   Second, for public policy, marriage, like all other things, needs to be defined through a non-religious, secular framework. The separation of church and state has always been an important tenet in American government. Allowing religious dogma to define marriage violates this tenet, setting up a dangerous precedent for further unification of church and state. If gay marriage were legalized, religions would still be allowed to distinguish what they do and do not see as "marriage." The Human Rights Campaign Web site provides the example of the Catholic church, which does not bless second marriages after divorce. Yet people can still file for divorce and then remarry if they see fit. In this case, the state recognizes a legal marriage that is not officially sanctioned by the church ("I Believe God Meant"). Also, while certain passages of the Bible prohibit sexual relationships between members of the same sex, others condone slavery and polygamy—both practices that would not be approved in American society today. Clearly, appeals to the Bible cannot be used to determine public policy. We would not only violate the important principle of separation between church and state, but by strict Biblical interpretation of morality, we could theoretically have a polygamous, slave-owning society.

6   Another compelling reason for legalizing same-sex marriage is the money that could actually be *saved* in state budgets every year. The FAQ section on marriage on the Human Rights Campaign Web site explains how government savings could add up through increased reliance between gay and lesbian couples on each other, reducing reliance on government assistance programs such as Temporary Assistance to Needy Families (welfare), Supplemental Security Income (disability), food stamps and Medicaid. The Web site cites two economic studies by professors at UCLA and the University of Massachusetts, Amherst, who examined possible savings to state governments in California and New Jersey if domestic benefits were extended to same-sex couples. According to these studies, the savings were projected to be $10.6 million in California and $61 million in New Jersey ("Won't This Cost"). Additionally, the legalization of gay marriage would provide medical insurance benefits for thousands of currently uninsured children. While gay and lesbian couples obviously cannot conceive children on their own, plenty raise children from previous, heterosexual marriages, adopt children, or use reproductive assistance such as surrogate mothers or

assisted insemination to bear their own children. The fact that many gay and lesbian partners are raising children shows the fallacy in claiming that gays should not be allowed to marry because they can't procreate. If we used the logic of procreation in determining whether to grant marriage rights, we would have to ban marriage between elderly couples, between sterile straight couples, and between those who plan to use birth control to prevent pregnancy. Of course, we would never ban such marriages because we recognize the value of having a life partner. Extending marriage benefits to gay partners brings the same benefits to them, with the additional benefit to the states of reducing reliance on state assistance programs and bringing medical insurance to many children.

7   My final reason for the legalization of gay marriage is that same-sex unions have existed across all cultures and time. This is important to recognize, because Judeo-Christian societies like ours tend to discount the legitimacy or even existence of such unions, and of so-called "sexual minorities." Such disregard can be explained by the histories of Judaism and Christianity, says Ted Fortier, Ph.D., a cultural anthropologist at Seattle University. In early Jewish societies, largely due to problems with underpopulation, he notes, any sexual activity without procreative power was considered taboo. Also, in Christian medieval Europe, disease and famine required that the people have all the labor possible to produce food. Again, all non-procreative sex was labeled taboo. For anthropological purposes, Fortier defines marriage as "a union between a woman and another person." This definition, however, can be quite broad, he says. The "woman" can actually be a man playing a feminine role. He explains that in our culture, we look at gender as a biological concept, instead of a socially determined one. He gives examples of different cultures that distinguish certain men who take on womanly roles as being a third gender, such as that of Tahiti, where every village has a man that takes on the role of a woman, or the Native American *berdache* role, another womanly role played by a man. These men raise children just like the other adults. For the most part, Fortier claims, throughout all societies and cultures marriage has always been about securing resources and property—known as "alliance theory" in anthropology. Looking at our own society with this concept in mind, we see that marriage is utilized in the same way—as a stabilizing combination of tangible and intangible resources that leads to benefits to society, often including the raising of children. Law professor Mark Strasser, in an essay entitled "State Interests in Recognizing Same-Sex Marriage," mentions that "there is no evidence that children will not thrive when raised by same-sex parents and, indeed, some evidence that children may be better off in certain ways when they are raised by same-sex parents than when they are raised by different-sex parents" (37). Strasser refers to the increased tolerance and appreciation of differences that children of gays and lesbians typically have and the innumerable studies over the years that show these children grow up just as well-adjusted and are no more likely to be homosexual than children living with

straight parents. The government, therefore, should recognize and extend marriage protections to same-sex couples as well. While there are some gay/lesbian/bisexual/transgender people who think gay marriage is just a futile attempt to copy mainstream, straight society, and that the government should not bother legalizing it, entering into any union is based on the mutual choice of two individuals. GLBT persons who find the institution of marriage unsavory would still not be forced by the government to marry if gay marriage were legalized.

8   The case for gay marriage is a strong one indeed, similar to earlier struggles for interracial marriage, which was legalized only relatively recently in American history. Gay marriage will result in an unprecedented addition of formal protections to America's last marginalized minority—the queer community. Studies suggest that it will save individual states millions of dollars in revenue on an annual basis. Gay marriage is not sick or a perversion—it exists across all cultures and times in one form or another and was stigmatized in Judeo-Christian traditions for the practical purpose of achieving as high of a population as possible. It is impossible to turn on a television set or open a newspaper now without seeing a reference to gay marriage. Legalizing gay marriage affirms both the "liberal" ideal of equality and the "conservative" value of community stability and individual rights. It also affirms the dignity of all of mankind.

Works Cited

Fortier, Ted. Personal interview. 26 Feb. 2004.

"I Believe God Meant Marriage for Men and Women." Human Rights Campaign 20 Feb. 2004. 15 Mar. 2004 <http://www.hrc.org>. Path: marriage; "I Believe God Meant."

Strasser, Mark. "State Interests in Recognizing Same-Sex Marriage." Marriage and Same Sex Unions: A Debate. Ed. Lynn D. Wardle, et al. Westport, CT: Praeger, 2003.

United States. General Accounting Office. Categories of Laws Involving Marital Status. Letter of transmittal. By Barry R. Bedrick. 31 Jan. 1997. 16 Mar. 2004 <http://www.gao.gov/archive/1997/og97016.pdf>.

"What If It Were a Gay World?" Advertisement. Human Rights Campaign. The Commercial Closet 2004. 2 Mar. 2004 <http://www.commercialcloset.org/cgi-bin/iowa/portrayals.html?record=1817>.

"Won't This Cost Taxpayers Too Much Money?" Human Rights Campaign 2004. 15 Mar. 2004 <http://www.hrc.org>. Path: marriage; "Won't This Cost."

Thinking Critically about "The Case for (Gay) Marriage"

1. In classical arguments there is often an overlap between the reasons used to support one's own claim and the reasons used to rebut opposing views. In such cases the distinction between support and rebuttal can become blurred (not a problem so long as the argument remains clear). In this essay, where does A. J. Chavez summarize the arguments opposing the legalization of gay

marriage? How many of these arguments does he respond to as the argument proceeds? Where does he add supporting reasons in favor of gay marriage that aren't initially framed as rebuttals?

2. How effectively does A. J. create appeals to *ethos* in this argument? How would you characterize his persona based on tone, reasonableness, and empathy for opposing views?

3. On the gay marriage issue, opponents of gay marriage can range from conservative audiences with strong religious arguments against same-sex marriage to very liberal gay audiences who believe that gays shouldn't imitate heterosexual relationships. How well does A. J. use appeals to *pathos* to connect with his imagined readers at both ends of this spectrum? How does he appeal to the values, beliefs, and emotions of his audiences? Point out specific passages where you think he is successful or unsuccessful.

4. How would you assess the appeals to *logos* in this argument? Are A. J.'s use of reasons and evidence persuasive?

5. What do you see as the major strengths and weaknesses of this argument?

Composing Your Essay

Writing arguments deepens our thinking by forcing us to consider alternative views and to question the assumptions underlying our reasons and claims. Consequently, it is not unusual for a writer's position on an issue to shift—and even to reverse itself—during the writing process. If this happens to you, take it as a healthy sign of your openness to change, complexity, and alternative points of view. If writing a draft causes you to modify your views, it will be an act of discovery, not a concession of defeat.

Generating and Exploring Ideas

The tasks that follow are intended to help you generate ideas for your argument. Our goal is to help you build up a storehouse of possible issues, explore several of these possibilities, and then choose one for deeper exploration before you write your initial draft.

Make an Inventory of Issues That Interest You
Following the lead of the For Writing and Discussion exercise on page 396, make a list of various communities that you belong to and then brainstorm contested issues in those communities. You might try a trigger question like this: "When members of [X community] get together, what contested questions cause disagreements?" What decisions need to be made? What values are in conflict? What problems need to be solved?

Explore Several Issues

For this task, choose two or three possible issues from your previous list and explore them through freewriting or idea mapping. Try responding quickly to the following questions:

1. What is my position on this issue and why?
2. What are alternative points of view on this issue?
3. Why do people disagree about this issue? (Do people disagree about the facts of the case? About key definitions? About underlying values, assumptions, and beliefs?)
4. If I were to argue my position on this issue, what evidence would I need to gather and what research might I need to do?

Brainstorm Claims and Reasons

Choose one issue that particularly interests you and work with classmates to brainstorm possible claims that you could make on the issue. Imagining different perspectives, brainstorm possible reasons to support each claim, stating them as *because* clauses.

For *because* clauses, see pp. 397–398.

Conduct and Respond to Initial Research

If your issue requires research, do a quick bibliographic survey of what is available and do enough initial reading to get a good sense of the kinds of arguments that surround your issue and of the alternative views that people have taken. Then freewrite your responses to the following questions:

1. What are the different points of view on this issue? Why do people disagree with each other?
2. Explore the evolution of your thinking as you did this initial reading. What new questions have the readings raised for you? What changes have occurred in your own thinking?

Conduct an In-Depth Exploration Prior to Drafting

The following set of tasks is designed to help you explore your issue in depth. Most students take one or two hours to complete these tasks; the time will pay off, however, because most of the ideas that you need for your rough draft will be on paper.

1. Write out the issue your argument will address. Try phrasing your issue in several different ways, perhaps as a yes/no question and as an open-ended question. Try making the question broader, then narrower. Finally, frame the question in the way that most appeals to you.
2. Now write out your tentative answer to the question. This will be your beginning thesis statement or claim. Put a box around this answer. Next, write out one or more different answers to your question. These will be alternative claims that a neutral audience might consider.

See the discussion of issue questions on pp. 395–396.

3. Why is this a controversial issue? Is there insufficient evidence to resolve the issue, or is the evidence ambiguous or contradictory? Are definitions in dispute? Do the parties disagree about basic values, assumptions, or beliefs?

4. What personal interest do you have in this issue? How does the issue affect you? Why do you care about it? (Knowing why you care about it might help you get your audience to care about it.)

5. What reasons and evidence support your position on this issue? Freewrite everything that comes to mind that might help you support your case. This freewrite will eventually provide the bulk of your argument. For now, freewrite rapidly without worrying whether your argument makes sense. Just get ideas on paper.

6. Imagine all the counterarguments your audience might make. Summarize the main arguments against your position and then freewrite your response to each of the counterarguments. What are the flaws in the alternative points of view?

7. What kinds of appeals to *ethos* and *pathos* might you use to support your argument? How can you increase your audience's perception of your credibility and trustworthiness? How can you tie your argument to your audience's beliefs and values?

8. Why is this an important issue? What are the broader implications and consequences? What other issues does it relate to? Thinking of possible answers to these questions may prove useful when you write your introduction or conclusion.

Shaping and Drafting

Once you have explored your ideas, create a plan. Here is a suggested procedure:

Begin your planning by analyzing your intended audience. You could imagine an audience deeply resistant to your views or a more neutral, undecided audience acting like a jury. In some cases, your audience might be a single person, as when you petition your department chair to take an upper-division course when you are a sophomore. At other times, your audience might be the general readership of a newspaper, church bulletin, or magazine. When the audience is a general readership, you need to imagine from the start the kinds of readers you particularly want to sway. Here are some questions you can ask:

- *How much does your audience know or care about your issue?* Will you need to provide background? Will you need to convince them that your issue is important? Do you need to hook their interest? Your answers to these questions will particularly influence your introduction and conclusion.

For Rogerian approaches, see pp. 411–412.

- *What is your audience's current attitude toward your issue?* Are they deeply opposed to your position? If so, why? Are they neutral and undecided? If so, what other views will they be listening to? Classical argument works best with neutral or moderately dissenting audiences. Deeply skeptical audiences are best addressed with delayed-thesis or Rogerian approaches.

- *How do your audience's values, assumptions, and beliefs differ from your own?* What aspects of your position will be threatening to your audience? Why? How does your position on the issue challenge your imagined reader's worldview or identity? What objections will your audience raise toward your argument? Your answers to these questions will help determine the content of your argument and alert you to the extra research you may have to do to respond to audience objections.

- *What values, beliefs, or assumptions about the world do you and your audience share?* Despite your differences with your audience, where can you find common links? How might you use these links to build bridges to your audience?

Your next step is to plan out an audience-based argument by seeking audience-based reasons or reasons whose warrants you can defend. Here is a process you can use:

1. Create a skeleton, tree diagram, outline, or flowchart for your argument by stating your reasons as one or more *because* clauses attached to your claim. Each *because* clause will become the head of a main section or *line of reasoning* in your argument.

2. Use the planning schema on pages 404–406 to plan each line of reasoning. If your audience accepts your warrant, concentrate on supporting your reason with grounds. If your warrant is doubtful, support it with backing. Try to anticipate audience objections by exploring conditions for rebuttal, and brainstorm ways of addressing those objections.

3. Using the skeleton you created, finish developing an outline or tree diagram for your argument. Although the organization for each part of your argument will grow organically from its content, the main parts of a classical argument are as follows:

   a. *An introduction,* in which you engage your reader's attention, introduce your issue, and state your own position.

   b. *Background and preliminary material,* in which you place your issue in a current context and provide whatever background knowledge and definitions of key terms or concepts that your reader will need. (If this background is short, it can often be incorporated into the introduction.)

   c. *Arguments supporting your own position,* in which you make the best case possible for your views by developing your claim with reasons and evidence. This is usually the longest part of your argument, with a separate section for each line of reasoning.

   d. *Anticipation of objections and counterarguments,* in which you summarize fairly key arguments against your position. This section not only helps the reader understand the issue more clearly, but also establishes your *ethos* as a fair-minded writer willing to acknowledge complexity.

   e. *Response to objections through refutation or concession,* in which you point out weaknesses in opposing arguments or concede to their strengths.

    f. *A conclusion,* in which you place your argument in a larger context, perhaps by summarizing your main points and showing why this issue is an important one or by issuing a call to action.

This classical model can be modified in numerous ways. A question that often arises is where to summarize and respond to objections and counterarguments. Writers generally have three choices: One option is to handle opposing positions before you present your own argument. The rationale for this approach is that skeptical audiences may be more inclined to listen attentively to your argument if they have been assured that you understand their point of view. A second option is to place this material after you have presented your argument. This approach is effective for neutral audiences who don't start off with strong opposing views. A final option is to intersperse opposing views throughout your argument at appropriate moments. Any of these possibilities, or a combination of all of them, can be effective.

Another question often asked is, "What is the best way to order one's reasons?" A general rule of thumb when ordering your own argument is to put your strongest reason last and your second-strongest reason first. The idea here is to start and end with your most powerful arguments. If you imagine a quite skeptical audience, build bridges to your audience by summarizing alternative views early in the paper and concede to those that are especially strong. If your audience is neutral or undecided, you can summarize and respond to possible objections after you have presented your own case.

Revising

As you revise your argument, you need to attend both to the clarity of your writing (all the principles of closed-form prose described in Chapter 18) and also to the persuasiveness of your argument. As always, peer reviews are valuable, and especially so in argumentation if you ask your peer reviewers to role-play an opposing audience. The following Guidelines for Peer Reviews can both assist your peer reviewers and help you with revision.

GUIDELINES FOR PEER REVIEWS

Instructions for peer reviews are provided in Chapter 17 (pp. 519–520).

For the Writer
Prepare two or three questions you would like your peer reviewer to address while responding to your draft. The questions can focus on some aspect of your draft that you are uncertain about, on one or more sections where you particularly seek help or advice, on some feature that you particularly like about your draft, or on

some part you especially wrestled with. Write out your questions and give them to your peer reviewer along with your draft.

For the Reviewer

I. Read the draft at a normal reading speed from beginning to end. As you read, do the following:

A. Place a wavy line in the margin next to any passages that you find confusing, that contain something that doesn't seem to fit, or that otherwise slow down your reading.

B. Place a "Good!" in the margin next to any passages where you think the writing is particularly strong or interesting.

II. Read the draft again slowly and answer the following questions by writing brief explanations of your answers.

A. Introduction

1. How could the title be improved so that it announces the issue, reveals the writer's claim, or otherwise focuses your expectations and piques interest?

2. What strategies does the writer use to introduce the issue, engage your interest, and convince you that the issue is significant and problematic? What would add clarity and appeal?

3. How could the introduction more effectively forecast the argument and present the writer's claim? What would make the statement of the claim more focused, clear, or risky?

B. Arguing for the claim

1. Consider the overall structure: What strategies does the writer use to make the structure of the paper clear and easy to follow? How could the structure of the argument be improved?

2. Consider the support for the reasons: Where could the writer provide better evidence or support for each line of reasoning? Look for the grounds in each line of reasoning by noting the writer's use of facts, examples, statistics, testimony, or other evidence. Where could the writer supply more evidence or use existing evidence more effectively?

3. Consider the support for the warrants: For each line of reasoning, determine the assumptions (warrants) that the audience needs to grant for the argument to be effective. Are there places where these warrants need to be stated directly and supported with backing? How could the use of backing be improved?

4. Consider the writer's summary of and response to alternative viewpoints: Where does the writer treat alternative views? Are there additional alternative views that the writer should consider? What strategies does the writer use to respond to alternative views? How could the writer's treatment of alternative views be improved?

C. Conclusion: How might the conclusion more effectively bring completeness or closure to the argument?

III. Rhetorical considerations

A. *Purpose, audience,* and *genre:* How well has the writer achieved his or her persuasive purpose? Were you persuaded by this argument? Why or why not? How effective is the writer at imagining a neutral or skeptical audience (as opposed to preaching to the choir)? How effective is this writer at meeting the constraints of the classical argument genre?

B. *Logos, ethos,* and *pathos:* Overall, how could the writer improve the reasoning of this argument? How effective is the writer at gaining the reader's confidence and trust? How effective is the writer at appealing to the audience's values, beliefs, and emotions? How could the argument be made more vivid or gripping?

IV. If the writer has prepared questions for you, respond to his or her inquiries.

V. Sum up what you see as the main strengths and problem areas of the draft.

A. Strengths

B. Problem areas

VI. Read the draft one more time. Place a check mark in the margin wherever you notice problems in grammar, spelling, or mechanics (one check mark per problem).

Making an Evaluation

About Evaluative Writing

In everyday life you make evaluations all the time. You do so through a critical thinking process in which you match the thing being evaluated against criteria that you deem important. Consider how you might choose between two elective courses for your class schedule next term. You'll decide by matching each course against criteria that matter to you, such as the course's projected interest level, the course's workload and level of difficulty, the reputation of the teacher, the course's usefulness to your future career, or the attractiveness of the course's time slot.

In many evaluative decisions, the stakes will be high. In professional life you may have to write evaluations of a subordinate's work performance or create an argument for investing substantial company funds into Project A or Project B—decisions with enormous consequences. In fact, making evaluative arguments may be among the most important writing you will ever do.

This chapter instructs you in a systematic procedure for evaluating an object, person, or other phenomenon. Research suggests that most college assignments require some form of evaluative thinking. According to one study, college assignments often take the form of "good/better/best" questions:

Good: Is X good or bad? (Based on your current perspective, how effective was the U.S. response to the terrorist acts of September 11, 2001?)

Better: Which is better—X or Y? (Which is the better theoretical model for designing a treatment program for social anxiety disorder—a medical/biological model or an environmental model?)

Best: Among available options, which is the best solution to the problem? (For this engineering application, what is the best solution: conventional steel roller bearings, ceramic bearings, air bearings, or magnetic bearings? Why?)

You can write evaluations for different rhetorical aims such as an informative aim, an analytic aim, or a persuasive aim. A typical informative evaluation might be an article in *Consumer Reports,* where, for example, a prospective buyer of a used car might find independent data about a car's reliability, fuel economy, safety, and other factors. Typical analytical evaluations include movie, book, or restaurant reviews. In a typical restaurant review, for example, the writer might describe the good and bad features of Elvis's House of Chili using such criteria as quality of cuisine, seating and atmosphere, friendliness of service, cost, and so forth.

Table 3.1, pp. 49–50, discusses the different aims writers can have.

447

In this book we have chosen to treat evaluative writing as persuasion, in which case you imagine a skeptical audience with some degree of initial resistance to your evaluation. Because evaluation issues frequently cause the most disagreements within communities, many students writing classical arguments for Chapter 14 may have already addressed an evaluation issue in their arguments. (The starling case used as an example in Chapter 14 is an evaluation issue.) All the classical arguing skills covered in Chapter 14 apply as well to this chapter, which simply looks at this specific kind of argument in more depth. (The next chapter looks in depth at proposal arguments, which are another very common kind of argument.) Because evaluative arguments help communities make choices about actions, beliefs, or values, they are among the most important kinds of arguments to understand.

Exploring Evaluative Writing

To introduce you to evaluative thinking, we ask you to resolve a provocative evaluative question that at first looks innocuous. As you apply the principles of truth seeking and persuasion to this issue, be aware of your thinking processes.

> Situation: You are a tenth-grade social studies teacher. In your school building, the history and social studies classrooms have a large map of the world prominently displayed on a side wall. At a teacher's meeting, one of your colleagues proposes that in the history and social studies classrooms, this traditional map of the world be replaced with an equivalent-sized *inverted map* like the "What's Up? South!" map shown in Figure 15.1. The question becomes, "Which of these two kinds of maps—the traditional one or the inverted one—is better for the front of a social studies classroom?" (As a class you may wish to establish a fuller context for this discussion by stipulating the size and location of the high school, thereby giving you more information about the class, ethnicity, and politics of its community.)

1. Freewrite your initial thoughts on this question and then share your freewrites in small groups or as a whole class.
2. Working in small groups or as a whole class, create the best arguments you can in favor of each map, framing each argument as a claim with reasons. State each reason as a *because* clause (for example, "The traditional map is better because ... , because ... ," etc.; then do the same for the inverted map).
3. Role-playing the teachers in this high school, reach consensus on this issue by holding a truth-seeking discussion in which participants make their best persuasive cases for their points of view but listen empathically to other points of view.
4. When the class reaches consensus on the issue, write the frame of the deciding argument on the chalkboard as a claim with *because* clauses. If you wish, you can also write a dissenting argument on the board. Then write out the warrant that links each reason to the claim (that is, the unstated assumption that the audience has to accept for the reason to have any force). As we show in the next section, these warrants are actually statements of evaluative criteria for the argument.

The concept of underlying assumptions or warrants is explained in Chapter 14, pp. 398–399.

FIGURE 15.1 An Inverted Map

Mapmakers have traditionally placed north at the top of maps and south at the bottom. However, putting north on top is an arbitrary and conventional decision that has a subtle rhetorical effect. Because words like *top*, *above*, and *up* suggest superiority over words like *bottom*, *below*, and *down*, a conventional map makes the northern hemisphere seem more important than the southern. An inverted map reverses this effect, placing the southern hemisphere in the privileged "upper" position. Geographically, the inverted map is completely accurate. All that changes is the viewer's perspective. Map © 2002, www.odt.org

WRITING PROJECT

Write an argument in which you use evaluative thinking to persuade your audience to see the value (or lack of value) of the person, place, thing, event, or phenomenon that you are evaluating. The introduction to your argument should hook your audience's interest in your evaluation question. The body of your argument should establish criteria for evaluating your chosen subject, and then show how your subject meets or does not meet the criteria. Depending on the degree of controversy surrounding your subject, follow the procedure for other arguments by summarizing alternative views and responding to them through either concession or refutation.

For this assignment you need to pose an evaluative question that is important to your audience and invites multiple views. This question can arise from any of the various communities to which you belong: family, school, work, social or religious communities, or the civic communities of town, city, region, or nation. For example: What telephone plan (automobile, method of paying for your college education, day care facility) is best for your family? How effective is your school's general studies curriculum (intramural sports program, service-learning program, writing center, online registration system)? How effective is your employer's incentive program (office layout, customer relations office, dress code)? Is establishing a national ID system (profiling airline passengers, federalizing airport security) a good way to combat terrorism? Which movie deserves an Academy Award? Is art therapy a valuable contribution to clinical psychological practice?

In some cases, you may choose to evaluate a controversial person, event, thing, or phenomenon—something that engenders lively disagreement within a particular community. (For example: Is "Nimbletoes" Nelson a good quarterback?) When your subject is controversial, you need to consider alternative evaluations and show why yours is better.

In other cases, you may choose to evaluate something that is not directly controversial. Your purpose might be to help a specific audience determine how to spend their time or money. For example, is taking an art gallery walk a good way for students to spend a Saturday afternoon in your city? You might consider writing your evaluation within a specific genre. For example, you might write a review for a parents magazine evaluating whether *Lord of the Rings* is a good family movie. Or you might write an editorial for your school newspaper explaining why tutoring with the local children's literacy project is a good experience for education majors.

Understanding Evaluation Arguments

The Criteria-Match Process of Evaluation Arguments

Evaluation arguments involve what we call a *criteria-match* process. The first step in this process is to establish criteria; the second step is to show how well your subject matches these criteria. Here are several examples:

- Which students should be awarded the prestigious presidential scholarships?

  Criteria task: What are the criteria for the presidential scholarship?

  Match task: Which of the candidates best meets the criteria?

- Is hospitalization an effective treatment program for eating disorders?

  Criteria task: What are the criteria for an effective treatment for eating disorders?

  Match task: Does hospitalization meet these criteria?

- Is *Nightmare on Elm Street* a great horror film?

  Criteria task: What are the criteria for a great horror film?

  Match task: Does *Nightmare on Elm Street* meet these criteria?

- Which is the better map for this high school's social studies classroom—a traditional map or an inverted one?

  Criteria task: What are the criteria for a better map in this context?

  Match task: Which map best meets the criteria?

In each of these cases, it is possible to articulate criteria, even though stakeholders in each issue might argue for different criteria or weight the criteria differently. For example, on the map issue, one set of stakeholders might have argued this way:

ARGUMENT IN FAVOR OF TRADITIONAL MAP

The traditional map is the better choice

- because it follows standard conventions for mapmaking.
- because it is easier to comprehend quickly and will facilitate more thorough learning.
- because no costs are involved (we already own these maps and don't have to buy replacements).

The unstated assumptions (warrants) behind these reasons are that in choosing a map it is good to follow standard conventions, it is good to facilitate ease of comprehension, and it is good to keep costs low. In other words, this argument states that a good map should meet three criteria: (1) standard conventions, (2) ease of comprehension, and (3) minimal cost. Based on these criteria, the traditional map wins the argument hands down.

But another group of stakeholders might present a different argument:

Chapter 14, p. 400, introduces *warrant* as one of Toulmin's terms for the structure of an argument.

ARGUMENT IN FAVOR OF INVERTED MAP

The inverted map is the better choice

- because it reveals how certain arbitrary conventions of mapmaking (e.g., putting north on top) can have a rhetorical effect on how we read the map.
- because it exposes our ethnocentric assumptions about the "top" being superior to the "bottom."
- because it better promotes multicultural awareness and respect.

The warrants behind this argument establish a quite different set of criteria. To these stakeholders, a good map (1) reveals the rhetorical effect of arbitrary map conventions; (2) exposes ethnocentric assumptions; and (3) promotes multiculturalism. Based on these criteria, the inverted map wins hands down. Clearly, what is at issue in this dispute are the criteria themselves.

In other evaluation disputes, it is the application of criteria (the match argument) that causes disagreement. Consider a family deciding what used car to buy. They might agree on the criteria—let's say, (1) low cost, (2) safety, and (3) reliability. But they might disagree whether a specific car meets the criteria. In terms of cost, Car A may be initially cheaper than Car B but may get lower gas mileage and have a higher frequency-of-repair record. It would not be clear, then, whether Car A or Car B best meets the cost criterion.

For Writing and Discussion

Whenever you evaluate something you first need to establish criteria—that is, for any given class of items, you have to determine the qualities, traits, behaviors, or features that constitute excellence for members of that class. Then you need to match those criteria to a single member of that class—the thing you are evaluating. The following simple exercise will give you practice in thinking in this systematic, two-stage way:

1. Working individually, make a list of criteria that are important to you in choosing a career. These criteria are apt to differ from person to person. Some people might place "high income" at the top of their list, while others might put "adventure" or "being outdoors" or "time for family and leisure" at the top. Then rank your criteria from highest to lowest priority.
2. Share your criteria lists in small groups or as a whole class. Then write on the chalkboard two or three representative lists of criteria.
3. Finally, write several different careers on the board and match them to the lists of criteria. Which possible careers come out on top for you? Which ones come out on top based on the criteria lists placed on the board? Possible careers to consider include these: grade school/high school teacher, lawyer, auto mechanic, airplane pilot, bus driver, military officer, engineer, computer technician, insurance salesperson, accountant, small business owner, plumber, commercial artist, homemaker, nurse/physician/dentist, chiropractor/optometrist, social worker, police officer.
4. When disagreements arise, try to identify whether they are disagreements about criteria or disagreements about the facts of a given career.

The Role of Purpose and Context in Determining Criteria

Ordinarily, criteria are based on the purpose of the class to which the thing being evaluated belongs. For example, if you asked a professor to write a recommendation for you, he or she would need to know what you were applying for—A scholarship? Internship in a law office? Peace Corps volunteer? Summer job in a national park? The qualities of a successful law office intern differ substantially from those of a successful Peace Corps worker in Uganda. The recommendation isn't about you in the abstract but about you fulfilling the purposes of the class "law office intern" or "Peace Corps volunteer." Similarly, if you were evaluating a car, you would need to ask, "a car for what purpose?"—Reliable family transportation? Social status (if so, what social group?)? Environmental friendliness?

Decisions about purpose are often affected by context. For example, a union member, in buying a car, might specify an American-made car while a subscriber to *Mother Jones* magazine might specify high gas mileage and low pollution. To see how context influences criteria, consider a recent review of Seattle's soup kitchens appearing in a newspaper produced by homeless people. In most contexts, restaurant reviews focus on the quality of food. But in this review the highest criterion was the sense of dignity and love extended to homeless people by the staff.

Or consider the wider context of the map issue discussed earlier. The teachers might well pay attention to how administrators, parents, and school board members would react to a change of maps in the history classrooms. Would some people ridicule the teachers for their politically correct agenda? Would others applaud the teachers for championing multiculturalism and diversity? Would new, untenured teachers, drawn into the conflict, risk alienating key administrators or powerful senior teachers? Sometimes a tiny act that seems inconsequential at the time can become a symbolic battleground for clashing political forces.

For Writing and Discussion

1. Working in small groups or as a whole class, decide how you would evaluate a local eatery as a place to study. How would you evaluate it as a place to take a date, a place to hang out with friends, or a place to buy a nutritious meal?

2. Working in small groups or as a whole class, decide how you would evaluate Barry Bonds in the class "baseball player." How about the class "role model for young athletes"?

3. Working individually, identify several different classes that you belong to such as the class "son or daughter," "math student," "employee," "party animal," "friend." Choose one category in which you would rate yourself high or low. What are the criteria for excellence in that category? How do you meet or not meet these criteria? (You do not need to share your results unless you want to.)

4. As a whole class or in small groups, discuss how this individual exercise helped you realize how criteria for excellence vary when you place the same item into different classes with different purposes.

Other Considerations in Establishing Criteria

Establishing the criteria for evaluation arguments can entail other considerations besides purpose and context. We examine these considerations in this section.

The Problem of Apples and Oranges

To avoid the problem of mixing apples and oranges, try to place the thing you are evaluating into the smallest applicable class. That way, apples compete only with other apples, not with other members of the next-larger class, "fruit," where they have to go head-to-head against bananas, peaches, and oranges. You would therefore evaluate Kobe Bryant against other basketball players rather than against golfers and race car drivers. And if you were to evaluate a less talented basketball player, you might do so within the subclass of "point guard" or "power forward" or "off-the-bench scorer" rather than the general class "basketball player."

In the readings for this chapter, the student writer evaluating the film *Shanghai Noon* had to place it in the narrow class of "revisionist film western" to distinguish it from classic film westerns, dramas, and Academy Award winners or other subclasses of film. Clearly, the criteria for a successful revisionist film western are different from those of a horror film, dramatic comedy, or blockbuster film.

The Problem of Standards: What's Commonplace Versus What's Ideal

When we determine criteria, we often encounter the problem of what's commonplace versus what's ideal. Do we praise something because it is better than average, or do we condemn it because it is less than ideal? Do we hold it to absolute standards or to common practice? Do we censure someone for paying a housekeeper under the table to avoid taxes (failure to live up to an ideal), or do we overlook this behavior because it is so common? Is it better for high schools to pass out free contraceptives because teenagers are having sex anyway (what's *commonplace*), or is it better not to pass them out in order to support abstinence (what's *ideal*)?

There is no easy way to decide which standard to use. The problem with the "ideal" is that nothing may ever measure up. The problem with the "commonplace" is that we may lower our standards and slip into a morally dangerous relativism. In deciding which standard to follow, we need to recognize the limitations of each, to make the best choice we can, and to use the same standard for all items being evaluated.

The Problems of Necessary, Sufficient, and Accidental Criteria

In identifying criteria, we often recognize that some are more important than others. Suppose you said, "I will be happy with any job as long as it puts food on my table and gives me time for my family." In this case the criteria "adequate income" and "time for family," taken together, are *sufficient*, meaning that once these criteria are met, the thing being rated meets your standard for excellence. Suppose you said instead, "I am hard to please in my choice of a career, which must meet many criteria. But I definitely will reject any career that doesn't put enough food on my table or allow me time for my family." In this case the criteria of "adequate income" and "time for family" are *necessary* but not *sufficient*, meaning that these two criteria have to be met for a career to meet your standards, but that other criteria must be met also.

Besides necessary and sufficient criteria, there are also *accidental* criteria, which are added bonuses but not essential. For example, you might say something like, "Although it's not essential, having a career that would allow me to be outside a lot would be nice." In this case "being outside" is an *accidental* criteria (nice but not required).

The Problem of Seductive Empirical Measures

Empirical data can help you evaluate all sorts of things. If you are buying an automobile, you can be helped a great deal by knowing the numbers for its horsepower and acceleration, for its fuel economy and frequency-of-repair record, and for its potential resale value. But sometimes the need to make defensible evaluative decisions leads people to empirical measures that disastrously oversimplify complex matters. Every year, for example, new crops of potential professional athletes are scrutinized minutely for their records in the forty-yard dash, the bench press, the vertical jump, and so forth. Every year, some of the people who max out on these empirical measures flop ingloriously in actual competition because they lack qualities that are difficult if not impossible to measure empirically, whereas other athletes, with more modest scores, achieve great success thanks to these same invisible qualities.

Quantifiable measures can be helpful, of course. But they are so concrete and they make comparisons so easy that they can seduce you into believing that you can make complex judgments by comparing numbers. It's all too easy to fall into the trap of basing college admissions on SAT scores, scholarships on grade point averages, or the success of a government policy on tax dollars saved.

The Problem of Cost

A final problem in establishing criteria is cost. A given X may be far superior to any other Xs in its class, but it may also cost far more. Before you move from evaluating an X to acting on your evaluation (by buying, hiring, or doing X), you must consider cost, whether it is expressed as dollars, time, or lost opportunity. There's little question, for example, that a Lexus is superior to a Nissan Sentra according to most automotive criteria. But are the differences sufficient to justify the additional thirty thousand or so dollars that the Lexus costs?

Using Toulmin's System to Develop Evaluation Arguments

In Chapter 14, we presented a language for talking about argument based on the terminology of philosopher Stephen Toulmin. We explained how you can examine any claim with reason from the perspective of *grounds* (evidence to support the reason), *warrant* (the unstated assumption that links the reason to your claim), *backing* (an argument to support the warrant if needed), *conditions of rebuttal* (ways that a skeptical audience might refute your argument by attacking your reason and grounds or your warrant), and *qualifier* (a limiting phrase to reduce the sweep of your claim). Because the warrants for an evaluation argument are typically statements of your criteria, this system can easily be applied to evaluation arguments.

Let's say that you are the student member of a committee to select a professor for an outstanding teaching award. Several members of the committee want to give the award to Professor M. Mouse, a popular sociology professor at your institution. You are opposed. One of your lines of reasoning is that Professor Mouse's courses aren't rigorous. Here is how you could develop this line of reasoning using the planning schema explained in Chapter 14.

Chapter 14, pp. 404–406, explains how the Toulmin system can help writers map out and structure an argument to connect with their audience.

CLAIM WITH REASON

Professor Mouse does not deserve the teaching award because his courses aren't rigorous.

GROUNDS

I need to provide evidence that his courses aren't rigorous. From the dean's office records, I have discovered that eighty percent of his students get As or high Bs; a review of his syllabi shows that he requires little outside reading and only one short paper; he has a reputation in my dorm of being fun and easy.

WARRANT

Having rigorous academic standards is a necessary criterion for the university teaching award.

BACKING

I need to show why I think rigorous academic standards are necessary. Quality of teaching should be measured by the amount that students learn. Good teaching is more than a popularity contest. Good teachers draw high-level performance from their students and motivate them to put time and energy into learning. High standards lead to the development of skills that are demanded in society.

CONDITIONS OF REBUTTAL

How could someone attack my reason and grounds? Might a person say that Mouse has high standards? Could someone show that students really earned the high grades? Are the students I talked to not representative? Could someone say that Mouse's workload and grading patterns meet or exceed the commonplace behavior of faculty in his department? *How could someone attack my warrant?* Could someone argue that rigorous academic standards aren't as important as other criteria—that this is an accidental not a necessary criterion? Could a person say that Mouse's goal—to inspire interest in sociology—is best achieved by not loading students down with too many papers and too much reading, which can appear like busywork? (I'll need to refute this argument.) Could someone say that the purpose of giving the university teaching award is public relations and it is therefore important to recognize widely popular teachers who will be excellent speakers at banquets and other public forums?

QUALIFIER

Rather than saying that Professor Mouse doesn't deserve the award, perhaps it would be better for me to say that he is a weak candidate or even a generally strong candidate except for one notable weakness.

Conducting an Evaluation Argument: An Extended Example of Evaluating a Museum

For an extended example of how to evaluate Web sites for academic purposes, see Chapter 21, pp. 631–637.

Now that we have explored some potential difficulties in establishing and defending criteria for an evaluation, let's consider in more detail the process of making an evaluation argument.

The student examples in this section focus on the evaluation of a rock and roll museum in Seattle, Washington, called Experience Music Project (EMP). Designed by world-famous architect Frank Gehry (who is known for his creation of the Guggenheim Museum in Bilbao, Spain, the Aerospace Hall in Los Angeles, and other famous buildings around the world), EMP was sponsored by Microsoft

WRITING
PROJECTS

FIGURE 15.2 Experience Music Project, Seattle, Washington

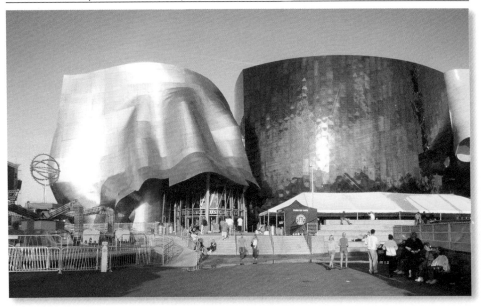

cofounder Paul Allen as a tribute to rock singer Jimi Hendrix and to rock music itself, especially in the Pacific Northwest. In Figure 15.2, you can see this innovative structure which has sparked much controversy (is it a wonder or an eyesore?). Sharing some characteristics with the Rock and Roll Hall of Fame and Museum in Cleveland, Ohio, EMP features some permanent exhibits—the Hendrix Gallery, the Guitar Gallery (tracing the development of guitars from the 1500s to the electric guitars of today), Milestones (including displays from rhythm and blues to hip-hop and current rap artists), and Northwest Passage (focusing on popular music in Seattle, from jazz and rhythm and blues to heavy metal, punk, grunge, and the contemporary music scene). EMP also includes Sound Lab (where visitors can play instruments using interactive technology), On Stage (where visitors can pretend to be rock stars playing before a cheering crowd), Artist's Journey (a ride involving motion platform technology), three restaurants, and a store. (To see for yourself what EMP is and how it looks on the inside, you can go to its Web site at www.emplive.com. A Web search on Frank Gehry will show you photos of his prizewinning architecture.)

Let's now turn to the specific steps of making an evaluation argument.

Step 1: Determining the Class to Which X Belongs and the Purposes of That Class

When you conduct an evaluation argument, you must first assign your person/object/phenomenon (the X you are evaluating) to a category or class and then determine the purposes of that class. Often people disagree about an evaluation because they disagree about the arguer's choice of category for X. EMP, as students soon discovered, could be placed in several different categories, leading to different criteria for evaluation. Here are typical classes proposed by students:

- A tourist attraction (for an audience of visitors to Seattle)
- A museum of rock history (for people interested in the development of rock as an art form)
- A rock and roll shrine (for rock fans who want to revere their favorite artists and feel part of the rock scene for a day)

Clearly these classes have different purposes. The purpose of a tourist attraction is to offer a unique, fun place to spend the day during a visit to Seattle. The purpose of a rock museum is to teach about the history of its subject in an informative, interesting, and accessible way. The purpose of a rock and roll shrine is to honor famous rock stars, bring visitors into their lives and work, and let them experience the music scene.

Step 2: Determining and Weighting Criteria

The criteria for your evaluation are directly connected to the purposes of the class to which X belongs. The following lists show typical criteria chosen by different students for each of the classes listed in Step 1:

- A good *tourist attraction* should
  - be entertaining and enjoyable.
  - be affordable and worth the price, not simply out to gouge tourists' wallets.
  - be unique—something the tourist wouldn't find in another city.
- A good *museum of rock history* should
  - have a clear, well-organized layout that is easy to navigate.
  - display objects of clear aesthetic or historical significance.
  - teach the public by providing clear, meaningful information about rock music.
  - arouse interest in rock as an art form and encourage the public's appreciation and involvement.
- A good *rock and roll shrine* should
  - take fans up close and personal into the lives of major artists.
  - encourage fans to appreciate the complexity of rock and the skills of artists.
  - help fans experience the rock scene and fantasize about being rock stars themselves.

In addition to identifying criteria, you should arrange them in order of importance so that you build to your most important criterion. In each of the preceding examples, students placed their most important criterion last.

Step 3: Determining the Extent to Which X Meets Your Criteria for the Class

A third step in constructing an evaluation argument is to make your match argument: To what extent does X meet or not meet the criteria you have formulated? The following examples show how three students framed the match part of their evaluation arguments on EMP. Note how each student matches EMP to the specific criteria he or she has selected.

- Experience Music Project is a tourist trap rather than an attraction because

- the headphones and heavy computerized MEGs (Museum Exhibit Guides) keep everyone isolated, making companionship difficult.
- the arrangement of exhibits is chaotic, leading to frustration and repetition of the same experiences.
- it doesn't give any substance, just endless music trivia.
- it's too expensive and commercial, leaving the tourist feeling ripped-off.
- Experience Music Project is a good museum of rock and roll history because
  - it covers a range of popular music styles from jazz and blues to reggae, punk, grunge, and hip-hop.
  - it provides interesting information on musicians, musical styles, and key moments in popular music history.
  - it makes people excited about popular music and its history through the museum's interactive exhibits and technologically advanced museum guide devices.
- For rock fans, Experience Music Project is a good rock and roll shrine because
  - it gives illuminating insights into the lives and artistry of many rock musicians.
  - it gives an in-depth look at some of the greats like Jimi Hendrix and helps fans really appreciate the talent of these musicians.
  - the "onstage" room lets fans fulfill a fantasy by pretending they are rock stars.

Step 4: Determining What Alternative Views You Must Respond to in Your Evaluation Argument

Finally, in constructing your evaluation argument you need to determine whether your intended audience is likely to object to (1) the class in which you have placed your object; (2) the criteria you have developed for assessing your object; or (3) the degree to which your object matches the criteria you have chosen. You have numerous options for accommodating your audience's doubts or objections. For example, if your proposed class is controversial, you might choose to justify it in your introduction. If your criteria might be controversial, you could address objections before you start the match part of your argument. If you think your match argument will raise doubts, you could intersperse alternative views throughout or treat them separately near the end of your argument. Any of these methods can work.

In the readings section of this chapter, we include a student writer's complete evaluation argument on the Experience Music Project.

For Writing and Discussion

Consider how student writer Katie Tiehen confronts and responds to alternative views. After reading this typical passage from her argument, answer these questions:

1. What objections to her argument does Katie anticipate (doubts about her proposed class for EMP, her criteria, or her match argument)?

(continued)

2. How does Katie respond to alternative views—by conceding points and shifting back to her own perspective or by refuting alternative views with counterreasons and counterexamples?

> . . . Some may challenge my contention that EMP is an ineffective museum of rock history by arguing that a day spent at EMP is entertaining and fun. I'll be the first to admit that EMP is fun. From a rock and roll fan's perspective, EMP is nonstop entertainment, a musical paradise. I felt like a five-year-old on Christmas morning when I saw Eric Clapton's guitar, Jimi Hendrix's personal journals, and walls plastered in punk memorabilia. These items, coupled with video documentaries and hands-on activities, provided hours of enjoyment. Because of the fun factor, it's easy for people to jump to EMP's defense. However, it is not the entertainment value of EMP that I am questioning. There's no doubt that it is a fun and amusing place to visit. The problem arises when one tries to classify EMP as an historical museum, which should provide visitors with access to objects of lasting historical significance. Some entertainment is fine, but not to the point that it clouds the true purpose of the museum as it does in EMP's case. After two visits, I still couldn't tell you where rock and roll originated, but I could tell you that the line to play the drums in Sound Lab is really long. Entertainment is the main purpose of EMP and it shouldn't be.

READINGS

The first reading is a student essay by Jackie Wyngaard evaluating the Experience Music Project in Seattle, Washington.

Jackie Wyngaard (student)
EMP:
Music History or Music Trivia?

1   Along with other college students new to Seattle, I wanted to see what cultural opportunities the area offers. I especially wanted to see billionaire Paul Allen's controversial Experience Music Project (known as EMP), a huge, bizarre, shiny, multicolored structure that is supposed to resemble a smashed guitar. Brochures say that EMP celebrates the creativity of American popular music, but it has prompted heated discussions among architects, Seattle residents, museumgoers, and music lovers, who have questioned its commercialism and the real value of its exhibits. My sister recommended this museum to me because she knows I am a big music lover and a rock and roll fan. Also, as an active choir member since the sixth grade, I have always been intrigued by the history of music. I went to EMP expecting to learn more about music history from exhibits that showed a range of popular musical styles, that traced historical connections and influ-

ences, and that enjoyably conveyed useful information. However, as a museum of rock history, EMP is a disappointing failure.

2   EMP claims that it covers the history of rock and roll from its roots to the styles of today, but it fails at this task because it isolates musicians and styles without explaining historical progressions or cultural influences. For instance, the museum doesn't show how Elvis Presley's musical style was influenced by his predecessors like Chuck Berry and Muddy Waters. It doesn't show how early folk and blues influenced Bob Dylan's music. It doesn't show how early jazz paved the way for rock and roll. How are these isolated and separate EMP exhibits connected? How did rock and roll progress from the '50s "Let's Go to the Hop" beats to the laid-back guitar riffs of the '60s and '70s? How did '70s music become the heavy metal, head-banger rock of the '80s and '90s? How did these styles lead to rap? The exhibits show the existence of these different styles, but they don't help viewers understand the historical developments or historical context. While it is interesting to see a peace patch once owned by Janis Joplin, this exhibit does not explain either the social and political events of the time or Joplin's political views.

3   Another fault of EMP is that it omits many influential groups and musicians, particularly women. For example, there is no display about the Beatles, the Rolling Stones, Led Zeppelin, or the Doors. The exhibits also exclude many major female artists who made substantial contributions to popular music. I found nothing about Joan Baez, Ella Fitzgerald, Aretha Franklin, Carly Simon, or Joni Mitchell. I was also surprised that there were few women mentioned in the Northwest Passage exhibit. Weren't more women involved in the Seattle music scene? As a woman interested in music, I felt left out by EMP's overall neglect of women musicians.

4   Perhaps most frustrating about EMP is the way exhibits are explained through the awkward, difficult-to-use handheld computer called a Museum Exhibit Guide (MEG). The explanations are hard to access and then disappointing in their content. I wanted to hear a landmark song that an artist wrote or an interesting analysis of the artist's musical style. Instead, I listened to "how Elvis made the leather jacket famous" and other random trivia. The MEG also offers too many choices for each exhibit, like a Web page with a dozen links. But after all the time and effort, you learn nothing that increases your understanding or stimulates your thinking about music history. The MEGs themselves are very heavy, clunky, and inconvenient. If you don't point this gadget exactly at the activator, nothing happens. It took me a good ten minutes to figure out how to get the device to play information for me, and many of my classmates had to keep going back to the booth to get new batteries or other repairs. The museum would be much more effective if visitors had the option of just reading about the displays from plaques on the walls.

5   I know that many people will disagree with my assessment of EMP. They'll point to the fun of the interactive exhibits and the interesting collection of album covers, crushed velvet costumes, concert clips, famous

guitars, and old jukeboxes. But a good museum has to be more than a display of artifacts and an array of hands-on activities. Pretending you're a rock star by performing on stage with instruments doesn't tell you how a certain style of music came about. Displaying trivial information about Elvis's leather jacket or Janis Joplin's feather boa doesn't help you appreciate the importance of their music. Devoting half an exhibit to punk rock without any analysis of that style doesn't teach you anything. In short, the museum displays frivolous trivia tidbits without educational substance.

6   Music lovers hoping for an educational experience about the rock and roll era of musical history will be disappointed by EMP. And this is without the additional insult of having to shell out $19.95 to get in the door. Speaking for serious music lovers and students of music history, I have to say that EMP is a failure.

Thinking Critically about "EMP: Music History or Music Trivia?"

1. What strategies particularly appropriate for evaluation arguments does Jackie Wyngaard use in her introduction?
2. How has Jackie chosen to classify Experience Music Project? What criteria does she choose?
3. In the match part of her argument, what evidence does Jackie use to support her assessment of Experience Music Project?
4. What alternative views does she acknowledge and where in her argument does she choose to treat them? Does she anticipate objections to her criteria or to the match part of her argument? What other objections might people raise to her argument?
5. What do you find persuasive about her arguments? How might this evaluation argument be improved?

The second reading aims at changing its readers' assessment of the children's television program *Sesame Street*. It posits just one criterion—a good children's program should not be sexist—and then focuses exclusively on demonstrating that *Sesame Street* is sexist. Its authors are both attorneys and mothers of young children.

Diane Helman and Phyllis Bookspan
Sesame Street:
Brought to You by the Letters M-A-L-E

1   A recent report released by the American Association of University Women, "How Schools Shortchange Women," finds that teachers, textbooks, and tests are, whether intentionally or unintentionally, giving preferential treatment to elementary-school boys. As a result, girls who enter school with equal or better academic potential than their male counterparts lose confidence and do not perform as well.

2   An earlier study about law students, published in the *Journal of Legal Education*, found a similar disparity. "Gender Bias in the Classroom" found that male law students are called upon in class more frequently than females, speak for longer periods of time, and are given more positive feedback by law professors.

3   The article raised some disturbing questions about whether women and men receive truly equal education in American law schools.

4   Unfortunately, this insidious gender bias appears long before our children enter school and pervades even the television show *Sesame Street*. Yes, *Sesame Street* is sexist! But, just as in the story of the emperor and his new clothes, many of us do not notice the obvious.

5   The puppet stars of the show, Bert and Ernie, and all the other major *Sesame Street* animal characters—Big Bird, Cookie Monster, Grover, Oscar the Grouch, Kermit the Frog, and Mr. Snuffleupagus—are male. Among the secondary characters, including Elmo, Herry Monster, Count VonCount, Telemonster, Prairie Dawn, and Betty Lou, only a very few are girls.

6   The female Muppets always play children, while the males play adult parts in various scenes. In a recently aired skit "Squeal of Fortune," this disparity is evident when the host of the show introduces the two contestants. Of Count VonCount of Transylvania the host asks, "What do you do for a living?" to which the count responds authoritatively, "I count!" Of Prairie Dawn, he inquires, "And how do you spend your day?" Sure, it would be silly to ask a schoolgirl what she does for a living. But none of the female Muppets on *Sesame Street* are even old enough to earn a living.

7   Further, almost all the baby puppet characters on *Sesame Street* are girls. For example, Snuffie's sibling is Baby Alice; in books, Grover's baby cousin is a girl, and when Herry Monster's mother brings home the new baby—it's a girl. Since babies are totally dependent and fairly passive, the older (male) relatives take care of them and provide leadership.

8   Also, the female Muppets almost never interact with each other. In sharp contrast, consequential and caring friendships have been fully developed between male Muppets: Ernie and Bert; Big Bird and Snuffie; even Oscar the Grouch and his (male) worm, Squirmy.

9   Any parent of toddlers or preschoolers can testify that the "girls" on *Sesame Street* are not very popular. Children ask their parents for Bert and Ernie dolls, not Baby Alice. Is this just because the girls are not marketed via books, tapes, placemats and toy dolls the same way the boys are? Or is it that the *Sesame Street* writers simply have not developed the girls into the same types of lovable, adorable personalities that belong to the main characters?

10   Interestingly and peculiarly, the minor "girls" look more human than most of the well-loved animal roles. They are not physically cuddly, colorful or bizarre, as are the more important male characters. Prairie Dawn has ordinary blonde hair and brown eyes—nothing even remotely similar to Big Bird's soft yellow feathers or Cookie Monster's wild, bright blue, mane.

11   Yes, we believe that *Sesame Street* is one of the best shows on television for small children. Our children—boys and girls—are regular viewers. In addition to its educational value, lack of violence and emphasis on cooperation, the adult characters on the show are admirably balanced in terms of avoiding sexual stereotypes.

12   But even the best of the bunch has room for improvement. Just as elementary through professional school educators must learn to be more sensitive to subtle and unintentional gender bias, so too should the folks at Children's Television Network. We can stop sexism from seeping into our children's first "formal" educational experience.

13   The message was brought to you by the letter F: fairness for females.

Thinking Critically about "Sesame Street"

1. This essay spends no time on the criteria part of the argument ("Sexism is bad") and all its time on the match argument ("*Sesame Street* exhibits sexism"). Why do the authors feel no need to defend the criterion?
2. Do the authors convince you that *Sesame Street* is sexist?
3. If you agree with the argument that *Sesame Street* is sexist, should that criterion be sufficient for undermining the popular assessment of *Sesame Street* as a model educational program for children?

The final essay, by student writer Cecily Ballou, evaluates the film *Shanghai Noon.* Cecily's evaluation argument was written for a composition class that included a film unit connected to the class's thematic focus on the myth of the old west and contemporary violence.

Cecily Ballou (Student)
<u>Shanghai Noon</u> Is Not the Same Old West

1   The film <u>Shanghai Noon</u> has generally been regarded as lightweight entertainment. Some of my friends thought it was a funny Jackie Chan-slap-stick-martial-arts film. Others thought it was just a bad movie. However, in the context of my composition class's focus on classic film westerns and more recent film westerns, <u>Shanghai Noon</u> becomes more interesting. My class posed the question, "Do contemporary films about the American West merely repackage the themes of classic western films, or are they revisionist westerns that tell a different story of the West?" If they revise the old western formulas, are they good revisionist westerns or half-hearted attempts? What appeals to me about classic westerns are the sweeping views of open plains and towering rock formations, the handsome horses, and the stern, independent gunfighters and cowboys who ride off into the sunset. But I and most of my class concluded that classic film westerns perpetuate some negative images and harmful ideas. Classic film westerns devalue and stereotype minorities and women and promote violence, guns, and killing as the solution to every problem. Although I expected <u>Shanghai Noon,</u> a comic western made in 2000, to be bad as a film and bad as a revisionist western, this film actually has some merit. It gives minorities important roles, features strong women characters, and replaces the deadly seriousness of classic film westerns with funny, playful satire, making it a good revisionist film western.

2   Someone might say that the plot of <u>Shanghai Noon</u> sounds similar to the plots of many classic film westerns in its focus on rescuing a woman and on fights between good guys and bad guys; however, the plot has different twists throughout. The film begins in 1881 in China and then moves to the American West. Princess Pei Pei (Lucy Liu) runs away from her restricted life in the royal family and thinks she has escaped her arranged marriage but finds herself betrayed, kidnapped, and held captive in Carson City, Nevada. Her father, the Emperor, sends gold and three of his Imperial Guards to ransom her. Another guard of questionable reputation, Chon Wang (Jackie Chan), manages to join the rescue mission. Once in the West, a series of misadventures, including a train robbery, separate Chon Wang from his countrymen. As he struggles to carry out his duty to the princess, Chon Wang gains a resourceful Native American wife, Falling Leaves (Brandon Merrill), and a partner, an easy-going, inept bandit, Roy O'Bannon (Owen Wilson). In the big confrontation at the end of the film, the princess, Chon Wang, and Roy O'Bannon defeat her captors, and Falling Leaves and her tribe disarm Roy's old gang.

3   The first feature that makes this movie a good revisionist film western is its choice of a Chinese hero, who is actually a person of little importance in the Chinese court who knows nothing about life in the American West. The film begins in the Forbidden City in China, and the Emperor's reluctance to

let Chon Wang accompany his specially picked Imperial Guards implies that Chon Wang doesn't fit the mold for Imperial Guards. Throughout the film, though, Chon Wang shows that he is intensely loyal to Princess Pei Pei, never giving up his quest to find her despite many obstacles. Chon Wang also possesses dignity and pride, compassion, courage, stamina, and amazing martial arts skills. When Roy O'Bannon tries to cut off his queue, Chon Wang fiercely objects and fights to maintain this symbol of ethnic pride and identity. He also does not let Roy get away with lying to him or snubbing him because he is Chinese. Chon Wang shows bravery by saving the Native American boy who is being hunted down by an enemy tribe. Often western heroes are motivated by revenge and goaded into action by personal insults. Chon Wang stands up for himself but he is also driven by honor and devotion. Because he uses martial arts and ingenious methods of fighting and because he wins although he is outnumbered, Chon Wang seems more heroic than the typical hired gun, outlaw, cowboy, and sheriff who are simply fast on the draw. Also, his talent with martial arts makes Asian ways appear superior to the fighting styles of the Old West.

4   In its main women characters, <u>Shanghai Noon</u> changes conventional classic film westerns' depiction of both minorities and women. Often in film westerns, there aren't any women characters; it's a male world. For example, in <u>The Good, the Bad, and the Ugly</u> (a Clint Eastwood film from 1968), the only woman is beaten up. Often, if women do appear, they are left on the sidelines, helpless and useless, or are classified by their sexuality into one of two categories—"good" respectable women fit for marrying or "bad" fallen women who work as bar maids and whores in brothels. In <u>Stagecoach</u> (a John Wayne film from 1939), the whore with a good heart can cook but she can't defend herself. In contrast, in <u>Shanghai Noon</u>, the two main women characters—Princess Pei Pei and the Native American chief's daughter, Falling Leaves—are bold, willful, independent, and very active. They defy all strict gender roles. Princess Pei Pei is tricked by her white tutor, who takes advantage of Pei Pei's desire to escape her rigid society and pre-arranged marriage, but she resists her captors, refuses to be bent to their will, and courageously works beside the Chinese laborers. In the end of the film, she uses martial arts herself and helps Chon Wang and Roy defeat her captors. Falling Leaves is particularly resourceful. She is at home on a horse, can rope, and is very accurate with a rifle. She engineers the jailbreak for Chon Wang and Roy, using a stampeding herd of steers to break down the jail. She also shoots the ropes about to hang Chon Wang and Roy, an act traditionally performed by men in westerns. She summons her tribe to appear at the end of the film where they save Chon Wang and Roy from being gunned down by Roy's crazy former gang. Beautiful and lusty, Falling Leaves chooses to help Chon Wang and Roy because it amuses her and because she finds them attractive. In order to survive, the heroes in the film need these women's cleverness, courage, and skill.

5   Some viewers might say that this film exhibits many of the flaws of classic film westerns. Even though only three people die—the corrupt, mean

marshal; Princess Pei Pei's captor; and Chon Wang's uncle—the film is full of violent combat. Chon Wang by himself and later with Roy are always fighting someone. However, these fights are choreographed to show off Chon Wang's ingenuity and prowess at martial arts and are physical combats, not gunfights. They are comic because Chon Wang uses whatever is handy— pine trees, a rope with a horseshoe at the end, and antlers from the saloon wall—to win the fight, making them funny, thrilling acts of self-defense.

6   Some students in class questioned the women's roles. I admit that the only white women in this film are buxom whores in the brothel and there's nothing new about that. Also, the main women characters—Princess Pei Pei and Falling Leaves—are on screen much less than Chon Wang and Roy O'Bannon. In addition, a case could be made that in her kidnapping, Princess Pei Pei is the helpless, passive maiden in need of rescue. Yet, the film complicates that idea by endowing Pei Pei with the boldness to run away in the first place and by making her active in fighting her captors. She also refuses to go back to her restricted life in China, preferring to stay in Nevada to help the Chinese laborers.

7   Some viewers might also say this film is a comedy but not a western. In fact, some viewers thought this movie was mainly silliness and slapstick. Indeed, it is written to show off Jackie Chan's physical comedy, his funny facial expressions, and comic battles; however, the whole film employs classic western conventions in order to take them apart and challenge them. The more viewers know about westerns, the funnier the film is.

8   Finally, <u>Shanghai Noon</u> is a good revisionist western partly because it makes fun of the seriousness of classic film westerns, which are often tense and somber as the hero heads for his big test, the inevitable final showdown. By giving power to minorities, women, and two often-awkward men, <u>Shanghai Noon</u> challenges the classic western formulas. It makes such classic western scenes as the train robbery, the capture by Native Americans, the saloon fight, the jailbreak, the near-hanging, and the shoot-out into humorous misadventures. Shaking up conventions makes viewers laugh and makes them wonder why we have come to think of the West in these terms anyway: Why are classic film westerns dominated by white males and filled with violence when the West of history was much more complex and multicultural? Roy O'Bannon, Chon Wang's partner, uses contemporary speech with lots of psychological lingo ("Relax. You're too tense") that seems humorously out of place and mocks the typical anti-social western heroes who bear their pain, fear, and all their feelings in silence. The film also points out and mocks racist assumptions. For instance, at the end of the film, Falling Leaves reveals she has been a fluent English speaker all along. Finally, the names in this film such as "Chon Wang" and "Shanghai Noon" are humorous and satirical. In their laughable reference to important parts of the classic western tradition—John Wayne and the film <u>High Noon</u>—they make viewers begin to question the traditional characters and conflicts.

9   <u>Shanghai Noon</u> is certainly not the only way to create a revisionist western. There are problems with classic film westerns that we should confront,

not simply laugh at and brush off. Even this film suggests some serious social questions it doesn't deal with: What about all those exploited Chinese laborers who built the railroads? What about the Native American tribes who weren't able to hold on to their territory and their culture? In choosing light comedy over realism, this film ducks some of the big issues. Still, it plants different views of the West, minorities, women, the western hero, and violence in viewers' minds, and in making fun of classic film westerns, it weakens the power of those old images.

Thinking Critically about "*Shanghai Noon* Is Not the Same Old West"

1. Cecily Ballou's introduction highlights her composition class as the rhetorical context for this essay. What other ways could she introduce her evaluation argument?
2. To argue that *Shanghai Noon* is not a classic film western but is a good revisionist western, Cecily must set up two sets of related criteria: the features that make a good classic western and the features that make a good revisionist western. What criteria does she use for each?
3. What evidence is persuasive in the match part of the argument?
4. What objections and alternative views does she address? How effective do you find her rebuttal and her choice of where she handles these views? What other alternative views can you think of?
5. Where do you find this evaluation argument persuasive? Where could it be made stronger?

For Writing and Discussion

An important part of writing evaluation arguments is deciding on criteria by considering the attributes and purpose of a class: What features or criteria constitute excellence within that class? Another main move in an evaluation argument is matching your X (the subject of your evaluation) to the criteria: Does your X meet or fail to meet the criteria? This exercise asks you to use Cecily Ballou's evaluation essay and the movie poster in Figure 15.3 to practice thinking about the criteria and match parts of arguments.

1. In her evaluation of *Shanghai Noon*, Cecily Ballou places this film into the class of "revisionist film western" and argues that it is a good example of its class. This film could also be evaluated in other terms:

FIGURE 15.3 Movie Poster of *Bad Girls*

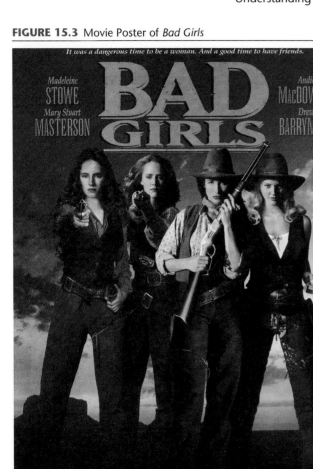

    a. as a good buddy film
    b. as a good action thriller
    c. as a good family comedy
    d. as good in-flight entertainment (a good movie to watch on a plane).

Construct criteria for each of these classes. If you and your group are familiar with *Shanghai Noon*, sketch out the match argument for one of these classes, showing how you would evaluate this film against your criteria for that class.

(continued)

2. One of Cecily's main criteria for a good revisionist film western is that the film positively transforms the view of women. She explains that classic film westerns portray the American West as a tough man's world in which women are either (a) absent; (b) depicted as helpless and useless or passive and dependent; or (c) classified according to their sexuality as either proper and fit for marrying or as whores. The 1994 film *Bad Girls* was one of a group of 1990s film westerns (some others were *The Ballad of Little Jo* [1993] and *The Quick and the Dead* [1995]) with women heroes. *Bad Girls* tells the story of four prostitutes who become outlaws after one shoots a violent customer and the women lose their savings in a bank robbery. Study the poster for the film *Bad Girls* in Figure 15.3 and consider the way the women are portrayed. In classic film westerns, poster advertisements often show the gunfighter hero in a climactic shootout in the desert or on the main street of a dusty western town, emphasizing the hero's skill with a gun, his independence and bravery in facing death, and his acceptance of violence as an ultimate test and final solution. With these ideas in mind, consider the way the women characters are posed in this poster. What are they wearing, holding, and doing? What is their hair like? What is the background? How does the angle of the camera affect the appearance of the women? How do the words on the poster contribute to the visual effect? (Why does the poster designer use the word *woman* in the first sentence of the verbal copy instead of word *girls* from the title?) From the poster alone, what view of women seems to emerge? What case could be made that this film might meet Cecily's criteria for a good revisionist film western?

Composing Your Essay

Generating and Exploring Ideas

For your evaluation essay, you will try either to change your readers' assessment of a controversial person, event, thing, or phenomenon or help your readers decide whether an event or thing is worth their time or money.

If you have not already chosen an evaluation issue, try thinking about evaluation questions within the various communities to which you belong:

Local civic community: evaluative questions about transportation, land use, historical monuments, current leaders, political bills or petitions, housing, parking policies, effectiveness of police

National civic community: evaluative questions about public education, environmental concerns, economic policies, responses to terrorism, Supreme Court decisions, foreign policies, political leaders

Your university community: evaluative questions about academic or sports programs, campus life programs, first-year or transfer student orientation, clubs, dorm life, campus facilities, financial-aid programs, campus security, parking, cultural programs

Your scholarly community or disciplinary community in your major: evaluative questions about internships, study abroad programs, general studies programs, course requirements, first-year studies, major curriculum, advising, course sequences, teaching methods, homework requirements, academic standards, recent books or articles, new theories in a field, library resources, laboratory facilities, Web site sources of primary documents or numerical data in a field

Culture and entertainment issues within your social or family communities: evaluative questions about restaurants, movies, plays, museums, TV shows, musicians, video games, entertainment Web sites, concerts, books, paintings, sports figures, buildings

Consumer issues within your social or family communities: evaluative questions about computer systems, CDs, cars, clothing brands, stores, products, e-commerce

Work communities: Evaluative questions about supervisors or subordinates, office efficiency, customer relations, advertising and marketing, production or sales, record keeping and finance, personnel policies

Another good strategy for finding a topic is to think about a recent review or critique with which you disagree—a movie or restaurant review, a sportswriter's assessment of a team or player, an op-ed column assessing a government official or proposed legislation. How would you evaluate this controversial subject differently?

Once you have chosen a possible topic, freewrite your response to each of the following questions as a means of exploring ideas for your argument.

1. For the audience you have in mind, what is the most meaningful and most specific category in which you can place your X? Choose the smallest relevant class. (Instead of asking, "Is the Super Eye 2000 a good digital camera?", ask "Is the Super Eye 2000 a good low-cost digital camera for novices?")
2. Determine the criteria you will use to make your evaluation meaningful and helpful to your audience. Begin by listing the purposes of the class you have placed your subject in and then use freewriting or idea mapping to explore the qualities a member of that class needs to have to achieve those purposes. If your subject is highly disputed, what objections might your audience raise about your criteria? How will you justify your criteria?
3. Which of your criteria is the most important? Why?

4. Evaluate your subject by matching it to each of the criteria. Explore why your subject does or does not match each of the criteria. Your freewriting for this exercise will yield most of the ideas you need for your argument.

Shaping and Drafting

For your first draft, consider trying the following format. Many evaluation arguments follow this shape, and you can always alter the shape later if it seems too formulaic for you.

1. Introduce your issue and show why evaluating X is problematic or controversial.
2. Summarize and respond to opposing or alternative views.
3. Present your own argument.
   a. State criterion 1 and defend it if necessary.
   b. Show that X meets/does not meet the criterion.
   c. State criterion 2 and defend it if necessary.
   d. Show that X meets/does not meet the criterion.
   e. Continue with additional criteria and match arguments.
4. Sum up your evaluation.

Revising

If your essay is an evaluation intended to help your audience make a decision, think about the clarity and usefulness of your criteria and the match part of your evaluation for that audience.

If you have written about a controversial topic, a good way to revise an evaluation argument, as well as other kinds of arguments, is to analyze your lines of reasoning using Toulmin's system. Look particularly at your reasons and grounds (the match part of your argument) and your warrants (your criteria in an evaluation argument) to determine how persuasively you have structured and supported these parts for your chosen audience.

GUIDELINES FOR PEER REVIEWS

Instructions for peer reviews are provided in Chapter 17 (pp. 519–520).

For the Writer
Prepare two or three questions you would like your peer reviewer to address while responding to your draft. The questions can focus on some aspect of your draft that you are uncertain about, on one or more sections where you particularly seek help or advice, on some feature that you particularly like about your draft, or on

some part you especially wrestled with. Write out your questions and give them to your peer reviewer along with your draft.

For the Reviewer

I. Read the draft at a normal reading speed from beginning to end. As you read, do the following:

   A. Place a wavy line in the margin next to any passages that you find confusing, that contain something that doesn't seem to fit, or that otherwise slow down your reading.

   B. Place a "Good!" in the margin next to any passages where you think the writing is particularly strong or interesting.

II. Read the draft again slowly and answer the following questions by writing brief explanations of your answers.

   A. Introduction

      1. What expectations does the title set up for you? How does it grab your interest?

      2. What does the introduction do to capture your interest, provide needed background, and identify the controversy or importance of the subject?

      3. What is the evaluative question being addressed? Who is the intended audience? What is the writer's claim?

      4. How might the writer improve the introduction or make the claim more focused?

   B. The criteria-match argument

      1. What criteria does the writer use for evaluating X? How could the writer establish or defend these criteria more clearly or persuasively?

      2. Do you accept the writer's criteria and agree with the way the writer has weighted their relative importance? How could the writer improve the criteria argument?

      3. What evidence does the writer present to show that the X being evaluated meets or fails to meet each criterion? How could the writer make the evidence more compelling? How could the writer improve the match argument?

      4. Where does the writer anticipate and summarize alternative views? Is the summary fair? How does the writer respond to these alternative views? How could the writer's refutation or response be improved?

      5. How might the writer better apply the ideas from Chapter 18 to achieve more clarity?

III. Rhetorical considerations

   A. *Purpose, audience,* and *genre*: How well has the writer made this evaluation argument achieve its persuasive aim? How does this draft meet the demands of its genre and the needs of its audience?

   B. *Logos, ethos,* and *pathos:* Where does the writer do well making a case for his or her evaluative claim? What could the writer do to improve the reasoning in this piece? Where does the writer do well at seeming reliable, fair, and knowledgeable about his or her subject? What further attention to the appeal to *ethos* could strengthen this draft? How does the writer connect this evaluation to the interests and values of the audience?

IV. If the writer has prepared questions for you, respond to his or her inquiries.

V. Sum up what you see as the chief strengths and problem areas of this draft.
  A. Strengths
  B. Problem areas

VI. Read the draft one more time. Place a check mark in the margin wherever you notice problems in grammar, spelling, or mechanics (one check mark per problem).

CHAPTER

16

Proposing a Solution

About Proposal Writing

Proposal arguments call an audience to action. They make a claim that some action *should* or *ought* to be taken. Sometimes referred to informally as *should arguments,* proposals are among the most common kinds of arguments that you will write or read.

Some proposals aim to solve local, practical matters. For example, Rebekah Taylor's proposal in this chapter (pp. 487–491) advocates that campus stores carry products that are not tested on animals. Practical proposals generally target a specific audience (usually the person with the power to act on the proposal) and are typically introduced with a "letter of transmittal," in which the writer briefly summarizes the proposal, explains its purpose, and courteously invites the reader to consider it.

The rhetorical context of practical proposals makes effective document design essential. An effective design (appropriate layout, overall neatness, clear headings, flawless editing) helps establish the writer's *ethos* as a quality-oriented professional and makes reading the proposal as easy as possible. In business and industry, effective practical proposals are crucial for financial success. Many kinds of businesses—construction and engineering firms, ad agencies, university research teams, nonprofit agencies, and others—generate most of their revenue from effective, competitive proposals.

Another kind of proposal (often called a *policy proposal*) is aimed at more general audiences instead of specific decision makers. These proposals typically address issues of public policy with the aim of swaying public support toward the writer's proposed solution. Policy proposals might address the problems of prison overcrowding, out-of-control health costs, children's access to Internet pornography, national security and terrorism, and so forth.

A third kind of proposal argument takes the form of condensed *public affairs advocacy advertisements*. These are usually very focused arguments making direct appeals to an audience to take action. These arguments appear as flyers, one-page advertisements in newspapers and magazines, posters, brochures, and Web pages in advocacy Web sites. Because advocacy advertisements are brief and must be catchy, clear, and lively, they often employ document design—type, layout, graphic images, and color—to maximum advantage.

If the problem you are addressing is already known to your audience, then proposal arguments can follow the shape of classical arguments described in Chapter 14, in which you introduce the issue, present the claim, provide supporting reasons for the claim, summarize and respond to alternative views, and provide a

475

conclusion. If you wrote an argument for Chapter 14, you may have chosen a proposal issue. A. J. Chavez's argument in that chapter, in which he argues that gay marriages should be legalized, is a proposal argument (pp. 435–439).

In many cases, however, the problem you wish to address is not known to your audience (or the audience doesn't take the problem seriously). The writer, in effect, must *create* the issue being addressed by calling the readers' attention to the problem and then proposing a course of action. The rest of this chapter focuses on strategies for the second type of proposal, in which part of the writer's task is to convince readers that a problem exists, that it is serious, and that some action should be taken to resolve it.

Exploring Proposal Writing

The following activity introduces you to the thinking processes involved in writing a proposal argument.

1. In small groups, identify and list several major problems facing students in your college or university.
2. Decide among yourselves which problems are most important and rank them in order of importance.
3. Choose your group's number-one problem and explore answers to the following questions. Group recorders should be prepared to present answers to the class as a whole.
   a. Why is the problem a problem?
   b. For whom is the problem a problem?
   c. How will these people suffer if the problem is not solved? Give specific examples.
   d. Who has the power to solve the problem?
   e. Why hasn't the problem been solved up to this point?
   f. How can the problem be solved? Create a proposal for a solution.
   g. What are the probable benefits of acting on your proposal?
   h. What costs are associated with your proposal?
   i. Who will bear these costs?
   j. Why should this proposal be enacted?
   k. What makes this proposal better than alternative proposals?
4. As a group, draft an outline for a proposal argument in which you do the following:
   a. Describe the problem and its significance.
   b. Propose your solution to the problem.
   c. Justify your proposal by showing how the benefits of adopting it outweigh the costs.
5. Recorders for each group should write the group's outline on the board and be prepared to present the group's argument orally to the class.

WRITING PROJECT

Call your audience's attention to a problem, propose a solution to that problem, and present a justification for your solution. You have three choices (your instructor may limit you to just one): (a) create a *practical proposal,* with a letter of transmittal, proposing a nuts-and-bolts solution to a local problem; (b) write a more general *policy proposal,* addressing a public issue, in the form of a feature editorial for a particular (state, local, or college) newspaper; or (c) create a *public affairs advocacy advertisement* that takes a proposed stand on a public issue. If you choose (b), your instructor might ask you to do substantial research and model your proposal after a magazine or journal article.

All proposals have one feature in common—they offer a solution to a problem. For every proposal, there is always an alternative course of action, including doing nothing. Your task as a proposal writer is threefold: You must demonstrate that a significant problem exists; propose a solution to the problem; and justify the solution, showing that benefits outweigh costs and that the proposed solution will fix the problem better than alternative solutions would. Accordingly, a proposal argument typically has three main parts:

1. *Description of the problem.* The description often begins with background. Where does the problem show up? Who is affected by the problem? How long has the problem been around? Is it getting worse? You may add an anecdote or some kind of startling information or statistics to give the problem *presence.* Typically, this section also analyzes the problem. What are its elements? What are its causes? Why hasn't it been solved before? Why are obvious solutions not adequate or workable? Finally, the description shows the problem's significance. What are the negative consequences of not solving the problem?
2. *Proposal for a solution.* This section describes your solution and shows how it would work. If you don't yet have a solution, you may choose to generate a *planning proposal,* calling for a committee or task force to study the problem and propose solutions at a later date. The purpose of a planning proposal is to call attention to a serious problem. In most cases, however, this section should propose a detailed solution, showing step-by-step how it would solve the problem and at what cost.
3. *Justification.* Here you persuade your audience that your proposal should be enacted. Typically you show that the benefits of your proposal outweigh the costs. You also need to show why your proposed solution is better than alternatives. Point out why other possible approaches would not solve the problem, would provide fewer benefits, or would cost significantly more than your proposal.

Understanding Proposal Writing

As we have noted, proposal arguments focus on identifying a problem and then proposing and justifying a solution. In this section we look first at some of the distinctive demands of proposal writing. We then show you a powerful strategy for developing the justification section of a proposal.

Special Demands of Proposal Arguments

To get the reader to take action—the ultimate purpose of a proposal—requires you to overcome some difficult challenges. Here we examine the special demands that proposal arguments make on writers and offer suggestions for meeting them.

Creating Presence
To convince readers that a problem really exists, you must give it *presence;* that is, you must help readers *see* and *feel* the problem. Writers often use anecdotes or examples of people suffering from the problem or cite startling facts or statistics to dramatize the problem. For example, a student proposing streamlined check-out procedures in the hotel where she worked gave presence to her problem by describing a family that missed its flight home because of a slow checkout line. Her description of this family's frustration—including angry complaints over-heard by people waiting to check in—convinced her boss that the problem was worth solving. To persuade your readers to act on your proposal, you need to involve them both mentally *and* emotionally in your argument.

Appealing to the Interest and Values of Decision Makers
Proposal writers sometimes appeal directly to readers' idealism, urging them to do the right thing. But writers also need to show how doing the right thing con-verges with their readers' own best interests. Show decision makers how acting on your proposal will benefit *them* directly. The author of the hotel checkout pro-posal argued that her solution would enhance customer satisfaction, an idea that her boss would find more compelling than the notion of making life easier for desk clerks.

Overcoming Inherent Conservatism
People are inherently resistant to change. One of the most famous proposals of all time, the Declaration of Independence, is notable for the way in which it antici-pates its audience's resistance to change: "Prudence, indeed, will dictate that gov-ernments long established should not be changed for light and transient causes; and accordingly, all experience hath shown, that mankind are more disposed to suffer, while evils are sufferable, than to right themselves by abolishing the forms to which they are accustomed."

To restate this passage as folk wisdom, "Better the devil you know than the one you don't know." Most people expect the status quo to have its problems, flaws, and frustrations. They live with and adapt to familiar imperfections. Unless they can be persuaded that change will make things markedly better, they will "suffer, while evils are sufferable" rather than risk creating new, possibly insufferable evils.

The challenge of proving that something needs to be changed is compounded by the fact that the status quo often appears to be working. If its shortcomings were readily apparent, people would probably already have fixed them. It is much harder to stir an audience to action when the problem you depict entails lost potential (things could be better), rather than palpable evil (look at all the suffering).

Predicting Consequences

People also resist change because they fear unforeseen bad consequences and doubt predictions of good consequences. Everyone has experienced the disappointment of failed proposals: your favorite sports team makes a major trade—and then does worse; a company you invested in went through a major reorganization—and promptly went into the red; voters elect a new leader who promises major reforms—and nothing happens. Although most people do not become true cynics, they are understandably cautious about accepting the rosy scenarios contained in most proposals.

The more uncertain your proposal's consequences, the more clearly you must show *how* the proposal will bring about those consequences. To persuade your audience that your predictions are realistic, identify the links in the chain and show how each one leads to the next. Whenever possible, cite similar proposals that yielded the sorts of results you are predicting.

Evaluating Consequences

Compounding the problem of predicting consequences is the difficulty of figuring out whether those consequences are good or bad and for whom. For example, any alternative to the current health care system will contain changes that simultaneously advantage one segment of your audience (say, patients) and disadvantage another (say, doctors, insurance companies, or taxpayers). Indeed, if any health care proposal benefited all segments of your audience, it would probably have been adopted long ago.

It can also be difficult to identify the appropriate standard of measurement to use in calculating a proposal's costs and benefits. Often you must try to balance benefits measured in apples against costs measured in oranges. For instance, suppose that a health care proposal will reduce the cost of insurance by limiting coverage. How would you balance the dollars saved on your insurance bill against the suffering of persons denied a potentially lifesaving medical procedure? Some cost-benefit analyses try to reduce all consequences to one scale of measure—usually money. This scale may work well in some circumstances, but it can lead to grotesquely inappropriate conclusions in others.

With these challenges in mind, we now set forth some strategies for making proposals as effective as possible.

Developing an Effective Justification Section

The distinctions between proposals and other kinds of arguments dictate a special variety of support for proposals. Experienced proposal writers often use a *three-approach* strategy to help them develop their justification sections. They brainstorm justifying reasons by focusing sequentially on principles, consequences, and precedents or analogies. Figure 16.1 explains each element in the sequence.

Each of these argumentation strategies was clearly evident in a public debate in Seattle, Washington, over a proposal to raise county sales taxes to build a new baseball stadium. Those favoring the stadium put forth arguments such as these:

> We should build the new stadium because preserving our national pastime for our children is important (*argument from principle*), because building the stadium will create new jobs and revitalize the adjacent Pioneer Square district (*argument from consequence*), and because building the stadium will have the same beneficial effects on the city that building Camden Yards had in Baltimore (*argument from precedent*).

Those opposing the stadium created arguments using the same strategies:

> We should not build the stadium because it is wrong to subsidize rich owners and players with tax dollars (*argument from principle*), because building a stadium diverts tax money from more important concerns such as low-income housing (*argument from consequence*), and because Toronto's experience with Skydome shows that once the novelty of a new stadium wears off, attendance declines dramatically (*argument from precedent*).

For Writing and Discussion

Working individually or in small groups, use the strategies of principle, consequence, and precedent/analogy to create *because* clauses that support (or oppose) the following proposals. Try to have at least one *because* clause from each of the strategies, but generate as many reasons as possible.

Example:

Claim	Spanking children should be made illegal.
Principle	Because it is wrong to cause bodily pain to children.
Consequence	Because it teaches children that it is okay to hit someone out of anger; because it causes children to obey rules out of fear rather than respect; because it can lead children to be abusive parents.
Precedent/ analogy	Because spanking a child is like throwing dishes or banging your fists against a wall—it relieves your anger but turns the child into an object.

(*continued*)

FIGURE 16.1 The Three-Approach Strategy for a Justification Section

Approach 1: Argument from Principle

Using this strategy, you argue that a particular action should be taken because doing so is right according to some value, assumption, principle, or belief that you share with your audience. For example, you might argue, "We should create publicly financed jobs for poor people because doing so is both charitable and just." The formula for this strategy is as follows:

We should (should not) do (this action) because (this action) is

_____ .

Fill in the blank with an appropriate adjective or noun specifying a belief or value that the audience holds: good, just, right, ethical, honest, charitable, equitable, fair, and so forth.

Approach 2: Argument from Consequence

Using this strategy, you argue that a particular action should (should not) be taken because doing so will lead to consequences that you and your audience believe are good (bad). For example, you might say, "We should create publicly financed jobs for poor people because doing so will provide them money for food and housing, promote a work ethic, and produce needed goods and services." The formula for this strategy is as follows:

We should (should not) do (this action) because (this action) will lead to these good (bad) consequences: _____ , _____ , _____ , etc.

Think of consequences that your audience will agree are good or bad, as your argument requires.

Approach 3: Argument from Precedent or Analogy

Using a precedent strategy, you argue that a particular action should (should not) be taken because doing so is similar to what was done in another case, which proved to be successful (unsuccessful). For example, you might say, "We should create publicly financed jobs for poor people because doing so will alleviate poverty in this country just as a similar program has helped poor people in Upper Magnesia." Using an analogy strategy, you compare the proposed action with a similar action that your audience already accepts as good or bad. For example, "We should create publicly financed jobs for poor people because doing so is like teaching the poor how to fish rather than giving them fish." The formula for either strategy is as follows:

We should (should not) do (this action) because doing (this action) is like _____ , which turned out to be good (bad).

Think of precedents or analogies that are similar to your proposed action and that have definite good (bad) associations for your audience.

(continued)

1. Service-learning courses should/should not be required for graduation.
2. Medical insurance should/should not cover psychological counseling for eating disorders.
3. Marijuana should/should not be legalized.
4. The school year for grades K through 12 should/should not be extended to eleven months.

Proposal Arguments as Public Affairs Advocacy Advertisements

Understanding the Power of Condensed Advocacy Arguments

As the volume of information bombarding us grows, we are increasingly met by condensed, attention-grabbing advocacy ads promoting a cause and seeking our support. These condensed arguments appear as posters or flyers, as paid advertisements in newspapers or magazines, as brochures filling our mailboxes, and as Web pages in advocacy Web sites.

These condensed advocacy ads are marked by their bold, abbreviated, tightly planned format. The creators of these arguments know they must work fast to capture our attention, give presence to a problem, advocate a solution, and enlist our support. These advocacy ads frequently use photographs, images, or icons that are arresting or in some way memorable and that appeal to a reader's emotions and imagination.

As examples of one-page advocacy ads, consider Figures 16.2 and 16.3. As part of a campaign to decriminalize drugs, the ad shown in Figure 16.2 is sponsored by an organization calling itself "Common Sense for Drug Policy." Note how the advocacy advertisement makes its view of the problem real and urgent to readers by using disturbing black-and-white drawings, varied type sizes and fonts, and powerful lists of evidence. It also gains credibility through its documentation of sources, presented at the bottom of the page. Taking a somewhat different approach, the "World Vision" ad appealing for charitable donations to feed children in Afghanistan (Figure 16.3) uses lots of color, including a plaintive photograph of a young girl leaning against her mother's lap. This ad, which appeared on the Web site of World Vision, offers a convenient way for viewers to make a donation over the Internet.

FIGURE 16.2 A One-Page Advocacy Advertisement from a Magazine

WHITE KIDS ARE MUCH MORE LIKELY TO BE USING (AND SELLING) DRUGS!

CAN YOU FIND ANYTHING WRONG WITH THESE PICTURES??

According to the federal Centers for Disease Control, he's 4 times more likely than his African-American classmate to be a regular cocaine user.

White high-school students who are current users of cocaine: 4.1%[1]

Chance of a white person ever trying an illicit drug in their lifetime: 42%[2]

Percent of felony drug defendants in state courts who are white: 37%[3]

Percent of white drug felons given probation or nonincarceration sentence by state courts: 32%[4]

Percent of white drug felons sentenced to prison by state courts each year: 27%[5]

According to the Justice Department, if he's arrested on drug charges, he's 1-1/2 times more likely than his white classmate to be sent to prison.

African-American high-school students who are current users of cocaine: 1.1%[1]

Chance of an African-American person ever trying an illicit drug in their lifetime: 37.7%[2]

Percent of felony drug defendants in state courts who are black: 61%[3]

Percent of black drug felons given probation or nonincarceration sentence by state courts: 25%[4]

Percent of black drug felons sentenced to prison by state courts each year: 43%[5]

BLACK KIDS ARE MORE LIKELY TO GO TO PRISON!

Note:
According to the US Justice Department and the Office of National Drug Control Policy, drug users typically buy their drugs from sellers of their own racial or ethnic background. Research of Ethnicity & Race of Drug Sellers and Users: US Dept. of Justice National Institute of Justice & the Office of National Drug Control Policy, "Crack, Powder Cocaine, and Heroin: Drug Purchase and Use Patterns in Six U.S. Cities, " December 1997, p.1, 16, and p. 15, Table 16.

Sources:
[1] Data on drug use by high-school students: Youth Risk Behavior Survey 1999, Centers for Disease Control, reported in Morbidity and Mortality Weekly Report, Vol. 49, No. SS-5, p. 66, Table 24.
[2] Data on lifetime prevalence of drug use: US Dept. of HHS Substance Abuse and Mental Health Services Administration, "Summary of Findings from the 1999 National Household Survey on Drug Abuse," August 2000, p. G-13, Table G-13.
[3] Demographic data on felony drug defendants in state courts: US Dept. of Justice Bureau of Justice Statistics. "Felony Defendants in Large Urban Counties, 1996," October 1999, p.4, Table 3
[4] Demographic data on felony drug defendants in state courts: US Dept. of Justice Bureau of Justice Statistics, "State Court Sentencing of Convicted Felons, 1996," February 2000, p. 13, Table 2.5
[5] Demographic data on felony drug defendants in state courts: US Dept. of Justice Bureau of Justice Statistics, "State Court Sentencing of Convicted Felons, 1996," February 2000, p. 13, Table 2.5

Kevin B. Zeese, President, Common Sense for Drug Policy
3220 "N" Street, NW, #141, Washington, D.C. 20007 * 703-354-9050 * fax 703-354-5695 * info@csdp.org
For more information, visit www.csdp.org and www.drugwarfacts.org

FIGURE 16.3 One-Page Advocacy Advertisement from a Web Site

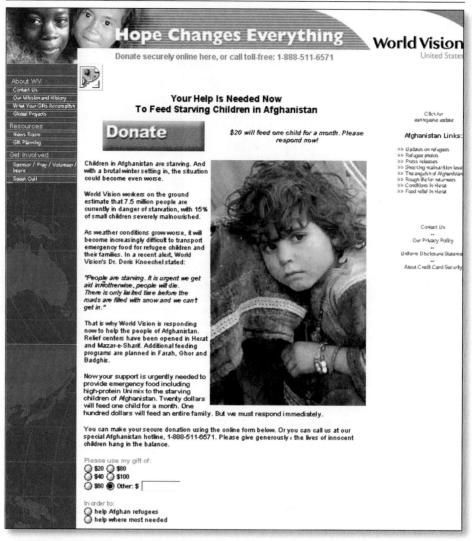

Document Design Features of Advocacy Advertisements

To interpret and drive home the problem presented in photos or drawings, advocacy ads employ different type sizes and fonts. Large-type text in these documents frequently takes the form of slogans or condensed thesis statements written in an

6   If enacted, this proposal would provide students with cruelty-free options for such products as toothpaste, deodorant, shampoo, soap, shaving products, laundry detergent, dish soap, and all-purpose cleaner. One cruelty-free brand of each of these products would be sufficient. This proposal would not prevent students from buying the products they normally do because it would add new products to the store inventories; it would not replace any existing products.

7   To enact this proposal, the campus store can select among numerous producers of cruelty-free brands. _____ could provide toothpaste and floss, shampoos, deodorants, and soap. _____ offers excellent shaving products that are cruelty free. A conscientious company called "_____" could provide laundry detergent, dish soap, and cleaning sprays.

8   Perhaps one of the university's many purveyors could be persuaded to carry brands like these. If that is the case, providing cruelty-free products would only require adding new inventory from an already existing source. This situation would be ideal because the products could be easily delivered to campus along with other goods that the store already provides. If the university's purveyors will not offer such brands, they might still be easily acquired from a new purveyor, or from a local warehouse store. Based on phone calls I have made, I know of several warehouse stores in our area that offer natural and cruelty-free products in bulk. These companies might provide delivery services just as the university's current purveyors do.

9   If a new purveyor could not be found, and if the warehouse stores in the area could not deliver, concerned students might volunteer to personally obtain cruelty-free products from neighborhood stores and transport them to the school.

10   An important part of my proposal is that designated areas on campus store shelves would be provided for cruelty-free products. These areas would be clearly identified with a sign so that compassionate students would know which products are cruelty free. This aspect of the proposal is very important because it would draw the attention of students to the issue of animal testing and encourage them to consider seriously which products they want to buy. The hope is not only to offer cruelty-free products on campus, but to create a dialogue on the issue of animal testing.

Justification

11   There are four important reasons why _____ University should act on this proposal.

Success at Other Universities

12   First, other colleges and universities have enacted similar proposals to help combat animal testing and have had great success with the new products. I have researched two such places—_____ College and _____ College—and have discovered that cruelty-free products are very popular with students.

13   For example, the campus stores at _____ College in Iowa underwent a massive product change about five years ago in response to student protests against the _____ products sold on campus. These students knew that _____ is one of the corporate world's most ardent supporters of animal testing. The cruelty-free products that replaced _____ sold exceedingly well. Similarly, at _____ College in Colorado students raised an outcry when one of these cruelty-free products was almost pulled from the shelves. Our university should look to success stories such as these when considering whether or not to offer cruelty-free products on campus.

In Line with University Mission

14   Second, offering cruelty-free products on campus would be an action in line with our university's efforts to be a progressively minded, service- and value-oriented school. In many ways, _____ University has shown itself to be a leader in social change. This university has proved eager to become involved in struggles against all kinds of injustice. The most recent examples are the mission to Iraq to help people impoverished by U.N. sanctions and the addition of environmentally friendly, shade-grown coffee in the university coffee shops. These actions challenged current social practices and demonstrated clearly that many of our students are willing to fight for human rights and for the global ecosystem and endangered species. These actions are consistent with _____ University's official mission "to look critically at the society in which we live and at its institutions" (Mission Statement). It is time now to look critically at corporations that contribute to the suffering of animals by subjecting them to cruel, unnecessary experiments. At the very least, _____ University should allow its students the right to choose not to support such corporations.

Student Convenience and Safety

15   Third, offering cruelty-free products would allow students to purchase needed items on campus and to use the money on their University One Cards to do so. Simply put, if cruelty-free products were offered on campus, students would be safer and less inconvenienced because they would not have to worry about off-campus transportation or security. In addition, the ability to purchase such products with the One Card would allow numerous students who otherwise could not have afforded to do so to buy what they need.

Promise of Economic Success

16   Finally, many students at this university would choose cruelty-free products over other brands if they were available on campus. In a short survey I conducted winter quarter, many students said they would support a proposal to introduce cruelty-free products to the stores on campus. This survey of fifty randomly selected students revealed that over half (56%) are more than

"somewhat concerned" about animal testing. The survey also showed that almost three-quarters (72%) would buy cruelty-free products instead of products tested on animals if they were offered on campus. Additionally, compassionate students who have gone off-campus to buy cruelty-free products would start spending their money at the campus store.

Conclusion

17   Past social actions by the students, faculty, and administration of _____University reveal a long-held belief that real progress means real change. In hope of bettering the school and society, this university has always been willing to challenge the status quo. It is time to challenge the status quo again. To continue the university's efforts to fight injustice in the world, to take conscientious action on the issue of animal testing as other respected colleges have, and to honor the wishes of many students, the university's campus store should offer cruelty-free products. Taking this action would help our university remain faithful to its mission.

Thinking Critically about "A Proposal to Provide Cruelty-Free Products on Campus"

1. What strategies does Rebekah Taylor use to convince the Director of Residence Life that a problem exists?
2. What strategies (including arguments from principle, consequence, and precedent) does Rebekah employ to persuade university administrators that her proposal is workable and that the benefits outweigh the costs?
3. How does Rebekah tie her proposal to the values and beliefs of her audience—the Director of Residence Life in particular and university administrators in general?
4. If you were Mr. Charles Ramos, the Director of Residence Life to whom this proposal is addressed, how effective would you find this proposal? What are its chief strengths and weaknesses?

Our second reading, an op-ed piece from the *New York Times* (February 20, 2004), proposes that competitive cheerleading be recognized as a varsity sport. It was written by Jennifer Allen, the daughter of former Washington Redskins football coach George Allen. She has also written a memoir about growing up female in a football family, *Fifth Quarter: The Scrimmage of a Football Coach's Daughter.*

Jennifer Allen
The Athlete on the Sidelines

1   It's midseason in cheer nation. This winter, thousands of girls will travel on college all-star teams to take part in competitions across the country. Practicing more than 20 hours a week, they will refine a routine of back flips, handsprings, round-offs and splits—all perfectly synchronized and timed to an Olympic second. Their goal: first place. Their game: competitive cheerleading, one of the fastest-growing sports for women in America.

2   Last year, the University of Maryland became the first Division I N.C.A.A. institution to recognize competitive cheerleading as a varsity sport. That means team members are accorded the same benefits as other campus athletes—a coaching and medical staff; locker rooms; help with academics; help dealing with the press. By the 2005–06 academic year, Maryland will provide 12 full scholarships to competitive cheerleaders. The question is this: What took so long?

3   (Time out for a definition. Competitive cheerleading overlaps with but is not identical to the spirit squads you see, say, on the sidelines of a Saturday afternoon college football game. The teams we're talking about do cheer at school games, but they also compete against other schools in cheerleading competitions where they perform high-risk routines under high-pressure circumstances.)

4   For too many years, cheerleading has been the subject of derision. Sports Illustrated has lampooned it. Many Americans fail to distinguish it from the sideline shows the Dallas Cowboy cheerleaders put on. Back when I was a cheerleader in high school in the late 70's, we were called a sideshow. In those days, we performed at every sporting event—football, basketball and baseball. We practiced three days a week; purchased our own uniforms (skirts, sweaters, trunks, socks, saddle shoes) and were responsible for our own steady supply of bandages. Ace bandages. There were plenty of injuries, mostly to ligaments. After a big game, my knee would swell. My dad would offer a diagnosis—water on the knee—bandage it up, and then prescribe 50 reps on the knee machine. But cheerleaders weren't allowed in the school weight room.

5   Today, more than 200,000 high-school and college students attend cheerleading camps each year; at least 15 percent of them participate in competitions. The Universal Cheerleading Association feeds its competitions to ESPN for lively weekend fare. When these events were televised last year, they drew an average audience of 334,000 homes.

6   For all its popularity, though, the sport is governed—or not governed—by a patchwork of entities. Schools may treat cheerleaders as athletes—but they don't have to. Some offer little more than a uniform and a game-day parking pass; others offer scholarships; none offer the full-range of support and benefit that Maryland does for competitive cheerleading. What's more, cheerleading is not even recognized by the N.C.A.A. as a sport.

7   Given the nature of competitive cheerleading, this seems like a risky proposition. Think about it: in what other sport is an athlete tossed more than 30 feet in the air—smiling—before spiraling down into the arms of a trusted teammate? Lifts and tosses and catches are the mainstay of competitive cheerleading. "Fliers" do not wear hip pads or kneepads or helmets. There is little to protect a cheerleader from awkward or poor landings on the gym floor.

8   Not surprisingly, cheerleading is the No. 1 cause of serious sports injuries to women, according to the National Center for Catastrophic Sport Injury Research, ahead of gymnastics and track. From 1980 to 2001, emergency room visits for cheerleading injuries rose fivefold.

9   Pushing colleges to recognize competitive cheerleading as a sport will surely help to cut down on injuries. Right now, the American Association of Cheering Coaches and Advisers publishes a manual and administers a safety certification program, but only a fraction of coaches have been certified. Many cheerleaders try dangerous stunts without proper training, coaching and supervision.

10   Of course, convincing other schools to make competitive cheerleading an official sport won't be easy. According to Deborah Yow, Maryland's athletic director, it took more than a year to make sure that the university's cheerleading squad would meet all the guidelines set forth by the Department of Education's Office of Civil Rights. While the department does not define what is or is not a "sport," it does determine whether a university's given activity—such as cheerleading—can be considered a sport in order to comply with Title IX.

11   Is Maryland's action entirely altruistic? Probably not. It doubtless relieves some Title IX pressure. But what's wrong with that? And would it be so wrong to ask the N.C.A.A. to sponsor and govern the sport? After all, when the big collegiate cheerleading competitions begin next month, hundreds of thousands of people will tune in, acknowledging the importance of cheerleading. More N.C.A.A. colleges would be wise to follow suit.

Thinking Critically about "The Athlete on the Sidelines"

1. As in most proposal arguments, Allen's first task is to convince readers that a problem exists. She has to persuade readers to take competitive cheerleading seriously and to show them why it is problematic for competitive cheerleaders not to be granted varsity sport status. What are her strategies for convincing us that a problem exists? How effective is she?

2. How does Allen justify her claim that cheerleading should be recognized as a sport? According to her argument, what are the benefits that will come from making cheerleading a varsity sport? What costs does she acknowledge? What additional costs might you point to if you were skeptical of her claim?

3. Overall, how persuasive is her argument? In your response to this question, focus on the strengths and weaknesses of her appeals to *logos, ethos,* and *pathos.*

4. If you are persuaded by her argument and if you are attending an institution where competitive cheerleading could exist, how might you persuade the administration on your campus to make cheerleading a varsity sport? (Who are the decision makers for this issue? What arguments would most motivate them? What are the constraints that must be overcome?)

Our last reading, by student writer Dylan Fujitani, is a researched policy argument that addresses the problem of civilian contractors taking military roles in Iraq. To appreciate the origins of Dylan Fujitani's argument, read his exploratory essay in Chapter 8 (pp. 203–207).

Dylan Fujitani (Student)
"The Hardest of the Hardcore":
Let's Outlaw Hired Guns in Contemporary American Warfare

1   On March 31, 2004, America was shocked by the news that four civilians had been brutally killed, mutilated, and hung up on a bridge in Falluja, Iraq. This horrific event publicized the little-known role of civilian "contractors" in the Iraq war. The public's unawareness that some of these contractors are armed to the teeth is hardly surprising, however, because the language used to refer to non-military personnel in Iraq is often so vague that one can scarcely tell whether a reference to a contractor means a truck driver working for Halliburton or a South African mercenary with a history of killing blacks under the apartheid government working for a private security company. These personnel are often referred to using such broad and mundane terms as "security consultants" or simply "civilian contractors." But in reality, the jobs involved and the kinds of people doing them vary so greatly that these catchall labels are inaccurate. Persons referred to as "civilian contractors" are often well-armed ex-military personnel who took an early retirement to double their pay by working for one of many private security firms hired by the Pentagon. With their obvious training and heavy weaponry, these contractors bear a striking resemblance to soldiers, but one enormous difference sets them apart from the regular troops of the U.S. military: They are actually civilians who can be hired without even the symbolic approval of Congress. Without the need for approval, contractors give the

Pentagon the flexibility of outsourcing certain military jobs to private security companies. Despite being paid much more than regular troops, contractors may actually cost less when military benefits and retirement are taken into account.

2   Soldiers for hire have historically been called mercenaries. A case could be made that this term is inapplicable in Iraq because contractors in Iraq are being hired to *support* the military's operations, not to fight the war itself. It is true that many of these civilians are support personnel who should not be called mercenaries—for example, highly specialized technicians or drivers of supply trucks—even though these persons may carry a weapon in case of an attack. But some of these personnel replace soldiers in combat roles historically filled by the military. According to Joshua Hammer of <u>The New Republic</u>, these jobs include guarding the Baghdad airport, protecting oil fields, escorting convoys, training local police, and serving as prison interrogators (18). The use of these mercenaries circumvents public and congressional scrutiny of some aspects of war. Their non-military status gives virtual legal immunity to heavily armed individuals who often have questionable backgrounds, who profit from violent conflict, and who ultimately have responsibility to no one but their employers. In light of these dangerous developments, the use of mercenary soldiers must be halted or brought under intense congressional scrutiny.

3   Using mercenaries in war is problematic for six major reasons. First, the deployment of mercenaries disguises the true cost of war to the American public. According to <u>New York Times</u> reporter David Barstow, there are roughly 20,000 mercenaries on the ground in Iraq supporting U.S. military operations, and these numbers are not included in reports of the number of American soldiers in Iraq. These 20,000 private contractors make up the second largest contingent in Iraq, surpassing even the British deployment ("Privatizing Warfare"), yet they have received relatively little media attention even as their numbers continue to increase. The use of contractors enables the Pentagon to get by with a smaller number of actual troops through outsourcing to private military companies. Only the deployments of actual troops are reported, so the Pentagon appears to have done more with less. According to a Baghdad-based security consultant, "If you're going to keep the number of troops down, this is the way to do it. . . . The expense is the same or more. But politically it's much less expensive" (qtd. in Daragahi). The use of mercenaries in Iraq blurs the high cost of war in the public eye, both in terms of dollars and in terms of human lives. Contractors have suffered casualties, yet the public scarcely hears of their death toll unless they are mutilated and publicly exhibited. Furthermore, with the service of a civilian mercenary in Iraq costing as much as $1,500 dollars a day ("Privatizing Warfare"), contractor use is consuming an enormous portion of the funding allocated for reconstruction. <u>New York Times</u> reporter David Barstow asserts that "security costs could claim up to 25

percent of the $18 billion budgeted for reconstruction," diverting capital from important reconstruction projects like school and road construction. Thus, the use of mercenaries in Iraq makes it more difficult for the American public to determine the true cost of war.

4   The second major problem with use of mercenaries is that as a group they have no national loyalties and ultimately answer to their employers, not the armed forces. According to the Brookings Institution's P. W. Singer, "during the Persian Gulf War, a 'very small number' of private contractors working at an air base in Saudi Arabia fled from fear that chemical weapons might be used" (qtd. in Bredemeier). In using mercenaries, the Pentagon is outsourcing what the New York Times calls its "core responsibilities" ("Privatizing Warfare"), and despite the importance of these tasks, the jobs are being assigned to people who can basically leave whenever they want to. As P. W. Singer has pointed out, a soldier faces a court-martial for refusing to face battle, whereas a contractor merely loses his job (Bredemeier). In addition, the mercenaries and regular military personnel sometimes have poor working relationships. Since contractors are not required to abide by normal military procedures, mercenaries can pretty much operate any way they want, sometimes to the armed forces' disliking. Writing in The New Republic, Joshua Hammer explains the attitudes of the Marines who had been with the four contractors killed in Falluja the day before their deaths. Quoting a Marine officer, Hammer writes, "We would have told them not to do it [take an unauthorized shortcut through Baghdad]." According to Hammer, the officer "angrily called the contractors 'cowboys' and said they had failed to inform anyone on the base of their plans, a direct violation of military policy" (19). Relying on such a large number of poorly supervised and unaccountable mercenaries to fill crucial roles leaves the United States dangerously vulnerable to the future uncertainties of war.

5   Another problem with the use of mercenaries is their civilian status, creating legal ambiguity and making discipline extremely difficult if not impossible. Phillip Carter, a former U.S. Army officer, writing for the e-magazine Slate, commented that the involvement of private contractors in the Abu Ghraib prison abuse scandal brought the issue of discipline to the forefront ("How to Discipline"). According to Carter, mercenaries don't fit the Geneva convention definition of "non-combatants" (since they are armed), or of "lawful combatants" (since they don't wear uniforms or fit within a military chain of command). Rather, "they fall into an international legal gray zone" ("Hired Guns"). This problem is highlighted in an editorial from The Economist, which pointed out that the "great sanction on wrongdoing—the law—does not really operate. Regular soldiers are subject to courts-martial or international law. But it is not clear what law applies to private security firms" ("Dangerous Work"). Borzou Daragahi, in a piece for the Post-gazette.com, wrote that contractors are not subject to the Uniform Code of Military Justice and that there are military personnel who are very uncomfortable with their

seemingly untouchable status. Contractors' fuzzy legal status with regard to military justice and international law is highly problematic.

6   Some have argued against these claims of virtual immunity, saying that in reality a lot can be done to discipline law-breaking private contractors. Carter, says that possible disciplinary measures include termination of contracts, prohibition from bidding for future contracts, criminal prosecution, and civil suits ("How to Discipline"). All of these penalties, however, are at "the discretion of the agency that issued the original contract," or in this case, presumably the Pentagon. Although Carter effectively makes the point that contractors are not entirely immune from discipline, many of these forms of punishment ultimately amount to nothing more than loss of the job. Carter admits that government contractors are "shielded" from civil suits by a legal doctrine called the "government contractor" defense. Under the current circumstances in Iraq where offensive and defensive roles are becoming increasingly muddied, the only form of punishment contractors are concerned with is financial. This virtual legal immunity is striking considering the strict rules that govern the actions of military personnel. The threat of mere financial punishment cannot be expected to deter mercenaries from possible abusive and criminal behavior. Their legal status must be clarified as soon as possible in both domestic and international law.

7   The fourth major problem with mercenaries is that private military companies frequently hire employees with questionable backgrounds. Inadequate governmental oversight has allowed private companies to hire known war criminals who have been or continue to be paid with American taxpayer dollars. According to journalist Louis Nevaer, writing for the <u>National Catholic Reporter</u>, roughly 1,500 South African mercenaries are now in Iraq, many of them former Apartheid-era mercenaries, some of whom have even confessed to killing blacks. Nevaer states that there are "terrorists . . . and war criminals on the payrolls of companies contracted by the Pentagon." He gives the example of a former South African police officer who was "a member of the Vlakplass death squad that terrorized blacks under apartheid." Not only are the personal histories of the mercenaries questionable, but their motivations are also dubious. Joshua Hammer in his <u>New Republic</u> article "Cowboy Up" describes what he observed of these private contractors in Baghdad:

[M]ost of the contractors are the hardest of the hard core—veterans of such elite outfits as the U.S. Special Forces; the Rhodesian Selous Scouts, the former special forces of the Rhodesian white regime; and Executive Outcomes, the now-disbanded South African mercenary army that fought in Sierra Leone and Angola. These men thrive on the danger of working in war zones. (19)

Given the current uncertainty about the legal status of private contractors, and given the fact that actual American military personnel could be targeted in retaliation for the behavior of mercenaries, Congress must quickly act to regulate hiring practices of private military companies to screen against the hiring of terrorists, war criminals, or anyone who would potentially misrepresent the United States.

8   The fifth problem with the use of mercenaries is that the growth of the private security industry entices many of America's most experienced soldiers to leave the military for higher paying contractor jobs. Eric Schmitt and Tom Shanker, writing in the <u>New York Times</u>, explain the lure of contractors' salaries:

> Senior enlisted members of the Army Green Berets or Navy Seals with 20 years or more experience now earn about $50,000 in base pay, and can retire with a $23,000 pension. But private security companies . . . are offering salaries of $100,000 to nearly $200,000 a year to the most experienced of them.

The military is losing some of its finest soldiers to the private sector where their expertise goes to the highest bidder. The use of mercenaries must be swiftly restrained and eventually halted lest the military be gradually stripped of its edge and become further reliant upon the expertise of private military companies.

9   Finally, the sixth major problem regarding the use of mercenaries is that the rapid increase in their numbers is creating large international interest groups who will *want war* in the long run. For mercenaries, war means fortune and excitement, and peace means a boring period of unemployment. The creation of such groups who thrive off violent conflict is dangerous on a very fundamental level. In the interests of peace, mercenaries and any other war profiteers must not be encouraged through governmental employment. The business of war has proven lucrative, and the free market must not be allowed to encourage war any more than it already does.

10   The expanded use of mercenaries in American warfare has given rise to numerous problems that must be addressed immediately. Among the obvious, their use hides the true cost of war from the American people; contractors' backgrounds and loyalties are questionable; and they have been given a great reason to hope for war in the world. These problems must be addressed swiftly and immediately, particularly by Congress. Mercenaries are used because they are cheaper, both economically and politically, but they also serve the critical purpose of circumventing the scrutiny of Congress and the people of the United States. Action must be taken now to disable this circumvention of democracy and to protect legitimate uses of war from market forces, lawlessness, and the abuse of power.

Works Cited

Barstow, David. "Security Companies: Shadow Soldiers in Iraq." <u>New York Times</u> 19 Apr. 2004: A1+. Lexis-Nexis. Lemieux Lib., Seattle U. 19 May 2004 <http://search.epnet.com>.

Bredemeier, Kenneth. "Thousands of Private Contractors Support U.S. Forces in Persian Gulf." <u>Washington Post</u> 3 Mar. 2003: E01. 19 May 2004 <http://www.washingtonpost.com>.

Carter, Phillip. "Hired Guns: What to Do about Military Contractors Run Amok." Slate 9 Apr. 2004. 12 June 2004 <http://slate.msn.com/id/2098571>.

---. "How to Discipline Private Contractors." Slate 4 May 2004. 19 May 2004 <http://slate.msn.com/id/2099954>.

"Dangerous Work." Economist 10 Apr. 2004: 22-23. Academic Search Premier. EBSCO. Lemieux Lib., Seattle U. 23 May 2004 <http://www.epnet.com>.

Daragahi, Borzou. "In Iraq, Private Contractors Lighten Load on U.S. Troops." Post-gazette.com 28 Sept. 2003. 19 May 2004 <http://www.post-gazette.com/pg/pp/03271/226368.stm>.

Hammer, Joshua. "Cowboy Up." New Republic 24 May 2004: 18-19. Academic Search Premier. EBSCO. Lemieux Lib., Seattle U. 23 May 2004 <http://www.epnet.com>.

Nevaer, Louis. "Many Hired Guns in Iraq Have War Crimes Pasts." National Catholic Reporter 14 May 2004: 10.

"Privatizing Warfare." Editorial. New York Times 21 Apr. 2004: A22. Lexis-Nexis. Reed Elsevier. Lemieux Lib., Seattle U. 19 May 2004 <http://www.lexisnexis.com/>.

Schmitt, Eric, and Tom Shanker. "Big Pay Luring Military's Elite to Private Jobs." New York Times 30 Mar. 2004: A1+. Lexis-Nexis. Reed Elsevier. Lemieux Lib., Seattle U. 19 May 2004 <http://www.lexisnexis.com/>.

Thinking Critically about "'The Hardest of the Hardcore': Let's Outlaw Hired Guns in Contemporary American Warfare"

1. Most people are unaware that a problem might exist with civilian contractors in Iraq. Dylan's major rhetorical task, therefore, is to persuade readers that a problem exists. To what extent do you think he convinces readers that the use of civilian contractors to fulfill military roles constitutes a problem? Point to passages that you think are or are not persuasive in building his case.

2. The structure of Dylan's paper is almost entirely devoted to showing that a problem exists. However, his proposed solution is vague: either to eliminate the use of contractors in military roles entirely or to demand more congressional oversight. Dylan's strategy is typical for "planning proposals" (see p. 477) where the writer points out a problem but is unable to propose a clear plan for solving it. Does this strategy work for you? Do you think Dylan needs to propose a more specific solution or is it enough that he simply identifies a problem?

3. Overall, how would you evaluate the *logos* of this argument? How effective is Dylan's use of reasons and evidence to convince you that the continued use of civilian contractors in military roles is a problem that requires some action?

4. How effective are Dylan's appeals to *ethos* and *pathos?* To what extent does Dylan project a credible and trustworthy persona? To what extent does he connect his argument to the values and beliefs of his audience, appealing to readers' emotions and sympathies as well as to their minds?

Composing Your Essay

Generating and Exploring Ideas

If you are having trouble thinking of a proposal topic, try making an idea map of local problems you would like to see solved. For your spokes, consider some of the following starting points:

Finding a Proposal Issue

> ***Problems at your university:*** dorm, parking, registration system, grading system, campus appearance, clubs, curriculum, intramural program
>
> ***Problems in your city or town:*** dangerous intersections, ugly areas, inadequate lighting, a poorly designed store, a shopping center that needs a specific improvement
>
> ***Problems at your place of work:*** office design, flow of customer traffic, merchandise display, company policies, customer relations
>
> ***Problems related to other aspects of your life:*** hobbies, recreational time, life as a consumer, and so forth

Another approach is to freewrite your response to these trigger statements:

> I would really like to solve the problem of _____.
> I believe that X should _____. (Substitute for X words such as *my instructor, the president, the school administration, Congress, my boss,* and so forth.)

Note that the problem you pose for this paper can be personal, but shouldn't be private; that is, others should be able to benefit from a solution to your personal problem. For example, your inability to find child care for your daughter is a private problem. But if you focus your proposal on how zoning laws discourage development of in-home day care—and propose a change in those zoning laws to permit more in-home day care centers—then your proposal will benefit others.

Using Stock Issues to Explore Your Problem
Once you have decided on a proposal issue, explore it by freewriting your responses to the following questions. These questions are often called *stock issues,* since they represent generic, or stock, questions that apply to almost any kind of proposal.

1. Is there a problem here that has to be solved?
2. Will the proposed solution really solve this problem?
3. Can the problem be solved in a simpler way without disturbing the status quo?
4. Is the proposed solution practical enough that it really stands a chance of being implemented?
5. What will be the positive and negative consequences of the proposal?

You might also try freewriting your responses to the questions in the exploratory exercise on page 476. Although these questions cover much the same territory as the stock issues, their different presentation might stimulate additional thought.

Finally, try thinking of justifications for your solution by using the three-approach strategy described in Figure 16.1, page 481.

Avoid Presupposing Your Solution in Your Problem Statement

A common mistake of inexperienced proposal writers is to write problem statements that presuppose their solutions. As a restaurant server, suppose you notice that customers want coffee refills faster than servers can provide them. To solve this problem, you propose placing carafes of hot coffee at each table. When describing your problem, don't presuppose your solution: "The problem is that we don't have carafes of hot coffee at the tables." Rather, describe the problematic situation itself: annoyed customers clamoring for coffee and harassed servers trying to bring around refills. Only by giving presence to the original problem can you interest readers in your proposed solution, which readers will compare to other possible approaches (including doing nothing).

Here are some more examples:

> Weak: The problem is that our medical office doesn't have an answering machine during closed hours.

> Actual Problem: The problem is that (1) we are overwhelmed with calls from patients canceling appointments during the first few hours every morning; (2) employees can't phone in emergency messages early in the morning (illness, car trouble); and (3) because we are on the West Coast, East Coast insurance companies can't communicate with us until after 12:00 p.m. their time.

> Weak: Our supermarket doesn't give new employees a location index for store items.

> Actual Problem: Customers often ask employees where to find an item and are given a bad first impression when a new employee doesn't know the answer; it wastes valuable time when the new employee walks with the customer to find an experienced employee to actually answer the question.

> Weak: The Campus Coffee House doesn't stay open late enough at night.

> Actual Problem: Students who study late at night don't have an attractive, convenient place to socialize or study; off-campus coffee houses are too far to walk to at night; dorm lounges aren't attractive or conducive to study; late-nighters make noise in the dorms instead of going to a convenient place.

Shaping and Drafting

The following is a typical organizational plan for a proposal argument that you might turn to if you get stuck in composing the first draft of your essay.

1. Presentation of a problem that needs solving
   a. Description of the problem (give it presence)
   b. Additional background, including previous attempts to solve the problem
   c. Argument that the problem is solvable (optional)
2. Presentation of the proposed solution
   a. Succinct statement of the proposed solution
   b. Explanation of specifics for the proposed solution

3. Summary and rebuttal of opposing views (in practical proposals, this section is often a summary and rejection of alternative ways of solving the problem)
4. Justification—persuades reader that proposal should be enacted
   a. Reason 1 presented and developed
   b. Reason 2 presented and developed
   c. And so forth
5. Conclusion—exhorts audience to act (sometimes incorporated into the last sentences of the final supporting reason)

Revising

After you have completed your first draft and begun to clarify your argument for yourself, you are ready to start making your argument clear and persuasive for your readers. Use the strategies for clear closed-form prose outlined in Chapter 18. At this stage, feedback from peer readers can be very helpful. Use the following guidelines for peer reviews:

GUIDELINES FOR PEER REVIEWS

Instructions for peer reviews are provided in Chapter 17 (pp. 519–520).

For the Writer

Prepare two or three questions you would like your peer reviewer to address while responding to your draft. The questions can focus on some aspect of your draft that you are uncertain about, on one or more sections where you particularly seek help or advice, on some feature that you particularly like about your draft, or on some part you especially wrestled with. Write out your questions and give them to your peer reviewer along with your draft.

For the Reviewer

I. Read the draft at a normal reading speed from beginning to end. As you read, do the following:
   A. Place a wavy line in the margin next to any passages that you find confusing, that contain something that doesn't seem to fit, or that otherwise slow down your reading.
   B. Place a "Good!" in the margin next to any passages where you think the writing is particularly strong or interesting.
II. Read the draft again slowly and answer the following questions by writing brief explanations of your answers.
   A. Introduction and statement of problem:
      1. How could the title more effectively focus the paper and pique your interest? How could the title be improved?
      2. How does the writer convince you that a problem exists and that it is significant (worth solving) and solvable? How does the writer give the

problem presence? How could the writer improve the presentation of the problem?

  B. Proposed solution:

    1. How could the writer's thesis more clearly propose a solution to the problem? Could the thesis be made more precise?

    2. Could the writer give you more details about the solution so that you can understand it and see how it works? How could the writer make the solution clearer?

  C. Justification:

    1. In the justification section, how could the writer provide stronger reasons for acting on the proposal? Where could the reasons be better supported with more details and evidence? How could the reasons appeal more to the values and beliefs of the audience?

    2. Can you help the writer think of additional justifying arguments (arguments from principle, from consequences, from precedent or analogy)? How could the writer improve support for the proposal?

    3. Where does the writer anticipate and address opposing views or alternative solutions? How does the writer convince you that the proposed solution is superior to alternative solutions?

    4. Has the writer persuaded you that the benefits of this proposal will outweigh the costs? Who will pay the costs and who will get the benefits? What do you think the gut reaction of a typical decision maker will be to the writer's proposal?

    5. Can you think of other unforeseen costs that the writer should acknowledge and address? What unforeseen benefits could the writer mention?

    6. How might the writer improve the structure and clarity of the argument? Where might the writer better apply the principles of clarity from Chapter 18?

III. Rhetorical considerations

  A. *Purpose, audience,* and *genre:* How well has the writer achieved his or her persuasive purpose? How effective is the writer at imagining a neutral or skeptical audience (as opposed to preaching to the choir)? How effective is this writer at meeting the constraints of the proposal argument genre? Were you persuaded by this argument? Why or why not?

  B. *Logos, ethos,* and *pathos:* Overall, how could the writer improve the reasoning of this argument? How effective is the writer at gaining the reader's confidence and trust? How effective is the writer at appealing to the audience's values, beliefs, and emotions? How could the argument be made more vivid or gripping?

IV. If the writer has prepared questions for you, respond to his or her inquiries.

V. Sum up what you see as the main strengths and problem areas of the draft.

  A. Strengths

  B. Problem areas

VI. Read the draft one more time. Place a check mark in the margin wherever you notice problems in grammar, spelling, or mechanics (one check mark per problem).

A Guide to Composing and Revising

According to its Web site, Lockheed Martin Corporation is "an advanced technology company" that produces aeronautics, electronic systems, integrated systems, space systems, and technology services primarily for the United States Department of Defense and other federal government agencies. This Lockheed Martin ad depicts the splendor of outer space and the impressive power of high-tech equipment in an arrangement of images that has a surreal quality. Consider how the optimistic, challenging message of the verbal text works with the visual elements of this ad to make it compelling. This advertisement is part of the For Writing and Discussion exercise on army recruitment and military contractors in Chapter 8, on page 208.

Part 3   A Guide to Composing and Revising

Writing as a Problem-Solving Process

I rewrite as I write. It is hard to tell what is a first draft because it is not determined by time. In one draft, I might cross out three pages, write two, cross out a fourth, rewrite it, and call it a draft. I am constantly writing and rewriting. I can only conceptualize so much in my first draft—only so much information can be held in my head at one time; my rewriting efforts are a reflection of how much information I can encompass at one time. There are levels and agenda which I have to attend to in each draft.*

—DESCRIPTION OF REVISION BY AN EXPERIENCED WRITER

I read what I have written and I cross out a word and put another word in; a more decent word or a better word. Then if there is somewhere to use a sentence that I have crossed out, I will put it there.*

—DESCRIPTION OF REVISION BY AN INEXPERIENCED WRITER

Blot out, correct, insert, refine,
Enlarge, diminish, interline;
Be mindful, when invention fails,
To scratch your head, and bite your nails.

—JONATHAN SWIFT

I n Part One of this text we focused on writing as a problem-solving process in which writers pose and solve both subject-matter problems and rhetorical problems. Part Three shows you how to translate these basic principles into effective strategies for composing and revising your writing along the continuum from closed to open forms. The three self-contained chapters, which can be read in whatever sequence best fits your instructor's course plan, will help you compose and revise the essays you write for the assignments in Part Two.

This chapter explains how experienced writers use multiple drafts to manage the complexities of writing and suggests ways for you to improve your own writing processes. Chapter 18, which takes the form of ten self-contained lessons, focuses on key strategies for composing and revising closed-form prose. Chapter

*From Nancy Sommers, "Revision Strategies of Student Writers and Experienced Adult Writers," *College Composition and Communication* 31 (October 1980): 291–300.

19 switches from closed to open forms, showing you how, when appropriate, to open your prose by creating surprises of style and structure that engage readers and involve them in the process of completing your text's meaning.

Understanding How Experts Compose and Revise

We begin this chapter with a close look at how experienced writers compose, explaining what they think about when they write and why they often need multiple drafts. Composition theorist Peter Elbow has asserted that "meaning is not what you start out with" but "what you end up with." Thus composing is a discovery process. In the early stages of writing, experienced writers typically discover what they are trying to say, often deepening and complicating their ideas rather than clarifying them. Only in the last drafts will such writers be in sufficient control of their ideas to shape them elegantly for readers.

It's important not to overgeneralize, however, because no two writers compose exactly the same way; moreover, the same writer may use different processes for different kinds of prose. Some writers outline their ideas before they write; others need to write extensively before they can outline. Some write their first drafts very slowly, devoting extensive thought and planning to each emerging paragraph; others write first drafts rapidly, to be sure to get all their ideas on paper, and then rework the material part by part. Some prefer to work independently, without discussing or sharing their ideas; others seek out classmates or colleagues to help them hash out ideas and rehearse their arguments before writing them down. Some seek out the stillness of a library or private room; others do their best writing in noisy cafeterias or coffee shops.

The actual mechanics of composing differ from writer to writer as well. Some writers create first drafts directly at a keyboard, whereas others require the reassuring heft of a pen or pencil. Among writers who begin by planning the structure of their work, some make traditional outlines (perhaps using the flexible outline feature on their word processors), whereas others prefer tree diagrams or flowcharts. Some of those who use word processors revise directly at the computer, whereas others print out a hard copy, revise with pen, and then type the changes into the computer.

Also, writers often vary their composing processes from project to project. A writer might complete one project with a single draft and a quick editing job, but produce a half dozen or more drafts for another project.

What experienced writers do have in common is a willingness to keep revising their work until they feel it is ready to go public. They typically work much harder at drafting and revising than do inexperienced writers, taking more runs at their subject. And experienced writers generally make more substantial alterations in their drafts during revision. (Compare the first two quotations that open this chapter—one from an experienced and one from an inexperienced writer.) An experienced writer will sometimes throw away a first draft and start over; a beginning writer tends to be more satisfied with early drafts and to think of revision as primarily cleaning up errors. Figure 17.1 shows the first page of a first draft for a magazine article written by an experienced writer.

FIGURE 17.1 Draft Page of Experienced Writer

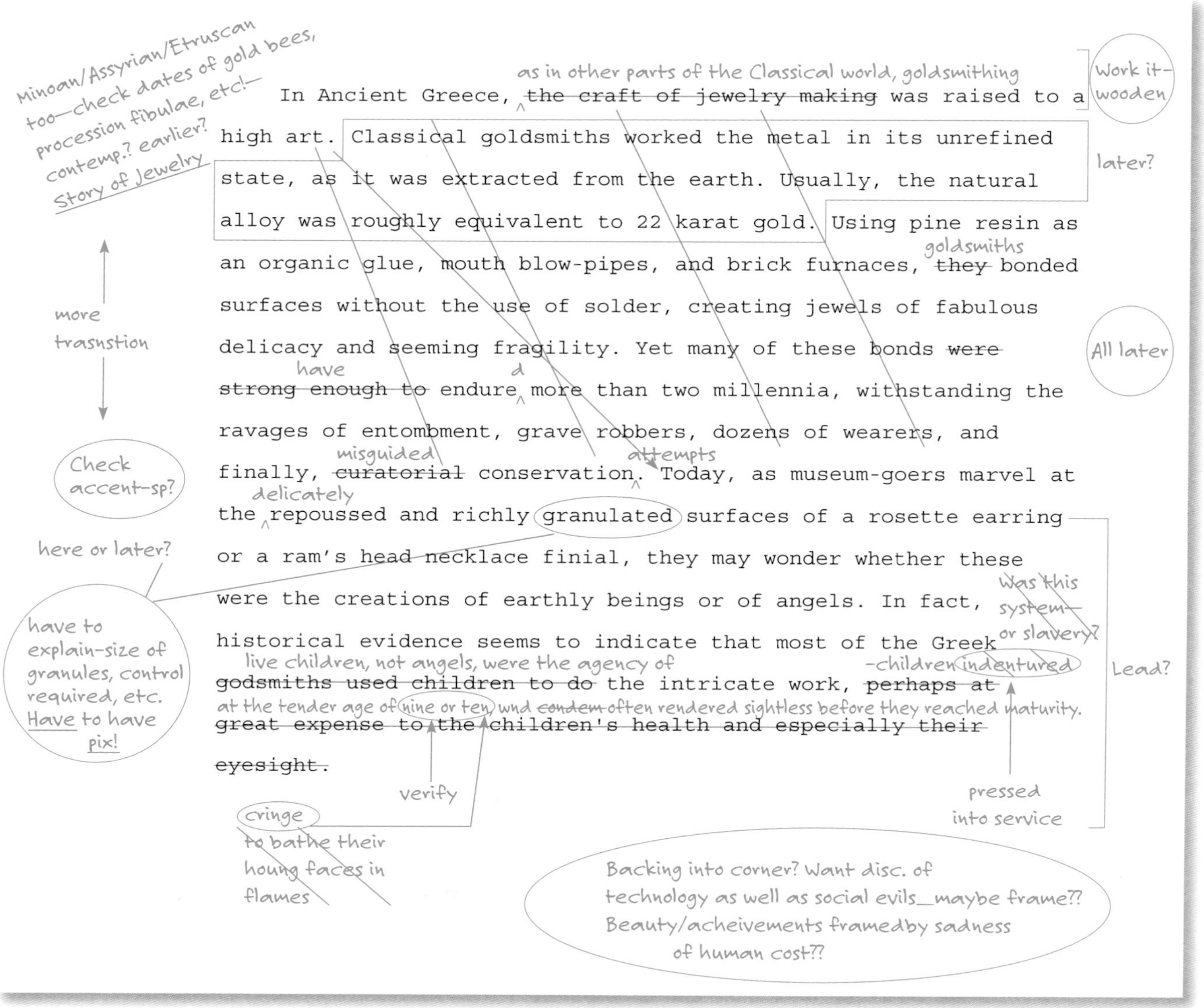

In Ancient Greece, the craft of jewelry-making was raised to a high art. Classical goldsmiths worked the metal in its unrefined state, as it was extracted from the earth. Usually, the natural alloy was roughly equivalent to 22 karat gold. Using pine resin as an organic glue, mouth blow-pipes, and brick furnaces, they bonded surfaces without the use of solder, creating jewels of fabulous delicacy and seeming fragility. Yet many of these bonds were strong enough to endure more than two millennia, withstanding the ravages of entombment, grave robbers, dozens of wearers, and finally, curatorial conservation. Today, as museum-goers marvel at the repoussed and richly granulated surfaces of a rosette earring or a ram's head necklace finial, they may wonder whether these were the creations of earthly beings or of angels. In fact, historical evidence seems to indicate that most of the Greek goldsmiths used children to do the intricate work, perhaps at great expense to the children's health and especially their eyesight.

Handwritten annotations:

Work it in wooden later?

All later

Lead?

as in other parts of the Classical world, goldsmithing

Minoan/Assyrian/Etruscan too—check dates of gold bees, procession fibulae? earlier? contemp.? earlier?
Story of jewelry

move transition

Check accent-sp?

here or later?

have to explain—size of granules, control required, etc. Have to have pix!

goldsmiths

have

a

misguided
delicately

attempts

Was this system—
or slavery?
child indentured

—children, not angels, were the agency of
live
at the tender age of nine or ten and condemn—often rendered sightless before they reached maturity.

pressed into service

cringe
to bathe their young faces in flames

verify

Backing into corner? Want disc. of technology as well as social evils _ maybe frame??
Beauty/acheivements framed by sadness of human cost??

A Working Description of the Writing Process

The writing process we have just described may be considerably different from what you have previously been taught. For many years—before researchers began studying the composing processes of experienced writers—writing teachers typically taught a model something like this:

OLD MODEL OF THE WRITING PROCESS

1. Choose a topic
2. Narrow it
3. Write a thesis
4. Make an outline
5. Write a draft
6. Revise
7. Edit

The major problem with this model is that hardly anyone writes this way. We know of no writers who being by choosing a topic and narrowing it. Rather, as we explained in Part One, writers begin with a sense of a problem or of a conversation that isn't quite satisfactory. Writers identify questions that impel them to add their own voice to a conversation. Nor is the process neatly linear, as the old model implies. Sometimes writers settle on a thesis early in the writing process. But just as frequently they formulate a thesis during an "Aha!" moment of discovery later in the process, perhaps after several drafts. (So *this* is my point! Here is my argument in a nutshell!) Even very late in the process, while checking spelling and punctuation, experienced writers are apt to think of new ideas, thus triggering more revision.

Rather than dividing the writing process into distinct, sequential steps, let's review the kinds of things experienced writers are likely to do early, midway, and late in the process of writing an essay.

More Accurate View of the Writing Process

Early in the process	•	*Writers become aware of a question or problem.* Initially the question may not be well defined, but writers identify something unknown about the topic, feel dissatisfied with someone else's view of it, or wish to add something new or different to the conversation.
	•	*Writers explore the problem.* Through research, critical thinking, and exploratory writing and talking, writers search for an effective response to the problem. They consider what different audiences might already know about the problem, what these audiences believe, and how they might be surprised by the writer's view. Writers might take time off from the problem and let ideas cook in the subconscious.

More Accurate View of the Writing Process *continued*

- *Writers begin conceptualizing the paper in terms of purpose, audience, and genre.* As ideas for a paper take shape—through outlining or early drafting—writers try to imagine a purpose for writing in terms of the change they want to bring about in the audience. They also consider the conventions and constraints of their intended genre.

- *Writers complete a first draft.* At some point writers put ideas on paper in a whole or partial draft. Some writers make an informal outline prior to writing. Others discover direction as they write, putting aside concerns about form and coherence until later. One of the major causes of writer's block among less experienced writers is the desire to make the paper perfect the first time. Experienced writers know their first drafts are often messy and unfocused, and they lower their expectations accordingly. Some writers even like to call their first drafts "zero drafts" or "garbage drafts" to emphasize these lower expectations.

Midway through the process

- *Writers begin to revise and reformulate.* The real work of actual composing now begins. Once they have written a first draft, writers can start to see the whole territory. The second draft may be quite different from the first. Some writers actually discard the first draft, reshaping their initial insights into a different structure. Others go slowly through the first draft, adding, deleting, reordering, or completely rewriting passages.

- *Writers increasingly consider the needs and expectations of readers.* As writers clarify their ideas for themselves, they increasingly reorganize for readers. Using knowledge of "reader expectation theory," which we describe in detail in Chapter 18, writers build into their text mapping statements, transitions, and structural cues. They also create unity and coherence by following the "old/new contract" explained in Chapter 18.

- *Writers seek feedback from readers.* Experienced writers regularly ask trusted colleagues to read their drafts and offer feedback. Composition instructors often try to create the same experience for students by organizing peer review workshops.

- *Writers often go through many additional drafts.* It is not unusual for an experienced writer to go through numerous drafts, making both large-scale "global revisions" (different structure, complete rewriting of sections, revised purpose) as well as small-scale "local revisions" (unifying or developing paragraphs, rewriting sentences).

Late in the process

- *Writers edit for style and correctness.* Eventually the writer's sense of purpose and audience stabilizes, and the ideas become increasingly clear, well organized, and developed. At this point writers begin shifting their attention to the craft of writing—getting each word, phrase, sentence, and paragraph just right so that the prose is clear, graceful, and correct.

- *Writers edit for manuscript form and genre considerations.* Writers also edit to meet the genre conventions of document design, citation style, and so forth. The professional appearance of a manuscript creates the audience's first impression of the writer's *ethos*.

We should emphasize again that the writing process is recursive, rather than linear. A writer might be "early in the process" for one part of a draft and "late in the process" for another. Frequently, a writer can also reconceptualize the argument late in the process and seemingly "start over"—but the time has not been wasted since the whole process has led to the writer's new ideas.

For Writing and Discussion

When you write, do you follow a process resembling the one we just described? Have you ever

- had a writing project grow out of your engagement with a problem or question?
- explored ideas by talking with others or by doing exploratory writing?
- made major changes to a draft because you changed your mind or otherwise discovered new ideas?
- revised a draft from a reader's perspective by consciously trying to imagine and respond to a reader's questions, confusions, and other reactions?
- road-tested a draft by trying it out on readers and then revising it as a result of what they told you?

Working in groups or as a whole class, share stories about previous writing experiences that match or do not match the description of experienced writers' processes. To the extent that your present process differs, what strategies of experienced writers might you like to try?

Improving Your Own Writing Processes

The previous section describes the many ways in which experienced writers compose. In this section we'll show you how to use this knowledge to improve your own writing processes. We'll begin with an overview list of expert composing strategies that you can start to practice right away. We'll then explain techniques for exploratory writing followed by some advice on drafting and global revision.

Practice the Composing Strategies of Experienced Writers

One of the best ways to improve your composing processes is to practice strategies used by experienced writers.

- *Use exploratory writing and talking to discover and clarify ideas.* Don't let your first draft be the first time you put your ideas into written words. Use exploratory writing to generate ideas and deepen thinking. (Later in this section we explain the techniques of freewriting, focused freewriting, and idea-mapping.) Also seek out opportunities to talk about your ideas with classmates or friends in order to clarify your own thinking and appreciate alternative points of view. Whenever possible, talk through your draft with a friend; rehearse your argument in conversation as practice for putting it in writing.

- *Schedule your time.* Plan for exploration, drafting, revision, and editing. Don't begin your paper the night before it is due. Give ideas time to ruminate in your mind. Recognize that your ideas will shift, branch out, even turn around as you write. Allow some time off between writing the first draft and beginning revision. Experienced writers build in time for revision.

- *Discover what methods of drafting work best for you.* Some people compose rough drafts directly on the computer; others write longhand. Some make outlines first; others plunge directly into drafting and make outlines later. Some revise extensively on the computer as they are drafting; others plough ahead until they have a complete draft before they start revising. Some people sit at their desk for hours at a time; others need to get up and walk around every couple of minutes. Some people need a quiet room; others work best in a coffee shop. Discover the methods that work best for you.

- *Occasionally revise on double- or triple-spaced hard copy.* Because many experienced writers revise on the screen without going through paper drafts, it is hard to say when one draft ends and another begins. Nevertheless, there are powerful advantages in printing off occasional paper drafts. Research suggests that writers are apt to make more large-scale changes in a draft if they work from hard copy. Because they can see the whole draft at once without having to scroll through a file, they can see more easily how the parts connect to the whole. They can look back at page two while revising page six. We suggest that you occasionally print out a double- or triple-spaced hard copy of your draft and then mark it up aggressively. Cross out text to be changed and write new text in the blank spaces between the lines. Make inserts. Draw arrows. (See again Figure 17.1, which shows how a professional writer marks up a draft.) When your draft gets too messy, type your changes in your computer and begin another round of revision.

- *Exchange drafts with others.* Get other people's reactions to your work in exchange for your reactions to theirs. Experienced writers regularly seek critiques of their drafts from trusted readers. Later in this chapter we explain procedures for peer review of drafts.

- *Save correctness for last.* To revise productively, concentrate first on the big questions: Do I have good ideas in this draft? Am I responding appropriately to the assignment? Are my ideas adequately organized and developed? Save questions about exact wording, grammar, and mechanics for later. These concerns are important, but they cannot be efficiently attended to until after higher-order concerns are met. Your first goal is to create a thoughtful, richly developed draft.

Explore Ideas through Freewriting, Idea-Mapping, and Good Talking

Another way to improve your writing processes is to explore ideas through informal writing and talking. Composition theorists sometimes refer to this stage of writing as *prewriting* or *invention*. When you use exploratory writing, such as writing in a journal or doing regular "thinking pieces," you'll have a record of your thinking that you can draw on later. Moreover, the very act of recording your thoughts on paper—or articulating them to others orally—stimulates more ideas. In this section, we will briefly describe four exploratory strategies that will help you learn to think like an experienced writer: freewriting, focused freewriting, idea-mapping, and dialectic discussion.

Freewriting

Freewriting, also sometimes called *nonstop writing* or *silent, sustained writing*, asks you to record your thinking directly. To freewrite, put pen to paper (or sit at your computer screen, perhaps turning *off* the monitor so that you can't see what you are writing) and write rapidly, *nonstop*, for ten to fifteen minutes at a stretch. Don't worry about grammar, spelling, organization, transitions, or other features of edited writing. The object is to think of as many ideas as possible. Some freewriting looks like stream of consciousness. Some is more organized and focused, although it lacks the logical connections and development that would make it suitable for an audience of strangers.

Many freewriters find that their initial reservoir of ideas runs out in three to five minutes. If this happens, force yourself to keep your fingers moving. If you can't think of anything to say, write, "Relax" over and over (or "This is stupid" or "I'm stuck") until new ideas emerge.

What do you write about? The answer varies according to your situation. Often you will freewrite in response to a question or problem posed by your instructor. Sometimes you will pose your own questions and use freewriting to explore possible answers or simply generate ideas. Here is an example of a student's freewrite in response to the prompt "What puzzles you about homelessness?"

> Let's see, what puzzles me about homelessness? Homeless homeless. Today on my way to work I passed a homeless guy who smiled at me and I smiled back though he smelled bad. What are the reasons he was out on the street? Perhaps an extraordinary string of bad luck. Perhaps he was pushed out onto the street. Not a background of work ethic, no place to go, no way to get someplace to live that could be afforded, alcoholism. To what extent do government assistance, social spending, etc, keep people off the street? What benefits could a person get that stops "the cycle"? How does welfare affect homelessness, drug abuse programs, family planning? To what extent does the individual have control over homelessness? This question of course goes to the depth of the question of how community affects the individual. Relax, relax. What about the signs that I see on the way to work posted on the windows of businesses that read, "please don't give to panhandlers it only promotes

drug abuse etc" a cheap way of getting homeless out of the way of business? Are homeless the natural end of unrestricted capitalism? What about the homeless people who are mentally ill? How can you maintain a living when haunted by paranoia? How do you decide if someone is mentally ill or just laughs at society? If one can't function obviously. How many mentally ill are out on the street? If you are mentally ill and have lost the connections to others who might take care of you I can see how you might end up on the street. What would it take to get treatment? To what extent can mentally ill be treated? When I see a homeless person I want to ask, How do you feel about the rest of society? When you see "us" walk by how do you think of us? Do you possibly care how we avoid you?

Note how this freewrite rambles, moving associatively from one topic or question to the next. Freewrites often have this kind of loose, associative structure. The value of such freewrites is that they help writers discover areas of interest or rudimentary beginnings of ideas. When you read back over one of your freewrites, try to find places that seem worth pursuing. Freewriters call these places "hot spots," "centers of interest," "centers of gravity," or simply "nuggets" or "seeds." The student who wrote the preceding freewrite discovered that he was particularly interested in the cluster of questions beginning "What about the homeless people who are mentally ill?" and he eventually wrote a research paper proposing a public policy for helping the mentally ill homeless. Because we believe this technique is of great value to writers, we suggest that you use it to generate ideas for class discussions and essays.

Focused Freewriting

Freewriting, as we have just described it, can be quick and associational, like brainstorming aloud on paper. Focused freewriting, in contrast, is less associational and aimed more at developing a line of thought. You wrestle with a specific problem or question, trying to think and write your way into its complexity and multiple points of view. Because the writing is still informal, with the emphasis on your ideas and not on making your writing grammatically or stylistically polished, you don't have to worry about spelling, punctuation, grammar, or organizational structure. Your purpose is to deepen and extend your thinking on the problem. Some instructors will create prompts or give you specific questions to ponder, and they may call this kind of exploratory writing "focused freewriting," "learning log responses," "writer's notebook entries," or "thinking pieces." You can see examples of focused freewriting in students' responses to the learning log tasks in Chapter 13.

Examples of these learning log entries are found on pp. 367–373.

Idea Mapping

Another good technique for exploring ideas is *idea mapping*, a more visual method than freewriting. To make an idea map, draw a circle in the center of a page and write down your broad topic area (or a triggering question or your thesis) inside the circle. Then record your ideas on branches and subbranches that extend out from the center circle. As long as you pursue one train of thought, keep recording your ideas on subbranches off the main branch. But as soon as that chain of ideas runs dry, go back and start a new branch.

Often your thoughts will jump back and forth between one branch and another. This technique will help you see them as part of an emerging design rather than as strings of unrelated ideas. Additionally, idea mapping establishes at an early stage a sense of hierarchy in your ideas. If you enter an idea on a subbranch, you can see that you are more fully developing a previous idea. If you return to the hub and start a new branch, you can see that you are beginning a new train of thought.

An idea map usually records more ideas than a freewrite, but the ideas are not as fully developed. Writers who practice both techniques report that they can vary the kinds of ideas they generate depending on which technique they choose. Figure 17.2 shows a student's idea map made while he was exploring issues related to the grading system.

Dialectic Discussion

Another effective way to explore the complexity of a topic is through face-to-face discussions with others, whether in class, over coffee in the student union, or late at night in bull sessions. Not all discussions are productive; some are too superficial and scattered, others too heated. Good ones are *dialectic*—participants with differing views on a topic try to understand each other and resolve their differences by examining contradictions in each person's position. The key to dialectic conversation is careful listening, made possible by an openness to each other's views. A dialectic discussion differs from a talk show shouting match or a pro/con debate in which proponents of opposing positions, their views set in stone, attempt to win the argument. In a dialectic discussion, participants assume that each position has strengths and weaknesses and that even the strongest position contains inconsistencies, which should be exposed and examined. When dialectic conversation works well, participants scrutinize their own positions more critically and deeply, and often alter their views. True dialectic conversation implies growth and change, not a hardening of positions.

For more discussion of dialectic conversation, see the criteria for class discussions in Chapter 4, p. 77; for more discussion on how to work cooperatively with others through dialectic discussion, see Chapter 23 on oral communication.

Draft Purposefully

When you sit down to compose your first draft, write purposefully by thinking of your rhetorical context: What is the question or problem you are addressing? Who is your audience? What change do you want to bring about in your audience's thinking? Sometimes you will know the answers to these questions before you start drafting. At other times, the act of drafting helps you discover ideas. Have confidence that the revising process will help you eventually make your ideas well structured, clear, and surprising to your readers. When writing your first draft, lower your expectations. (We said earlier that many experienced writers think of the first draft as their *zero draft* or *garbage draft*.) For more specific advice on drafting and revising, see Chapters 18 and 19 on composing and revising

FIGURE 17.2 Idea Map on Problems with the Grading System

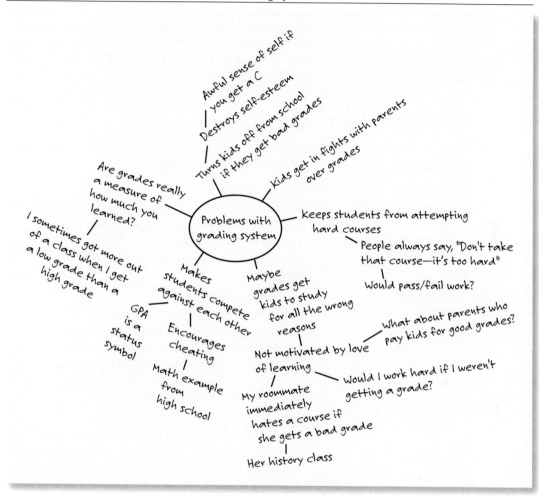

closed-form and open-form prose. If you are writing closed-form prose, pay particular attention at the drafting stage to Chapter 18's advice on planning and visualizing your structure (Lesson 3, pp. 535–541) and on writing introductions (Lesson 4, pp. 542–548). We have found that these lessons particularly help writers get started on a draft.

After Drafting, Revise Globally

As we explained at the start of this chapter, experienced writers revise their drafts much more extensively than do inexperienced writers. Inexperienced writers tend to revise *locally*; experienced writers revise *globally*. By *local revision*, we mean small-scale revisions at the level of the sentence—correcting spelling, finding a different word, perhaps adding a short example. By *global revision*, we mean large-scale revision at the level of ideas and structure—reshaping a whole section, crossing out a series of paragraphs, and rewriting from scratch in the light of new ideas.

To appreciate the significance of both global and local revision, consider the changes that experienced writers typically make in their drafts.

Recognize Kinds of Changes Typically Made in Drafts

We begin by classifying the kinds of changes writers typically make in drafts and explaining their reasons for making each sort of change.

Kinds of Changes	Reasons for Change
Crossing out whole passage and rewriting from scratch	Original passage was unfocused; ideas have changed.
	New sense of purpose or point meant that whole passage needed reshaping.
	Original passage was too confused or jumbled for mere editing.
Cutting and pasting; moving parts around	Original was disorganized.
	Points weren't connected to particulars.
	Conclusion was clearer than introduction; part of conclusion had to be moved to introduction.
	Rewriting introduction led to discovery of more effective plan of development; new forecasting required different order in body.
Deletions	Material not needed or irrelevant.
	Deleted material was good but went off on a tangent.
Additions	Supporting particulars needed to be added: examples, facts, illustrations, statistics evidence (usually added to bodies of paragraphs).
	Points and transitions needed to be supplied (often added to openings of paragraphs).
	New section needed to be added or a brief point expanded.
Recasting of sentences (crossing out and rewriting portions of sentences; combining sentences; rephrasing; starting sentences with a different grammatical structure)	Passage violated old/new contract (see pp. 556–562).
	Passage was wordy or choppy.
	Passage lacked rhythm and voice.
	Grammar was tangled, diction odd, meaning confused.
Editing sentences to correct mistakes	Words were misspelled or mistyped.
	Comma splices, fragments, dangling participles, other grammatical errors were found.

For Writing and Discussion

Choose an important paragraph in the body of a draft you are currently working on. Then write out your answers to these questions about that paragraph.

1. Why is this an important paragraph?
2. What is its main point?
3. Where is that main point stated?

Now—as an exercise only—write the main point at the top of a blank sheet of paper, put away your original draft, and, without looking at the original, write a new paragraph with the sole purpose of developing the point you wrote at the top of the page.

When you are finished, compare your new paragraph to the original. What have you learned that might help you revise your original?

Here are some typical responses of writers who have tried this exercise:

> I recognized that my original paragraph was unfocused. I couldn't find a main point.
> I recognized that my original paragraph was underdeveloped. I had a main point but not enough particulars supporting it.
> I began to see that my draft was scattered and that I had too many short paragraphs.
> I recognized that I was making a couple of different points in my original paragraph and that I needed to break it into separate paragraphs.
> I recognized that I hadn't stated my main point (or that I had buried it in the middle of the paragraph).
> I recognized that there was a big difference in style between my two versions and that I had to choose which version I liked best. (It's not always the "new" version!)

Using Peer Reviews to Stimulate Revision

One of the best ways to become a better reviser is to see your draft from a *reader's* rather than a *writer's* perspective. As a writer, you know what you mean; you are already inside your own head. But you need to see what your draft looks like to someone outside your head.

The best way to learn this skill is to practice reading your classmates' drafts and have them read yours. In this section we offer advice on how to respond candidly to your classmates' drafts and how to participate in peer reviews.

Becoming a Helpful Reader of Classmates' Drafts

When you respond to a writer's draft, learn to make readerly rather than writerly comments; describe your mental experience in trying to understand the draft rather than pointing out problems or errors in the draft. For example, instead of saying, "Your draft is disorganized," say, "I got lost when. . . ." Instead of saying,

"This paragraph needs a topic sentence," say, "I had trouble seeing the point of this paragraph."

When you help a writer with a draft, your goal is both to point out where the draft needs more work and to brainstorm with the writer possible ways to improve the draft. Begin by reading the draft all the way through at a normal reading speed. As you read, take mental notes to help focus your feedback. We suggest that you make wavy lines in the margin next to passages that you find confusing; write "Good!" in the margin where you like something; and write "?" in the margin where you want to ask questions.

After you have read the draft, use the following strategies for making helpful responses:

IF THE IDEAS IN THE DRAFT SEEM THIN OR UNDEVELOPED, OR IF THE DRAFT IS TOO SHORT:

- help the writer brainstorm for more ideas.
- help the writer add more examples, better details, more supporting data or arguments.

IF YOU GET CONFUSED OR LOST:

- have the writer talk through ideas to clear up confusing spots.
- help the writer sharpen the thesis: suggest that the writer view the thesis as the answer to a controversial or problematic question; ask the writer to articulate the question that the thesis answers.
- help the writer create an outline, tree diagram, or flowchart.

See Chapter 18 for a detailed explanation of these revision strategies.

- help the writer clarify the focus by asking him or her to complete these statements about purpose:
  My purpose in this paper is —————————————.
  My purpose in this section (paragraph) is —————————————.
  Before reading my paper, the reader will have this view of my topic: —————————————; after reading my paper, my reader will have this different view of my topic: —————————————.
- show the writer where you got confused or miscued in reading the draft ("I started getting lost here because I couldn't see why you were giving me this information" or "I thought you were going to say X, but then you said Y").

IF YOU CAN UNDERSTAND THE SENTENCES BUT CAN'T SEE THE POINT:

- help the writer articulate the meaning by asking "So what?" questions, making the writer bring the point to the surface by stating it directly. ("I can understand what you are saying here but I don't quite understand why you are saying it. I read all these facts, and I say, 'So what?' What do these facts have to do with your thesis?")

IF YOU DISAGREE WITH THE IDEAS OR THINK THE WRITER HAS AVOIDED ALTERNATIVE POINTS OF VIEW:

- play devil's advocate to help the writer deepen and complicate ideas.
- show the writer specific places where you had queries or doubts.

For Writing and Discussion

In the following exercise, we ask you to respond to a student's draft ("Should the University Carpet the Dorm Rooms?" below). The assignment asked students to take a stand on a local campus issue. Imagine that you have exchanged drafts with this student and that your task is to help this student improve the draft.

Read the draft carefully; make wavy lines in the margins where you get confused, write "Good!" for something you like, and write "?" where you want to ask questions.

On your own, complete the following tasks:

1. Identify one specific place in the draft where you got confused. Freewrite a brief explanation for why you got confused. Make readerly rather than writerly comments.
2. Identify one place in the draft where you think the ideas are thin or need more development.
3. Identify one place where you might write "So what?" in the margins. These are places where you understand the sentences but don't see the point the writer is getting at.
4. Identify at least one place where you could play devil's advocate or otherwise object to the writer's ideas. Freewrite your objections.

In groups or as a whole class, share your responses. Then turn to the following tasks:

1. With the instructor serving as a guide, practice explaining to the writer where or how you got confused while reading the draft. Readers often have difficulty explaining their reading experience to a writer. Let several class members role-play being the reader. Practice using language such as "I like the way this draft started because . . . ." "I got confused when . . . ." "I had to back up and reread when . . . ." "I saw your point here, but then I got lost again because . . . ." Writing theorist Peter Elbow calls such language a "movie of your mind."
2. Have several class members role-play being devil's advocates by arguing against the writer's thesis. Where are the ideas thin or weak?

Should the University Carpet the Dorm Rooms?

Tricia, a university student, came home exhausted from her work-study job. She took a blueberry pie from the refrigerator to satisfy her hunger and a tall glass of milk to quench her thirst. While trying to get comfortable on her bed, she tipped her snack over onto the floor. She cleaned the mess, but the blueberry and milk stains on her brand-new carpet could not be removed.

(continued)

Tricia didn't realize how hard it was to clean up stains on a carpet. Luckily this was her own carpet.

A lot of students don't want carpets. Students constantly change rooms. The next person may not want carpet.

Some students say that since they pay to live on campus, the rooms should reflect a comfortable home atmosphere. Carpets will make the dorm more comfortable. The carpet will act as insulation and as a soundproofing system.

Paint stains cannot be removed from carpets. If the university carpets the rooms, the students will lose the privilege they have of painting their rooms any color. This would limit students' self-expression.

The carpets would be an institutional brown or gray. This would be ugly. With tile floors, the students can choose and purchase their own carpets to match their taste. You can't be an individual if you can't decorate your room to fit your personality.

According to Rachel Jones, Assistant Director of Housing Services, the cost will be $300 per room for the carpet and installation. Also the university will have to buy more vacuum cleaners. But will vacuum cleaners be all that is necessary to keep the carpets clean? We'll need shampoo machines too.

What about those stains that won't come off even with a shampoo machine? That's where the student will have to pay damage deposit costs.

There will be many stains on the carpet due to shaving cream fights, food fights, beverage parties, and smoking, all of which can damage the carpets.

Students don't take care of the dorms now. They don't follow the rules of maintaining their rooms. They drill holes into the walls, break mirrors, beds, and closet doors, and leave their food trays all over the floor.

> If the university buys carpets our room rates will skyrocket.
>
> In conclusion, it is a bad idea for the university to buy carpets.

Conducting a Peer Review Workshop

If you are willing to respond candidly to a classmate's draft—in a readerly rather than a writerly way—you will be a valuable participant in peer review workshops. In a typical workshop, classmates work in groups of two to six to respond to each other's rough drafts and offer suggestions for revisions. These workshops are most helpful when group members have developed sufficient levels of professionalism and trust to exchange candid responses. A frequent problem in peer review workshops is that classmates try so hard to avoid hurting each other's feelings that they provide vague, meaningless feedback. Saying, "Your paper's great. I really liked it. Maybe you could make it flow a little better" is much less helpful than saying, "Your issue about environmental pollution in the Antarctic is well defined in the first paragraph, but I got lost in the second paragraph when you began discussing penguin coloration."

Chapter 23 (pp. 697–705) discusses additional ways to use groups and improve group dynamics.

Responsibilities of Peer Reviewers and Writers

Learning to respond conscientiously and carefully to others' work may be the single most important thing you can do to improve your own writing. When you review a classmate's draft, you should prepare as follows:

1. **Understand how experienced writers revise their drafts.** Prior to reviewing a classmate's draft, review the material in this chapter. Pay particular attention to pages 519–520, which provide general guidelines about what to look for when reading a draft, and to page 518, which summarizes the kinds of changes writers often make in response to reviews: additions, deletions, reordering, complete refocusing and rewriting, and so forth.

2. **Understand the assignment and the guidelines for peer reviewers.** For assignments in Part Two of this text, carefully read both the assignment itself and the Guidelines for Peer Reviews at the end of the chapter in which the assignment appears. These guidelines will help both the writer and you, as peer reviewer, to understand the demands of the assignment and the criteria on which it should be evaluated.

3. **Understand that you are not acting as a teacher.** A peer reviewer's role is that of a fresh reader. You can help the writer appreciate what it's like to encounter his or her text for the first time. Your primary responsibility is to articulate your understanding of what the writer's words say to you and to identify places where you get confused, where you need more details, where you have doubts or queries, and so on. Although the specific kinds of evaluations called for in the Guidelines for Peer Reviews will be helpful, you don't need to be an expert offering solutions to every problem.

When you play the role of writer during a workshop session, your responsibilities parallel those of your peer reviewers. You need to provide a legible rough draft, preferably typed and double-spaced, that doesn't baffle the reader with illegible handwriting, crossouts, arrows, and confusing pagination. Your instructor may ask you to bring photocopies of your draft for all group members. During the workshop, your primary responsibility is to *listen*, taking in how others respond to your draft without becoming defensive. Many instructors also ask writers to formulate two or three specific questions about their drafts—questions they particularly want their reviewers to address. These questions might focus on something writers particularly like about their drafts or on specific problem areas or concerns.

Exchanging Drafts

An excellent system for exchanging drafts is to have each writer read his or her draft aloud while group members follow along in their own photocopies. We value reading drafts aloud when time allows. Reading expressively, with appropriate emphasis, helps writers distance themselves from their work and hear it anew. When you read your work silently to yourself, it's all too easy to patch up bits of broken prose in your head or to slide through confusing passages. But if you stumble over a passage while reading aloud, you can place a check mark in the margin to indicate where further attention is needed. Another benefit to reading aloud is perhaps more symbolic than pragmatic: Reading your work to others means that you are claiming responsibility for it, displaying your intention to reach a range of readers other than the teacher. And knowing that you will have to read your work aloud will encourage you to have that work in the best possible shape before bringing it to class.

Types of Peer Review Workshops

After you've read your draft aloud, the next stage of your peer review may take one of several forms, depending on your instructor's preference. We describe here two basic strategies: response-centered workshops, and advice-centered workshops. Additional strategies often build on these approaches.

Response-Centered Workshops

This process-oriented, non-intrusive approach places maximum responsibility on the writer for making decisions about what to change in a draft. After the writer reads the draft aloud, group members follow this procedure:

1. All participants take several minutes to make notes on their copies of the manuscript. We recommend using the wavy line, "Good!", "?" system described in the Guidelines for Peer Reviews.
2. Group members take turns describing to the writer their responses to the piece—where they agreed or disagreed with the writer's ideas, where they got confused, where they wanted more development, and so forth. Group members do not give advice; they simply describe their own personal response to the draft as written.
3. The writer takes notes during each response but does not enter into a discussion. The writer listens without trying to defend the piece or explain what he or she intended.

No one gives the writer explicit advice. Group members simply describe their reactions to the piece and leave it to the writer to make appropriate changes.

Advice-Centered Workshops

In this more product-oriented and directive approach, peer reviewers typically work in pairs. Each writer exchanges drafts with a partner, reviews the draft carefully, and then writes specific advice on how to improve the draft. This method works best when peer reviewers use the Guidelines for Peer Reviews that conclude each chapter in Part Two, either addressing all the questions in the guidelines or focusing on specific questions identified by the instructor.

A variation on this approach, which allows peer reviewers to collaborate in pairs when analyzing a draft, uses the following process:

1. The instructor divides the class into initial groups of four.
2. Each group then divides into pairs; each pair exchanges drafts with the other pair.
3. The members of each pair collaborate to compose jointly written reviews of the two drafts they have received.
4. The drafts and the collaboratively written reviews are then returned to the original writers. If time remains, the two pairs meet to discuss their reviews.

When two students collaborate to review a draft, they often produce more useful and insightful reviews than when working individually. In sharing observations and negotiating their responses, they can write their reviews with more confidence and reduce the chances of idiosyncratic advice.

However, because each pair has received two drafts and has to write two peer reviews, this approach takes more class time. Instructors can speed this process by setting up the groups of four in advance and asking pairs to exchange and read drafts prior to the class meeting. Class time can then be focused on collaborative writing of the reviews.

Responding to Peer Reviews

After you and your classmates have gone over each other's papers and walked each other through the responses, everyone should identify two or three things about his or her draft that particularly need work. Before you leave the session, you should have some notion about how you want to revise your paper.

You may get mixed or contradictory responses from different reviewers. One reviewer may praise a passage that another finds confusing or illogical. Conflicting advice is a frustrating fact of life for all writers, whether students or professionals. Such disagreements reveal how readers cocreate a text with a writer: Each brings to the text a different background, set of values, and way of reading.

It is important to remember that you are in charge of your own writing. If several readers offer the same critique of a passage, then no matter how much you love that passage, you probably need to follow their advice. But when readers disagree, you have to make your own best judgment about whom to heed.

Once you have received advice from others, reread your draft again slowly and then develop a revision plan, allowing yourself time to make sweeping, global changes if needed. You also need to remember that you can never make your draft perfect. Plan when you will bring the process to a close so that you can turn in a finished product on time and get on with your other classes and your life.

Chapter Summary

This chapter has focused on the writing processes of experts, showing how experienced writers use multiple drafts to solve subject-matter and rhetorical problems. We have also offered advice on how to improve your own writing processes. Particularly, beginning college writers need to understand the kinds of changes writers typically make in drafts, to role-play a reader's perspective when they revise, and to practice the revision strategies of experts. Because peer reviewing is a powerful strategy for learning how to revise, we showed you how to make "readerly" rather than "writerly" comments on a rough draft and how to participate productively in peer review workshops.

Composing and Revising Closed-Form Prose

[Form is] an arousing and fulfillment of desires. A work has form insofar as one part of it leads a reader to anticipate another part, to be gratified by the sequence.

—KENNETH BURKE, *RHETORICIAN*

I think the writer ought to help the reader as much as he can without damaging what he wants to say; and I don't think it ever hurts the writer to sort of stand back now and then and look at his stuff as if he were reading it instead of writing it.

—JAMES JONES, *WRITER*

Chapter 17 explained the composing processes of experienced writers and suggested ways that you can improve your own writing processes. In this chapter we present ten lessons in composing and revising closed-form prose. This chapter is not intended to be read in one sitting, lest you suffer from information overload. To help you learn the material efficiently, we have made each lesson a self-contained unit that can be read comfortably in half an hour or less and discussed in class as part of a day's session. You will benefit most from these lessons if you focus on one lesson at a time and then return to the lessons periodically as you progress through the term. Each lesson's advice will become increasingly meaningful and relevant as you gain experience as a writer.

The first lesson—on reader expectations—is intended as a theoretical overview to the rest of the chapter. The remaining nine lessons can then be assigned and read in any order your instructor desires. You will learn how to convert loose structures into thesis/support structures (Lesson 2); how to plan and visualize your structure (Lesson 3); how to create effective titles and introductions (Lesson 4); how to use topic sentences, transitions, and the old/new contract to guide your readers through the twists and turns of your prose (Lessons 5–7); how to perform several common writer's "moves" for developing your ideas (Lesson 8); how to write good conclusions (Lesson 9); and, finally, how to create effective document design (Lesson 10). Together these lessons will teach you strategies for making your closed-form prose reader-friendly, well structured, clear, and persuasive.

Lesson 1: Understanding Reader Expectations

In this opening lesson, we show you how to think like a reader. Imagine for a moment that your readers have only so much *reader energy,* which they can use either to follow and respond to your ideas (the result you want) or to puzzle over what you are trying to say (the result you don't want).* Skilled readers make predictions about where a text is heading based on clues provided by the writer. When readers get lost, the writer has often failed to give clues about where the text is going or has failed to do what the reader predicted. "Whoa, you lost me on the turn," a reader might say. "How does this passage relate to what you just said?" To write effective closed-form prose, you need to help readers see how each part of your text is related to what came before. (Sometimes with open-form prose, surprise or puzzlement may be the very effect you want to create. But with closed-form prose this kind of puzzlement is fatal.)

In this lesson we explain what readers of closed-form prose need in order to predict where a text is heading. Specifically we show you that readers need three things in a closed-form text:

- They need unity and coherence.
- They need old information before new information.
- They need forecasting and fulfillment.

Let's look at each in turn.

Unity and Coherence

Together the terms *unity* and *coherence* are defining characteristics of closed-form prose. *Unity* refers to the relationship between each part of an essay and the larger whole. *Coherence* refers to the relationship between adjacent sentences, paragraphs, and parts. The following thought exercise will illustrate your own expectations for unity and coherence:

THOUGHT EXERCISE 1

Read the following two passages and try to explain why each fails to satisfy your expectations as a reader:

A. Recent research has given us much deeper—and more surprising—insights into the father's role in childrearing. My family is typical of the east side in that we never had much money. Their tongues became black and hung out of their mouths. The back-to-basics movement got a lot of press, fueled as it was by fears of growing illiteracy and cultural demise.

B. Recent research has given us much deeper—and more surprising—insights into the father's role in childrearing. Childrearing is a complex process that is frequently

---

*For the useful term *reader energy,* we are indebted to George Gopen and Judith Swan, "The Science of Scientific Writing," *American Scientist* 78 (1990): 550–559. In addition, much of our discussion of writing in this chapter is indebted to the work of Joseph Williams, George Gopen, and Gregory Colomb. See especially Gregory G. Colomb and Joseph M. Williams, "Perceiving Structure in Professional Prose: A Multiply Determined Experience," in Lee Odell and Dixie Goswamie (eds.), *Writing in Nonacademic Settings* (New York: The Guilford Press, 1985), pp. 87–128.

investigated by psychologists. Psychologists have also investigated sleep patterns and dreams. When we are dreaming, psychologists have shown, we are often reviewing recent events in our lives.

If you are like most readers, Passage A comically frustrates your expectations because it is a string of random sentences. Because the sentences don't relate either to each other or to a larger point, Passage A is neither unified nor coherent.

Passage B frustrates expectations in a subtler way. If you aren't paying attention, Passage B may seem to make sense because each sentence is linked to the one before it. But the individual sentences don't develop a larger whole: the topics switch from a father's role in childrearing to psychology to sleep patterns to the function of dreams. This passage has coherence without unity.

To fulfill a reader's expectations, then, a closed-form passage must be both unified and coherent:

> C. (*Unified and coherent*) Recent research has given us much deeper—and more surprising—insights into the father's role in childrearing. It shows that in almost all of their interactions with children, fathers do things a little differently from mothers. What fathers do—their special parenting style—is not only highly complementary to what mothers do but is by all indications important in its own right. [The passage continues by showing the special ways that fathers contribute to childrearing.]

This passage makes a unified point—that fathers have an important role in childrearing. Because all the parts relate to that whole (unity) and because the connections from sentence to sentence are clear (coherence), the passage satisfies our expectations: It makes sense.

Because achieving unity and coherence is a major goal in revising closed-form prose, we'll refer frequently to these concepts in later lessons.

Old before New

One dominant way that readers process information and register ideas is by moving from already known (old) information to new information. In a nutshell, this concept means that new material is meaningful to a reader only if it is linked to old material that is already meaningful. To illustrate this concept, consider the arrangement of names and numbers in a telephone directory. Because we read from left to right, we want people's names in the left column and the telephone numbers in the right column. A person's name is the old, familiar information we already know and the number is the new, unknown information that we seek. If the numbers were in the left column and the names in the right, we would have to read backward.

You can see the same old-before-new principle at work in the following thought exercise:

THOUGHT EXERCISE 2

You are a passenger on an airplane flight into Chicago and need to transfer to Flight 29 to Memphis. As you descend into Chicago, the flight attendant announces transfer gates. Which of the following formats is easier for you to process? Why?

Option A		Option B	
To Atlanta on Flight 29	Gate C12	Gate C12	Flight 29 to Atlanta
To Dallas on Flight 35	Gate C25	Gate C25	Flight 35 to Dallas
To Memphis on Flight 16	Gate B20	Gate B20	Flight 16 to Memphis

If you are like most readers, you prefer Option A, which puts old information before new. In this case, the old/known information is our destination (cities arranged alphabetically) and perhaps our flight number (To Memphis on Flight 16). The new/unknown information is Gate B20. Option B causes us to expend more energy than does Option A because it forces us to hold the number of each gate in memory until we hear its corresponding city and flight number. Whereas Option A allows us to relax until we hear the word "Memphis," Option B forces us to concentrate intensely on each gate number until we find the meaningful one.

The principle of old before new has great explanatory power for writers. At the level of the whole essay, this principle helps writers establish the main structural frame and ordering principle of their argument. An argument's frame derives from the writer's purpose to change some aspect of the reader's view of the topic. The reader's original view of the topic—what we might call the common, expected, or ordinary view—constitutes old/known/familiar material. The writer's surprising view constitutes the new/unknown/unfamiliar material. The writer's hope is to move readers from their original view to the writer's new and different view. By understanding what constitutes old/familiar information to readers, the writer can determine how much background to provide, how to anticipate readers' objections, and how to structure material by moving from the old to the new. We discuss these matters in more depth in Lesson 4, on writing effective introductions.

At the sentence level, the principle of old before new also helps writers create coherence between adjacent parts and sentences. Most sentences in an essay should contain both an old element and a new element. To create coherence, the writer begins with the old material, which links back to something earlier, and then puts the new material at the end of the sentence. (See the discussion of the old/new contract in Lesson 7.)

Forecasting and Fulfillment

Finally, readers of closed-form prose expect writers to forecast what is coming and then to fulfill those forecasts. To appreciate what we mean by forecasting and fulfillment, try one more thought exercise:

THOUGHT EXERCISE 3

Although the following paragraph describes a simple procedure in easy-to-follow sentences, most readers still scratch their heads in bewilderment. Why? What makes the passage difficult to understand?

The procedure is actually quite simple. First, you arrange things into different groups. Of course, one pile may be sufficient depending on how much there is to do. If you have to go somewhere else due to lack of facilities, that is the next step; otherwise, you are pretty well set. Next you operate the machines according to the instructions. After the procedure is completed, one arranges the materials into different groups again. Then they can be put in their appropriate places. Eventually, they will be used once more and the whole cycle will have to be repeated. However, that is part of life.

Most readers report being puzzled about the paragraph's topic. Because the opening sentence doesn't provide enough context to tell them what to expect, the paragraph makes no forecast that can be fulfilled. Now try rereading the paragraph, but this time substitute the following opening sentence:

> The procedure for washing clothes is actually quite simple.

With the addition of "for washing clothes," the sentence provides a context that allows you to predict and understand what's coming. In the language of cognitive psychologists, this new opening sentence provides a schema for interpretation. A *schema* is the reader's mental picture of a structure for upcoming material. The new opening sentence allows you as reader to say mentally, "This paragraph will describe a procedure for washing clothes and argue that it is simple." When the schema proves accurate, you experience the pleasure of prediction and fulfillment. In the language of rhetorician Kenneth Burke, the reader's experience of form is "an arousing and fulfillment of desires."

What readers expect from a closed-form text, then, is an ability to predict what is coming as well as regular fulfillment of those predictions. Writers forecast what is coming in a variety of ways: by writing effective titles and introductions, by putting points at the beginning of paragraphs, by creating effective transitions and mapping statements, and by using effective headings and subheadings if appropriate for the genre. To meet their readers' needs for predictions and fulfillment, closed-form writers start and end with the big picture. They tell readers where they are going before they start the journey, they refer to this big picture at key transition points, and they refocus on the big picture in their conclusion.

Lesson 2: Converting Loose Structures into Thesis/Support Structures

In Lesson 1 we described readers' expectations for unity and coherence, old information before new, and forecasting and fulfillment. In academic contexts, readers also expect closed-form prose to have a thesis/support structure. As we explained in Chapter 2, most closed-form academic writing—especially writing with the aim of analysis or persuasion—is governed by a contestable or risky thesis statement. Because developing and supporting a thesis is complex work requiring much critical thought, writers sometimes retreat into loose structures that are easier to compose than a thesis-based argument with points and particulars.

In this lesson we help you better understand thesis-based writing by contrasting it with prose that looks like thesis-based writing but isn't. We show you three common ways in which inexperienced writers give the appearance of writing thesis-based prose while actually retreating from the rigors of making and developing an argument. Avoiding the pitfalls of these loose structures can go a long way toward improving your performance on most college writing assignments.

And Then Writing, or Chronological Structure

Chronological structure, often called "narrative," is the most common organizing principle of open-form prose. It may also be used selectively in closed-form prose to support a point. But sometimes the writer begins recounting the details of a story until chronological order takes over, driving out the thesis-based structure of points and particulars.

To a large degree, chronological order is the default mode we fall into when we aren't sure how to organize material. For example, if you were asked to analyze a fictional character, you might slip into a plot summary instead. In much the same way, you might substitute historical chronology ("First A happened, then B happened . . .") for historical analysis ("B happened because A happened . . ."); or you might give a chronological recounting of your research ("First I discovered A, then I discovered B . . .") instead of organizing your material into an argument ("I question A's account of this phenomenon on the grounds of B's recent findings . . .").

The tendency toward loose chronological structure is revealed in the following example from a student's essay on Shakespeare's *The Tempest*. This excerpt is from the introduction of the student's first draft:

PLOT SUMMARY—*AND THEN* WRITING

Prospero cares deeply for his daughter. In the middle of the play Prospero acts like a gruff father and makes Ferdinand carry logs in order to test his love for Miranda and Miranda's love for him. In the end, though, Prospero is a loving father who rejoices in his daughter's marriage to a good man.

Here the student seems simply to retell the play's plot without any apparent thesis. (The body of her rough draft primarily retold the same story in more detail.) However, during an office conference, the instructor discovered that the student regarded her sentence about Prospero's being a loving father as her thesis. In fact, the student had gotten in an argument with a classmate over whether Prospero was a good person or an evil one. The instructor helped her convert her draft into a thesis/support structure:

REVISED INTRODUCTION—THESIS/SUPPORT STRUCTURE

Many persons believe that Prospero is an evil person in the play. They claim that Prospero exhibits a harsh, destructive control over Miranda and also, like Faust, seeks superhuman knowledge through his magic. However, I contend that Prospero is a kind and loving father.

This revised version implies a problem (What kind of father is Prospero?), presents a view that the writer wishes to change (Prospero is harsh and hateful), and asserts a contestable thesis (Prospero is a loving father). The body of her paper can now be converted from plot summary to an argument with reasons and evidence supporting her claim that Prospero is loving.

This student's revision from an *and then* to a thesis/support structure is typical of many writers' experience. Because recounting events chronologically is a natural way to organize, many writers—even very experienced ones—lapse into long stretches of *and then* writing in their rough drafts. However, experienced writers have learned to recognize these *and then* sections in their drafts and to rework this material into a closed-form, thesis-based structure.

All About Writing, or Encyclopedic Structure

Whereas *and then* writing turns essays into stories by organizing details chronologically, *all about* writing turns essays into encyclopedia articles by piling up details in heaps. When *all about* writing organizes these heaps into categories, it can appear to be well organized: "Having told you everything I learned about educational opportunities in Cleveland, I will now tell you everything I learned about the Rock and Roll Hall of Fame." But the categories do not function as points and particulars in support of a thesis. Rather, like the shelving system in a library, they are simply ways of arranging information for convenient retrieval, not a means of building a hierarchical structure.

To illustrate the differences between *all about* writing and thesis-based writing, consider the case of two students choosing to write term papers on the subject of female police officers. One student is asked simply to write "all about" the topic; the other is asked to pose and investigate some problem related to female police officers and to support a thesis addressing that problem. In all likelihood, the first student would produce an initial outline with headings such as the following:

   I. History of women in police roles
      A. Female police or soldiers in ancient times
      B. 19th century (Calamity Jane)
      C. 1900s–1960
      D. 1960–present
  II. How female police officers are selected and trained
 III. A typical day in the life of a female police officer
 IV. Achievements and acts of heroism of female police officers
  V. What the future holds for female police officers

Such a paper is a data dump that places into categories all the information the writer has uncovered. It is riskless, and, except for occasional new information, surpriseless. In contrast, when a student focuses on a significant question—one that grows out of the writer's own interests and demands engagement—the writing can be quite compelling.

Consider the case of a student, Lynnea, who wrote a research paper entitled "Women Police Officers: Should Size and Strength Be Criteria for Patrol Duty?" Her essay begins with a group of male police officers complaining about being assigned to patrol duty with a new female officer, Connie Jones (not her real name), who is four feet ten inches tall and weighs ninety pounds. Here is the rest of the introduction to Lynnea's essay.

> Connie Jones has just completed police academy training and has been assigned to patrol duty in _____. Because she is so small, she has to have a booster seat in her patrol car and has been given a special gun, since she can barely manage to pull the trigger of a standard police-issue .38 revolver. Although she passed the physical requirements at the academy, which involved speed and endurance running, situps, and monkey bar tests, most of the officers in her department doubt her ability to perform competently as a patrol officer. But nevertheless she is on patrol because men and women receive equal assignments in most of today's police forces. But is this a good policy? Can a person who is significantly smaller and weaker than her peers make an effective patrol officer?

Lynnea examined all the evidence she could find—through library and field research (interviewing police officers) and arrived at the following thesis: "Because concern for public safety overrides all other concerns, police departments should set stringent size and strength requirements for patrol officers, even if these criteria exclude many women." This thesis has plenty of tension because it sets limits on equal rights for women. Because Lynnea considers herself a feminist, it caused her considerable distress to advocate setting these limits and placing public safety ahead of gender equity. The resulting essay is engaging precisely because of the tension it creates and the controversy it engenders.

Engfish Writing, or Structure without Surprise

Unlike the chronological story and the *all about* paper, the *engfish* essay has a thesis.* But the thesis is a riskless truism supported with predictable reasons—often structured as the three body paragraphs in a traditional five-paragraph theme. It is fill-in-the-blank writing: "The food service is bad for three reasons. First, it is bad because the food is not tasty. Blah, blah, blah about tasteless food. Second, it is bad because it is too expensive. Blah, blah, blah about the expense." And so on. The writer is on autopilot and is not contributing to a real conversation about a real question. In some situations, writers use *engfish* intentionally: bureaucrats and politicians may want to avoid saying something risky; students may want to avoid writing about complex matters that they fear they do not fully understand. In the end, using *engfish* is bad not because what you say is *wrong*, but because what you say couldn't *possibly be* wrong. To avoid *engfish*, stay focused on the need to surprise your reader.

---

*The term *engfish* was coined by the textbook writer Ken Macrorie to describe a fishy kind of canned prose that bright but bored students mechanically produce to please their teachers. See Ken Macrorie, *Telling Writing* (Rochelle Park, NJ: Hayden Press, 1970).

For Writing and Discussion

As a class, choose a topic from popular culture such as TV talk shows, tattooing, eating disorders, rock lyrics, or something similar.

1. Working as a whole class or in small groups, give examples of how you might write about this topic in an *and then* way, an *all about* way, and an *engfish* way.
2. Then develop one or more questions about the topic that could lead to thesis/support writing. What contestable theses can your class create?

Lesson 3: Planning and Visualizing Your Structure

As we explained in Lesson 2, closed-form writing supports a contestable thesis through a hierarchical network of points and particulars. One way to visualize this structure is to outline its skeleton, an exercise that makes visually clear that not all points are on equal levels. The highest-level point is an essay's thesis statement, which is usually supported by several main points that are in turn supported by subpoints and sub-subpoints, all of which are supported by their own particulars. In this lesson we show you how to create such a hierarchical structure for your own papers and how to visualize this structure through an outline, tree diagram, or flowchart.

At the outset, we want to emphasize two important points. First, structural diagrams are not rigid molds, but flexible planning devices that evolve as your thinking shifts and changes. The structure of your final draft may be substantially different from your initial scratch outline. In fact, we want to show you how your outlines or diagrams can help you generate more ideas and reshape your structure.

Second, outlines or diagrams organize *meanings,* not topics. Note that in all our examples of outlines, diagrams, and flowcharts, we write *complete sentences* rather than phrases in the high-level slots. We do so because sentences can make a point, which conveys meaning, unlike a phrase, which identifies a topic but doesn't make an assertion about it. Any point—whether a thesis, a main point, or a subpoint—is a contestable assertion that requires its own particulars for support. By using complete sentences rather than phrases in an outline, the writer is forced to articulate the point of each section of the emerging argument.

With this background, we now proceed to a sequence of steps you can take to plan and visualize a structure.

Use Scratch Outlines Early in the Writing Process

Many writers can't make a detailed outline of their arguments until they have written exploratory drafts. At these early stages, writers often make brief scratch outlines that list the main ideas they want to develop initially or they make a list of points that emerged from a freewrite or a very early draft. Here is student writer Christopher Leigh's initial scratch outline for his argument against metal detectors in schools:

Schools should not use metal detectors as a way of reducing violence.

- Media have created a panic.
- Metal detectors are easily defeated.
- Students hate them.
- Should I put in a section on whether they violate rights???
- Poland article shows we should put the money into creating better school atmosphere.

We first introduced Christopher's research problem in Chapter 1, p. 9. Christopher's final paper is shown in Chapter 22, pp. 675–686.

Before Making a Detailed Outline, "Nutshell" Your Argument

As you explore your topic and begin drafting, your ideas will gradually become clearer and more structured. You can accelerate this process through a series of short exercises that will help you "nutshell" your argument (see Figure 18.1).

The six exercises in this figure cause you to look at your argument from different perspectives, helping you clarify the question you are addressing, articulate

FIGURE 18.1 Exercises for Nutshelling Your Argument

Exercise 1   What puzzle or problem initiated your thinking about X?

Exercise 2   *(Paradigm: Many people think X, but I am going to argue Y.)*

Before reading my paper, my readers will think this about my topic:

_____ .

But after reading my paper, my readers will think this new way about my topic:

_____ .

Exercise 3   The purpose of my paper is _____ .

Exercise 4   My paper addresses the following question: _____ .

Exercise 5   My one-sentence summary answer to the above question is this:

_____

Exercise 6   A tentative title for my paper is this: _____

_____ .

the kind of change you want to make in your audience's view of your topic, and directly state your purpose, thesis, and tentative title. The authors of this text often use this exercise in one-on-one writing conferences to help students create an initial focus from a swirl of ideas. We recommend that you write out your responses to each exercise as a preliminary step in helping you visualize your structure. Here are Christopher Leigh's responses to these questions:

> Exercise 1: I was initially puzzled by how best to reduce school violence. When I found that many schools were using metal detectors, I wondered whether this was a good approach.
> Exercise 2: Before reading my paper, my readers will believe that metal detectors are a good way to reduce school violence. After reading my paper, my readers will realize that there are many problems with metal detectors and will want to put money instead into improving the school environment.
> Exercise 3: The purpose of my paper is to argue against metal detectors and to argue for a better school environment.
> Exercise 4: Should schools use metal detectors? Are metal detectors a good way to reduce school violence?
> Exercise 5: Metal detectors should not be used in schools because there are other, more effective, and less costly alternatives for violence prevention.
> Exercise 6: The Case Against Metal Detectors in Schools.

Articulate a Working Thesis and Main Points

Once you have nutshelled your argument, you are ready to visualize a structure containing several sections, parts, or chunks, each of which is headed by a main point and supported with particulars. Try answering these questions:

1. My working thesis statement is:
2. The main sections or chunks needed in my paper are:

Here are Christopher Leigh's answers to these questions:

1. Metal detectors should not be used in schools because there is no basis for panic about violence and because there are other, more effective, and less costly alternatives for violence prevention.
2. (a) A section on the media's having created a panic; (b) a big section on the arguments against metal detectors; (c) a section on my solution, which is to improve the school atmosphere.

Sketch Your Structure Using an Outline, Tree Diagram, or Flowchart

At this point you can make an initial structural sketch of your argument and use the sketch to plan out the subpoints and particulars necessary to support the main points. We offer you three different ways to visualize your argument: outlines, tree diagrams, and flowcharts. Use whichever strategy best fits your way of thinking and perceiving.

Outlines

The most common way of visualizing structure is the traditional outline, which uses letters and numerals to indicate levels of points, subpoints, and particulars. If you prefer outlines, we recommend that you use the outlining feature of your word processing program, which allows you to move and insert material and change heading levels with great flexibility. What follows is Christopher Leigh's detailed outline of his argument. Note that Chris uses complete sentences rather than phrases for each level.

The importance of complete sentences is explained at the beginning of this lesson, p. 535.

Thesis: Except for schools with severe threats of danger, metal detectors should not be used because there is no basis for panic and because there are other, more effective, and less costly alternatives for violence prevention in schools.

I. Media have created panic over school violence.
   A. School violence is actually quite rare.
   B. Frequency of weapons being brought to school has declined since 1993.
II. There are many strong arguments against use of metal detectors.
   A. Metal detectors may violate student rights.
      1. Quotations from students reveal belief that metal detectors violate their rights.
      2. Court rulings leave gray areas.
   B. Metal detectors are easily defeated.
      1. They can't close off all entrances.
      2. A shooter can always find a way to get guns inside.
   C. Metal detectors are costly.
   D. Metal detectors have bad psychological consequences for students.
      1. Quotations from students show students' dislike of prison atmosphere.
      2. Metal detectors create feeling of distrust and humiliation.
III. A better solution is to use the money spent on metal detectors to provide a better school atmosphere.
   A. Quotation from high school senior Malik Barry-Buchanan shows need to create respect and caring in the schools.
   B. Article by Poland shows need to make schools more personal and to provide more counseling.
      1. Teachers should make efforts to know each student as an individual.
      2. Extracurricular activities should not be cut.
      3. Schools should provide more counseling.
IV. Conclusion

Tree Diagrams

A tree diagram displays a hierarchical structure visually, using horizontal and vertical space instead of letters and numbers. Figure 18.2 shows Christopher's argument as a tree diagram. His thesis is at the top of the tree. His main reasons, written as point sentences, appear as branches beneath his claim. Supporting evidence and arguments are displayed as subbranches beneath each reason.

FIGURE 18.2 Christopher's Tree Diagram

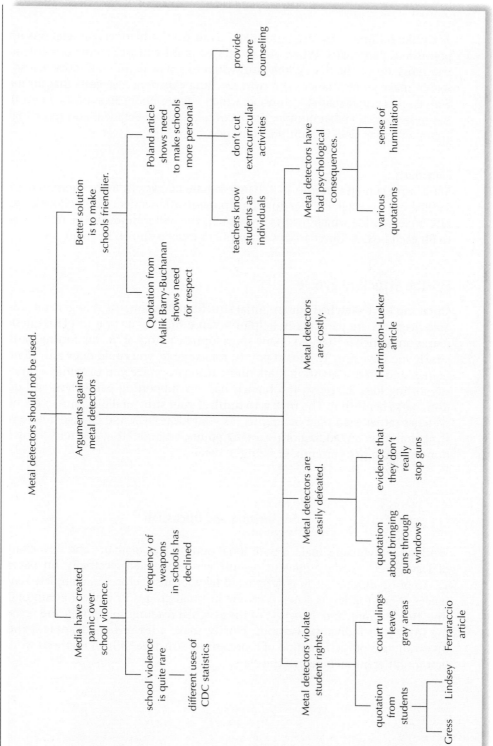

Unlike outlines, tree diagrams allow us to *see* the hierarchical relationship of points and particulars. When you develop a point with subpoints or particulars, you move down the tree. When you switch to a new point, you move across the tree to make a new branch. Our own teaching experience suggests that for many writers, this visual/spatial technique, which engages more areas of the brain than the more purely verbal outline, produces fuller, more detailed, and more logical arguments than does a traditional outline.

Flowcharts

Many writers prefer an informal, hand-sketched flowchart as an alternative to an outline or tree diagram. The flowchart presents the sequence of sections as separate boxes, inside which (or next to which) the writer notes the material needed to fill each box. A flowchart of Christopher's essay is shown in Figure 18.3.

Let the Structure Evolve

Once you have sketched out an initial structural diagram, use it to generate ideas. Tree diagrams are particularly helpful because they invite you to place question marks on branches to "hold open" spots for new points or for supporting particulars. If you have only two main points, for example, you could draw a third main branch and place a question mark under it to encourage you to think of another supporting idea. Likewise, if a branch has few supporting particulars, add question marks beneath it. The trick is to think of your structural diagrams as evolving sketches rather than rigid blueprints. As your ideas grow and change, revise your structural diagram, adding or removing points, consolidating and refocusing sections, moving parts around, or filling in details.

For Writing and Discussion

Working individually, make a traditional outline, tree diagram, and flow chart of David Rockwood's argument against wind-generated electricity on pages 17–18 or of another reading designated by your instructor. Use complete sentences at the top levels. Then convene in small groups to make a group outline, tree diagram, and flowchart of the assigned reading, combining and revising from your individual versions. Finally, make a list of the advantages and disadvantages of each method of representing structure. Which methods work best for different members of the class?

FIGURE 18.3 Christopher's Flowchart

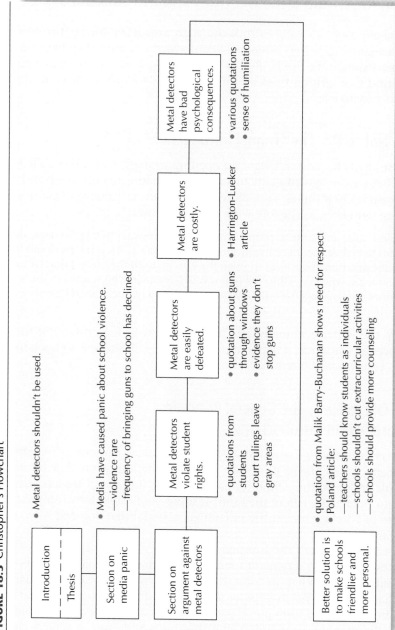

Introduction

Thesis

Section on media panic

Section on argument against metal detectors

Better solution is to make schools friendlier and more personal.

- Metal detectors shouldn't be used.

- Media have caused panic about school violence.
  —violence rare
  —frequency of bringing guns to school has declined

Metal detectors violate student rights.

- quotations from students
- court rulings leave gray areas

Metal detectors are easily defeated.

- quotation about guns through windows
- evidence they don't stop guns

Metal detectors are costly.

- Harrington-Lueker article

Metal detectors have bad psychological consequences.

- various quotations
- sense of humiliation

- quotation from Malik Barry-Buchanan shows need for respect
- Poland article:
  —teachers should know students as individuals
  —schools shouldn't cut extracurricular activities
  —schools should provide more counseling

Lesson 4: Writing Effective Titles and Introductions

Because effective titles and introductions give readers a big-picture overview of a paper's argument, writers often can't compose them until they have finished one or more exploratory drafts. But as soon as you know your essay's big picture, you'll find that writing titles and introductions follows some general principles that are easy to learn.

What Not to Do: The "Funnel Introduction"

Some students have been taught an opening strategy, sometimes called the "funnel," that encourages students to start with broad generalizations and then narrow down to their topics. This strategy often leads to vapid generalizations in the opening sentences, as the following example shows:

> Since time immemorial people have pondered the question of freedom. What it means to be free was asked by the great philosophers of ancient Greece and Rome, and the question has echoed through the ages up until the present day. One modern psychologist who asked this question was B. F. Skinner, who wanted to study whether humans had free will or were programmed by their environment to act the way they did. . . .

Here the writer eventually gets to his subject, B. F. Skinner. But the opening sentences are snoozers. A better approach, as we will show, is to hook immediately into your readers' interests.

From Old to New: The General Principle of Closed-Form Introductions

We introduced the principle of old before new in Lesson 1. See pp. 529–530.

Whereas the broad-to-narrow strategy is mechanical, the strategy we show you in this lesson, based on the principle of old information before new information, is dynamic and powerful. Old information is something your readers already know and find interesting before they start reading your essay. New information is the surprise of your argument, the unfamiliar material that you add to your readers' understanding.

See the explanation of a prototypical academic introduction in Chapter 2, pp. 32–34.

Because the writer's thesis statement forecasts the new information the paper will present, a thesis statement for a closed-form essay typically comes *at the end of the introduction*. What precedes the thesis is typically the old, familiar information that the reader needs in order to understand the conversation that the thesis joins. In most closed-form prose, particularly in academic prose, this old information is the problem or question that the thesis addresses. A typical closed-form introduction has the following shape:

PROBLEM
[old information]

↓

THESIS
[new information]

The length and complexity of your introduction is a function of how much your reader already knows and cares about the question or problem your paper addresses. The function of an introduction is to capture the reader's interest in the first few sentences, to identify and explain the question or problem that the essay addresses, to provide any needed background information, and to present the thesis. You can leave out any of the first three elements if the reader is already hooked on your topic and already knows the question you are addressing. For example, in an essay exam you can usually start with your thesis statement because you can assume the instructor already knows the question and finds it interesting.

To illustrate how an effective closed-form introduction takes the reader from the question to the thesis, consider how the following student writer revised his introduction to a paper on Napster.com:

ORIGINAL INTRODUCTION (CONFUSING)

Napster is all about sharing, not stealing, as record companies and some musicians would like us to think. Napster is an online program that was released in October of '99. Napster lets users easily search for and trade mp3s—compressed, high-quality music files that can be produced from a CD. Napster is the leading file sharing community; it allows users to locate and share music. It also provides instant messaging, chat rooms, an outlet for fans to identify new artists, and a forum to communicate their interests.

> *Thesis statement*
>
> *Background on Napster*

Most readers find this introduction confusing. The writer begins with his thesis statement before the reader is introduced to the question that the thesis addresses. He seems to assume that his reader is already a part of the Napster conversation, and yet in the next sentences, he gives background on Napster. If the reader needs background on Napster, then the reader also needs background on the Napster controversy. In rethinking his assumptions about old-versus-new information for his audience, this writer decides he wants to reach general newspaper readers who may have heard about a lawsuit against Napster and are interested in the issue but aren't sure of what Napster is or how it works. Here is his revised introduction:

REVISED INTRODUCTION (CLEARER)

Several months ago the rock band Metallica filed a lawsuit against Napster.com, an online program that lets users easily search for and trade mp3s—compressed, high-quality music files that can be produced from a CD. Napster.com has been wildly popular among music lovers because it creates a virtual community where users can locate and share music. It also provides instant messaging, chat rooms, an outlet for fans to identify new artists, and a forum to communicate their interests. But big-name bands like Metallica, alarmed at what they see as lost revenues, claim that Napster.com is stealing their royalties. However, Napster is all about sharing, not stealing, as some musicians would like us to think.

> *Triggers readers' memory of lawsuit*
>
> *Background on Napster*
>
> *Clarification of problem (Implied question: Should Napster be shut down?)*
>
> *Thesis*

This revised introduction fills in the old information the reader needs in order to recall and understand the problem; then it presents the thesis.

Typical Elements of a Closed-Form Introduction

Now that you understand the general principle of closed-form introductions, let's look more closely at its four typical features or elements:

An Opening Attention-Grabber.   The first few sentences in an introduction have to capture your reader's interest. If you aren't sure your reader is already interested in your problem, you can begin with an attention-grabber (what journalists call the "hook" or "lead"), which is typically a dramatic vignette, a startling fact or statistic, an arresting quotation, an interesting scene, or something else that taps into your reader's interests. Attention-grabbers are uncommon in academic prose (where you assume your reader will be initially engaged by the problem itself) but frequently used in popular prose. The student writer of the Napster paper initially toyed with the following attention-grabber to begin his essay:

> How many times have you liked one or two songs on a CD but thought the rest of it was garbage? How many times have you burned your own customized CDs by finding your favorite music on Napster.com? Well, that opportunity is about to be lost if Metallica wins its lawsuit against Napster.

He decided not to use this attention-grabber, however, because he wanted to reach audiences who weren't already users of Napster. He decided that these general readers were already interested in the lawsuit and didn't need the extra zing of an attention-grabber.

The brief writing project in Chapter 1 teaches you how to show that a question is problematic and significant. See pp. 24–25.

Explanation of the Question to Be Investigated.   If you assume that your reader already knows about the problem and cares about it, then you need merely to summarize it. This problem or question is the starting point of your argument. Closed-form writers often state the question directly in a single sentence ending with a question mark, but sometimes they imply it, letting the reader formulate it from context. If you aren't sure whether your audience fully understands the question or fully cares about it, then you need to explain it in more detail, showing why it is both problematic and significant.

Background Information.   In order to understand the conversation you are joining, readers sometimes need background information—perhaps a definition of key terms, a summary of events leading up to the problem you're presenting, factual details needed for basic understanding of the problem, and so forth. In scientific papers, this background often includes a review of the preexisting literature on the problem. In the Napster introduction, the writer devotes several sentences to background on Napster.com.

A Preview of the Whole.   The final element of a closed-form introduction sketches the big picture of your essay by giving readers a sense of the whole. This preview is initially new information for your readers (this is why it comes at the end of the introduction). Once stated, however, it becomes old information that readers will use to locate their position in their journey through your argument. By predicting what's coming, this preview initiates the pleasurable process of forecasting/fulfillment that we discussed in Lesson 1. Writers typically forecast the whole by stating their thesis, but they can also use a purpose statement or a blueprint statement to accomplish the same end. These strategies are the subject of the next section.

See this chapter's opening epigraph from rhetorician Kenneth Burke, p. 527.

Forecasting the Whole with a Thesis Statement, Purpose Statement, or Blueprint Statement

The most succinct way to forecast the whole is to state your thesis directly. Student writers often ask how detailed their thesis statements should be and whether it is permissible, sometimes, to delay revealing the thesis until the conclusion—an open-form move that gives papers a more exploratory, mystery-novel feel. It is useful, then, to outline briefly some of your choices as a writer. To illustrate a writer's options for forecasting the whole, we use Christopher Leigh's essay on metal detectors in schools that we discussed in Lesson 3.

To see the choices Christopher Leigh actually made, see his complete essay on pp. 675–686.

Options for Forecasting the Whole

Option	Explanation	Example
Short thesis	State claim without summarizing your supporting argument or forecasting your structure.	Schools should not use metal detectors to reduce school violence.
Detailed thesis	Summarize whole argument; may begin with an *although* clause that summarizes the view you are trying to change.	Although metal detectors may be justified in schools with severe threats of danger, they should generally not be used because there is no basis for panic and because there are other, more effective, and less costly alternatives for violence prevention in schools.
Purpose statement	State your purpose or intention without summarizing the argument. A purpose statement typically begins with a phrase such as "My purpose is to . . ." or "In the following paragraphs I wish to . . .:"	My purpose in this essay is to make a case against using metal detectors in schools.
Blueprint or mapping statement	Describe the structure of your essay by announcing the number of main parts and describing the function or purpose of each one.	First I show that the media have created a false panic about school violence. Next I present four reasons metal detectors have bad consequences. Finally I outline a better approach—making schools friendlier and more personal.

In addition you have at least two other options:

- *Multisentence summary.* In long articles, academic writers often use all three kinds of statements—a purpose statement, a thesis statement, and a blueprint statement. While this sort of extensive forecasting is common in academic and business writing, it occurs less frequently in informal or popular essays. Christopher decided that his paper wasn't complex enough to justify an extensive multisentence overview.
- *Thesis question.* When writers wish to delay their thesis until the middle or the end of their essays, letting their arguments slowly unfold and keeping their stance a mystery, they often end the introduction with a question. This open-form strategy invites readers to join the writer in a mutual search for the answer.

> Although I would prefer having no metal detectors in schools, I am strongly in favor of making schools safer. So the question of whether metal detectors are justified leaves me baffled and puzzled. Should schools use them or not? [This approach would have required a very different structure from the paper Christopher actually wrote.]

Which of these options should a writer choose? There are no firm rules to help you answer this question. How much you forecast in the introduction and where you reveal your thesis is a function of your purpose, audience, and genre. The more you forecast, the clearer your argument is and the easier it is to read quickly. You minimize the demands on readers' time by giving them the gist of your argument in the introduction, making it easier to skim your essay if they don't have time for a thorough reading. The less you forecast, the more demands you make on readers' time: You invite them, in effect, to accompany you through the twists and turns of your own thinking process, and you risk losing them if they become confused, lost, or bored. For these reasons, academic writing is generally closed form and aims at maximum clarity. In many rhetorical contexts, however, more open forms are appropriate.

Chapter 3, pp. 56–57, gives more advice on when to choose closed or open forms.

If you choose a closed-form structure, we can offer some advice on how much to forecast. Readers sometimes feel insulted by too much forecasting, so include only what is needed for clarity. For short papers, readers usually don't need to have the complete supporting argument forecast in the introduction. In longer papers, however, or in especially complex ones, readers appreciate having the whole argument forecast at the outset. Academic writing in particular tends to favor explicit and often detailed forecasting.

Writing Effective Titles

The strategies we have suggested for a closed-form introduction apply equally well to a closed-form title. A good title needs to have something old (a word or phrase that hooks into a reader's existing interests) and something new (a hint of the writer's thesis or purpose). Here is an example of an academic title:

"Style as Politics: A Feminist Approach to the Teaching of Writing" [This title attracts scholars interested either in style or in feminist issues in writing (old); it promises to analyze the political implications of style (new).]

As this example shows, your title should provide a brief but detailed overview of what your paper is about. Academic titles are typically longer and more detailed than are titles in popular magazines. They usually follow one of four conventions:

1. Some titles simply state the question that the essay addresses:

   "Will Patriarchal Management Survive Beyond the Decade?"

2. Some titles state, often in abbreviated form, the essay's thesis:

   "The Writer's Audience Is Always a Fiction"

3. Very often the title is the last part of the essay's purpose statement:

   "The Relationship between Client Expectation of Improvement and Psychotherapy Outcome"

4. Many titles consist of two parts separated by a colon. To the left of the colon the writer presents key words from the essay's issue or problem or a "mystery phrase" that arouses interest; to the right the author places the essay's question, thesis, or summary of purpose:

   "Money and Growth: An Alternative Approach"
   "Deep Play: Notes on a Balinese Cockfight"
   "Fine Cloth, Cut Carefully: Cooperative Learning in British Columbia"

Although such titles might seem overly formal to you, they indicate how much a closed-form writer wishes to preview an article's big picture. Although their titles may be more informal, popular magazines often use these same strategies. Here are some titles from *Redbook* and the business magazine *Forbes*:

   "Is the Coffee Bar Trend About to Peak?" (question)
   "A Man *Can* Take Maternity Leave—And Love It" (abbreviated thesis)
   "Why the Department of Education Shouldn't Take Over the Student Loan Program" (last part of purpose statement)
   "Feed Your Face: Why Your Complexion Needs Vitamins" (two parts linked by colon)

Composing a title for your essay can help you find your focus when you get bogged down in the middle of a draft. Thinking about your title forces you to *nutshell* your ideas by seeing your project's big picture. It causes you to reconsider your purpose and to think about what's old and what's new for your audience.

For Writing and Discussion

Individual task: Choose an essay you are currently working on or have recently completed and examine your title and introduction based on the advice in this lesson. Ask yourself these questions:

- What audience am I imagining? What do I assume are my readers' initial interests that will lead them to read my essay (the old information I must hook into)? What is new in my essay?
- Do I have an attention-grabber? Why or why not?
- Where do I state or imply the question or problem that my essay addresses?
- Do I explain why the question is problematic and significant? Why or why not?
- For my audience to understand the problem, do I provide too much background information, not enough, or just the right amount?
- What strategies do I use to forecast the whole?

Based on your analysis of your present title and introduction, revise as appropriate.

Group task: Working with a partner or in small groups, share the changes you made in your title or introduction and explain why you made the changes.

Lesson 5: Placing Points before Particulars

In our lesson on outlining (Lesson 3), we suggested that you write complete sentences rather than phrases for the high-level slots of the outline in order to articulate the *meaning* or *point* of each section of your argument. In this lesson we show you how to place these points where readers expect them: near the beginning of the sections or paragraphs they govern.

When you place points before particulars, you follow the same principle illustrated in Lesson 1 with the flight attendant announcing the name of the city before the departure gate (the city is the old information, the departure gate the new information). When you first state the point, it is the new information that the next paragraph or section will develop. Once you have stated it, it becomes old information that helps readers understand the meaning of the particulars that follow. If you withhold the point until later, the reader has to keep all the particulars in short-term memory until you finally reveal the point that the particulars are supposed to support or develop.

Place Topic Sentences at the Beginning of Paragraphs

Readers of closed-form prose need to have point sentences (usually called "topic sentences") at the beginnings of paragraphs. However, writers of rough drafts often don't fulfill this need because, as we explained in Chapter 17, drafting is an exploratory process in which writers are often still searching for their points as they compose. Consequently, in their rough drafts writers often omit topic sentences entirely or place them at the ends of paragraphs, or they write topic sentences that misrepresent what the paragraphs actually say. During revision, then, you should check your body paragraphs carefully to be sure you have placed accurate topic sentences near the beginning.

What follow are examples of the kinds of revisions writers typically make. We have annotated the examples to explain the changes the writer has made to make the paragraphs unified and clear to readers. The first example is from a later draft of the essay on dorm room carpets from Chapter 17 (pp. 521–523).

Revision—Topic Sentence First

Another reason for the university not to buy carpets is the cost.
ʌAccording to Rachel Jones, Assistant Director of Housing   *Topic sentence*
                                                                                       placed first
Services, the initial purchase and installation of carpeting would

cost $300 per room. Considering the number of rooms in the three

residence halls, carpeting amounts to a substantial investment.

Additionally, once the carpets are installed, the university would

need to maintain them through the purchase of more vacuum cleaners

and shampoo machines. This money would be better spent on other

dorm improvements that would benefit more residents, such as

expanded kitchen facilities and improved recreational space. ~~Thus~~

~~carpets would be too expensive.~~

In the original draft, the writer states the point at the end of the paragraph. In his revision he states the point in an opening topic sentence that links back to the thesis statement, which promises "several reasons" that the university should not buy carpets for the dorms. The words "another reason" thus link the topic sentence to the argument's big picture.

Revise Paragraphs for Unity

In addition to placing topic sentences at the heads of paragraphs, writers often need to revise topic sentences to better match what the paragraph actually says, or revise the paragraph to better match the topic sentence. Paragraphs have unity when all their sentences develop the point stated in the topic sentence. Paragraphs in rough drafts are often not unified because they reflect the writer's shifting, evolving, thinking-while-writing process. Consider the following paragraph from an early draft of an argument against euthanasia by student writer Dao Do. Her peer reviewer labeled it "confusing." What makes it confusing?

We look at more examples from Dao's essay later in this chapter.

Early Draft—Confusing

First, euthanasia is wrong because no one has the right to take the life of another person. Some people say that euthanasia or suicide will end suffering and pain. But what proofs do they have for such a claim? Death is still mysterious to us; therefore, we do not know whether death will end suffering and pain or not. What seems to be the real claim is that death to those with illnesses will end our pain. Such pain involves worrying over them, paying their medical bills, and giving up so much of our time. Their deaths end our pain rather than theirs. And for that reason, euthanasia is a selfish act, for the outcome of euthanasia benefits us, the nonsufferers, more. Once the sufferers pass away, we can go back to our normal lives.

The paragraph opens with an apparent topic sentence: "Euthanasia is wrong because no one has the right to take the life of another person." But the rest of the paragraph doesn't focus on that point. Instead, it focuses on how euthanasia benefits the survivors more than the sick person. Dao had two choices: to revise the paragraph to fit the topic sentence or to revise the topic sentence to fit the paragraph. Here is her revision, which includes a different topic sentence and an additional sentence midparagraph to keep particulars focused on the opening point. Dao unifies this paragraph by keeping all its parts focused on her main point: "Euthanasia . . . benefits the survivors more than the sick person."

Revision for Unity

First, euthanasia is wrong because it benefits the survivors more than the sick person.

~~First, euthanasia is wrong because no one has the right to~~

Revised topic sentence better forecasts focus of paragraph

~~take the life of another person.~~ Some people say that euthanasia

the sick person's ←———————————————

or suicide will end ˬsuffering and pain. But what proofs do they

Keeps focus on "sick person"

have for such a claim? Death is still mysterious to us;

therefore, we do not know whether death will end suffering and

Moreover, modern pain killers can relieve most most of the pain a sick person has to endure. ←———————

pain or not. ˬWhat seems to be the real claim is that death to

Concludes subpoint about sick person

those with illnesses will end <u>our</u> pain. Such pain involves

worrying over them, paying their medical bills, and giving up so

Supports subpoint about how euthanasia benefits survivors

much of our time. Their deaths end our pain rather than theirs.

And for that reason, euthanasia is a selfish act, for the outcome

of euthanasia benefits us, the nonsufferers, more. Once the

sufferers pass away, we can go back to our normal lives.

A paragraph may lack unity for a variety of reasons. It may shift to a new direction in the middle, or one or two sentences may simply be irrelevant to the point. The key is to make sure that all the sentences in the paragraph fulfill the reader's expectations based on the topic sentence.

Add Particulars to Support Points

Just as writers of rough drafts often omit point sentences from paragraphs, they also sometimes leave out the particulars needed to support a point. In such cases, the writer needs to add particulars such as facts, statistics, quotations, research summaries, examples, or further subpoints. Consider how adding additional particulars to the following draft paragraph strengthens student writer Tiffany Linder's argument opposing the logging of old-growth forests.

DRAFT PARAGRAPH: PARTICULARS MISSING

One reason that it is not necessary to log old-growth forests is that the timber industry can supply the world's lumber needs without doing so. For example, we have plenty of new-growth forest from which timber can be taken (Sagoff 89). We could also reduce the amount of trees used for paper products by using other materials besides wood for paper pulp. In light of the fact that we have plenty of trees and ways of reducing our wood demands, there is no need to harvest old-growth forests.

REVISED PARAGRAPH: PARTICULARS ADDED

Added particulars support subpoint that we have plenty of new-growth forest

Added particulars support second subpoint that wood alternatives are available

One reason that it is not necessary to log old-growth forests is that the timber industry can supply the world's lumber needs without doing so. For example, we have plenty of new-growth forest from which timber can be taken as a result of major reforestation efforts all over the United States (Sagoff 89). In the Northwest, for instance, Oregon law requires every acre of timber harvested to be replanted. According to Robert Sedjo, a forestry expert, the world's demand for industrial wood could be met by a widely implemented tree farming system (Sagoff 90). We could also reduce the amount of trees used for paper products by using a promising new innovation called Kenaf, a fast-growing annual herb which is fifteen feet tall and is native to Africa. It has been used for making rope for many years, but recently it was found to work just as well for paper pulp. In light of the fact that we have plenty of trees and ways of reducing our wood demands, there is no need to harvest old-growth forests.

For Writing and Discussion

Individual Task: Bring to class a draft-in-progress for a closed-form essay. Pick out several paragraphs in the body of your essay and analyze them for "points-first" structure. For each paragraph, ask the following questions:

- Does my paragraph have a topic sentence near the beginning?
- If so, does my topic sentence accurately forecast what the paragraph says?
- Does my topic sentence link to my thesis statement or to a higher-order point that my paragraph develops?
- Does my paragraph have enough particulars to develop and support my topic sentence?

Group Task: Then exchange your draft with a partner and do a similar analysis of your partner's selected paragraphs. Discuss your analyses of each other's paragraphs and then help each other plan appropriate revision strategies. If time permits, revise your paragraphs and show your results to your partner. [Note: Sometimes you can revise simply by adding a topic sentence to a paragraph, rewording a topic sentence, or making other kinds of local revisions. At other times, you may need to cross out whole paragraphs and start over, rewriting from scratch after you rethink your ideas.]

Lesson 6: Signaling Relationships with Transitions

As we have explained in previous lessons, when readers read closed-form prose, they expect each new sentence, paragraph, and section to link clearly to what they have already read. They need a well-marked trail with signposts signaling the twists and turns along the way. They also need resting spots at major junctions where they can review where they've been and survey what's coming. In this lesson, we show you how transition words as well as summary and forecasting passages can keep your readers securely on the trail.

Use Common Transition Words to Signal Relationships

Transitions are like signposts that signal where the road is turning and limit the possible directions that an unfolding argument might take. Consider how the use of "therefore" and "nevertheless" limits the range of possibilities in the following examples:

> While on vacation, Suzie caught the chicken pox. Therefore, _____.
> While on vacation, Suzie caught the chicken pox. Nevertheless, _____.

"Therefore" signals to the reader that what follows is a consequence. Most readers will imagine a sentence similar to this one:

> Therefore, she spent her vacation lying in bed itching, feverish, and miserable.

In contrast, "nevertheless" signals an unexpected or denied consequence, so the reader might anticipate a sentence such as this:

> Nevertheless, she enjoyed her two weeks off, thanks to a couple of bottles of calamine lotion, some good books, and a big easy chair overlooking the ocean.

Here is a list of the most common transition words and phrases and what they signal to the reader:*

Words or Phrases	What They Signal
first, second, third, next, finally, earlier, later, meanwhile, afterward	*sequence*—First we went to dinner; then we went to the movies.
that is, in other words, to put it another way,—(dash), :(colon)	*restatement*—He's so hypocritical that you can't trust a word he says. To put it another way, he's a complete phony.
rather, instead	*replacement*—We shouldn't use the money to buy opera tickets; rather, we should use it for a nice gift.
for example, for instance, a case in point	*example*—Mr. Carlysle is very generous. For example, he gave the janitors a special holiday gift.

---

*Although all the words on the list serve as transitions or connectives, grammatically they are not all equivalent, nor are they all punctuated the same way.

Words or Phrases	What They Signal
because, since, for	*reason*—Taxes on cigarettes are unfair because they place a higher tax burden on the working class.
therefore, hence, so, consequently, thus, then, as a result, accordingly, as a consequence	*consequences*—I failed to turn in the essay; therefore I flunked the course.
still, nevertheless	*denied consequence*—The teacher always seemed grumpy in class; nevertheless, I really enjoyed the course.
although, even though, granted that (*with* still)	*concession*—Even though the teacher was always grumpy, I still enjoyed the course.
in comparison, likewise, similarly	*similarity*—Teaching engineering takes a lot of patience. Likewise, so does teaching accounting.
however, in contrast, conversely, on the other hand, but	*contrast*—I disliked my old backpack immensely; however, I really like this new one.
in addition, also, too, moreover, furthermore	*addition*—Today's cars are much safer than those of ten years ago. In addition, they get better gas mileage.
in brief, in sum, in conclusion, finally, to sum up, to conclude	*conclusion or summary*—In sum, the plan presented by Mary is the best choice.

For Writing and Discussion

This exercise is designed to show you how transition words govern relationships between ideas. Working in groups or on your own, finish each of the following statements using ideas of your own invention. Make sure what you add fits the logic of the transition word.

1. Writing is difficult; therefore _____.
2. Writing is difficult; however, _____.
3. Writing is difficult because _____.
4. Writing is difficult. For example, _____.
5. Writing is difficult. To put it another way, _____.
6. Writing is difficult. Likewise, _____.
7. Although writing is difficult, _____.
8. _____. In sum, writing is difficult.

In the following paragraph, various kinds of linking devices have been omitted. Fill in the blanks with words or phrases that would make the paragraph coherent. Clues are provided in brackets.

> Writing an essay is a difficult process for most people. _____ [contrast] the process can be made easier if you learn to practice three simple techniques. _____ [sequence] learn the technique of nonstop writing. When you are first trying to think of ideas for an essay, put your pen to your paper and write nonstop for ten or fifteen minutes without letting your pen leave the paper. Stay loose and free. Let your pen follow the waves of thought. Don't worry about grammar or spelling. _____ [concession] this technique won't work for everyone, it helps many people get a good cache of ideas to draw on. A _____ [sequence] technique is to write your rough draft rapidly without worrying about being perfect. Too many writers try to get their drafts right the first time. _____ [contrast] by learning to live with imperfection, you will save yourself headaches and a wastepaper basket full of crumpled paper. Think of your first rough draft as a path hacked out of the jungle—as part of an exploration, not as a completed highway. As a _____ [sequence] technique, try printing out a triple-spaced copy to allow space for revision. Many beginning writers don't leave enough space to revise. _____ [consequence] these writers never get in the habit of crossing out chunks of their rough draft and writing revisions in the blank spaces. After you have revised your rough draft until it is too messy to work from anymore, you can _____ [sequence] enter your changes into your word processor and print out a fresh draft, again setting your text on triple-space. The resulting blank space invites you to revise.

Write Major Transitions between Parts

In long closed-form pieces, writers often put *resting places* between major parts—transitional passages that allow readers to shift their attention momentarily away from the matter at hand to a sense of where they've been and where they're going. Often such passages sum up the preceding major section, refer back to the essay's thesis statement or opening blueprint plan, and then preview the next major section. Here are three typical examples:

> So far I have looked at a number of techniques that can help people identify debilitating assumptions that block their self-growth. In the next section, I examine ways to question and overcome these assumptions.

> Now that the difficulty of the problem is fully apparent, our next step is to examine some of the solutions that have been proposed.

> These, then, are the major theories explaining why Hamlet delays. But let's see what happens to Hamlet if we ask the question in a slightly different way. In this next section, we shift our critical focus, looking not at Hamlet's actions, but at his language.

Signal Transitions with Headings and Subheadings

In many genres, particularly scientific and technical reports, government documents, business proposals, textbooks, and long articles in magazines or scholarly journals, writers conventionally break up long stretches of text with headings and subheadings. Headings are often set in different type sizes and fonts and mark transition points between major parts and subparts of the argument. We discuss headings in detail in Lesson 10 on document design.

Lesson 7: Binding Sentences Together by Following the Old/New Contract

In the previous lesson we showed you how to mark the reader's trail with transitions. In this lesson we show you how to build a smooth trail without potholes or washed-out bridges.

An Explanation of the Old/New Contract

A powerful way to prevent gaps is to follow the old/new contract—a writing strategy derived from the principle of old before new that we explained and illustrated in Lesson 1. Simply put, the old/new contract asks writers to begin sentences with something old—something that links to what has gone before—and then to end sentences with new information.

To understand the old/new contract more fully, try the following thought exercise. We'll show you two passages, both of which explain the old/new contract. One of them, however, follows the principle it describes; the other violates it.

THOUGHT EXERCISE

Which of these passages follows the old/new contract?

VERSION 1

The old/new contract is another principle for writing clear closed-form prose. Beginning your sentences with something old—something that links to what has gone before—and then ending your sentences with new information that advances the argument is what the old/new contract asks writers to do. An effect called *coherence,* which is closely related to *unity,* is created by following this principle. Whereas the clear relationship between the topic sentence and the body of the paragraph and between the parts and the whole is what *unity* refers to, the clear relationship between one sentence and the next is what *coherence* relates to.

VERSION 2

Another principle for writing clear closed-form prose is the old/new contract. The old/new contract asks writers to begin sentences with something old—something that links to what has gone before—and then to end sentences with new information that advances the argument. Following this principle creates an effect called *coherence,* which is closely related to unity. Whereas *unity* refers to the clear relationship between the body of a paragraph and its topic sentence and between the parts and the whole, *coherence* refers to the clear relationship between one sentence and the next, between part and part.

If you are like most readers, you have to concentrate much harder to understand Version 1 than Version 2 because it violates the old-before-new way that our minds normally process information. When a writer doesn't begin a sentence with old material, readers have to hold the new material in suspension until they have figured out how it connects to what has gone before. They can stay on the trail, but they have to keep jumping over the potholes between sentences.

To follow the old/new contract, place old information near the beginning of sentences in what we call the *topic position* and new information that advances the argument in the predicate or *stress position* at the end of the sentence. We associate topics with the beginnings of sentences simply because in the standard English sentence, the topic (or subject) comes before the predicate—hence the notion of a "contract" by which we agree not to fool or frustrate our readers by breaking with the "normal" order of things. The contract says that the old, backward-linking material comes at the beginning of the sentence and that the new, argument-advancing material comes at the end.

For Writing and Discussion

What follow are two more passages, one of which obeys the old/new contract while the other violates it. Working in small groups or as a whole class, reach consensus on which of these passages follows the old/new contract. Explain your reasoning by showing how the beginning of each sentence links to something old.

PASSAGE A

Play is an often-overlooked dimension of fathering. From the time a child is born until its adolescence, fathers emphasize caretaking less than play. Egalitarian feminists may be troubled by this, and spending more time in caretaking may be wise for fathers. There seems to be unusual significance in the father's style of play. Physical excitement and stimulation are likely to be part of it. With older children more physical games and teamwork that require the competitive testing of physical and mental skills are also what it involves. Resemblance to an apprenticeship or teaching relationship is also a characteristic of fathers' play: Come on, let me show you how.

PASSAGE B

An often-overlooked dimension of fathering is play. From their children's birth through adolescence, fathers tend to emphasize play more than caretaking. This may be troubling to egalitarian feminists, and it would indeed be wise for

(*continued*)

most fathers to spend more time in caretaking. Yet the fathers' style of play seems to have unusual significance. It is likely to be both physically stimulating and exciting. With older children it involves more physical games and teamwork that require the competitive testing of physical and mental skills. It frequently resembles an apprenticeship or teaching relationship: Come on, let me show you how.

How to Make Links to the "Old"

To understand how to link to "old information," you need to understand more fully what we mean by "old" or "familiar." In the context of sentence-level coherence, we mean everything in the text that the reader has read so far. Any upcoming sentence is new information, but once the reader has read it, it becomes old information. For example, when a reader is halfway through a text, everything previously read—the title, the introduction, half the body—is old information to which you can link to meet your readers' expectations for unity and coherence.

In making these backward links, writers have three targets:

1. They can link to a key word or concept in the immediately preceding sentence (creating coherence).
2. They can link to a key word or concept in a preceding point sentence (creating unity).
3. They can link to a preceding forecasting statement about structure (helping readers map their location in the text).

Writers have a number of textual strategies for making these links. In Figure 18.4 our annotations show how a professional writer links to old information within the first five or six words of each sentence. What follows is a compendium of these strategies:

- *Repeat a key word.* The most common way to open with something old is to repeat a key word from the preceding sentence or an earlier point sentence. In our example, note the number of sentences that open with "father," "father's," or "fathering." Note also the frequent repetitions of "play."
- *Use a pronoun to substitute for a key word.* In our example, the second sentence opens with the pronouns "it," referring to "research," and "their," referring to "fathers." The last three sentences open with the pronoun "It," referring to "father's style of play."
- *Summarize, rephrase, or restate earlier concepts.* Writers can link to a preceding sentence by using a word or phrase that summarizes or restates a key concept. In the second sentence, "interactions with children" restates the concept of childrearing. Similarly, the phrase "an often-overlooked dimension" refers to a concept implied in the preceding paragraph—that recent

FIGURE 18.4 How a Professional Writer Follows the Old/New Contract

Refers to "fathers" in previous sentence

Transition tells us new paragraph will be an example of previous concept

Refers to fathers

New information that becomes topic of this paragraph

Repeats words "father" and "play" from the topic sentence of the paragraph

Recent research has given us much deeper—and more surprising—insights into the father's role in childrearing. It shows that in almost all of their interactions with children, fathers do things a little differently from mothers. What fathers do—their special parenting style—is not only highly complementary to what mothers do but is by all indications important in its own right.

For example, an often-overlooked dimension of fathering is play. From their children's birth through adolescence, fathers tend to emphasize play more than caretaking. This may be troubling to egalitarian feminists, and it would indeed be wise for most fathers to spend more time in caretaking.

Yet the fathers' style of play seems to have unusual significance. It is likely to be both physically stimulating and exciting. With older children it involves more physical games and teamwork that require the competitive testing of physical and mental skills. It frequently resembles an apprenticeship or teaching relationship: Come on, let me show you how.

Refers to "research" in previous sentence

Rephrases idea of "childrearing"

Repeats "fathers" from previous sentence

Rephrases concept in previous paragraph

Pronoun sums up previous concept

"It" refers to fathers' style of play

David Popenoe, "Where's Papa?" from *Life Without Father: Compelling New Evidence that Fatherhood and Marriage Are Indispensable for the Good of Children and Society.*

research reveals something significant and not widely known about a father's role in childrearing. An "often-overlooked dimension" sums up this idea. Finally, note that the pronoun "this" in the second paragraph sums up the main concept of the previous two sentences. (But see our warning on page 560 about the overuse of "this" as a pronoun.)

- *Use a transition word.* Writers can also use transition words such as *first . . .*, *second . . .*, *third . . .* or *therefore* or *however* to cue the reader about the logical relationship between an upcoming sentence and the preceding ones. Note how the second paragraph opens with "For example," indicating that the upcoming paragraph will illustrate the concept identified in the preceding paragraph.

These strategies give you a powerful way to check and revise your prose. Comb your drafts for gaps between sentences where you have violated the old/new contract. If the opening of a new sentence doesn't refer back to an earlier word, phrase, or concept, your readers could derail, so use what you have learned to repair the tracks.

For Writing and Discussion

Individual Task: Bring to class a draft-in-progress for a closed-form essay. On a selected page, examine the opening of each sentence. Place a vertical slash in front of any sentence that doesn't contain near the beginning some backward-looking element that links to old, familiar material. Then revise these sentences to follow the old/new contract.

Group Task: Working with a partner, share the changes you each made on your drafts. Then on each other's pages, work together to identify the kinds of links made at the beginning of each sentence. (For example, does the opening of a sentence repeat a key word, use a pronoun to substitute for a key word, rephrase or restate an earlier concept, or use a transition word?)

As we discussed in Lesson 1, the principle of old before new has great explanatory power in helping writers understand their choices when they compose. In this last section, we give you some further insights into the old/new contract.

Avoid Ambiguous Use of "This" to Fulfill the Old/New Contract

Some writers try to fulfill the old/new contract by frequent use of the pronoun *this* to sum up a preceding concept. Occasionally such usage is effective, as in our example passage on fathers' style of play when the writer says: "*This* may be troubling to egalitarian feminists." But frequent use of *this* as a pronoun creates lazy and often ambiguous prose. Consider how our example passage might read if many of the explicit links were replaced by *this:*

LAZY USE OF *THIS* AS PRONOUN

Recent research has given us much deeper—and more surprising—insights into **this.** It shows that in doing **this,** fathers do things a little differently from mothers. **This** is not only highly complementary to what mothers do but is by all indications important in its own right.

For example, an often-overlooked dimension of **this** is play.

Perhaps this passage helps you see why we refer to *this* (used by itself as a pronoun) as "the lazy person's all-purpose noun-slot filler."*

---

*It's acceptable to use *this* as an adjective, as in "this usage"; we refer only to *this* used by itself as a pronoun.

How the Old/New Contract Modifies the Rule "Avoid Weak Repetition"

Many students have been warned against repetition of the same word (or *weak repetition,* as your teacher may have called it). Consequently, you may not be aware that repetition of key words is a vital aspect of unity and coherence. The repeated words create what linguists call "lexical strings" that keep a passage focused on a particular point. Note in our passage about the importance of fathers' style of play the frequent repetitions of the words *father* and *play.* What if the writer worried about repeating *father* too much and reached for his thesaurus?

UNNECESSARY ATTEMPT TO AVOID REPETITION

Recent research has given us much deeper—and more surprising—insights into the **male parent's** role in childrearing. It shows that in almost all of their interactions with children, **patriarchs** do things a little differently from mothers. What **sires** do. . . .

For example, an often-overlooked dimension of **male gender parenting** is. . . .

You get the picture. Keep your reader on familiar ground through repetition of key words.

How the Old/New Contract Modifies the Rule "Prefer Active over Passive Voice"

Another rule that you may have learned is to use the active voice rather than the passive voice. In the active voice the doer of the action is in the subject slot of the sentence, and the receiver is in the direct object slot, as in the following examples:

The dog caught the Frisbee.
The women wrote letters of complaint to the boss.
The landlord raised the rent.

In the passive voice the receiver of the action becomes the subject and the doer of the action either becomes the object of the preposition *by* or disappears from the sentence:

The Frisbee was caught by the dog.
Letters of complaint were written (by the women) to the boss.
The rent was raised (by the landlord).

Other things being equal, the active voice is indeed preferable to the passive because it is more direct and forceful. But in some cases, other things *aren't* equal, and the passive voice is preferable. *What the old/new contract asks you to consider is whether the doer or the receiver represents the old information in a sentence.* Consider the difference between the following passages:

| Second Sentence, Active Voice | My great-grandfather was a skilled cabinetmaker. He made this dining room table near the turn of the century. |
| Second Sentence, Passive Voice | I am pleased that you stopped to admire our dining room table. It was made by my great-grandfather near the turn of the century. |

In the first passage, the opening sentence is about *my great-grandfather*. To begin the second sentence with old information ("He," referring to "great-grandfather"), the writer uses the active voice. The opening sentence of the second passage is about the *dining room table*. To begin the second sentence with old information ("It," referring to "table"), the writer must use the passive voice, since the table is the receiver of the action. In both cases, the sentences are structured to begin with old information.

Lesson 8: Learning Four Expert Moves for Organizing and Developing Ideas

In this lesson we show you that writers of closed-form prose often employ a conventional set of moves to organize parts of an essay. In using the term *moves,* we are making an analogy with the "set moves" or "set plays" in such sports as basketball, volleyball, and soccer. For example, a common set move in basketball is the "pick," in which an offensive player without the ball stands motionless in order to block the path of a defensive player who is guarding the dribbler. Similarly, certain organizational patterns in writing occur frequently enough to act as set plays for writers. These patterns set up expectations in the reader's mind about the shape of an upcoming stretch of prose, anything from a few sentences to a paragraph to a large block of paragraphs. As you will see, these moves also stimulate the invention of ideas. Next, we describe four of the most powerful set plays.*

The *For Example* Move

An earlier example of Dao's paragraphs is on p. 551.

Perhaps the most common set play occurs when a writer makes an assertion and then illustrates it with one or more examples, often signaling the move explicitly with transitions such as *for example, for instance,* or *a case in point is.* . . . Here is how student writer Dao Do used the *for example* move to support her third reason for opposing euthanasia:

*You might find it helpful to follow the set plays we used to write this section. This last sentence is the opening move of a play we call "division into parallel parts." It sets up the expectation that we will develop four set plays in order. Watch for the way we chunk them and signal transitions between them.

FOR EXAMPLE MOVE

My third objection to euthanasia is that it fails to see the value in suffering. ◄——————— *Topic sentence*
Suffering is a part of life. We see the value of suffering only if we look deeply within   *Transition signaling*
our suffering. <u>For example,</u> I never thought my crippled uncle from Vietnam was a   *the move*
blessing to my grandmother until I talked to her. My mother's little brother was
born prematurely. As a result of oxygen and nutrition deficiency, he was born crippled. His tiny arms and legs were twisted around his body, preventing him from any
normal movements such as walking, picking up things, and lying down. He could
only sit. Therefore, his world was very limited, for it consisted of his own room and
the garden viewed through his window. Because of his disabilities, my grandmother   *Extended example*
had to wash him, feed him, and watch him constantly. It was hard, but she man-   *supporting point*
aged to care for him for forty-three years. He passed away after the death of my
grandfather in 1982. Bringing this situation out of Vietnam and into Western society shows the difference between Vietnamese and Western views. In the West, my
uncle might have been euthanized as a baby. Supporters of euthanasia would have
said he wouldn't have any quality of life and that he would have been a great burden. But he was not a burden on my grandmother. She enjoyed taking care of him,
and he was always her company after her other children got married and moved
away. Neither one of them saw his defect as meaningless suffering because it
brought them closer together.

This passage uses a single, extended example to support a point. You could also
use several shorter examples or other kinds of illustrating evidence such as facts
or statistics. In all cases the *for example* move creates a pattern of expectation and
fulfillment. This pattern drives the invention of ideas in one of two ways: It urges
the writer either to find examples to develop a generalization or to formulate a
generalization that shows the point of an example.

For Writing and Discussion

Working individually or in groups, develop a plan for supporting one or more
of the following generalizations using the *for example* move:

1. Another objection to state sales taxes is that they are so annoying.
2. Although assertiveness training has definite benefits, it can sometimes get
   you into real trouble.
3. Sometimes effective leaders are indecisive.

The *Summary/However* Move

This move occurs whenever a writer sums up another person's viewpoint in order
to qualify or contradict it or to introduce an opposing view. Typically, writers use
transition words such as *but, however, in contrast,* or *on the other hand* between the
parts of this move. This move is particularly common in academic writing, which

often contrasts the writer's new view with prevailing views. Here is how Dao uses a *summary/however* move in the introduction of her essay opposing euthanasia:

SUMMARY/HOWEVER MOVE

Issue over which there is disagreement

Summary of opposing viewpoint

Transition to writer's viewpoint

Statement of writer's view

> Should euthanasia be legalized? My classmate Martha and her family think it should be. Martha's aunt was blind from diabetes. For three years she was constantly in and out of the hospital, but then her kidneys shut down and she became a victim of life support. After three months of suffering, she finally gave up. Martha believes this three-month period was unnecessary, for her aunt didn't have to go through all of that suffering. If euthanasia were legalized, her family would have put her to sleep the minute her condition worsened. Then, she wouldn't have had to feel pain, and she would have died in peace and with dignity. However, despite Martha's strong argument for legalizing euthanasia, I find it wrong.

The first sentence of this introduction poses the question that the essay addresses. The main body of the paragraph summarizes Martha's opposing view on euthanasia, and the final sentence, introduced by the transition "However," presents Dao's thesis.

For Writing and Discussion

For this exercise, assume that you favor development of wind-generated electricity. Use the *summary/however* move to acknowledge the view of civil engineer David Rockwood, whose letter opposing wind-generated electricity you read in Chapter 1 (pp. 17–18). Assume that you are writing the opening paragraph of your own essay. Follow the pattern of Dao's introduction: (a) begin with a one-sentence issue or question; (b) summarize Rockwood's view in approximately one hundred words; and (c) state your own view, using *however* or *in contrast* as a transition. Write out your paragraph on your own, or work in groups to write a consensus paragraph. Then share and critique your paragraphs.

The *Division-into-Parallel-Parts* Move

Among the most frequently encountered and powerful of the set plays is the *division-into-parallel-parts* move. To initiate the move, a writer begins with an umbrella sentence that forecasts the structure and creates a framework. (For example, "Freud's theory differs from Jung's in three essential ways" or "The decline of the U.S. space program can be attributed to several factors.") Typical overview sentences either specify the number of parts that follow by using phrases such as "two ways," "three differences," or "five kinds," or they leave the number unspecified, using words such as *several, a few,* or *many.* Alternatively, the writer may ask a rhetorical question that implies the framework: "What are some main differences, then, between Freud's theory and Jung's? One difference is. . . ."

To signal transitions from one part to the next, writers use two kinds of signposts in tandem. The first is a series of transition words or bullets to introduce each of the parallel parts. Here are typical series of transition words:

First . . . Second . . . Third . . . Finally . . .

First . . . Another . . . Still another . . . Finally . . .

One . . . In addition . . . Furthermore . . . Also

The second kind of signpost, usually used in conjunction with transitions, is an echolike repetition of the same grammatical structure to begin each parallel part.

> I learned several things from this course. First, *I learned that* [development]. Second, *I learned that* [development]. Finally, *I learned that* [development].

The division-into-parallel parts move can be used within a single paragraph, or it can control larger stretches of text in which a dozen or more paragraphs may work together to complete a parallel series of parts. (For example, you are currently in the third part of a parallel series introduced by the mapping sentence on page 562: "Next we describe four of the most powerful set plays." Here is an example of a student paragraph organized by the division-into-parallel-parts move.

DIVISION-INTO-PARALLEL-PARTS MOVE

In this paper I will argue that political solutions to homelessness must take into account four categories of homeless people. A first category is persons who are out of work and seek new jobs. Persons in this category may have been recently laid off, unable to meet their rental payments, and forced temporarily to live out of a car or van. They might quickly leave the ranks of the homeless if they can find new jobs. A second category includes the physically disabled or mentally ill. Providing housing for these persons addresses only part of their problems since they also need medical care and medication. For many, finding or keeping a job might be impossible. A third category is the street alcoholic or drug addict. These persons need addiction treatment as well as clothing and shelter and will not become productive citizens until they become sober or drug free. The final category includes those who, like the old railroad "hobo," choose homelessness as a way of life.

Mapping statement forecasts "move"

Transition to first parallel part

Transition to second parallel part

Transition to third parallel part

Final transition completes "move"

Instead of transition words, writers can also use bullets followed by indented text:

USE OF BULLETS TO SIGNAL PARALLEL PARTS

The Wolf Recovery Program is rigidly opposed by a vociferous group of ranchers who pose three main objections to increasing wolf populations:

- They perceive wolves as a threat to livestock. [development]
- They fear the wolves will attack humans. [development]
- They believe ranchers will not be compensated by the government for their loss of profits. [development]

For Writing and Discussion

Working individually or in small groups, use the *division-into-parallel-parts* move to create, organize, and develop ideas to support one or more of the following point sentences.

1. To study for an exam effectively, a student should follow these (specify a number) steps.
2. Why do U.S. schoolchildren lag so far behind European and Asian children on standardized tests of mathematics and science? One possible cause is . . . (continue).
3. Constant dieting is unhealthy for several reasons.

The *Comparison/Contrast* Move

A common variation on the *division-into-parallel-parts* move is the *comparison/contrast* move. To compare or contrast two items, you must first decide on the points of comparison (or contrast). If you are contrasting the political views of two presidential candidates, you might choose to focus on four points of comparison: differences in their foreign policy, differences in economic policy, differences in social policy, and differences in judicial philosophy. You then have two choices for organizing the parts: the *side-by-side pattern,* in which you discuss all of candidate A's views and then all of candidate B's views; or the *back-and-forth pattern,* in which you discuss foreign policy, contrasting A's views with B's views, then move on to economic policy, then social policy, and then judicial philosophy. Here is how these two patterns would appear on a tree diagram:

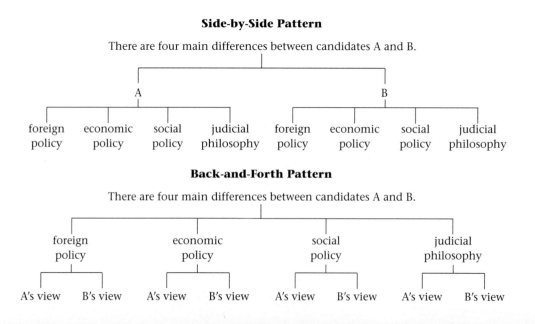

Side-by-Side Pattern

There are four main differences between candidates A and B.

A

foreign policy   economic policy   social policy   judicial philosophy

B

foreign policy   economic policy   social policy   judicial philosophy

Back-and-Forth Pattern

There are four main differences between candidates A and B.

foreign policy   economic policy   social policy   judicial philosophy

A's view   B's view   A's view   B's view   A's view   B's view   A's view   B's view

There are no cut-and-dried rules that dictate when to use the *side-by-side pattern* or the *back-and-forth pattern*. However, for lengthy comparisons, the *back-and-forth pattern* is often more effective because the reader doesn't have to store great amounts of information in memory. The *side-by-side pattern* requires readers to remember all the material about A when they get to B, and it is sometimes difficult to keep all the points of comparison clearly in mind.

For Writing and Discussion

Working individually or in groups, create tree diagrams for stretches of text based on one or more of the following point sentences, all of which call for the *comparison/contrast* move. Make at least one diagram follow the *back-and-forth pattern* and at least one diagram follow the *side-by-side pattern*.

1. To understand U.S. politics, an outsider needs to appreciate some basic differences between Republicans and Democrats.
2. Although they are obviously different on the surface, there are many similarities between the Boy Scouts and a street gang.
3. There are several important differences between closed-form and open-form writing.

Lesson 9: Writing Effective Conclusions

Conclusions can best be understood as complements to introductions. In both the introduction and the conclusion, writers are concerned with the essay as a whole more than with any given part. In a conclusion, the writer attempts to bring a sense of completeness and closure to the profusion of points and particulars laid out in the body of the essay. The writer is particularly concerned with helping the reader move from the parts back to the big picture and to understand the importance or significance of the essay.

If you are having trouble figuring out how to conclude an essay, consider the following guide questions, which are designed to stimulate thought about how to conclude and to help you determine which model best suits your situation.

1. How long and complex is your essay? Is it long enough or complex enough that readers might benefit from a summary of your main points?
2. What's the most important point (or points) you want your readers to remember about your essay? How long ago in the essay did you state that point? Would it be useful to restate that point as succinctly and powerfully as possible?
3. Do you know of an actual instance, illustration, or example of your main point that would give it added weight?
4. What larger principle stands behind your main point? Or what must your audience accept as true in order to accept your main point? How would you defend that assumption if someone were to call it into question?

5. Why is your main point significant? Why are the ideas in your paper important and worth your audience's consideration? What larger issues does your topic relate to or touch on? Could you show how your topic relates to a larger and more significant topic? What might that topic be?

6. If your audience accepts your thesis, where do you go next? What is the next issue or question to be examined? What further research is needed? Conversely, do you have any major reservations, unexpressed doubts, or "All bets are off if X is the case" provisos you'd like to admit? What do you *not* know about your topic that reduces your certainty in your thesis?

7. How much antagonism or skepticism toward your position do you anticipate? If it's a great deal, would it be feasible to delay your thesis, solution, or proposal until the very end of the paper?

Because many writers find conclusions challenging to write, we offer the following six possible models:

The *Simple Summary* Conclusion

The most common, though often not the most effective, kind of conclusion is a simple summary, in which the writer recaps what has just been said. This approach is useful in a long or complex essay or in an instructional text that focuses on concepts to be learned. We use *summary* conclusions for most of the chapters in this text. In a short, easy-to-follow essay, however, a *summary* conclusion can be dull and may even annoy readers who are expecting something more significant, but a brief summary followed by a more artful concluding strategy can often be effective.

The *Larger Significance* Conclusion

A particularly effective concluding strategy is to draw the reader's attention to the *larger significance* of your argument. In our discussion of academic problems (see Chapter 1), we explained that a good academic question needs to be significant (worth pursuing). Although readers need to be convinced from the outset that the problem investigated in your paper is significant, the conclusion is a good place to elaborate on that significance by showing how your argument now leads to additional benefits for the reader. For example, you might explain how your proposed solution to a question leads to potential understanding of a larger, more significant question or brings practical benefits to individuals or society. If you posed a question about values or about the interpretation of a confusing text or phenomenon, you might show how your argument could be applied to related questions or to related texts or phenomena. Your goal in writing this kind of conclusion is to show how your answer to the question posed in your paper has larger applications or significance.

The *Proposal* Conclusion

Another option, often used in analyses and arguments, is the *proposal* conclusion, which calls for action. A *proposal* conclusion states the action that the writer believes needs to be taken and briefly demonstrates the advantages of this action over alternative actions or describes its beneficial consequences. If your paper analyzes the negative consequences of shifting from a graduated to a flat-rate income tax, your conclusion may recommend an action such as modifying or opposing the flat tax. A slight variation is the *call-for-future-study* conclusion, which indicates what else needs to be known or resolved before a proposal can be offered. Such conclusions are especially common in scientific writing.

The *Scenic* or *Anecdotal* Conclusion

Popular writers often use a *scenic* or *anecdotal* conclusion, in which a scene or brief story illustrates the theme's significance without stating it explicitly. A paper opposing the current trend against involuntary hospitalization of the homeless mentally ill might end by describing a former mental patient, now an itinerant homeless person, collecting bottles in a park. Such scenes can help the reader experience directly the emotional significance of the topic analyzed in the body of the paper.

The *Hook and Return* Conclusion

A related variety of conclusion is the *hook and return*, in which the ending of the essay returns to something introduced in the opening hook or lead. If the lead of your essay is a vivid illustration of a problem—perhaps a scene or an anecdote—then your conclusion might return to the same scene or story, but with some variation to illustrate the significance of the essay. This sense of return can give your essay a strong feeling of unity.

The *Delayed-Thesis* Conclusion

This type of conclusion delays the thesis until the end of the essay. Rather than stating the thesis, the introduction merely states the problem, giving the body of the essay an open, exploratory, "let's think through this together" feel. Typically, the body of the paper examines alternative solutions or approaches to the problem and leaves the writer's own answer—the thesis—unstated until the end. This approach is especially effective when writing about highly complex or divisive issues on which you want to avoid taking a stand until all sides have been fairly presented.

For Writing and Discussion

Choose a paper you have just written and write an alternative conclusion using one of the strategies discussed in this lesson. Then share your original and revised conclusions in groups. Have group members discuss which one they consider most effective and why.

Lesson 10: Using Document Design Effectively

Throughout this text, we have suggested that choices about document design are linked to the writer's rhetorical context of purpose, audience, and genre. In Chapter 3, we examined four visual components of document design: fonts (size and style of type), spacing on the page, color, and images or graphics (pp. 62–65). In this chapter, we ask you to consider how document design can play an important role in the effectiveness of closed-form prose. Our advice is eminently practical: Good document design serves the whole communication, enhancing the writer's ethos and the impact of the writer's message.

Match Your Document Design to the Genre Expectations of Your Audience

In Chapter 3 (pp. 54–55), we explained how different genres of writing have their own conventions for approaching subject matter, structure, and style. These conventions function as agreements with readers that a particular kind of writing will meet certain reader expectations, including expectations for the way a document will look.

The closed-form genres you are likely to be assigned in college include academic research papers, experimental/scientific reports, various civic genres (letters to the editor, op-ed pieces, proposals), and various academic or workplace genres inside your major. In this textbook, we have included student examples of several different closed-form genres, each with a different "look" or appearance:

- MLA style research paper (pp. 675–686)
- APA style experimental report (pp. 277–289)
- Practical proposal with headings (pp. 487–491)
- Desk-top published informational piece designed to look like a magazine article (p. 230)
- Advocacy poster and Web page (pp. 483 and 484)

In addition, the text includes many professional examples exhibiting different document designs, including a variety of Web sites (see especially Chapter 21).

A common principle of document design for closed-form genres is to keep the design functional—not decorative—with an emphasis on what you are communicating. In academic papers, follow the design specifications provided by appropriate disciplinary style manuals. In writing for workplace or popular genres, find successful examples to use as models. (Many businesses or corporations produce in-house style manuals for their documents.) Familiarizing yourself in advance with the specific document design requirements of a genre can help you throughout the invention, drafting, and revising stages of your writing by letting you envision the structure and appearance of your final document.

Consider Document Design an Important Part of Your *Ethos*

The appearance of your document also communicates your professional *ethos*. As you prepare your final document, ask yourself these questions: Does the appearance of my document reveal my professionalism? Does it convey that I am responsible, serious, and credible? Does it show that I am knowledgeable about this genre? Does my document design show consideration for my audience's time and appreciation of their background and expectations?

Use Document Design Components for Clarity and Emphasis

You can often increase the clarity and persuasiveness of documents through effective use of headings, graphics, or other visuals.

Headings and subheadings can add clarity to your documents by providing readers with a mental frame for processing your ideas. Some genres, such as the experimental report, employ standard headings. In other genres, writers often create their own headings, especially in papers more than six pages long. These headings show readers at a glance not only the structure of the paper but also a capsule of the argument. For example, here are the headings used by one of our students in an argument that coastal Indian tribes should not be allowed to hunt whales. (For first-level heads, she typed the words flush-left, bold-face, and all-caps; for second level heads she used flush-left, bold-face, and title-case.)

See page 250 for an explanation of the headings in an APA experimental report.

ILLUSTRATION OF HEADINGS IN STUDENT PAPER OPPOSING TRIBAL WHALING

THE NATIVE PERSPECTIVE: WHALING AS A CULTURAL TRADITION
[The paper's first section summarized the tribal perspective that a resumption of whaling would revive cultural traditions.]

CULTURAL WHALING AS A STEP TOWARD COMMERCIAL WHALING
[In this section the writer argued that allowing any cultural whaling promotes increases commercial whaling.]

THE HARM OF COMMERCIAL WHALING
[This heading marked the start of a long section providing three main arguments against commercial whaling.]

Increase in the Demand for Whale Meat
[This subsection provided evidence that whale meat will grow in popularity, increasing demand.]

Difficulty in Sustaining Whale Stocks
[This subsection showed that commercial whaling will lead toward gradual extinction of whales.]

Decrease in Biodiversity
[This subsection showed the harm of losing biodiversity.]

INTRINSIC VALUE OF WHALES
[In her final main section, the writer argued for the intrinsic value of whales.]

As you can see, these headings give readers an immediate overview of the structure and content of the paper.

When creating heads, develop and follow the same font style for each level of head and make all the heads at each level grammatically parallel. (All the headings in the previous example are noun phrases.)

For discussion of visual rhetoric see Chapter 3, pp. 85–88, and all of Chapter 11. For strategies for creating effective graphics, see Chapter 10, pp. 261–266.

Like headings, graphics and images can enhance clarity and emphasize ideas by creating a visually interesting contrast to the written text, by focusing the readers' attention on the points you are making, and by giving your points presence and impact. Graphics and images should contribute to your intended rhetorical effect rather than show off the bells and whistles of your computer's graphics program. To avoid decorative and distracting use of graphics, ask yourself these main questions: What point or story do I want this graph or image to emphasize? What does this graphic add to my written text?

Use Design Components to Highlight and Reinforce—But Not Replace—Transitions, Points, and Key Explanations in the Text Itself

See Chapter 10, pp. 264–265 on independent redundancy of text and graphics.

Graphics and design elements should enhance a written text but never replace your verbal explanations of the same points. While headings and subheadings can guide readers through a document and direct them to particular points, you need to repeat the point, key explanation, or transition in the text itself. Your text should make complete sense with headings and graphics removed.

For Writing and Discussion

Consider the following writing scenario.

Spencer works in a drug rehabilitation center as an aide. He has become convinced that the United States should decriminalize possession of drugs, empty prisons of those convicted of victimless drug offenses, and divert money currently being spent on the "War on Drugs" into rehabilitation programs. Spencer wants to write a paper influencing readers to legalize drugs and focus on rehabilitation rather than punishment.

What document design features can you imagine Spencer using for each of the following genres and implied rhetorical contexts?

1. An academic research paper in a sociology class
2. A desktop-published article for a Web site (to be downloadable in pdf format)
3. A one-page newspaper advertisement (purchased space)
4. A newspaper op-ed column?

Working in groups or as a whole class, arrive at possible answers to the questions just posed. How do differences in genres and rhetorical contexts lead to different decisions about document design?

Composing and Revising Open-Form Prose

Good writing is supposed to evoke sensation in the reader—not the fact that it's raining, but the feel of being rained upon.

—E. L. DOCTOROW, *NOVELIST*

Much of this book focuses on closed-form prose where "good writing" means having a surprising thesis supported with effective points and particulars arranged hierarchically into unified and coherent paragraphs. But there are many kinds of good writing, and we probably all share the desire at times to write in ways other than tightly argued, thesis-governed, closed-form prose. In our epigraph, novelist E. L. Doctorow suggests another way to think of "good writing": Writing that evokes sensations, that triggers in the reader's imagination the very feel of the rain.

In this chapter, we shift our attention from closed- to open-form writing. Open-form prose differs from closed-form prose in its basic features, in the challenges and options it presents writers, in the demands it places on its readers, and in the mental and emotional pleasures it creates. Open-form writing, of the kind we discuss here, is often called *literary nonfiction* because it uses literary techniques and strategies such as story, plot, characterization, setting, and theme.

Of course, it should be remembered that writing exists on a continuum from closed to open forms and that many features of open-form prose can appear in primarily closed-form texts. In fact, many of the example essays in this book combine elements of both open and closed styles. At the extremes of the continuum, closed- and open-form writing are markedly different, but the styles can be blended in pleasing combinations.

As we have discussed throughout this text, writing at the closed end of the spectrum seeks to be efficient and reader-friendly. By forecasting what's coming, placing points first, using clear transitions, and putting old information before new, closed-form writers place maximum emphasis on delivering clear ideas that readers can grasp quickly. In contrast, open-form writers, by violating or simply stretching those same conventions, set up a different kind of relationship with readers. They often provide more pleasure in reading, but just as often demand more patience and tolerance of ambiguity. They are likely to take readers backstage to share the process of their thinking. They often cast themselves in the role

Chapter 7 on autobiographical narrative discusses plot, characterization, setting, and theme.

For essays that blend open and closed elements, see Cheryl Carp's "Behind Stone Walls" (pp. 231–232), Florence King's "I'd Rather Smoke than Kiss" (pp. 144–149), or Edward Abbey's "The Damnation of a Canyon" (pp. 157–161).

of narrators or characters reporting their quest for understanding and all the coincidences, disappointments, puzzling advice, and confusion they experienced along the way. In this process of sharing, they make readers codiscoverers of ideas and insights.

Open-form prose is also characterized by its emphasis on an aesthetic use of language—that is, language used to please and entertain. Without the benefit of a thesis or points appearing first to convey meaning, open-form prose depends on the very specificity of words, the ability of words to create mental pictures, to appeal to readers' senses and emotions, and to conjure up memories.

Our goal in this chapter is to give you some practical lessons on how to write effective open-form prose. But we need to acknowledge at the outset that, whereas closed-form prose is governed by a few widely accepted conventions, one of the main features of open-form prose is its freedom to play with conventions in a bewildering variety of ways. Consequently, our discussion of open-form writing seeks more to introduce you to guiding principles rather than to treat open-form writing exhaustively.

Lesson 1: Make Your Narrative a Story, Not an *and Then* Chronology

And then writing is also discussed in Chapter 18, pp. 532–533.

We have said that open-form prose is narrative based and uses the strategies of a story. In this first lesson we want you to think more deeply about the concept of a story—particularly how a story differs from an *and then* chronology. Both a story and an *and then* chronology depict events happening in time. But there are important differences between them. At the start of this lesson, we'd like you to try your own hand at articulating the differences between a story and an *and then* chronology. Read the following example of a student's autobiographical narrative and then respond to the questions that follow.

READINGS

Patrick Klein (student)
Berkeley Blues

1   It was a cold night. That is nothing new in San Francisco, but something made this night particularly frigid. It was early February and the whole city, including the Berkeley section where we were staying, was still held tight in the firm grip of winter. It had also rained that afternoon and the air, having been cleared by the storm, was cold and sharp. It hurt the back of your throat when you inhaled and turned into mist when you exhaled. As the six of us hurriedly walked in a huddled mass, the water that was lying in puddles on the dimly lit sidewalk jumped out of our way as we slammed our dress shoes down into its dregs. We silently decided on our destination and

slipped into the grungy, closet-like pizza joint. We took the only seats the place had and as we pulled them into a circle, we all breathed a sigh of relief.

2   This was our first night at Berkeley. We were there for a debate tournament to be held the next day at the university. On this night, however, we were six high school sophomores in search of food. So, dressed in our suits and ties (we were required to wear them) and heavy coats, we ventured out of the university and entered the city of Berkeley.

3   Berkeley is an interesting place. Many might have romantic notions of a bunch of shaggy intellectuals discussing French existentialism while sipping cappuccino, but while this might have been the case a few decades ago, the reality is that Berkeley is a ghetto. The place is filled with grungy closet shops while newspapers cover the sidewalks and the people lying on them. The university is divided from this ghetto by a two-lane street.

4   As the six of us crossed the two-lane street that fateful night, my thoughts drifted to my own neighborhood, which up until that moment had been the extent of my world.

5   McCormick Ranch, Arizona, is a sheltered place. To a certain extent it's mostly white, with little crime and few domestic problems. Everybody has a pool, at least two cars, and a beautiful desert sunset every night. I had everything I ever wanted. It seemed very gentle and dreamlike compared to the harsh slum we found ourselves in.

6   When we made it into the pizza place and moved the chairs into a protective circle around a square table, anxiety about our "hostile" environment was quickly swept away with hot, greasy pizza. We ate until we were content and were trying to decide how to divide the few remaining pieces among ourselves when it happened.

7   The pizza place was separated from the rest of humanity by a large window. Our table was directly in front of that window and two feet from the door. People had been passing the window and probably remarking on the six well-dressed kids inside, but we paid them no mind and they all walked by without incident. Still, our hearts were seized with terror every time a human being would pass that window, and we hoped with all that we could muster that every one of them would continue on. We were almost right.

8   On this night, when six young yuppie kids from an upper middle-class world decided to risk it and go eat pizza in a ghetto, he walked by. He didn't look any different from others we'd seen that night. Black. Dirty. Tired. Cold. His clothes consisted of a grimy, newspaper-stained jacket, a T-shirt with who-knows-how-old dirt on it, flimsy pants with holes at the knees, and tattered excuses for shoes. He was not quite up to par with our Gucci loafers and Armani jackets.

9   He shuffled past the window and glanced in. We didn't notice. He stopped. We noticed. Twelve eyes glanced up as casually as they could and six hearts stopped beating for a second. Yep, still there. All eyes went back to the floor, except for two. Those eyes belonged to Chad, and in some act of defiance, his eyes met the poor man's eyes and glared.

10 The man opened the door. "We're all going to die," I thought. "All my hopes and dreams are going to end here, in a stupid pizza place, at the hands of a crazy black bum."

11 He took something out of his pocket.

12 It was shiny.

13 I couldn't look.

14 A knife.

15 No. It was a flask. He took a swig from it, and, still propping the door open with his sagging frame, spoke the most jolting, burning words I've ever heard.

16 "I love you," he said. "All of you." He glanced at Chad, "Even you." He stepped back and said, "I know what you think of me, but I still love you." I will probably never forget those words or how he said them with a steady, steely voice.

17 Then he left. That was it. Gone. It took about five minutes for anyone to talk. When the talking started, we exchanged jokes and responded with empty, devastating laughter.

18 We soon left the shop. It had grown colder outside and we quickly returned to our climate-controlled hotel room. We had just eaten a filling meal and paid for it with our own money. We were all about fifteen. The man we had encountered was probably in his fifties. He had no roof, no money, or food. It seemed strange that I owned more than an adult, but in truth, he had more than I. He was able to love us when we ostracized him and thought stereotypically about him.

19 I remember later trying to rationalize my sickening behavior by thinking that there is nothing wrong with being and acting afraid in a strange environment. I tried to use my age as an excuse. Nothing worked. I was guilty of fearing a fellow human being because of his color and my preset notions of bums.

20 To this day I still think about what difference, if any, it would have made if we had given him our leftover pizza. It might have eased my conscience. It was a very cold night and we had made it colder.

For Writing and Discussion

Individual task: Now that you have read "Berkeley Blues," read the following autobiographical narrative entitled "The Stolen Watch," which was submitted by a student as a draft for an assignment on narrative writing.

The Stolen Watch

Last fall and winter I was living in Spokane with my brother, who during this time had a platonic girlfriend come over from Seattle and stay for a weekend. Her name was Karen, and we became interested in each other and I went over to see her at the first of the year. She then invited me to, supposedly, the biggest party of the year, called the Aristocrats' Ball. I said sure and made my way back to Seattle in February. It started out bad on Friday, the day my brother and I left Spokane. We left town an hour late, but what's new. Then my brother had to stop along the way and pick up some parts; we stayed there for an hour trying to find this guy. It all started out bad because we arrived in Seattle and I forgot to call Karen. We were staying at her brother's house and after we brought all our things in, we decided to go to a few bars. Later that night we ran into Karen in one of the bars, and needless to say she was not happy with me. When I got up the next morning I knew I should have stayed in Spokane, because I felt bad vibes. Karen made it over about an hour before the party. By the time we reached the party, which drove me crazy, she wound up with another guy, so her friends and I decided to go to a few bars. The next morning when I was packing, I could not find my watch and decided that someone had to have taken it. We decided that it had to have been the goon that Karen had wound up with the night before, because she was at her brother's house with him before she went home. So how was I going to get my watch back?

We decided the direct and honest approach to the problem would work out the best. We got in contact and confronted him. This turned out to be quite a chore. It turned out that he was visiting some of his family during that weekend and lived in Little Harbor, California. It turned out that Karen knew his half brother and got some information on him, which was not pretty. He had just been released by the army and was trained in a special forces unit, in the field of Martial Arts. He was a trained killer! This information did not help matters at all,

(continued)

```
but the next bit of information was just as bad if not worse.
Believe it or not, he was up on charges of attempted murder and
breaking and entering. In a way, it turned out lucky for me,
because he was in enough trouble with the police and did not
need any more. Karen got in contact with him and threatened him
that I would bring him up on charges if he did not return the
watch. His mother decided that he was in enough trouble and sent
me the watch. I was astounded, it was still working and looked
fine. The moral of the story is don't drive 400 miles to see a
girl you hardly know, and whatever you do, don't leave your
valuables out in the open.
```

Group task: Share your responses to the following questions:

1. How does your experience of reading "Berkeley Blues" differ from your experience of reading "The Stolen Watch"? Try to articulate the different ways you reacted to the two pieces while in the process of reading them.
2. Based on the differences between these two pieces, how would you define a "story"? Begin by brainstorming all the ways that the two pieces differ. Then try to identify the essential differences that make one a "story" and the other an *and then* chronology.

Now that you have tried to define a story for yourselves, we would like to explain our own four criteria for a story: depiction of events through time, connectedness, tension, and resolution. If we combine these criteria into a sentence, it would read like this: A story depicts events that are connected causally or thematically to create a sense of tension that is resolved through action, insight, or understanding. These four criteria occurring together turn a chronology into a story.

Depiction of Events Through Time

The essence of storytelling is the depiction of events through time. Whereas thesis-based writing descends from problem to thesis to supporting reasons and evidence, stories unfold linearly, temporally, from event to event. You may start in the middle of the action and then jump backward and forward, but you always encounter some sequence of events happening in time. This temporal focus creates a sense of "onceness." Things that happen at a point in time happen only once, as the classic fairy-tale opening "Once upon a time" suggests. When you compose and revise a narrative, you want to try to capture the "onceness" of that experience. As the essayist E. B. White once advised a young writer, "Don't write about Man but about a man."

Consider how Val Plumwood, a professor of women's studies and author of the book *Feminism and the Mastery of Nature,* depicts the events leading up to a disturbing encounter with a crocodile. (Later in the story, the reader sees how this encounter shapes her understanding of humans' place in the food chain and the need for a respectful, rather than a dominating, attitude toward other animals.)

> In the early wet season, Kakadu's paper-bark wetlands are especially stunning, as the water lilies weave white, pink, and blue patterns of dreamlike beauty over the shining thunderclouds reflected in their still waters. Yesterday, the water lilies and the wonderful bird life had enticed me into a joyous afternoon's idyll as I ventured onto the East Alligator Lagoon for the first time in a canoe lent by the park service. "You can play about on the backwaters," the ranger had said, "but don't go onto the main river channel. The current's too swift, and if you get into trouble, there are the crocodiles. Lots of them along the river!" I followed his advice and glutted myself on the magical beauty and bird life of the lily lagoons, untroubled by crocodiles.
>
> Today, I wanted to repeat the experience despite the drizzle beginning to fall as I neared the canoe launch site. I set off on a day trip in search of an Aboriginal rock art site across the lagoon and up a side channel. The drizzle turned to a warm rain within a few hours, and the magic was lost. The birds were invisible, the water lilies were sparser, and the lagoon seemed even a little menacing. I noticed now how low the 14-foot canoe sat in the water, just a few inches of fiberglass between me and the great saurians, close relatives of the ancient dinosaurs. . . .
>
> After hours of searching the maze of shallow channels in the swamp, I had not found the clear channel leading to the rock art site, as shown on the ranger's sketch map. When I pulled my canoe over in driving rain to a rock outcrop for a hasty, sodden lunch, I experienced the unfamiliar sensation of being watched. Having never been one for timidity, in philosophy or in life, I decided, rather than return defeated to my sticky trailer, to explore a clear, deep channel closer to the river I had traveled the previous day.
>
> The rain and wind grew more severe, and several times I pulled over to tip water from the canoe. The channel soon developed steep mud banks and snags. Farther on, the channel opened up and was eventually blocked by a large sandy bar. I pushed the canoe toward the bank, looking around carefully before getting out of the shallow and pulling the canoe up. I would be safe from crocodiles in the canoe—I had been told—but swimming and standing or wading at the water's edge were dangerous. Edges are one of the crocodile's favorite food-capturing places. I saw nothing, but the feeling of unease that had been with me all day intensified.

In this example of literary nonfiction, Plumwood persuades readers to appreciate the beauties of the exotic Australian rain forest as well as its dangers. Note how her method includes the depicting of events that happen once in time—her wondrous first day of exploration, the ranger's warning to stay away from the main river, her second day's unsuccessful search by canoe for a site of Aboriginal rock art, and then her emerging discovery that in the increasing intensity of the rainstorm, she had reached the junction with the main river. Plumwood's powerful narrative becomes the basis for a profound concluding reflection on what she calls humans' "ecological identity."

Connectedness

The events of a story must also be connected, not merely spatially or sequentially, but causally or thematically. When discussing "The Stolen Watch" in the previous exercise, you might have asked yourselves, "What does all that stuff about forgetting to call Karen and stopping for parts, etc., have to do with the stolen watch? Is this story about the watch or about confronting a potential killer?" If so, you instinctively understood the concept of connectedness. Stories are more than just chronicles of events. Novelist E. M. Forster offered the simplest definition of a story when he rejected "The king dies and then the queen died," but accepted "The king died and then the queen died . . . of grief." The words "of grief" connect the two events to each other in a causal relationship, converting a series of events into a patterned, meaningfully related sequence of events. Now examine this passage to see the connections the writer establishes between the scenes.

THEMATIC AND CAUSAL CONNECTEDNESS

I have been so totally erased from nature lately, like a blackboard before school starts, that yesterday when I was in the Japanese section of San Francisco, Japantown, I saw the sidewalk littered with chocolate wrappers.

There were hundreds of them. Who in the hell has been eating all these chocolates? I thought. A convention of Japanese chocolate eaters must have passed this way.

Then I noticed some plum trees on the street. Then I noticed that it was autumn. Then I noticed that the leaves were falling as they will and as they must every year. Where had I gone wrong?

—Richard Brautigan, "Leaves"

Brautigan's narrative becomes a story only when you realize that the "chocolate wrappers" are really plum leaves; the two images are connected by the writer's changed perception, which illuminates the thematic question raised at the beginning and end: Why has he become "so totally erased from nature"? As you write, connect the elements of your narrative causally and thematically.

Tension or Conflict

The third criterion for a story—tension or conflict—creates the anticipation and potential significance that keep the reader reading. In whodunit stories, the tension follows from attempts to identify the murderer or to prevent the murderer from doing in yet another victim. In many comic works, the tension is generated by confusion or misunderstanding that drives a wedge between people who would normally be close. Tension always involves contraries, such as those between one belief and another, between opposing values, between the individual and the environment or the social order, between where I am now and where I want to be or used to be. In the following passage, see how the contraries create dramatic tension that engages readers.

DRAMATIC TENSIONS

Straddling the top of the world, one foot in China and the other in Nepal, I cleared the ice from my oxygen mask, hunched a shoulder against the wind, and stared absently down at the vastness of Tibet. I understood on some dim, detached level that the sweep of earth beneath my feet was a spectacular sight. I'd been fantasizing about this moment, and the release of emotion that would accompany it, for many months. But now that I was finally here, actually standing on the summit of Mount Everest, I just couldn't summon the energy to care.

It was early in the afternoon of May 10, 1996. I hadn't slept in fifty-seven hours. The only food I'd been able to force down over the preceding three days was a bowl of ramen soup and a handful of peanut M&M's. Weeks of violent coughing had left me with two separated ribs that made ordinary breathing an excruciating trial. At 29,028 feet up in the troposphere, so little oxygen was reaching my brain that my mental capacity was that of a slow child. Under the circumstances, I was incapable of feeling much of anything except cold and tired.

—Jon Krakauer, *Into Thin Air*

Notice how this passage presents several contraries or conflicts: the opposition between the narrator's expectation of what it would be like to stand on the top of Mount Everest and the actuality once he's there; and the opposition between the physical strength and stamina of the climber and the extreme danger of climbing this mountain. The reader wonders how Krakauer reached the summit with no sleep, almost no food, and a violent and agonizing cough; more important, the reader wonders why he kept on climbing. We can ask this important query of any narrative: What conflicts and tensions are prompting readers' ongoing questions and holding their interest?

Resolution, Recognition, or Retrospective Interpretation

The final criterion for a story is the resolution or retrospective interpretation of events. The resolution may be stated explicitly or implied. Fables typically sum up the story's significance with an explicit moral at the end. In contrast, the interpretation of events in poetry is almost always implicit. Note how the following haiku collapses events and resolution.

RESOLUTION

A strange old man
stops me,
Looking out of my deep mirror.

—Hitomaro, *One Hundred Poems from the Japanese*

In this tiny story, two things happen simultaneously. The narrator is stopped by a "strange old man" and the narrator looks into a mirror. The narrator's *recognition* is that he is that same old man. This recognition—"That's me in the mirror; when I wasn't looking, I grew old!"—in turn ties the singular event of the story back to more universal concerns and the reader's world.

The typical direction of a story, from singular event(s) to general conclusion, reverses the usual points-first direction of closed-form essays. Stories force readers to read inductively, gathering information and looking for a pattern that's confirmed or unconfirmed by the story's resolution. This resolution is the point *toward* which readers read. It often drives home the significance of the narrative.

Typically, a reader's satisfaction or dissatisfaction with a story hinges on how well the resolution manages to explain or justify the events that precede it. Writers need to ask: How does my resolution grow out of my narrative and fit with the resolution the reader has been forming?

For Writing and Discussion

1. Working as a whole class or in small groups, return to Patrick Klein's essay "Berkeley Blues" and explain how it qualifies as a story rather than an *and then* chronology. How does it meet all four of the criteria: depiction of events through time, connectedness, tension, and resolution?
2. Consider again "The Stolen Watch." It seems to meet the criterion of "depiction of events through time," but it is weak in connectedness, tension, and resolution. How could the writer revise the chronology to make it a story? Brainstorm several different ways that this potentially exciting early draft could be rewritten.
3. If you are working on your own open-form narrative, exchange drafts with a classmate. Discuss each others' drafts in light of this lesson's focus on story. To what extent do your drafts exhibit the features of a story rather than of an *and then* chronology? Working together, develop revision plans that might increase the story elements in your narratives.

Lesson 2: Write Low on the Scale of Abstraction

In Chapter 3 we introduced the concept of "scale of abstraction," in which words can be arranged from the very abstract (living creatures, clothing) down to the very specific (our dog Charley, a Rhodesian Ridgeback with floppy ears; my hippie Birkenstocks with the saltwater stains; see pp. 60–61). In this lesson we show why and how open-form writers stay low on the scale of abstraction through their use of concrete words, revelatory words, and memory-soaked words.

Concrete Words Evoke Images and Sensations

To appreciate the impact of specific, concrete language, look again at the opening sentence of Val Plumwood's narrative about her encounter with crocodiles (p. 579):

> In the early wet season, Kakadu's paper-bark wetlands are especially stunning, as the water lilies weave white, pink, and blue patterns of dreamlike beauty over the shining thunderclouds reflected in their still waters.

For further discussion of specific, sensory words, see Chapter 5, pp. 112–113, on *show* words versus *tell* words.

Here is how that same passage might sound if rewritten a level higher on the scale of abstraction:

> In the early wet season the Kakadu landscape is especially stunning as the water plants weave their colorful patterns of dreamlike beauty over the clouds reflected in the water's surface.

This is still quite a nice sentence. But something is lost when you say "landscape" rather than "paper-bark wetlands," "clouds" rather than "thunderclouds," or "colorful" rather than "white, pink, and blue." The lower you write on the scale of abstraction, the more you tap into your readers' storehouse of particular memories and images.

The power of concrete words has been analyzed by writer John McPhee in a widely quoted and cited interview. When asked why he wrote the sentence "Old white oaks are rare because they had a tendency to become bowsprits, barrel staves, and queen-post trusses" instead of a more generic sentence such as, "Old white oaks are rare because they were used as lumber," he responded in a way that reveals his love of the particular:

> There isn't much life in [the alternative version of the sentence]. If you can find a specific, firm, and correct image, it's always going to be better than a generality, and hence I tend, for example, to put in trade names and company names and, in an instance like this, the names of wood products instead of a general term like "lumber." You'd say "Sony" instead of "tape recorder" if the context made it clear you meant to say tape recorder. It's not because you're on the take from Sony, it's because the image, at least to this writer or reader, strikes a clearer note.

Some readers might complain that the particulars "bowsprits, barrel staves, and queen-post trusses" don't help readers' understanding, as do particulars in closed-form prose, but instead give most readers a moment's pause. Today most barrel staves and bowsprits are made of metal, not oak, and few contemporary readers encounter them on a regular basis no matter what they're made of. Furthermore, few readers at any time could readily identify "queen-post trusses," a technical term from the building trade. Instead of smoothly completing the reader's understanding of a point, McPhee's particulars tend to arrest and even sidetrack, sending the reader in pursuit of a dictionary.

But if McPhee's examples momentarily puzzle, it's the sort of puzzlement that can lead to greater understanding. Precisely because they are exotic terms, these words arouse the reader's curiosity and imagination. "Exotic language is of value," says McPhee. "A queen-post truss is great just because of the sound of the words and what they call to mind. The 'queen,' the 'truss'—the ramifications in everything."

For McPhee, the fact that these words trip up the reader is a point in their favor. If McPhee had said that old white oaks are rare these days because they became parts of "ships, barrels, and roofs," no one would blink or notice. If you were to visualize the items, you'd probably call up some ready-made pictures that leave little trace in your mind. You also wouldn't hear the sounds of the words. (In this regard, notice McPhee's emphasis on images sounding "a clearer note.") Your forward progress toward the point would be unimpeded, but what would be lost? A new glimpse into a lost time when oak trees were used to make exotic items that today exist mostly in old books and memories.

Another quality also recommends words that readers trip over, words such as *bowsprit, barrel stave,* and *queen-post truss:* their power to persuade the reader to believe in the world being described. Tripping over things, whether they're made of steel or words, forces the reader to acknowledge their independence, the reality of a world outside the reader's own head. For this reason, writers of formula fiction—

thrillers, westerns, romances, and the like—will load their texts with lots of little details and bits of technical information from the time and place they describe. Because their stories are otherwise implausible (e.g., the description of the Evil Empire's doomsday machine), they need all the help they can get from their details (the size of the toggle bolts used to keep the machine in place while it's blasting out intergalactic death rays) to convince readers that the story is real.

Using Revelatory Words and Memory-Soaked Words

As we have seen, concrete language, low on the scale of abstraction, can evoke imaginative experiences for readers. Two particularly powerful kinds of concrete language are revelatory words and memory-soaked words. By *revelatory* words we mean specific details that reveal the social status, lifestyle, beliefs, and values of people. According to writer Tom Wolfe, carefully chosen details can reveal a person's *status life*—"the entire pattern of behavior and possessions through which people express their position in the world or what they think it is or hope it to be." Wolfe favors writing that records "everyday gestures, habits, manners, customs, styles of furniture, clothing, decoration, styles of traveling, eating, keeping house, modes of behaving toward children, servants, superiors, inferiors, peers, plus the various looks, glances, poses, styles of walking and other symbolic details that might exist within a scene." Thus subtle differences in a person's status life might be revealed in details about fast food (a Big Mac versus a Subway turkey wrap), body piercing (pierced ears versus pierced tongue), a watch (a Timex versus a Taghauer) or music (Kenny Chesney versus Busta Rhymes). In "Berkeley Blues," Patrick Klein and his classmates are economically revealed as upper-middle-class people by their attire—"Armani jackets" and "Gucci loafers."

Another way to create powerful concrete language is through *memory-soaked* words. Such words trigger a whole complex of ideas, emotions, and sensations in readers who share memories from a particular era. People who grew up in the 1950s, for example, might have deep associations with 45-rpm records, the Ed Sullivan show, or the words "duck tail" or "tail fins." For Vietnam veterans, Nancy Sinatra's "These Boots Were Made for Walking" or the whirr of helicopter blades might evoke strong memories. Persons growing up in the 1970s or 1980s might remember "Cookie Monster," "Pez guns," or 8-track tapes. In recent years, our students have come up with these memory-soaked words from their own childhoods: American Girl dolls, Power Rangers, Ghostbuster action figures, Super Nintendo, and Uno (card game).

For Writing and Discussion

1. Working in small groups or as a whole class, try your own hand at using revelatory words to reveal status life. Create a list of specific details that you might associate with each of the following: junior high girls at a slumber party; friends at a tailgate party before a football game; the kitchen of

an upscale urban apartment of a two-profession couple who subscribe to *Gourmet* magazine; the kitchen of a middle-class, middle America family with three kids and a collection of *Good Housekeeping* magazines; the kitchen of an apartment shared by college students. (If you are describing kitchens, for example, consider the different *status life* signaled by ketchup versus stone ground mustard or by an iceberg lettuce salad with ranch dressing versus an almond mandarin salad.)

2. Also try your hand at finding memory-soaked words. Make a list of specific words and names associated with your childhood that you now rarely hear or see. Share your list with others in your group and identify the items that have the strongest associations.

3. If you are working on your own open-form narrative, exchange drafts with a classmate and, working together, find specific examples where each of you have successfully used concrete, revelatory, or memory-soaked words. Then find passages that could be profitably revised by moving down a level on the scale of abstraction or by adding concrete details that follow the advice in this lesson.

Lesson 3: Disrupt Your Reader's Desire for Direction and Clarity

The epigraph to Chapter 18 by the philosopher Kenneth Burke speaks about form as "an arousing and fulfillment of desires." In closed-form prose, we can easily see this process at work: The writer previews what he or she is going to say, arousing the reader's desire to see the general outline fleshed out with specifics, and then fulfills that desire speedily through a presentation of pertinent points and particulars.

In more open-form prose, the fulfillment of desire follows a less straightforward path. Writers offer fewer overviews and clues, leaving readers less sure of where they're headed; or writers mention an idea and then put it aside for a while as they pursue some other point whose relevance may seem tenuous. Rather than establish the direction or point of their prose, writers suspend that direction, waiting until later in the prose to show how the ideas are meaningfully related. In other words, the period of arousal is longer and more drawn out; the fulfillment of desire is delayed until the end, when the reader finally sees how the pieces fit together.

Open-form prose gives you the opportunity to overlay your narrative core with other patterns of ideas—to move associatively from idea to idea, to weave a complex pattern of meaning in which the complete picture emerges later. Often the way you achieve these surprising twists and turns of structure and meaning is by playing with the conventions of closed-form prose. For example, in the autobiographical narrative "Berkeley Blues," Patrick Klein breaks the cardinal closed-form rule that pronouns should refer only to previously stated antecedents; he introduces the stranger only as *he* and gradually reveals that person's identity. This violation creates an aura of mystery and suspense. Here in this lesson we describe some of your open-form options for surprising your readers and delaying their fulfillment of desires.

Disrupting Predictions and Making Odd Juxtapositions

Open-form writers frequently violate the principle of forecasting and mapping that we stressed in Chapter 18. Consider the following introduction to an essay:

PASSAGE WITH DISRUPTED PREDICTIONS AND ODD JUXTAPOSITIONS

Whose bones?
What feathers?

Birds? What birds?
What do birds have to do with how the brain works? Where is this writer going?

I suppose their little bones have years ago been lost among the stones and winds of those high glacial pastures. I suppose their feathers blew eventually into the piles of tumbleweed beneath the straggling cattle fences and rotted there in the mountain snows, along with dead steers and all the other things that drift to an end in the corners of the wire. I do not quite know why I should be thinking of birds over the *New York Times* at breakfast, particularly the birds of my youth half a continent away. It is a funny thing what the brain will do with memories and how it will treasure them and finally bring them into odd juxtapositions with other things, as though it wanted to make a design, or get some meaning out of them, whether you want it or not, or even see it.

—Loren Eisley, "The Bird and the Machine"

Note the sequence of ideas from bones to birds to breakfast over *The New York Times* to comments about the workings of the brain. In fact, in this essay it takes Eisley six full paragraphs in which he discusses mechanical inventions to return to the birds with the line: ". . . or those birds, I'll never forget those birds. . . ."

Throughout these paragraphs, what drives the reader forward is curiosity to discover the connections between the parts and to understand the meaning of the essay's title "The Bird and the Machine." Actually, Eisley's comment about the brain's "odd juxtapositions" of memories with "other things, as though it wanted to make a design, or get some meaning out of them" could be a description of this open-form technique we've called "disrupting predictions and making odd juxtapositions." Open-form writers can choose when "odd juxtapositions" are an appropriate strategy for inviting the reader to accompany the discovering, reflecting writer on a journey toward meaning.

Leaving Gaps

An important convention of closed-form prose is the old/new contract, which specifies that the opening of every sentence should link in some way to what has gone before. Open-form prose often violates this convention, leaving *gaps* in the text, forcing the reader to puzzle over the connection between one part and the next.

The following passage clearly violates the old/new contract. This example recounts the writer's thoughts after startling a weasel in the woods and exchanging glances with it.

PASSAGE WITH INTENTIONAL GAPS

Gap caused by unexplained or unpredicted shift from weasel to philosophic musing

What goes on in [a weasel's brain] the rest of the time? What does a weasel think about? He won't say. His journal is tracks in clay, a spray of feathers, mouse blood and bone: uncollected, unconnected, loose-leaf, and blown.

> I would like to learn, or remember, how to live. I come to Hollins Pond not so much to learn how to live as, frankly, to forget about it.
>
> —Annie Dillard, "Living Like Weasels"

Dillard suddenly switches, without transition, from musing about the mental life of a weasel to asserting that she would like to learn how to live. What is the connection between her encounter with the weasel and her own search for how to live? Dillard's open-form techniques leave these gaps for readers to ponder and fill in, inviting us to participate in the process of arriving at meaning. Just as open-form writers can deliberately avoid predicting or mapping statements, they also have the liberty to leave gaps in a text when it suits their purpose.

For Writing and Discussion

If you are currently working on an open-form narrative, exchange drafts with a classmate. Discuss in what way the strategies explained in this lesson might be appropriate for your purposes. Where might you currently "explain too much" and benefit by juxtaposing scenes without explanatory filler? Where might you use other strategies from this lesson?

Lesson 4: Tap the Power of Figurative Language

Open-form writers often use figurative language in situations in which closed-form writers would use literal language. In this brief lesson, we show you some of the power of figurative language.

When journalist Nicholas Tomalin describes a captured Vietnamese prisoner as young and slight, the reader understands him in a literal way, but when, a moment later, he compares the prisoner to "a tiny, fine-boned wild animal," the reader understands him in a different way; the reader understands not only what the subject looks like—his general physical attributes—but how that particular boy appears in that moment to those around him—fierce, frightened, trapped.

Metaphors abound when literal words fail. When writers encounter eccentric people or are overwhelmed by the strangeness of their experiences, they use *figurative language*—imaginative comparisons—to explain their situation and their reactions to it. Figurative language—similes, metaphors, and personifications—enables the writer to describe an unfamiliar thing in terms of different, more familiar things. The surprise of yoking two very unlike things evokes from the reader a perception, insight, or emotional experience that could not otherwise be communicated. The originality and vividness of the imaginative comparison frequently resonates with meaning for readers and sticks in their minds long afterward.

In the following passage, Isak Dinesen describes an experience that most of us have not had—seeing iguanas in the jungle and shooting one. After reading this passage, however, we have a striking picture in our minds of what she saw and a strong understanding of what she felt and realized.

PASSAGE USING FIGURATIVE LANGUAGE

In the Reserve I have sometimes come upon the Iguana, the big lizards, as they were sunning themselves upon a flat stone in a riverbed. They are not pretty in shape, but nothing can be imagined more beautiful than their coloring. They shine *like a heap of precious stones or like a pane cut out of an old church window*. When, as you approach, they swish away, there is a flash of azure, green and purple over the stones, the color seems to be standing behind them in the air, *like a comet's luminous tail*.

Once I shot an Iguana. I thought that I should be able to make some pretty things from his skin. A strange thing happened then, that I have never afterwards forgotten. As I went up to him, where he was lying dead upon his stone, and actually while I was walking a few steps, he faded and grew pale, all color *died out of him as in one long sigh*, and by the time that I touched him he was *gray and dull like a lump of concrete*. It was the live impetuous blood pulsating within the animal, which had radiated out all that glow and splendor. Now that *the flame was put out*, and the soul had flown, the Iguana was as *dead as a sandbag*.

—Isak Dinesen, "The Iguana"

Similes heaped up

Simile

Metaphor of dying applied to color

Simile

Metaphor

Simile

The figurative language in this passage enables readers to share Dinesen's experience. It also compacts a large amount of information into sharp, memorable images.

For Writing and Discussion

1. Figurative language can fall flat when it takes the form of clichés ("I stood transfixed like a bump on a log") or mixed metaphors ("Exposed like a caterpillar on a leaf, he wolfed down his lunch before taking flight"). But when used effectively, figurative language adds powerfully compressed and meaningful images to a passage. Working individually or in small groups, find examples of figurative language in one or more of the example essays in this chapter or in Chapter 7 (pp. 176–185). See if you can reach consensus on what makes a particular instance of figurative language effective or ineffective. As an initial example, consider this passage from the student essay "Masks" (pp. 181–183): "She was so elusive, like a beautiful perfume you smell but can't name, like the whisper that wakes you from a dream and turns out to belong to the dream."
2. If you are currently working on an open-form narrative, exchange drafts with a classmate. See if you can find instances of figurative language in your current drafts and analyze their effectiveness. Perhaps you can also discover places where figurative language could be profitably added to the text.

Lesson 5: Expand Your Repertoire of Styles

In Chapter 3, we introduced you to the concept of style, which is a combination of sentence structure, word choice, and rhythm that allows writers to vary their emphasis and tone in a variety of ways. In this lesson, we show you how to expand your repertoire of styles through a classic method of teaching in which you try to imitate other writers' styles. This rhetorical practice—called "creative imitation"—has a long history beginning with the rhetoricians of classical Greece and Rome. When you do creative imitation, you examine a passage from an expert stylist and try to emulate it. You substitute your own subject matter, but you try to imitate the exact grammatical structures, lengths and rhythms of the sentences, and the tones of the original passage. The long-range effect of creative imitation is to expand your stylistic choices; the more immediate effect is to increase your skill at analyzing a writer's style. Most practitioners find that creative imitation encourages surprising insights into their own subject matter (when seen through the lens of the original writer's style) as well as a new understanding of how a particular piece of writing creates its special effects.

See pp. 57–59 for a discussion of style.

You begin a creative imitation by asking questions such as these: What is distinctive about the sentences in this passage of writing? How do choices about sentence length and complexity, kinds of words, figures of speech, and so forth create a writer's voice? After close examination of the passage, you then think of your own subject matter that could be appropriately adapted to this writer's style.

To help you understand creative imitation, we provide the following example. In this passage, the writer, Victoria Register-Freeman, is exploring how relations between young men and women today threaten to undo some of the twentieth century's progress toward gender equality. In the section of her article that precedes this passage, Register-Freeman explains how she, as a single mother, taught her boys to cook, sew, do laundry, and "carry their weight domestically." But then, as she explains in this passage, teenage girls undid her attempts at creating gender equality:

REGISTER-FREEMAN PASSAGE

Then came puberty and hunkhood. Over the last few years, the boys' domestic skills have atrophied because handmaidens have appeared en masse. The damsels have driven by, beeped, phoned and faxed. Some appeared so frequently outside the front door they began to remind me of the suction-footed Garfields spread-eagled on car windows. While the girls varied according to height, hair color and basic body type, they shared one characteristic. They were ever eager to help the guys out.

—Victoria Register-Freeman, "My Turn: Hunks and Handmaidens"

Register-Freeman's voice projects the image of a concerned mother and feminist social critic. Her tone includes a range of attitudes: serious, personal, factual, ironic, frustrated. Note how this passage begins and ends with short, clipped sentences. The second sentence states a problem that the next three sentences develop with various kinds of details. The third sentence includes a series of colorful verbs; the fourth uses a metaphor (the ever-present girls compared to Garfields on car windows). The fifth sentence builds to the point in the sixth sentence, which is delivered bluntly and simply.

Here is one writer's attempt at a creative imitation:

CREATIVE IMITATION OF REGISTER-FREEMAN

Then came prosperity and popularity. Over the last ten years, Seattle's special charms have faded because expansion has occurred too rapidly. Traffic has multiplied, thickened, amplified, and slowed. Traffic jams appeared so often on the freeways and arterials they began to remind me of ants swarming over spilled syrup. While the congestion varied according to time, seasons, and weather conditions, it had one dominant effect. It increasingly threatened to spoil the city's beauty.

For Writing and Discussion

1. Do your own creative imitation of the passage from Register-Freeman.
2. Choose one or both of the following passages for creative imitation. Begin by jotting down all the specific observations you can make about the stylistic features of the passage. Then choose a topic that matches the topic of the original in its degree of lightness or seriousness and its depth. Explore your topic by presenting it using the sentence structures and kinds of words used in the original. Try to imitate the original phrase by phrase and sentence by sentence. You may find it helpful to use a dictionary and thesaurus.

   a. Africa is mystic; it is wild; it is a sweltering inferno; it is a photographer's paradise, a hunter's Valhalla, an escapist's Utopia. It is what you will, and it withstands all interpretations. It is the last vestige of a dead world or the cradle of a shiny new one. To a lot of people, as to myself, it is just "home." It is all of these things but one thing—it is never dull.

      —Beryl Markham, "Flying Elsewhere," *West with the Night*

   b. The disease was bubonic plague, present in two forms: one that infected the bloodstream, causing the buboes and internal bleeding, and was spread by contact; and a second, more virulent pneumonic type that infected the lungs and was spread by respiratory infection. The presence of both at once caused the high mortality and speed of contagion. So lethal was the disease that cases were known of persons going to bed well and dying before they woke, of doctors catching the illness at bedside and dying before the patient.

      —Barbara Tuchman, "This Is the End of the World," *A Distant Mirror*

Lesson 6: Use Open-Form Elements to Create "Voice" in Closed-Form Prose

So far we have been talking about features of open-form prose in its purer forms. Sometimes, however, writers wish simply to loosen basically closed-form prose by combining it with some features of open-form prose. If, for example, an academic wanted to share new developments in a field with a popular audience, he or she would be well-advised to leaven his or her prose with some elements of open-form writing. In this final lesson, we offer several pieces of advice for loosening up closed-form prose.

Introducing Some Humor

Humor is rare in tightly closed prose because humor is nonfunctional—it doesn't *have* to be there for a writer to make a point—and closed-form prose values efficiency, getting what you have to say said in the most economical fashion.

Humor is closely related to one of the mainsprings of open-form style, surprise. Humor typically depends on sudden twists and abrupt changes in direction. In physical comedy, pratfalls are funny in direct proportion to the audience's inability to see them coming. In verbal humor, the less clearly the audience sees the punch line coming, the more it makes the audience laugh.

Humor is particularly valuable in that it can make imposing subjects more manageable for readers. Just as humor can deflate pretensions and bring down the high and the mighty in an instant, it can make difficult and foreign subjects less anxiety producing. Formal, abstract language can put readers off, estranging them from the subject; humor has the power to "de-strange" a subject, to allow the audience to look at it long enough to understand it. Many popular books on science and many of the best instructional books on car repair, cooking, money management, and others of life's drearier necessities use a humorous style to help their phobic readers get on with life.

To appreciate the effect of humor, consider the following passages from two different instructional books on how to operate the database program Paradox. The first passage, from *Windows in 21 Days,* uses a clear, humor-free, closed-form style.

> In this book, you learn by following detailed step-by-step exercises based on real-world problems in database application design. Every exercise leads you further into the power of "Paradox for Windows" as you develop the components of an automated application. This section does the following: explains the assumptions and conventions used in this book; lists the hardware and software requirements and setup needed to run Paradox for Windows and use this book efficiently; and offers some suggestions for strategies to get the most from this book. The step-by-step exercises make it easy.

Now note the different effect produced by the following passage from one of the hugely popular *For Dummies* books:

> Welcome to *Paradox for Windows for Dummies,* a book that's not afraid to ask the tough questions like "When's lunch?" and "Who finished the cookie dough ice cream?" If you're more interested in food (or Australian Wombats, for that matter) than you are in Paradox for Windows, this book is for you. If you're more interested in Paradox for Windows, please get some professional help before going out into society again.
>
> My goal is to help you get things done despite the fact that you're using Paradox. Whether you're at home, in your office, or at home in your office (or even if you just *feel* like you live at work) *Paradox for Windows for Dummies* is your all-in-one guidebook through the treacherous, frustrating, and appallingly technical world of the relational database.

For Writing and Discussion

1. Which of these two instructional books would you prefer to read?
2. The second passage says that the world of relational databases is "treacherous, frustrating, and appallingly technical," whereas the first stresses that the "step-by-step exercises [in the book] make it easy." Why do you suppose the humorous passage stresses the difficulty of databases whereas the humorless passage stresses the ease of a step-by-step approach? Is it good strategy for the humorous writer to stress the difficulty of Paradox?
3. Under what rhetorical circumstances are humorous instructions better than strictly serious instructions? When is a strictly serious approach better?

Using Techniques from Popular Magazines

Writers who publish regularly for popular audiences develop a vigorous, easy-reading style that differs from the style of much academic writing. The effect of this difference is illustrated by the results of a famous research study conducted by Michael Graves and Wayne Slater at the University of Michigan. For this study, teams of writers revised passages from a high school history textbook.* One team consisted of linguists and technical writers trained in producing closed-form texts using the strategies discussed in Chapter 18 (forecasting structure, putting points first, following the old/new contract, using transitions). A second team consisted of two *Time-Life* book editors.

Whereas the linguists aimed at making the passages clearer, the *Time-Life* writers were more concerned with making them livelier. The result? One hundred eleventh-grade students found the *Time-Life* editors' version both more comprehensible and more memorable. Lack of clarity wasn't the problem with the original textbook; unbearable dryness was the problem. According to the researchers, the *Time-Life* editors did not limit themselves

> to making the passages lucid, well-organized, coherent, and easy to read. Their revisions went beyond such matters and were intended to make the texts interesting, exciting, vivid, rich in human drama, and filled with colorful language.

To see how they achieved this effect, let's look at their revision. Here is a passage about the Vietnam War taken from the original history text:

ORIGINAL HISTORY TEXT

The most serious threat to world peace developed in Southeast Asia. Communist guerrillas threatened the independence of the countries carved out of French Indo-China by the Geneva conference of 1954. In South Vietnam, Communist guerrillas (the Viet Cong) were aided by forces from Communist North Vietnam in a struggle to overthrow the American-supported government. . . .

*The study involved three teams, but for purposes of simplification we limit our discussion to two.

Shortly after the election of 1964, Communist gains prompted President Johnson to alter his policy concerning Vietnam. American military forces in Vietnam were increased from about 20,000 men in 1964 to more than 500,000 by 1968. Even so, North Vietnamese troops and supplies continued to pour into South Vietnam.

Here is the *Time-Life* editors' revision:

HISTORY PRESENTED IN POPULAR MAGAZINE STYLE

In the early 1960's the greatest threat to world peace was just a small splotch of color on Kennedy's map, one of the fledgling nations sculpted out of French Indo-China by the Geneva peacemakers of 1954. It was a country so tiny and remote that most Americans had never uttered its name: South Vietnam. . . .

Aided by Communist North Vietnam, the Viet Cong guerrillas were eroding the ground beneath South Vietnam's American-backed government. Village by village, road by road, these jungle-wise rebels were waging a war of ambush and mining: They darted out of tunnels to head off patrols, buried exploding booby traps beneath the mud floors of huts, and hid razor-sharp bamboo sticks in holes. . . .

No sooner had Johnson won the election than Communist gains prompted Johnson to go back on his campaign promise. The number of American soldiers in Vietnam skyrocketed from 20,000 in 1964 to more than 500,000 by 1968. But in spite of GI patrols, leech-infested jungles, swarms of buzzing insects, and flash floods that made men cling to trees to escape being washed away—North Vietnamese troops streamed southward without letup along the Ho Chi Minh Trail.

What can this revision teach you about envigorating closed-form prose? What specifically are the editors doing here?

First, notice how far the level of abstraction drops in the revision. The original is barren of sensory words; the revision is alive with them ("South Vietnam" becomes a "small splotch of color on Kennedy's map"; "a struggle to overthrow the American-supported government" becomes "[They] buried exploding booby traps beneath the mud floors of huts, and hid razor-sharp bamboo sticks in holes").

Second, notice how much more dramatic the revision is. Actual scenes, including a vision of men clinging to trees to escape being washed away by flash floods, replace a chronological account of the war's general progress. According to the editors, such scenes, or "nuggets"—vivid events that encapsulate complex processes or principles—are the lifeblood of *Time-Life* prose.

Finally, notice how the revision tends to delay critical information for dramatic effect, moving information you would normally expect to find early on into a later position. In the first paragraph, the *Time-Life* writers talk about "the greatest threat to world peace" in the early 1960s for five lines before revealing the identity of that threat—South Vietnam.

For Writing and Discussion

Here is a passage from a student argument opposing women's serving on submarines. Working individually or in small groups, enliven this passage by using some of the techniques of the *Time-Life* writers.

(continued)

Not only would it be very expensive to refit submarines for women personnel, but having women on submarines would hurt the morale of the sailors. In order for a crew to work effectively, they must have good morale or their discontent begins to show through in their performance. This is especially crucial on submarines, where if any problem occurs, it affects the safety of the whole ship. Women would hurt morale by creating sexual tension. Sexual tension can take many forms. One form is couples' working and living in a close space with all of the crew. When a problem occurs within the relationship, it could affect the morale of those directly involved and in the workplace. This would create an environment that is not conducive to good productivity. Tension would also occur if one of the women became pregnant or if there were complaints of sexual harassment. It would be easier to deal with these problems on a surface ship, but in the small confines of a submarine these problems would cause more trouble.

READING

To conclude this chapter, we present a famous short example of open-form prose—Annie Dillard's "Living Like Weasels." The exercises that follow the reading will help you review the lessons in this chapter.

Annie Dillard
Living Like Weasels

1   A weasel is wild. Who knows what he thinks? He sleeps in his underground den, his tail draped over his nose. Sometimes he lives in his den for two days without leaving. Outside, he stalks rabbits, mice, muskrats, and birds, killing more bodies than he can eat warm, and often dragging the carcasses home. Obedient to instinct, he bites his prey at the neck, either splitting the jugular vein at the throat or crunching the brain at the base of the skull, and he does not let go. One naturalist refused to kill a weasel who was socketed into his hand deeply as a rattlesnake. The man could in no way pry the tiny weasel off, and he had to walk half a mile to water, the weasel dangling from his palm, and soak him off like a stubborn label.

2   And once, says Ernest Thompson Seton—once, a man shot an eagle out of the sky. He examined the eagle and found the dry skull of a weasel fixed by the jaws to his throat. The supposition is that the eagle had pounced on the weasel and the weasel swiveled and bit as instinct taught him, tooth to neck, and nearly won. I would like to have seen that eagle from the air a few weeks or months before he was shot: was the whole weasel still attached to his feathered throat, a fur pendant? Or did the eagle eat what he could reach, gutting the living weasel with his talons before his breast, bending his beak, cleaning the beautiful airborne bones?

3   I have been reading about weasels because I saw one last week. I startled a weasel who startled me, and we exchanged a long glance.

4   Twenty minutes from my house, through the woods by the quarry and across the highway, is Hollins Pond, a remarkable piece of shallowness, where I like to go at sunset and sit on a tree trunk. Hollins Pond is also called Murray's Pond; it covers two acres of bottomland near Tinker Creek with six inches of water and six thousand lily pads. In winter, brown-and-white steers stand in the middle of it, merely dampening their hooves; from the distant shore they look like miracle itself, complete with miracle's nonchalance. Now, in summer, the steers are gone. The water lilies have blossomed and spread to a green horizontal plane that is terra firma to plodding blackbirds, and tremulous ceiling to black leeches, crayfish, and carp.

5   This is, mind you, suburbia. It is a five-minute walk in three directions to rows of houses, though none is visible here. There's a 55 mph highway at one end of the pond, and a nesting pair of wood ducks at the other. Under every bush is a muskrat hole or a beer can. The far end is an alternating series of fields and woods, fields and woods, threaded everywhere with motorcycle tracks—in whose bare clay wild turtles lay eggs.

6   So. I had crossed the highway, stepped over two low barbed-wire fences, and traced the motorcycle path in all gratitude through the wild rose and poison ivy of the pond's shoreline up into high grassy fields. Then I cut down through the woods to the mossy fallen tree where I sit. This tree is excellent. It makes a dry, upholstered bench at the upper, marshy end of the pond, a plush jetty raised from the thorny shore between a shallow blue body of water and a deep blue body of sky.

7   The sun had just set. I was relaxed on the tree trunk, ensconced in the lap of lichen, watching the lily pads at my feet tremble and part dreamily over the thrusting path of a carp. A yellow bird appeared to my right and flew behind me. It caught my eye. I swiveled around—and the next instant, inexplicably, I was looking down at a weasel, who was looking up at me.

8   Weasel! I'd never seen one wild before. He was ten inches long, thin as a curve, a muscled ribbon, brown as fruitwood, soft-furred, alert. His face was fierce, small and pointed as a lizard's; he would have made a good arrowhead. There was just a dot of chin, maybe two brown hairs' worth, and then the pure white fur began that spread down his underside. He had two black eyes I didn't see, any more than you see a window.

9   The weasel was stunned into stillness as he was emerging from beneath an enormous shaggy wild rose bush four feet away. I was stunned into stillness twisted backward on the tree trunk. Our eyes locked, and someone threw away the key.

10   Our look was as if two lovers, or deadly enemies, met unexpectedly on an overgrown path when each had been thinking of something else: a clearing blow to the gut. It was also a bright blow to the brain, or a sudden beating of brains, with all the charge and intimate grate of rubbed balloons. It emptied our lungs. It felled the forest, moved the fields, and drained the pond; the world dismantled and tumbled into that black hole of eyes. If you and I looked at each other that way, our skulls would split and drop to our shoulders. But we don't. We keep our skulls. So.

11   He disappeared. This was only last week, and already I don't remember what shattered the enchantment. I think I blinked, I think I retrieved my brain from the weasel's brain, and tried to memorize what I was seeing, and the weasel felt the yank of separation, the careening splashdown into real life and the urgent current of instinct. He vanished under the wild rose. I waited motionless, my mind suddenly full of data and my spirit with pleadings, but he didn't return.

12   Please do not tell me about "approach-avoidance conflicts." I tell you I've been in that weasel's brain for sixty seconds, and he was in mine. Brains are private places, muttering through unique and secret tapes—but the weasel and I both plugged into another tape simultaneously, for a sweet and shocking time. Can I help it if it was a blank?

13   What goes on in his brain the rest of the time? What does a weasel think about? He won't say. His journal is tracks in clay, a spray of feathers, mouse blood and bone: uncollected, unconnected, loose-leaf, and blown.

14   I would like to learn, or remember, how to live. I come to Hollins Pond not so much to learn how to live as, frankly, to forget about it. That is, I don't think I can learn from a wild animal how to live in particular—shall I suck warm blood, hold my tail high, walk with my footprints precisely over the prints of my hands?—but I might learn something of mindlessness, something of the purity of living in the physical senses and the dignity of living without bias or motive. The weasel lives in necessity and we live in choice, hating necessity and dying at the last ignobly in its talons. I would like to live as I should, as the weasel lives as he should. And I suspect that for me the way is like the weasel's: open to time and death painlessly, noticing everything, remembering nothing, choosing the given with a fierce and pointed will.

15   I missed my chance. I should have gone for the throat. I should have lunged for that streak of white under the weasel's chin and held on, held on through mud and into the wild rose, held on for a dearer life. We could live under the wild rose wild as weasels, mute and uncomprehending. I could very calmly go wild. I could live two days in the den, curled, leaning on mouse fur, sniffing bird bones, blinking, licking, breathing musk, my hair tangled in the roots of grasses. Down is a good place to go, where the mind is single. Down is out, out of your ever-loving mind and back to your careless senses. I remember muteness as a prolonged and giddy fast, where every moment is a feast of utterance received. Time and events are merely poured, unremarked, and ingested directly, like blood pulsed into my gut through a jugular vein. Could two live that way? Could two live under the wild rose, and explore by the pond, so that the smooth mind of each is as everywhere present to the other, and as received and as unchallenged, as falling snow?

16   We could, you know. We can live any way we want. People take vows of poverty, chastity, and obedience—even of silence—by choice. The thing is

to stalk your calling in a certain skilled and supple way, to locate the most tender and live spot and plug into that pulse. This is yielding, not fighting. A weasel doesn't "attack" anything; a weasel lives as he's meant to, yielding at every moment to the perfect freedom of single necessity.

17   I think it would be well, and proper, and obedient, and pure, to grasp your one necessity and not let it go, to dangle from it limp wherever it takes you. Then even death, where you're going no matter how you live, cannot you part. Seize it and let it seize you up aloft even, till your eyes burn out and drop; let your musky flesh fall off in shreds, and let your very bones unhinge and scatter, loosened over fields, over fields and woods, lightly, thoughtless, from any height at all, from as high as eagles.

For Writing and Discussion

Working in small groups or as a whole class, use the questions that follow to guide your close examination of Dillard's structural and stylistic choices.

1. How does Dillard's essay meet the criteria for a story—events depicted in time, connectedness, tension, and resolution? What final resolution or interpretation does Dillard offer?
2. Find ten examples of Dillard's use of specific words and concrete language. Try rewording some of these examples at a higher level of abstraction and then compare Dillard's "low on the scale" version with your "higher on the scale" version.
3. Choose three consecutive paragraphs in this essay and examine how Dillard employs gaps between sentences to stimulate readers to think actively about the questions she is raising. Try tracking her ideas from sentence to sentence in these paragraphs. Where does she disrupt readers' expectations by violating conventions of closed-form prose?
4. Find ten examples of figurative language and explain how these are particularly effective in holding the reader's interest and portraying the intensity or meaning of her experience.
5. Suppose that you were going to do a stylistic imitation of one of Dillard's passages. Choose a passage that you think is particularly interesting stylistically and explain why you have chosen it.
6. Imagine the entry on "weasels" in an encyclopedia. How could you use some of Dillard's strategies to make a typical closed-form encyclopedia article more lively?

A Rhetorical Guide to Research

This screen capture shows the home page of Women Against Gun Control (www.wagc.com), a grassroots organization dedicated to supporting women's right to defend themselves. This organization participates in pro-gun political activism, legislative research, media awareness, distribution of print resources, and gun-related education. The Web site itself uses color, images, other design features, and bold text to stake out its position in the complex controversy over women's role in the hotly contested, larger issue of gun control. This Web site home page is featured in a class discussion exercise in Chapter 21.

Ladies of High-Caliber

Protect Your Rights!

Join Now!

Click Here for the 10 Commandments of gun safety!

- Home
- WAGC Information
- WAGC Features
- WAGC Boycotts
- WAGC Links
- WAGC Site map
- WAGC Contact

Get your pin in honor of WAGC!

Women Against Gun Control

"The Second Amendment IS the Equal

Click here to sign and read our new forum board!

WAGC sends amicus brief to the U.S. Supreme Court!

Click Here (Opens New Window)

Click here to read a press release regarding this hearing.

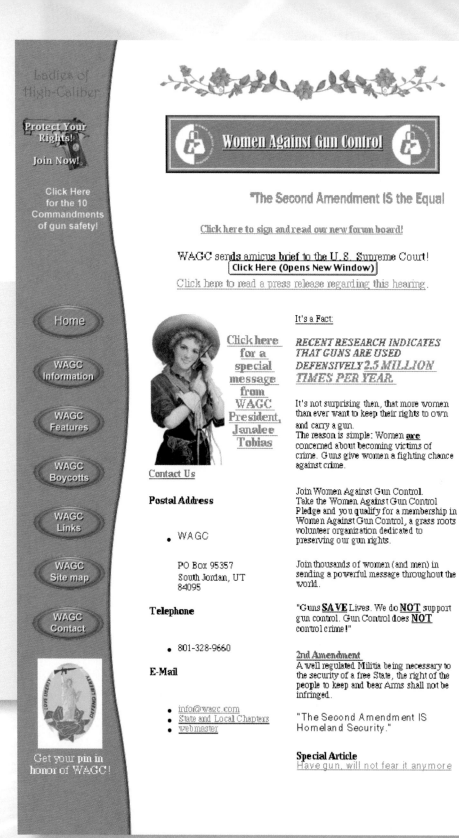

Click here for a special message from WAGC President, Janalee Tobias

Contact Us

Postal Address

- WAGC

  PO Box 95357
  South Jordan, UT
  84095

Telephone

- 801-328-9660

E-Mail

- info@wagc.com
- State and Local Chapters
- webmaster

It's a Fact:

RECENT RESEARCH INDICATES THAT GUNS ARE USED DEFENSIVELY 2.5 MILLION TIMES PER YEAR

It's not surprising then, that more women than ever want to keep their rights to own and carry a gun.
The reason is simple: Women **are** concerned about becoming victims of crime. Guns give women a fighting chance against crime.

Join Women Against Gun Control.
Take the Women Against Gun Control Pledge and you qualify for a membership in Women Against Gun Control, a grass roots volunteer organization dedicated to preserving our gun rights.

Join thousands of women (and men) in sending a powerful message throughout the world.

"Guns **SAVE** Lives. We do **NOT** support gun control. Gun Control does **NOT** control crime!"

<u>2nd Amendment</u>
A well regulated Militia being necessary to the security of a free State, the right of the people to keep and bear Arms shall not be infringed.

"The Second Amendment IS Homeland Security."

Special Article
Have gun, will not fear it anymore

Rosie O'Donnel

Hillary Clinton

Janet Reno

Diane Feinstein

Want Americans to believe all women support gun control...

Let's BLOW HOLES in this MYTH!

If women are disarmed, a rapist will never hear...

"STOP OR I'LL SHOOT!"

Looking for Pro-Second Amendment and Pro-Freedom Books? Check Out These Book Reviews and Help Support This Site!

THE UTAH GIRAFFE SOCIETY

Support WAGC Efforts with the Utah GIRAFFE Society!

Part 4 A Rhetorical Guide to Research

An Introduction to Research

An Overview of Part Four, "A Rhetorical Guide to Research"

Our goal in Part Four is to help you become an effective writer of college-level research papers. This chapter, "An Introduction to Research," gives you a big-picture overview of how to approach research writing using rhetorical skills. It explains some of the challenges research writing poses for college students who are new to academic scholarship. It ends by identifying seven essential skills that you should develop in order to become a successful writer of research papers across the curriculum.

Chapters 21 and 22, "Finding and Evaluating Sources" and "Using, Citing, and Documenting Sources," help you learn these skills through a sequence of seven self-contained sections or lessons. Each one focuses on a specific aspect of the research process and forms a discrete unit for class discussion or for application to your own research writing.

Introduction to Research Writing

Although the research paper is a common writing assignment in college, students are often baffled by their professor's expectations. Many students think of research writing as finding information on a topic or as finding quotations to support a thesis rather than as wrestling with a question or problem. One of our colleagues calls these sorts of papers "data dumps": The student backs a truckload of data up to the professor's desk, unloads it, and says, "Here's what I found out about sweatshops, Professor Jones. Enjoy!" Another colleague calls papers full of long quotations "choo-choo train papers": big boxcars of quotations coupled together with little patches of a student's own writing.

But a research paper shouldn't be a data dump or a train of boxcar quotations. Instead, it should follow the same principles of writing discussed throughout this text. A research paper should pose an interesting and significant problem and respond to it with a contestable thesis. That thesis, in turn, must be supported by material from reputable research sources that are documented in a formal, academic style.

Much of the writing you encounter in popular magazines has the characteristics of a research paper—a thesis and support—but not the documentation that college professors expect. That documentation makes all the difference because new knowledge is inevitably built on the work of others. In academic culture, authors who hope to gain credibility for new findings and ideas must explain the roots of their work as well as show how they reached their conclusions. To consider more closely the difference between the public face of research when it reaches most of us in general circulation media and the research papers valued at colleges and universities, consider this excerpt from a brief article in *Parenting* magazine:

> Another reason to think twice before you park your baby in front of the screen: The more TV he watches between ages 1 and 3, the greater the chance he'll develop attention problems as a 7-year-old. For each hour watched per day, on average, the risk rises 10 percent. In the study, 1-year-olds averaged 2.2 hours of daily TV viewing; 3-year-olds, 3.6 hours. Since kids this age are awake for only about 12 hours, that's 20 to 30 percent of their day!
>
> TV may affect the "wiring" of the brain, which develops very quickly in the first three years, researchers believe. Their theory: If a child gets used to lots of rapidly changing images on the screen, his brain may not be as well suited to quieter, slower tasks like listening to a teacher and reading. "And TV can replace such developmental experiences as reading and playing," says study head Dimitri Christakis, M.D., director of the Child Health Institute at the University of Washington. (Having your programs on, even in the background, may also be distracting to toddlers, according to other studies.)

The article's remaining two paragraphs inform readers of the American Academy of Pediatrics' guidelines for limiting young children's exposure to TV and provide reassuring suggestions from Dr. Christakis about alternative activities. As does a good research paper, this article has a thesis (i.e., television watching can be harmful to young children), detailed numbers supporting the main point, and comments from an expert. Notice, however, that a parent who decides to limit TV viewing on the basis of this article would be doing so out of trust in *Parenting*'s reporting and editorial processes, not out of any understanding or appreciation of Dr. Christakis's research. Readers are justified in assuming that the research was published in a peer-reviewed scholarly journal where impartial experts had scrutinized and endorsed it. Busy parents rely on magazines like this one to digest such reports for them. But an academic writer who wants to know how the Christakis team arrived at the numbers indicating risk must hunt down the article on the basis of very few clues. Ten minutes of searching on the American Academy of Pediatrics Web site eventually led us to a press release about the study and a link to an abstract of the article. Full text was available only to subscribers of *Pediatrics*, the organization's official journal, but the linked page offered a valuable glimpse inside the culture of scientific research: It included links to two journal articles that had cited the study and to twenty-some posts at Pediatrics Online responding to the article. Most of these questioned whether the reported results were a matter of causation or correlation—fascinating reading for an undergraduate writing a paper about the question of how detrimental television viewing might be for young children.

The genre of the scientific research paper, including correlation versus causation, is discussed in Chapter 10.

Our point here is that academic research paper assignments call not for quick distillations of advice to a busy parent but for multifaceted examination of a question. Furthermore, your professors will expect your final product to include in-text citations referring to a bibliography so that your readers can follow the trail of your research. To meet these expectations for research papers, you need to know how academic discourse works. Out of our own desire to bring you into the kitchen of academic life, we invite you to explore for a moment some of the difficulties of undergraduate research.

Why Research Writing Poses Difficulties for Novice Writers

Many of you reading this text—as first-year college students—are novices standing outside the research culture of your professors. Our goal is to help you begin to enter that culture. Once you are inside it, you'll learn habits of critical reading and thinking that will help you excel in your careers as well as in college. In the interest of full disclosure, here is a list of difficulties almost all new researchers face:

Learning How to Ask Research Questions

Unless your previous teachers have emphasized question asking and inquiry in a variety of courses, you may be new to this text's emphasis on problem posing as the starting point of the writing process. To complicate your initiation into academic culture, each new discipline you encounter in college asks different kinds of questions and frames them in different ways. The first section in Chapter 21 explains how to pose a good research question for your particular project.

Learning How to Find Sources

We live in an information-saturated culture. Novice researchers are often overwhelmed by the sheer volume of information that is available on many topics. They are often unaware of how the print and video resources of a library differ significantly from cyberspace resources or of how searching the licensed databases that libraries subscribe to is different from searching the World Wide Web. Moreover, material retrieved from both types of sources often has the same basic appearance when it emerges from your printer. To separate the gold of good material from the gravel of everything available, you need to understand how sources differ and how the different kinds are stored, indexed, and searched. The sequenced sections in Chapter 21 teach you these skills. They show you how to conduct efficient searches by thinking rhetorically about the whole search process.

Learning *Why* to Find Sources

Perhaps the most subtle problem is learning *why* an academic writer needs to find sources. For people outside the culture of scholarship, research can seem like a mechanical process of jumping through the professor's hoops. For many students, research has meant paraphrasing an encyclopedia, padding a term paper to include "five required sources," or scouring articles to find quotations to support a thesis.

But all these views reveal confusion about how academic discourse works. Once you are inside the culture, you will recognize that research is propelled by genuine curiosity and intellectual wrestling. In looking for sources, skilled researchers have two kinds of goals:

- First, they conduct research to uncover information, data, and evidence that bear on their research problems. They seek raw material that they can analyze and synthesize to build a thesis and an argument.
- Second, they conduct research to position themselves in the conversation surrounding the topic, trying to figure out how their views relate to what others have written about the same problem.

In other words, a scholar doesn't do research to *find* an answer to her research question. She does research to *make* an answer. Scholars always see themselves as critical thinkers working toward something new, surprising, or challenging for their intended readers. You will see this point emphasized throughout Chapters 21 and 22.

Learning How to Read Sources Rhetorically

Beginning researchers often treat all sources as having equal and objective status—a quotation from writer A is as good as a quotation from writer B. But, as we have shown throughout this text, all writers have an angle of vision (or interpretive filter) that causes them to choose and present data in ways that advance their own purposes and points of view. You therefore need to think rhetorically about your research sources. You need to ask of each source: Who wrote this piece, for what audience, and for what purpose?

"Angle of vision" is first introduced in Chapter 4, pp. 80–82.

To analyze a source's bias and perspective, you typically need to determine its writer's original context. This process can be troublesome with sources retrieved from the Web. Chapter 21 deals specifically with reading sources rhetorically and evaluating their biases.

Learning How to Work Sources into Your Own Writing

Another major difficulty is figuring out what to do with your sources—when to quote, when to paraphrase, and when to summarize a part of or the whole of an argument. Moreover, you need to work these quotations and paraphrases into the texture of your own prose so that you carry the argument in your own voice and make it easy for readers to distinguish between your ideas and those of your sources. If you quote long passages or include extensive paraphrasing, you are not in control of your sources but are simply reproducing them. In contrast, after you learn how to use sources purposefully, your own voice will dominate your writing. The first section of Chapter 22 focuses on these skills.

Learning How to Cite and Document Sources

From a mechanical point of view, the problems of citing and documenting sources should be relatively easy to solve. In actual practice, however, documentation can seem bewildering. First of all, conventions for citing sources differ from discipline to discipline. Literature teachers prefer the MLA (Modern Language Association) system, social scientists the APA (American Psychological Association) system, historians the University of Chicago *Manual of Style,* and chemists the ACS (American Chemical Society) system. As students move from discipline to discipline, they have to shift formats.

Additionally, citing Web sources can be frustrating. These sources often come and go, disembodied and free-floating in cyberspace. It is often hard to tell who wrote a Web document, when, under what circumstances, and for what audience.

Finally, the details of citing can seem nitpicky. Does it really matter, you might ask, whether you put a period after the parenthesis? As we try to show, carefully following citation conventions is as much a matter of a writer's projected *ethos* as of objective correctness. Are you trying to project yourself as an insider or an outsider to this discipline? The last section in Chapter 22 deals with these skills.

Seven Essential Skills for Novice Researchers

Now that we have laid out some of the problems you can expect to encounter as a researcher, we want to reassure you that you can develop skills to deal with them. In fact, you could probably develop these skills on your own through trial and error over a period of several years. What we hope to do in the next chapters is to accelerate your learning.

As you study this material, keep foremost in mind your twofold purpose as you do research for an academic research paper:

1. To find information and data relevant to your research question
2. To position yourself in a conversation with other voices that have addressed the same question

In the following list, we identify seven essential skills that will help you produce an accomplished research paper. The next two chapters devote one section to each skill.

- **Skill 1: Compose and argue your own thesis.** Arguing your own thesis requires the ability to pose a research question, to create your own answer, and to build an argument for it in your own voice, using your research as support. Your thesis will evolve as you increase your understanding of the larger conversation addressing your question and as you find materials relevant to answering it.
- **Skill 2: Understand the different kinds of sources.** As you look at books, periodicals, and Web sites, you need to understand how scholarly books

differ from trade books, how peer-reviewed journals differ from magazines, and how print sources differ from cyberspace-only sources.

- **Skill 3: Use purposeful strategies for searching libraries, databases, and Web sites.** By using your rhetorical knowledge during a search, you can efficiently tap the resources of libraries and the Internet to find books, articles, and Web sites relevant to your research question. Specifically, you need to learn how to use your library's online catalog, how to search a licensed database such as ProQuest or Lexis-Nexis Academic Universe, and how to search the World Wide Web using a search engine such as Yahoo! or Google.

- **Skill 4: Use rhetorical knowledge to read and evaluate sources.** Reading sources rhetorically will enable you to evaluate sources for angle of vision, degree of advocacy, credibility, and reliability.

- **Skill 5: Understand the rhetoric of Web sites.** In the nearly two decades since the World Wide Web was formed, its store of information has expanded exponentially. It is now an indispensable resource for almost all researchers, but it can also be a conundrum. To use the Web with sophistication, you need to know how its welter of advocacy sites, its images and hypertext structure, and its democratic openness make the Web substantively and rhetorically different from print media. Understanding the rhetoric of Web sites will help you make expert decisions when you evaluate and use Web sources.

- **Skill 6: Use sources purposefully through clearly attributed summary, paraphrase, or quotation.** Incorporating sources into your own prose through purposeful summary, paraphrase, or quotation is a hallmark of an experienced writer. To help your reader separate your own voice from the voice of your sources, you need to write effective attributive tags and use in-text citations. Together these skills protect you from any hint of plagiarism.

- **Skill 7: Cite and document sources effectively according to appropriate conventions.** A final skill you need is the ability to cite and document sources according to the conventions appropriate to your purpose, genre, and audience. Chapter 22 explains two common systems—the Modern Language Association (MLA) and the American Psychological Association (APA). When you use appropriate citation conventions, you help your readers follow the track of your research while you project a competent and professional image.

Finding and Evaluating Sources

The previous chapter explained some of the difficulties that novice research writers regularly encounter and introduced seven essential skills you need to become an effective research writer. This chapter focuses on the first five of these skills. To help you avoid information overload, we cover each skill in a relatively short, self-contained section that can be read comfortably in one sitting.

These seven skills are listed on pp. 605–606.

Skill 1: Compose and Argue Your Own Thesis

This skill, which enables you to take charge of your own writing, means that you need to pose your own research question and write a thesis-based argument in your own voice. In doing so, you use research for two connected purposes: to find information and data relevant to your research question and to position yourself in a conversation with other voices.

Formulating a Research Question

The best way to avoid writing a data dump or a jumble of quotations is to begin with a good research question. A good question keeps you in charge of your writing. It reminds you that your task is to answer this question for yourself, in your own voice, through your own critical thinking, applied to your own research sources. Skilled researchers don't seek the "perfect source" that answers their question. Rather, they know that they must create an answer themselves out of a welter of data and conflicting points of view.

See the discussion of data dumps and "choo-choo train papers" on p. 601. Question asking is introduced in Chapter 1.

To stay in charge of your writing, you need to focus your research on a question rather than on a topic. Suppose a friend sees you doing research in the library and asks what your research paper is about. Consider differences in the following answers:

Topic Focus: I am doing a paper on eating disorders.
Question Focus: I'm trying to sort out what the experts say is the best way to treat severe anorexia nervosa. Is inpatient or outpatient treatment more effective?

Topic Focus: I am doing my paper on gender-specific toys for children.
Question Focus: I am puzzled about some of the effects of gender-specific toys. Do boys' toys, such as video games, toy weapons, and construction sets, develop intellectual and physical skills more than girls' toys do?

As these scenarios suggest, a topic focus invites you to collect information without a clear purpose—a sure road toward data dumping. In contrast, a question focus requires you to be a critical thinker who must assess and weigh data and understand multiple points of view. A topic focus encourages passive collection of information. A question focus encourages active construction of meaning.

How do you arrive at a research question? Ideally, good research questions arise from your own intellectual curiosity—a desire to resolve something that truly puzzles you. Often questions emerge from conflicting points of view in class discussions or from controversies or unknowns you encounter while reading. In most cases your initial research question will evolve as you do your research. You may make it broader or narrower, or refocus it on a newly discovered aspect of your original problem. You can test the initial feasibility of your research question by considering the following prompts:

For a discussion of problematic and significant questions, see Chapter 1, pp. 7–11.

- Are you personally interested in this question?
- Is the question both problematic and significant?
- Is the question limited enough for the intended length of your paper?
- Is there a reasonable possibility of finding information on this question based on the time and resources you have available?
- Is the question appropriate for your level of expertise?

Establishing Your Role as a Researcher

After you have formulated your research question, you need to consider the possible roles you might play as a researcher. Your role is connected to the aim or purpose of your paper—to explore, to inform, to analyze, or to persuade. To help you see more fully what we mean by "role," here are some of the typical roles that writers of academic research papers might take:

- **Reporter of the Current Best Thinking on a Problem:** In this role, the writer researches the current thinking of experts on some important problem and reports what the experts think. The paper has primarily an informative aim. For example, *What are the current views of experts on the causes of homosexuality?*
- **Reviewer of a Controversy:** In this role, the writer investigates and reports the differing arguments on various sides of a controversy. If the writer simply reports alternative arguments, the aim is informative. If the writer decides to evaluate these arguments, the paper takes on an analytical or persuasive aim. A typical example is, *What are the arguments for and against creating a five-year undergraduate engineering curriculum?*
- **Advocate in a Controversy:** Here the writer shifts from an informative or analytical to a persuasive aim. The paper asserts a position using research data for support, with the aim of persuading skeptical readers toward the writer's position: *What role(s) should the U.S. government play in providing health care for American citizens?* This purpose and role are particularly common in civic discourse where writers use reason and argument to influence decision making in a democratic society.

- **Analyzer/Synthesizer Positioned within a Conversation:** When writers adopt this role, they devote much of their paper to their own original analyses of a text, phenomenon, or data source, but they must also relate their views to what others have said about the same or similar questions. *How does Hobbes's view of the effective prince differ from Machiavelli's? What view of the self emerges from inventing identities in a cyberspace chatroom?* This is perhaps the most common role taken by scholars in academic discourse.
- **Original Field or Laboratory Researcher:** Here the writer poses a problem that requires field or laboratory research. In this case, research papers often take the form of a five-section scientific report. Field research, particularly common in the social sciences, involves collecting data through observation, interviews, and questionnaires. A typical field research question might be: *How has the war on terrorism following the September 11, 2001, disaster affected the lives of Muslim students on our campus?* A typical laboratory question might be: *Does topsoil downwind from a copper refinery show dangerous levels of heavy metals?* For questions of this kind, library research is often also required in order to determine what others have said about the same or similar problems (often called a "review of the literature"). Papers in this category generally combine an informative and an analytic aim.
- **Narrator of One's Research Process:** Most academic research papers follow a closed-form, question-thesis-support structure. Occasionally, however, readers may be interested in the researcher's thinking processes (exploratory aim), so the paper will read like a detective story with the thesis or further questions emerging at the end. In adopting an exploratory stance, the researcher narrates chronologically his or her engagement with the problem. Although this role is rare in academic and professional writing, it is becoming more common in some academic disciplines and is frequently used in popular writing aimed at showing the process of discovery. It is also an effective tool for generating complex thought about a question.

The structure of experimental reports is explained on p. 250.

See Chapter 10 for advice about conducting field research.

For Writing and Discussion

Working individually or in small groups, develop research questions on one general topic area such as music, health, sports, use of fossil fuels, or some other topic specified by your instructor. Develop questions that would be appropriate for each of the following roles:

1. Reporter of the current best thinking on a problem
2. Reviewer of a controversy
3. Advocate in a controversy
4. Analyzer/synthesizer positioned within a conversation
5. Original field or laboratory researcher
6. Miscellaneous (good questions that don't fit neatly into any of these roles)

A Case Study: Christopher Leigh's Research on School Violence

To illustrate how a student writer stays in charge of his writing by arguing his own thesis, let's return to Christopher Leigh's research on school violence, which we introduced in Chapter 1. Christopher's concern, as you will recall, grew out of his distress from the Columbine High School massacre in April 1999, which led to a nationwide debate: What causes school violence? How can we prevent it? Dozens of possible causes were bandied about in the media, such as unsupervised teenagers, violent video games, rap lyrics, a proliferation of guns, Internet chat rooms, the overuse of psychotropic medications, bullying, cliquish high schools, and the disintegration of the two-parent family. Likewise, promoted solutions ranged from banning violent video games to putting metal detectors in schools. As he began reading about this controversy, trying to make sense of it for himself, Christopher read an article on psychological profiling. His initial reaction to this article was recorded in a journal entry, which we reprinted on page 9.

At the start of his research project, Christopher narrowed the broad question, "How can school violence be reduced?" down to the more limited question, "Is psychological profiling an effective means of reducing school violence?" He knew he was opposed to psychological profiling, but he also knew that something needed to be done to reduce school violence. Christopher's research process is narrated in his exploratory essay (pp. 197–202), in which he wrestles with different points of view on school violence.

As the exploratory essay makes clear, Christopher's center of interest gradually shifts from psychological profiling to the use of metal detectors in schools. Throughout this process you can observe Christopher thinking for himself, questioning different points of view, searching for different perspectives, struggling to find his own position.

In the conclusion of his exploratory narrative, Christopher sums up what he has learned so far in his research:

> I believe that this exploratory paper has helped me clarify my own thinking about school violence. I am now convinced that the media have instigated a panic about school violence, leading in many cases to counterproductive approaches like psychological profiling and metal detectors. When it comes time to write my major argument paper, I plan to show that these approaches only increase students' sense of alienation and hostility. The most important approach is to make schools more friendly, communal, and personal. We must ensure that troubled students are provided with help they need, rather than treating them like criminals.

Christopher's exploratory research gave him a solid background on school violence, allowing him to explore his own point of view against those of other voices in the conversation. In order to convert his exploratory narrative into a closed-form, question-thesis-support research paper, he decided to create an argument against metal detectors in schools. He had already clarified his own beliefs that schools need to be made more personal, so his remaining research primarily involved finding arguments in favor of metal detectors, in order to build a well-structured argument that attended to opposing views. You can read his final research paper in Chapter 22, pages 675–686.

For Writing and Discussion

Working individually, read Christopher's exploratory paper (pp. 197–202) and his final research paper (pp. 675–686). Then, working in small groups or as a whole class, try to reach consensus answers to the following questions:

1. Trace the steps in Christopher's thinking from the time he first becomes interested in psychological profiling until he finally settles on metal detectors as the topic of his final paper. What were the key moments that shaped his thinking? How did his thinking evolve?
2. We have used Christopher's story as an example of a student in charge of his own writing. Where do you see Christopher doing active critical thinking? Where do you see instances of what we have called "rhetorical reading"—that is, places where Christopher asks questions about an author's purpose, angle of vision, and selection of evidence? How is his final paper different from a data dump or a choo-choo train paper?

Skill 2: Understand the Different Kinds of Sources

To be an effective researcher, you need to understand the differences among the many kinds of books, articles, and Web sites you are apt to encounter—for example, the differences between scholarly books and trade books, between peer-reviewed journals and popular magazines, and between print sources and cyberspace-only sources. Before we describe strategies for finding sources (covered in the section devoted to Skill 3), we want to explain these differences, which are important for the following reasons:

- Different kinds of sources are found through different kinds of searches.
- For any particular research question, some kinds of sources are more useful than others.
- Knowing the differences among kinds of sources speeds your learning of search strategies, making you a more efficient and sophisticated researcher.
- Knowing what kind of source something is helps you read it rhetorically.

Looking at Sources Rhetorically

The best way to understand different kinds of sources is to view them rhetorically. Table 21.1, "A Rhetorical Overview of Print Sources," shows how print sources (books, scholarly journals, magazines, newspapers) can be categorized according to genre, publisher, author, and angle of vision. The last column in Table 21.1

TABLE 21.1 A Rhetorical Overview of Print Sources

Genre and Publisher	Author and Angle of Vision	How to Recognize Them
Books		
SCHOLARLY BOOKS • University/academic presses • Nonprofit • Selected through peer review	**Author:** Professors, researchers **Angle of vision:** Scholarly advancement of knowledge	• University press on title page • Specialized academic style • Documentation and bibliography
TRADE BOOKS (NONFICTION) • Commercial publishers (for example, Penguin Putnam) • Selected for profit potential	**Author:** Journalists, freelancers, scholars aiming at popular audience **Angle of vision:** Varies from informative to persuasive; often well researched and respected, but sometimes shoddy and aimed for quick sale	• Covers designed for marketing appeal • Popular style • Usually documented in an informal rather than academic style
REFERENCE BOOKS—MANY IN ELECTRONIC FORMAT • Publishers specializing in reference material • For-profit through library sales	**Author:** Commissioned scholars **Angle of vision:** Balanced, factual overview	• Titles containing words such as *encyclopedia, dictionary,* or *guide* • Found in reference section of library or online through library Web site
Periodicals		
SCHOLARLY JOURNALS • University/academic presses • Nonprofit • Articles chosen through peer review • Examples: *Journal of Abnormal Psychology, Review of Metaphysics*	**Author:** Professors, researchers, independent scholars **Angle of vision:** Scholarly advancement of knowledge; presentation of research findings; development of new theories and applications	• Not sold on magazine racks • No commercial advertising • Specialized academic style • Documentation and bibliography • Cover often has table of contents
PUBLIC AFFAIRS MAGAZINES • Commercial, "for-profit" presses • Manuscripts reviewed by editors • Examples: *Harper's, Commonweal, National Review*	**Author:** Staff writers, freelancers, scholars, for general audiences **Angle of vision:** Aims to deepen public understanding of issues; magazines often have political bias of left, center, or right	• Long, well-researched articles • Ads aimed at upscale professionals • Often has reviews of books, theater, film, and the arts
TRADE MAGAZINES • Commercial, "for-profit" presses • Focused on a profession or trade • Examples: *Advertising Age, Automotive Rebuilder, Farm Journal*	**Author:** Staff writers, industry specialists **Angle of vision:** Informative articles for practitioners; advocacy for the profession or trade	• Title indicating trade or profession • Articles on practical job concerns • Ads geared toward a particular trade or profession

TABLE 21.1 continued

Genre and Publisher	Author and Angle of Vision	How to Recognize Them
	Periodicals (continued)	
NEWSMAGAZINES AND NEWSPAPERS • Newspaper chains and publishers • Examples: *Time, Newsweek, Washington Post, Los Angeles Times*	**Author:** Staff writers and journalists; occasional freelance pieces **Angle of vision:** News reports aimed at balance and objectivity; editorial pages reflect perspective of editors; op-ed pieces reflect different perspectives	• Readily familiar by name, distinctive cover style • Widely available on newsstands and by subscription • Ads aimed at broad, general audience
POPULAR NICHE MAGAZINES • Large conglomerates or small presses with clear target audience • Focused on special interests of target audience • Examples: *Seventeen, People, TV Guide, Car and Driver, Golf Digest*	**Author:** Staff or freelance writers **Angle of vision:** Varies—in some cases content and point of view are dictated by advertisers or the politics of publisher	• Glossy paper, extensive ads, lots of visuals • Popular, often distinctive style • Short, undocumented articles • Credentials of writer often not mentioned

identifies contextual clues that will help you recognize what category a print source belongs to. Later in this chapter, when we discuss strategies for understanding the rhetoric of Web sites (Skill 5), we provide a similar "Rhetorical Overview of Web Sites" in Table 21.6 (p. 633). We suggest that you take a few moments now to peruse the information in these tables so that you can begin to appreciate the distinctions we are making among types of research sources.

Books Versus Periodicals Versus Web Sites

The simple physical differences among these three types of sources are obvious—books are substantial physical objects that libraries store on shelves. Magazines and scholarly journals—categorized together as periodicals—are similarly printed on paper and kept on library shelves, typically in bound volumes that combine a year's worth of issues. (*Periodical* indicates that a publication appears at regular intervals—that is, periodically, usually more often than once a year.) What's important to know as a researcher is that the contents of print publications are stable—in great contrast to materials published on Web sites, which might change hourly. If you work from print sources, you can be sure that others will be able to track down your sources for their own projects. Furthermore, print publications generally go through an editorial review process that helps ensure accuracy and reputability. In contrast, Web-only documents from individuals or small organizations may be unedited and thus unreliable. The stability and reputability of print sources is good, but the editing, fact-checking, shipping, and storage that make them possible all cost money. Furthermore, in a world of rapidly changing circumstances and ideas, periodicals and reference books are increasingly being published in electronic formats, sometimes in conjunction with paper issues, sometimes in electronic form only. These changes mean that when evaluating and citing sources, researchers must now pay attention to matters not even imagined just a decade ago. It used to be as obvious as the paper in front of you what kind of source you were using. Now, for students and faculty alike, the evidence of time well spent on research is an armload of downloaded printouts or photocopies. Does each of your sources have markers that show its origin? Was it photocopied from a print resource? Printed from a reference CD? Downloaded from a database? Printed from the Web (and if so, who wrote it when and why?). All these matters will impact the credibility of your sources as well as the citation formats you use to document these sources.

Details about licensed databases and how they differ from the Web are covered later in this chapter, pp. 617–620.

If you download and print material from a periodical that is unfamiliar to you, whether from a database or directly from the Web, be aware that you may lose important contextual clues about the author's purpose and angle of vision—clues that would be immediately apparent in the original journal or magazine through the table of contents, statement of editorial policy, or advertisements targeting specific audiences. (The increasing availability of *.pdf* or *portable document format* files, which reproduce the appearance of the original print page, makes understanding publication contexts much easier. When .pdf format is available, take advantage of it.) The more savvy you become at recognizing distinctions among different kinds of sources—especially electronic ones—the more you can read sources rhetorically and document them accurately.

Scholarly Books Versus Trade Books

Note in Table 21.1 the distinction between scholarly books, which are peer-reviewed and published by nonprofit academic presses, and trade books, which are published by for-profit presses with the intention of making money. By "peer review," which is a highly prized concept in academia, we mean the selection process by which scholarly manuscripts get chosen for publication. When manuscripts are submitted to an academic publisher, the editor sends them for independent review to experienced scholars who judge the rigor and accuracy of the research and the significance and value of the argument. The process is highly competitive and weeds out much shoddy or trivial work.

In contrast, trade books are not peer-reviewed by independent scholars. Instead, they are selected for publication by editors whose business is to make a profit. Fortunately, it can be profitable for popular presses to publish superbly researched and argued intellectual material because college-educated people, as lifelong learners, create a demand for intellectually satisfying trade books written for the general reader rather than for the highly specialized reader. These can be excellent sources for undergraduate research, but you need to separate the trash from the treasure. Trade books are aimed at many different audiences and market segments and can include sloppy, unreliable, and heavily biased material.

Scholarly Journals Versus Magazines
Like scholarly books, scholarly journals are academic, peer-reviewed publications. Although they may look like magazines, they almost never appear on news-stands; they are nonprofit publications subsidized by universities for disseminating high-level research and scholarship.

In contrast, magazines are intended to make a profit through sales and advertising revenues. Fortunately for researchers, a demand exists for intellectually satisfying magazines, just as for sophisticated trade books. Many for-profit magazines publish highly respectable, useful material for undergraduate or professional researchers, but many magazines publish shoddy material. As Table 21.1 shows, magazines fall into various categories aimed at different audiences.

Print Sources Versus Cyberspace Sources
Another crucial distinction exists between print sources and cyberspace sources. Much of what you can retrieve from a computer was originally published in print. What you download is simply an electronic copy of a print source, either from a library-leased database or from someone's Web site. (The next section shows you how to tell the difference.) In such cases, you often need to consider the article's original print origins for appropriate cues about its rhetorical context and purpose. But much cyberspace material, having never appeared in print, may never have undergone either peer review or editorial review. To distinguish between these two kinds of cyberspace sources, we call one kind a "print/cyberspace source" (something that has appeared in print and is made available on the Web or through library-leased databases) and the other a "cyberspace-only source." When you use a cyberspace-only source, you've got to take special care in figuring out who wrote it, why, and for what audience. Also, you need to document cyberspace-only material differently from print material retrieved electronically.

For Writing and Discussion

Your instructor will bring to class a variety of sources—different kinds of books, scholarly journals, magazines, and downloaded material. Working individually or in small groups, try to decide which category in Table 21.1 each piece belongs to. Be prepared to justify your decisions on the basis of the cues you used to make your decision.

Skill 3: Use Purposeful Strategies for Searching Libraries, Databases, and Web Sites

In the previous section, we explained differences among the kinds of sources you may encounter in a research project. In this section, we explain how to find these sources by using your campus library's online catalog (for locating books and other library resources, including paper copies of periodicals), library-leased electronic databases (for finding articles in journals and magazines), and Web search engines for finding material on the World Wide Web.

Perusing Your Library's Homepage

We begin by focusing on the specialized resources provided by your campus library. Your starting place and best initial research tool will be your campus library's homepage. This portal will lead you to two important resources: (1) the library's online catalog and (2) direct links to the periodicals and reference databases leased by the library. Here you will find indexes to a wide range of articles in journals and magazines and direct access to frequently used reference materials, including statistical abstracts, biographies, dictionaries, and encyclopedias. Furthermore, many academic library sites post lists of good research starting points, organized by discipline, including Web sites librarians have screened.

In addition to perusing your library's home page, make a personal visit to your library to learn its features and especially to note the location of a researcher's best friend and resource: the reference desk. Make use of reference librarians—they are there to help you.

Finding Books: Searching Your Library's Online Catalog

Your library's holdings are listed in its online catalog. Most of the entries are for books, but an academic library also has a wealth of other resources such as periodical collections, government records and reports, newspapers, video and audio recordings, maps, encyclopedias, and hundreds of specialized reference works that your reference librarian can help you use.

Indexed by subject, title, and author, the online catalog gives you titles of books and other library-owned resources relevant to your research area. Note that the catalog lists the titles of journals and magazines in the library's periodical collection (for example, *Journal of Abnormal Psychology, Atlantic Monthly*), but does *not* list the titles of individual articles within these periodicals. As we explain later in this section, you can search the contents of periodicals by using a licensed database. Methods of accessing and using online catalogs vary from institution to institution, so you'll need to learn the specifics of your library's catalog through direct experience.

Subject Searches Versus Keyword Searches

At the start of a research project, before researchers know the names of specific authors or book titles, they typically search by subject or by keywords. Your own research process will be speedier if you understand the difference between these kinds of searches.

- *Subject searches.* Subject searches use predetermined categories published in the reference work *Library of Congress Subject Headings*. This work informs you that, for example, material on "street people" would be classified under the heading "homeless persons." If the words you use for a subject search don't yield results, seek help from a librarian, who can show you how to use the subject heading guide to find the best word or phrase.

- *Keyword searches.* Keyword searches are not based on predetermined subject categories. Rather, the computer locates the keywords you provide in titles, abstracts, introductions, and sometimes bodies of text. Keyword searches in online catalogs are usually limited to finding words and phrases in titles. We explain more about keyword searches in the upcoming section on using licensed databases, whose search engines look for keywords in bodies of text as well as in titles.

Learning Your Library's Shelving System

With a little experience you will find yourself efficiently jotting down call numbers and following wall or elevator signs to locate what you need within your library's shelving system. Most college and university libraries use the Library of Congress classification system, but some may have an older section organized by the Dewey Decimal System, which is often used in public libraries. When you are looking for a periodical, you will need to consult the "location" notes on a catalog entry so that you can determine where your library shelves its scholarly journals and magazines.

Finding Print Articles: Searching a Licensed Database

For many research projects, useful sources are print articles from your library's periodical collection, including scholarly journals, public affairs magazines, newspapers or newsmagazines, and niche magazines related to your research area. Some of these articles are available through the free-access portions of the World Wide Web, but many of them are not. Rather, they may be located physically in your library's periodical collection (or in that of another library and available through interlibrary loan) or located electronically in vast databases leased by your library.

What Is a Licensed Database?

Electronic databases of periodical sources are produced by for-profit companies that index articles in thousands of periodicals and construct engines that can search the database by author, title, subject, keyword, date, genre, and other characteristics. In most cases the database contains an abstract of each article, and in many cases it contains the complete text of the article that you can download and print. These databases are referred to by several different generic names: "licensed databases" (our preferred term), "periodicals databases," or "subscription services." Because access to these databases is restricted to fee-paying customers, they can't be searched through Web engines like Yahoo! or Google. Most university libraries allow students to access these databases from a remote computer by using a password. You can therefore use the Internet to connect your computer to licensed databases as well as to the World Wide Web (see Figure 21.1).

Although the methods of accessing licensed databases vary from institution to institution, we can offer some widely applicable guidelines. Most likely your library has online one or more of the following databases:

FIGURE 21.1 Licensed Database Versus Free-Access Portions of Internet

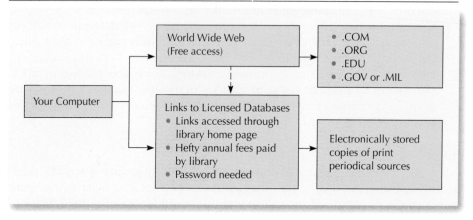

- *EBSCOhost:* Includes citations and abstracts from journals in most disciplines as well as many full-text articles from thousands of journals.
- *ProQuest:* Gives access to full text of articles from magazines and journals in many subject areas; may include full-text articles from newspapers.
- *FirstSearch Databases:* Incorporates multiple specialized databases in many subject areas, including WorldCat, which contains records of books, periodicals, and multimedia formats from libraries worldwide.
- *Lexis-Nexis Academic Universe:* Is primarily a full-text database covering current events, business and financial news; includes company profiles and legal, medical and reference information.
- *JSTOR:* Offers full text of scholarly journal articles across many disciplines; you can limit searches to specific disciplines.

MLA and APA formats for citing information and texts retrieved from licensed electronic databases are presented in Chapter 22, pp. 666 (MLA) and 691 (APA).

Given the variability of these and many other resources, we once again refer you to your campus library's Web site and the librarians at the reference desk (who often answer questions by e-mail). There you will find the best advice about where to look for what. Then, when you decide to use a specific source for your research project, be sure to include in your notes the names of both the database and the database company because, as we explain in the next chapter, you will need to include that information when you cite your sources.

More on Keyword Searching

To use an online database, you need to be adept at keyword searching, which we introduced on page 617. When you type a word or phrase into a search box, the computer will find sources that contain the same words or phrases. If you want the computer to search for a phrase, put it in quotation marks. Thus if you type *"street people"* using quotation marks, the computer will search for those two words occurring together. If you type in *street people* without quotation marks, the computer will look for the word *street* and the word *people* occurring in the same document but not necessarily together. Use your imagination to try a number of

TABLE 21.2 Boolean Search Commands

Command and Function	Research Example	What to Type	Search Result
X OR Y (Expands your search	You are researching Barbie dolls and decide to include G.I. Joe figures.	"Barbie doll" OR "G.I. Joe"	Articles that contain either phrase
X AND Y (Narrows your search)	You are researching the psychological effects of Barbie dolls and are getting too many hits under *Barbie dolls*.	"Barbie dolls" AND psychology	Articles that include both the phrase "Barbie dolls" and the word *psychology*
X NOT Y (Limits your search)	You are researching girls' toys and are tired of reading about Barbie dolls. You want to look at other popular girls' toys.	"girl toys" NOT Barbie	Articles that include the phrase "girl toys" but exclude *Barbie*

related terms. If you are researching gendered toys and you get too many hits using the keywords *toys,* try *gender toys, Barbie, G.I. Joe, girl toys, boy toys, toys psychology,* and so forth. You can increase the flexibility of your searches by using Boolean terms to expand, narrow, or limit your search (see Table 21.2 for an explanation of Boolean searches).

Illustration of a Database Search

As an illustration, Figure 21.2 shows a screen from the Results List for a search under the keywords *school violence AND "metal detectors"* in the database EBSCOhost. In the third column, the appearance of a page icon followed by "Full Text" (for example, Records 2 and 3) indicates that the full text of the article is available on the database. The line marked "**Note**" under each entry indicates whether your particular library subscribes to the magazine or journal. If you click on a specific article in the Results list, you will get a full display page showing complete publication data about that article. Figure 21.3 shows a full display page for the fifth article, "Girl's Slaying Elicits Calls for Metal Detectors." This page provides an abstract of the article—useful for helping you decide whether you want to read the entire text. But note that the article is only three-quarters of a page long (one column), indicating that it won't give you an in-depth discussion. Note also that a box at the top of the page lets you refine the search. With a little practice you will learn how to limit the search in useful ways—either by asking only for articles in peer-reviewed journals or only for articles of certain lengths.

After you've identified articles you'd like to read, locate physically all those available in your library's periodical collection. (This way you won't lose important contextual cues for reading them rhetorically.) For those unavailable in your library, print them from the database, if possible, or order them from interlibrary loan.

FIGURE 21.2 Sample Results List from a Search Using EBSCOhost

Record	Mark	Select Result For More Detail
1.	☐	*Schools* Get the Sales Pitch: Better Safe Than Sorry. By: Walsh, Mark; Education Week, 03/21/2001, Vol. 20 Issue 27, p8, 1p, 1c **Note:** Lemieux Library Subscribes to this title
2.	☐	Using Students as *Metal Detectors* . By: Reno, Jamie; Smalley, Suzanne; Figueroa, Ana; Rogers, Adam; Newsweek, 03/19/2001, Vol. 137 Issue 12, p28, 2p, 1c **Note:** Lemieux Library Subscribes to this title 📄 Full Text
3.	☐	Searching for Safe *Schools* : Legal Issues in the Prevention of *School Violence* . By: Yell, Mitchell L.; Rozalski, Michael E.; Journal of Emotional & Behavioral Disorders, Fall2000, Vol. 8 Issue 3, p187, 10p, 3 charts **Note:** This title is not held locally 📄 Full Text
4.	☐	House Unit Approves *School* Safety Grants. (cover story) By: Rigsby, Deborah; Nation's Cities Weekly, 06/05/2000, Vol. 23 Issue 22, p1, 1/6p **Note:** This title is not held locally
5.	☐	Girl's Slaying Elicits Calls for *Metal Detectors* . By: Portner, Jessica; Education Week, 03/15/2000, Vol. 19 Issue 27, p3, 3/4p, 1 graph, 1c **Note:** Lemieux Library Subscribes to this title

Finding Cyberspace Sources: Searching the World Wide Web

Another valuable resource is the World Wide Web. Before we offer suggestions for searching the Web, we need to explain in more detail the logic of the Internet—the difference between restricted portions of the Internet, such as licensed databases, and the amorphous, ever-changing, "free-access" portion, commonly called the "World Wide Web" (see again Figure 21.1).

The Logic of the Internet

To understand the logic of Web search engines, you need to know that the Internet is divided into restricted sections open only to those with special access rights and a "free-access" section. Web engines such as Yahoo! or Google search only the free-access portion of the Internet. When you type keywords into a Web search engine, it searches for matches in material made available on the Web by all the users of the world's network of computers—government agencies, corporations, advocacy groups, information services, individuals with their own Web sites, and many others.

The following example will quickly show you the difference between a licensed database search and a Web search. When we entered the keywords *school violence AND "metal detectors"* into EBSCOhost, we received twenty-two "hits"—the titles of twenty-two recent articles on the subject of metal detectors in schools (see Figure 21.2). In contrast, when we entered the same keywords into the Web search engine AltaVista, we received 5,934 hits—all the files available to AltaVista that had the words *school, violence,* and *metal detectors* appearing somewhere in the file.

FIGURE 21.3 Sample Full Display for an Article on EBSCOhost

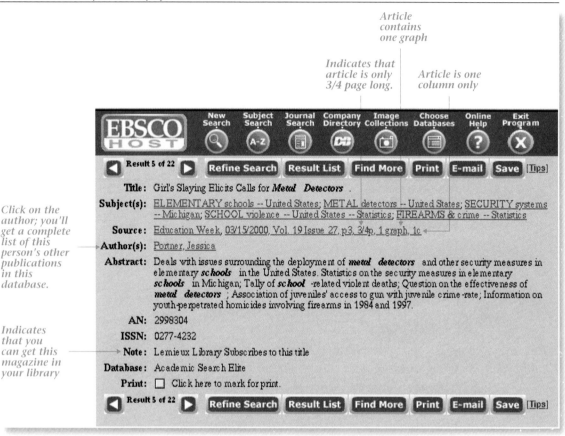

When we plugged the same words into Google, we received 11,400 hits, but none of the first ten hits from AltaVista matched the first ten hits from Google.

For Writing and Class Discussion

Figure 21.4 shows the first screen of hits for the keywords *school violence AND "metal detectors"* retrieved by the search engine AltaVista. Working in small groups or as a whole class, compare these items with those retrieved from the equivalent search using the licensed database EBSCOhost (Figure 21.2). Using just the results that appear on each of the screens, try to predict what you would find in the full article or on the full site. Then explain in your own words why the results for the Web searches are different from the licensed database search.

Questions for reading potential sources rhetorically and evaluating their usefulness for your projects are discussed in the next section of this chapter.

FIGURE 21.4 First Screen of Hits from AltaVista

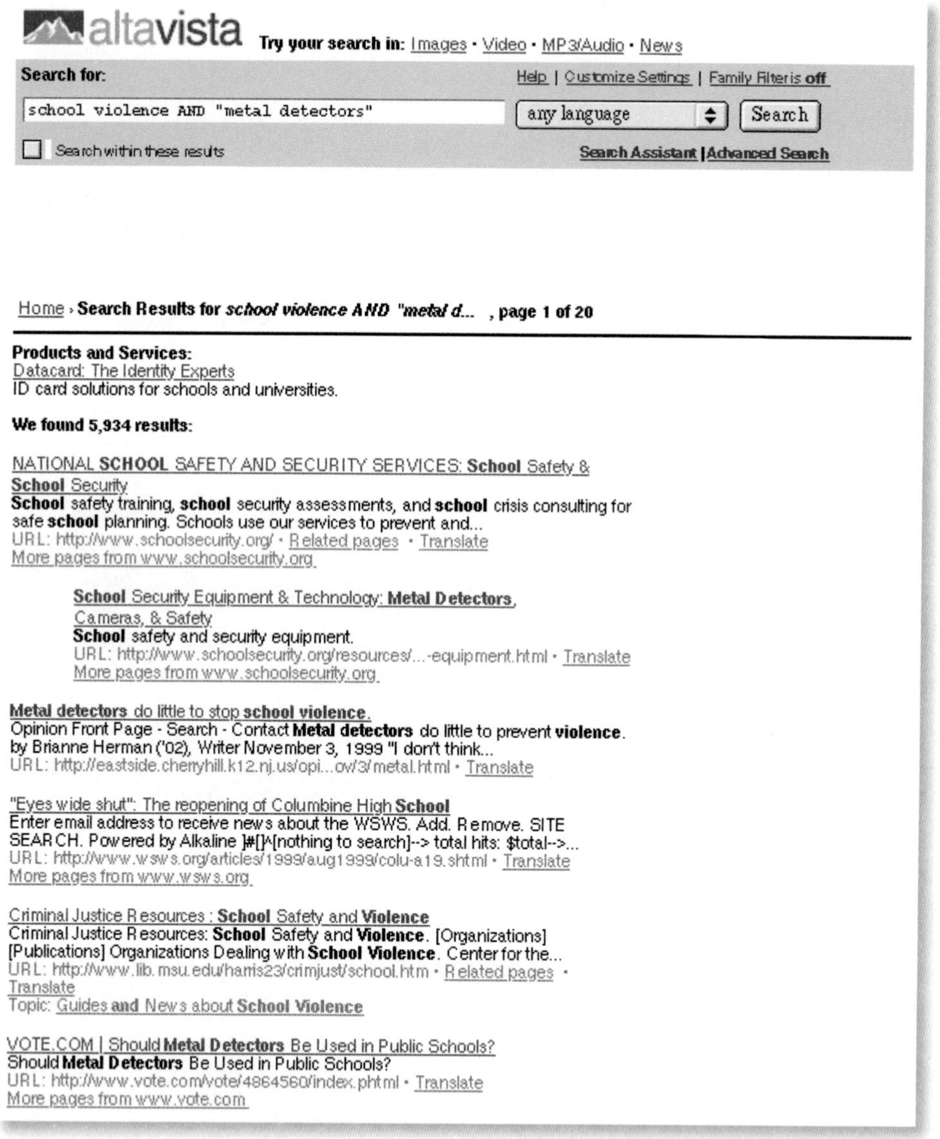

Using Web Search Engines

Although the hits you receive from a Web search frequently include useless, shoddy, trivial, or irrelevant material, the Web's resources for researchers are breathtaking. At your fingertips you have access to government documents and statistics, legislative and corporate white papers, court cases, persuasive appeals of advocacy groups, consumer information—the list is almost endless.

The World Wide Web can be searched by a variety of engines that collect and categorize individual Web files and search them for keywords. Most of these engines will find not only text files but also graphic, audio, and video files. Different engines search the Web in different ways, so it is important that you try a variety of search engines when you look for information. For example, a recent service offered by Google is "Google Scholar," with which you can limit a Web search to academic or scholarly sources. (But you will still need to turn to your library's collection or licensed databases for a full text of the source.) On campus, reference librarians and disciplinary experts can give you good advice about what has worked well in the past for particular kinds of searches. On the Web, an additional resource is NoodleTools.com, which offers lots of good advice for choosing the best search engine. (See the link "Choose the Best Search for Your Information Need.")

Determining Where You Are on the Web

As you browse the Web looking for resources, clicking from link to link, try to figure out what site you are actually in at any given moment. This information is crucial, both for properly documenting a Web source and for reading the source rhetorically.

To know where you are on the Web, begin by recognizing typical designations for home pages. A typical home page URL (universal resource locator) looks like this:

www.monash.com (home page of Monash, Inc., an information technology firm)

www.avma.org (home page of the American Veterinary Medical Association)

www.usdoj.gov (home page of the U.S. Department of Justice)

The site designer then creates hyperlinks that branch off the home page. Each hyperlink opens a new file, which is identified by the home page URL followed by extension codes that are separated by slashes. The generic structure of a typical URL looks like this: http://www.servername.domain/directory/subdirectory/filename.filetype

Here is a specific example, the URL for the NINDS (National Institute of Neurological Disorders and Stroke) Cerebral Aneurysm Information Page:

Stands for "hypertext transfer protocol"

Server name (NINDS is part of the National Institutes of Health)

Domain type   *Directory & Subdirectory*   *File name*   *File type*

http://www.ninds.nih.gov/health_and_medical/disorders/ceraneur_doc.htm

In some URLs, the domain name will be followed by an abbreviation signaling that the Web site is located in a country other than the United States, as in this URL for the home page of the National Institute for Research Advancement in Japan:

Country abbreviation

http://www.nira.go.jp

When you click on a link in one site, you may be sent to a totally different site. To determine the home page of this new site, simply note the root URL immediately following the "www."* To view the home page directly, delete the codes to the right of the initial home page URL in your computer's location window and hit Enter. You will then be linked directly to the site's home page, where you may be able to find an "About" link through which you can gather information about the purpose and sponsors of the page. As we discuss later in this chapter and in Chapter 22, being able to examine a site's home page helps you read the site rhetorically and document it properly.

Skill 4: Use Rhetorical Knowledge to Read and Evaluate Sources

Now that you know expert strategies for searching library catalogs, licensed databases, and the Web, we turn in this section to strategies for reading and evaluating sources. Specifically, we focus on reading sources rhetorically, taking useful and efficient notes, and evaluating sources for credibility and bias.

Reading Your Sources Rhetorically

Even when you have a research question that interests you, it's easy to feel overwhelmed when you return from a library with a stack of books and magazine or journal articles. How do you begin reading all this material? There is no one right answer to this question. At times you need to read slowly with analytical closeness, as we discussed in Chapter 6. At other times you can skim a source, looking only for its gist or for a needed piece of information.

See our discussion of Leigh's process on pp. 610–611. See also his exploratory paper on pp. 197–202.

Reading with Your Own Goals in Mind
How you read a source depends to a certain extent on where you are in the research process. Early in the process, when you are in the thesis-seeking, exploratory stage, your goal is to achieve a basic understanding about your

---

*Not all URLs begin with "www" after the first set of double slashes. Our description doesn't include variations from the most typical URL types. You can generally find the home page of a site by eliminating all codes to the right of the first slash mark after the domain or country name.

research problem. You need to become aware of different points of view, learn what is unknown or controversial about your research question, see what values or assumptions are in conflict, and build up your store of background knowledge. As we saw in the case of Christopher Leigh, your initial research question often evolves as your knowledge increases and your interests shift.

Given these goals, at the early stages of research you should select, where possible, easy-to-read, overview kinds of sources to get you into the conversation. In some cases, even an encyclopedia or specialized reference work can be a good start for getting general background.

As you get deeper into your research, your questions become more focused, and the sources you read become more specialized. Once you formulate a thesis and plan a structure for your paper, you can determine more clearly the sources you need and read them with purpose and direction. For example, after Christopher Leigh decided to argue against metal detectors in the schools, he knew that he needed to find research sources in three different areas:

- Arguments in favor of metal detectors (He knew he would need to summarize opposing views and respond in some way to their arguments.)
- Testimony, data, research studies, and other information that would help him support his own case against metal detectors
- Ideas and supporting data for ways of reducing school violence other than metal detectors

Reading with Rhetorical Awareness

To read your sources rhetorically, you should keep two basic questions in mind: (1) What was the source author's purpose in writing this piece?; and (2) What might be my purpose in using this piece? Table 21.3 sums up the kinds of questions a rhetorical reader typically considers.

This chart reinforces a point we've made throughout this text: All writing is produced from an angle of vision that privileges some ways of seeing and filters out other ways. You should guard against reading your sources as if they present hard, undisputed facts or universal truths. For example, if one of your sources says that "Saint-John's-wort [an herb] has been shown to be an effective treatment for depression," some of your readers might accept that statement as fact; but many wouldn't. Skeptical readers would want to know who the author is, where his views have been published, and what he uses for evidence. Let's say the author is someone named Samuel Jones. Skeptical readers would ask whether Jones is relying on published research, and if so, whether the studies have been peer-reviewed in reputable, scholarly journals and whether the research has been replicated by other scientists. They would also want to know whether Jones has financial connections to companies that produce herbal remedies and supplements. Rather than settling the question about Saint-John's-wort as a treatment for depression, a quotation from Jones might open up a heated controversy about medical research.

Reading rhetorically is thus a way of thinking critically about your sources. It influences the way you take notes, evaluate sources, and shape your argument.

TABLE 21.3 Questions Asked by Rhetorical Readers

What was the source author's purpose in writing this piece?	What might be my purpose in using this piece in my own argument?

• Who is this author? What are his or her credentials and affiliations?
• What audience was this person addressing?
• What is the genre of this piece? (If you downloaded the piece from the World Wide Web, did it originally appear in print?)
• If this piece appeared in print, what are the reputation and bias of the journal, magazine, or press? Was the piece peer-reviewed?
• If this piece appeared only on the Web, who or what organization sponsors the Web site (check the home page)? What are the reputation and bias of the sponsor?
• What is the author's thesis or purpose?
• How does this author try to change his or her audience's view?
• What is this writer's angle of vision or bias?
• What is omitted or censored from this text?
• How reliable and credible is this author?
• What facts, data, and other evidence does this author use and what are the sources of these data?
• What are this author's underlying values, assumptions, and beliefs?
	• How has this piece influenced or complicated my own thinking?
	• How does this piece relate to my research question?
	• How will my own intended audience react to this author?
	• How might I use this piece in my own argument?
	   ◦ Is it an opposing view that I might summarize?
	   ◦ Is it an alternative point of view that I might compare to other points of view?
	   ◦ Does it have facts and data that I might use?
	   ◦ Would a summary of all or part of this argument support or oppose one or more of my own points?
	   ◦ Could I use this author for testimony? (If so, how should I indicate this author's credentials?)
	   ◦ If I use this source, will I need to acknowledge the author's bias and angle of vision?

Taking Effective Notes

Taking good research notes serves two functions: First, it encourages you to read actively because you must summarize your sources' arguments, record usable information, and extract short quotations. Second, taking notes encourages you to do exploratory thinking—to write down ideas as they occur to you, to analyze sources as you read them, and to join your sources in conversation.

Double-entry research notes are explained on p. 210; for an example of double-entry note taking, see pp. 212–213.

There are many ways to take notes, but we can offer several techniques that have worked especially well for other writers. First of all, you can try using a dialectic or double-entry journal. Divide a page in half; enter your informational notes on one side and your exploratory writing on the other. Another system is to record notes on index cards or in a computer file and then write out your exploratory thinking in a separate research journal. Still another method is to record informational notes on your computer in a regular font and then to use a boldfaced font for exploratory writing. Your objective here is to create a visual way to distinguish your informational notes from your exploratory thinking.

A common practice of beginning researchers—one that experienced researchers almost never use—is *not* taking notes as they read and *not* doing any exploratory writing. We've seen students photocopy a dozen or more articles, but then write nothing as they read (sometimes they highlight passages with a marker), planning to rely later on memory to navigate through the sources. This practice reduces your ability to synthesize your sources and create your argument. When you begin drafting your paper, you'll have no notes to refer to, no record of your thinking-in-progress. Your only recourse is to revisit all your sources, thumbing through them one at a time—a practice that leads to passive cutting and pasting.

To make your notes purposeful, you need to imagine how a given source might be used in your research paper. Table 21.4 shows how notes are a function of your purpose.

When you use a source's exact words, be meticulous in copying them exactly and marking the quoted passage with prominent quotation marks. If you record information without directly quoting it, be sure that you restate it completely in your own words to avoid later problems with plagiarism. Next, check that you have all the bibliographic information you need for a citation, including the page numbers for each entry in your notes. (Citing page numbers for articles downloaded from the Web or a licensed database is problematic—see Chapter 22, p. 669.)

For a discussion of plagiarism, see Chapter 22, pp. 656–657.

TABLE 21.4 Note Taking According to Purpose

How Source Might Be Used in Your Paper	Notes to Take
Background information about research problem or issue	Summarize the information; record specific data.
Part of a section reviewing different points of view on your question	Summarize the source's argument; note its bias and perspective. In exploratory notes, jot down ideas on how and why different sources disagree.
As an opposing view that you must summarize and respond to	Summarize the argument fully and fairly. In exploratory notes, speculate about why you disagree with the source and whether you can refute the argument, concede to it, or compromise with it.
As data, information, or testimony to be used as evidence to support your thesis	Record the data or information; summarize or paraphrase the supporting argument with occasional quotations of key phrases; directly quote short passages for supporting testimony; note the credentials of the writer or person quoted. In exploratory notes, record new ideas as they occur to you.
As data, information, or testimony that counters your position or raises doubts about your thesis	Take notes on counterevidence. In exploratory notes, speculate on how you might respond to the counterevidence.

Evaluating Sources

When you read sources for your research project, you need to evaluate them as you go along. As you read each potential source, ask yourself questions about the author's reliability, credibility, angle of vision, and degree of advocacy.

Reliability

"Reliability" refers to the accuracy of factual data in a source as determined by external validation. If you check a writer's "facts" against other sources, do you find that the facts are correct? Does the writer distort facts, take them out of context, or otherwise use them unreasonably? In some controversies, key data are highly disputed—for example, the number of homeless people in the United States, the frequency of date rape, or the risk factors for many diseases. A reliable writer acknowledges these controversies and doesn't treat disputed data as fact. Furthermore, if you check out the sources used by a reliable writer, they'll reveal accurate and careful research—respected primary sources rather than hearsay or secondhand reports. Journalists of reputable newspapers (not tabloids) pride themselves in meticulously checking out their facts, as do editors of serious popular magazines. Editing is often minimal for Web sources, however, and they can be notoriously unreliable. As you gain knowledge of your research question, you'll develop a good ear for writers who play fast and loose with data.

Credibility

"Credibility" is synonymous with the classical term *ethos*. See pp. 79 and 408–409.

"Credibility" is similar to "reliability" but is based on internal rather than external factors. It refers to the reader's trust in the writer's honesty, goodwill, and trustworthiness and is apparent in the writer's tone, reasonableness, fairness in summarizing opposing views, and respect for different perspectives. Audiences differ in how much credibility they will grant to certain authors. Nevertheless a writer can achieve a reputation for credibility, even among bitter political opponents, by applying to issues a sense of moral courage, integrity, and consistency of principle.

Angle of Vision

The concept of "angle of vision" was first introduced in Chapter 4, pp. 80–82. See also Chapter 5, which is devoted to a fuller analysis of angle of vision, and Chapter 6, which shows how an analysis of angle of vision helps you read a text with and against the grain.

How to analyze a writer's underlying assumptions is discussed in Chapter 6; the role of assumptions in argument is discussed in Chapter 14.

By "angle of vision," we mean the way that a piece of writing gets shaped by the underlying values, assumptions, and beliefs of its author, resulting in a text that reflects a certain perspective, worldview, or belief system. A text's angle of vision becomes apparent through both internal and external factors. Internally, factors such as the author's word choices (especially notice the connotations of words), selection and omission of details, figurative language, and grammatical emphasis combine with overt statements to reveal angle of vision. Of paramount importance are the assumptions that the writer assumes his or her readers will share. Externally, the politics and reputation of the author, along with the genre, market niche, and political reputation of the publication in which the material appears, will also provide useful clues about a writer's angle of vision and about the audience to whom she or he hopes to appeal and persuade.

To get at these external factors when you are evaluating a source, it is important to consider the writer's credentials, including any biographical information, which is often presented at the end of articles. Is the writer affiliated with an advocacy group or known for a certain ideology? (If you want more information about an author, try typing the author's name into a Web search engine. You will probably discover useful facts about her or his reputation and other publications.) Also note publishing data. If the source is an article, did it appear in a peer reviewed scholarly journal or in a for-profit magazine or newspaper? What is the publication's reputation and editorial slant?

Your awareness of angle of vision is especially important if you are doing research on contemporary cultural or political issues. In Table 21.5, we have categorized some well-known political commentators, publications, and policy research institutes (commonly known as *think tanks*) across the political spectrum from left/liberal to right/conservative.

Although the terms *liberal* and *conservative* or *left* and *right* often have fuzzy meanings, they provide a convenient shorthand for signaling a person's overall political stance or for pigeon-holing opponents. (The "left" and "right" labels originated as references to the seating arrangements for radicals, who sat on the left, and nobility, who sat on the right, in the French National Assembly at the time of the French Revolution.) In the contemporary United States, "left–right" identities provide insight into views about the proper role of government in relation to the economy and social values. Liberals, tending to sympathize with labor and environmentalists, are typically comfortable with government regulation of economic matters while conservatives, who tend to sympathize with business interests, typically assert faith in free markets and favor a limited regulatory role for government. Some conservatives identify themselves as economic conservatives but social liberals; others side with workers' interests on many issues but are conservative on social issues. Social conservatives espouse traditional family values and advocate laws that would maintain these values (for example, a Constitutional amendment limiting marriage to a bond between a man and a woman). Liberals, on the other hand, tend to espouse individual choice regarding marital partnerships, abortion rights, and a wide range of other issues. Some issues will inevitably confound the distinction between liberals and conservatives. For example, in debates over immigration laws, liberals and conservatives have both found themselves agreeing with former opponents and clashing with former allies. Advocates for relatively open borders include liberals interested in protecting civil rights and conservatives interested in increasing the pool of low cost labor. Meanwhile, their opposition includes liberals concerned about protecting organized labor and conservatives who oppose increased government spending for bilingual education and health care. Also, many persons regard themselves as "centrists." In Table 21.5 the column labeled "Center" includes commentators who seek out common ground between the left and the right and who often believe that the best civic decisions are compromises between opposing views. Likewise, centrist publications and institutes often approach issues from multiple points of view, looking for the most workable solutions.

Degree of Advocacy

By "degree of advocacy" we mean the extent to which an author unabashedly takes a persuasive stance on a contested position as opposed to adopting a more neutral, objective, or exploratory stance. For example, publications affiliated with advocacy organizations (the Sierra Club, the National Rifle Association) will have

TABLE 21.5 Angles of Vision in U.S. Media and Think Tanks: A Sampling Across the Political Spectrum[1]

Commentators				
Left	**Left Center**	**Center**	**Right Center**	**Right**
Barbara Ehrenreich	E. J. Dionne	David Broder	David Brooks	Pat Buchanan
Al Franken	Ellen Goodman	Amitai Etzioni	Midge Decter	Tucker Carlson
Bob Herbert	Nicholas Kristof	Thomas Friedman	William Kristol	Linda Chavez
Molly Ivins	William Raspberry	Kathleen Hall Jamieson	William Safire	Ann Coulter
Michael Moore	Mark Shields	Kevin Phillips	Andrew Sullivan	John Leo
Bill Moyers	Fareed Zakaria	Leonard Pitts	George Will	Rush Limbaugh
Salim Muwakkil		William Saletan		Bill O'Reilly
Daniel Schorr		Bob Woodward		Kathleen Parker
Gloria Steinem				Cal Thomas

Newspapers and Magazines[2]		
Left/Liberal	**Center**	**Right/Conservative**
The American Prospect	*Atlantic Monthly*	*American Enterprise*
Harper's	*Business Week*	*American Spectator*
Los Angeles Times	*Christian Science Monitor*	*Reader's Digest*
Mother Jones	*Commentary*	*Fortune*
The Nation	*Commonweal*	*National Journal*
The New Yorker	*Foreign Affairs*	*National Review*
New York Times	*New Republic*	*Reason*
Salon	*Slate*	*Wall Street Journal*
Sojourners	*Washington Post*	*Washington Times*
Utne		*Weekly Standard*

Think Tanks		
Left/Liberal	**Center**	**Right/Conservative**
Center for Defense Information	The Brookings Institution	American Enterprise Institute
Center for Media and Democracy (sponsors *Disinfopedia.org*)	Carnegie Endowment for International Peace	Cato Institute (Libertarian)
Institute for Policy Studies	Council on Foreign Relations	Center for Strategic and International Studies
Institute for Women's Policy Research	Jamestown Foundation	Heritage Foundation (sponsors *Townhall.com*)
Open Society Institute (Soros Foundation)	National Bureau of Economic Research	Project for the New American Century
Urban Institute	Progressive Policy Institute	Rand Corporation

[1]*For further information about the political leanings of publications or think tanks, ask your librarian about* Gale Directory of Publications and Broadcast Media *or* NIRA World Directory of Think Tanks.

[2]*Newspapers are categorized according to positions they take on their editorial page; any reputable newspaper strives for objectivity in news reporting and includes a variety of views on its op-ed pages. Magazines do not claim and are not expected to present similar breadth and objectivity.*

a clear editorial bias. When a writer has an ax to grind, you need to weigh carefully the writer's selection of evidence, interpretation of data, and fairness to opposing views. Although no one can be completely neutral, it is always useful to seek
out authors who offer a balanced assessment of the evidence. Evidence from a

more detached and neutral writer may be more trusted by your readers than the arguments of a committed advocate. For example, if you want to persuade corporate executives on the dangers of global warming, evidence from scholarly journals may be more persuasive than evidence from an environmentalist Web site or from a freelance writer for a leftist popular magazine such as *Mother Jones*.

Skill 5: Understand the Rhetoric of Web Sites

In the previous section we focused on reading sources rhetorically by asking questions about a source's reliability, credibility, angle of vision, and degree of advocacy. In this section we turn to the skills of evaluating and using Web sources by understanding the special rhetoric of Web sites. The evaluation strategies we discussed in the previous section will also help you evaluate sources in the unique rhetorical environment of cyberspace.

The Web as a Unique Rhetorical Environment

The resources available on the World Wide Web are mind-boggling. Dozens of entertainment and commercial sites are no doubt familiar to you, but many people don't realize that Web sites can provide highly specialized data banks, historical archives, or scholarly portals useful for serious researchers. Some Web sites function like major research libraries. For example, without having to travel to Paris or Madrid, medieval historians can use Web portals to examine thousands of rare documents scanned into digital files, the originals of which are stored deep in European vaults.

But the Web is also a great vehicle for democracy, giving voice to the otherwise voiceless. Anyone with a cause and a rudimentary knowledge of Web design can create a site. Millions log on to their favorite blog nearly every day to share the minutia of their lives. For that matter, it's easy to download blogging software, register a link at your favorite blog portal, and become a political commentator or gossip columnist. Before the invention of the Web, people with a message had to stand on street corners passing out flyers or put money into newsletters or advocacy advertisements. The Web, in contrast, is cheap. The result is a rhetorical medium that differs in significant ways from print.

Consider, for example, the difference in the way writers attract readers. Magazines displayed on racks attract readers through interest-grabbing covers and teaser headlines inviting readers to look inside. Web sites, however, can't begin attracting readers until the readers have found them through links from another site or through a "hit" on a Web search. Research suggests that Web surfers stay connected to a site for no more than thirty seconds unless something immediately attracts their interest; moreover, they seldom scroll down to see the bottom of a page. The design of a home page—the arrangement and size of the print, the use of images and colors, the locations and labels of navigational buttons—must hook readers immediately and send a clear message about the purpose and contents of the site. If the home page is a confused jumble or simply a long, printed text, the average surfer will take one look and move on.

The biggest difference between the Web and print is the Web's hypertext structure. Users click from link to link rather than read linearly down the page. Users often "read" a Web page as a configuration of images and strategically arranged text that is interspersed with bullets, boxes, and hot links. Long stretches of straight text are effective only deep within a site where a user purposefully chooses to read something in a conventional, linear way.

Analyzing the Purpose of a Site

For instructions on how to find a site's home page, see pp. 623–624.

As a researcher, your first question when you arrive at a potentially useful Web site should be, Who placed this piece on the Web and why? You can begin answering this question by analyzing the site's home page, where you will often find navigational buttons linking to "Mission," "About Us," or other identifying information about the site's sponsors. You can also get hints about the site's purpose by asking, What kind of Web site is it? Different kinds of Web sites have different purposes, often revealed by the domain identifier following the server name (for example, .com, .net, .org, .edu, .gov, or .mil). Table 21.6, "A Rhetorical Overview of Web Sources," describes key rhetorical elements of different types of sites. Knowing who sponsors a site and analyzing the sponsor's purpose for creating the site will prepare you to read the site rhetorically. In the next section, we illustrate this process by examining the rhetoric of Web sites that address the issue of gun control and are aimed at women.

Reading Web Sites Rhetorically: An Illustration

To illustrate the rhetorical analysis of Web sites, we imagined ourselves as student researchers exploring the following research question: How are women represented and involved in the public controversy over gun control and Second Amendment rights? We launched our search by typing *"gun control" women* into Google. As we clicked on links from the first screen of our Google results, we began encountering a vigorous national conversation on gun control by women's groups and by traditionally male-dominated groups seeking support or membership from women.

Our next step was to analyze these sites rhetorically to understand the ways that women frame their interests and represent themselves on sites for or against gun control. We discovered that the angle of vision of each kind of site—whether pro–gun control or anti–gun control—filters evidence in distinctive ways. For example, women's groups advocating gun control emphasize accidental deaths from guns (particularly of children), suicides from easy access to guns, domestic violence turned deadly, guns in schools, and gun-related crime (particularly juvenile crime). In contrast, women's groups opposing gun control emphasize armed resistance to assaults and rapes, inadequate police responses to crime, the right of individuals to protect themselves and their families, and the Second Amendment right to keep and bear arms. (Women's anti–gun control sites often frame the gun control issue as pro-self-defense versus anti-self-defense.) We also noted that most of these sites make powerful use of visual elements—icons, colors (bright pink in

TABLE 21.6 A Rhetorical Overview of Web Sites

Type of Site	Author/Sponsor and Angle of Vision	Characteristics
.COM OR .BIZ (A COMMERCIAL SITE CREATED BY A BUSINESS OR CORPORATION)		
• Either of these suffixes signals a for-profit operation; this group includes major periodicals and publishers of reference materials • Purpose is to enhance image, attract customers, market products and services, provide customer service • Creators are paid by salary or fees and often motivated by desire to design innovative sites • Also in the business category: specialized suffixes .aero (for sties related to air travel), .pro (for professionals—doctors, lawyers, accountants)	**Author:** Difficult to identify individual writers; sponsoring company often considered the author **Angle of vision:** Purpose is to promote the point of view of the corporation or business; links are to sites that promote same values	• Links are often to other products and services provided by company • Photographs and other visuals used to enhance corporate image
.ORG (NONPROFIT ORGANIZATIONS OR ADVOCACY GROUPS)		
• Note: Sites with the ".museum" suffix have similar purposes and feel. • Sometimes purpose is to provide accurate, balanced information (for example, the American Red Cross site) • May function as a major information portal, such as NPR.org, PBS.org, a think tank, or a museum (for example, the Heritage Foundation, the Art Institute of Chicago, or the Museum of Modern Art) • Frequently, purpose is to advocate for or explain the organization (for example, the Ford Foundation or local charity sites); thus, advocacy for fund-raising or political views is likely (for example, Persons for the Ethical Treatment of Animals [PETA] site or blog portals [Cursor.org])	**Author:** Often hard to identify individual writers; sponsoring organization often considered the author; some sites produced by amateurs with passionate views; others produced by well-paid professionals **Angle of vision:** Purpose is to promote views of sponsoring organization and influence public opinion and policy; many encourage donations through the site	• Advocacy sites sometimes don't announce purpose on home page • You may enter a node of an advocacy site through a link from another site and not realize the political slant • Facts/data selected and filtered by site's angle of vision • Often uses visuals for emotional appeal
.EDU (AN EDUCATIONAL SITE ASSOCIATED WITH A COLLEGE OR UNIVERSITY)		
• Wide range of purposes • Home page aimed at attracting prospective students and donors • Inside the site are numerous subsites devoted to research, pedagogy, libraries, student employment, and so forth	**Author:** Professors, staff, students **Angle of vision:** Varies enormously from personal sites of professors and students to organizational sites of research centers and libraries; can vary from scholarly and objective to strong advocacy on issues	• Often an .edu site has numerous "subsites" sponsored by the university library, art programs, research units • Links to .pdf documents may make it difficult to determine where you are in the site—e.g., professor's course site, student site, administrative site

(*continued*)

TABLE 21.6 continued

Type of Site	Author/Sponsor and Angle of Vision	Characteristics
.GOV OR .MIL (SPONSORED BY GOVERNMENT AGENCIES OR MILITARY UNITS)		
• Provides enormous range of basic data about government policy, bills in Congress, economic forecasts, and so forth • Aims to create good public relations for agency or military unit	**Author:** Development teams employed by the agency; sponsoring agency is usually considered the author **Angle of vision:** Varies—informational sites publish data and government documents with an objective point of view; agency sites also promote agency's agenda—e.g., Dept. of Energy, Dept. of Labor	• Typical sites (for example, www.energy.gov, the site of the U.S. Dept. of Energy) are extremely layered and complex and provide hundreds of links to other sites • Valuable for research • Sites often promote values/assumptions of sponsoring agency
PERSONAL WEB SITES (.NAME OR .NET)		
• An individual contracts with server to publish the site; many personal Web sites have .edu affiliation • Promotes hobbies, politics; provides links according to personal preferences	**Author:** Anyone can create a personal Web site **Angle of vision:** Varies from person to person	• Credentials/bias of author often hard to determine • Irresponsible sites might have links to excellent sites; tracing links is complicated • Probably not designed for fast download
.INFO (INFORMATION PROVIDERS—UNRESTRICTED, SO BECOMING A CATCHALL)		
• Libraries and library information materials • Regulations, hours, procedures, resources from local governments (e.g., www.lowermanhattan.info) • Publicity brochures for local organizations (e.g., Celtic Heritage Society, hobby groups) • Consumer alerts • Lodging, restaurants, bike rental, hiking trails, or other travel advice from tourist bureaus • Privately authored materials	**Author:** Varies widely from small public and private offices with an information mandate to individuals or groups with an ax to grind **Angle of vision:** Varies from genuinely helpful (Where can bicycles be loaded onto the ferry?) to business motives (Where can you find books or movies about bicycles?) to thinly disguised advocacy (e.g., "Debunking the Myths about Gun Control")	• Makes some information easier to find through advanced searches that specify the domain type • If author is identified, credentials difficult to determine • Information will be filtered through author(s) and sponsor(s) • Quality of editing and fact-checking will vary

particular), and well-known symbols—to enhance their emotional appeals. For instance, anti–gun control sites often have patriotic themes with images of waving American flags, stern-eyed eagles, and colonial patriots with muskets. Pro–gun control sites often have pictures of children about to find a gun in Mommy's or Daddy's dresser drawer.

Most of the sites we examined tailor their appeals directly to women. We started our analysis with the site of the most well-known women's group advocating gun control—the Million Mom March (Figure 21.5). This page, like many others on both sides of the issue at the time, drew attention to the 1994 ban on assault weapons, which was set to expire on September 13, 2004, unless Congress renewed it. (Politically oriented Web sites change quickly, so as you read this, the current page undoubtedly emphasizes a different issue.) We were initially struck by the site's heavy use of pink, a perennially feminine color. As we considered the diverse but eye-catching images strewn across the busy page, we noted that they created an *ethos* of grassroots action, of women working together to protect children. From the verbal image of moms seeking "to halt the assault" by traveling cross-country in a "big pink rig" (a twenty-six-foot pink RV, we learned from the news clips) to the many opportunities for making the page interactive, this Web site was working harder at promoting specific action, and more types of action, than the others we studied. As you examine the page, note how the theme of grassroots action becomes explicit in the lower half. Note, too, how a change in color brings a change in mood in the bottom boxes, which link to more aggressive sites sponsored by "StoptheNRA.com."

A careful look at the list of links in the purple box near the bottom of the page reveals how the Million Mom March (MMM) has branded itself with connotations of motherhood. "Meet a mom," reads one of the links; "a million stories . . . ," offers another. In this homespun spirit, the organization gives a monthly award called "Mom's Apple Pie Award" to a person or organization that advances the cause of gun legislation. It also gives a "Time Out" award to individuals who set back the cause. (Note that these moms have time-outs rather than spankings.) A click on "About Us" took us to a history of the organization, which describes itself as "the nation's largest national, non-partisan, grassroots organization leading the fight to prevent gun violence . . . dedicated to creating an America free from gun violence." Its mission statement lists specific legislative actions that the MMM advocates and then closes with this memorable sentence: "With one loud voice, we will continue to cry out that we love our children more than the gun lobby loves its guns!"

At this point, we wondered: How do women who oppose gun control represent themselves? Do they also portray themselves as nurturing mothers or as something else? We invite you now to consider the Web sites of Women Against Gun Control (see p. 599) and the Northern Colorado Chapter of the Second Amendment Sisters (Fig. 21.6).

FIGURE 21.5 Million Mom March home page

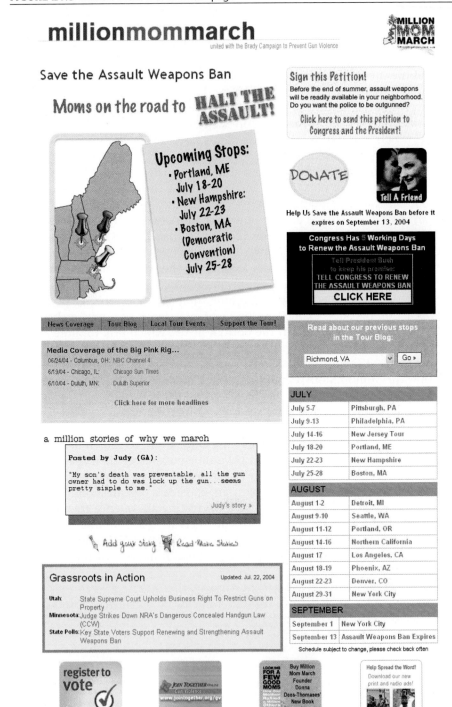

FIGURE 21.6 Home Page of Northern Colorado Chapter of Second Amendment Sisters

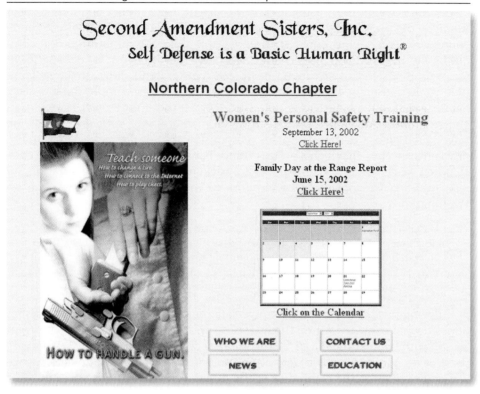

For Writing and Discussion

Working in small groups or as a whole class, try to reach consensus answers to the following questions about how these Web sites seek to draw in readers.

1. How are the visual images of women in each of these home pages different from that evoked by the Million Mom March page?
2. What images of women are conveyed in the "Teach someone . . . How to handle a gun" poster in the Second Amendment Sisters (SAS) page or the phrases "Ladies of High-Caliber" and "Let's Blow Holes in the Myth!" in the Women Against Gun Control page?
3. In the Women Against Gun Control (WAGC) page, what seems to be the Web designer's intention in the use of color, curved background lines, and images?
4. How do these pages use appeals to *ethos* and *pathos* as part of the argument they are making?

Appeals to *ethos* and *pathos* are discussed in Chapter 4, p. 79, and Chapter 14, pp. 408–410.

Now that you have had an opportunity to consider these sites, we offer our own rhetorical analysis. We were struck by the fact that both the Million Mom March and Northern Colorado SAS pages portray women as protectors of children, but in different ways. One projects the image of activist mothers for whom lobbying for gun control legislation is part of being a good parent. The other portrays combative mothers using firearms to defend their homes and families. For example, the photograph on the Northern Colorado SAS Web page of the gentle young girl being taught how to handle a pistol argues by implication that combining motherhood and guns is not unnatural—that it is, indeed, necessary. On the Web site itself, this picture is one of four that rotate to show attractive, feminine women, usually with children, handling guns. A fifth simply shows a sleek handbag with bullets next to it, and asks, "My Mother Can Protect Herself. Can Yours?" Another caption reads, "A Strong Woman and Well-Armed. Her Kids Are Safe." "In Defense of Family Values. Responsible People Protect Their Family," proclaims another, in which a mother stands behind a teenage son holding a rifle.

When we clicked on "Who We Are" for background about the organization, we read that SAS was organized in response to the first Million Mom March on Washington:

> SECOND AMENDMENT SISTERS Inc. was founded in 1999 by five women who got together on the internet. . . . [because] they didn't want the anti-rights Million Mom March to speak for them. [These founding sisters made] a powerful statement on May 12, 2000—that there were women to whom the Second Amendment meant something, and to whom "gun control" was a false promise.

Knowing this history helped us appreciate the extent to which many Web sites opposing gun control position themselves against the Million Mom March organization with competing images as well as messages. On the days we were studying these pages, for example, we were not surprised to see that the national SAS page was advocating for the expiration of the assault weapons ban as strenuously as the Million Mom March page was advocating for its renewal.

When we looked at the Women Against Gun Control home page, we noticed that it, too, talks back to the Million Mom March activists and takes ironic delight in antagonizing feminists. Its bold, pink colors and provocatively curved lines use traditional symbols of coy seductiveness to create an in-your-face, Annie Oakley-style message: This gun-toting cowgirl won't take any guff. The messages are complex: Women can be sexy and feminine while simultaneously being powerful and independent if they own and carry a gun. The language in the home page is vigorous and powerful, associating women with self-defense and protection of Second Amendment rights. This home page purports to "BLOW HOLES" in the myth that all women support gun control. Instead, these women seek, through guns, "a fighting chance against crime" and yell "STOP OR I'LL SHOOT" at burglars. The statistic next to the Annie Oakley figure says that "guns are used defensively 2.5 million times per year"—a factoid evidently meant to startle the reader into getting a gun for self-defense. The gritty realism of these no-nonsense women is brought out in the caption at the bottom of the home page:

> Gun Control: The theory that a woman found dead in an alley, raped and strangled with her panty hose, is somehow morally superior to a woman explaining to police how her attacker got that fatal bullet wound.

Whereas the home page of the Million Mom March site ends with defiant links to "Stop the NRA" Web sites, the WAGC home page ends with the verbal image of a raped woman dead in the street (an implied consequence of gun control) versus the image of a heroic woman shooting an assailant dead (the implied consequence of empowering women with guns). These sites are in conversation both with gun control sites and with feminist sites—redefining the gun-carrying woman as defiant, sexy, and independent, and yet protective of the family.

Just as we have done here, when you conduct your own research on the Web, you need to be aware that you might be stepping into a heated controversy. To read a site rhetorically, you've got to understand its position within the larger social conversation in order to interpret its use of both visual and textual elements.

Evaluating a Web Source

Once you've considered your reasons for using a source and the rhetorical context of your issue on the Web, you are ready to evaluate a site's reliability, credibility, angle of vision, and degree of advocacy. As we show, part of evaluating a source is evaluating the site in which it is posted. In Table 21.7 we offer five criteria developed by scholars and librarians as points to consider when you are evaluating Web sites.

An Example: Applying Evaluation Criteria

In this section we offer a brief example of the thinking processes used to evaluate a potential Web source. Suppose, for illustrative purposes, that you are trying to determine your own stance on gun control from a woman's perspective. In doing a Web search, you click on a link that takes you to the following site: http://www.armedandsafe.com/women.htm. What appears on your screen is an article entitled "Women Are the Real Victims of Handgun Control" by Kelly Ann Connolly, who is identified as the director of the Nevada State Rifle and Pistol Association. (See Figure 21.7 which shows the first screen of this article.) The site includes a biographical note indicating that she is a public school teacher with a master's degree and that her husband is a former California Deputy Sheriff and police officer.

Connolly argues that a woman can walk confidently down any street in America if she is carrying a concealed weapon and is skilled in using it. She offers as support anecdotal cases of women who fought off rapists and cites numerous statistics, attributing the sources to "Bureau of Justice Statistics (1999)." Here are some examples from later screens in the article:

- "3 out of 4 American women *will* be a victim of violent crime at least once in their lifetime."
- 2 million women are raped each year, one every 15 seconds.
- Rapists know they have only a 1 in 605 chance of being caught, charged, convicted, and sentenced to serving time.

The effect of these statistics is to inform women about the prevalence of rape and to reduce women's confidence in the police or justice system to protect them. The implied solution is to buy a pistol and learn how to use it.

How might you evaluate such an article for your own research purposes? A first step is to evaluate the site itself. We found the home page by deleting "/women.htm" from the URL and looking directly at www.armedandsafe.com.

TABLE 21.7 Criteria for Evaluating Web Sites

Criteria	Questions to Ask
1. Authority	• Is the document author or site sponsor clearly identified? • Does the site identify the occupation, position, education, experience, or other credentials of the author? • Does the home page or a clear link from the home page reveal the author's or sponsor's motivation for establishing the site? • Does the site provide contact information for the author or sponsor such as an e-mail or organization address?
2. Objectivity or Clear Disclosure of Advocacy	• Is the site's purpose clear (for example, to inform, entertain, or persuade)? • Is the site explicit about declaring its point of view? • Does the site indicate whether the author is affiliated with a specific organization, institution, or association? • Does the site indicate whether it is directed toward a specific audience?
3. Coverage	• Are the topics covered by the site clear? • Does the site exhibit a suitable depth and comprehensiveness for its purpose? • Is sufficient evidence provided to support the ideas and opinions presented?
4. Accuracy	• Are the sources of information stated? • Do the facts appear to be accurate? • Can you verify this information by comparing this source with other sources in the field?
5. Currency	• Are dates included in the Web site? • Do the dates apply to the material itself, to its placement on the Web, or to the time the site was last revised and updated? • Is the information current, or at least still relevant, for the site's purpose? For your purpose?

The screen that appeared is shown in Figure 21.8. This is the commercial site of a husband-and-wife team who run a firing range and give lessons in the use of rifles, pistols, and machine guns. The site obviously advocates Second Amendment rights and promotes gun ownership as a means of domestic and personal security. The fierce eagle emerging from a collage of the American flag, the burning World Trade Center towers, and an aircraft carrier appeals to the patriotic sentiments that tend to dominate pro-gun Web sites. (On the day we accessed it, the site also played a John Wayne rendition of "America the Beautiful.") It is easy to evaluate this site against the five criteria:

1. *Authority:* You can clearly tell who created the site and is responsible for its contents.
2. *Advocacy:* The site clearly advocates Second Amendment rights and gun ownership.
3. *Coverage:* The site will not cover gun control issues in a complex way. Every aspect of the site will be filtered to support its pro-gun vision.

FIGURE 21.7 First Screen of "Women Are the Real Victims of Handgun Control"

Women are the Real Victims of Handgun Control

By Kelly Ann Connolly
Director, Nevada State Rifle and Pistol Assoc.

Women are 100 times more likely to be raped than men and 3 out of 4 American women <u>will</u> be a victim of violent crime at least once in their lifetime.* Women, by far, have the greatest need for self-defense.

Handgun control, laws designed to limit legal access to handguns, are also more likely to limit women's access to guns, as a group, than men or criminals because women are less likely to knowingly break laws.

And the most effective form of self-defense is a handgun. Ask any law enforcement official if he would trade his firearm in for pepper spray alone.

Personal devices used exclusively as a safety strategy (mace, alarms and objects used to jab or poke) offer little resistance to an attacker who usually outweighs and has greater strength than most women. Traditional self-defense techniques, while increasing strength and confidence, are ineffective for most women in hand-to-hand street fighting.

Developing and practicing Personal Safety Strategies* to avoid falling prey to an attack and learning a trained counterattack, such as Model Mugging *are excellent ways to help women. Those who use them have a better shot at being that 1 in 4 who remain free of personal tragedy, but we need access to handguns for a real fighting chance if we hope to really change the odds that are stacked against women. Even the originator of Model Mugging, Matthew Thomas agrees, "Firearms are our most efficient tool for defending life and freedom."

Highlighting a well-known case, albeit dated, illustrates the effectiveness of armed women in reducing crime. In Orlando, Florida in 1966, a series of brutal rapes caused a dramatic increase in handgun purchases by female residents. The local newspaper (as usual) had an anti-gun editorial policy and some of its staff tried to persuade the chief of police to halt the sale of handguns to women. Since Orlando law protected the right to buy handguns, the newspaper and police department sponsored a
one day gun-training course. With an overwhelming response of over 2,500 women, they organized classes over a five-month period resulting in the training of more than 6,000 women. For the next five years, Orlando's incidents of rape, violent assault and burglary decreased dramatically while it sky-rocketed in every other city in the country. Additionally, there hadn't been a single accidental shooting, misuse of handguns against family or intimates nor even reported use of a firearm for defense by any of the women. Experts who have studied this situation attribute the decrease in crime to the media publicity of women who were armed and trained.

Criminals prefer easy targets.

4. *Accuracy:* You still need to check its facts against other sources, but you can predict that the information will be rhetorically filtered and selected to promote the site's position.

5. *Currency:* Because the site supports a pro-gun stance, it will use data that are most effective in promoting its view. Dates are included in the material and the Web site. Some dates cited are not recent (1996 Florida example), but appear relevant to the issue presented.

How might you therefore use Connolly's article posted on the site? The article could be very useful to you as one point of view on the gun control controversy. It is a fairly representative example of the argument that guns can increase a woman's sense of confidence and well-being, and it clearly shows the kinds of

FIGURE 21.8 Home Page of armedandsafe.com

rhetorical strategies such articles use—statistics on rape, descriptions of guns as equalizers in empowering women, and so forth.

As a source of factual data, however, the article is questionable. The sources used are not well documented, and the data appear to be filtered through the writer's pro-gun lens. As a responsible researcher, you need to find primary sources of statistics about gun usage and crime. You will also want to see how data are used in other sites, including those that support gun-control.

Using, Citing, and Documenting Sources

The previous chapter focused on the first five of seven research skills listed at the end of Chapter 20 (see pp. 605–606). In Chapter 21, you learned how to conduct an argument in your own voice, how to use appropriate search engines to find different kinds of research sources, and how to read and evaluate those sources using the skills of rhetorical reading emphasized throughout this text. We also examined the special problems of evaluating Web sources.

In this chapter we turn to the final two skills on our list: how to incorporate sources into your writing and how to cite and document them properly.

Skill 6: Use Sources Purposefully Through Clearly Attributed Summary, Paraphrase, or Quotation

One of the essential skills you need as a researcher is the ability to incorporate research sources purposefully into your prose. This section shows you how to do so. Specifically we show you how to use sources for your own purposes and how to weave them gracefully into your prose through effective summary, paraphrase, and quotation. We also show you how to shape your readers' response to these sources through rhetorically effective attributive tags. Finally, we show you how to recognize and scrupulously avoid plagiarism.

Using Sources for Your Own Purposes

In Chapter 21, we explained how you should remain aware of your research goals when you take notes and evaluate sources. To use sources purposefully, you need to understand why you are using any given source and how it functions in your argument. Keep in mind the following reasons for using research sources:

See Table 21.4, "Note Taking According to Purpose" on p. 627.

- To provide direct evidence, such as facts, information, statistics, and other data, in support of your reasons and points
- To provide indirect evidence through testimony of experts
- To show conflicting or puzzling data that you will analyze or interpret
- To show your understanding of alternative views

- To provide big-picture overviews and background
- To convey your general knowledge, credibility, and authority

The most typical way that inexperienced researchers use sources is through block quotations—a method that often seems amateurish because it simply reproduces a source without foregrounding the writer's voice and purpose.

To illustrate the difference between reproducing a source and using a source purposefully, we show you the hypothetical case of three writers using the same article for different purposes. Read carefully the following short article about violence in the Old West. Then proceed to the examples of three writers who use this article for their own different purposes.

READING

Roger D. McGrath
The Myth of Violence in the Old West

1   It is commonly assumed that violence is part of our frontier heritage. But the historical record shows that frontier violence was very different from violence today. Robbery and burglary, two of our most common crimes, were of no great significance in the frontier towns of the Old West, and rape was seemingly nonexistent.

2   Bodie, one of the principal towns on the trans-Sierra frontier, illustrates the point. Nestled high in the mountains of eastern California, Bodie, which boomed in the late 1870s and early 1880s, ranked among the most notorious frontier towns of the Old West. It was, as one prospector put it, the last of the old-time mining camps.

3   Like the trans-Sierra frontier in general, Bodie was indisputably violent and lawless, yet most people were not affected. Fistfights and gunfights among willing combatants—gamblers, miners, and the like—were regular events, and stagecoach holdups were not unusual. But the old, the young, the weak, and the female—so often the victims of crime today—were generally not harmed.

4   Robbery was more often aimed at stagecoaches than at individuals. Highwaymen usually took only the express box and left the passengers alone. There were eleven stagecoach robberies in Bodie between 1878 and 1882, and in only two instances were passengers robbed. (In one instance, the highwaymen later apologized for their conduct.)

5   There were only ten robberies and three attempted robberies of individuals in Bodie during its boom years, and in nearly every case the circumstances were the same: the victim had spent the evening in a gambling den, saloon, or brothel; he had revealed that he had on his person a significant sum of money; and he was staggering home drunk when the attack occurred.

6   Bodie's total of twenty-one robberies—eleven of stages and ten of individuals—over a five-year period converts to a rate of eighty-four robberies per 100,000 inhabitants per year. On this scale—the same scale used by the FBI to index crime—New York City's robbery rate in 1980 was 1,140, Miami's was 995, and Los Angeles's was 628. The rate for the United States as a whole was 243. Thus Bodie's robbery rate was significantly below the national average in 1980.

7   Perhaps the greatest deterrent to crime in Bodie was the fact that so many people were armed. Armed guards prevented bank robberies and holdups of stagecoaches carrying shipments of bullion, and armed homeowners and merchants discouraged burglary. Between 1878 and 1882, there were only thirty-two burglaries—seventeen of homes and fifteen of businesses—in Bodie. At least a half-dozen burglaries were thwarted by the presence of armed citizens. The newspapers regularly advocated shooting burglars on sight, and several burglars were, in fact, shot at.

8   Using the FBI scale, Bodie's burglary rate for those five years was 128. Miami's rate in 1980 was 3,282, New York's was 2,661, and Los Angeles's was 2,602. The rate of the United States as a whole was 1,668, thirteen times that of Bodie.

9   Bodie's law enforcement institutions were certainly not responsible for these low rates. Rarely were robbers or burglars arrested, and even less often were they convicted. Moreover, many law enforcement officers operated on both sides of the law.

10   It was the armed citizens themselves who were the most potent—though not the only—deterrent to larcenous crime. Another was the threat of vigilantism. Highwaymen, for example, understood that while they could take the express box from a stagecoach without arousing the citizens, they risked inciting the entire populace to action if they robbed the passengers.

11   There is considerable evidence that women in Bodie were rarely the victims of crime. Between 1878 and 1882 only one woman, a prostitute, was robbed, and there were no reported cases of rape. (There is no evidence that rapes occurred but were not reported.)

12   Finally, juvenile crime, which accounts for a significant portion of the violent crime in the United States today, was limited in Bodie to pranks and malicious mischief.

13   If robbery, burglary, crimes against women, and juvenile crime were relatively rare on the trans-Sierra frontier, homicide was not: thirty-one Bodieites were shot, stabbed, or beaten to death during the boom years, for a homicide rate of 116. No U.S. city today comes close to this rate. In 1980, Miami led the nation with a homicide rate of 32.7; Las Vegas was a distant second at 23.4. A half-dozen cities had rates of zero. The rate for the United States as a whole in that year was a mere 10.2.

14   Several factors contributed to Bodie's high homicide rate. A majority of the town's residents were young, adventurous, single males who adhered to a code of conduct that frequently required them to fight even if, or perhaps especially

15   if, it could mean death. Courage was admired above all else. Alcohol also played a major role in fostering the settlement of disputes by violence.

15   If the men's code of conduct and their consumption of alcohol made fighting inevitable, their sidearms often made it fatal. While the carrying of guns probably reduced the incidence of robbery and burglary, it undoubtedly increased the number of homicides.

16   For the most part, the citizens of Bodie were not troubled by the great number of killings; nor were they troubled that only one man was ever convicted of murder. They accepted the killings and the lack of convictions because most of those killed had been willing combatants.

17   Thus the violence and lawlessness of the trans-Sierra frontier bear little relation to the violence and lawlessness that pervade American society today. If Bodie is at all representative of frontier towns, there is little justification for blaming contemporary American violence on our frontier heritage.

There is no one right way to use this article in your research paper. What you use depends on your research question and your purpose in using the source. Sometimes you will summarize a source's whole argument; sometimes you will summarize only a part; at other times you will use an isolated fact or statistic from the source or quote a sentence or two as testimonial evidence. In what follows we show how three hypothetical writers, addressing three different research questions, use this source in different ways.

Writer 1: Summary for an Analytical Paper on Causes of Violence

For an explanation of the numbers in parentheses, see the discussion of MLA in-text documentation on pp. 661–662.

The first hypothetical writer is analyzing the causes of violence in contemporary U.S. society. She wants to reject one possible cause—that contemporary violence grows out of our violent past. To make this point in her argument, she summarizes McGrath's article.

> Many people believe that violence is part of our Wild West heritage. But Roger McGrath, in his article "The Myth of Violence in the Old West," shows that frontier violence was very different from contemporary violence. He explains that in a typical frontier town, violence involved gunslingers who were "willing combatants," whereas today's typical victims—"the old, the young, the weak, and the female"—were unaffected by crime (644). Because the presence of an armed populace deterred robbery and burglary, theft was much less common in the Old West than today. On the other hand, McGrath explains, killings were fueled by guns, alcohol, and a code of conduct that invited fighting, so murders were much more frequent than in any U.S. city today (645). Thus, according to McGrath, there is little resemblance between violence on the frontier and violence in today's cities, so we cannot blame current violence on our tumultuous frontier past.

In this passage the author summarizes McGrath's argument in order to refute the violent frontier theory about the causes of contemporary violence. Presumably, this author will proceed to other causes of violence and will not return again to McGrath.

Writer 2: Partial Summary for a Persuasive Paper in Support of Gun Control

In our next case, the hypothetical writer uses McGrath's article in an argument supporting gun control. He wants to refute the popular anti–gun control argument that law-abiding citizens need to be armed to protect themselves against crime.

> Opponents of gun control often argue that guns benefit society by providing protection against intruders. But such protection is deadly, as Roger McGrath shows in his study of violence in the frontier town of Bodie, California. Although guns reduced theft, as seen in the low rate of theft in the well-armed town of Bodie, the presence of guns also led to a homicide rate far above that of the most violent city in the U.S. today. The homicide rate in the frontier town of Bodie, California, for example, was 116 per 100,000, compared to the current national average of 10.2 per 100,000 (645). True, Bodie citizens reduced the theft rate by being heavily armed, but at a cost of a homicide rate more than ten times the current national average. To protect our consumer goods at the cost of so much human life is counter to the values of most Americans.

McGrath's article contains data that could be used on either side of the gun control debate. This writer acknowledges the evidence showing that gun possession reduces theft and then works that potentially damaging information into an argument for gun control. How might you use the McGrath article to oppose gun control?

Writer 3: Partial Summary for an Analytical Paper on Shifting Definitions of Crime

Looking at another facet of McGrath's article, the last hypothetical writer summarizes part of McGrath's article to support her thesis that a community's definition of crime is constantly shifting.

> Our notion of criminal activity shifts over time. For example, only a short time ago on the American frontier, murder was often ignored by law enforcement. Roger McGrath, in his discussion of violence in the frontier town of Bodie, California, during the 1870s and 1880s, showed that the townspeople accepted homicides as long as both the murderer and the victim were "willing combatants" who freely participated in gunfights (646). These young males who were the "willing combatants" in Bodie share many characteristics with modern gang members in that they were encouraged to fight by a "code of conduct": "A majority of the town's residents were young, adventurous, single males who adhered to a code of conduct that frequently required them to fight even if . . . it could mean death" (645–646). Today's gang members also follow a code of conduct that requires violence—often in the form of vengeance. Although joining a gang certainly makes youths "willing combatants," that status doesn't prevent prosecution in court. Today's "willing combatants" are criminals, but yesterday's "willing combatants" were not.

This writer uses McGrath's article to make a point completely different from McGrath's. But by extending and applying information from McGrath's article to a new context, the writer gathers fuel for her own argument about shifting definitions of the word *criminal*.

For Writing and Discussion

Each of the hypothetical writers uses McGrath's article for a different purpose. Working individually or in groups, answer the following questions. Be ready to elaborate on and defend your answers.

1. What are the differences in the ways the writers use the original article? How are these differences related to differences in each writer's purpose?
2. What differences would you expect to find in the research notes each writer took on the McGrath article?
3. What makes each writer's paragraph different from a purposeless listing of random information?

Working Sources into Your Own Prose

As a research writer, you need to incorporate sources gracefully into your own prose so that your paper's focus stays on your own argument. In this section we examine some of the techniques that the three hypothetical writers used to adapt the McGrath article to their own purposes: summarizing a source's argument, paraphrasing a relevant portion of a source, or quoting the source directly. Let's look at each of these options.

Summarizing

See Chapter 6, pp. 126–130, for detailed advice on summary writing.

Writing a summary of a source's argument (either of the whole argument or of a relevant section) is an appropriate strategy when the source represents an opposing or alternative view or when it supports or advances one of your own points. Summaries can be as short as a single sentence or as long as a paragraph. Writer 1's summary of the McGrath article is a good example of a graceful summary.

Paraphrasing

We explain how to cite sources later in this chapter; see pp. 658–693.

Unlike a summary, which is a condensation of a source's whole argument, a paraphrase translates a short passage from a source's words into the writer's own words. You should paraphrase when you are using brief, specific information from a source and don't want to interrupt the flow of your own voice with a quotation. Of course, you must still acknowledge the source through a citation.

When you paraphrase, be careful to avoid the original writer's grammatical structure and syntax. If you mirror the original sentence structure while replacing some words with synonyms, you are plagiarizing rather than paraphrasing. Here is an acceptable paraphrase of a short passage from the McGrath article:

ORIGINAL

There is considerable evidence that women in Bodie were rarely the victims of crime. Between 1878 and 1882 only one woman, a prostitute, was robbed, and there were no reported cases of rape. (There is no evidence that rapes occurred but were not reported.)

PARAPHRASE

According to McGrath, women in Bodie seldom suffered at the hands of criminals. Between 1878 and 1882, the only female robbery victim in Bodie was a prostitute. Also rape seemed nonexistent, with no reported cases and no evidence that unreported cases occurred (645).

Note that to avoid plagiarism, the writer has changed the sentence structure substantially. However, the writer still acknowledges the original source with the phrase "According to McGrath" and provides the page number.

Quoting Directly

Occasionally, you will want to quote an author's words directly. Avoid quoting too much because the effect, from your reader's perspective, is a collage of quotations rather than an argument. Quote only when doing so strengthens your argument. Here are some occasions when a direct quotation is appropriate:

- When the quotation comes from a respected authority and, in a pithy way, supports one of your points. (Your use of the quotation is like expert testimony in a trial.)
- When you are summarizing an opposing or alternative view and want to use brief quotations to show that you have listened carefully and accurately.
- When you want to give readers the flavor of a source's voice, particularly if the language is striking or memorable.
- When you want to analyze the writer's choice of words or metaphors. (You would first quote the passage and then begin your analysis.)

When you quote, you must be meticulous in copying the passage *exactly,* including punctuation. When the quoted material takes up more than four lines in your paper, use the following block quotation method:

EXAMPLE OF A BLOCK QUOTATION

McGrath describes the people most affected by violence in the frontier town of Bodie:

> Fistfights and gunfights among willing combatants—gamblers, miners, and the like—were regular events, and stagecoach holdups were not unusual. But the old, the young, the weak, and the female—so often the victims of crime today—were generally not harmed. (644)

EXPLANATION*

- The block quotation is indented one inch.
- There are *no quotation marks.* The block indentation itself signals a quotation.

*This and subsequent examples follow the guidelines of the MLA (Modern Language Association) style. We explain this style in detail in the last half of this chapter (Skill 7), where we also explain APA (American Psychological Association) style.

- The number in parentheses indicates the page number where the quotation is found in the original source. Note that in block quotations the parentheses come after the closing period.
- Block quotations are usually introduced with a colon.

If the quoted passage is fewer than four typed lines in your own text, insert it directly into your paragraph using quotation marks. How you punctuate depends on whether the inserted quotation is a complete sentence or part of a sentence.

EXAMPLE OF AN INSERTED QUOTATION WHEN THE QUOTATION IS A COMPLETE SENTENCE

According to McGrath, "It was the armed citizens themselves who were the most potent—though not the only—deterrent to larcenous crime" (645).

EXPLANATION

- The page number in parentheses is inserted *after* the quotation mark but *before* the closing period.
- Because the quotation is a complete sentence, it starts with a capital letter and is separated from the introductory phrase by a comma.

Often you won't want to quote a complete sentence but instead work brief words and phrases from your source into your own grammatical structure.

EXAMPLE OF AN INSERTED QUOTATION WHEN THE QUOTATION IS NOT A COMPLETE SENTENCE

McGrath contrasts frontier violence to crime today, pointing out that today's typical crime victims are "the old, the young, the weak, and the female" and showing that these groups were not molested in Bodie (644).

EXPLANATION

- Because the quoted material is not a complete sentence, it is worked into the grammar of the writer's own sentence.
- No comma introduces the quotation; commas should be used only to fit the grammar of the writer's own sentence.
- The number in parentheses is the page number where the quotation is found in the original source. Note that it comes wherever the borrowed idea ends.

Modifying Quotations to Fit Your Grammatical Structure

Occasionally the grammar of a desired quotation doesn't match the grammatical structure of your own sentence, or the meaning of a quoted word will not be clear because the passage has been removed from its original context. In these cases, use brackets to modify the quotation's grammar or to add a clarifying explanation: Change the quotation, placing your changes in brackets to indicate that the bracketed material is not part of the original wording. You should also use brackets to show a change in capitalization.

ORIGINAL PASSAGE

The newspapers regularly advocated shooting burglars on sight, and several burglars were, in fact, shot at.

QUOTATION MODIFIED TO FIT THE GRAMMAR OF THE WRITER'S SENTENCE

In Bodie, an armed citizenry successfully eliminated burglaries, aided by newspapers "regularly advocat[ing] shooting burglars on sight" (McGrath 645).

ORIGINAL PASSAGE

Highwaymen, for example, understood that while they could take the express box from a stagecoach without arousing the citizens, they risked inciting the entire populace to action if they robbed the passengers.

USE OF BRACKETS TO CHANGE THE CAPITALIZATION AND EXPLAIN MISSING REFERENTS

Public sentiment influenced what laws were likely to be broken. According to McGrath, "[W]hile they [highwaymen] could take the express box from a stagecoach without arousing the citizens, they risked inciting the entire populace to action if they robbed the passengers" (645).

Perhaps the most frequent modification writers make is omitting portions of a quotation. To indicate an omission in a quotation in MLA style, use three spaced periods, called an *ellipsis*. Placement of the ellipsis depends on where the omitted material occurs. In the middle of a sentence, each of the periods should be preceded and followed by an additional space.

ORIGINAL PASSAGE

Finally, juvenile crime, which accounts for a significant portion of the violent crime in the United States today, was limited in Bodie to pranks and malicious mischief.

USING ELLIPSES TO INDICATE OMISSION

"Finally, juvenile crime . . . was limited in Bodie to pranks and malicious mischief" (McGrath 645).

When your ellipsis comes at the boundary between sentences, use an additional period to mark the end of the sentence. Do not leave an extra space before the sentence-ending period. When a parenthetical page number must follow the ellipsis, insert it before the final (fourth) period in the sequence.

| **Original** | Bodie's law enforcement institutions were certainly not responsible for these low rates. Rarely were robbers or burglars arrested, and even less often were they convicted. Moreover, many law enforcement officers operated on both sides of the law. |

Omitting Sentence within Quotation	According to McGrath, "Bodie's law enforcement institutions were certainly not responsible for these low rates. . . . Moreover, many law enforcement officers operated on both sides of the law" (645).
Omitting End of Quoted Sentence	According to McGrath, "Bodie's law enforcement institutions were certainly not responsible for these low rates. Rarely were robbers or burglars arrested. . . . Moreover, many law enforcement officers operated on both sides of the law" (645).
Placing Parenthetical Citation after Ellipsis	According to McGrath, "Bodie's law enforcement institutions were certainly not responsible for these low rates. Rarely were robbers or burglars arrested . . ." (645).

Quotations within Quotations

Occasionally a passage that you wish to quote will already contain quotation marks. If you use block indentation, keep the quotation marks exactly as they are in the original. If you set the passage within your own quotation marks, however, change the original double marks (") into single marks (') to indicate the quotation within the quotation. The same procedure works whether the quotation marks are used for quoted words or for a title.

ORIGINAL PASSAGE: ROBERT HEILBRONER QUOTING WILLIAM JAMES

And finally, we tend to stereotype because it helps us make sense out of a highly confusing world, a world which William James once described as "one great, blooming, buzzing confusion."

QUOTED PASSAGE: WRITER QUOTING HEILBRONER

Robert Heilbroner explains why people tend to create stereotypes: "And finally, we tend to stereotype because it helps us make sense out of a highly confusing world, a world which William James once described as 'one great, blooming, buzzing confusion' " (22).

Creating Rhetorically Effective Attributive Tags

As we have shown in this section, whenever you use sources in your writing, you need to distinguish your source's words and ideas from your own. The most precise way of doing so is to use strategically placed attributive tags—short phrases like "according to McGrath," "McGrath says," "in McGrath's view," and so on. As we show in a moment, attributive tags can have a powerful rhetorical effect by letting you create the angle of vision from which you want your readers to view a source.

Using Attributive Tags to Separate Your Ideas from Your Source's
The previous examples of citing, summarizing, paraphrasing, and quoting use attributive tags to signal which ideas are the writer's and which are taken from another source. Here, for example, are excerpts from Writer 1's summary of McGrath, in which we have highlighted the attributive tags with boldfaced font. (The complete summary appears on p. 646.)

USE OF ATTRIBUTIVE TAGS

Many people believe that violence is part of our Wild West heritage. But **Roger McGrath, in his article "The Myth of Violence in the Old West,"** shows that frontier violence was very different from contemporary violence. **He explains** that . . . . On the other hand, **McGrath explains,** killings were fueled . . . . Thus, **according to McGrath,** there is little resemblance between violence on the frontier and violence in today's cities. . . .

Using Parenthetical Citations without Attributive Tags and the Resulting Ambiguities
You can also indicate borrowed material by inserting the source author's name and appropriate page number in a parenthetical citation at the end of the borrowed material:

(McGrath 645)

However, this approach—which is common in some academic writing, particularly in the social sciences—can introduce two kinds of ambiguity. First, it does not clearly mark where the borrowed material begins or how far it extends. Second, it tends to imply that the borrowed material is a "fact" as opposed to an author's argument filtered through that author's angle of vision. Note these ambiguities in the following passage, where parenthetical citations are used without attributive tags:

AMBIGUOUS ATTRIBUTION

There are many arguments in favor of preserving old-growth forests. First, it is simply unnecessary to log these forests to supply the world's lumber. We have plenty of new-growth forest from which lumber can be taken (Sagoff 89–90). Recently there have been major reforestation efforts all over the United States, and it is common practice now for loggers to replant every tree that is harvested. These new-growth forests, combined with extensive planting of tree farms, provide more than enough wood for the world's needs. Tree farms alone can supply the world's demand for industrial lumber (Sedjo 90).

When confronted with this passage, skeptical readers might ask, "Who are Sagoff and Sedjo? I've never heard of them." It is also difficult to tell how much of the passage is the writer's own argument and how much is borrowed from Sagoff and Sedjo. Is this whole passage a paraphrase? Finally, the writer tends to treat Sagoff's and Sedjo's assertions as uncontested facts rather than as professional opinions. Compare the preceding version with this one, in which attributive tags are added:

CLEAR ATTRIBUTION

There are many arguments in favor of preserving old-growth forests. First, it is simply unnecessary to log these forests to supply the world's lumber. **According to environmentalist Carl Sagoff**, we have plenty of new-growth forest from which lumber can be taken (89–90). Recently there have been major reforestation efforts all over the United States, and it is common practice now for loggers to replant every tree that is harvested. These new-growth forests, combined with extensive planting of tree farms, provide more than enough wood for the world's needs. **According to forestry expert Robert Sedjo**, tree farms alone can supply the world's demand for industrial lumber (90).

We can now see that most of the paragraph is the writer's own argument, into which she has inserted the expert testimony of Sagoff and Sedjo, whose views are treated not as indisputable facts but as the opinions of authorities in this field.

Using Attributive Tags to Create Context and Shape Reader Response

When you introduce a source for the first time, you can use the attributive tag not only to introduce the source but also to shape your readers' attitudes toward the source. In the previous example, the writer wants readers to respect Sagoff and Sedjo, so she identifies Sagoff as an "environmentalist" and Sedjo as a "forestry expert." If the writer favored logging old-growth forests and supported the logging industry's desire to create more jobs, she might have used different tags: "Carl Sagoff, an outspoken advocate for spotted owls over people," or "Robert Sedjo, a forester with limited knowledge of world lumber markets."

When you compose an initial tag, you can add to it any combination of the following kinds of information, depending on your purpose, your audience's values, and your sense of what the audience already knows or doesn't know about the source:

Add to Attributive Tag	Example
Author's credentials or relevant specialty (enhances credibility)	Civil engineer David Rockwood, a noted authority on stream flow in rivers
Author's lack of credentials (decreases credibility)	City Council member Dilbert Weasel, a local politician with no expertise in international affairs
Author's political or social views	Left-wing columnist Alexander Cockburn [has negative feeling]; Alexander Cockburn, a longtime champion of labor [has positive feeling]
Title of source if it provides context	In her book *Fasting Girls: The History of Anorexia Nervosa,* Joan Jacobs Brumberg shows that [establishes credentials for comments on eating disorders]

Add to Attributive Tag	Example
Publisher of source if it adds prestige or otherwise shapes audience response	Dr. Carl Patrona, in an article published in the prestigious *New England Journal of Medicine*
Historical or cultural information about a source that provides context or background	In his 1960s book popularizing the hippie movement, Charles Reich claims that
Indication of source's purpose or angle of vision	Feminist author Naomi Wolfe, writing a blistering attack on the beauty industry, argues that

Our point here is that you can use attributive tags rhetorically to help your readers understand the significance and context of a source when you first introduce it and to guide your readers' attitudes toward the source.

For Writing and Discussion

What follow are four different ways that a writer can use the same passage from a source to support a point about the greenhouse effect. Working in groups or as a whole class, rank the four methods from "most effective" to "least effective." Assume that you are writing a researched argument addressed to your college classmates.

1. *Quotation without attributive tag*
   The greenhouse effect will have a devastating effect on the earth's environment: "Potential impacts include increased mortality and illness due to heat stress and worsened air pollution, as in the 1995 Chicago heat wave that killed hundreds of people. . . . Infants, children and other vulnerable populations—especially in already-stressed regions of the world—would likely suffer disproportionately from these impacts" (Hall 19).

2. *Quotation with attributive tag*
   The greenhouse effect will have a devastating effect on the earth's environment. David C. Hall, president of Physicians for Social Responsibility, claims the following: "Potential impacts include increased mortality and illness due to heat stress and worsened air pollution, as in the 1995 Chicago heat wave that killed hundreds of people. . . . Infants, children and other vulnerable populations—especially in already-stressed regions of the world—would likely suffer disproportionately from these impacts" (19).

3. *Paraphrase without attributive tag*
   The greenhouse effect will have a devastating effect on the earth's environment. One of the most frightening effects is the threat of diseases

(continued)

stemming from increased air pollution and heat stress. Infants and children would be most at risk (Hall 19).

4. *Paraphrase with attributive tag*

The greenhouse effect will have a devastating effect on the earth's environment. One of the most frightening effects, according to David C. Hall, president of Physicians for Social Responsibility, is the threat of diseases stemming from increased air pollution and heat stress. Infants and children would be most at risk (19).

Avoiding Plagiarism

Before we proceed to the nuts and bolts of documenting sources, we'd like you to understand the ethical issue of plagiarism. As you know from writing your own papers, developing ideas and putting them into words is hard work. *Plagiarism* occurs whenever you take someone else's work and pass it off as your own. Plagiarism has two forms: borrowing another person's ideas without giving credit through proper citation and borrowing another writer's language without giving credit through quotation marks or block indentation.

The second kind of plagiarism is far more common than the first, perhaps because inexperienced writers don't appreciate how much they need to change the wording of a source to make the writing their own. It is not enough just to change the order of phrases in a sentence or to replace a few words with synonyms. In the following example, compare the satisfactory paraphrase of a passage from McGrath's piece with a plagiarized version.

Original	There is considerable evidence that women in Bodie were rarely the victims of crime. Between 1878 and 1882 only one woman, a prostitute, was robbed, and there were no reported cases of rape. (There is no evidence that rapes occurred but were not reported.)
Acceptable Paraphrase	According to McGrath, women in Bodie rarely suffered at the hands of criminals (645). Between 1878 and 1882, the only female robbery victim in Bodie was a prostitute. Also rape seemed nonexistent, with no reported cases and no evidence that unreported cases occurred.
Plagiarism	According to McGrath, there is much evidence that women in Bodie were seldom crime victims (645). Between 1878 and 1882 only one woman, a prostitute, was robbed, and there were no reported rapes. There is no evidence that unreported cases of rape occurred (645).

For Writing and Discussion

The writer of the plagiarized passage perhaps assumed that the accurate citation of McGrath is all that is needed to avoid plagiarism. Yet this writer is
guilty of plagiarism. Why? How has the writer attempted to change the wording of the original? Why aren't these changes enough?

The best way to avoid plagiarism is to be especially careful at the note-taking
stage. If you copy from your source, copy exactly, word for word, and put quotation marks around the copied material or otherwise indicate that it is not your
own wording. If you paraphrase or summarize material, be sure that you don't
borrow any of the original wording. Also be sure to change the grammatical structure of the original. Lazy note taking, in which you follow the arrangement and
grammatical structure of the original passage and merely substitute occasional
synonyms, leads directly to plagiarism.

Also remember that you cannot borrow another writer's ideas without citing
them. If you summarize or paraphrase another writer's thinking about a subject,
you should indicate in your notes that the ideas are not your own and be sure to
record all the information you need for a citation. If you do exploratory reflection
to accompany your notes, then the distinction between other writers' ideas and
your own should be easy to recognize when it's time to incorporate the source
material into your paper.

For Writing and Discussion

The following exercise asks you to apply all the research and writing skills that
you have learned in this part of the chapter. After reading Edward Abbey's article "The Damnation of a Canyon" (pp. 157–161), imagine that you are going
to use Abbey's article in an essay of your own. Working individually or in small
groups, write an appropriate passage for each of the following scenarios. You
will need to decide how much you will quote from Abbey's article and how
you will use attributive tags to create a context and to shape your readers'
responses to your source.

Scenario 1 You are a supporter of dams and wish to write an article supporting
the Glen Canyon Dam and opposing Abbey's article. Write a one-paragraph summary of Abbey's views to include in your own essay.

Scenario 2 You are doing research on the ecological effects of dams and want to
use Abbey's article as one source. For your essay, write a paragraph, citing Abbey's
article, on how building the Glen Canyon Dam changed the river's ecology.

(*continued*)

Scenario 3 You are investigating the socioeconomic status of people who use Lake Powell for recreation. You particularly want to investigate Abbey's claim that the lake is used only by the wealthy. For your essay, write a short passage that reports Abbey's view of the socioeconomic status of the lake's recreational users.

Skill 7: Cite and Document Sources Effectively According to Appropriate Conventions

In this final section we focus on the nuts and bolts of documentation that is appropriate for your purpose, audience, and genre. As we have explained, proper documentation not only helps other researchers locate your sources but also con- tributes substantially to your own *ethos* as a writer. Specifically, this section helps you understand the general logic of parenthetical citation systems, the MLA and APA methods for in-text citations, the MLA and APA methods for documenting sources in a "Works Cited" and "References" list, respectively, and the MLA and APA styles for formatting academic papers.* As you use one or both of these methods in papers for various classes, your familiarity with the type of informa- tion expected in citations will make it easier to follow the formatting details in the models we provide as well as in other systems your professors may expect you to use.

Understanding the Logic of Parenthetical Citation Systems

An example of a research paper written in MLA style is Christopher Leigh's paper on pp. 675–686. An example of a research paper written in APA style is Brittany Tinker et al.'s on pp. 277–289.

Not too many years ago, most academic disciplines used footnotes or endnotes to document sources. Today, however, both the MLA (Modern Language Association) system, used primarily in the humanities, and the APA (American Psychological Association) system, used primarily in the social sciences, use par- enthetical citations instead of footnotes or endnotes. Before we examine the details of MLA and APA styles, we want to explain the logic of parenthetical cita- tion systems.

Connecting the Body of the Paper to the Bibliography
In both the MLA and APA systems, the writer places a complete bibliography at the end of the paper. In the MLA system this bibliography is called "Works Cited." In the APA system it is called "References." The bibliography is arranged alphabetically by author or by title (if an author is not named). The key to the systems' logic is this:

---

*Our discussion of MLA style is based on Joseph Gibaldi, *MLA Handbook for Writers of Research Papers,* 6th ed. (New York: Modern Language Association of America, 2003). Our discussion of APA style is based on the *Publication Manual of the American Psychological Association,* 5th ed. (Washington, D.C.: American Psychological Association, 2001).

- Every source in the bibliography must be mentioned in the body of the paper.
- Conversely, every source mentioned in the body of the paper must be listed in the bibliography.
- There must be a one-to-one correspondence between the first word in each bibliographic entry (usually, but not always, an author's last name)* and the name used to identify the source in the body of the paper.

Suppose a reader sees this phrase in your paper: "According to Debra Goldstein . . . ." The reader should be able to turn to your bibliography and find an alphabetized entry beginning with "Goldstein, Debra." Similarly, suppose that in looking over your bibliography, your reader sees an article by "Guillen, Manuel." This means that the name "Guillen" has to occur in your paper in one of two ways:

- As an attributive tag: "Economics professor Manuel Guillen argues that. . . ."
- As a parenthetical citation, probably following a quotation: ". . . changes in fiscal policy" (Guillen 49).

Because this one-to-one correspondence is so important, let's illustrate it with some complete examples using the MLA formatting style:

If the body of your paper has this:	Then the "Works Cited" list must have this:
According to linguist Deborah Tannen, political debate in America leaves out the complex middle ground where most solutions must be developed. [author cited in an attributive tag]	Tannen, Deborah. <u>The Argument Culture: Moving From Debate to Dialogue</u>. New York: Random, 1998.
In the 1980s, cigarette advertising revealed a noticeable pattern of racial stereotyping (Pollay, Lee, and Carter-Whitney). [authors cited in parentheses]	Pollay, Richard W., Jung S. Lee, and David Carter-Whitney. "Separate, but Not Equal: Racial Segmentation in Cigarette Advertising." <u>Journal of Advertising</u> 21.1 (1992): 45–57.
In its award-winning Web site, the National Men's Resource Center offers advice to parents whose teenagers want to get a nose stud or other form of body piercing ("Ouch!"). [shortened title used to identify source in "Works Cited" list]	"Ouch! Body Piercing." <u>Menstuff</u>. 1 Feb. 2001. National Men's Resource Center. 17 July 2004 <http://www.menstuff.org/ issues/byissue/ fathersgeneral.html#bodypiercing>.

*Sometimes a source won't have a named author. In such cases your parenthetical citation should identify the source by title, shortened for efficiency, and your bibliographic entry should begin with those title words (for example, "Guidelines for School Safety" could be shortened to "Guidelines" as long as no other sources begin with that title). To cite a source from a Web site identified by a corporation or group's name (for example, "Centers for Disease Control"), you have the choice of beginning the entry with the title of the document you are citing or with the corporate author, whichever you think will make more sense in your text and will help readers find the source more easily.

Citation Problems with Downloaded Sources

Now that you understand the concept of connecting the body of your text to your bibliography, you need to understand some special citation problems associated with sources downloaded from a licensed database or the Web. It is easy to cite a print source that you read in its original form (books, articles from the actual magazine or journal) because these sources can be retrieved in the same paper format from library to library all over the world. Both the MLA and APA systems have a basic format for citing books and articles. Although you'll encounter variations on the basic formats—more than one author, a revised edition, a translation, and so forth—in general, you simply find a bibliographic model that matches your source and plug the information into the correct slots.

The case is more difficult when you download an article from a licensed database or the Web. First of all, scholarly organizations usually expect researchers to find the original print version rather than use the downloaded version. But for college students, it is often difficult to locate the original print source if their libraries don't have it. There are three main problems with relying on downloaded articles: (1) you can't be sure the electronic article is a completely accurate version of the print article; (2) the downloaded version often doesn't reproduce the visual images that appear in the print version and that may be important; (3) the downloaded version usually doesn't reproduce the page numbering of the original source, so there is no clear way to cite pages.* Because downloaded versions are unstable, you must include in your bibliographic entry all the publication information about the original print version of the article *plus* information about the electronic source.

You will encounter the most difficulty when citing Web sources, where material often is ephemeral. (There are important exceptions. For example, totally electronic, peer-reviewed scholarly journals are now being published online. The publisher archives all accepted articles, making them stable and electronically available to future scholars.) In general, though, you can't be sure that material available today from the Web will still be available tomorrow, not to mention twenty or more years from now. Another problem with Web sources, as we saw in Chapter 21, is that it is often hard to determine publication dates and authorship of material. Also, as with licensed database sources, page numbers are usually impossible to specify for Web sites. Sometimes the only certain thing you'll know about a Web site is the URL in your computer's location window and the date you accessed the site. At the very minimum, you have to include this information in the citation.

From this point on, we separate our discussions of the MLA and APA systems. We begin with the MLA system because it is the one most commonly used in writing courses. We then explain the APA system.

---

*Databases are increasingly offering some sources in .pdf format, which reproduces the original look of the article. In these cases, images are usually reproduced, and the original page formatting is maintained.

Understanding the MLA Method of In-Text Citation

To cite sources in your text using the MLA system, place the author's last name and the page reference in parentheses immediately after the material being cited. If an attributive tag already identifies the author, give only the page number in parentheses. Once you have cited the author and it is clear that the same author's material is being used, you need cite only the page references in parentheses. The following examples show parenthetical documentation with and without an attributive tag. Note that the citation precedes the period. If you are citing a quotation, the parenthetical citation follows the quotation mark but precedes the final period.

> The Spanish tried to reduce the status of Filipina women who had been able to do business, get divorced, and sometimes become village chiefs (Karnow 41).
> According to Karnow, the Spanish tried to reduce the status of Filipina women who had been able to do business, get divorced, and sometimes become village chiefs (41).
> "And, to this day," Karnow continues, "women play a decisive role in Filipino families" (41).

A reader who wishes to look up the source will find the bibliographic information in the Works Cited section by looking for the entry under "Karnow." If more than one work by Karnow was used in the paper, the writer would include in the in-text citation an abbreviated title of the book or article following Karnow's name.

> (Karnow, "In Our Image" 41)

Citing from an Indirect Source

Occasionally you may wish to use a quotation that you have seen cited in one of your sources. You read Jones, who has a nice quotation from Smith, and you want to use Smith's quotation. What do you do? Whenever possible, find the quotation in its original source and cite that source. But if the original source is not available, cite the source indirectly by using the term "qtd. in" and list only the indirect source in your "Works Cited" list. In the following example, the writer wishes to quote a Buddhist monk, Thich Nhat Hanh, who has written a book entitled *Living Buddha, Living Christ*. However, the writer is unable to locate the actual book and instead has to quote from a review of the book by newspaper critic Lee Moriwaki. Here is how he would make the in-text citation:

> A Buddhist monk, Thich Nhat Hanh, stresses the importance of inner peace: "If we can learn ways to touch the peace, joy, and happiness that are already there, we will become healthy and strong, and a resource for others" (qtd. in Moriwaki C4).

The "Works Cited" list will have an entry for "Moriwaki" but not for "Thich Nhat Hanh."

Citing Page Numbers for Downloaded Material

As we discussed earlier, unless the downloaded materials you are citing are available in .pdf format, it is very difficult to provide accurate page numbers for parenthetical citations. If you are working with text or HTML files, do not use the page numbers on a printout because they will not be consistent from printer to printer. However, you can be confident in citing page numbers when a downloaded article indicates the source's original page breaks or has numbered paragraphs. Cite paragraphs with the abbreviation *par.* or *pars.*—for example, (Jones, pars. 22–24). In the typical case of the absence of reliable page numbers for the original material, MLA says to omit page references from the parenthetical citation. When researchers locate the source through the database or via its URL, they can use a software search function to pinpoint a specific quotation or passage.

Documenting Sources in a "Works Cited" List (MLA)

To see what citations look like when typed in a manuscript, see Christopher Leigh's Works Cited list on pp. 685–686. The MLA example citations on pp. 663–673 show the correct elements, sequence, and punctuation, but not typing formats.

In the MLA system, you place a complete bibliography, titled "Works Cited," at the end of the paper. The list includes all the sources that you mention in your paper. However, it does not include works you read but did not use. Entries in the Works Cited list are arranged alphabetically by author, or by title if there is no author.

Here are some general formatting guidelines for a works cited list:

- Begin the list on a new sheet of paper with the words "Works Cited" centered one inch from the top of the page.
- Sources are listed alphabetically, the first line flush with the left margin and succeeding lines indented one-half inch, known as a "hanging indentation."
- MLA formatting style uses abbreviations for months of the year (except for May, June, and July) and for publishers' names (for example, Random House is shortened to "Random" and "University Press" is shortened to "UP"). For a complete list of abbreviations, consult the sixth edition of the *MLA Handbook for Writers of Research Papers.*
- Author entries include the name as it appears in the article by-line or on the book's title page.
- MLA style recommends underlining rather than italicizing book titles and names of journals and magazines (because underlines stand out better on the page). Do not underline any punctuation marks following an underlined title.

Here is a typical example of a work, in this case a book, cited in MLA form.

> Karnow, Stanley. <u>In Our Image: America's Empire in the Philippines</u>. New York: Random, 1989.

Two or More Listings for One Author

When two or more works by one author are cited, the works are listed alphabetically by title. For the second and all additional entries, type three hyphens and a period in place of the author's name.

Dombrowski, Daniel A. <u>Babies and Beasts: The Argument from Marginal Cases</u>.
  Urbana: U of Illinois P, 1997.

---. <u>The Philosophy of Vegetarianism</u>. Amherst: U of Massachusetts P, 1984.

The remaining pages in this section show examples of MLA formats for different kinds of sources, provide explanations as needed, and give examples of the most frequently encountered variations and source types.

MLA Citation Models

Books

General Format for Books

Author. <u>Title</u>. City of publication: Publisher, year of publication.

One author

Brumberg, Joan J. <u>The Body Project: An Intimate History of American Girls</u>. New York:
  Vintage, 1997.

Two or more authors

Dombrowski, Daniel A., and Robert J. Deltete. <u>A Brief, Liberal, Catholic Defense of
  Abortion</u>. Urbana: U of Illinois P, 2000.

Belenky, Mary, et al. <u>Women's Ways of Knowing: The Development of Self, Voice, and
  Mind</u>. New York: Basic, 1986.

If there are four or more authors, you have the choice of listing all the authors in the order in which they appear on the title page or using "et al." (meaning "and others") to replace all but the first author. Make the same decision for the works cited entry and the parenthetical citation so they match.

Second, later, or revised edition

Montagu, Ashley. <u>Touching: The Human Significance of the Skin</u>. 3rd ed. New York:
  Perennial, 1986.

In place of "3rd ed.," you can include abbreviations for other kinds of editions: "Rev. ed." (for "Revised edition") or "Abr. ed." (for "Abridged edition").

Republished book (for example, a paperback published after the original hardback edition or a modern edition of an older work)

Hill, Christopher. <u>The World Turned Upside Down: Radical Ideas During the English
  Revolution</u>. 1972. London: Penguin, 1991.

Wollstonecraft, Mary. <u>The Vindication of the Rights of Woman, with Strictures on
  Political and Moral Subjects</u>. 1792. Rutland: Tuttle, 1995.

The date immediately following the title is the original publication date of the work.

Multivolume work

Churchill, Winston S. <u>A History of the English-Speaking Peoples</u>. 4 vols. New York: Dodd, 1956–58.

Churchill, Winston S. <u>The Great Democracies</u>. New York: Dodd, 1957. Vol. 4 of <u>A History of the English-Speaking Peoples</u>. 4 vols. 1956–58.

Use the first method when you cite the whole work; use the second method when you cite one specific volume of the work.

Article in familiar reference work

"Mau Mau." <u>The New Encyclopedia Britannica</u>. 15th ed. 2002.

Article in less familiar reference work

Ling, Trevor O. "Buddhism in Burma." <u>Dictionary of Comparative Religion</u>. Ed. S. G. F. Brandon. New York: Scribner's, 1970.

Translation

De Beauvoir, Simone. <u>The Second Sex</u>. 1949. Trans. H. M. Parshley. New York: Bantam, 1961.

Corporate author (a commission, committee, or other group)

American Red Cross. <u>Standard First Aid</u>. St. Louis: Mosby Lifeline, 1993.

No author listed

<u>The </u>New Yorker<u> Cartoon Album: 1975–1985</u>. New York: Penguin, 1987.

Edited Anthologies

An edited anthology looks like a regular book but has an editor rather than an author, and the contents are separate articles written by individual scholars. Anthology editors might also produce collections of short stories, poems, artwork, cartoons, or other kinds of documents. When you refer to the whole book, you cite the editor. When you refer to an individual work within the anthology, you cite the author of that work.

Citing the editor

O'Connell, David F., and Charles N. Alexander, eds. <u>Self Recovery: Treating Addictions Using Transcendental Meditation and Maharishi Ayur-Veda</u>. New York: Haworth, 1994.

Citing an individual article

Royer, Ann. "The Role of the Transcendental Meditation Technique in Promoting Smoking Cessation: A Longitudinal Study." <u>Self Recovery: Treating Addictions Using Transcendental Meditation and Maharishi Ayur-Veda</u>. Eds. David F. O'Connell and Charles N. Alexander. New York: Haworth, 1994. 221–39.

When you cite an individual article, the inclusive page numbers for the article come at the end of the citation.

Articles in Scholarly Journals Accessed in Print

The differences between a scholarly journal and a magazine are explained on page 615. When citing scholarly journals, you need to determine how the journal numbers its pages. Typically, separate issues of a journal are published four times per year. The library then binds the four separate issues into one "annual volume." Some journals restart the page numbering with each issue, which means that during the year there would be four instances of, say, page 31. Other journals number the pages consecutively throughout the year. In such a case, the fall issue might begin with page 253 rather than page 1. When pages are numbered sequentially throughout the year, you need to include only the volume number in the volume slot (for example, "25"). When page numbering starts over with each issue, you need to include in the volume slot both the volume and the issue number, separated by a period (for example, "25.3").

General Format for Scholarly Journals

Author. "Article Title." Journal Title volume number.issue number (year): page numbers.

Scholarly journal that numbers pages continuously

Barton, Ellen L. "Evidentials, Argumentation, and Epistemological Stance." College
    English 55 (1993): 745–69.

Scholarly journal that restarts page numbering with each issue

Pollay, Richard W., Jung S. Lee, and David Carter-Whitney. "Separate, but Not Equal:
    Racial Segmentation in Cigarette Advertising." Journal of Advertising 21.1 (1992):
    45–57.

Articles in Magazines and Newspapers Accessed in Print

Magazine and newspaper articles are easy to cite. If no author is identified, begin the entry with the title or headline. Distinguish between news stories and editorials by putting the word "Editorial" after the title. If a magazine comes out weekly or biweekly, include the complete date (27 Sept. 1998). If it comes out monthly, then state the month only (Sept. 1998).

General Format for Magazines and Newspapers

Author. "Article Title." Magazine Title [day] Month year: page numbers.

Note: If the article continues in another part of the magazine or newspaper, add "+" to the number of the first page to indicate the nonsequential pages.

Magazine article with named author

Snyder, Rachel L. "A Daughter of Cambodia Remembers: Loung Ung's Journey." Ms.
    Aug.—Sept. 2001: 62–67.

Hall, Stephen S. "Prescription for Profit." New York Times Magazine 11 Mar. 2001: 40+.

Magazine article without named author

"Daddy, Daddy." <u>New Republic</u> 30 July 2001: 2–13.

Review of book, film, or performance

Schwarz, Benjamin. "A Bit of Bunting: A New History of the British Empire Elevates
      Expediency to Principle." Rev. of <u>Ornamentalism: How the British Saw Their
      Empire</u>, by David Cannadine. <u>Atlantic Monthly</u> Nov. 2001: 126–35.

Kaufman, Stanley. "Polishing a Gem." Rev. of <u>The Blue Angel</u>, dir. Josef von Sternberg.
      <u>New Republic</u> 30 July 2001: 28–29.

Lahr, John. "Nobody's Darling: Fascism and the Drama of Human Connection in
      <u>Ashes to Ashes</u>." Rev. of <u>Ashes to Ashes</u>, by Harold Pinter. The Roundabout
      Theater Co. Gramercy Theater, New York. <u>New Yorker</u> 22 Feb. 1999: 182–83.

Follow this general model: Name of reviewer. "Title of Review." Rev. of <u>book, film,
or play</u>, by Author/Playwright [for films, use name of director preceded by "dir.";
for play, add production data as in last example]. <u>Periodical Title</u> [day] month
year: inclusive pages. Include company and theater information only for live performances.

Newspaper article

Henriques, Diana B. "Hero's Fall Teaches Wall Street a Lesson." <u>Seattle Times</u> 27 Sept.
      1998: A1+.

Page numbers in newspapers are typically indicated by a section letter or number
as well as a page number. Include these designations exactly as they appear in the
source. The "+" indicates that the article is completed on one or more pages later
in the newspaper.

Newspaper editorial

"Dr. Frankenstein on the Hill." Editorial. <u>New York Times</u> 18 May 2002: A22.

Letter to the editor of a magazine or newspaper

Tomsovic, Kevin. Letter. <u>New Yorker</u> 13 July 1998: 7.

Print Articles or Books Downloaded from a Database

Because of the difficulty in determining original page numbers for downloaded
articles, citations in this category must begin with complete print information,
followed by the electronic information.

General Format for Material from Licensed Databases

Author. "Title." <u>Periodical Name</u> Print publication data including date and
      volume/issue numbers: pagination. <u>Database</u>. Database company (if different).
      Library information. Date of access <URL of the database service's home page, if
      known>.

Note that there is no punctuation between the date of access and the URL; the
intended effect is a statement that on that date, the material was found at that
location or via that service.

Print article retrieved from licensed database

Lanza, Robert P., Betsy L. Dresser, and Philip Damiani. "Cloning Noah's Ark." <u>Scientific American</u> Nov. 2000: 84- . <u>Academic Search Elite</u>. EBSCO. Alexandria (Va.) Lib. 14 Sept. 2003 <http://www.epnet.com/>.

Watanabe, Myrna. "Zoos Act as Sentinels for Infectious Diseases." <u>Bioscience</u> 53 (2003): 792. <u>ProQuest</u>. Raynor Lib., Marquette U. 26 July 2004 <http://www.il.proquest.com/proquest/>.

Follow the formats for print magazines or scholarly journals, as relevant. When the database text provides only the starting page number of a multipage article, insert a hyphen and a space after the number, before the period. Providing only one number (as in the Watanabe citation above) indicates that the article has only one page.

Broadcast transcript retrieved from licensed database

Conan, Neal. "Arab Media." <u>Talk of the Nation</u>. With Shibley Telhami. 4 May 2004. Transcript. <u>LexisNexis</u>. Reed Elsevier. Raynor Lib., Marquette U. 31 July 2004 <http://www.lexisnexis.com/>.

The label "Transcript" after the broadcast date shows that a print copy was used.

Reference material retrieved from licensed database

"Cicada." <u>Encyclopaedia Britannica</u>. 2004. Encyclopaedia Britannica Online. Raynor Lib., Marquette U. 31 July 2004 <http://0search.eb.com.libus.csd.mu.edu:80/eb/article?eu=84788>.

This example uses the MLA citation provided at the end of the Britannica article. The URL is unique to the database license for the academic library through which we accessed it.

"Toni Morrison." <u>American Decades 1990–1999</u>. Ed. Tandy McConnell. Detroit: Gale Group, Inc., 2001. <u>Biography Resource Center</u>. Seattle Public Lib. 14 Sept. 2003 <http://www.galegroup.com/BiographyRC/>.

For MLA-approved alternatives to providing URLs, see p. 670.

Because the URL for the Toni Morrison article was long and unwieldy, we inserted the URL for the Biography Resource Center's home page, which we found quickly via a Google search.

Papers and monographs from an information service

Information services such as ERIC (Educational Resources Information Center) or NTIS (National Technical Information Service) provide material to your library on microfiche or online with indexes on CD-ROM or online. Much of the material from these services has not been published in major journals or magazines. Frequently they are typescripts of conference papers or other scholarly work disseminated on microfiche. Cite microfiche copies as you would cite print materials, adding an identifying phrase instead of publication information, and then an accession number at the end.

Coll, Richard K., Sara Tofield, Brent Vyle, and Rachel Bolstad. "Free-Choice Learning at a Metropolitan Zoo." Paper presented at the Annual Meeting of the National Association for Research in Science Teaching, Philadelphia, PA, 23–26 Mar. 2003. ERIC ED 477832.

For electronic versions, follow the format for periodical articles from a licensed database, adding the database information after the descriptive phrase and the accession number.

Coll, Richard K., Sara Tofield, Brent Vyle, and Rachel Bolstad. "Free-Choice Learning at a Metropolitan Zoo." Paper presented at the Annual Meeting of the National Association for Research in Science Teaching, Philadelphia, PA, 23–26 Mar. 2003. ERIC ED 477832. <u>Ovid</u>. Raynor Lib., Marquette U. 26 July 2004 <www.ovid.com>.

E-book

Hanley, Wayne. <u>The Genesis of Napoleonic Propaganda, 1796–1799</u>. Columbia UP, 2002. <u>Gutenberg-e</u>. 31 July 2004 <http://www.gutenberg-e.org>.

Machiavelli, Niccolo. <u>Prince</u>. [1513.] <u>Bibliomania</u>. 31 July 2004 <http://www.bibliomania.com>.

Information about the original print version, including a translator if relevant and available, should be provided. Use brackets for adding information not provided in the source.

Web and Internet Sources

Because Web and Internet sources vary widely in design and in the ways they approach content, creating citations for them can sometimes be a puzzling process. To help you create useful, accurate citations, we provide a general format followed by some general principles you can apply when creating Web citations; we then devote the rest of this section to model citations for types of sources that students frequently use.

General Format for Web Sources

Author of the page or document, if available. "Title of page or document." <u>Title of the overall site, usually taken from the home page</u>. Date of publication online or last update of the site, if available. Total range of paragraphs or pages, if they are numbered within the site itself (as in a .pdf document). Name of site sponsor, if available and not already stated in the Web site title. Date you accessed the site <URL of the specific document>.

Note that the main divisions are separated by periods except that no punctuation is used between the date of access and the URL.

Here is an illustration that contains nearly all of the elements listed above:

Smith, Anne-Marie. "Advances in Understanding International Peacemaking." <u>United States Institute of Peace</u>. 2000. 76 pp. 25 May 2004 <http://www.usip.org/pubs/summaries/advances.pdf>.

This citation indicates a seventy-six-page .pdf document by Anne-Marie Smith titled "Advances in Understanding International Peacemaking" and published in 2000. It was posted on the Web site of the United States Institute of Peace, which uses its name as the title of the site. The researcher accessed this document on 25 May 2004 at the URL given.

The next example shows a citation for which not all the information elements were available:

"Nuclear Power Plant Accidents." <u>Infoplease</u>. Pearson Education. 21 Sept. 2004
    <http://www.infoplease.com/ipa/A0001457.html>.

This citation begins with the article title because there is no named author. We
learned by clicking on the "About" link that the Web site <u>Infoplease</u> is sponsored
by Pearson Education. There is no entry for the date of the article because none
was provided; also, there is no entry for number of pages because the site doesn't
indicate page breaks. The researcher accessed the site on 21 Sept. 2004 at the
URL given.

General Principles for Web Sources

As with print sources, the fundamental rule is to give your readers enough
details to find the source you used. Since Web sites are frequently updated,
altered, or dropped, it is important to provide the date that you accessed the
material. In light of this variability, MLA advises that you print or download
your Web and Internet sources so that you can ensure your ability to verify the
material later. Here are a few additional useful principles for using the formats
we provide:

- Always include the date on which you retrieved the material.
- Always include either a URL or, if the URL is too long or unwieldy, an alternative means of finding the source (see p. 670 for how to cite a search page or give path designations).
- Provide the title of the overall Web site. These are usually available at the top of your browser page on the site's home page. Also identify the name of the organization sponsoring the site (often available through an "About us" link) to see if it is different from the Web site title. For example, the Web site shown on page 599 is titled <u>Women Against Gun Control</u>, which is also the name of the sponsoring organization; a citation for this site would include only the Web site title (underlined). In contrast, the Web site of the National Men's Resource Center is entitled <u>Menstuff</u>. A citation for that site would include both names (the title underlined, the sponsor not underlined).
- If you wish to cite an entire Web site rather than a specific page or document, you need to provide only the title of the Web site, the sponsoring organization if different from the title, the date of latest update, the date you accessed the Web site, and the URL.
- When you wish to cite a specific section or document within a Web site, you need to provide the section or document's title and, if available, its author. (As with print sources, if an author is not named, the citation starts with the title of the section or document.)
- When you are citing a specific document or section, include the date on which it was written, published, or posted to the site. If these are unavailable, omit this element of the citation.
- When citing a specific document, include its length in pages or paragraphs if these are indicated in the document itself. For example, .pdf documents show page numbers from paper publication, and some other documents indicate pagination from a print source. However, in most cases, you will not be able to provide the number of pages or paragraphs because they

won't be specified. Do not include data about number of pages based on printouts because different computers and printers will process pages in different ways.

- Some sites provide model citations for use in a research paper. These may not be in MLA style, so be sure to convert them to MLA format.

Alternatives to providing a URL

In MLA style, the preferred way to show Web location is to copy the source's URL directly into the citation. In some cases, however, this is difficult if not impossible. Some URLs are so long that they are unwieldy and prone to transcription errors, and some Web sites seek to simplify access by using just a primary URL with internal links that do not appear in the URL window. MLA suggests the following three alternatives to providing specific URLs:

1. Provide the URL of the site's search page (if available).

> Gidley, Cheryl. "The Best of Both Worlds." *Philanthropy News Digest* 2004. The
> Foundation Center. 15 Aug. 2004 <http://fdncenter.org/pnd/archives/
> index.jhtml>.

(This URL takes you immediately to the site's search box. Enter "Gidley" in the search box to locate the source.)

2. Provide the URL of the site's home page.
3. Indicate the sequence of links a reader can follow from the site home page.

> "Myths and Realities about Antibiotic Resistance." *Union of Concerned Scientists.*
> <http://www.ucsusa.org>. Path: Food and Environment; Antibiotic
> Resistance; FAQs.

(This citation tells the user to start at the UCSUSA home page, click on "Food and Environment," then "Antibiotic Resistance," and finally "FAQs.")

Entire Web site

BlogPulse. Intelliseek. 24 July 2004 <http://www.blogpulse.com/>.

William Faulkner on the Web. Ed. John B. Padgett. 26 Mar. 2004. U of Mississippi. 25
June 2004 <http://www.mcsr.olemiss.edu/~egjbp/faulkner/faulkner.html>.

Agatucci, Cora. Culture and Literature of Africa. Course home page. Humanities
Department, Central Oregon Community College. 31 July 2004
<http://web.cocc.edu/cagatucci/classes/hum211/>.

African Studies Program. Home page. School of Advanced International Study, Johns
Hopkins U. 31 July 2004 <http://www.sais-jhu.edu/programs/africa/index.html>.

Sharpe, William F. Home page. May 2004. 31 July 2004
<http://www.stanford.edu/~wfsharpe/>.

These examples show typical variations in the way to cite an entire Web site. The easiest case is the first, where you provide the site's title, its sponsoring organization, your date of access, and the URL. (If a "last updated" date is available for the entire site, it should be included, but BlogPulse dates and time-stamps individual entries, not the overall site.) The second citation adds the name of the site's editor and the date the site was last updated. The next two examples add the term "Home page" (not underlined) to signal the site's relation to a university course or program, and the final example refers to a personal home page that doesn't have a separate title.

Documents within a Web site

Marks, John. "Overview: Letter from the President." <u>Search for Common Ground</u>. 25 June 2004 <http://www.sfcg.org>. Path: About SFCG; Overview.

Bailey, Ronald. "The Impact of Science on Public Policy. Testimony before House Subcommittee on Energy and Mineral Resources. 108th Congress." <u>Reason Public Policy Institute</u>. 4 Feb. 2004. 10 pp. 18 Sept. 2004 <http://www.rppi.org/impact.pdf>.

The first example uses the "path method" rather than a URL to indicate Web access. The second includes data about the length of the document, available from a quick check of the .pdf document.

Article from a newspaper or newswire site

Thevenot, Brian. "Once in a Blue Moon." <u>Times Picayune</u> [New Orleans] 31 July 2004. 31 July 2004 <http://www.nola.com/news/t-p/frontpage/index.ssf?/base/news-1/1091264442208250.xml>.

"Great Lakes: Rwanda backed dissident troops in DRC-UN panel." <u>IRIN News.org</u>. 21 July 2004. 31 July 2004 <http://www.irinnews.org/advsearch.asp>.

Broadcast transcript from a Web site

Michels, Spencer, and Margaret Warner. "The Politics of 9/11." <u>Online NewsHour</u>. 28 July 2004. Transcript: background and discussion. PBS. 31 July 2004 <http://www.pbs.org/newshour/bb/terrorism/july-dec04/9-11_7-28.html>.

Article from a scholarly e-journal

Welch, John R., and Ramon Riley. "Reclaiming Land and Spirit in the Western Apache Homeland." <u>American Indian Quarterly</u> 25 (2001): 5–14. 19 Dec. 2001 <http://muse.jhu.edu/journals/american_indian_quarterly/v025/25.1welch.pdf>.

E-mail

Daffinrud, Sue. "Scoring Guide for Class Participation." E-mail to the author. 12 Dec. 2001.

Use the subject line as the title of the e-mail.

Online posting to a Listserv, bulletin board, newsgroup, or blog*

CalEnergyGuy. "Energy Crisis Impacts on the Economy: Changes since 2001." Blog posting. 27 July 2004. California Energy Blog. 1 Aug. 2004 <http://calenergy.blogspot.com/2004_07_01_calenergy_archive.html>.

Follow the format for citing an e-mail, using the appropriate label before the date of posting. After the posting date, add these elements: name of the forum, your

---

*Forums for blog entries are not listed in the *MLA Handbook,* so we have interpolated a format based on the formats given for other types of Internet forums.

date of access, a URL for—in order of preference—an archived version of the post, the forum home page, or the posting itself. It may be helpful to insert the name of a sponsoring organization, if available, after the name of the forum.

Miscellaneous Sources

Television or radio program

"Lie Like a Rug." <u>NYPD Blue</u>. Dir. Steven Bochco and David Milch. ABC. KOMO, Seattle. 6 Nov. 2001.

For a program with episodes, begin with the episode name in quotation marks followed by the program name, underlined. If the program is part of a series (such as Masterpiece Theatre), add the series name without quotation marks or underlining after the program title.

Film or video recording

<u>Shakespeare in Love</u>. Dir. John Madden. Perf. Joseph Fiennes and Gwyneth Paltrow. Screenplay by Marc Norman and Tom Stoppard. Universal Miramax, 1998.

A minimal citation begins with the name of the film, underlined, and includes the name of the film company or the distributor and distribution date. Most citations also include the name of the director and may include the names of major performers and writers.

<u>Shakespeare in Love</u>. Dir. John Madden. Perf. Joseph Fiennes and Gwyneth Paltrow. Screenplay by Marc Norman and Tom Stoppard. 1998. Videocassette. Universal Miramax, 1999.

Cite the original film data. Then cite the recording medium (videocassette, laser disc, or DVD), name of recording company, and date of the videocassette or disc.

Sound recording

Dylan, Bob. "Rainy Day Woman." <u>Bob Dylan MTV Unplugged</u>. Columbia, 1995.

For sound recordings begin the entry with what your paper emphasizes—for example, the artist's name, composer's name, or conductor's name—and adjust the elements accordingly.

Cartoon or advertisement

Trudeau, Garry. "Doonesbury." Comic strip. <u>Seattle Times</u> 19 Nov. 2001: B4.

Banana Republic. Advertisement. <u>Details</u> Oct. 2001: 37.

Interview

Castellucci, Marion. Personal interview. 7 Oct. 2001.

Lecture, speech, or conference presentation

Sharples, Mike. "Authors of the Future." Conference of European Teachers of Academic Writing. U of Groningen. Groningen, Neth. 20 June 2001.

Government publications

Government publications are often difficult to cite because there are so many varieties. In general, follow these guidelines:

- Usually cite as author the government agency that produced the document. Begin with the highest level and then branch down to the specific agency:

    United States. Dept. of Justice. FBI

    Idaho. Dept. of Motor Vehicles

- Follow this with the title of the document, underlined.
- If a specific person is clearly identified as the author, you may begin the citation with that person's name, or you may list the author (preceded by the word "By") after the title of the document.
- Follow standard procedures for citing publication information for print sources or retrieval information for Web sources.

    United States. Dept. of Justice. FBI. <u>The School Shooter: A Threat Assessment</u>
        <u>Perspective</u>. By Mary O'Toole. 2000. 16 Aug. 2001
        <http://www.fbi.gov/publications/school/school2.pdf>.

The in-text citation would be: (United States). If you have more than one U.S. government document, continue to narrow down the in-text citation: (United States. Dept. of Justice. FBI. <u>School Shooter</u>). Had this document been published in print rather than online, you would list the standard publishing information found on the title page. Typically the press would be the GPO (Government Printing Office).

Formatting an Academic Paper in MLA Style

An example research paper in MLA style is shown on pages 675–686. Here are the distinctive formatting features of MLA papers:

- Double-space throughout including block quotations and the Works Cited list.
- Use one-inch margins top and bottom, left and right. Indent one-half inch or five spaces from the left margin at the beginning of each paragraph.
- Number pages consecutively throughout the manuscript including the Works Cited list, which begins on a new page. Page numbers go in the upper right-hand corner, flush with the right margin, and one-half inch from the top of the page. The page number should be preceded by your last name. The text begins one inch from the top of the page.
- Do *not* create a separate title page. Type your name, professor's name, course number, and date in the upper left-hand corner of your paper (all double-spaced), beginning one inch from the top of the page; then double-space and type your title, centered, without underlining or any distinctive

fonts (capitalize the first word and important words only); then double-space and begin your text.

- Start a new page for the Works Cited list. Type "Works Cited" centered, one inch from the top of the page in the same font as the rest of the paper; do not enclose it in quotation marks. Use hanging indentation of five spaces or one-half inch for each entry longer than one line. Format entries according to the instructions on page 662.

Student Example of an MLA-Style Research Paper

As an illustration of a student research paper written in MLA style, we present Christopher Leigh's paper on metal detectors in schools. Christopher's process in producing this paper has been discussed in various places throughout the text.

Leigh 1

Christopher Leigh

Professor Grosshans

English 110

September 1, 2001

The Case Against Metal Detectors in Public Schools

One of the most watched news stories of the last decade took place on April 20, 1999, when two students walked into their suburban Colorado high school and shot twelve students and one teacher before shooting themselves. The brutal slayings sent shock waves around the country, leaving everyone asking the same questions. What drove them to commit such a horrible crime? What can we do to prevent something like this from happening again?

Panic over school safety has caused school boards from coast to coast to take action. Though their use is far from widespread, many schools are installing metal detectors to keep guns and knives out of school. Unfortunately, such measures do not address the causes of violence and are simply an ill-considered quick fix that may do more harm than good. Except for schools with very severe threats of danger, metal detectors should not be used because there is no basis for panic and because there are other more effective and less costly alternatives for violence prevention in schools.

An important point to realize about school violence is that the media have created a public outcry over

Leigh 2

school safety when in fact violent incidents are
extremely rare. The media have taken uncommon incidents
like the one at Columbine High and, according to school
psychologist Tony Del Prete, "overanalyze[d] and
sensationalize[d] them to the point of hysteria" (375).

Statistics and studies regarding school violence
are astonishingly conflicting and reported in
sensationalized ways. For example, one study conducted
by the Centers for Disease Control and Prevention
(United States) reports percentages of youths who
carried a gun or weapon to school from 1993 to 1999
(Table 1).

Table 22.1
Percentage of Youths Carrying Weapon or Gun to School,
1993-1999

	1993	1995	1997	1999
Carried a weapon	11.8%	9.8%	8.5%	6.9%
Carried a gun	7.9%	7.6%	5.9%	4.9%

Source: United States. Dept. of Health and Human
Services. Centers for Disease Control and Prevention.

These numbers can be cited in a frightening way ("In
1993 nearly 8 percent of teenagers reported carrying a
gun to school"). But it is also possible to display
these numbers in a graph (see Figure 1 and report them
in a more comforting way: "As shown in Figure 1,

Leigh 3

between 1993 and 1999 the number of students who carried a gun to school has dropped 38 percent from 7.9 percent to 4.9 percent." Proponents of metal detectors generally cite the figures in the most alarming way. For example, advocates of metal detectors claim that 100,000 students carry guns to school each day (Wilson and Zirkel 32), but they fail to note that these statistics are based on data before 1993. Since 1993, violence incidents in schools have declined steadily each year, and youth homicide has dropped by over 50 percent (Barr 44). Of course it is true that weapons and violence are undeniably present in schools. But the percentage of schools in which violence is a recurring problem is perceived to be exponentially larger than it actually is. As a result, metal detectors have been installed in schools that have had no problems with weapons and violence simply to appease a panicked and irrational public.

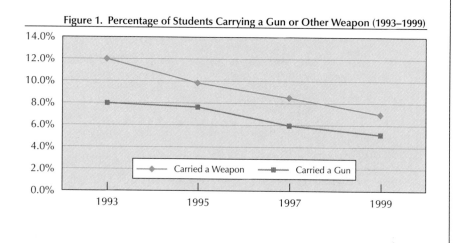

Figure 1. Percentage of Students Carrying a Gun or Other Weapon (1993–1999)

Leigh 4

Although metal detectors may seem like a quick and
tangible way to fight violence in schools, there are
many strong arguments against them based on students'
rights, the ease of defeating metal detectors, the
cost, and the psychological consequences that the
devices have on the school environment.

Many students believe that metal detectors violate
their rights. According to Arizona student Jon Gress,
the use of metal detectors

> invades the student's personal space,
> permitting anyone to see into their bags and
> purses. And if the detector went off, they
> would be required to subject their bags and
> body to a more thorough search. This act alone
> seems to infringe on the Fourth Amendment
> right of unwarranted search and seizure.

Another student, Lindsey, in a message posted on the
juvenile.net message board, says,

> [L]earning in such a threatening environment is
> not good for the students. . . . Does anyone
> else believe [besides me] that [use of metal
> detectors] disrupts the 'good' students and is
> [a] violation against student's rights . . . ?

So far the few court cases involving metal
detectors have ruled in favor of the schools, saying
that the benefit of public safety outweighs the right to
privacy. According to Michael Ferraraccio, the Supreme

Leigh 5

Court has said metal detectors in schools are legal. However, he says, the Supreme Court decision "seemed to indicate that generally some level of individualized suspicion is necessary for a search to be reasonable under the Fourth Amendment" (215). Although this case does not address generalized metal detector searches, legal experts believe that minimally invasive "administrative" searches will be permitted by the courts (Stefkovich and O'Brien 155). Judges liken them to searches used in airports where people are searched for weapons without reasonable suspicion. But I think there is a key distinction between the two situations. People are not required to travel through airports and may walk away from a search, but students are required by law to attend school and do not have the option of refusing a search. Despite court rulings so far, many students will continue to believe their constitutional rights are being violated.

Besides possibly violating students' rights, metal detectors have another serious problem: they can be easily defeated. As American School Board Journal contributor Donna Harrington-Lueker points out, schools have many entrances that can't be locked due to fire codes, windows that can be opened, "and legions of youngsters arriving en masse at the same time each day" (26). As she forcefully puts it, a "permanent, full time metal detector at the front door isn't going to

stop a youngster from passing a gun to a buddy through
the side window" (26).

Also, metal detectors are often used only at the
beginning of the day and sometimes not every day, which
creates a false sense of security. In 1992, a student
in a New York school was shot and killed on a day when
the metal detectors were not in use (Yarbrough 586).
Other shootings have taken place in schools despite the
use of metal detectors. In Los Angeles, ten shooting
incidents occurred after the school district began
using metal detectors in schools, and not a single gun
was confiscated through the searches (Stecklow A1).
Similar conditions exist in a Washington, D.C., school
district, which left one security guard "convinced that
the [metal] detectors were useless" (Stecklow A6).
Dennis Cunningham, a spokesman for a metal detector
manufacturer, notes that the devices are a " 'Band Aid'
solution that 'an innovative student' could foil 'very
easily' " (qtd. in Stecklow A1). Some students
interviewed note that "anyone could sneak in a
knife . . . or a gun" (Stecklow A6). Even organizations
that strongly advocate metal detectors, such as the
National School Safety and Security Services, warn on
their Web site that metal detectors are "not a panacea
for solving safety concerns." Yet schools continue to
use the devices despite the compelling evidence that
indicates that they are not working.

Leigh 7

Another major concern surrounding the use of metal
detectors is cost. Airport-style units cost anywhere
between four and ten thousand dollars (Harrington-
Lueker 27). Handheld units are cheaper and therefore
considerably more common, but they are much more time
consuming and much less effective. Personnel are also
required to operate the machinery, and large schools
will often require upwards of fifteen officers to conduct
the searches. According to Harrington-Lueker, it is not
unusual for school districts to spend several million
dollars to implement a comprehensive metal detector
system in their schools (27). Parents and citizens
argue that the safety of our children shouldn't carry a
price tag, but when metal detectors prove ineffective,
alternatives need to be investigated.

Perhaps the most harmful effect of metal detectors
is their psychological impact on students subjected to
daily searches. Student essays posted on the Web, along
with dozens of postings on electronic message boards,
show students' dismay at being subjected to metal
detectors. "Guards, cameras, scanners, and metal
detectors every day take over our schools," a
Philadelphia high school senior complained to Venture
Lee. Another student, using the nickname "ummm" on a
message board, says:

> It's not actually walking through the metal
> detectors that I'm against. . . . It's much

Leigh 8

more the principle of the thing. These damn

things, and the people the school board has

hired to run them, cost so much freaking money

that could be used for useful things. Metal

detectors will not stop a shooting in [this

high school]. If someone wanted to kill people

then they could just as well shoot people in

the damn line to get through them.

Metal detectors not only reinforce the feeling that

schools are unsafe, but they also instill a sense of

humiliation in students and, as a result, a feeling of

distrust between students and school administrators.

These feelings of distrust and susceptibility erode the

atmosphere of learning that is so important to a

student's education, and schools begin to feel more

like prisons than schools.

If metal detectors are an inappropriate means to

curb violence in our schools, what is a better

approach? If we look again at student postings on the

Web, we see a consistently recurring suggestion:

friendlier schools, personal relationships, and better

counseling. As one student told Lee, "City kids get

metal detectors, suburban kids get counselors." Atlanta

high school senior Malik Barry-Buchanan was asked how

the school environment can be changed "so people don't

feel the need to bring a weapon to school." Here is his

answer:

Leigh 9

> Well, for starters, we need to find ways for
> students to respect each other, have teachers
> go through training to encourage them to make
> even the smallest attempt at getting in touch
> with the students, and have school
> administrators look at students as
> independent, free-thinking young adults and
> not 5-year-old rug rats.

In order to combat the problem of school violence head-on, it is essential to provide students with better counseling and to work towards improving the overall school environment. Scott Poland, the president of the National Association of School Psychologists, writes that administrators need to do more to personalize schools and provide better counseling services to students who may be troubled (45). He writes that most counselors are already overworked and are required to do things such as scheduling that take away from their attention to the students. Poland also emphasizes that it is important for teachers to form strong relationships with each and every student. He suggests that teachers set aside a small amount of time each day to interact with students, and discourages schools from cutting extracurricular programs that may help students feel connected to the school (46).

In my opinion, Poland's article offers the most encouraging and perhaps the best advice for the

Leigh 10

prevention of school violence. Teachers might complain that they do not have the time to spend getting to know every student. But getting to know each student should be part of the job requirement. If teachers know their students on a personal level, they will be able to sense when a student is in trouble, reach out to that student, and create an atmosphere of care and trust rather than suspicion and surveillance.

Violence does undoubtedly exist in schools, but the percentage of schools where the level of violence justifies metal detectors is extremely small. The problem of school violence is simply a reflection of the high level of violence in American society in general, and the problem is not the schools, but society as a whole. Metal detectors may deter some students from bringing weapons to school, but they can't prevent violence and they create an atmosphere of fear and suspicion rather than trust and community. The key to preventing school violence is to focus on improving students' relationships with teachers and, more importantly, themselves, rather than treat them like potential criminals.

Leigh 11

Works Cited

Barr, Bob. "Liberal Media Adored Gun-Control Marchers."
    <u>Insight on the News</u> 5 June 2000: 44- . <u>ProQuest</u>.
    Lemieux Lib., Seattle U. 15 Aug. 2001
    <http://proquest.umi.com>.

Barry-Buchanan, Malik. "More Rules + More Security =
    Feelings of Safety." <u>Alternet.org</u> 16 Aug. 2001
    <http://alternet.org/print.html?StoryID=9623>.

Del Prete, Tony. "Unsafe Schools: Perception or
    Reality?" <u>Professional School Counseling</u> 3 (2000):
    375-76.

Ferraraccio, Michael. "Metal Detectors in the Public
    Schools: Fourth Amendment Concerns." <u>Journal of Law
    and Education</u> 28 (1999): 209-29.

Gress, Jon. "School Violence: How to Stop the Crime of
    Today's Youth." <u>Gecko--The Student Server</u> 5 May
    2000. 16 Aug. 2001 <http://gecko.gc.maricopa.edu/
    ~jtgress/argue2.htm>.

Harrington-Lueker, Donna. "Metal Detectors." <u>American
    School Board Journal</u> 179.5 (1992): 26-27.

Lee, Venture. "Detectors Alarm Some Students." <u>Said &
    Done</u>. Urban Journalism Workshop. Summer 2000. 16
    Aug. 2001 <http://ujw.philly.com/
    2000/detector.htm>.

Lindsey. "Re: School Security." Online posting. 23 Oct.
    1999. Juvenile Information Network. 16 Aug. 2001
    <http://www.juvenilenet.org/messages/27.html>.

Leigh 12

National School Safety and Security Services. "School
        Security Equipment and Technology." 23 Aug. 2001
        <http://www.schoolsecurity.org/
        resources/security-equipment.html>.

Poland, Scott. "The Fourth R--Relationships." <u>American
        School Board Journal</u> 187.3 (2000): 45-46.

Stecklow, Steve. "Metal Detectors Find a Growing
        Market, But Not Many Guns." <u>Wall Street Journal</u> 7
        Sept. 1993: A1+.

Stefkovich, Jacqueline, and G. M. O'Brien. "Students'
        Fourth Amendment Rights and School Safety."
        <u>Education and Urban Society</u> 29 (1997): 149-59.

Ummm. "Alright." Online posting. 27 May 2000. ezboard.
        16 Aug. 2001 <http://pub6.ezboard.com/
        fmastermanschool.showMessage?topicID=99.topic>.

United States. Dept. of Health and Human Services. Centers
        for Disease Control and Prevention. "Youth Risk
        Behavior Trends from CDC's 1991, 1993, 1995, 1997,
        and 1999 Youth Risk Behavior Surveys." <u>Adolescent and
        School Health</u> 6 Aug. 2001. 11 Aug. 2001
        <http://www.cdc.gov/nccdphp/dash/yrbs/trend.htm>.

Wilson, Joseph M., and Perry Zirkel. "When Guns Come to
        School." <u>American School Board Journal</u> 181.1
        (1994): 32-34.

Yarbrough, Jonathan W. "Are Metal Detectors the Answer
        to Handguns in Public Schools?" <u>Journal of Law and
        Education</u> 22 (1993): 584-87.

Understanding APA Style and Formatting

In many respects, the APA style and the MLA style are similar and the basic logic is the same. In the APA system, the list where readers can find full bibliographic information is titled "References"; as in MLA format, it includes only the sources cited in the body of the paper. Pay careful attention to possibly unfamiliar punctuation and format details in the models we present in this section. The most distinguishing features of APA style are highlighted in the following list:

- APA style emphasizes dates of books and articles and de-emphasizes the names of authors. Therefore the date of publication appears in parenthetical citations and is the second item mentioned in each entry in the "References" list.
- Only published or retrievable documents are included in the "References" list. Personal correspondence, e-mail messages, interviews, and lectures or speeches are referenced only through in-text citations.
- APA style uses fewer abbreviations and spells out the complete names of university presses. It uses an ampersand (&) instead of the word *and* for items in a series in both the reference list and in-text citations.
- APA style uses italics rather than underlining for titles and capitalizes only the first word of titles and subtitles of books and articles. It doesn't place titles of articles in quotation marks.
- APA style uses only an initial for authors' or editors' first names in citations.
- APA style calls for every page of a periodical article to be listed in a reference, even when the pages are not continuous.
- APA style streamlines the presentation of information about electronic documents into sentence-like statements at the end of a citation, requiring inclusion of a URL for Web documents but not for databases.
- For electronic documents without page numbers, APA suggests citing material by heading labels if they are available, and permits the writer to count paragraphs within a section. Paragraphs are cited with a ¶ symbol before the number. A parenthetical citation might then read: (Elrod, 2005, Introduction section, ¶ 7).
- APA style has a distinctive format for title pages and frequently includes an "Abstract" of the paper immediately following the title page.
- Page numbers are placed at the top right-hand margin and are preceded by a "running head" (a short version of the title).
- APA uses block indentation for quotations when they are longer than forty words. Quotations shorter than forty words are worked into your own text using quotation marks as in other systems.

For an example of a student paper in APA style, see the experimental report by Brittany Tinker, Trevor Tsuchikawa, and Tatiana Whizar on pp. 277–289.

APA Formatting for In-Text Citations

When you make an in-text citation in APA style, you place inside the parentheses the author's last name and the year of the source as well as the page number if a particular passage or table is cited. The elements in the citation are separated by commas, and a "p." or "pp." precedes the page number(s). If a source has more than one author, use an ampersand (&) to join their names. When the author is mentioned in an attributive tag, include only the date (and page if applicable) in the parenthetical citation. The following examples show parenthetical documentation with and without attributive tags according to APA style:

> The Spanish tried to reduce the status of women who had been able to do business, get divorced, and sometimes become village chiefs (Karnow, 1989, p. 41).
> According to Karnow (1989), the Spanish tried to reduce the status of women who had been able to do business, get divorced, and sometimes become village chiefs (p. 41).

Citing from an Indirect Source

Ideally, if you want to use a quotation or data cited by one of your sources, you should track down the original source. When this isn't possible, APA style calls for using the phrase "as cited in" within the parenthetical reference. Only the indirect source would appear in the list of references. Here is an example:

> Morrison's data from the 1980s provides multiple examples of the phenomenon (as cited in Stephanbach, 2004, p. 828).

Documenting Sources in a "References" List (APA)

The APA "References" list at the end of a paper presents entries alphabetically in a hanging indentation format like that of MLA style. A typical entry would look like this:

Smith, R. (1995). *Body image in Western cultures, 1750–present.* London: Bonanza Press.

Two or more listings for one author

If you cite more than one item for an author, repeat the author's name each time and arrange the items in chronological order, beginning with the earliest. In cases where two works by an author appeared in the same year, arrange them in the list alphabetically by title, and then add a lowercase "a" or "b" (etc.) after the date so that you can distinguish between them in the in-text citations. As illustration, the following parenthetical citations refer to the hypothetical book and article cited in the sample entries that follow them:

(Smith, 1999a)

(Smith, 1999b)

Smith, R. (1999a). *Body image in non-Western cultures.* London: Bonanza Press.

Smith, R. (1999b). Eating disorders reconsidered. *Journal of Appetite Studies, 45,* 295–300.

APA Citation Models

Books

One author

Brumberg, J. J. (1997). *The body project: An intimate history of American girls.* New York: Vintage.

Two or more authors

Dombrowski, D. A., & Deltete, R. J. (2000). *A brief, liberal, Catholic defense of abortion.* Urbana: University of Illinois Press.

Belenky, M., Clinchy, B. M., Goldberger, N. R., & Tarule, J. M. (1986). *Women's ways of knowing: The development of self, voice, and mind.* New York: Basic Books.

APA style uses "et al." only for books with more than six authors.

Second, later, or revised edition

Montagu, A. (1986). *Touching: The human significance of the skin* (3rd ed.). New York: Perennial Press.

The number of the edition goes in parentheses. One could also say "Rev. ed." for "Revised edition."

Republished book (for example, a paperback published after the original hardback edition or a modern edition of an older work)

Hill, C. (1991). *The world turned upside down: Radical ideas during the English revolution.* London: Penguin. (Original work published 1972)

The in-text citation should read: (Hill, 1972/1991).

Wollstonecraft, M. (1995). *The vindication of the rights of woman, with strictures on political and moral subjects.* Rutland, VT: Tuttle. (Original work published 1792)

The in-text citation should read: (Wollstonecraft, 1792/1995).

Multivolume work

Churchill, W. S. (1956–1958). *A history of the English-speaking peoples* (Vols. 1–4). New York: Dodd, Mead.

Citation for all the volumes together. The in-text citation should read: (Churchill, 1956–1958).

Churchill, W. S. (1957). *A history of the English-speaking peoples: Vol. 4. The great democracies.* New York: Dodd, Mead.

Citation for a specific volume. The in-text citation should read: (Churchill, 1957).

Article in reference work

Ling, T. O. (1970). Buddhism in Burma. In S. G. F. Brandon (Ed.), *Dictionary of comparative religion.* New York: Scribner's.

Translation

De Beauvoir, S. (1961). *The second sex* (H. M. Parshley, Trans.). New York: Bantam Books. (Original work published 1949)

The in-text citation should read: (De Beauvoir, 1949/1961).

Corporate author (a commission, committee, or other group)

American Red Cross. (1993). *Standard first aid.* St. Louis, MO: Mosby Lifeline.

Anonymous author

The New Yorker cartoon album: 1975–1985. (1987). New York: Penguin Books.

The in-text citation may be a shortened version of the title such as: (*New Yorker,* 1987).

Edited Anthologies

Citing the editor

O'Connell, D. F., & Alexander, C. N. (Eds.). (1994). *Self recovery: Treating addictions using transcendental meditation and Maharishi Ayur-Veda.* New York: Haworth Press.

Citing an individual article

Royer, A. (1994). The role of the transcendental meditation technique in promoting smoking cessation: A longitudinal study. In D. F. O'Connell & C. N. Alexander (Eds.), *Self recovery: Treating addictions using transcendental meditation and Maharishi Ayur-Veda* (pp. 221–239). New York: Haworth Press.

The pattern is as follows: Author of article. (Year of publication). Title of article. In Name of editor (Ed.), *Title of anthology* (pp. inclusive page numbers of article). Place of publication: Name of press.

Articles in Scholarly Journals Accessed in Print

Scholarly journal that numbers pages continuously

Barton, E. L. (1993). Evidentials, argumentation, and epistemological stance. *College English, 55,* 745–769.

The pattern is as follows: Author. (Year of publication). Article title. *Name of Journal, volume number,* inclusive page numbers. Note that the volume number is italicized along with the title of the journal.

Scholarly journal that restarts page numbering with each issue

Pollay, R. W., Lee, J. S., & Carter-Whitney, D. (1992). Separate, but not equal: Racial segmentation in cigarette advertising. *Journal of Advertising, 21*(1), 45–57.

The citation includes the issue number in parentheses as well as the volume number. Note that the issue number and the parentheses are *not* italicized.

Articles in Magazines and Newspapers Accessed in Print

Magazine article with named author

Snyder, R. L. (2001, August—September). A daughter of Cambodia remembers: Loung Ung's journey. *Ms., 12,* 62–67.

Hall, S. S. (2001, March 11). Prescription for profit. *New York Times Magazine,* 40–45, 59, 91–92, 100.

The pattern is as follows: Author. (Year, Month [Day]). Title of article. *Name of Magazine, volume number [if stated in magazine],* inclusive pages. If page numbers are discontinuous, identify every page, separating numbers with a comma.

Magazine article without named author

Daddy, daddy. (2001, July 30). *New Republic, 225,* 12–13.

Review of book or film

Schwarz, B. (2001, November). A bit of bunting: A new history of the British empire
elevates expediency to principle [Review of the book *Ornamentalism: How the
British saw their empire*]. *Atlantic Monthly, 288,* 126–135.

Kaufman, S. (2001, July 30). Polishing a gem [Review of the motion picture *The blue
angel*]. *New Republic, 225,* 28–29.

Newspaper article

Henriques, D. B. (1998, September 27). Hero's fall teaches Wall Street a lesson. *Seattle
Times,* pp. A1, A24.

Newspaper editorial

Dr. Frankenstein on the hill [Editorial]. (2002, May 18). *The New York Times,* p. A22.

Letter to the editor of a magazine or newspaper

Tomsovic, K. (1998, July 13). Culture clash [Letter to the editor]. *The New Yorker,* p. 7.

Print Articles or Books Downloaded from a Database

Print article downloaded from licensed database

Watanabe, M. (2003). Zoos act as sentinels for infectious diseases. *Bioscience, 53,* 792.
Retrieved July 26, 2004, from ProQuest database.

Note the commas before and after the year in the retrieval statement.

Broadcast transcript retrieved from licensed database

Conan, N. (Anchor), & Telhami, S. (Guest). (2004, May 4). Arab media [Radio
transcript]. *Talk of the nation.* Retrieved July 31, 2004, from LexisNexis database.

Reference material retrieved from licensed database

Cicada. (2004). *Encyclopaedia Britannica.* Retrieved July 31, 2004, from Britannica
Online database.

The *Publication Manual of the American Psychological Association,* 5th ed., has no
model format for an online reference database, so we followed the manual's
advice to adapt the format of similar items.

Papers and monographs from an information service

Information services such as ERIC (Educational Resources Information Center) or
NTIS (National Technical Information Service) provide material to your library on
microfiche or online, offering indexes on CD-ROM or online. Much of the material from these services has not been published in major journals or magazines.
Frequently they are typescripts of conference papers or other scholarly work disseminated on microfiche.

Coll, R. K., Tofield, S., Vyle, B., & Bolstad, R. (2003, March). *Free-choice learning at a metropolitan zoo*. Paper presented at the annual meeting of the National Association for Research in Science Teaching, Philadelphia, PA. (ERIC Document Reproduction Service No. ED477832)

If you retrieve the document online, add a retrieval statement indicating the name of the database and the date retrieved, as in the preceding examples.

Web and Internet Sources

Documents within a Web site

Provide corporate authors when a document does not list an individual author. Use "n.d." if no publication date is provided.

Marks, J. (n.d.). Overview: Letter from the president. Retrieved June 25, 2004, from the Search for Common Ground Web site: http://www.sfcg.org/sfcg/ sfcg_overview.html

United States Institute of Peace. (2000). Advances in understanding international peacemaking. Retrieved May 25, 2004, from http://www.usip.org/pubs/summaries/adv_intl.html

Article from a newspaper site

Thevenot, B. (2004, July 31). Once in a blue moon. *Times Picayune* [New Orleans]. Retrieved July 31, 2004, from http://www.nola.com/t-p/

Broadcast transcript from a Web site

Michels, S. (Correspondent), & Warner, M. (Anchor). (2004, July 28). The politics of 9/11 [Television transcript]. *Newshour with Jim Lehrer*. Retrieved July 31, 2004, from the Online Newshour Website: http://www.pbs.org/newshour/bb/terrorism/july-dec04/9-11_7-28.html

Because the APA *Manual* doesn't have a model for broadcast transcripts, we modified the format for television broadcasts by adding identifying labels.

Article from a scholarly E-journal

Welch, J. R., & Riley, R. (2001). Reclaiming land and spirit in the western Apache homeland. *American Indian Quarterly, 25*, 5–14. Retrieved December 19, 2001, from http://muse.jhu.edu/journals/american_indian_quarterly/v025/25.1welch.pdf

E-book

Hoffman, F. W. (1981). *The literature of rock: 1954–1978*. Retrieved December 19, 2001, from http://www.netlibrary.com/ebook_info.asl?product_id=24355

The *Publication Manual of the American Psychological Association*, 5th ed., has no example of an E-book. We followed the manual's advice about how to proceed when an unusual case arises.

E-mail, interviews, and personal correspondence
APA guidelines limit the "References" list to published or retrievable information. Cite personal correspondence in the body of your text, but not in the References list: "Daffinrud (personal communication, December 12, 2001) claims that. . . ."

Online posting to a Listserv, bulletin board, newsgroup, or blog
CalEnergyGuy. (2004, July 27). Energy crisis impacts on the economy: Changes since 2001 [Blog posting]. Retrieved August 1, 2004, from the Web site of the California Energy Blog: http://calenergy.blogspot.com/2004_07_01_calenergy_archive.html

We have again followed the APA's advice to interpolate a format from similar models.

Miscellaneous Sources

Television program
Bochco, S., & Milch, D. (Directors). (2001, November 6). Lie like a rug [Television series episode]. In *NYPD blue*. New York: American Broadcasting Company.

Film
Madden, J. (Director). (1998). *Shakespeare in love* [Motion picture]. United States: Universal Miramax.

Sound recording
Dwarf Music. (1966). Rainy day woman [Recorded by B. Dylan]. On *Bob Dylan MTV unplugged* [CD]. New York: Columbia. (1995)

Follow this format: Writer of song or copyright holder. (Date of copyright). Title of song [Recorded by artist if different from writer]. On *Title of album* [Medium such as CD, record, or cassette]. Location: Label. (Date of album if different from date of song)

Unpublished paper presented at a meeting
Sharples, M. (2001, June 20). *Authors of the future*. Keynote address presented at Conference of European Teachers of Academic Writing, Groningen, the Netherlands.

Government publications
O'Toole, M. (2000). *The school shooter: A threat assessment perspective*. Washington, DC: U.S. Federal Bureau of Investigation. Retrieved August 16, 2001, from http://www.fbi.gov/publications/school/school2.pdf

Student Example of an APA-Style Paper

An example of a paper in APA style is shown on pages 277–289.

PART

5

A Guide to Special Writing and Speaking Occasions

This energy poster is part of a series produced by Energy Conservation Awareness Products (www.energyconservationposters .com). These posters are intended to make people conscious of how they use and waste energy and of alternative energy sources that can lessen the use of fossil fuels. Consider how the poster's words, the features of this image, and the use of color all work together to attract viewers and make them think about their energy habits. This poster relates to various readings on energy and various For Writing and Discussion exercises throughout Parts One and Two of this text.

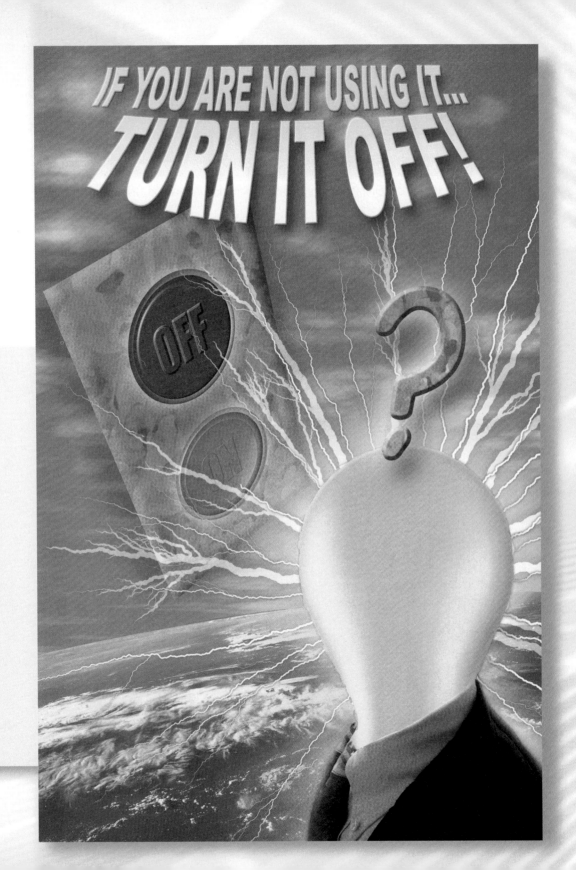

Part 5 A Guide to Special Writing and Speaking Occasions

696

Oral Communication
Working in Groups and Giving Speeches

The consensual process of truth seeking is based on the simple assumption that all
of us thinking together are smarter than any one of us thinking alone.

—PARKER PALMER, *EDUCATOR*

I n this chapter we focus on thinking, writing, and speaking as social activities that involve specific kinds of interaction. The first half of this chapter encourages you to discover how working in groups can deepen your thinking and enrich your writing. The second half shows you how preparing and giving formal—and sometimes impromptu—speeches can build on and extend what you have learned about effective writing for audiences.

About Working in Groups

Although images of the solitary writer are part of the cultural mystique of writing, most writers, as we have stressed throughout this book, seek out communities of peers with whom they test and share ideas and exchange drafts.

Writing communities are especially important in academic, business, and professional settings. The vast majority of scientific and technical articles are written by a team, often with three or more authors. And increasingly, professional proposals, research reports, legal briefs, ad campaigns, brochures to stockholders, and other documents in the academic and business worlds are team-produced efforts.

The reasons for this trend are readily apparent. First, much contemporary work is so complex and technical that no single person has enough expertise to compose a nonroutine document. Second, many large businesses now use self-directed teams without middle managers, and these teams are responsible for multiple tasks, many of which require the production of documents. And perhaps most important, much professional writing is now produced on networked computers, making joint authorship of documents procedurally convenient. Clearly, the ability to write effectively as part of a team is an increasingly critical skill for career advancement. Many businesses now regard group skills as one of the three or four most important determinants of employee success.

Besides these economic and career reasons, the ability to participate in writing communities is important for other reasons. Humans construct knowledge through interaction with others. Throughout this text, we have said that to write an essay is to join a conversation about a question; the back-and-forth dialogue involved in group work is a real-time version of the conversations embodied in printed texts. Through discourse with others, you gather multiple perspectives on phenomena, which you synthesize through the filter of your own perspective. In other words, you construct your knowledge by exposing yourself to alternative views. Moreover, purposeful, thoughtful group interaction is a source not only of knowledge of the world around you, but also of self-knowledge because groups enable you to see the products of your mind the way that others see them. The kind of thinking that you practice in groups, therefore, is the kind you must exhibit in writing.

Basic Principles of Successful Group Interaction

If the thought of group work makes you uncomfortable, you are not alone. Experiences of unpleasant or unproductive groups and unwieldy, time-consuming committees have generated such jokes as "A zebra is a horse designed by a committee" and "Committees keep minutes and waste hours." However, we suggest a different vision of groups. We prefer to think of groups as problem-solving teams like engineering design teams or the marketing teams that plan new sales strategies. You might also recall that one of the world's most influential documents—the Declaration of Independence—was written as a small-group project.

To help you form efficient and productive teams, we recommend that you and your group members practice the following principles.

Avoid Clone-Think and Ego-Think

Many group tasks ask you to propose and justify a solution to a problem. A group consensus is not the same as a majority view. Although a consensus is a form of agreement, a good one grows out of respectful and productive *disagreement*. The best small groups build solutions thoughtfully, beginning with different points of view and encouraging dissent along the way. Weak groups either reach closure too early or bicker endlessly, never building on disagreement to reach consensus.

To steer a middle ground between early closure and endless bickering, you need to avoid two common problems of group interaction: clone-think and ego-think. When groups lapse into *clone-think*, discussions degenerate into "feel-good sessions" guaranteed to produce safe, superficial solutions. Everyone agrees with the first opinion expressed to avoid conflict and difficult work. At the other extreme is the *ego-think* group, in which group members go their own way, producing a collection of minority views. Whereas clone-thinkers view their task as conformity to a norm, ego-thinkers see their goal as safeguarding the autonomy of individual group members. At both extremes, group members fail to take one another's ideas seriously.

When we talk about taking other people's ideas seriously or about reaching consensus, we don't mean that group discussions should transform people's fundamental values and attitudes. But we do mean that they should bring about realistic changes: softening a position, complicating an understanding, or simply acknowledging an alternative possibility. These sorts of changes in understanding happen only when people learn how to present and consider alternative views in a constructive, nonthreatening manner. One approach to avoiding both clone-thinking and ego-thinking is to practice our next principle, empathic listening.

Listen Empathically

Sometimes called "Rogerian listening," after the psychologist Carl Rogers, who popularized the technique, empathic listening is a powerful strategy for helping people resolve conflicts. To be *empathic* is to try to stand in the other person's shoes—to understand the values, beliefs, and fears underlying that person's position. Empathic listeners are *active*, not passive; they interpret not only the speaker's words, but also the speaker's tone of voice, body language, and even silences. Empathic listeners invite speech from others by maintaining eye contact, avoiding disapproving frowns or gestures, asking clarifying questions, and nodding or taking notes.

The rules of empathic listening are simple. Before you respond to someone else's position on an issue, summarize that person's viewpoint fairly in your own words. Carl Rogers discovered that when negotiating parties in a dispute (or couples in marital therapy) were required to summarize each other's views, the experience often defused their anger and encouraged them toward compromise or synthesis. In small groups, empathic listening can deepen conversation. If there is a dispute, the acting group leader might ask one disputant to summarize the other's position. For example: "Irwin, what do you understand Beth's position to be here and how do you see your position differing from hers?" Once Irwin and Beth understand their differences, they will be better able to reconcile them.

When a group becomes skilled at listening, here's what happens:

1. *There are fewer interruptions*. Group members have more "space" in which to complete their thoughts. They take turns speaking. To get the floor, one person doesn't have to interrupt another.
2. *Participation is more equitable*. Group discussions are less apt to be dominated by one or two group members. The group draws out shy or quiet group members and values their contributions.
3. *Discussions are more connected*. Speakers are apt to begin their contributions by referring to what previous speakers have said. "I really liked Pam's point about . . ." or "I see what Paul was saying when. . . , but. . ."

For Writing and Discussion

Freewrite your response to the following questions:

1. In the group work we have done so far in this class, how well do I think the group members have listened to and understood my views?

(continued)

2. How good a listener have I been?

3. What might our group do differently to promote better listening?

Then share your freewrites in groups and take turns summarizing each other's views. Reach consensus on several ways in which the group might improve its listening skills.

Play Assigned Roles

Writing groups accomplish tasks more efficiently when members take turns playing two distinct roles.

1. *Leader/Coordinator*. This person's job is to ensure that the assigned task is clearly understood by all, to set clear goals for the session, to monitor the time, to keep the group on task, and to make sure that the group has its assigned product completed in the time allocated by the instructor. To prevent early closure or endless bickering, the leader/coordinator must draw out divergent views, promote good listening, and help the group achieve a consensus, without ever being dictatorial.

2. *Recorder/Reporter*. The recorder keeps notes on the group's decision-making process, constantly asking group members for clarification, and reads back what he or she understands group members to have said and decided. The recorder also synthesizes the group's deliberations and reports the results to the class.

In writing classrooms, we have found that groups work best when each student takes a rotation in each of these roles. Some instructors prefer to combine the two roles so that a group recorder serves as both leader and note taker.

Be Sensitive to Body Language

Groups can often learn to function more effectively by reading body language. Groups that draw their chairs close together are more effective than groups that maintain distance from each other or marginalize some members through irregular placement of chairs. Group members should note potential problems signaled by body language. A person who sits with arms folded across the chest staring out a window is signaling alienation. Other signs of dysfunction include side conversations, division of the group into subgroups, and domination of the discussion by one or two people who ignore others.

Invest Time in Group Maintenance

Group members periodically need to reflect on and think critically about their performance, a process called *group maintenance*. Group maintenance may be as simple as taking several minutes at the completion of a task to discuss the things the group did well or not so well and to identify steps for improvement.

Occasionally a more extensive and formal sort of group-maintenance task is required. One such task calls for each member to do a self-assessment by freewriting responses to questions such as the following:

Our group performs best when _____.

Our group's effectiveness could be improved if _____.

My greatest strength as a group member is _____.

Another thing I could contribute is _____.

The members then share these self-assessments with the whole group.

Recognize How Personality and Culture Affect Group Participation

Group interaction can often be improved if group members understand the influence of personality and culture on a person's behavior in a group. Psychologists have discovered that people with different personality types have different reactions to working in groups. According to interpreters of the Myers-Briggs Type Indicator,* one of the most highly regarded personality assessment tests, people who test as *extroverts* like to think through an issue by talking out their ideas with others; they tend to be vocal and highly engaged during group discussions. People who test as *introverts* prefer thinking privately about an issue before talking about it and are often uncomfortable discussing their ideas in groups, although they listen carefully and take in what everyone is saying. Often, quiet group members are listening more carefully and thinking more deeply than more-vocal people realize. Until the group gently encourages them to contribute, however, they may be silent.

Judgers like to reach decisions rapidly, and they often grow impatient if the group wants to extend discussion of an issue. In contrast, *perceivers* resist early closure and want to talk through all possible points of view on an issue before reaching a decision. If you understand such personality differences, then you might better tolerate classmates' behaviors that are different from your own.

Other important differences are related to culture. Most U.S.-born students are used to talking in class, holding class debates, and even disagreeing with the teacher. In many cultures, however, it is disrespectful to argue with the teacher or to speak in class unless called on. Students are socialized to listen and not to talk. They can find group work in a North American college extremely painful.

Speech habits also vary widely. Typically, North Americans state their desires bluntly and assertively in ways that would seem rude to people from Asian cultures, who are taught to mask their statements of desire in roundabout conversation. Some cultures have a strong oral tradition of storytelling or speech making, whereas others have a tradition of silence. If your institution has a diverse student

---

*The Myers-Briggs Type Indicator locates persons along four different continuums: introversion/extroversion, thinking/feeling, sensing/intuition, perceiving/judging. Composition researchers have used the Myers-Briggs inventory to reveal fascinating differences among writers that throw valuable light on students' behavior in groups. See G.H. Jensen and J.K. DiTiberio, *Personality and the Teaching of Composition* (Norwood, NJ: Ablex, 1989).

body that includes members of ethnic minority groups and international students, then group work can be a fascinating laboratory for the study of cultural differences.

Manage Conflict by Dealing with an "Impossible Group Member"

Occasionally groups face a critical test of their ability to manage conflict: the Impossible Group Member, or IGM. IGMs may dominate group discussions; they may be rude or intimidating, trying to turn every discussion into a conflict; they may sit sullenly, draining off group enthusiasm; or they may be generally unprepared or fail to do the work assigned to them outside class.

Although it's not easy to deal with an IGM (sometimes the instructor has to intervene), most impossible group members may simply need encouragement and direction. The root of most IGMs' problems is their difficulty in recognizing the effects they're having on other people. Direct criticism of their behaviors will likely surprise them—they won't see it coming—and cause them to react defensively. IGMs need to see the consequences of their actions and they need to see positive behaviors modeled for them. If IGMs dominate discussions, they need to learn to listen. If they are sullenly silent, they need to have their input actively solicited and their responses taken seriously. They have to take their turns in leadership positions and learn to appreciate the difficulties of consensus building and decision making. And they must be made aware that their actions are bothering the other group members.

The best way to deal with IGMs is to discuss the problem candidly, perhaps during a group-maintenance session (see pp. 700–701). If group members reflect on and evaluate *how* the group did its task, focusing on group shortcomings ("What could we do better next time?") rather than on individuals' failures ("Martine, you drive me crazy!"), then it becomes easier for errant group members to accept responsibility for their actions. In explaining a problem to an IGM, try using what communication experts call *I statements* rather than *you statements*. Keep the focus on your own feelings and avoid launching accusations. Note the different tones in the following examples:

You Statement	Martine, you're always insulting us by looking out the window.
I Statement	Martine, when you look out the window, it makes me feel like I'm a boring person.
You Statement	Pete and Valencia are always dominating the discussion.
I Statement	On some days I want to say something in the group but there is never a break in the conversation where I can join.

Using *I* statements helps defuse defensiveness by calling attention to the consequences of behaviors without attaching blame or censure.

We are now ready to turn to productive group strategies for addressing three kinds of tasks: consensus seeking, brainstorming, and orally rehearsing drafts.

Thinking in Groups

Group work is one of the most effective ways to practice critical thinking. This section examines three ways that groups can think together.

Seeking Consensus

Most of the problems posed in the For Writing and Discussion exercises in this text have alternative solutions—there is no single "right" answer. Seeking a consensus answer—especially when group members have different views—can lead to highly productive critical thought. When different group members propose different answers to the same problem, how does a group reach a consensus?*

First, don't assume that every group member has to be completely satisfied with the group's final solution. Instead, everyone should agree that the proposed solution is feasible and rationally supportable. Your solution must be achieved through *consensus* rather than through majority vote, coin flip, or taking turns. This approach means that each group member has veto power over the final solution. But this option should be used sparingly, and only if a person truly cannot live with the proposed solution. After an initial discussion to be sure that everyone understands the task, you can use the following guidelines to embark on a problem-solving procedure that encourages consensus:

1. *Ask every group member to propose at least one tentative solution for discussion.* Members should present justifying arguments as well so that group members can appreciate the reasoning behind each approach.
2. *Once you have presented a possible solution, avoid arguing for it a second time.* Your goal now is to be flexible and listen to other viewpoints rather than to press for adoption of your own position. Remember, however, not to give up your viewpoint quickly just to avoid conflict. Yield only if you see legitimate strengths in other approaches.
3. *If none of the proposed solutions wins everyone's approval, begin brainstorming for alternatives that synthesize good features from various proposals.* Sometimes you can formulate a lowest-common-denominator solution—one that everyone grudgingly accepts but that no one really likes—and brainstorm ways to improve it.
4. *Don't think in terms of winners and losers* ("If Lenore's solution wins, then Pete's must lose"). Rather, try to negotiate win/win solutions in which all parties give up something but also retain something.
5. *Accept disagreement and conflict as a strength rather than a weakness.* Chances are that the disagreements in your group mirror disagreements in the larger community to which your solution must appeal. From these disagreements you can forge a synthesis that is much stronger than any individual's private

---

*The discussion of consensus making is adapted from Parker Palmer, *To Know as We Are Known: Education as a Spiritual Journey* (San Francisco: Harper & Row, 1983), pp. 94–96.

solution. As Parker Palmer says in the epigraph to this chapter, "The consensual process of truth seeking is based on the simple assumption that all of us thinking together are smarter than any one of us thinking alone."

Brainstorming

Group brainstorming uses intuitive, unstructured thinking. During a brainstorming session, everyone is encouraged to suggest ideas, however outlandish they may seem on the surface, and to build on, without criticizing or questioning, all other suggestions generated by group members. Groups often begin brainstorming by asking individual members to take turns offering ideas. Frequently, a high energy, almost frantic atmosphere develops. In its zanier moments, brainstorming crosses over into free association.

For a writer exploring topic ideas, brainstorming sessions can provide a variety of options to consider as well as clues about an audience's potential reaction to a topic and ideas about how the writer might change those views. Brainstorming can also generate arguments in support of a thesis. When the class is assigned a persuasive paper, playing the believing and doubting game with each group member's proposed thesis can help writers anticipate alternative possibilities and counterevidence as well as think of new support for a position.

The believing and doubting game is explained on pp. 42–46.

Oral Rehearsal of Drafts

Rehearsing a draft orally is an excellent way to generate and clarify ideas. A good procedure for doing so is to interview one another in pairs or in groups of three early in the writing process. One-on-one or one-on-two interviews that enable writers to talk through their ideas can help clarify the writers' sense of direction and stimulate new ideas. When you are the interviewer, use the following set of generic questions, modifying them to fit each assignment.

- What problem or question is your paper going to address?
- Why is this an interesting question? What makes it problematic and significant?
- How is your paper going to surprise your readers?
- What is your thesis statement? (If the writer doesn't have a good thesis statement yet, go on to the next question and then come back to this one. Perhaps you can help the writer figure out a thesis.)
- Talk me (us) through your whole argument or through your ideas so far.

When you conduct your interview, get the writer to do most of the talking. Respond by offering suggestions, bringing up additional ideas, playing devil's advocate, and so forth. The goal is for the writer to rehearse the whole paper orally. Whenever the writer gets stuck for ideas, arguments, or supporting details, help brainstorm possibilities.

During these sessions, it is best for writers not to look at notes or drafts. They should try to reformulate their ideas conversationally. We recommend that each student talk actively for fifteen to twenty minutes as the interviewer asks probing questions, plays devil's advocate, or helps the writer think of ideas.

We now turn to a more formal kind of social interaction, that of making a speech in front of an audience.

About Oral Presentations

This section explains how to prepare and deliver the kinds of oral presentations that you are most likely to give in academic, business, or professional settings. We focus mostly on formal speeches, but we also provide tips for handling impromptu speeches that you might have to produce on the spot.

The idea that oral communication is spoken instead of written might seem too obvious to mention; less apparent, however, is the difference from the audience's perspective: heard versus seen. That difference points to the special needs of an audience of listeners. What kinds of messages can listeners really follow? The answer to that question will guide the adjustments you should make to your writing as you compose speeches.

Just as you can use writing for a wide variety of purposes, you can also use speaking for a wide variety of purposes; however, the range of oral presentations that people actually deliver in academic and professional settings is quite limited. Formal speeches are usually arguments, reports, or ceremonial orations. Less formal speech opportunities include giving input at an open forum and answering questions. We start by explaining the process of preparing a formal speech and then show how to accelerate that process for impromptu speaking.

Preparing Formal Speeches

Most formal speeches are delivered extemporaneously. That means that the speaker has spent ample time preparing a well-arranged speech, but does not end up reading from a script or reciting from memory. Instead, the speaker talks directly to the audience with the aid of note cards or an outline that may be projected from transparencies or a computer.

Long before the delivery of the speech, the speaker should have engaged in the same sort of writing process that precedes a finished essay, including the production of multiple drafts to solve subject-matter and rhetorical problems. However, in the case of a speech, the drafts may consist mostly of revised versions of a sentence outline, with very few fully composed paragraphs written out in detail. That does not mean that you should draft an outline and then wing it. Effective speakers regularly spend an hour of preparation time per minute of speaking time; that preparation includes revising the outline and saying aloud the details that flesh out the skeleton. Such spoken composition helps keep a speech "oral" and prevents you from accidentally composing a text that is too "written" and therefore begs for an audience of readers.

One way that well-composed speeches accommodate the needs of listeners is that the closed forms associated with written discourse close up even more when the message is to be spoken. The most common formula for a speech is sometimes called the "tell 'em rule." It says: Tell 'em what you are about to say, say it, then tell 'em what you just said. While such redundancy may seem ridiculous, it greatly enhances an audience's ability to follow a spoken argument without a text. This "tell 'em rule" serves audience-based needs for unity and coherence, for receiving old information before new information, and for forecasting and fulfillment. These essentials are especially valuable to listeners, who, unlike readers, cannot back up to reread a sentence or a whole paragraph.

Speech Outlines as Multipurpose Tools

While an outline may be optional for an essay consisting of several paragraphs of polished prose, it is vital for a formal speech delivered extemporaneously. A speech outline serves as a composing tool and as an essential aid to your delivery, and it may, in fact, be the only "finished" text that the audience ever sees—if they see any written text at all. It, plus some note cards for reading exact quotations or precise figures, often represents the fullest "written" form that some speeches ever take, as most formal speaking rarely requires a full text of polished prose—just a polished delivery of a well-planned talk.

Whether you use traditional outlines or different fonts and indentations to indicate a hierarchy of main points and subpoints, you should be aware of the two essential features of any well-arranged message: coordination and subordination. What are your main points, and what other points are subordinate to them? Often speakers provide outlines of their speeches through a handout or slide projection. However, even if the only thing your audience gets is the sound of your voice, you can still clearly indicate coordinate and subordinate ideas by using parallel sentence structures. When you do this, your audience "sees" the structure of your message through what they hear.

The following simple outline uses parallel syntactic structures so that the relationships of coordination and subordination can be heard:

- The proposed amendment will cost too much.
  - It will increase expenses.
  - It will decrease revenues.
- The proposed amendment will worsen conditions.
  - It will not eliminate the old problems.
    - The noise problem
    - The safety problem
  - It will add new problems.
    - The problem of accountability
    - The problem of sustainability
    - The problem of legality

While the outline above may take only twenty seconds to read aloud, it could represent the entire structure of a ten-minute speech. The speaker fills the rest of the airtime by fleshing out each of the points. For example, the claim that the proposed amendment will increase expenses could be sustained first with a quotation from a financial expert, followed by dollar amounts comparing current expenses with projected increases. Both the quotation and the figures can be printed on an index card clearly labeled "Increased Expenses" to be read at the appropriate moment. Remember, however, that every time you read from a text, you lose eye contact with your audience while also running the risk of presenting some of that "writerly" prose that may not suit an audience of listeners.

Contents and Arrangement

What your speech has to include depends upon the rhetorical situation. If you are making an argument, then the classical form suggests that you not only provide support for your claim but that you also anticipate objections, rebut those that you can, and concede what you must. If you are delivering a report, then you need to determine what your audience already knows and provide the information they lack. In addition to a global structure, your speech will probably include several local structures, each with its own arrangement of ideas and information: problem/solution, cause/effect, cost/benefit, or past/present/future.

See Chapter 14 for an explanation of classical argument.

If you are concerned about boring your audience by keeping your arrangement utterly predictable, you can always choose to defy some of their expectations. Just remember that each time you do, you increase the information-processing burden upon your audience while simultaneously drawing attention to your arrangement itself rather than to your message. Yes, some of the best stories are told through multiple flashbacks instead of using chronological order. However, whenever you employ an unusual arrangement, you also create the need for more signposting with phrases like "as I stated earlier." Such convoluted messages are harder for your audience to follow and harder for you to give. So, rather than relying on artful twists to maintain the audience's interest, keep the structure simple, and maintain their interest with strong content and an enthusiastic delivery.

For Writing and Discussion

Working in groups or as a whole class, examine the full text of the speech by former attorney general John Ashcroft delivered at the Federalist Society National Convention in November 2003 (pp. 419–425). Then answer the following questions about the speech.

1. To what extent can you "see" the structure of this speech?
2. To what extent does Ashcroft follow the "tell 'em rule"?
3. How does Ashcroft adapt the presentation of his points to the needs of listeners? In other words, how can you tell that this piece is a speech?

(continued)

4. Create an after-the-fact outline for this speech.
5. Do you think this speech would be more or less effective if he announced his structure more explicitly?

Using Visual Aids to Support Your Presentation

Long before the arrival of presentation software such as Microsoft PowerPoint, speakers developed simple rules for the effective use of visual aids. Nowadays, these commonsense rules are programmed into the software: Your visuals should be simple, neat, and big enough for everyone to see clearly; additionally, any single slide should contain only a few lines of text. The default settings in PowerPoint guarantee that you adhere to these rules. If you find yourself wanting to reduce the font size so that you can fit more text onto a slide, resist the temptation, because it indicates that you are trying to use the program as a word processor, not a slide processor. Figure 23.1 shows a portion of the simple outline used earlier as it would appear in Slide View.

If a computer projection system is not available in the room where you will give your speech, PowerPoint and similar programs let you print attractive transparencies for use with an overhead projector. With either approach, you need to remember to look at and talk to your audience, not the slide projected on the

FIGURE 23.1 "Slide View" in PowerPoint lets you edit all aspects of a slide while simultaneously displaying the visual effects that will result.

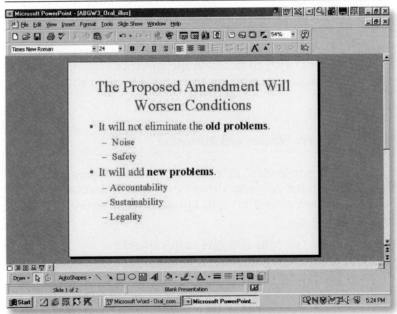

screen, and to be sure to familiarize yourself with any equipment you will be using well before you start your speech.

Delivering a Formal Speech

When the moment finally arrives to give your speech, you will be delivering much of it for the umpteenth time, because your composing process included saying it aloud while timing yourself, preferably in front of a mirror. If possible, you have recorded it on audio-or videotape and practiced it in front of a group of friends, revising all the way. Now it's show time, so you need to attend to what will show—what the audience will see and hear. The aspects of delivery that you need to consider are volume and pace, posture and gesture, eye contact, enthusiasm, use of notes, and integration of presentation aids if you use any.

Because delivery style has become less dramatic and more natural over the years, the only vocal aspects you need to control are your volume and pace. As long as you speak loud enough to be heard, you can add emphasis by speaking louder or softer. You can speed up to get through details quickly and slow down for points you want to stress.

Like delivery style, conventions for posture and gesture have also become more natural, but you should hold yourself as straight and as open as you can. Nervousness might make you try to shrink down to a smaller target, but a slouching form will weaken your delivery by interfering with your breathing and projection. No one is ever going to criticize a speaker for standing too straight or projecting too well.

Gestures, however, are another matter. The sweeping gestures of yesteryear now look contrived, but a death grip on the podium doesn't help either. Some people use their hands a lot when they speak, while others rarely move them. Too many gestures can be distracting, but if you tend not to talk with your hands, then a few planned gestures, even something as simple as holding up two fingers when you turn to your second main point, can help your delivery.

The most important visible aspect of your delivery is your eye contact. You should try to make as much eye contact as possible and be sure to spread it around. Don't deliver your entire speech to just one member of the audience or glance around so quickly that you never actually meet anyone's gaze.

Your enthusiasm counts for a lot. If, out of nervousness or a desire to look cool, you appear not to care about your message, your audience probably won't care about it either. Rather than claim that your topic is important, show that by the energy you put into your delivery.

Finally, your delivery will be affected by how well you use your notes and any presentation aids you might include. If you read more than a very small amount, you are going to lose contact with your audience. If you have handouts, transparencies, or PowerPoint slides, you need to control the flow of information so that your supports match what you say when you say it. If you want your audience to listen to what you have to say, it is a bad idea to give them something to read unless it repeats, summarizes, or exemplifies your point. And you certainly don't want your audience looking at the slide that summarizes an opposing viewpoint five minutes after you have dispensed with that argument.

Preparing and Delivering Impromptu Speeches

Impromptu speaking, where you receive little or no warning that you have to deliver some remarks, is considered so challenging that some textbooks recommend that you avoid it. That may be good advice when you have a choice in the matter, but when a professor calls on you with a question, you probably shouldn't say, "Sorry, I don't do impromptus."

The real challenge with impromptu speaking is that the preparation and delivery stages get collapsed into one, and you literally have to be inventing much of your speech as you give it. However, if you can remember three simple techniques, you should be able to produce impromptu speeches that are clear and intelligible, instead of a series of awkward pauses punctuated mostly by "um."

First, use the "tell 'em rule." While short speeches may not need an organizational preview and a follow-up summary, it never hurts to announce what your point is going to be before you actually make it.

Second, try the principle of "define and divide." By "define" we mean that you should specify the scope of your remarks by asserting what you will address and what you will not. ("I will limit my remarks to the economic causes of this problem and not attempt to address the more complex personnel issues at this time.")

The "divide" principle refers again to your audience's need for structure. Give your remarks a structure with obvious divisions like problem/solution, cause/effect, or past/present/future. By quickly choosing such an arrangement, you buy yourself time to invent the solution portion while you are articulating some aspect of the problem.

Finally, we come to the "vocalized pause." When called upon to speak, most people keep making sounds even when they don't have something to say. Consequently, they often fill the air with a series of linguistic tics such as "ya know," "like," "really," and the ubiquitous "um." Rather than fill the void with "*um*'s," use a silent pause or two. If a moment's silence could cost you the floor, hold up your index finger to indicate that your next point is about to be uttered, while you use that moment to come up with it. Furthermore, effective impromptu speakers regularly use a whole series of vocalized pauses to buy time to discover their next point, while sounding fairly articulate in the process. For example, say "actually" in lieu of "really" and substitute "as you may be aware" for "ya know." Combine the "tell 'em rule" with the articulate pause and you can buy ten seconds of thinking time: "If we consider, now, for a moment, what some solutions to this problem might actually be, I am confident that some of you may well be aware that they would most probably include at least these two."

Handling Speech Anxiety

If you are like most people, giving a formal presentation will make you nervous; however, there are things you can do to minimize the jitters. Remember that speech anxiety is a universal phenomenon; also realize that your nervousness is largely invisible. Your racing pulse, the butterflies in your stomach, and that knot in your shoulders all feel very intense to you, but the audience can't see any of them. So, instead of letting the slight tremor in your hands become magnified by holding a visibly trembling outline, rest your paper on the podium and gently grasp its sides. Instead of letting your voice get high and reedy because you are taking short, shallow breaths, take deep breaths and speak slightly louder than usual. Finally, you should know that the path that connects your psychological state of anxiety to your physical reactions of discomfort is a two-way street. You can engage in breathing exercises that relax all the major muscle groups in your body, making them less able to tense up involuntarily, and you can be doing this quite invisibly as you sit awaiting your turn to speak. The net result will be an overall physical relaxation that will also reduce your level of anxiety. But the most effective thing you can do about speech anxiety is to use that nervousness about your performance as an incentive to prepare your presentation diligently and practice it repeatedly.

For Writing and Discussion

Convert one of your writing projects for this course from an essay to a speech. Using the principles in this chapter, prepare a speech outline and drafts of appropriate slides or transparencies. Then, working in groups, do a practice run-through of your speech, using your outline. Group members who are playing the role of audience should answer the following questions on each practice speech:

1. How could the speaker help the audience "see" the structure of the speech more clearly with their ears using the "tell 'em rule" and parallel syntactic structures for parallel points? How could the speaker's thesis and hierarchy of coordinate points and subordinate points be clearer?
2. What other ways could the speaker accommodate the audience's ability to process information delivered orally?
3. How could the visual aids better help the audience understand and enjoy this speech? How could these be more effectively integrated?
4. How could the speaker improve his or her volume, emphasis, posture, gestures, eye contact, use of notes, and use of visual aids?

Chapter Summary

This chapter has focused on oral communication in small groups and in speeches given before an audience. In the group section, we explained basic principles for successful group interaction: avoiding clone-think and ego-think, listening empathically, playing assigned roles, being sensitive to body language, investing time in group maintenance, recognizing how personality and culture affect group participation, and managing conflict by dealing with "an impossible group member." We have also showed you how to use groups for seeking consensus, brainstorming ideas, and rehearsing drafts orally. In the speech section, we explained similarities and differences between speeches and writing and showed you how to prepare and deliver a formal speech using speech outlines and visual aids designed to meet the needs of your audience. We also offered suggestions for impromptu speaking and for overcoming speech anxiety.

Essay Examinations
Writing Well Under Pressure

I'm pretty good at writing research essays, but when I have to write under pressure,
I freeze. Last time I took an essay test, I wrote two pages before I realized that I'd
left out an important piece of my argument. By the time I had scratched out, made
additions, and drawn arrows all over the page, my paper was such a mess that I
couldn't decipher it. Needless to say, the instructor couldn't either.

—STUDENT A

For me, the worst thing about exams is trying to figure out what the professor
wants. The final in my European literature course was a perfect example: There
was only one question. It started with a difficult-to-follow quotation from an
author we hadn't studied, which we were supposed to apply to a whole slew of
questions about novels we had read during the semester. The question went on for
half a page (single-spaced!) and had at least five or six subsections. By the time I
finished reading it, I didn't have a clue about where to start or how to cover so
much ground in a single essay.

—STUDENT B

(Anonymous undergraduate students at the University of Oklahoma, paraphrased
from responses written when asked to comment on their experiences with essay
examinations)

As these students' comments about essay exams indicate, taking essay
exams, with the extra demands that exams place on writers, can be
stressful and frustrating experiences. When instructors give essay exams,
they want to see how well students can restate, apply, and assess course
material. Just as important, they want to see whether students can discuss in their
own words what they have studied—whether they can participate in that discipline's discourse community. These twin demands make essay exams doubly
challenging. Furthermore, not only must students master course material, but
they must also write about it quickly and confidently.

Although you will rarely take exams after you leave college (unless you plan to
attend graduate school), writing essay tests can help you develop skills relevant to
many real-world situations. For example, in such fields as journalism, advertising,

marketing, publishing, engineering, and teaching, you will need to compose documents on tight deadlines.

Even when you accept that it's important to learn how to write essay exams, you may wonder how you can possibly prepare for the kinds of exams you will face in all your college courses. These diverse courses will require that you adapt your exam essays to the course, instructor, and test question at hand. However, we can give you some useful guidelines and strategies that you can apply. This chapter shows you how to plan and draft an essay exam and how to adapt to the unique requirements of in-class essay writing.

How Exams Written Under Pressure Differ from Other Essays

Essay exams do share similarities to other assignments. Most of the instructions in this book apply to exam writing. For instance, you have learned how to respond to rhetorical context—audience, purpose, and genre—as you write an essay. Your audience for an essay exam is your instructor, so you need to ask yourself what your instructor values and wants. Does your instructor stress analysis of material or application of roles? Does your instructor encourage individual interpretations? Just as analyzing an audience helps you focus an out-of-class essay, so too analyzing your instructor's expectations can help you focus an exam response.

You also know the importance of knowing what you're talking about. Even the most brilliant writers will stumble on a test if they haven't bothered to attend class regularly, take notes, participate in class discussions, and keep up with the reading. Familiarity with the material lays the groundwork for a successful exam performance, just as thorough research and exploratory writing grounds a good paper.

However, not all the writing strategies you use for papers will serve you well in a test situation. Writing researcher Randall Popken, after reviewing more than two hundred sample exams in various disciplines, identified three skills unique to essay exam writing:

1. The ability to store, access, and translate appropriate knowledge into an organized essay
2. The ability to analyze quickly the specific requirements of an exam question and formulate a response to those requirements
3. The ability to deal with time pressure, test anxiety, and other logistical constraints of the exam situation

We examine each of these skills in the next section.

Preparing for an Exam: Learning and Remembering Subject Matter

One of the biggest differences between writing a paper and writing an exam essay involves how you access material. For essays written outside of class, in addition to your own personal knowledge of the topic, you have access to other sources—the library, course readings, your classmates' and instructors' input. But in an exam, you're on your own. You won't know beforehand which of the many pages of material you have studied in a class you'll be asked to synthesize and comment on. Although you may have studied hard and learned a great deal, you will have to display your knowledge in rapid, on-the-spot writing. Preparing for an exam involves finding efficient ways to organize and recall your knowledge so that you can easily construct an intelligent discussion on paper.

Identifying and Learning Main Ideas

No instructor will expect you to remember every single piece of information covered in class. Most instructors are happy if you can remember main ideas and theories, key terminology, and a few supporting examples. The best strategy when you study for an essay exam is to figure out what is most important and learn it first.

How do you determine the main ideas and key concepts? Sometimes they're obvious. Many professors outline their lectures on the board or distribute review sheets before each exam. If your professor does not provide explicit instructions, listen for a thesis statement, main points, and transitions in each lecture to determine the key ideas and relationships among them. For example,

> The *most important critics* of the welfare state are . . .
> *Four developments* contributed to the reemergence of the English after the Norman invasion . . .
> Hegel's dialectic was *most influenced by* Kant . . .

Look for similar signals in your textbook and pay special attention to chapter summaries, subheadings, and highlighted terms. If the course involves a lot of discussion or if your professor prefers informal remarks to highly structured lectures, you may have to work harder to identify major points. But streamlining and organizing your knowledge in this way will keep you from feeling overwhelmed when you sit down to study.

Most instructors expect you to master more than the information they cover in class. Essay exams in humanities, social science, and fine arts courses often ask for an individual interpretation, argument, or critique. To prepare for such questions, practice talking back to course readings by developing your own positions

Chapter 18, Lesson 8, explains some of the main organizing moves writers use in the bodies of essays to clarify and develop their points.

on the viewpoints they express. If the professor has lectured on factors involved in mainstreaming schoolchildren with physical disabilities, look at your notes and try to define your own position on mainstreaming. If the textbook identifies salient features of Caravaggio's art, decide how you think his paintings compare to and differ from his contemporaries' work. Questioning texts and lectures in this way will help you personalize the material, expand your understanding, and take ownership of your education. Remember, though, that professors won't be impressed by purely subjective opinions; as you explore your views, search for evidence and arguments, not just from your own experience but the course as well, that you can use to support your ideas in the exam.

For specific strategies to help you understand and respond to reading material, review Chapter 6 and Chapter 13.

Applying Your Knowledge

In business, science, social science, and education courses, professors may ask you to apply a theory or method to a new situation; for example, they might ask you to show how "first in, last out" accounting might work in bookkeeping for a washing machine factory or how you might use Freudian concepts to analyze a hypothetical psychiatric case. If you suspect that such a question might appear, use some study time to practice this kind of thinking. Brainstorm two or three current situations to which you could apply the theories or concepts you've been learning. Check local newspapers or browse the Web for ideas. Then freewrite for a few minutes on how you might organize an essay that puts the theory to work. For instance, if you've studied federal affirmative action law in a public administration course, you might ask the following questions: How has the recent decision by the U.S. Supreme court in regard to the University of Michigan's affirmative action policies affected the use of race as a factor in college admissions? How might it apply to a local college trying to attract a diverse student body? You won't be able to predict exactly what will appear on the exam, but you can become skilled at transferring ideas into new settings.

Making a Study Plan

Once you've identified crucial subject matter, you need to develop a study plan. If you're a novice at studying for a major exam, try following some tried-and-true approaches. Review your instructor's previous exams. Don't be afraid to ask your instructor for general guidelines about the type, length, and format of questions he or she normally includes on tests. Then generate your own practice questions and compose responses. If you can, organize group study sessions with two to four classmates. Meet regularly to discuss readings, exchange practice questions, test each other informally, and critique each other's essays.

Avoid study techniques that are almost universally ineffective: Don't waste time trying to reread all the material or memorize passages word for word (unless the exam will require you to produce specific formulas or quotations). Don't set an unreasonable schedule. You can seldom learn the material adequately in one or two nights, and the anxiety produced by cramming can hurt your performance even more. Most important, don't stay up all night studying. Doing so can be worse than not studying at all, since sleep deprivation impairs your ability to recall and process information.

No matter how you decide to study, remember that the point of developing exam-preparation strategies isn't simply to do well on a single test, but to become comfortable with learning difficult, complex material and to acquire a level of intellectual confidence that will help you grow as a writer.

Analyzing Exam Questions

Whereas paper assignments typically ask you to address broad problems that can be solved in numerous possible ways, essay exams usually require much more narrowly focused responses. Think about some of your paper assignments. They might have read, "Write a persuasive research paper in which you propose a solution to a current local controversy" or "Write a ten-page essay exploring an ethical issue in the field of vertebrate biology"; they might have called for either closed-or open-form prose; but in virtually all cases you were free to choose from among several possible approaches to your topic. Essay exams, in contrast, feature well-defined problems with a very narrow range of right answers. They require you to recall a particular body of information and present it in a highly specific way. However, what your instructors are asking you to recall and how they want it presented will not always be clear to you. Exam questions often require interpretation.

Although the language of essay exams varies considerably across disciplines, professors typically draw on a set of conventional moves when they write exam prompts. Consider the following question from an undergraduate course in the history of the English language:

> Walt Whitman once wrote that English was not "an abstract construction of dictionary makers" but a language that had "its basis broad and low, close to the ground." Whitman reminds us that English is a richly expressive language because it comes from a variety of cultural sources. One of these is African-American culture. Write an essay discussing the major ways in which African-American culture and dialect have influenced the English language in the United States. Identify and illustrate at least three important influences: What were the historical circumstances? What important events and people were involved? What were the specific linguistic contributions?

This question presents an intimidating array of instructions, but it becomes manageable if you recognize some standard organizational features.

Outside Quotations. First, like many exam questions, this sample opens with a quotation from an author or work not covered in the course. Many students panic when they encounter such questions. "Whitman?! We didn't even study Whitman. What am I supposed to do now?" Don't worry. The primary function of such quotations is to encapsulate a general issue that the instructor wants you to address in your response. When you encounter an unfamiliar quotation, look carefully at the rest of the question for clues about what role the quotation should play in your essay. The point of the Whitman quotation is restated in the very next sentence—English is shaped by numerous cultural influences—and the function of the quotation is simply to reinforce that point. Because the rest of the question tells you specifically what kinds of cultural influences your response should address (African-American culture, three major linguistic contributions), you don't need to consider this quotation when you write your essay.

Sometimes professors will ask you to take a position on an unfamiliar quotation and support your argument with material covered in the course. Suppose that the question was, "What is your position on Whitman's view? Do you believe that English is enriched or corrupted by multicultural influences?" In this case the quotation is presented as the basis for a thesis statement, which you would then explain and support. A successful response might begin, "Whitman believes that multicultural influences make our language better, but this view is hopelessly naive for the following reasons . . ." or "Whitman correctly argues that the contributions of different cultures enrich our language. Take these three examples. . . ."

Organizational Cues.   The question itself can show you the best way to organize your response. Questions tend to begin with general themes that often suggest a thesis statement. Subsequent divisions tell you how to organize the essay into sections and in what order to introduce supporting points. For example, a successful response that follows the organization of our sample might be arranged as follows:

- A thesis stating that several contributions from African-American language and culture have enriched English
- Three supporting paragraphs, each discussing a different area of influence by
  1. summarizing historical circumstances
  2. noting important people and events
  3. providing one or two examples of linguistic contributions

Key Terms.   As do all exam questions, this one asks you to write about a specific body of information in a specific way. When you encounter a lengthy question such as this, first pick out the *noun phrases* that direct you to specific areas of knowledge: "African-American culture," "major influences on the English language in the United States," "historical circumstances," "important events and people," "linguistic contributions." Pay careful attention to words that modify these noun phrases. Does the question tell you how many influences to discuss? What kinds of examples to cite? Does the instructor include conjunctions, such as *or*, to give you a choice of topics, or does he or she use words such as *and* or *as well as* that require you to address all areas mentioned? Words such as *who, what, where,* and *why* also point to particular kinds of information.

After you've determined the specific areas you need to address, look for *directive verbs* that tell you what to do: *discuss, identify,* or *illustrate,* for example. These verbs define the horizons of your response. Table 24.1 defines some key directives that frequently appear in essay exams and provides sample questions for each. Meanings vary somewhat according to the course, the context of the

TABLE 24.1 Strategies for Responding to Common Essay-Question Verbs

Verb	How to Respond	Example
Analyze	Break an argument, concept, or approach into parts and examine the relations among them; discuss causes and effects; evaluate; or explain your interpretation. Look at the rest of the question to determine which strategies to pursue.	*Analyze* the various technical, acoustic, and aesthetic factors that might lead a musician to choose analog over digital recording for a live performance. Be sure to include the strengths and weaknesses of both methods in your discussion.
Apply	Take a concept, formula, theory, or approach and adapt it to another situation.	Imagine that you've been hired to reengineer the management structure of a major U.S. automaker. How might you *apply* the principles of Total Quality Management in your recommendations?
Argue	Take a position for or against an issue and give reasons and evidence to support that position.	*Argue* whether or not cloning should be pursued as a method of human reproduction. Be sure to account for the relationship between cloning and mitosis in your discussion.
Compare/ Contrast	Note the similarities (compare) or differences (contrast) between two or more objects or ideas.	*Compare* and *contrast* the leadership styles of Franklin Delano Roosevelt, John F. Kennedy, and Ronald Reagan, focusing on their uses of popular media and political rhetoric.
Construct	Assemble a model, diagram, or other organized presentation of your knowledge about a subject.	*Construct* a model of the writing process that illustrates the major stages writers go through when developing an idea into a finished text.
Critique	Analyze and evaluate an argument or idea, pointing out and explaining both strengths and weaknesses.	Dinesh D'Souza's "Illiberal Education" sparked widespread controversy when it was published in 1991. Write an essay *critiquing* D'Souza's arguments against affirmative action, identifying both the strengths and weaknesses of his position. Use examples from the text, class discussion, and other class readings to illustrate your points.
Define	Provide a clear, concise, authoritative meaning for an object or idea. The response may include describing the object or idea, distinguishing it clearly from other objects or ideas, and providing one or more supporting examples.	How was "equality" *defined* by the Supreme Court in *Plessy v. Ferguson* (1896)? How did that definition influence subsequent educational policy in the United States?
Discuss	Comprehensively present and analyze important concepts, supported by examples or evidence. Cover several key points or examine the topic from several perspectives. Check the question for guidelines about what to include in your response.	*Discuss* the controversy that surrounded Stanley Milgram's studies of authority and state your own position on the relevance and validity of the experiments.
Enumerate (or List)	List steps, components, or events pertaining to a larger phenomenon, perhaps briefly explaining and commenting on each item.	A two-year-old child falls from a swing on the playground and lies unconscious. As the head preschool teacher, *enumerate* the steps you would take from the time of the accident until the ambulance arrives.

(continued)

TABLE 24.1 continued

Verb	How to Respond	Example
Evaluate	Make a judgment about the worth of an object or idea, examining both strengths and weaknesses.	*Evaluate* William Whyte's "Street Corner Society" as an ethnographic study. What are its methodological strengths and weaknesses? Do you believe the weaknesses make Whyte's research obsolete?
Explain	Clarify and state reasons to show how some object or idea relates to a more general topic.	*Explain* the relationship of centripetal force to mass and velocity and give an example to illustrate this relationship.
Identify	Describe some object or idea and explain its significance to a larger topic.	*Identify* the major phonetic characteristics of each of the following language groups of Africa, and provide illustrative examples: Koisan, Niger-Kordofanian, and Nilo-Saharan.
Illustrate	Give one or more examples, cases, or other concrete instances to clarify a general concept.	Define "monopoly," "public utility," and "competition," and give specific *illustrations* of each.
Prove	Produce reasons and evidence to establish that a position is logical, supportable, or factual.	Use your knowledge about the findings of the National Assessment of Educational Progress to *prove* that public schools either are or are not doing an adequate job of educating children to become productive U.S. citizens.
Review	Briefly survey or summarize something.	*Review* the major differences between Socrates' conception of ethics and the ethical theories of his contemporaries in the fifth century B.C.E.
Summarize	Lay out the main points of a theory, argument, or event in a concise and organized manner.	*Summarize* Mill's definition of justice and explain how it differs from Kant's. Which definition comes closest to your own, and why?
Trace	Explain chronologically a series of events or the development of an idea.	Write an essay that *traces* the pathway of a nerve impulse through the nervous system, being sure to explain neuron structure, action potential, and the production and reception of neurotransmitters.

Our thanks to Michael C. Flanigan, who suggested some of the terms for this table, in "Processes of Essay Exams," manuscript. University of Oklahoma, 1991.

question, and the professor's expectations, but you'll feel more confident if you have basic working definitions.

In some questions, directives are implied rather than stated directly. If a question asks, "Discuss the effects of Ronald Reagan's tax policies on the U.S. economy during the 1980s," you'll need to summarize what those policies were before you can assess their effects. Before you can take a position on an issue, you have to define what the controversy is about. In general, when you answer any question, you should include sufficient background information about the topic to convince your instructor that you're making an informed argument, whether or not the question specifically asks for background information.

For Writing and Discussion

This exercise will hone your ability to analyze essay questions. The following student essay, which received an A, was a response to one of the four closely related questions that follow it. The essay may address issues raised in two or more questions, but it is an A response to only one. Your task is to figure out which question the essay answers best. Although you have not read the specific material from which the essay draws, you should nonetheless be able to match the responses to the questions based on the kinds of information included and how the information is used.

Decide on your answer independently; then compare answers in small groups. Try to come to a group consensus, referring to Table 24.1 to help resolve disagreements. As you discuss your responses, note any successful strategies that you may be able to adapt to your own writing.

From a British Literature Course

Gulliver's Travels and *Frankenstein* portray characters whose adventures bring them face to face with the innate weaknesses and limitations of humankind. Victor Frankenstein and Lemuel Gulliver find out during their travels that humans are limited in reasoning capacity and easily corruptible, traits that cause even their best-intentioned projects to go awry. These characters reflect the critical view that Swift and Shelley take of human nature. Both believe that humans have a "dark side" that leads to disastrous effects.

In *Gulliver's Travels,* Gulliver's sea voyages expose him to the best and worst aspects of human civilization. Through Gulliver's eyes, readers come to share Swift's perception that no matter how good people's original intentions, their innate selfishness corrupts everything they attempt. All the societies Gulliver visits give evidence of this. For example, Lilliput has a system of laws once grounded on justice and morality, but that slowly were perverted by greedy politicians into petty applications. Even the most advanced society, Brobdingnag, has to maintain a militia even though the country is currently peaceful—since they acknowledge that because humans are basically warlike, peace can't last forever. By showing examples of varied cultures with common faults, Swift demonstrates what he believes to be innate human weaknesses. He seems to believe that no matter how much progress we make, human societies will eventually fall back into the same old traps.

Victor Frankenstein also experiences human limitations, this time in his own personality, as he pushes to gain knowledge beyond what any human has ever possessed. When he first begins his experiments to manufacture life in the laboratory, his goals are noble—to expand scientific knowledge and to help people. As he continues, he becomes more concerned with the power that his discovery will bring him. He desires to be a "god to a new race of men." Later, when the creature he creates wreaks havoc, Frankenstein's pride and selfishness keep him from confessing and preventing further deaths. Like the societies Gulliver observed, Frankenstein is a clear example of how human frailties corrupt potentially good projects.

(continued)

Even though Swift and Shelley wrote during two different historical periods, they share a critical view of human nature. However, several unambiguously good characters in *Frankenstein*—including the old man and his daughter—suggest that Shelley feels more optimism that people are capable of overcoming their weaknesses, while Swift seems adamant that humans will eternally backslide into greed and violence. Basically, however, both works demonstrate vividly to readers the ever present flaws that prevent people and their societies from ever attaining perfection.

Which question does this essay address most successfully?

1. Contrast Swift's and Shelley's views of human nature, illustrating your points with specific examples from *Gulliver's Travels* and *Frankenstein.*
2. Analyze the use Swift and Shelley make of scientific knowledge to show the limits of human progress in *Gulliver's Travels* and *Frankenstein,* citing specific illustrations from each work.
3. Discuss the characters of Lemuel Gulliver in *Gulliver's Travels* and Victor Frankenstein in *Frankenstein:* What purpose does each serve in the text? How does each author use the character to illustrate important traits or concepts?
4. Many of the writers we've studied this semester explored the limitations of human potential in their work. Write an essay showing how any two of the following works deal with this idea: William Blake's *Songs of Innocence and Experience,* Jonathan Swift's *Gulliver's Travels,* Mary Shelley's *Frankenstein,* Percy Shelley's "Prometheus Unbound." Does each writer suggest a pessimistic or optimistic view of human nature? Be sure to support your argument with specific illustrations from each text.

Dealing with Constraints: Taking an Essay Exam

Suppose that you've organized the course material, studied faithfully, analyzed the exam questions, and know generally how you'll respond. You still need one more skill to succeed: the ability to thrive within the limits of a test situation. Here are some suggestions for handling the pressure.

First, you need to minimize test anxiety. Many students feel anxious if a test question looks unfamiliar or difficult. Others freeze up if they lose their train of thought midway through an essay. Still others panic when time begins to run out. But you can learn to anticipate potential disasters and brainstorm ways to handle them. If you tend to panic when a test question looks impossible on first reading, make a deal with yourself to close your eyes and count to ten and then read it again and try to block off the parts that you don't have to consider. If you usually run out of time, set a time limit when writing some practice questions so that you can get used to performing under pressure. Finally, make sure that you're in top form to take the exam: organize your supplies—including extra exam booklets and scratch paper, pens, and any testing aids your instructor allows—the night before; get plenty of sleep; eat breakfast; arrive at class a few minutes early;

give yourself a pep talk. These measures will increase your confidence and head off debilitating nerves.

Lack of time when writing an essay exam is perhaps the hardest constraint for most people to deal with. Most writers produce their best work only after writing several drafts. You won't be able to compose a perfectly polished essay in an exam—there simply isn't time—so you will need to streamline your writing process through planning. After you have analyzed the exam question carefully, take a few minutes to jot down a quick outline or a list of key concepts you want to discuss. Exploratory writing techniques, such as tree diagrams and freewriting, can help you generate and arrange ideas. Prewriting gives you a sense of direction and helps you remember where the essay is going as you write.

For example, one undergraduate student jotted down this five-minute scratch outline in response to the following exam question in a Texas government course:

> What are the relative advantages and disadvantages of the district method versus the at-large method in municipal elections? Analyze the strengths and weaknesses of each and then either argue in favor of one method over the other or propose a different plan that avoids the limitations of both.

> Thesis
> District method
> Advantages—history of discrimination and underrepresentation of minorities (examples)
> —race consciousness important for overcoming injustice
> Disadvantages—encourages racial divisions
> —not necessary because much racism has been overcome; minorities may now be freely elected (ex. Sen. Barrientos, Ann Richards) BUT
> At-large
> Advantages—all citizens can work together for common good, not just concerned with narrow group interests
> Disadvantages—majority rule may ignore important minority needs (ex. East Austin)
> THESIS—B/c minories have been and are still underrepresented in local government, the district method of local elections, while flawed, offers the best chance for these communities' voices to be heard.

Once you have a plan, you need to determine how much time to give to each answer. Many students' grades suffer because they blow all their time on the first question and then race through the rest of the exam. To determine how much time to allot each response, you need to solve a quick ratio problem. Divide the points assigned to a given question by the points for the whole exam; the result equals the percentage of time you should spend on that question. When you write your answer, follow the example of journalists and load critical information into your lead. Write a first paragraph that summarizes your whole answer (the student response in the For Writing and Discussion exercise on pp. 721–722 does this beautifully). Add examples and details to the extent that you have time, moving from more important to less important. If you can't finish a response in time, stop, but don't panic. You may have time to return to it later. If not, write a brief note directing the professor to your original notes or outline;

let your professor know that you intended to write more but ran out of time. Many instructors will award partial credit for outlined responses.

You can save time by focusing only on elements important to your grade. Instructors don't expect dramatic, polished introductions and conclusions or artistically constructed sentences in an exam. They would rather you provide a clear thesis statement and explain your main points fully. Most instructors also value organization, although some grade almost entirely on content.

Instructors differ in how they treat errors in grammar, spelling, and punctuation. Some believe it's unfair to expect students to edit their work thoroughly in a short time and don't penalize such errors unless they interfere with the argument (as do garbled or fragmented sentences, for example). Other instructors deduct points for grammatical errors on the grounds that correct usage is always important. If your instructor is a stickler for these details, you may want to save the last five or ten minutes of the exam period for proofreading.

Even if you know a lot about a question, avoid writing more than it asks—unless, perhaps, you know absolutely nothing about one question and want to demonstrate extreme depth of understanding about the others to compensate. Extraneous material may make it difficult for your instructor to find the core of your argument.

Guidelines for Producing Successful Responses

No matter how committed you are to studying, planning, analyzing exam questions, and managing time constraints, your worries about essay tests probably come down to a single, inevitable question: What does an A response look like? Research suggests that most professors want closed-form, thesis-based prose that develops key ideas fully, drawing on supporting facts and examples. Although your essay's shape will be influenced by your individual writing style and the particular rhetorical context, the following summary of the points covered in this chapter can serve as a template for a successful essay:

Clear Thesis Statement. Show your professor that you understand the big picture that the question addresses by including a thesis statement early on. Many professors recommend that you state your thesis clearly, though not necessarily stylishly, in the very first sentence.

Coherent Organization. Although a few instructors will read your essay only to see whether you've included important facts and concepts, most expect a logical presentation. Each paragraph should develop and illustrate one main point. Use transition words and phrases to connect each paragraph clearly to the thesis of the essay: "Another factor that led to the economic decline of the South was . . ."; "In contrast to Hegel, Mill believed . . . ." Show your instructor that you know where the essay's going, that you're developing your thesis.

Support and Evidence. When the question calls for supporting facts and examples, be specific. Don't assert or generalize unless you present names, dates, studies, examples, diagrams, or quotations from your reading as support.

Independent Analysis and Argument. Your response should not be a pedestrian rehash of the textbook. When the question allows, present your own insights, criticisms, or proposals, making sure to support these statements with course material and relate them clearly to your thesis.

Conclusion. Even if you're running short of time, write a sentence or two to tie together main points and restate your thesis. Your conclusion, even if brief, serves an important rhetorical function. It confirms that you've dealt adequately with the question and proved your point.

Clearly we can't teach you everything you need to know about exam writing in one chapter. Becoming comfortable with any genre of writing requires patience and experience. Practicing the suggestions in this chapter for preparing for essay exams, comprehending exam questions, and organizing your answers will help you build your mastery of this kind of writing.

For Writing and Discussion

To gain some practical experience, your instructor may ask you to write an essay exam on one of the following topics. Use the preparation and prewriting strategies you've practiced in this chapter and any other strategies you find useful to prepare for the exam. Review the guidelines for writing a successful response presented on pages 724–725 and, if possible, organize and conduct group study sessions with your classmates.

Exam Option 1   Imagine that you've been appointed to a campus committee charged with developing minimum requirements for writing assignments in undergraduate courses. Specifically, the committee is trying to decide whether to require professors to assign a final essay exam or a major research paper in core-curriculum courses. Write an essay in which you argue in favor of mandatory essay exams or mandatory research papers, using examples from your own experience and material from Chapters 1 through 4 and this chapter to support your position. You may want to consider some or all of the following questions in your discussion: Which kind of writing helps students learn the most? Which kind of writing most accurately gauges how well students know course material? Which kind of writing develops skills students are most likely to need in the future?

Exam Option 2   Explain the difference between closed-form and open-form prose as presented in Chapter 1 and Chapters 18 and 19. Illustrate your answer with examples taken from Ross Taylor's "Paintball" (pp. 414–417) and Annie Dillard's "Living Like Weasels" (pp. 594–597). Why does Linder choose to write near the closed end of the closed-to-open continuum, whereas Dillard chooses to write near the open end?

Exam Option 3   Write an essay on a topic of your instructor's choice.

Chapter Summary

This chapter has discussed strategies for writing effective examination essays under time pressure. We have shown how exam essays differ from essays written outside class and have suggested strategies for learning and remembering subject matter, for analyzing exam questions, and for dealing with the constraints of an exam situation. We have also provided guidelines for producing successful examination essays: a clear thesis statement, coherent organization, specific support and evidence, independent analysis and argument, and an effective conclusion.

Assembling a Portfolio and Writing a Reflective Self-Evaluation

Reflection becomes a habit of mind, one that transforms.

—Kathleen Blake Yancey, *Writing and Composition Theorist*

Being an adult student, returning after a twelve-year layoff, working full-time and taking a twelve-credit load, I found that I really had to make time to reinvent my writing. These were times of incredible discovery and frustration. Odd as it seems, frustration breeds discovery.

—William Jensen, *Student*

Before we explain in detail what we mean by a reflective self-evaluation, let's begin with some examples. Consider the following scenarios:

Scenario 1: Your boss sends you to a one-week professional development seminar in Chicago. Upon your return, she asks you to write a memo reflecting on what you learned from the seminar, how you might apply it to your current job, and how it has helped you grow professionally.

Scenario 2: Your history professor has assigned a major term paper and is willing to read and comment on a rough draft. When you submit your draft, the professor asks you to write out your answers to three questions: What do you like best about this draft? What has been your greatest difficulty in composing this draft? If you were on your own, how would you revise this current draft?

Scenario 3: The composition program at your college requires students to submit a portfolio of their work at the end of the term. You have been given the following assignment:

Write a reflective letter, addressed to other instructors of this course, that will introduce you and your portfolio. It may describe and compare the process used in creating the out-of-class essays contained in your portfolio, explain why you chose these pieces as your best work for the semester, assess the strengths and weaknesses of your writing, discuss how the writing for this course fits in with previous or future writing, or combine these approaches. Your letter should provide readers with a clearer understanding of who you are as a writer. It should be approximately 500 to 750 words.

All these assignments ask you to look back over a recently completed process; to think reflectively about that process; and to evaluate critically what went well, what didn't go well, what you might have done differently, and how you might change in the future. Our aim in this chapter is to explain in more detail this kind of reflective, self-evaluative writing. We begin by explaining what we mean by reflective writing, how reflective writing is assigned in writing courses, and why reflective writing is important. We then give examples of different kinds of reflective assignments and describe strategies for composing good reflections. We conclude this chapter by explaining how to assemble a writing portfolio and compose an accompanying reflective self-evaluation.

Understanding Reflective Writing

What Is Reflective Writing?

Broadly defined, reflective writing is writing that describes, explains, interprets, and evaluates any past performance, action, belief, feeling, or experience. To *reflect* is to turn or look back, to reconsider something thought or done in the past from the perspective of the present.

Whether or not you record your thinking on paper, you think reflectively all the time. Suppose you ask your boss for a raise and get turned down. An hour later, as you cool your anger over coffee and a doughnut, you think of a particular point you could have made more effectively. On a larger scale, this kind of informal reflective thinking can be made more formal, systematic, and purposeful. Consider, for example, a football team that systematically reviews game tapes to evaluate their own and their opponents' strategies and patterns of play. The camera's eye offers players and coaches new perspectives on their performance; it enables them to isolate, analyze, and evaluate specific moves that were unconsciously performed in the heat of the game.

Similar ways of thinking can be applied to any past performance. Writing reflectively encourages you to train your own camera's eye, metaphorically speaking, on the past. Reflective writing is now required in many jobs where employees are asked to write an annual self-reflective review of their job performance. The following example comes from the performance review of a student who worked for a health maintenance organization. In this excerpt, she describes how she plans to make herself more productive in her job and then considers how this improvement will help the company's efficiency generally:

EXCERPT FROM A SELF-EVALUATION OF JOB PERFORMANCE

To improve my claims processing knowledge, I signed up to take a CPT4 coding class. This will allow me to answer coding questions quickly without having to contact our Cost Containment Department. The Cost Containment Department will have more time to work on their projects if our department does not have to continually call to get answers to simple coding questions.

Similarly, a writer can look back reflectively on a writing performance. The following example is from an e-mail message sent by student writer Susan Meyers to her writing instructor concerning his comments on a draft of a paper she had written about the causes of anorexia. On the draft, the instructor had puzzled over a confusing sentence and suggested a revised version. Here is her e-mail response:

EXCERPT FROM A STUDENT REFLECTION ON A DRAFT

I think that your suggested revision changes what I intended. I'd like that sentence to read: "Perhaps anorexics don't pursue desirability but are rather avoiding it." I am arguing not that anorexics want to be "undesirable" (as your sentence suggests) but rather that they want to avoid the whole issue; they want to be neutral. Sexuality and desire can be tremendously scary if you're in a position that places the value of your body over the value of your self/personage; one can feel that, by entering the sexual world of mature adults, one will lose hold of one's essential self. This is the idea I'm trying to express. Perhaps I should try to draft it some more. . . . At any rate, thank you for pointing out the inadequacies of the topic sentence of this paragraph. I struggled with it, and I think your impulse is right: it needs to encompass more of a transition.

As these examples suggest, reflection involves viewing your writing from different perspectives, looking back on the past from the present, achieving a critical distance. Just as light waves are thrown or bent back from the surface of a mirror, so, too, reflective writing throws our experience, action, or performance back to us, allowing us to see it differently.

This process resembles the kind of dialectical thinking introduced in Chapter 8 on exploratory writing, where we explained how juxtaposing one thesis against its opposite can lead to synthesis that incorporates some aspects of each of the opposing views. Similarly, the process of reexamining one's writing from a new perspective yields new insights and an enriched, more complicated understanding of a particular action, question, problem, or choice.

The synthesizing strategies in Chapter 13 for responding to multiple readings and arriving at your own enlarged views can also be applied to your own pieces of writing.

For Writing and Discussion

Working individually, think of a past experience that you can evaluate reflectively. This experience could be your performance in a job; participation in a sport, play, music recital, or other activity; development of a skill (learning to play the piano, juggle a soccer ball, perform a complex dance movement); or problem with an institution (a coach, your dorm resident assistant, job supervisor). To encourage you to think about the past from the perspective of the

(continued)

present, try the formula, "How do I see the experience differently now from the way I saw it then?" Imagine you are doing a debriefing of your participation in the experience. Working on your own for ten minutes, freewrite reflectively about your performance. What did you do well? What wasn't working for you? What could you have done better?

Then in groups or as a whole class, share what you have learned through your reflective freewrites. How did the process of looking back give you a new perspective on your experience? How might reflective writing help you bring about changes and improvements in future performances?

Reflective Writing in the Writing Classroom

Reflective writing in college writing courses can take several forms. One common type of reflective assignment asks you to write a brief, informal reflection on a particular draft-in-progress or a recently completed essay. Susan Meyers's e-mail reflection on her anorexia draft is an example of this type of reflective writing.

Perhaps the type most frequently assigned is the reflective letter or essay that accompanies a writing portfolio handed in at the end of a term. This final portfolio is a collection of representative work produced for a particular course. Sometimes this work includes rough drafts and informal writing such as freewrites and journal entries as well as polished final drafts; at other times, it includes just the polished final products. Almost always, however, writers have some or complete say in what goes into the final portfolio. Just as architects select their best designs or photographers their best photographs to put into a portfolio to show a potential employer, so, too, do student writers assemble their best writing to demonstrate to the instructor or portfolio readers what they have learned and accomplished during the term. The role of the accompanying reflective letter or essay is to offer the author's perspective on the writing in the portfolio, to give a behind-the-scenes account of the thinking and writing that went into the work, and to assess the writer's struggles and achievements during the term. The last section of this chapter discusses writing portfolios further and offers suggestions for assembling such a portfolio.

To distinguish the two types of reflective writing, we use the terms *single reflection* and *comprehensive reflection*. When you write a single reflection, you focus on one piece of writing, either recently completed or in-process; you formulate your ideas primarily for yourself and perhaps for a friendly, nonjudgmental audience. When you write a comprehensive reflection, you offer your perspective on a series of completed writing projects for presentation to an outside audience, either your instructor or a portfolio reader. The aim of a single reflection is to learn about a particular piece of writing in order to understand and often to revise it in the present or near future. The aim of a comprehensive reflection is to demonstrate what you have learned from your writing over the course of the term in order to transfer that learning to future writing situations.

Why Is Reflective Writing Important?

According to learning theorists, reflective writing can substantially enhance both your learning and your performance.* Reflective writing helps you gain the insights needed to transfer current knowledge to new situations. For example, one of our students recently reported that the most important thing she had learned in her first-year writing course was that research could be used in the service of her own argument. In high school, she had thought of research as merely assembling and reporting information she had found in various sources. Now she realized that writers must make their own arguments, and she saw how research could help her do so. Clearly, this new understanding of the relationship between argument and research will help this student do the kind of research writing expected in upper-level college courses.

Learning theorists call this kind of thinking "metacognition": the ability to monitor consciously one's intellectual processes or, in other words, to be aware of how one "does" intellectual work. Reflection enables you to control more consciously the thinking processes that go into your writing, and it enables you to gain the critical distance you need to evaluate and revise your writing successfully.

Reflective Writing Assignments

In this section we describe the kinds of reflective writing that your instructors across the disciplines may ask of you.

Single Reflection Assignments

Single reflection assignments are usually informal, exploratory pieces, similar to other kinds of informal writing you have done. Like the exploratory writing described in Chapter 2, single reflections are conversational in tone, open in form, and written mainly for yourself and, perhaps, a friendly, nonjudgmental audience. However, single reflections differ from most other kinds of exploratory writing in timing, focus, and purpose.

Whereas exploratory writing helps you generate ideas early in the writing process, single reflection writing is usually assigned between drafts or after you have completed an essay. Its focus is your writing itself, both the draft and the processes that produced it. Its aim is critical understanding, usually for the purpose of revision. In it, you think about what's working or not working in the

---

*Learning theorists who have made this general claim include J. H. Flavel, "Metacognitive Aspects of Problem-Solving," in L. B. Resnick (ed.), *The Nature of Intelligence* (Hillsdale, NJ: Erlbaum, 1976); Donald Schon, *Educating the Reflective Practitioner* (San Francisco: Jossey-Bass, 1987); and Stephen Brookfield, *Becoming a Critically Reflective Teacher* (San Francisco: Jossey-Bass, 1995). Throughout this chapter we are indebted to Kathleen Blake Yancey, *Reflection in the Writing Classroom* (Logan, UT: Utah State UP, 1998), who has translated and extended this work on reflection for writing instructors. We are also indebted to Donna Qualley, *Turns of Thought: Teaching Composition as Reflexive Inquiry* (Portsmouth, NH: Boynton/Cook, Heinemann, 1997), who draws on feminist and other critical theorists to argue for the value of reflexive approaches to writing instruction.

draft, what thinking and writing processes went into producing it, and what possibilities you see for revising it.

Instructors use a variety of assignments to prompt single reflections. Some examples of assignments are the following:

- *Process log:* Your instructor asks you to keep a process log in which you describe the writing processes and decisions made for each essay you write throughout the term. In particular, you should offer a detailed and specific account of the problems you encountered (your "wallowing in complexity") and the rhetorical and subject-related alternatives considered and choices made.
- *Writer's memo:* Your instructor asks you to write a memorandum to turn in with your draft. In it, you answer a series of questions: How did you go about composing this draft? What problems did you encounter? What do you see as this draft's greatest strengths? What are its greatest weaknesses? What questions about your draft would you like the instructor to address?
- *Companion piece:* Less structured than a formal memorandum, a companion piece asks you to reflect briefly on one or two questions. A typical assignment might be this: "Please turn over your draft and on the back tell me what you would do with this draft if you had more time."
- *Talk-To:* In this type of companion piece, your instructor asks you to do four things: (1) believe this is the best paper you've ever written and explain why; (2) doubt that this paper is any good at all and explain why; (3) predict your instructor's response to this paper; and (4) agree or disagree with what you expect your instructor's response to be.
- *Talk-Back:* In another type of companion piece, the instructor asks you to respond to his or her comments after you get the paper back: (1) What did I value in this text as a reader? (2) Do you agree with my reading? and (3) What else would you like for me to know?*

Guidelines for Single Reflection Assignments

If you are inexperienced with reflective writing, your tendency at first may be to generalize about your writing. That is, you may be tempted to narrate your writing process in generic, blow-by-blow procedural terms ("First I took some notes. Then I wrote a first draft and showed it to my roommate, who gave me some suggestions. Then I revised") or to describe your rhetorical choices in general, pre-

---

*We are indebted to Kathleen Blake Yancey and Donna Qualley for a number of the definitions, specific assignments, and suggestions for single and comprehensive reflection tasks that are discussed in the rest of this chapter. Yancey explains the "Talk-To" and "Talk-Back" assignments in her book *Reflection in the Writing Classroom* (Logan, UT: Utah State UP, 1998). Donna Qualley draws on feminist and other critical theorists to argue for the value of reflexive approaches to writing instruction. See her book *Turns of Thought: Teaching Composition as Reflexive Inquiry* (Portsmouth, NH: Boynton/Cook, Heinemann, 1997).

scriptive terms ("I started with a catchy introduction because it's important to grab your reader's attention").

To write an effective single reflection, select only a few ideas to focus on, look at specific aspects of a specific paper, explore dialectically your past thinking against your present thinking, and support your analysis with adequate details. We suggest the following questions as a guide to producing such reflections. But don't answer them all. Rather, pick out the two or three questions that best apply to your performance and text. (Try to select your questions from at least two different categories.) Your goal should be depth, not a broad survey. The key criteria are these: be *selective*, be *specific*, show *dialectic thinking*, and include *adequate details*.

Process questions: What specific writing strategies did I use to complete this paper?

- Which strategies were the most or least productive?
- Did this writing project require new strategies or did I rely on past strategies?
- What was the biggest problem I faced in writing this paper, and how successful was I in solving that problem?
- What was my major content-level revision so far?
- What were my favorite sentence- or word-level revisions?
- What did I learn about myself as a writer or about writing in general by writing this paper?

Subject-related questions: How did the subject of my paper cause me to "wallow in complexity"?

- What tensions did I encounter between my ideas/experiences and those of others? Between the competing ideas about the subject in my own mind?
- Did I change my mind or come to see something differently as a result of writing this paper?
- What passages in the paper show my independent thinking about the subject? My unresolved problems or mixed feelings about it?
- What were the major content problems I had with this paper, and how successful was I in solving them?
- What did writing about this subject teach me?

Rhetoric-related questions: How did the audience I imagined influence me in writing this paper?

- What do I want readers to take away from reading my paper?
- What rhetorical strategies please me most (my use of evidence, my examples, my delayed thesis, etc.)? What effect do I hope these strategies have on my audience?
- How would I describe my voice in this paper? Is this voice appropriate? Similar to my everyday voice or to the voices I have used in other kinds of writing?
- Did I take any risks in writing this paper?

- What do readers expect from this kind of paper, and did I fulfill those expectations?

Self-assessment questions: What are the most significant strengths and weaknesses in this essay?

- Do I think others will also see these as important strengths or weaknesses? Why or why not?
- What specific ideas and plans do I have for revision?

READING

In the following companion piece, student Jaime Finger writes about what she sees as the strengths and weaknesses of an exploratory essay in which she was asked to pose a question raised but not clearly answered in a collection of essays on issues of race and class. (She posed the question: "What motivates people to behave as they do?") She was then asked to investigate various perspectives on the question that were offered by the readings, to consider other perspectives drawn from her own knowledge and experience, and to assess the strengths and weaknesses of differing points of view.

Jaime Finger (Student)
A Single Reflection on an Exploratory Essay

1   Although this paper was harder than the first one, I believe I have a good opening question. I like how I divided her [the author of the essays] ideas about motivation into two parts—individual and social. I also like how I used examples from many different essays (this proves I really read the whole book!). Another thing I like about this essay is how I include some examples of my own, like the Michael Jordan example of how he did not make the basketball team in his freshman year and that motivated him to practice every day for a year before making the team his sophomore year. I wonder if he ever would have been as good as he is if he had made the team his freshman year? I wish I could or would have added more of my own examples like this one.

2   What I'm not sure about is if I later ask too many other questions, like when I ask, "If someone is doing something because of society's pressures, is he responsible for that behavior?" and "How much are we responsible to other people like the homeless?" I felt that I piled up questions, and also felt I drifted from my original questions. The paper was confusing for me to write, and I feel that it jumps around. Maybe it doesn't, but I don't know.

3   Since *Alchemy* [the title of the essay collection] was such a hard book, I'm kind of happy with my paper (although after hearing some of the others in my peer group, I don't know if it's up to par!!).

Thinking Critically about "A Single Reflection on an Exploratory Essay"

1. To what extent does this reflection show that Jaime has deepened her thinking about the question "What motivates people to behave as they do?"

2. Where does Jaime show an awareness of audience and purpose in her self-reflection on her essay?

3. To what extent does Jaime show us that she can identify strengths and weaknesses of her essay?

4. What are Jaime's most important insights about her essay?

5. How would you characterize Jaime's voice in this reflection? Does this voice seem appropriate for this kind of reflective writing? Why or why not?

6. What are the greatest strengths and weaknesses in Jaime's single reflection?

Comprehensive Reflection Assignments

You may also be asked to write a final, comprehensive reflection on your development as a writer over a whole term. Although end-of-the-term reflective essays differ in scope and audience from single reflections, similar qualities are valued in both: selectivity, specificity, dialectical thinking, and adequate detail.

In some cases, the comprehensive reflective essay will introduce the contents of a final portfolio; in other cases, this will be a stand-alone assignment. Either way, your goal is to help your readers understand more knowledgeably how you developed as a writer. Most important, in explaining what you have learned from this review of your work, you also make new self-discoveries.

Guidelines for Comprehensive Reflection Assignments

Instructors look for four kinds of knowledge in comprehensive reflections: self-knowledge, content knowledge, rhetorical knowledge, and critical knowledge or judgment. Here we suggest questions that you can use to generate ideas for your comprehensive reflective letter or essay. Choose only a few of the questions to respond to, questions that allow you to explain and demonstrate your most important learning of the course. Also, choose experiences to narrate and passages to cite that illustrate more than one kind of knowledge.

Self-Knowledge

By *self-knowledge*, we mean your understanding of how you are developing as a writer. Think about the writer you were, are, or hope to be. You can also contemplate how the subjects you have chosen to write about (or the way you have approached your subjects) relate to you personally beyond the scope of your papers. Self-knowledge questions you might ask are the following:

- What knowledge of myself as a writer have I gained from the writing I did in this course?
- What changes, if any, have occurred in my writing practices or my sense of myself as a writer?
- What patterns or discontinuities can I identify between the way I approached one writing project versus another?
- How can I best illustrate and explain the self-knowledge I have gained through reference to specific writing projects?

Content Knowledge

Content knowledge refers to what you have learned by writing about various subjects. It also includes the intellectual work that has gone into the writing and the insights gained from considering multiple points of view and from grappling with your own conflicting ideas. Perhaps you have grasped ideas about your subjects that you have not shown in your papers. These questions about content knowledge can prod your thinking:

- What kinds of content complexities did I grapple with this semester?
- What *earned insights** did I arrive at through confronting clashing ideas?
- What new perspectives did I gain about particular subjects from my considerations of multiple or alternate viewpoints?
- What new ideas or perspectives did I gain that may not be evident in the essays themselves?
- What passages from various essays best illustrate the critical thinking I did in my writing projects for this course?

Rhetorical Knowledge

Our third category, *rhetorical knowledge*, focuses on your awareness of your rhetorical decisions—how your contemplation of purpose, audience, and genre affected your choices about content, structure, style, and document design. The following questions about rhetorical choices can help you assess this area of your knowledge:

- What important rhetorical choices did I make in various essays to accomplish my purpose or to appeal to my audience? What passages from my various essays best illustrate these choices? Which of these choices are particularly effective and why? About which choices am I uncertain and why?
- What have I learned about the rhetorical demands of audience, purpose, and genre, and how has that knowledge affected my writing and reading practices?
- How do I expect to use this learning in the future?

---

*Thomas Newkirk, in *Critical Thinking and Writing: Reclaiming the Essay* (Urbana, IL: NCTE, 1989), coined the phrase "earned insights," a phrase that Donna Qualley also refers to in *Turns of Thought: Teaching Composition as Reflexive Inquiry* (Portsmouth, NH: Boynton/Cook, Heinemann, 1997), pp. 35–37.

Critical Knowledge or Judgment

A fourth area of knowledge, *critical knowledge* or *judgment*, concerns your aware-ness of significant strengths and weaknesses in your writing. This area also encompasses your ability to identify what you like or value in various pieces of writing and to explain why. You could ask yourself these questions about your critical knowledge:

- Of the papers in my portfolio, which is the best and why? Which is the weakest paper and why?
- How has my ability to identify strengths and weaknesses changed during this course?
- What role has peer, instructor, or other reader feedback had on my assess-ments of my work?
- What improvements would I make in the enclosed papers if I had more time?
- How has my writing changed over the term? What new abilities will I take away from this course?
- What are the most important things I still have to work on as a writer?
- What is the most important thing I have learned in this course?
- How do I expect to use what I've learned from this course in the future?

The Writing Portfolio as an Opportunity for Reflective Self-Evaluation

Assembling a portfolio of your writing at the end of a composition course, in which you are invited to select and present what work you think best shows your progress or what work represents your best writing for the term, engages you deeply in reflective self-evaluation. Typically, writing portfolios include a reflective letter or essay in which you discuss your portfolio choices and the learning they represent.

Portfolios offer many advantages to writers. You have more time to revise before presenting your work for evaluation since many instructors who assign portfolios do not assign grades to individual drafts. Through your comprehensive reflection, you can assess and comment on your writing and learning before some-one else passes judgment. Further, the portfolio process helps you develop the metacognitive insights we mentioned earlier in this chapter, insights that can help you transfer this learning to new writing situations. Finally, this experience can prepare you for work-related tasks because portfolios are increasingly used in job applications as well as in assessments for job promotions or merit-based increases.

Specific guidelines for preparing a writing portfolio vary from course to course, so you will need to check with each individual instructor for directions about what to include and how to organize your portfolio. You may be given a lot of choice in what you include in your portfolio, or you may be required to submit a specific number or type of work. You may be asked to include only polished final essays, or you may be asked to include other work such as process work, multiple drafts, journal entries, peer responses, research notes, and so on. However, no matter what the specific requirements entail, the following general suggestions can help you manage the portfolio process.

Keeping Track of Your Work

Crucial to your success in assembling a portfolio is careful organization of your work throughout the term. This way, you will avoid the headache and wasted time caused by trying to hunt down lost or misplaced work. If you are in a conventional, non-computer-based course, we recommend that you purchase an accordion-type file folder to keep and organize all of your work for the course. You can use the dividers to separate your work for individual writing projects. Include everything that contributed to your work on a particular writing project: the original assignment sheet, process work, multiple drafts, peer response sheets, teacher comments, reflective writing about the project, research notes, photocopied research articles, and so on. In addition to careful organization and storage of your work, you need to date and label all work so that you can reconstruct your work on a particular project and identify which draft is second or third, which peer response goes with which draft, and so on.

If you are in a computer-based course where most of the work is submitted electronically, then your portfolio will take electronic form. In this case, you will need to develop an electronic storage system. Specifically, you will need to establish separate electronic files for all work related to specific writing projects and to save, label, and back up all of that work. You will probably want to save your work on a disk as well as on a hard drive. You may also have hard copy you need to save—say, of in-class handwritten peer responses. If this is the case, you will need to develop two storage systems.

Besides the practical need to keep track of all your work in order to review and select the writing that you will include in your portfolio, the process of saving and organizing your work causes you to attend to writing processes throughout the term, one of the key goals of portfolio teaching.

Selecting Work for Your Portfolio

Even if you are given explicit instructions about the number and type of writing to include in your portfolio, you will still have important choices to make about which completed pieces to include or which pieces to revise for inclusion. We suggest three general guidelines to consider as you review your writing and select work for your portfolio presentation.

- *Variety:* One purpose of portfolio assessment is to offer a fuller picture of a writer's abilities. Therefore, it is important that you choose work that demonstrates your versatility—your ability to make effective rhetorical choices according to purpose, audience, and genre. What combination of writing samples best illustrates your ability to write effectively for different rhetorical situations?
- *Course Goals:* A second consideration is course goals. The goals are likely to be stated in the course syllabus and may include such things as "ability to

demonstrate critical thinking in writing"; "ability to use multiple strategies for generating ideas, drafting, revising, and editing"; and "ability to demonstrate control over surface features such as syntax, grammar, punctuation, and spelling." Which pieces of writing most clearly demonstrate the abilities given as your course's goals or which pieces can be revised to offer such a demonstration?

- *Personal Investment:* Finally, be sure to consider which pieces of writing best reflect your personal investment and interest. If you are going to be revising the selected pieces multiple times during the last few weeks of class, you want to make sure you choose work that holds your interest and has ideas you care about. Which pieces are you proudest of? Which were the most challenging or satisfying to write? Which present ideas you'd like to explore further?

Writing a Comprehensive Reflective Letter

Because the letter (sometimes an essay) that you write to introduce your portfolio shows your insights not only about your writing abilities but also about your abilities as a reflective learner, it may be one of the most important pieces of writing you do for the course. Earlier in this chapter, we offered guidelines for writing a comprehensive reflection. Here we offer some additional suggestions geared specifically toward introducing your writing portfolio:

- Review the single reflections you have written about specific writing projects during the term. As you reread these process-log entries, writer's memos, companion pieces, and so on, what do you discover about yourself as a writer?
- Consider key rhetorical concepts and terms that you have learned in this course. Use this book's index to refresh your memory about these concepts. How can you show that you understand these terms and have applied them in your writing?
- Take notes on your own writing as you review your work and reconstruct your writing processes for particular writing projects. What patterns do you see? What surprises you? How can you show the process behind the product? How can you show your growth as a writer through specific examples?
- Be honest. Identifying weaknesses is as important as identifying strengths. How can you use this opportunity to discover more about yourself as a writer or learner?

READING

Now let's look at the draft of a reflective letter written by a student, Bruce Urbanik, for a second-semester composition course that involved a large-scale portfolio assessment. Bruce's portfolio as a whole will be read and scored (Pass or Fail) by two outside readers (and a third if the first two disagree). The contents of

Bruce's portfolio include two essays written outside of class and revised extensively and one essay written in class under test conditions. As his letter suggests, his two out-of-class essays were classical arguments (see Chapter 14) written in response to the nonfiction texts that his class read during the semester. The assignment he was given for this comprehensive reflection is similar to the one on pages 727–728.

Bruce Urbanik (Student)
A Comprehensive Reflective Letter

Dear Portfolio Reader:

1   This is my first college course in five years. I left school for financial reasons and a career opportunity that I couldn't pass up. I thought of contesting the requirement of this course because I had completed its equivalent back in 1993. But, as I reflected on the past few years, I realized that the only books I have read have been manuals for production machinery. My writing has consisted of shorthand, abbreviated notes that summarize a shift's events. Someday, after I finish my degree and move up in my company, I'm going to have to write a presentation to the directors on why we should spend millions of dollars on new machinery to improve productivity. I need this course if I expect to make a persuasive case.

2   I was very intimidated after I read the first book in the course, *No Contest: The Case Against Competition*, by Alfie Kohn. The author used what seemed to me a million outside sources to hammer home his thesis that competition is unhealthy in our society and that cooperation is the correct route. I felt very frustrated with Kohn and found myself disagreeing with him although I wasn't always sure why. I actually liked many of his ideas, but he seemed so detached from his argument. Kohn's sources did all the arguing for him. I tried to take a fresh perspective by writing about my own personal experience. I also used evidence from an interview I conducted with a school psychologist to back up my argument about the validity of my own experiences with cooperative education. The weakness of this paper is my lack of opposing opinions.

3   For my second essay, on Terry Tempest Williams's *Refuge: An Unnatural History of Family and Place*, I certainly could not use any personal experience. Williams, a Mormon woman, writes about the deaths of her mother, grandmother, and other female relatives from breast cancer, believed to be caused by the atomic testing in Utah. I argued that the author, Williams, unfairly blamed men and the role women play in the Mormon religion for the tragic death of her mother and other relatives. She thinks that if the Mormon Church had not discouraged women from questioning authority, maybe some of them would have protested the nuclear testing. But I think this reasoning ignores the military and government pressures at the time and the fact that women in general didn't have much power back in the 50s. Since I didn't know anything about the subject, I asked a Mormon woman that I know to comment on these ideas. Also, my critique group in

class was comprised of myself and three women. I received quite a bit of verbal feedback from them on this essay. I deal with men at work all day. This change, both for this essay and the entire semester, was welcome.

4   In-class, timed essay writing was my biggest downfall. I have not been trained to develop an idea and present support for it on the fly. Thoughts would race through my head as I tried to put them on paper. I thought I was getting better, but the in-class essay in this portfolio is just awful. I really wish I could have had more practice in this area. I'm just not comfortable with my writing unless I've had lots of time to reflect on it.

5   A few weeks ago, I found a disk that had some of my old papers from years ago stored on it. After reading some of them, I feel that the content of my writing has improved since then. I know my writing has leaped huge steps since my first draft back in September. As a student not far from graduation, I know I will value the skills practiced in this course.

Thinking Critically about "A Comprehensive Reflective Letter"

1. What kinds of self-knowledge does Bruce display in his reflective letter?

2. Does Bruce demonstrate dialectical thinking about himself as a writer? If so, where? What multiple writing selves does Bruce identify in his letter?

3. What has Bruce learned from writing about *No Contest* and *Refuge?* What specific examples does he give of "earned insights" or dialectical thinking regarding his subjects?

4. Does Bruce demonstrate his ability to make judgments about his essays' strengths and weaknesses?

5. What learning from this course do you think Bruce is likely to use in the future?

6. Which of the four kinds of writer's knowledge would you like Bruce to address more closely in revising this reflective letter? What kinds of questions does he overlook? Which points could he build up more? Where could his comments be more text specific and adequately detailed?

Chapter Summary

In this chapter, we have introduced you to the value of reflective thinking as a path to self-discovery and improvement as a writer. We have shown how single reflections enable you to reexamine your writing processes, subject-matter choices, and rhetorical choices for individual pieces of writing, often with the goal of targeting problems to resolve in your revision of that writing. We have explained how comprehensive reflections, in contrast, sum up and give you more of a long-range, wide-angle view of your writing over the course of a term, encouraging you to consider your growth as a writer, your intellectual and personal discoveries as you wrestled with subjects, your understanding of the effectiveness of rhetorical choices, and the development of your critical reading and writing skills. Finally, we have shown how writing portfolios work and how they emphasize reflective learning. We have suggested ways to manage the portfolio process by organizing, selecting, and presenting your writing to display your progress in the course. Throughout this chapter, we have shown you the value of making your reflective writing selective, specific, dialectical, and adequately detailed.

Acknowledgments
Index

This advocacy ad for National Public Lands Day, blending the themes of public responsibility, opportunity, and the power of cooperative hands to preserve this land for personal and public enjoyment, appeared in a popular general circulation magazine. Consider how the word "dirty" contrasts with the beauty of the land and sky glimpsed through the hand-shaped space as well as how words and images work together in this ad to move readers to action. This advertisement represents a genre of proposal arguments discussed in Chapter 16 on pages 482–486.

GET DOWN AND DIRTY FOR AMERICA.

One out of every three acres of America's land – 600 million acres – is public land, your land. Lands to hike, bike, climb, swim, explore, picnic or just plain relax. And when you get your hands dirty in programs like National Public Lands Day, you help spruce up your beautiful lands. Last year, on this day, nearly 80,000 volunteers built trails, bridges, planted native trees and removed trash.

To find out how you can help, go to www.npld.com or call 800-VOL-TEER (800-865-8337).

HELPING HANDS FOR AMERICA'S LANDS

Acknowledgments

Page 5. Rodney Kilcup, "A Modest Proposal for Reluctant Writers," *Newsletter of the Pacific Northwest Writing Consortium 2*, no. 3 (September 1982): 5.

Page 5. Stephen D. Brookfield, *Developing Critical Thinkers: Challenging Adults to Explore Alternative Ways of Thinking and Acting* (San Francisco: Jossey-Bass, 1987):5.

Page 6. Andrea Lunsford and Lisa Ede, *Singular Texts/Plural Authors: Perspective on Collaborative Writing* (Carbondale and Edwardsville, IL: Southern Illinois University Press, 1992): 21, 45–48.

Pages 7–8. Excerpts from a workshop for new faculty members, Jeffrey R. Stephens (Department of Chemistry, Seattle University) and Tomas Guillen (Department of Speech Communication and Journalism, Seattle University).

Pages 9. Christopher Leigh, journal entries, student writing. Reprinted with the permission of the author.

Page 11. Paulo Freire, *Pedagogy of the Oppressed* (New York: Continuum, 1989).

Page 12. Ron Gluckman, "Shifting into High Gear," *Silk Road* (April 2004).

Page 13. "Greenpeace Responds to the Bush/Cheney National Energy Policy Task Force." Copyright © Greenpeace.

Page 13. Danny Hakim, "A Fuel-Saving Proposal from Your Automaker: Tax the Gas," *The New York Times*, April 18, 2004. Copyright © 2004 New York Times Company, Inc. Used with permission.

Page 13. Ray Darby, "Energy Issues." Copyright © 2004 Ray Darby.

Page 15. Energy Information Administration, U.S. Department of Energy, Oil consumption graph.

Page 17. David M. Rockwood, letter to editor, *The Oregonian* (January 1, 1993): E4. Copyright © 1993 David Rockwood. Used with permission.

Page 18. Thomas Merton, "A Festival of Rain," from *Raids on the Unspeakable* by Thomas Merton. Copyright © 1966 by The Abbey of Gethsemani, Inc. Reprinted by permission of New Directions Publishing Corp.

Page 23. Noel Gaudette, "Questions about Genetically Modified Foods," student writing. Reprinted with the permission of the author.

Page 23. Brittany Tinker, "Can the World Sustain an American Standard of Living?" student writing. Reprinted with the permission of the author.

Page 27. A. Kimbrough Sherman, in *Thinking and Writing in College: A Naturalistic Study of Students in Four Disciplines* by Barbara E. Walvoord and Lucille P. McCarthy (Urbana, IL: NCTE, 1990): 51.

Page 28. William G. Perry, *Forms of Intellectual and Ethical Development in the College Years* (Troy, MO: Holt, Rinehart & Winston, 1970).

Page 32. Judy Cohen and John Richardson, "Pit Bull Panic," *Journal of Popular Culture*, Fall 2002, Vol. 36, Issue 2, pp. 285-333. Copyright © 2002 Blackwell Publishing. Used with permission.

Page 34. Peter Elbow, *Writing Without Teachers* (New York: Oxford University Press, 1973): 147–190.

Page 42. Peter Elbow, *Writing Without Teachers* (New York: Oxford University Press, 1973): 14–15.

Page 42. Paul Theroux, *Sunrise with Seamonsters* (Boston: Houghton Mifflin, 1985).

Page 47. James Moffett, *Active Voice: A Writing Program Across the Curriculum* (Montclair, NJ: Boynton/Cook Publishers, 1981).

Pages 58 and 66. Dale Kunkel, Kristie M. Cope, and Erica Biely, from "Sexual Messages on Television," *The Journal of Sex Research*, Vol. 36, No. 3 (August 1999): 230. Copyright © 1999 by The Society for the Study of Sexuality. Used with permission.

Pages 58 and 67. Deborah A. Lott, from "The New Flirting Game," *Psychology Today* (January/February 1999): 42. Copyright © 1999 Sussex Publishers. Reprinted with permission.

Page 59. Lisa Sussman and Tracey Cox, from "Flirting with Disaster," *Cosmopolitan* (Australian ed.) (January 2001): 108ff.

Page 71. Penny Parker, "For Teeth, Say Cheese," from *New Scientist* (April 6, 1991). Copyright © 1991 New Scientist. Used with permission.

Page 72. Carlo Patrono, "Aspirin as an Antiplatelet Drug," *The New England Journal of Medicine* 330, (May 5, 1994): 1287–1294. Copyright © 1994 Massachusetts Medical Society. Used with permission.

Page 73. Kenneth Burke, *Permanence and Change,* 3rd rev. ed. (Berkeley: University of California Press, 1984): 49.

Page 73. Nayan Chanda, quoted in Thomas Friedman, "Think Global, Act Local," *The New York Times* (June 6, 2004): WK13.

Page 75. Kenneth Burke, *A Rhetoric of Motives* (New York: Prentice Hall, 1950): 43.

Page 76. Kenneth Burke, "Rhetoric—Old and New," *Journal of General Education* 5 (April 1951): 63.

Page 91. Marianne Means, "Bush, Cheney Will Face Wall of Opposition if They Try to Resurrect Nuclear Power," (April 12, 2001). © 2001 Hearst Newspapers. Used with permission.

Page 98. From "ANWR Information Brief" from www.anwr.org/tech-facts.pdf, accessed September 24, 2001. Reprinted by permission of Arctic Power.

Page 100. From "Which One Is the Real ANWR" from www.anwr.org/features/pdfs/realanwr.pdf, accessed September 24, 2001. Reprinted by permission of Arctic Power.

Page 100. Randal Rubini, from "A Vicious Cycle," *The Seattle Times* (August 27, 1992): G1+. Copyright © 1992 Randal Rubini.

Page 104. Lorna Marshal, *The !Kung of Nyae Nyae* (Cambridge: Harvard University Press, 1976): 177–178.

Page 105. P. Draper, "!Kung Women: Contrasts in Sexual Egalitarianism in Foraging and Sedentary Contexts," in *Toward an Anthropology of Women,* ed. R. Reiter (New York: Monthly Review Press, 1975): 82–83.

Page 108. Henry Morton Stanley, "Henry Morton Stanley's Account" from "A Classroom Laboratory for Writing History" from *Social Studies Review* 31, no. 1 (1991). Copyright © 1991. Reprinted with permission.

Page 109. Donald C. Holsinger, "A Classroom Laboratory for Writing History," *Social Studies Review* 31, no. 1 (1991): 59–64.

Pages 118 and 142. Andrés Martin, M.D., "On Teenagers and Tattoos," *Journal of the American Academy of Child and Adolescent Psychiatry* 36, no. 6 (June 1997): 860–861. Copyright © 1997. Used with permission.

Page 124. Robert B. Cullen with Sullivan, "Dangers of Disarming," *Newsweek* (October 27, 1986). Copyright © 1986. All rights reserved. Reprinted by permission.

Page 125. Carl Rogers, *On Becoming a Person: A Therapist's View of Psychotherapy,* 3rd ed. (Boston: Houghton Mifflin, 1961).

Page 132. Sean Barry, "Why Do Teenagers Get Tattoos? A Response to Andrés Martin," student essay. Reprinted with the permission of the author.

Page 144. Florence King, "I'd Rather Smoke Than Kiss," *National Review* (July 9, 1990): 32, 34–36. Copyright © 1990 by National Review, Inc., 215 Lexington Avenue, New York, NY 10016. Reprinted by permission.

Page 150. Lyndon Haviland, "A Silence that Kills," *American Journal of Public Health,* Vol. 94, No. 2 (March 2004). Copyright © 2004 by APHA. Used with permission.

Page 157. Edward Abbey, "The Damnation of a Canyon" from *Beyond the Wall* by Edward Abbey, © 1971, 1976, 1977, 1979, 1984 by Edward Abbey. Reprinted by permission of Henry Holt and Company, LLC.

Page 161. Friends of Lake Powell, home page (www.lakepowell.org). © 2004 Friends of Lake Powell. Used with permission.

Page 172. Richard Wright, excerpt from *Black Boy* by Richard Wright, pp. 216–217. Copyright © 1937, 1942, 1944, 1945 by Richard Wright. Copyright renewed 1973 by Ellen Wright. Reprinted by permission of HarperCollins Publishers, Inc.

Page 176. Kris Saknussemm, "Phantom Limb Pain." Reprinted by permission of Kris Saknussemm.

Page 178. Patrick José, "No Cats in America?", student essay. Reprinted with the permission of the author.

Page 184. Sheila Madden, "Letting Go of Bart," *Santa Clara Magazine* (Summer 1994). Copyright © 1994. Reprinted by permission.

Page 192. Anonymous, "Essay A/Essay B" from "Inventing the University," in *When A Writer Can't Write* by David Bartholomae. Reprinted with the permission of The Guilford Press.

Page 197. Christopher Leigh, "An Exploration of How to Prevent Violence in Schools," student essay. Reprinted with the permission of the author.

Page 203. Dylan Fujitani, "Hired Guns: Uncovering the Nature of Private Militaries in the Iraq War," student essay. Reprinted with the permission of the author.

Page 209. "About the Army" web page, http://goarmy.com/about/index.jsp.

Pages 211 and 214. Stephen Bean, "Sam" journal entries and "Should Women Be Allowed to Serve in Combat Units?", student writing. Reprinted with the permission of the author.

Page 221. EnchantedLearning.com, "Tarantulas." www.enchantedlearning.com/subjects/arachnids/spider.

Page 222. Rod Crawford, "Myths About 'Dangerous' Spiders" from the Burke Museum web site. www.washington.edu/burkemuseum/spidermyth/index.html. Copyright © Burke Museum. Reprinted by permission of Burke Museum, Seattle, WA.

Page 227. Article abstract of "Reefer Madness" by Eric Schlosser (August 1994). Abstract reprinted with the permission of *The Atlantic Monthly.*

Page 227. Article abstract of "The Sex-Bias Myth in Medicine" by Andrew G. Kadar, M.D. (August 1994). Abstract reprinted with the permission of *The Atlantic Monthly.*

Page 227. Article abstract of "Midlife Myths" by Winifred Gallagher (May 1993). Abstract reprinted with the permission of *The Atlantic Monthly.*

Page 228. Dylan Loeb McClain, "Growing More Oil Dependent, One Vehicle at a Time," *The New York Times* (June 20, 2004). Copyright © 2004 New York Times Co., Inc. Used with permission.

Page 230. Kerri Ann Matsumoto, "How Much Does It Cost to Go Organic?" student essay. Reprinted with the permission of the author.

Page 231. Cheryl Carp, "Behind Stone Walls," student essay. Reprinted with the permission of the author.

Page 233. Shannon King, "Will the Hydrogen Economy Solve the Energy Crisis and Protect Our Environment?" student essay. Reprinted with the permission of the author.

Page 236. Jonathan Rauch, "Coming to America," *Atlantic Monthly* (July/Aug. 2003). Copyright © 2003 Jonathan Rauch. Used with permission.

Page 266. Robert H. Aseltine, Jr., and Ronald C. Kessler, "Marital Disruption and Depression in a Community

Sample," *Journal of Health and Social Behavior* 34 (Sept. 1993): 237–251; adapted from Russell K. Schutt, *Investigating the Social World: The Process and Practice of Research,* 2nd ed. (Thousand Oaks, CA: Pine Forge Press, 1999): 470.

Page 271. Gina Escamilla, Angie L. Cradock, and Ichiro Kawachi, "Women and Smoking in Hollywood Movies: A Content Analysis," *American Journal of Public Health,* Vol. 90, Issue 3 (March 2000): 412ff. Copyright © 2000 by APHA. Used with permission.

Page 277. Brittany Tinker, Trevor Tsuchikawa, and Tatiana Whizar, "Energy Literacy: A Comparative Study of Seattle University Students Against a National Sample," student essay. Reprinted with the permission of the authors.

Page 288. National Environmental Education and Training Foundation, "Americans' Low 'Energy IQ': A Risk to Our Energy Future," www.neetf.org/roper/Roper2002.pdf.

Page 293. John Berger, *About Looking* (New York: Vintage Books, 1980), p. 52.

Page 308. "Attention Advertisers: Real Men Do Laundry," *American Demographics* (March 1994): 13–14.

Page 309. Erving Goffman, *Gender Advertisements* (New York: Harper & Row, 1979).

Page 315. Paul Messaris, from *Visual Persuasion: The Role of Images in Advertising* by Paul Messaris (Thousand Oaks, CA: Sage, 1997). Copyright © 1997 Sage Publications. Used with permission.

Page 320. Stephen Bean, "How Cigarette Advertisers Address the Stigma Against Smoking: A Tale of Two Ads," student essay. Reprinted with the permission of the author.

Page 328. Evelyn Dahl Reed, "Medicine Man," from *Coyote Tales from the Indian Pueblos* by Evelyn Dahl Reed. Copyright © 1988 by Evelyn Dahl Reed. Reprinted with the permission of Sunstone Press, P.O. Box 2321, Sante Fe, NM 87504-2321.

Page 338. Alice Walker, "Everyday Use," from *In Love & Trouble: Stories of Black Women* by Alice Walker. Copyright © 1973 by Alice Walker. Reprinted by permission of Harcourt, Inc.

Page 345. David Updike, "Summer," from *Out on the Marsh* by David Updike. Reprinted by permission of David R. Godine, Publisher, Inc. Copyright © 1988 by David Updike.

Page 349. Elizabeth M. Weiler, "Who Do You Want to Be?", student essay. Reprinted with the permission of the author.

Page 359. John Gallagher, "Young Entrepreneurs' Disdain for Time Off," *The Seattle Times* (July 4, 2001): E1, E6. Copyright © 2001 Knight Ridder/Tribune. Reprinted by permission.

Page 361. Keith Goetzman, "The Late, Great Outdoors," *Utne Reader* (September/October 2001): 16–17. Copyright © 2001 Keith Goetzman. Used with permission.

Pages 367, 368, 370, 372, 373. Kara Watterson, student writings. Reprinted with the permission of the author.

Pages 367, 370, 372, 374. Kate MacAulay, student writings. Reprinted with the permission of the author.

Page 377. Ellen Goodman, "The Big Fat Case Against Big Macs," *The Washington Post* (Dec. 14, 2002): A25. Copyright © 2002, The Washington Post Writers Group. Reprinted with permission.

Page 378. Dale Buss, "Is the Food Industry the Problem or the Solution?" The New York Times (Aug. 29, 2004). Copyright © 2004 New York Times Co., Inc. Used with permission.

Page 381. Marilyn Larkin, "Can Cities Be Designed to Fight Obesity?" *The Lancet,* Vol. 362, Issue 9389 (Sept. 27, 2003): 1046. Reprinted with permission from Elsevier.

Page 400. Stephen Toulmin, *The Uses of Argument* (Cambridge: Cambridge University Press, 1958).

Page 402. Michael Levin, "The Case for Torture," *Newsweek* (June 7, 1982).

Page 407. Walter Wink, "Biting the Bullet: The Case for Legalizing Drugs," *The Christian Century* (August 8–15, 1990).

Page 414. Ross Taylor, "Paintball: Promoter of Violence or Healthy Fun?" student essay. Reprinted with the permission of the author.

Page 419. John Ashcroft, "Prepared Remarks of Attorney General John Ashcroft at the Federalist Society National Convention," November 15, 2003.

Page 426. James Bovard, "Surveillance State," *The American Conservative* (May 19, 2003). Copyright © 2003 The American Conservative. www.amconmag.com. All rights reserved. Reprinted with permission.

Page 433. Leonard A. Pitts, Jr., "Spare the Rod, Spoil the Parenting," *The Seattle Times* (September 6, 2001). Copyright © 2001 by the Miami Herald. Reprinted by permission.

Page 435. A. J. Chavez, "The Case for (Gay) Marriage," student essay. Reprinted with the permission of the author.

Page 460. Katie Tiehen, from "Some may challenge . . .," student essay. Reprinted with the permission of the author.

Page 460. Jackie Wyngaard, "EMP: Music History or Music Trivia?" student essay. Reprinted with the permission of the author.

Page 463. Diane Helman and Phyllis Bookspan, "*Sesame Street*: Brought to You by the Letters M-A-L-E," *The Seattle Times* (July 28, 1992). Reprinted with permission.

Page 465. Cecily Ballou, "*Shanghai Noon* Is Not the Same Old West," student essay. Reprinted with the permission of the author.

Page 487. Rebekah Taylor, "A Proposal to Provide Cruelty-Free Products on Campus," student essay. Reprinted with the permission of the author.

Page 492. Jennifer Allen, "The Athlete on the Sidelines," *New York Times* (February 20, 2004). Copyright © 2004 The New York Times. Reprinted by permission.

Page 494. Dylan Fujitani, "The Hardest of the Hardcore: Let's Outlaw Hired Guns in Contemporary

American Warfare," student essay. Reprinted with the permission of the author.

Page 507. Jonathan Swift, "A Modest Proposal," in *The Prose Works of Jonathan Swift* (London: Bell, 1914).

Page 508. Peter Elbow, *Writing Without Teachers* (New York: Oxford University Press, 1973): 14-15.

Page 514. Stephen Bean, "What Puzzles You About Homelessness?" student writing. Reprinted with the permission of the author.

Page 527. Kenneth Burke, *The Grammar of Motives* (Berkeley: University of California Press, 1969).

Page 527. James Jones, quoted in Jon Winokur (Ed.), *Writers on Writing* (Philadelphia: Running Press, 1986).

Pages 528–529. Adapted from J. D. Bransford and M. K. Johnson, "Conceptual Prerequisites for Understanding," *Journal of Learning Behavior* 11 (1972): 717–726.

Pages 533, 534. Lynnea Clark, excerpt and outline from "Women Police Officers: Should Size and Strength Be Criteria for Patrol Duty?", student essay.

Pages 550, 551, and 563. Dao Do, "Choose Life," student essay. Reprinted with the permission of the author.

Page 551. Tiffany Linder, excerpt from "Salvaging Our Old-Growth Forests," student essay. Reprinted with the permission of the author.

Pages 557, 559. David Popenoe, "Where's Papa?" from *Life Without Father: Compelling New Evidence that Fatherhood and Marriage Are Indispensable for the Good of Children and Society.* As published in "The Decline of Fatherhood," *Wilson Quarterly* (September/October 1996).

Page 574. Patrick Klein, "Berkeley Blues," in *University of Arizona First Year Composition Guide.* Copyright © 1995 by University of Arizona First Year Composition Program. Reprinted with the permission.

Page 579. Val Plumwood, excerpt from "Being Prey," *Utne Reader* (July/August 2000): 56–57. Originally published in *The Ultimate Journey* by Val Plumwood. Copyright © 2000 Val Plumwood. Used by permission of the author.

Page 580. Richard Brautigan, excerpt from "Leaves" from *The Tokyo-Montana Express* by Richard Brautigan. Copyright © 1979 by Richard Brautigan. Used with permission.

Page 580. Jon Krakauer, excerpt from *Into Thin Air.* Copyright © 1997 by Jon Krakauer. Publishing by Anchor Books.

Page 581. Hitomaro, "A Strange Old Man," by Hitomaro, translated by Kenneth Rexroth, from *One Hundred Poems from the Japanese,* copyright © New Directions Publishing Corp. Used with permission.

Page 583. *College Composition and Communication,* Viponid Interview with John McPhee (May 1991): 203–204.

Page 584. Tom Wolfe, "New Journalism," introduction to *New Journalism,* ed. Tom Wolfe and E. W. Johnson (New York: Harper & Row, 1973): 32. Nicholas Tomalin, in *New Journalism,* ed. Wolfe and Johnson: 201.

Page 588. Isak Dinesen, "The Iguana," *Out of Africa* (New York: Modern Library, 1952).

Page 589. Victoria Register-Freeman, from "My Turn: Hunks and Handmaidens," *Newsweek* (November 4, 1996): 16. Copyright © 1996 by Newsweek, Inc. Reprinted with the permission of *Newsweek.* All rights reserved.

Page 591. John Kaufeld, *Paradox 5 for Windows for Dummies* (San Mateo, CA: IDG Books Worldwide, Inc., 1994).

Pages 592–593. Michael F. Graves and Wayne H. Slater, "Could Textbooks Be Better Written and Would It Make a Difference?" *American Educator* (Spring 1986): 36–42.

Page 594. Annie Dillard, "Living Like Weasels," in *Teaching a Stone to Talk: Expeditions and Encounters:* 11–16. Copyright © 1982 by Annie Dillard. Reprinted by permission of HarperCollins Publishers, Inc.

Page 599. Women Against Gun Control home page, www.wagc.com. Used with permission.

Page 602. Laura Flynn McCarthy, "A New TV Risk" *Parenting,* Vol. 18, No. 6 (July 2004): 28. Used with permission.

Pages 620–621. EbscoHost search screen and full display. © EBSCO Publishing. Used with permission.

Page 622. AltaVista search results. © AltaVista. Reprinted by permission.

Page 636. Million Mom March home page. © Million Mom March United with the Brady Campaign to Prevent Gun Violence. Used with permission.

Page 637. Second Amendment Sisters, Northern Colorado Chapter, home page. Used with permission.

Page 641. Kelly Ann Connolly, "Women are the Real Victims of Gun Control," from armedandsafe.com. © 2002 Kelly Ann Connolly. Used with permission.

Page 642. Armed and Safe home page. © 2002 by armedandsafe.com. Used with permission.

Page 644. Roger D. McGrath, "The Myth of Violence in the Old West," in *Gunfighters, Highwaymen, and Vigilantes: Violence on the Frontier.* Copyright © 1984 by The Regents of the University of California.

Page 675. Christopher Leigh, "The Case Against Metal Detectors in Public Schools," student essay. Reprinted with the permission of the author.

Page 697. Parker Palmer, *To Know as We Are Known: Education as a Spiritual Journey* (San Francisco: Harper & Row, 1983).

Page 699. Carl Rogers, *On Becoming a Person: A Therapist's View of Psychotherapy,* 3rd ed. (Boston: Houghton Mifflin, 1961).

Page 713. Randall Popken, "Essay Exams and Papers: A Contextual Comparison," *Journal of Teaching Writing* 8 (1989): 51–65.

Page 729. Susan Meyers, excerpt from an e-mail message, student writing. Reprinted with the permission of the author.

Page 734. Jaime Finger, "A Single Reflection," student essay. Reprinted with the permission of the author.

Page 740. Bruce Urbanik, "A Comprehensive Reflective Letter." Reprinted with the permission of the author.

Illustrations

Page 45. Courtesy of Shell.

Page 46. Courtesy www.adbusters.org.

Page 67. Photography by Frank Veronsky.

Page 87. Allan H. Shoemake/Taxi/Getty Images.

Page 89. Bill Bachmann/The Image Works.

Page 90. Jeff Greenberg/The Image Works.

Page 91. Leland Bobbe/Taxi/Getty Images.

Page 92. Frank Micelotta/Getty Images.

Page 95. Courtesy of the U.S. Army.

Page 98. AP/Wide World Photos.

Page 99. Chuck Dial, on behalf of photographer John Benck.

Page 100. Patrick Endres/AlaskaStock.com.

Pages 154–155. All Courtesy of GASP (UK) www.gasp.org.uk.

Page 156. Courtesy www.adbusters.org.

Page 223. Courtesy of Manuel J. Cabrero.

Page 223. Photo Courtesy of Ron Taylor.

Page 299. Courtesy of Nikon.

Page 301. © DaimlerChrysler Corporation. Used with permission.

Page 302. © DaimlerChrysler Corporation. Used with permission.

Page 307. Coors Brewing Co.

Page 310. Courtesy of The Hoover Company.

Page 311. Courtesy Zenith Audio Products, a Division of S.D.I. Technologies.

Page 313. Courtesy of COTY US LLC.

Page 314. Courtesy of AT&T.

Page 318. Photography by Katrine Naleid.

Page 319. Courtesy of Vokal.

Page 382. Art Brewer/imagestate.

Page 383. SPL/Photo Researchers, Inc.

Page 449. For maps and other related teaching materials contact: ODT, Inc., PO Box 134, Amherst MA 01004 USA; (800-736-1293; Fax: 413-549-3503; E-mail: odtstore@aol.com). Web: www.odt.org.

Page 457. Douglas Peebles/CORBIS.

Page 483. Courtesy of Common Sense for Drug Policy, Washington, D. C.

Page 505. Courtesy of Lockheed Martin.

Page 695. Courtesy of MarketingSolutionsAndConservation.com.

Page 745. Courtesy of Plowshare Group for National Environmental Education & Training Foundation.

Index

READINGS AND VISUAL TEXTS IN
THE ALLYN & BACON GUIDE TO WRITING

The Allyn & Bacon Guide to Writing, Fourth Edition, contains 59 essays—34 by professional writers and 25 by student writers—from a wide variety of sources, as well as 42 visual texts.